	DATE DUE		
	REF.	REF.	
REF.	REF.	REF.	REF.
	REF.	REF.	

Encyclopedia of American Business History and Biography

Railroads in the Age of Regulation, 1900-1980

Encyclopedia of American Business History and Biography

Railroads in the Age of Regulation, 1900-1980

Edited by

Keith L. Bryant, Jr.
Texas A & M University

A Bruccoli Clark Layman Book

Facts On File Publications
New York   Oxford, England

Encyclopedia of American Business History and Biography:
Railroads in the Age of Regulation, 1900–1980

LC number 87-36493
ISBN 0-8160-1371-3 (v. 1)

Full CIP information available on request
British CIP information available on request

Designed by Quentin Fiore

Printed in the United States of America

10 9 8 7 6 5 4 3 2 1

To Richard C. Overton

He showed us the way

Contents

Foreword

The Encyclopedia of American Business History and Biography chronicles America's material civilization through its business figures and businesses. It is a record of American aspirations—of success and of failure. It is a history of the impact of business on American life. The volumes have been planned to serve a cross section of users: students, teachers, scholars, researchers, government and corporate officials. Individual volumes or groups of volumes cover a particular industry during a defined period; thus each *EABH&B* volume is freestanding, providing a history expressed through biographies and buttressed by a wide range of supporting entries. In many cases a single volume is sufficient to treat an industry, but certain industries require two or more volumes. When completed, the *EABH&B* will provide the fullest available history of American enterprise.

The editorial direction of *EABH&B* is provided by the general editor and the editorial board. The general editor appoints volume editors, whose duties are to prepare, in consultation with the editorial board, the list of entries for each volume, to assign the entries to contributors, to vet the submitted entries, and to work in close cooperation with the Bruccoli Clark Layman editorial staff so as to maintain consistency of treatment. All entries are written by specialists in their fields, not by staff writers. Volume editors are experienced scholars.

The publishers and editors of *EABH&B* are convinced that timing is crucial to notable careers. Therefore, the biographical entries in each volume of the series place businesses and their leaders in the social, political, and economic contexts of their times. Supplementary background rubrics on companies, inventions, legal decisions, marketing innovations, and other topics are integrated with the biographical entries in alphabetical order.

The general editor and the volume editors determine the space to be allotted to biographies as major entries, standard entries, and short entries. Major entries, reserved for giants of business and industry (e.g., Henry Ford, J. P. Morgan, Andrew Carnegie, James J. Hill), require approximately 10,000 words. Standard biographical entries are in the range of 3,500-5,000 words. Short entries are reserved for lesser figures who require inclusion and for significant figures about whom little information is available. When appropriate, the biographical entries stress their subjects' roles in shaping the national experience, showing how their activities influenced the way Americans lived. Unattractive or damaging aspects of character and conduct are not suppressed. All biographical entries conform to a basic format and have the same rubrics.

A significant part of each volume is devoted to concise background entries supporting and elucidating the biographies. These nonbiographical entries provide basic information about the industry or field covered in the volume. Histories of companies are necessarily brief and limited to key events. To establish a context for all entries, each volume includes an overview of the industry treated. These historical introductions are normally written by the volume editors.

We have set for ourselves large tasks and important goals. We aspire to provide a body of work that will help redress the imbalance in the writing of American history, the study of which too often slights business. Our hope is also to stimulate interest in business leaders, enterprises, and industries that have not been given the scholarly attention they deserve. By setting high standards for accuracy, balanced treatment, original research, and clear writing, we have tried to ensure that these works will commend themselves to those who seek a full account of the development of America.

—William H. Becker
General Editor

Acknowledgments

This book was produced by Bruccoli Clark Layman, Inc. Philip B. Dematteis was the in-house editor.

Art supervisor is Gabrielle Elliott. Copyediting supervisor is Patricia Coate. Production coordinator is Kimberly Casey. Typesetting supervisor is Kathleen M. Flanagan. Laura Ingram and Michael D. Senecal are editorial associates. The production staff includes Rowena Betts, David R. Bowdler, Charles Brower, Cheryl Crombie, Mary S. Dye, Charles Egleston, Sarah A. Estes, Cynthia Hallman, Judith K. Ingle, Maria Ling, Warren McInnis, Kathy S. Merlette, Sheri Neal, Joycelyn R. Smith, and Libby York. Jean W. Ross is permissions editor. Joseph Caldwell, photography editor, and Joseph Matthew Bruccoli did photographic copy work for the volume. Mary Louise Shevlin and Robert Shevlin supervised external production.

Walter W. Ross and Rhonda Marshall did the library research with the assistance of the staff at the Thomas Cooper Library of the University of South Carolina: Daniel Boice, Kathy Eckman, Gary Geer, Cathie Gottlieb, David L. Haggard, Jens Holley, Dennis Isbell, Jackie Kinder, Marcia Martin, Jean Rhyne, Beverley Steele, Ellen Tillet, Carole Tobin, and Virginia Weathers.

A portion of the Introduction taken from *A History of American Business* by Keith L. Bryant, Jr., and Henry C. Dethloff (Prentice-Hall, 1983) is reprinted with permission.

Introduction

The railroads were the nation's first big businesses. With their intricate network of lines, these companies gave inland points access to navigable waters and joined those waters to the seaboard, linked farms and villages to the rising industrial cities, opened millions of acres of land to cultivation, provided the means to ship raw materials and finished goods quickly and cheaply, and created billions of dollars in capital to be reinvested in the nation's economy. Railway managers designed administrative structures and accounting systems to control thousands of employees, hundreds of locomotives, and thousands of cars and to collect fares and freight bills from customers across the nation. These structures and procedures would be adopted by large-scale enterprises in the steel, petroleum, automobile, and other industries. The railroads provided a model for the basic units in the capitalistic system; they helped to create America's modern economy even as they moved freight and passengers across the continent.

Before the coming of the railroad, virtually no basic changes in transportation had taken place for 2,000 years. People and goods moved as they had during the Roman Empire—by packhorse, wagon, or boat. Beginning in the 1820s the railway revolutionized transportation in the United States and laid the basis for a modern industrial economy. The railroad was invented in western Europe—specifically, in England—but by 1840 European countries had only 1,818 miles of track whereas the United States had almost 3,000 miles. The United States became the leader in the development of the railroad because of the vast distances to be overcome and because it was not hampered by the entrenched vested interests, regional jealousies, and long-established customs that hindered European rail expansion. Although some opposition to railroads did exist—one Ohio school board held that the steam railroad was "a device of Satan to lead immortal souls down to Hell"—such sentiments were rare. The American people welcomed the railroad with unbounded enthusi-asm and invested their savings and supported the promoters who built the lines across the country.

The experience of three major commercial centers, Baltimore, Charleston, and Boston, illustrate America's fervor for railways. Each city sought to expand its hinterland to the west, and each pioneered in the construction of railroads. Baltimore built the Baltimore & Ohio Railroad (B&O) across the Alleghenies to tap markets in the Ohio Valley. The people of Charleston constructed a railroad inland to the Savannah River, hoping to divert the cotton trade to their port and away from their archrival Savannah. Frightened by the sudden rise of New York after the completion of the Erie Canal, Bostonians sought to build a railroad westward to Albany on the Hudson River and take away traffic going to the port of New York. These three cities initiated the railroad era in their respective regions.

On July 4, 1828, Charles Carroll, one of the signers of the Declaration of Independence, turned the first earth to initiate construction of the horsedrawn Baltimore & Ohio Railroad. Later that summer steam power came to the B&O when Peter Cooper, a part-time inventor from New York, brought the locomotive Tom Thumb to the line. The Tom Thumb was not a success, however, losing a race with a horse-powered vehicle. Not until 1831 did steam locomotives replace horse-drawn wagons on the railroad. The successful utilization of steam power and further construction to the west enhanced the profitability of the B&O, which soon had gross revenues of over a quarter of a million dollars per year. On Christmas Eve 1852 the B&O reached the Ohio River at Wheeling, Virginia, and traffic from the Ohio Valley began to flow east to Baltimore.

Meanwhile, the South Carolina Canal and Railroad Company constructed its line westward from Charleston. On Christmas Day 1830 the Best Friend of Charleston, the first locomotive built for sale in the United States, carried over 140 passengers on the first scheduled steam railroad in the country. When the 136-mile route to Hamburg, South

Carolina, was completed in 1833, it was the longest continuous railroad in the world.

Railroad promoters in Boston built three fledgling lines from that city to Lowell, Providence, and Worcester which formed the basis of a New England railway system. The subsequent success of these cities generated a wave of railway construction in the 1830s. Railroad enthusiasm became wild and boisterous railway *fever* when every town and city sought to emulate Baltimore, Charleston, and Boston.

The nation's rail system grew rapidly, although the panic of 1837 and the subsequent depression slowed the expansion of the railroads and some states, particularly those in the Old Northwest, suffered heavily because of their investments in railroad projects. The lines largely served cities along the Atlantic coast, and New England and the mid-Atlantic states had over 50 percent of the total mileage in the country. Nevertheless, by 1840 only four of the twenty-six states in the union were without railroads.

American railroads did not have a uniform track gauge, or distance between the rails. In England the standard gauge was 4 feet 8 1/2 inches; this measurement became the usual track gauge in New England and portions of the North, but some railways, the Erie, for example, were 6-foot gauge. Other railroads, particularly in the Southern states, had a 5-foot gauge. This confusion of gauges necessitated expensive and inefficient transshipments of goods where lines of different gauges intersected.

Throughout the 1830s and 1840s the companies constantly improved their trackage and rolling equipment. The first railroads had been built on tracks of iron straps or bars fastened to wooden rails that, in turn, were attached to blocks of granite or other heavy stones embedded in the earth. The iron straps, twenty to twenty-five feet long, often broke loose and curled under the weight of passing trains to form "snake-heads" which tore through the bottoms of cars. The solution to this problem appeared in 1831 when Robert L. Stevens, an engineer and president of the Camden & Amboy Railroad of New Jersey, designed the iron T-rail. Supporting the T-rail were wooden "sleepers" or ties, which replaced the stones or granite blocks under the rails. A roadbed surfaced with crushed stone or gravel supported the track. Locomotive design improved steadily. Originally most of the en-

gines were imported from England, but Philadelphia jewelry manufacturer Matthias Baldwin entered the business in 1832 and soon other locomotive builders emerged in the Northeast. Passenger cars, which had been nothing more than stagecoaches with railroad wheels, quickly evolved into longer, more comfortable accommodations. The diminutive freight cars, usually with only four wheels, were replaced by longer and heavier eight-wheeled cars with greater carrying capacity. Thus the railways spawned auxiliary enterprises in T-rail manufacturing, locomotive works, and car and wheel shops and gave impetus to the lumber industry, which furnished the wooden ties.

Railroad construction, which had rapidly expanded in the 1840s, turned into a veritable explosion of new tracks and rail lines in the prosperous 1850s. In 1850 the nation's railway mileage was 8,879; by 1860 the total exceeded 30,000 miles. During the 1850s many short rail lines were consolidated into large companies, particularly in the North and Northeast; while a few roads, such as the Erie and the Baltimore & Ohio, had been built as single companies, most trunk lines were created through mergers. Yet the nation did not have a unified rail system: the railways north of the Ohio River and those in the South connected in only three locations.

The proliferation of railways in the 1850s resulted in part from financial stimulation by government. State governments granted liberal railroad charters, and in a few cases they actually built the lines. State and local governments also supplied money and credit for many of the private railroads. Between 1845 and 1860 state governments borrowed more than $90 million, largely to finance railroad construction, and state and local governments often purchased securities of the railway corporations. The federal government contributed by making surveys at taxpayer expense and by reducing the tariff on iron used by the railroads.

The federal government also supported the railways by providing almost 25 million acres of land for railroad construction before the Civil War. Debates over the use of federal lands to aid railroads deeply divided Congress, with members from the Northeast generally opposed while those from the West and South strongly urged such help. On September 20, 1850, the government made its first significant railroad land grant: two companies would build a line from northern Illinois to Mobile, Alabama. The grant included a 200-foot right of way and alternate even-numbered sections of land on each side of the track for a depth of six miles. If the granted lands were occupied, the railroads could have other sections within fifteen miles of their track. The law provided that the railroads should transport the property or troops of the United States free from any toll or charge and that Congress would determine the rate for the mail the lines would carry. Additional grants before the Civil War benefited forty-five other railroads.

The federal land grant program expanded rapidly after the war. Many politicians believed that settlement would take place on a large scale in the West only if railroads already existed there; tracks had to be laid ahead of demand, they contended. The national government subsidized some of the western railroads because the state, territorial, and local governments were unable to provide the level of support which had existed in the South and the East before 1860. Between 1850 and 1871, 175 million acres of land were granted to various companies by Congress, although 35 million acres were eventually forfeited and returned when contracts were not fulfilled. While seventy railroads received federal land grants, four—the Northern Pacific, Atchison, Topeka & Santa Fe, Southern Pacific, and Union Pacific—received over 70 percent of the total. Altogether, the land grants covered only 20,000 miles, or 8 percent, of the nation's railroads.

In all cases the government required that railroads built with land grants reduce charges for federal shipments, the general reduction being 50 percent from ordinary rates; a congressional report in 1945 estimated that the government had saved $900 million because of this clause. Nevertheless, heated debate continued as to whether or not the land grants were justified. The major contribution of grants was to furnish a basis for credit so that construction could begin. The belief that the land grants would provide instant profits proved an illusion, but they did encourage the development of railroads in advance of settlement. On the other hand, they also encouraged the lines to be built quickly and often poorly. The economic consequences of the land grants did not bring a halt to them, however; rather, revelations of corruption and bribery caused public opinion to demand that such assistance be ended. Direct federal aid terminated early

in the 1870s, and most state and local support for railroads ceased during the next decade. But government aid, in any case, was relatively small in comparison with investment by private capital.

Private investors largely financed the construction of the nation's railway system. Merchants, farmers, manufacturers, and professional men and women bought stocks and bonds in rail companies. Boston, New York, and Philadelphia investors purchased the securities of railways in the West and South. Some railway bonds were sold in London before the Civil War, but most of the capital came from the United States. Investors were willing to purchase the securities because the railroad had triumphed over other forms of transportation. Turnpike and plank-road companies had largely disappeared, and canals were being abandoned even before the 1850s. The railroads could transport goods more cheaply than wagons and more efficiently than canal boats or riverboats.

By 1860 railways provided much of the nation with fast and economical transportation. Tonnage rates fell, and increased speeds reduced the financial burdens of other industries. Wagon rates for wheat had been as high as 30 cents per ton-mile in the Old Northwest, By the time of the Civil War, farmers could ship a bushel of wheat from Chicago to New York for only 1.2 cents per ton-mile. Only half of this decrease reflected the general price decline of the period. The consequences for domestic commerce were important indeed: the building of the railroads, more than any other factor, gave rise to industrialization. Markets for manufacturers, miners, and commercial firms expanded with the rail network, and additional outlets encouraged more complex machinery in manufacturing. In turn, machinery increased output even further, providing yet another impetus for expansion and continued growth.

The railroads proved to be important in war as well as in peace. When the Civil War broke out in April 1861, the rail systems of the Union and the Confederacy stood in sharp contrast. With 9,000 miles of track the eleven Confederate states claimed only one-third of the nation's total rail mileage. Railways in the South were more lightly constructed and less systematic in design and operation than those in the North; rolling stock and locomotives were smaller and less numerous. The South had few facilities for the construction and maintenance of equipment, and its modest locomotive-building shops were soon pressed into the production of ordnance. It quickly became evident that the American Civil War would be the first major conflict in which railroads were vital tactically and strategically, and that they had revolutionized warfare.

Shortages of basic commodities, such as lubricating oil and car wheels, soon made effective management of the railways in the South a virtual impossibility, but in the North the railroads prospered. The Illinois Central, for example, carried heavy trainloads of Union troops, animals, forage, and ammunition to Kentucky and Tennessee, while the Baltimore & Ohio moved troops from Maryland to western Virginia and Ohio. Traffic increased so rapidly that some Northern railway companies paid their first dividends in 1863-1864.

Both armies recognized that successful campaigns often depended on possession of major railroad junctions, and each engaged in widespread railroad destruction to deny its opponent use of these critical arteries. At the end of the war the railway system of the South was generally in ruins, and a rehabilitation program began almost immediately. The Northern system, however, was in excellent condition. War demands had resulted in greater cooperation among railways, and increased traffic led to the replacement of iron rails with steel and of wood with coal for fuel. The expansion of the 1850s and the consolidation of operations to meet the challenges of the war placed the railroads on the threshold of even more rapid growth after 1865.

Mileage doubled in the first eight years after the war and doubled again in the next fourteen years. Construction of the first transcontinental route dramatized this expansion. The Pacific Railway Act of 1862 authorized the building of the Union Pacific and Central Pacific railroads, which pushed toward each other from Omaha, Nebraska, and Sacramento, California. Completed in 1869, the Union Pacific-Central Pacific route proved to be the forerunner of additional transcontinentals. In 1883 the Northern Pacific, extending west from Minneapolis, reached Tacoma, Washington, and a few years later the Southern Pacific and the Santa Fe linked the west coast to New Orleans and Chicago.

To acquire new business and retain traditional traffic, the railroads engaged in developmental activities in their territories. They spent large sums recruiting farmers from the East and Europe for the new lands opened on the Great Plains and in the Northwest. The railroads operated free excursion trains, sold lands at low prices and with modest down payment, carried feed free or at low rates in times of drought, and moved settlers to the West in "Zulu" cars that hauled families, furniture, implements, and animals. Company land agents purchased advertising in farm journals lauding the fertility of western lands, mailed millions of brochures and pamphlets to prospective settlers, and gave lectures and magic lantern shows before farm audiences in the United States and in Europe. Industrial development was not neglected as the carriers built sidings and spur lines to new firms, discounted freight rates, and found locations for businesses seeking new sites in the South and West.

As the construction of the transcontinentals proceeded, the carriers improved and standardized their operations. Giant bridges spanned the Ohio, Mississippi, and Missouri rivers. In 1871 over twenty different track gauges still were in use, but by 1880, 80 percent of the mileage had been converted to "standard gauge" (4 feet 8 1/2 inches), and during the next decade virtually the entire network was rebuilt to this gauge. To further facilitate interchange of traffic railroads also standardized coupling devices, car trucks, bills of lading, and classification of products. Larger locomotives and freight cars with increased carrying capacities required the replacement of iron rails with steel, which provided a smoother, safer, and faster track and lasted up to twelve times as long as wrought iron, saving millions annually in maintenance costs. The link-and-pin couplers that had cost thousands of men fingers or even hands were replaced by effective automatic safety couplers. Similarly, the hand brake system that required men to run along the tops of cars to set the devices was replaced by an air brake system mandated by federal law in 1893. More apparent to the public than any of the technical changes was the division of the nation into four time zones to enhance the orderly movement of trains.

The most significant contribution of the railroads to the development of business enterprise in America was the establishment by the larger roads of complex but highly efficient managerial systems; the railroads, in fact, created the modern business structure. Management of canals, steamboats, and turnpikes had been relatively simple, but distance, complexity, and size required a larger and more systematic organization for the railroads. Before the 1840s American businesses used methods not unlike those practiced in fifteenth-century Venice, but the railways needed system and order to move freight and passengers efficiently, quickly, and safely and companies had to provide direct, scheduled, and reliable delivery of freight. Internal procedures had to be routinized and accounting, maintenance, and statistical controls devised.

The modern manager emerged to meet these needs. Railroad managers did not copy European models; rather, they designed rational responses to the problems they faced. They established divisions of responsibilities and assigned specific functions to employees throughout the corporation. They developed ways to discover costs and reduce expenditures, which involved daily detailed reports from all segments of the railroad. They devised new accounting procedures and billing systems. Many of the brightest and most promising young men in the country became part of these new railway enterprises, which offered both challenges and financial rewards. They formed structures to manage hundreds and then thousands of employees scattered across several states. As Alfred D. Chandler has written, "The railroad and the telegraph provided the fast, regular, and dependable transportation and communication so essential to high-volume production and distribution—the hallmark of large modern manufacturing or marketing enterprises. As important, the rail and telegraph companies were themselves the first modern business enterprises to appear in the United States."

Because of the scope and intricacy of their operations, railroads required absolute discipline of employees. Workers were placed on strict schedules, and detailed work rules were formulated and imposed. Workers often felt that the rules were arbitrary and against their interests; as a consequence, labor relations were extremely difficult and occasionally violent. Some railroad crew members joined one of the four principal brotherhoods—those of engineers, conductors, firemen and enginemen, and trainmen—but relatively few were members of unions before 1890. Nevertheless, in times of strife workers banded together in opposition to their employers. During July 1877, for example, in the midst of the depression that followed the panic of 1873, the Baltimore & Ohio Railroad twice cut wages by 10 percent; it also increased the length of freight trains without expanding crews. Its firemen and brakemen struck, and mobs in Baltimore and Pittsburgh attacked company property; in Pittsburgh alone damages exceeded $5 million. Violence spread, and soon police, the militia, and regular army regiments were called out. The strike was broken, but the public knew that while the workers suffered wage cuts, dividends were still being paid on the B&O and other railroads. Similarly, sympathy developed for the workers who struck George M. Pullman's carworks at Pullman, Illinois, in 1894, after he reduced wages but not the rents on their company-owned housing. Railroad employees in the Chicago area attempted to aid the Pullman workers by refusing to haul Pullman sleeping cars on passenger trains. The federal government and local courts intervened on the side of Pullman and the strike failed. Some railway companies exacerbated these situations by creating blacklists of workers who were members of or sympathetic to the brotherhoods. Undoubtedly these events played a large part in creating a negative public image of the corporations.

The public also resented the scandals that surrounded the construction and operation of some of the nation's railways. For example, during the building of the Union Pacific Railroad, a construction company, the Credit Mobilier, distributed shares of stock to members of Congress and even to the Vice President of the United States. The Credit Mobilier received contracts to build the Union Pacific that were far in excess of the value of the track the railroad acquired. Those involved in the Credit Mobilier pocketed an estimated $23 million. The public was also incensed by revelations that as much as half of the Union Pacific's capitalization of $110 million represented "watered stock." Railway companies often sold securities whose total face value was more than the lines were actually worth; the excess stock was called "watered." This practice was generally justified on the ground that investors would buy securities only if they received more in stocks and bonds than the cash they had actually paid. The result was overcapitalization, which made it extremely difficult for these companies to pay interest on bonds and dividends on stocks. This kind of corruption was primarily to be found in the South and the Far West, but a corruption of a different sort, the manipulation of the prices of securities, became a common practice in the money markets of the Northeast.

In 1867 Commodore Cornelius Vanderbilt attempted to add the Erie Railroad to his collection of lines in New York. Vanderbilt had created the New York Central and Hudson River Railroad, which had largely replaced the Erie Canal in moving goods from Lake Erie to New York City. The Erie Railroad, controlled by Daniel Drew, caused Vanderbilt enormous difficulty by reducing its rates. The Commodore proceeded to purchase Erie securities to rid himself of this competitor. Aided by Jim Fisk and Jay Gould, Drew provided Vanderbilt with 100,000 unauthorized shares of Erie stock. Vanderbilt obtained from a friendly judge a warrant to arrest Drew, Fisk, and Gould, but the trio, surrounded by armed guards fled across the Hudson River with $6 million in cash to safety in Jersey City. Gould then traveled secretly to Albany, where he spent half a million dollars bribing the legislature to legalize the issuance of the securities the Commodore had purchased. Vanderbilt said that fighting to gain control of the Erie and losing had "learned me it never pays to kick a skunk." Such capers angered the public, which came to believe that Vanderbilt, Drew, Fisk, and Gould were typical of all railroad leaders.

Where intense competition existed between railroads, a reduction in rates often resulted. The carriers employed the concept of charging on the basis of the value of the product carried, and they classified freight for rate-making purposes; but when competition arose, rates plunged and the carriers suffered. Economies of scale did allow the railroads to drastically reduce some charges. Between 1866 and 1897 the rate for carrying wheat, for example, fell by 70 percent and the rate for dressed beef decreased 55 percent; during that period general prices declined by only 43 percent. The expansion of lines in the Great Plains brought further reductions: between 1879 and 1889 the Santa Fe cut rates by 42 percent, the Chicago, Burlington & Quincy by almost 50 percent, and the Northern Pacific by 46 percent. These reductions were more substantial than the decline in agricultural prices: farmers received 37 percent less for their wheat and 25 percent less for their corn in this period. Nevertheless, farmers, small businessmen, and other shippers argued that the rates were still too high. The public believed that charging more for short hauls than

for long hauls was discriminatory, but such rates were necessary if the railroads were to have an equitable return on their investment: their fixed charges had to be paid, and terminal costs were the same, whether the haul was 100 or 1,000 miles. Large corporations had distinct advantages in dealing with the railways, and, where competing service was available, they threatened to move their traffic if the railroads did not reduce rates or give a rebate on part of the charges.

The debilitating effect of rate wars led the railroads to seek solutions, and they created pools which divided traffic and income between particular points among competing lines. For example, the three major railroads between Chicago and Omaha decided in 1870 to split the traffic by thirds. This arrangement, known as the Iowa Pool, gave rise to other freight associations in various regions of the country. These pools worked relatively well for a time but in the early 1880s a series of railroad wars broke out and many of these "gentlemen's agreements" collapsed.

Small shippers complained bitterly that the railroads granted rebates to larger customers. Standard Oil Company, for example, forced the railroads in its area to rebate over $10 million in only a year and a half. The railroads gave free passes to politicians, ministers, and community leaders to gain support. It became necessary for the railroads to seek such favor because of the rate-making philosophy which they had adopted. Most railroad managers firmly believed that they should, and could, "charge all the traffic will bear." The railroads moved people and products at a fraction of the rates which had prevailed in 1860, but their heavy indebtedness, wildly fluctuating stock prices, short-haul-long-haul discrimination, rebating, and granting of passes alienated the public.

Farmers in the West, small businessmen in upstate New York, grain elevator owners in Iowa, and other groups sought state regulation in response to what they perceived to be abuses of economic power by the railroads. In the 1870s several states in the upper Midwest passed statutes known as Granger Laws. Named after their sponsor, the National Grange of the Patrons of Husbandry, or Grangers, these laws created state railway commissions to establish maximum rates and to end discrimination. The railroads fought back in the courts, but in 1876, in *Munn* v. *Illinois*, the Supreme

Court upheld such regulation. Ratemaking by the states proved complex and difficult, and legislatures and railroad commissions were often uninformed about and uninterested in the plight of the companies being regulated. A series of appeals by the railways led to partial reversals of the earlier decisions, and in 1886 in the *Wabash* case, Supreme Court severely limited state regulation of railroads.

In 1887 the federal government responded to cries for national railroad regulation with the passage of the Interstate Commerce Act, which created the five-member Interstate Commerce Commission (ICC). The law said–vaguely–that rates should be "reasonable and just," that is, not so high as to destroy the traffic; it also prohibited rebates, pools, and higher rates for noncompetitive short hauls. The ICC which was to administer and enforce the act, could hear shipper complaints and examine witnesses, but it did not specifically receive the power to set maximum railroad rates, and it could enforce its decisions only through the federal courts. The first five commissioners proved to be capable people, but the federal judiciary undermined their efforts to implement the law. Between 1887 and 1905 the Supreme Court ruled in favor of the railroads and against the government in fifteen of sixteen cases. The courts found that the ICC had no ratemaking power and that it could not effectively prohibit discrimination. The Interstate Commerce Act did, however, create a regulatory precedent.

Perhaps more important than regulation was the impact of the depression of 1893 on the nation's rail system, and the subsequent reorganization of bankrupt carriers by investment bankers in New York and Chicago. Companies operating one-third of America's railroad mileage entered bankruptcy between 1873 and 1897. A federal court decision in 1882 made it possible for the management of a railroad to act as its receivers. This decision allowed the railroads to recover financially and pay creditors, but it also enabled investment-banking houses to play highly influential roles in their reorganization. By the late 1880s J. P. Morgan and Company and other banking houses were not only refinancing the railroads but were dominating their boards of directors. Morgan reorganized the Reading Railroad in 1886, the Chesapeake & Ohio two years later, and the Baltimore & Ohio in 1896. Following the Panic of 1893 many railroads declared bankruptcy, and in four years over 40,000 miles of

line with a capitalization (stocks and bonds) of more than $2.5 billion entered receivership. Morgan ultimately reorganized the Erie, the Northern Pacific, and the Richmond Terminal (which became the Southern Railway). Similar functions were provided by other banking houses, such as Kuhn, Loeb and J. and W. Seligman. The investment bankers reduced the debt structures and rationalized the distribution of routes; they also reduced competition.

Nearly two-thirds of the nation's rail mileage fell under the control of seven investment groups, and these transportation "communities of interest" received increasing criticism from reform-minded Progressives. After 1903 state and federal investigations of the financial manipulations of the railroad companies brought charges of "loose, extravagant and improvident" management. Higher railroad operating costs in a time of general inflation led to small increases in average freight rates after 1900, adding to the general public hostility. As a consequence, pressure developed for further federal regulation of the industry. President Theodore Roosevelt's attorney general sued under the Sherman Anti-Trust Act of 1890 to dissolve Northern Securities Company, a giant holding corporation put together in 1902 by E. H. Harriman and James J. Hill to control several of the major railways in the Pacific Northwest. Two years after its formation, the Supreme Court ordered Northern Securities dissolved. In its continuing effort to deal with railway "abuses," Congress passed the Elkins Act in 1903, which made both the giver and the receiver of a railroad rebate liable for prosecution.

Nevertheless, leading political figures, such as William Jennings Bryan, advocated federal ownership of the railroads, not regulation, as a solution. President Roosevelt, who opposed nationalization of the rail network, finally agreed to the Hepburn Act of 1906, which expanded the powers of the ICC to include express and sleeping-car companies and pipelines and abolished the granting of passes. More important, the Hepburn Act, by giving the ICC the power to establish "just and reasonable" maximum freight rates, became a landmark in the development of federal regulatory policy. During the administration of William Howard Taft the Mann-Elkins Act of 1910 further expanded the jurisdiction of the commission and placed the burden of proof as to the "reasonableness" of rates on the carriers. The Progressives capped their regulatory efforts with the Valuation Act of 1913. Strongly opposed by the railroads, this legislation ordered the Interstate Commerce Commission to evaluate the "true" worth of all railway property to provide a basis for establishing freight rates. Senator Robert M. La Follette had argued that the railroads were basing their rates on inflated values, or watered stock, rather than upon the actual value of their operating properties.

In their zeal, the Progressives limited the ability of the railroads to raise additional investment capital at the very time when hundreds of millions of dollars were needed to increase the output of the system. The railroads were investing in larger, more powerful locomotives; freight car fleets were being expanded; passenger cars were becoming longer, heavier, and more luxurious as steel replaced wood construction; and some railroads were building extensive new city terminals. The Pennsylvania Railroad dug a tunnel under the Hudson River to reach its new midtown New York City station, and both the Pennsylvania and the New York Central began to electrify major urban trackage. Most companies replaced lightweight steel or iron rails with steel rails of much heavier carrying capacity and installed new signal systems. The railroads also faced increasing demands from railroad workers for higher wages. Over a million rail employees in 1900 earned an average annual wage of $567; by 1916, 1.7 million workers were earning an average of more than $880 per year. Greater capital expenditures and increased wages brought the operating ratio (the ratio of operating expenses to operating revenue, multiplied by 100) of the railroads from an average of 66 in 1890 to almost 70 by World War I. When the railroads requested rate increases from the ICC, however, the commission denied them under the authority granted by the Hepburn and Mann-Elkins Acts.

Railroad mileage in the United States was near its peak with 260,000 miles of first main track in 1916, a year in which the companies were called upon to meet not only domestic demands but also preparations for entering World War I. Between 1900 and 1915 general price levels in the country had increased by 30 percent while average railroad wages rose by more than 50 percent. The taxes paid by the carriers had tripled in that decade and a half, yet total revenues only doubled and freight rates remained almost unchanged. As the railways

sought to cope with traffic conditions produced by the war, management found only public ill will. In 1916 the four operating brotherhoods demanded an eight-hour day instead of a ten-hour day; President Woodrow Wilson attempted to serve as mediator, but his compromise proved unacceptable to management. When the negotiations between the president and the railroad companies broke down, Wilson exclaimed bitterly, "I pray God to forgive you, I never can." Threatened with a nationwide strike, Wilson asked Congress to approve legislation creating the eight-hour day for railroad workers, and the Adamson Act became law. The immediate issue had been resolved, but labor relations remained highly unsatisfactory in the spring of 1917, when Wilson requested a special session of Congress to hear his appeal for a declaration of war.

When the United States entered the war in April, over 180,000 freight cars were blocked in American ports with no place for their cargoes to be unloaded. The carriers attempted to meet this problem by forming the Railroads' War Board, which organized car pools and coordinated operations. The board was hampered, however, by the Sherman Anti-Trust Act, which limited cooperation by the carriers. The ICC recommended that Wilson assume control of the railroads, and on December 26 the president issued a proclamation for government operations to begin within forty-eight hours.

Appointed director general of the railroads, William G. McAdoo formed the United States Railroad Administration (USRA) and brought the nation's railroads into one federalized system. Duplicate trains were terminated, stations closed, unnecessary civilian traffic eliminated, and competing routes coordinated. McAdoo imposed stringent controls on the utilization of freight cars and purchased 100,000 new cars and almost 2,000 locomotives built to standardized USRA specifications. McAdoo also granted a series of wage increases to workers, including one of almost 40 percent; total labor costs rose from $1.8 billion in 1917 to $2.7 billion in 1918, and in 1920 the average USRA employee's wage rose from $1,000 a year to $1,800. Average railroad wages by 1920 stood more than a third higher than those in manufacturing; the portion of each dollar the railroads earned that went to labor costs rose from 40 cents in 1917 to 55 cents in 1920. Along with the increase in wages, the cost of coal nearly doubled during the war years, although freight movements increased by only 11 percent. As a result, the average operating ratio of 65.5 in 1916 soared to 94.3 in 1920. Federal control of the nation's railroads cost the taxpayers over $1.1 billion before the government returned the companies to their owners on March 1, 1920. Some Americans proposed federal ownership of the railroads, and one labor leader, Glenn E. Plumb, urged the government to purchase the railroads and operate them with a fifteen-person board. This idea won little public support.

Instead Congress passed the Esch-Cummins Act, or Transportation Act of 1920. This legislation further increased the power and responsibilities of the Interstate Commerce Commission but did provide that the carriers should receive fair rates of return on their investment: the original figure was 5.5 percent. The act also gave the ICC greater control over new construction and abandonments; the latter power would be misused by the commission to prevent elimination of superfluous mileage. The act further empowered the ICC to encourage the consolidation of the nation's railroads into a small number of major systems, and the ICC hired Professor William Z. Ripley of Harvard University to design a national rail plan. Ripley's scheme was not well received by industry leaders, and the ICC rejected merger plans put forward by management. While the ICC had gained greater powers, it failed to create a national system of carriers.

Ironically, the federal government had expanded its regulatory authority just at a time when the railroads were facing increasing competition from other forms of transportation. The Transportation Act of 1920 was based on assumptions which had had some validity in the 1890s; Congress simply failed to perceive the major impact on the railroads of the automobile, pipelines, renewed barge traffic on major waterways, an expanding trucking industry, intercity buses, and the incipient airlines. The nation's rail industry had peaked in importance in 1920; afterwards, other transportation industries began to diminish the significance of the rail system.

The developmental activities begun by the railroads in the nineteenth century accelerated in the twentieth century when many carriers formed industrial and agricultural departments to manage and stabilize their freight business. The industrial arms purchased lands for factory sites and then sought firms to build on the properties. Agricultural agents toured farms, providing advice on new hybrid seeds, crop diversification, and erosion prevention. The roads put together traveling exhibitions that toured the line, showing modern agricultural techniques. Agents on the trains and the speakers hired by the companies were often drawn from the staffs of the land grant agricultural colleges. The railroads sponsored chapters of the Future Farmers of America and other youth-oriented programs in an effort to increase production and balance crop output so that agricultural traffic to ports on the Great Lakes, the Gulf of Mexico, and the Pacific would be enhanced. Carriers in the Northeast had long been deeply involved in coal mining, especially for export; in the West emphasis was placed on copper, lead, and zinc. Timber and lumber represented major industrial activities in the South and the Northwest. The carriers participated in the massive harvests of pine forests in the South, but also initiated large-scale reforestation programs to provide a continuous source of traffic.

A transitory aspect of railroad history from the 1890s to 1930s was the rapid rise, then gradual disappearance, of electric streetcar lines and interurban systems that linked many of the nation's major cities. Existing as a transitional form of transportation between the era of the steam railway and the coming of the automobile, the electric railways provided low-cost, rapid, and clean transportation in America's major cities, linking downtowns to suburban housing developments. Streetcar lines allowed the city to grow beyond the distances people would generally walk and freed the streets of part of the pollution created by horse-drawn vehicles. Developers then began to build lines connecting cities to their hinterlands, using steam railroad standards for roadbeds and equipment. In the Midwest some traction systems rivaled railroads in quality of service and a few, like the Illinois Terminal, had extensive freight traffic and even operated sleeping cars. When passenger traffic on the streetcars and interurban systems was lost to buses and private cars during the 1920s, many lines were abandoned. Others, such as the Cincinnati & Lake Erie, invested in high-speed equipment and improved schedules, but only the temporary rise in traffic generated by World War II would prevent the almost total demise of these companies. After 1945 the interurbans and most electric streetcar lines would be abandoned; some would be replaced by buses. In the 1960s the light rail concept would return to vogue, and cities with systems still in place—Boston, Philadelphia, and Pittsburgh—would improve and extend them, while some cities—Atlanta, Buffalo, and San Francisco—would build entirely new electrified transit systems at an enormous cost. Intense competition destroyed these lines in their prime in the 1920s, and only massive tax subsidization would allow their return forty years later.

Throughout the 1920s the railroads generally improved and modernized their operations. New steam locomotive designs were introduced by the major builders—Baldwin, Lima, and American Locomotive Company—and the modern motive power increased efficiency, raised average speeds for passenger and freight trains, and reduced the need for double-headed trains and pusher locomotives in mountainous terrain. In a nearly $7 billion capital improvement program between 1923 and 1930 the carriers increased freight car capacities, length of freight trains, and the net tons carried by the average train. Passing sidings were constructed, new yards built, and heavier rail laid. The automatic block signaling systems were expanded to cover over 50,000 miles of line, thereby increasing safety standards and improving operating efficiency. The railroads also initiated an extremely efficient electronic dispatching system, Centralized Traffic Control, which employed a central dispatcher to control train movements over a particular stretch of track; the system created a major time saving. The coming of the Great Depression after 1929 drastically reduced this capital program, but most of the nation's railroads were in good physical condition prior to the economic chaos of the 1930s.

The Depression hit the nation's railway system hard. The depressed price of agricultural commodities throughout the 1920s had already harmed the Granger railroads in the Midwest and the carriers dependent upon farm products for traffic in the South and Southwest. As farm prices fell to catastrophic levels in 1930-1931, marginally successful carriers faced ruin. Between 1929 and 1932 tonnage and revenues for all railroads fell by half, and where they had carried 1,419 million tons of freight before the stock market crash, they transported only 679 million tons three years later. Management reduced expenses, stored equipment, furloughed workers, and cut dividends by 75 percent.

White- and blue-collar workers took salary and wage cuts, but to no avail. A number of companies formed bus and truck subsidiaries to generate local traffic and to meet the rising competition from privately owned highway carriers. Soon one-third of the railway mileage in the nation was served by bankrupt carriers and half of the nation's locomotives were stored—many as unserviceable. The net income of $977 million in 1929 became a loss of $122 million in 1932. The New Deal created the Emergency Railroad Transportation Act in 1933 to coordinate rail services and to end waste, but the results were negligible.

The railroads had lost their dominant position in transportation, and with the nation's economy in ruins their vulnerability became readily apparent. By 1939 receivers operated over 77,000 miles of lines of bankrupt carriers. The Erie and the New Haven in the East; the Seaboard Air Line in the South; the Chicago & North Western, Milwaukee Road, and Rock Island in the Midwest; the Frisco, Missouri Pacific, and Katy in the Southwest; and the Denver & Rio Grande Western and Western Pacific in the West joined other companies in the hands of the courts. Bowing to public pressure, the ICC refused virtually all requests for rate increases and even the profitable carriers saw their return on investment decline. The Railroad Credit Corporation, created to aid the carriers, loaned over $75 million to prevent companies from defaulting, but clearly the problem surpassed such emergency legislation. The Reconstruction Finance Corporation provided much greater support with some $512 million dollars in loans to eighty-one railroads to refinance debt and purchase cars and locomotives. Nevertheless, most railways faced perilous times between 1929 and 1939, and some "strong" firms like the Southern Railway and the Southern Pacific narrowly averted financial disaster. Not until the very end of the decade did the railways find much hope for economic recovery.

World War II dramatically altered the role of the railroads in the national economy. The rearmament program initiated in 1938-1939 increased traffic as the demand for coal, steel, petroleum, and related products accelerated. The Lend-Lease Act brought military goods to eastern ports and renewed economic activity helped return the country's rail system to profitability. Operating ratios fell below those of 1929 and revenues rose by almost 25 percent in 1941. With the United States almost assuming belligerent status, freight tonnage, even before Pearl Harbor, exceeded the peak set in 1918. The entry of the United States into the conflict brought the greatest prosperity to the rails since before World War I. The managers, determined not to repeat the mistakes of the Great War, cooperated fully with Ralph Budd, president of the Chicago, Burlington & Quincy, who became director of transportation in the Office of Emergency Management; later the Office of Defense Transportation coordinated the operations of the railroads. Without federal control, the railroads moved more freight each year from 1942 through 1945 than they had in 1918, and they did so with fewer freight and passenger cars, locomotives, and employees. The carriers moved 737 billion ton-miles in 1944, 300 percent more than in 1932. The railroads transported over 90 percent of the military traffic during the war, including 1 million barrels of oil moved daily to the east coast. Even the loss of over 350,000 employees to military service failed to reduce the carrying capacity of the railroads as they hired replacements often women—and raised wages to avert a threatened strike in 1941. The vast increase in traffic produced record profits and an average rate of return just under 5 percent. Despite higher taxes, the railroads were able to reduce their debts by almost $2 billion and several carriers were able to terminate receiverships. Whereas federal operation of the railroads during World War I had cost taxpayers $2 million per day, between 1942 and 1945 the carriers paid more than $3 million in taxes daily. The operation of the nation's rail system in World War II owed much of its success to the dedication of employees and management and to the essentially sound physical state of the properties.

The most significant technological change on the railways immediately followed the end of the war. As a consequence of their experiences with a small number of diesel-electric locomotives in coping with war-generated traffic demands, railway managers, with a few exceptions, determined to dieselize their locomotive fleets. Rudolph Diesel had designed an oil-powered engine in the 1890s, but not until the 1920s was the concept adapted to railway use. Mechanical developments in marine transportation led several manufacturers to experiment with diesel engines in self-propelled rail cars. The engines created electricity by turning generators, and the current was conveyed to traction motors on the axles of the wheels. By 1925 the Central Railroad of New Jersey operated a diesel-powered switching locomotive which proved quieter, cleaner, and more efficient than steam switchers. Not until 1934, when the Chicago, Burlington & Quincy ordered an articulated, streamlined passenger train with diesel-electric power from the E. M. Budd Company, was the concept applied to road power. The Burlington Zephyr toured the nation and made a record-setting speed run from Denver to Chicago. Passenger response was excellent, and soon other Zephyrs joined the original unit. The Union Pacific ordered its City of Salina streamliner with distillate-fueled power, but other carriers adopted diesel fuel. The Electro-Motive Division of General Motors developed separate locomotive units for freight service which were used experimentally by several railroads. In 1941 the Santa Fe began regular use of diesel freight locomotives; it was soon joined by the Southern, Great Northern, and Milwaukee Road.

Diesel locomotives cost far more than steam power to acquire, but operational savings came quickly. The diesels did not need the vast amounts of water steam locomotives required, a significant factor in parts of the West where water was scarce and of poor quality. The railroads discovered that the diesels required far less maintenance, had a high level of availability, were fuel efficient, and could operate 1,000 miles without servicing. The diesel was at least one-third more efficient than steam and harmed the track far less than the steam locomotives did. The manufacturers and the carriers also found that reversing the traction motors on downgrades allowed the locomotives to act as brakes. Dynamic braking saved millions of dollars in freight car brake shoes and some companies ordered units so equipped.

The experiments of the war years led to massive orders of diesels in peacetime. Electro-Motive, American Locomotive Company, Fairbanks-Morse, and even Baldwin Locomotive Works began to manufacture a wide range of diesel locomotives for switching, passenger, and freight service. By 1955 the carriers had spent $3.3 billion for 21,000 new locomotives, 95 percent of which were diesel units. One major railroad after another proudly announced "100 percent dieselization," and even steam holdouts such as the coal-carrying Norfolk

& Western succumbed to the efficiency of the diesel. By 1960 the era of the steam locomotive in the United States had ended.

The introduction and adoption of diesel power exacerbated conflicts between labor and management. One of the major savings management projected from dieselization was the elimination of firemen from locomotive crews: the coal- and oil-powered steam locomotives had required a fireman to maintain the flow of fuel to the engine's firebox; the diesel engines had no such requirement. But when the carriers sought to terminate the redundant firemen, a battle raged for almost three decades as the firemen argued that they should retain their positions in the interest of "safety." The issue of the firemen in diesel engines came to epitomize the labor problem on the nation's railroads.

Management operated under two constraints in labor relations: stringent federal regulations and well-organized and tenacious railway brotherhoods. Federal railway labor legislation passed in the 1930s provided for detailed arbitration and mediation practices. The carriers wanted to use dieselization and mechanization of track maintenance to substantially reduce labor costs, while the unions fought to retain jobs, obtain wage increases, and maintain an intricate system of work rules that had been developed during the steam era. For example, a 1919 rule gave all locomotive crews a day's wages for each 100 miles covered, regardless of the time the trip took. Faster schedules gave full wages to crews who "labored" only three or four hours in a diesel locomotive; a Santa Fe freight train from Chicago to Los Angeles took fifty-one hours to make the trip, requiring seventeen crew changes and an average of more than three persons per crew. Management had agreed to such work rules in a time of labor shortage and had assumed that additional costs could always be passed along to shippers; with growing competition that assumption proved fallacious.

The Canadian railroads operated without firemen following a recommendation by a Royal Commission in 1957. The Florida East Coast Railway engaged in a long and sometimes bloody strike with the unions over the labor issue, and in 1963 began to operate with nonunion, two-person crews and 300-mile crew districts. In the 1950s and 1960s several committees and commissioners under federal auspices urged changes in work rules, including the

gradual elimination of firemen. In 1964 an agreement was reached to use attrition to end the presence of firemen and to offer younger firemen other job opportunities such as promotion to engineer. But other major labor issues remained unresolved.

As their membership declined from 1.7 million in 1916 to 841,000 in 1958, the major railroad unions reorganized, with the Brotherhood of Locomotive Engineers and the United Transportation Union becoming the leading bargaining units. Eleven smaller unions also had railway employees as members. The unions opposed work rule changes, particularly the elimination of cabooses from freight trains and the installation of rear signaling devices. Their refusal to bargain on some work rule issues meant that labor costs for the railroads remained high compared with general industrial wages: in 1985 the average railway worker earned $34,064 per year. Such labor-intensive operations led management to explore every technological advance that would reduce costs and bring higher levels of operating efficiency.

The revolution in transportation that occurred during the six decades after 1920 exceeded in magnitude that which took place between 1820 and 1920. The internal-combustion engine, inexpensive gasoline, and mass production placed the automobile in the hands of virtually every family, and, as a result, the long-distance passenger train and mass transit almost died. Expansion of the federal and state highway systems provided intercity trucks with the means to compete with, and then largely surpass, freight trains as carriers for all but bulk commodities. By the 1950s airlines provided expensive but speedy service between major cites, and with the advent of jet-powered aircraft they were able to fly millions of travelers at relatively low fares. Pipelines, barge operators, and intercoastal shipping companies carried larger and larger volumes of petroleum products, coal, and grain. The federal government subsidized these transportation forms with improved highways and waterways and often with direct cash subsidies, yet it developed no plan for an integrated national transportation system. As a consequence, large segments of the great rail network, which had pioneered in big business, fell into physical disarray and fiscal chaos.

After 1945 the ICC raised railroad freight rates only with great reluctance. An arcane and archaic rate structure was allowed to continue in the face of mounting competition from trucks, pipelines, and barges. Where the railroads were able to use efficiencies to produce lower costs, the ICC often refused to allow the carriers to *reduce* rates because of protests from operators of other modes of transportation about the negative impact it would have on them. The Transportation Act of 1958 sought to prevent this line of argument before the ICC, and it also gave the ICC, rather than the states, authority to approve discontinuance of passenger trains. These provisions offered only modest reform.

The plight of portions of the rail network and the success of other carriers can be seen in the divergent histories of the Pennsylvania Railroad and the Union Pacific Railroad. In the 1890s leading railway security analyst S. F. Van Oss declared, "The Pennsylvania is in every respect the standard railway of America." He praised its management, locomotives, cars, track, terminals, and operations. The Pennsylvania made large profits and came to control the Norfolk & Western, Wabash, Lehigh Valley, and other former competitors in the East. The Pennsylvania prospered in the 1920s and during the Great Depression electrified its mainlines from Washington and Harrisburg through Philadelphia to New York. World War II brought record traffic volume and even greater prosperity. But after 1945 problems developed. The Pennsylvania paid high state and local property taxes on its yards, terminals, and trackage; competing truck lines were taxed only on their trucks. Management spent hundreds of millions of dollars on new streamlined passenger trains even as the subsidized airlines took away passengers. The railroad remained labor intensive, and federally approved wage increases rose faster than freight rates. Industry fled the Northeast to the South and West, and traffic on the line declined drastically. Expensive terminal operations, short hauls for freight, the cost of dieselization, huge losses from passenger and commuter services, and managerial laxity caused the Pennsylvania to fail rapidly. By the 1960s the Pennsylvania was surviving only because of real estate holdings and dividends from securities of other companies.

The Pennsylvania divested itself of its holdings in other carriers so that it could merge with its longtime rival, the New York Central, but the Penn Central merger of 1968 proved disastrous. The former Pennsylvania management ("the Red Team") and the New York Central managers ("the Green Team") refused to cooperate; even their computers were incompatible. The merger agreement prevented a reduction in employees or significant changes in the work rules on the combined system, thus precluding savings in labor costs. Losses mounted, and bankruptcy came in 1970. The federal government, moving to prevent the collapse of the nation's largest railway, created Conrail (the Consolidated Rail Corporation) in 1976 to salvage the Penn Central and other bankrupt lines in the Northeast. Over $4 billion in federal loans and grants were required to keep Conrail operating. Yet the vastly expanded Norfolk & Western and the Chesapeake & Ohio System, operating in the same region, remained strong, profitable railroads, as did the Union Pacific in the West.

Even as Van Oss was calling the Pennsylvania the "standard" railroad in the 1890s, the Union Pacific seemingly stood in ruins. Debilitated financially, threatened competitively by the Southern Pacific, and blocked from reaching California, it appeared a hopeless wreck. But E. H. Harriman of the Illinois Central bought control of the Union Pacific after it entered bankruptcy in 1897 and rebuilt the property. New locomotives and cars moved over revamped tracks, and Harriman acquired a line to Los Angeles. Although Harriman's efforts to create a transportation monopoly in the West failed, he made the Union Pacific a rail showcase. The company prospered in the 1920s, and World War II brought greater profits. The postwar era saw dramatic changes in the corporation. Because of its land grant, the Union Pacific held substantial coal, petroleum, and timber reserves which the railway began to exploit. It purchased a large independent oil firm and created a holding company for both its rail and nonrail properties. The company ended most passenger services, took advantage of its long-haul freight lines, especially for piggyback trailer traffic, and by 1980 was earning 16 percent on its equity.

The relative success of the Union Pacific was repeated on the Santa Fe, Southern Pacific, Southern, Burlington Northern, and a few other railroads. The rail industry as a whole declined, however, and by 1980 some lines in the Midwest were following several northeastern carriers into the federal bankruptcy courts. The plight of the nation's railroads received considerable attention, but little was done.

In 1945 the railroads had hauled 60 percent of freight ton-miles; by 1980 they carried about 35 percent. The moribund Interstate Commerce Commission allowed a few freight rate increases, but the railroads' return on equity was still less than 1 percent; twenty-one of the seventy-one largest railroads in the United States lost money in 1970. The newly created Department of Transportation sought to devise a national rail plan, but political interference, labor opposition to consolidation, and bureaucratic ineptitude precluded meaningful efforts to rescue the weak elements in the industry and strengthen the profitable carriers. In the 1970s the federal government spent over $100 billion for highways and more than $15 billion for waterways, but the railroads could raise only $5 billion in private investment during the decade as capital became more difficult to obtain because of falling profit levels. The carriers invested heavily in new technology in an effort to regain lost traffic and profitability.

The great advantage of the railroads is the inherent efficiency of flanged wheels on steel rails: the railroads *pull* freight, they do not carry it. To exploit this efficient concept the Association of American Railroads, and the carriers individually, have developed research facilities to study and create new approaches for the industry. Two hundred standing committees of the AAR direct research on rails, roller bearings, safe transportation of hazardous materials, accounting procedures, and a myriad of related matters. As early as 1914 the railroads began to substitute the radio for their elaborate telegraph and telephone systems as their basic means of communication. They installed radios in locomotives, cabooses, and yard offices. Later television cameras were placed in yards to view passing freight cars for operating and safety problems. In the 1970s the railways installed thousands of miles of microwave communications to enhance operations. Electronic devices were used in yards and at points along mainlines to detect problems with brakes, wheels, and bearings. Other devices classified and sorted cars in yards and assembled trains. These improvements saved some operating dollars, but much energy was directed at mechanization of maintenance procedures.

Led by D. William Brosnan, president of the Southern Railway, the companies began to mechanize track maintenance in the 1950s. Equipment suppliers and the carriers themselves designed machines to lay rails and to reballast the roadbed. Automatic tie replacement and powered spike hammers reduced the size of track crews. The railroads put the crews in trucks and dispatched them by radio to work sites. Huge welding machines placed long ribbons of welded rail on the ties, providing smoother track and ending the problems of rail joints. The savings easily paid for the purchase of these machines. The railroads were also early users of computers. The companies dealt with mountains of paper-train orders, ICC reports, locomotive and freight car locations, and bills of lading. The managers saw computers as a means to reduce paper flow, keep track of equipment, improve accounting procedures, and discover cost and profit margins of traffic. Sophisticated information systems on the major railroads quickly led to greater efficiency and substantial reductions in costs.

Technological change altered dramatically the physical appearance of the railroads after 1960. The carriers began to eliminate small-town freight depots and place freight agents in mobile offices equipped with radios. As traffic changes took place, cattle cars and tank cars for crude oil disappeared from freight trains, and even the common boxcar became obsolete. In 1983 the United Transportation Union agreed to the gradual elimination of $80,000 cabooses and their replacement with "black boxes" attached to the last car to monitor braking systems, a saving of $400 million per year. The passing of a long freight train at a crossing in the mid 1980s produced a sight far different from that of the 1930s or 1940s.

As early as the 1920s railroads began to lose substantial volumes of traffic to trucks, especially less-than-carload (LCL) business. Taking a page from circus practices, the Chicago Great Western placed freight truck trailers on flatcars and moved them from Chicago to the Twin Cities in the mid 1930s. World War II halted this development, but in the 1950s several roads invested in specially designed flatcars for highway trailers. Trailers-on-Flatcars (TOFC)–or piggyback–traffic grew slowly, then soared with the oil embargo in 1974. Special freight trains on high-speed schedules moved TOFC loads to terminals where unloading ramps with highway cabs waited. The railroads then sought container traffic with Container-on-Flatcar (COFC) equipment and subsequently added double-stacked containers with intermodal service from docks on the Atlantic or Gulf of Mexico to the Pacific. The railroads became a "land bridge" between the Orient and Europe.

The carriers introduced unit trains dedicated to one cargo–coal, wheat, sulfur, or chemicals–that moved in continuous runs from the production site to docks, generators, or factories. The unit trains often utilized specially designed equipment, such as the "Big John" grain cars, that allowed for substantial reductions in freight rates. To win back traffic in new automobiles that had largely been lost to trucks, the railroads placed trilevel automobile racks in fast freight trains. Many of the delays in freight service occurred in yards or at interchanges from one line to another at gateway cities such as Chicago, Kansas City, St. Louis, and New Orleans; to move the new TOFC, COFC, and unit trains more rapidly, the carriers instituted "run through trains" that stopped only for crew changes and retained the locomotives of the originating carrier. A "run through" might originate in Seattle on the Burlington Northern and arrive in Atlanta on another carrier without the cars ever having been blocked in yards and reclassified en route.

Railroads had to adopt these new approaches to survive. Trucks carried 5.4 percent of intercity freight in 1944; with the interstate highway system nearly complete they had expanded their market share to 24.1 percent in 1984. The railways fought back with freight trains running at 65 to 70 miles per hour. They experimented with truck trailers having both highway tires and steel railroad wheels for total flexibility on the road and on the tracks. But it was obvious to some executives that the acquisition of new equipment had to be related to more effective marketing of transportation; the key to success lay with the selling of the product, not solely with technological innovation. A few railways opened traffic offices in London and Tokyo to solicit land-bridge business. And by the 1980s some carriers had acquired pipelines, barge lines, and trucking companies and had invested in air freight forwarding to obtain a total intermodal position.

America's railroads had learned from their experience with passenger service that markets could melt away and that the investment of millions of dollars in equipment did not guarantee success. After World War II the railroads purchased new diesel passenger locomotives and streamlined dome cars, dining cars, lounges, and sleeping cars and initiated

new trains on fast schedules. The Great Northern, for example, spent $9 million to upgrade its Empire Builder and Oriental Limited even as the New York Central spent millions more to modernize its vast fleet. The California Zephyr from Chicago to San Francisco epitomized the postwar streamliners that fewer and fewer passengers rode. Ticket sales plummeted as Americans turned to the highway and the air. The 897 million passengers of 1945 declined to 413 million in 1957. By 1959 dining cars alone lost $29 million for the railroads and company after company began to drop trains, reduce service, and eliminate equipment. The public howled, but did not purchase tickets. Some railroads, including the Chicago, Burlington & Quincy, Santa Fe, Kansas City Southern, and Atlantic Coast Line, refused to give up on the passenger train; but after investing millions with no profitable return in sight, other turned to the regulatory agencies for relief. When the states refused to grant requests for discontinuances, Congress in 1958 gave the ICC authority to approve the elimination of trains. Within a decade 60 percent of passenger service had ended and one-third of all passenger routes had been abandoned.

Edna St. Vincent Millay wrote "Yet there isn't a train I wouldn't take, no matter where it's going"; but the American traveler abandoned the rails, and in 1969 the Association of American Railroads asked the federal government to follow the lead of other industrial nations and subsidize the remaining passenger trains. The end of mail traffic by the Post Office in the 1960s had cost the lines their last major source of revenue. In 1971 Congress created the National Railroad Passenger Corporation, commonly known as Amtrak, to operate virtually all of the nation's remaining passenger service. Amtrak inherited a varied collection of locomotives, equipment, and depots, in generally poor condition. The federal government provided subsidies to Amtrak to buy a new generation of passenger locomotives and cars, to upgrade the Washington-New York-Boston corridor, and to build new depots or refurbish stations. By 1985 Amtrak carried 20.7 million passengers and had gross revenues of $650 million, but it produced annual losses which Congress had to defray. City, state, or regional transit authorities took over commuter train operations.

When World War II ended, the railroads stood on the brink of a new era of prosperity, or so management believed. The employment of diesel locomotives during the war proved that this new motive power was far more efficient. The huge number of passengers carried during the war and the great successes of the stainless steel streamliners introduced in late 1930s led management to invest millions of dollars in new equipment, but to no avail. The American love affair with the automobile became even more passionate as the federal highway system expanded and the automobile manufacturers retooled for postwar production. The sleeping car trade also melted away as scheduled airline service expanded, using surplus planes purchased at low cost from the federal government. Management also invested in improved physical plant, more CTC, and continued to replace wooden freight equipment with steel cars. The vast growth of the trucking industry took away less-than-carload business and much high-revenue traffic. The network of pipelines grew during the war, reducing petroleum traffic and giving the nation access to natural gas. As a consequence, coal traffic on the railroads tumbled drastically. By the 1960s the railroads carried only a quarter of intercity passengers and less than half of intercity freight. The industry was in serious trouble.

The federal, state, and local governments invested billions of tax dollars in competing transportation facilities and subsidies after 1946, and thus played a significant role in hastening the deterioration of the rail system. After the Federal Aid Road Act of 1916 was enacted, the state and federal governments extended paved roads across the nation. The number of privately owned automobiles, trucks, and buses grew as the highway network was improved. By 1929, three-fourths of intercity travelers moved by automobile. The Greyhound network and regional bus lines also drew away passenger traffic despite the introduction of air conditioning, low-priced tourist trains and accommodations, and faster train schedules. Over 3 million miles of highways opened every market to trucks, which provided greater flexibility, often lower rates, and less damage to delicate products and animals. The railroads had already lost 10 percent of intercity freight to trucks before World War II. The highways were paid for by user taxes and from general revenues. The same sources subsidized air and water traffic.

Dieselization, the utilization of new technologies, the introduction of new services, the renewed emphasis on marketing, and the end of money-losing passenger business failed to prevent a massive restructuring of the nation's railroads. Railway mileage had peaked at 254,000 in 1916; it declined to 211,459 in 1955 and to 151,988 in 1984. The shrinkage of the rail network reflected the "merger mania" of the 1970s and 1980s.

After the failure of the ICC to carry out a restructuring of the railways in 1920s, there were few successful mergers until the late 1940s. The ICC refused to allow mergers that were not end-to-end, arguing that parallel mergers reduced competition. But the competition after 1945 was not between railroads but between the railroads and other modes of transportation. The carriers pleaded for the opportunity to merge and thereby eliminate duplicate yards, reduce excess trackage, centralize accounting functions, and meld marketing operations. The savings generated would be, they asserted, the difference between profitability and bankruptcy.

Slowly the ICC approved a few mergers, and some rationalization of the nation's railways occurred. In 1947 the Gulf, Mobile & Ohio joined with the Alton to create a new Chicago-New Orleans route and the Chesapeake & Ohio was allowed to merge with the Pere Marquette, which it already controlled. The first major change in philosophy took place in 1959 when the Norfolk & Western and the Virginian, which paralleled each other from the coalfields of West Virginia to the Atlantic at Norfolk, were allowed to merge. A flood tide of mergers followed as the Erie married the Delaware, Lackawanna & Western, the Atlantic Coast Line and the Seaboard Air Line joined, and the Chesapeake & Ohio pulled the Baltimore & Ohio and Western Maryland into its Chessie System. But the ICC refused to allow some mergers, and the results proved devastating. The Union Pacific and Southern Pacific proposed to divide the Chicago, Rock Island & Pacific, with the Union Pacific gaining direct access to Chicago from Omaha and the Southern Pacific acquiring a line to Kansas City and St. Louis. For years the ICC held hearings, collected data, studied the scheme, and then said no. The Rock Island later declared bankruptcy and was dismembered.

The so-called Granger railroads of the Midwest competed for similar traffic, suffered the vagaries of American agricultural production, and lost revenues to independent truckers. Five railroads operated from Chicago to Omaha, at least three too many. The Chicago & North Western absorbed two other Grangers, formed a holding company, was spun off to become an employee-owned carrier, and then became a holding company again. The Illinois Central merged with the Gulf, Mobile & Ohio and subsequently sold or abandoned well over half its combined mileage.

These changes paled in comparison with the dramatic alteration of the railroads in the Northeast. In 1968 the Pennsylvania Railroad merged with its ancient rival, the New York Central, but merger proved not a panacea, but a disaster. A 21,000-mile system with 70,000 employees and $4 billion in assets could not generate revenues to pay for excess workers to operate trains of empty cars over deteriorating trackage on which it paid exorbitant state and local taxes. Some of its neighbors—the Erie Lackawanna, Lehigh Valley, Central of New Jersey, and Reading—also went under. The railway system serving much of industrialized America had failed.

In 1974 the federal government created the United States Railway Association, which formed the Consolidated Rail Corporation, or Conrail, to take over the Northeastern carriers in the hands of receivers. Conrail started with 24,000 miles of lines; the federal government spent $7 billion to rehabilitate Conrail and to cover its initial losses. Under L. Stanley Crane, Conrail shed redundant trackage, obtained work rule changes and agreements for reduced wages from employees, and benefited from a general economic recovery in its service area. In 1987 the federal government concluded a strenuous effort to return Conrail, which by then was down to 11,900 miles, to private ownership.

The Staggers Act of 1980 provided significant relief for the railroads in rate development as the federal government moved into an era of deregulation. Indeed, there were proposals to abolish the ICC itself, but the commission protested that not all of its policies had failed. The creation of the Burlington Northern and its subsequent merger with the St. Louis-San Francisco (Frisco) had been successful, as had the merger of the Chessie System with the Seaboard Coast Line. Two of the nation's most profitable carriers, the Southern and the Norfolk & Western, merged as the Norfolk Southern and then acquired a national moving company, a major position in Piedmont Airlines, and other intermodal interests. But in 1986 the ICC rejected a proposal to allow the Santa Fe to join with the Southern Pacific, despite the negative impact of other mergers on those two carriers.

The 1980s brought giant mergers, massive line abandonments, and shrinking locomotive and equipment fleets. There was also a significant resurgence of short-line carriers as entrepreneurs bought or leased lines slated for abandonment. Operating customer-oriented service with nonunion crews, the new short lines often proved profitable on trackage long operated at a loss by the trunk lines. Railway managers in an era of deregulation continued line rationalization, sought new technologies, and placed a major emphasis on marketing transportation. There had been a revolution in the railroad industry, and the revolutionary period had certainly not ended by the late 1980s.

—Keith L. Bryant, Jr.
Texas A&M University

Encyclopedia of American Business History and Biography

Railroads in the Age of Regulation, 1900-1980

Adamson Act

The Adamson Act grew out of a threatened national rail strike in 1916. The railroad brotherhoods demanded an eight-hour workday at a time when the standard was ten; management balked. At a White House conference, President Woodrow Wilson warned leaders of both sides that a strike could retard the administration's drive for military preparedness and bring on a general economic crisis. When management resisted a solution proposed by the White House, the brotherhoods' leadership issued an order for 400,000 workers to walk out nationwide in September. The president pressed Congress for legislation.

Introduced by Representative William C. Adamson of Georgia on August 31, the eight-hour bill passed the House by 239 to 56; subsequently, the Senate adopted it 43 to 28. Wilson signed it on September 3, averting the strike. The Adamson Eight-Hour Act provided that as of January 1, 1917, eight hours would "be deemed a day's work" on railroads in interstate commerce. A three-member commission, reporting to the president, would be appointed to "observe the operation and effects" of the eight-hour day. Meanwhile, wages would not fall despite the cut in hours. The measure became an item of major controversy in the 1916 presidential campaign.

Management's legal challenge to the act failed. The Supreme Court upheld the legislation by a five-to-four vote in *Wilson* v. *New* (March 19, 1917). For the first time in a great national industry, and as a consequence of direct federal intervention, eight hours became the standard workday.

References:

K. Austin Kerr, *American Railroad Politics 1914-1920: Rates, Wages, and Efficiency* (Pittsburgh: University of Pittsburgh Press, 1968), pp. 33-34, 49, 53;

Arthur S. Link, *Wilson: Campaigns for Progressivism and Peace: 1916-1917* (Princeton: Princeton University Press, 1965);

Albro Martin, *Enterprise Denied: Origins of the Decline of American Railroads, 1897-1917* (New York: Columbia University Press, 1971), pp. 311, 332-335.

—John J. Broesamle

Akron, Canton & Youngstown Railroad

by H. Roger Grant

University of Akron

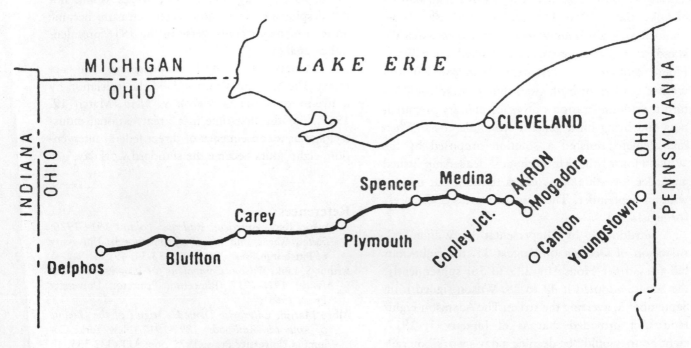

Map of the Akron, Canton & Youngstown Railroad (1930)

The Akron, Canton & Youngstown Railroad (AC&Y), an Ohio switching and bridge road (that is, a road with through traffic from one end to the other), was incorporated in June 1907 by a wealthy cement entrepreneur, Zebulon W. "Zeb" Davis, in order to connect the three northeastern Ohio cities of the company's corporate name. Track work did not begin until 1912, and then the AC&Y built only in the Akron area. Its 7.7 miles of east-west main line linked Mogadore and a connection with the Wheeling & Lake Erie (W&LE) to Copley Junction and the Northern Ohio Railway (NO).

By World War I Davis had lost interest in the property; the likelihood of the road reaching either Youngstown or Canton, the site of his cement plant, seemed remote. Thus an Akron group headed by rubber industrialist Frank A. Seiberling acquired the AC&Y and subsequently leased the Northern Ohio. The AC&Y-NO "system" ideally served the road's

principal shipper, Seiberling's Goodyear Tire & Rubber Company. Carloads of tires moved over the AC&Y-NO to Columbus Grove, Ohio, and from there over the Detroit, Toledo & Ironton to the "Motor City" and its automobile assembly plants. Also, unit coal trains rolled over the W&LE from Goodyear mines near Adena, Ohio, to the Akron rubber shops. On January 14, 1944, the AC&Y officially merged with the NO, although the companies had been operated as a single corporation since 1920.

The road generally prospered. Traffic consisted largely of Goodyear products; rock from quarries near Carey, Ohio; and interchange tonnage, much of which came from the New York, Chicago & St. Louis Railroad (Nickel Plate) at Delphos, Ohio, the AC&Y's western terminus. In 1964 the Nickel Plate entered the rapidly expanding Norfolk & Western (N&W); fearing the loss of bridge business, the AC&Y's owners, who included Seiberling's heirs, also sold out to the N&W. Until January 1, 1982, when the AC&Y corporation was dissolved, the N&W operated the road as a wholly owned subsidiary, although the AC&Y proudly claimed: "We're 100% locally managed."

Reference:

H. Roger Grant, "Land Development in the Middle West: The Case of the Akron, Canton & Youngstown Railroad, 1913-1925," *The Old Northwest,* 1 (December 1975): 359-373.

Alton Railroad

by John F. Stover

Purdue University

Map of the Alton Railroad (1930)

The first railroad projected as a route between Chicago and St. Louis was the Chicago & Mississippi, chartered in 1847. The first track on the line was laid in 1852, and under the direction of Henry Dwight the 220-mile road from Joliet to Alton, Illinois, was completed by 1854. South of Alton riverboats gave service downstream to St. Louis. In 1859 George Pullman provided some of the first sleeping cars for service on the line. The road never paid any dividends in the 1850s, and in 1857 it was reorganized as the St. Louis, Alton & Chicago, with Joel A. Matterson as president. Later the line was extended to East St. Louis and to Chicago; in 1861 it was reorganized as the Chicago & Alton Railroad. In 1868 the Chicago & Alton was a line of 280 miles with revenues of $4.5 million. In 1878 the Chicago & Alton leased the Kansas City, St. Louis & Chicago, which provided the shortest rail route from Chicago to Kansas City. During the 1880s and 1890s it was a prosperous road paying regular dividends, as high as 8 percent even during the depression of the mid 1890s. By 1898 the Chicago & Alton was a well-managed 840-mile line with revenues of $6.3 million, an operating ratio of 62, and a capital structure of $40 million.

Between 1888 and 1905 a syndicate led by E. H. Harriman, George J. Gould, and James Stillman acquired most of the common stock of the Chicago & Alton. Through financial manipulations the syndicate leaders increased the road's financial structure to about $114 million, spending very little of the money for improvements but keeping a major share for themselves as private profits. Beginning in 1912 the Chicago & Alton had annual deficits almost every year, finally going into receivership in 1922. The Baltimore & Ohio (B&O) purchased the road at a foreclosure sale in 1929, and in 1931 incorporated it as the Alton Railroad. For twelve years the Alton was operated under the management of the B&O but still had operating deficits nearly every year. During the early 1940s several midwestern lines considered purchasing the Alton but all finally decided against it. In 1945 the Gulf, Mobile & Ohio (GM&O) paid the B&O about $1.2 million for the Alton stock and all the B&O claims against the line. The acquisition, completed in May 1947, gave the GM&O connections to both Chicago and Kansas City. Twenty-five years later the GM&O merged with the Illinois Central to become the Illinois Central Gulf Railroad.

References:

George H. Drury, *The Historical Guide to North American Railroads* (Milwaukee: Kalmbach, 1985), p. 17;

Harold U. Faulkner, *The Decline of Laissez Faire, 1897-1917* (New York: Rinehart, 1951), pp. 199-200;

John F. Stover, *Iron Road to the West: American Railroads in the 1850s* (New York: Columbia University Press, 1978), p. 147.

Amtrak

by Arthur L. Lloyd

Amtrak

Amtrak's Empire Builder with Superliner bi-level cars (Courtesy Amtrak)

The National Railroad Passenger Corporation, trade name Amtrak, is a "hybrid" (private/public) corporation, the controlling stock held by the United States government through the U.S. Department of Transportation. Amtrak's business is the pro- vision of intercity rail passenger service, other than commuter service, in the major markets of the United States. Although it receives financial support from the federal government, Amtrak is not a govern- ment agency; it is a corporation structured and managed like other large companies, and successfully competes with other modes of transportation in the marketplace. The management of Amtrak is committed to a businesslike approach to the services provided.

Amtrak was started because the privately owned railroads were phasing out their passenger business, raising the possibility that the United States would be the only industrial nation in the world lacking an intercity rail passenger network. The railroad was created by the National Railroad Passenger Act of 1970 to take over the remaining routes and organize a rebuilding program. This program has been a success: ridership since 1971 has nearly doubled, and the system has been modernized and refitted with new cars and locomotives.

Out of a route system of over 24,000 miles, Amtrak owns the 2,611 track miles in the Northeast Corridor (Washington, D.C.-Boston; New Haven-Springfield; Philadelphia-Harrisburg); a 12-mile connection near Albany, New York; and track between Porter and Kalamazoo, Michigan. On all other routes, Amtrak operates over the tracks of twenty privately owned railroads and compensates the railroads for their services. Under contract, these railroads furnish maintenance services and are responsible for the condition of the roadbed and coordinating the flow of traffic.

In 1986 Amtrak employed approximately 24,000 persons; it operated an average of 240 trains per day serving 528 stations in 44 states. Almost 21 million passengers were carried that year, making Amtrak the sixth largest transporter of passengers in the United States.

Operation started on May 1, 1971, with an antiquated fleet of equipment inherited from the railroads; some cars were over thirty years old. In 1975 the company began receiving diesel locomotives with electric power for train heating and air conditioning and started to phase out its older diesel engines, which had used boilers to generate steam for heating the cars. Some 642 cars built by the Budd

Company of Philadelphia and 284 bi-level "Superliner" cars constructed by Pullman-Standard of Chicago had been delivered through 1986. Additionally, the company shops at Beech Grove, Indiana, had rebuilt the best of the older cars. By 1987 all trains west of Chicago operated with new cars, and all of the trains had new or completely refurbished all-electric equipment.

To further increase efficiency and productivity, reduce costs, and finance growth, Amtrak continually scrutinizes its largest area of expense–labor. In contracts signed in 1985, the various labor unions made concessions on the issues of antiquated work rules, dual bases of pay, and protective agreements were addressed. In 1986 the company took over the engineers, conductors, and crew members who had previously worked for the track-owning railroads; in the takeover, pay was changed from miles traveled to an hourly basis. This system had been set up in 1983 when the employees on the Amtrak-owned Northeast Corridor lines were taken over.

Amtrak's on-time performance has steadily improved to an average of 85 percent. Ridership continues to increase; the company is the only non airline member of the Airlines Reporting Corporation, which represents almost all travel agents in the United States.

In 1986 64% of Amtrak's budget came from passenger fares and 36% from Federal subsidy. This revenue/cost ratio has consistently improved since 1971. The company's goal is to decrease dependence on the taxpayers. Presidents of Amtrak have been: Roger Lewis from 1971 to 1975; Paul Reistrup from 1975 to 1977; Alan S. Boyd from 1977 to 1981; and W. Graham Claytor, Jr., since 1981.

References:
Harold A. Edmonson, *Journey to Amtrak* (Milwaukee: Kalmbach, 1972);

Fred W. Frailey, *Zephyrs, Chiefs & Other Orphans* (Godfrey, Ill.: RPC Publications, 1977).

Association of American Railroads

by Wallace W. Abbey

Association of American Railroads

The railroads of the United States are independent, separately—and, for the most part, privately—owned, competing entities. Because of the nature of the transportation services they provide and the cooperative manner in which they must provide them, the individual railroads must be able to function together as a system without violating laws that prohibit unfair or collusive business practices. The Association of American Railroads (AAR) is the "joint agent" through which the railroads coordinate their cooperation.

The AAR's predecessors go back to the Master Car Builders' Association, which was formed in 1867 to promote the standardization of freight car designs. In 1883 the railroads, working together but without a formal organization, spearheaded the successful effort to reduce the nation's 100 local time zones to today's four national zones.

The AAR was formed on October 12, 1934, on the recommendation of the Federal Coordinator of Transportation (appointed under the Emergency Railroad Transportation Act of 1933 to deal with railroad problems caused by the Great Depression) that the railroads form a "more perfect union." As of July 1987 the AAR had 121 members, including all major freight-carrying railroads in the United States and Amtrak. The principal railroads of Canada and Mexico and many foreign and small domestic railroads are associate or special members, although the principal coordinating organization for small railroads is the American Short Line Railroad Association. AAR member railroads do approximately 95 percent of the rail freight business in the United States on approximately 95 percent of the nation's trackage and employ 92 percent of all railroad workers.

AAR headquarters is in Washington, D.C. It has major research and test facilities in Pueblo, Colorado, where it operates the Transportation Test Center of the United States Department of Transportation as both a public and private testing facility, and in Chicago it also has a network of field representatives and inspectors. Its activities are governed by a board of directors consisting of chief executives of both large and small freight-carrying railroads in the United States. The chief executives of Amtrak and of one or the other of Canada's two principal railroads are ex officio members.

The AAR deals with the railroads' mutual concerns in the areas of operations, maintenance, safety, research and testings, economics, finance, accounting, data systems, and public affairs; represents the industry's position before Congress, regulatory agencies, and the federal courts; promotes favorable public attitudes about railroads; and encourages innovation on the part of suppliers of technology and equipment to the railroad industry. While it is not a decision-making body for the railroads, the AAR provides headquarters, staff, and continuity for the committees of railroad officers and executives that do guide the industry in joint matters.

The activities and services of the AAR affect all railroads, whether they are members or not. For example, 474 railroads subscribed to the AAR's code of freight car rental rules in 1985.

The AAR is a not-for-profit organization, but it has a wholly owned subsidiary, RAILINC Corporation, that operates as a profit-making business. RAILINC was formed in 1982 to provide the railroad industry with telecommunications networks, data clearinghouses, and data-processing services. RAILINC's facilities make it possible, for example, for a railroad to know the location and condition of its freight cars even when they are in service on another railroad.

Approximately 790 persons were employed by the AAR and RAILINC in 1985. The majority—435—worked in the AAR's Washington headquarters. Another 215 worked at the Transportation Test Center at Pueblo, 95 at the Chicago Technical Center, and the remainder across the United States and Canada.

Archives:

The only publicly available documents of the Association of American Railroads are the association's annual reports.

Atchison, Topeka & Santa Fe Railway

by Keith L. Bryant, Jr.

Texas A&M University

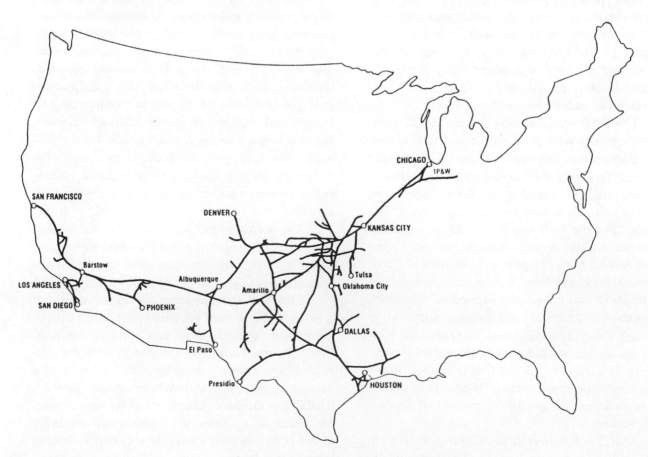

Map of the Atchison, Topeka & Santa Fe

Founded in Kansas in 1859 by Cyrus K. Holiday as the Atchison & Topeka Railroad, the Atchison, Topeka & Santa Fe Railway (ATSF) became one of the largest and most profitable railroads in the United States. Holiday dreamed of a line connecting Kansas with the Pacific Ocean in California, the Gulf of Mexico, Mexico City, and the legendary city of Santa Fe, New Mexico. While the Santa Fe, as it is popularly known, did not reach Mexico City, by 1888 it had built to the Pacific and the Gulf and expanded east to Chicago. Initially the ATSF built west from Topeka, Kansas, to capture the cattle trade from Texas at Wichita and Dodge City. The company encouraged the immigration of farmers to Kansas—especially farmers from Russia, who introduced winter wheat. The line reached Pueblo, Colorado, in 1876, and construction continued south into New Mexico and north to Denver. Colonel Holiday's original goal of building to Santa Fe was soon dwarfed by an ambitious management that drove the line west across New Mexico and Arizona on a land grant acquired through acquisition of the Atlantic & Pacific Railroad. The Southern Pacific (SP) blocked the firm's first efforts to reach California, though a connection with the SP had been made at Deming, New Mexico, forming a continuous route. The ATSF opened its own through line to Los Angeles in 1887.

Control of the Santa Fe rested largely in the hands of Boston investors until the early 1890s. The directors placed William Barstow Strong in the presidency of the company in 1877, and a major expansion program ensued. In addition to building the line from Kansas City to Chicago, Strong acquired the Gulf, Colorado & Santa Fe Railway (GC&SF), which extended north from Galveston and Houston into central Texas. A connecting line built south from Kansas across Indian Territory joined the ATSF with the GC&SF, which by then reached Dallas and Fort Worth. Other acquisitions proved less beneficial as the Santa Fe absorbed the Colorado Midland Railroad and the St. Louis & San Francisco Railroad (Frisco) and enormous debts. Financial reversals and overexpansion led to bankruptcy in 1893.

A reorganization shed the Colorado Midland and the Frisco, and under the conservative direction of Edward P. Ripley, who served as president from 1895 to 1919, the company began a gradual process of growth. A line to San Francisco was ac-

quired and cutoffs with lower grades were built across west Texas to link the Texas trackage to the route to California. An extensive branch line system was developed in central and western Oklahoma, east Texas, southern California, and central Arizona. Ripley's strong hand guided the company to substantial profitability by 1914.

The Santa Fe engaged in diverse nonrailroad activities from the beginning, buying and selling agricultural properties and coal mines. Later the railway explored for petroleum on company-owned lands in California and acquired mineral interests in Oklahoma and Texas. Urban properties were developed in Chicago, Dallas, and Los Angeles, and the railway acquired the Kirby Lumber Company in Texas in 1933. In addition, the Santa Fe conducted extensive efforts on behalf of agricultural advancement and industrial development in its territory.

Along with the rest of the railroads, the ATSF was federalized during World War I; it prospered after its return to private operation in 1920. In the 1920s, under William Benson Storey, who succeeded Ripley as president, additional branches were constructed, and in 1928 the company bought the Kansas City, Mexico & Orient Railway, extending southwest from Wichita, Kansas, to Alpine, Texas. In the face of rising competition, the railway created bus lines to serve smaller communities as well as an extensive truck subsidiary. Although the Depression and Dust Bowl of the 1930s hit the company's territory hard, the ATSF initiated a fleet of stainless steel passenger trains, and the process of dieselization began before the outbreak of war in 1941.

The carrier benefited substantially from traffic generated by World War II and emerged from the war, under President Fred G. Gurley, with reduced indebtedness and a commitment to expansion into other transportation modes. Efforts to form an airline were terminated, however, by negative federal regulatory decisions. The passenger train fleet was expanded even as traffic began to decline. Dieselization reduced the size of the work force and a gradual program of branch line abandonment was begun. An application for a route into St. Louis was denied by the Interstate Commerce Commission (ICC). The company developed traffic-building programs with unit trains for coal, wheat, and sulphur and trailers and containers on flatcars. As nonrail operations also expanded, management under Presi-

Atchison, Topeka & Santa Fe "mini-bridge" freight train near Kingman, Arizona (Santa Fe Railway Public Relations Department)

dent John S. Reed decided in 1967 to redeploy its resources.

In 1968 Santa Fe Industries was formed to provide a corporate umbrella for the railway and for separate firms in oil and natural gas exploration and extraction, pipelines, trucking, lumbering, coal mining, real estate development, and construction. By the mid 1970s nonrail business activities rivaled the railway as a source of profits, if not volume.

The Santa Fe largely stayed aloof from the merger "mania" of the 1960s. Its own efforts to acquire the Western Pacific were blocked by the ICC, and it successfully thwarted a takeover attempt by the Missouri Pacific. The merger of the Burlington Northern with the Frisco and the subsequent joining of the Union Pacific, Missouri Pacific, and Western Pacific, however, left the railway surrounded by larger carriers in an extraordinarily competitive situ-

ation. In 1983 management arranged a merger with the Southern Pacific Company, its long-time rival, to form the Santa Fe Southern Pacific Corporation. The Southern Pacific railroad was placed in trust pending ICC approval of the merger of the two systems. In 1986 the ICC rejected that proposal, and the firm was left with the choice of appealing the decision or disposing of one of the railroads.

References:

Glenn D. Bradley, *The Story of the Santa Fe* (Boston: Badger, 1920);

Keith L. Bryant, Jr., *History of the Atchison, Topeka and Santa Fe Railway* (New York: Macmillan, 1974);

William S. Greever, *Arid Domain: The Santa Fe Railway and Its Western Land Grant* (Stanford: Stanford University Press, 1954);

James L. Marshall, *Santa Fe: The Railroad That Built an Empire* (New York: Random House, 1945);

L. L. Waters, *Steel Trails to Santa Fe* (Lawrence: University of Kansas Press, 1950).

Archives:

The corporate archives of the Atchison, Topeka & Santa Fe Railway are housed in the company headquarters in Chicago and in warehouses in Topeka, Kansas.

Atlantic Coast Line Railroad

by James A. Ward

University of Tennessee at Chattanooga

The Atlantic Coast Line Railroad (ACL) was the product of a demand in northern cities for fresh fruits and vegetables in the winter, the sorry state of the Southern railroad industry during Reconstruction, and the ambitions of several prominent Baltimore capitalists with Wall Street financial backing. Created from the consolidation of over 100 separate lines, the ACL connected northern cities with farming areas tempered by the Gulf Stream, where crops matured earlier in the growing season.

At the end of the Civil War the state government of North Carolina held a controlling interest in the Wilmington & Weldon Railroad (W&W) and the Wilmington & Manchester Railroad, main arteries along the state's coastal area. In 1869 William Thompson Walters, a Baltimore produce commission merchant and former Confederate sympathizer, and his banker friend Benjamin Franklin Newcomer purchased the lines. When both men joined the Pennsylvania Railroad's infamous Southern Railway Security Company in the early 1870s, the roads became part of the Pennsylvania's Southern system. When that holding company broke up in the 1873 depression, the Baltimore financiers regained control of the two lines. In the 1870s five

Map of the Atlantic Coast Line Railroad (1930)

roads, including the W&W, that connected Richmond with Charleston, South Carolina, began working together calling themselves the Atlantic Coast Line, although they maintained their corporate identities. In 1884 Walters purchased another of the lines, the Petersburg Railroad; began to increase his investment in the other roads; and founded the Atlantic Coast Despatch, a fast freight line that specialized in refrigerator cars for the perishables business. With the standardization of gauges in 1886, Walters pushed his control farther south by purchasing the Wilmington, Columbia & Augusta. Finally, in 1889, he chartered a Connecticut holding company, the Atlantic Improvement Construction Company, to buy a majority of the stock in the companies within the Atlantic Coast Line system. The Atlantic Improvement Construction Company was renamed the Atlantic Coast Line Company in 1893.

The ACL's consolidation moved swiftly, engineered by Walters, who died in 1894, and his son Henry. In 1898 Henry Walters organized five railroads into the 700-mile Atlantic Coast Line Railroad of South Carolina and combined the Petersburg Railroad with the Richmond & Petersburg to form the Atlantic Coast Line Railroad of Virginia. In 1900 the Virginia legislature gave the Atlantic Coast Line Railroad of Virginia a new name, the Atlantic Coast Line Railroad Company; the right to purchase other railroads; and a capitalization limit of $100 million. In April 1900 the company purchased the other ACL roads to create a new system with over 2,000 miles of road, gross earnings of over $7.5 million, and a net of $3.2 million.

Two years later Henry Walters and his Baltimore supporters more than doubled the size of the ACL when they purchased the Plant roads. Henry B. Plant, with support from Walters and Newcomer, had begun buying lines in the 1873 depression and over the next two decades had put together a system that stretched from Charleston to Tampa, Florida. At Plant's death in 1899 he controlled fourteen railroads with over 2,100 miles of track. He ordered in his will that his system be held intact for his four-year-old great-grandson, but his wife broke the will in court and in 1902 sold the Plant roads to the ACL, bringing that system's mileage to 4,138. The road's offices were consolidated in Wilmington, North Carolina, where they remained until they were moved to Jacksonville, Florida, in 1960.

The ACL grew at a slower pace in the twentieth century; it had achieved its basic shape and reached its major markets. Nevertheless, Walters bought some local lines, including the Jacksonville & Southwestern, Florida Central, and the Conway Coast & Western, and constructed new roads in Florida connecting Tampa, Fort Meyers, Naples, and Collier City. The ACL also built several cut-offs to shorten Florida distances and attract a larger share of the tourist business. In 1919 the company began running its own trains into the new Broad Street Union Station in Richmond; its cars had been handled in Richmond by the Richmond, Fredericksburg & Potomac.

When World War I broke out in Europe in 1914, the ACL was earning in excess of $10 million in net profits on gross revenues of over $36 million on its 4,600 miles. When the road was restored to private hands after being federalized during the war, it embarked on another modest expansion effort, buying control of the Clinchfield Railroad, the Atlanta, Birmingham & Atlantic, and several smaller lines and operating all of them as subsidiaries. The road also installed automatic block signaling on its almost entirely double-tracked main line from Richmond to Jacksonville. These improvements, its strong financial base, and its size enabled the ACL to survive the Great Depression and carry the increased wartime tonnage during World War II.

When the war ended, however, economic conditions in the southeast began to change: the ACL lost much of its perishables traffic to trucks and many of its Florida passengers to airplanes. Although the firm was still financially healthy, in the 1950s it became clear to its president, W. Thomas Rice, that efforts would have to be made to ensure its future viability. When no government aid was forthcoming, Rice met with John Smith, president of rival Seaboard Air Line Railroad, to talk about a merger. The Interstate Commerce Commission (ICC) heard testimony on the proposal in 1961 and gave its approval in December 1963. The decision surprised many because the ICC had never before allowed two prosperous, parallel lines to merge; the commissioners had accepted the ACL's argument that it was not earning a fair return and that competition with other means of transport was more important than competition with other railroads. When the consolidation finally took place on July 1, 1967, the ACL, which had netted $22 million the previous year, swapped each of its shares for 1.42 shares in the new Seaboard Coast Line Company

(SCL). The new combination started business with assets of $1.2 billion, revenues of over $400 million, more than 1,000 locomotives, and 62,000 freight cars, making it the ninth largest railroad in the country. Baltimore financial interests, through the Safe-Deposit Trust Company of that city, maintained their preeminent position within the new amalgamation. On January 1, 1983, the SCL became the Seaboard System.

References:

Howard D. Dozier, *A History of the Atlantic Coast Line Railroad* (Boston: Houghton Mifflin, 1920);

Richard E. Prince, *Atlantic Coast Line Railroad* (Green River, Wyo.: Published by the author, 1966);

John F. Stover, *The Railroads of the South, 1865-1900* (Chapel Hill: University of North Carolina Press, 1955).

Archives:

The corporate records of the Atlantic Coast Line are at the CSX offices in Jacksonville, Florida.

W. W. Atterbury

(January 31, 1866-September 20, 1935)

by Michael Bezilla

Pennsylvania State University

CAREER: Road foreman of engines (1889-1892), assistant engineer of motive power, Lines West (1892-1895), master mechanic (1895-1896), superintendent of motive power, Lines East (1896- 1901), general superintendent of motive power (1901-1902), general manager, Lines East (1903-1909), fifth vice president (1909-1911), fourth vice president (1911-1912), vice president in charge of operations (1912-1917, 1919-1924), Pennsylvania Railroad; director general of transportation, American Expeditionary Force (1917-1919); vice president (1924-1925), president, Pennsylvania Railroad (1925-1935).

Upon W. W. Atterbury's retirement from the presidency of the Pennsylvania Railroad (PRR) in 1935, the *New York Times* hailed him as "a forceful and original figure in railroading." There is still probably no better way that he might be characterized. Atterbury was a dynamic, imaginative man—one of the ablest to head the Pennsylvania or any other railroad—and in engineering, finance, and operations he made significant contributions toward enhancing the PRR's reputation as "the Standard Railroad of the World."

William Wallace Atterbury was born on January 31, 1866, in New Albany, Indiana, the seventh son and twelfth child of John G. and Catherine Larned Atterbury. He was a descendant of Elias Boudinot, a member of the Continental Congress and the House of Representatives and director of the mint. His father had practiced law in Detroit before moving to Indiana to become a Presbyterian home missionary. John Atterbury eventually returned to Detroit as executive secretary of the American Bible Society, and that was where Wallace, as he was

W. W. Atterbury (Kalmbach Publishing Company)

known to his friends, spent most of his boyhood. In 1882 he enrolled at Yale's Sheffield Scientific School. Finances for the large Atterbury clan were limited, so Wallace paid most of his own way through school by tutoring other students.

After graduating in 1886, he began the mechanics apprentice course at the Altoona, Pennsylvania, shops of the Pennsylvania Railroad. A college degree offered no automatic advancement on the railroad, and in order to join the PRR's mechanical department Atterbury had to complete the same course requirements as all other students. His aptitude for engineering and his enormous appetite for hard work enabled him to finish the four–year pro-

Workers electrifying the Pennsylvania Railroad main line in 1937 (PRR)

gram in less than three years. During that time, although supported to some degree by his family, he earned extra income by renting the bed in his tiny flat during the day to a railroad policeman who worked nights.

Since 1871 the PRR had divided itself into two operating entities: the parent company, the Pennsylvania Railroad, operated as Lines East, while its subsidiary, the Pennsylvania Company, operated as Lines West, with Pittsburgh as the junction of the two systems. In 1889 Atterbury was appointed road foreman of engines, an assignment that over the next three years took him to several operating divisions on both Lines East and Lines West.

He received a promotion in 1892 to assistant engineer of motive power for all of Lines West. Three years later he became the Pennsylvania Company's master mechanic at Fort Wayne, Indiana, site of a large locomotive and car shop. He entered the upper echelon of the mechanical department in 1896 when he was named superintendent of motive power for Lines East, with offices in Altoona. Barely thirty years old, he had responsibility for the efficient utilization and maintenance of all locomotives in the area bounded by Pittsburgh, Buffalo, Jersey City, and Washington, D.C. The entire railroad became his domain in 1901 when he was made general superintendent of motive power. At this time Atterbury was also participating in the design of new steam locomotives, nearly all of which the PRR built in its own shops. Pennsylvania engines were noted for their standard designs (that is, the use in

large quantities of a few basic locomotive designs having as many interchangeable parts as possible) that were developed through careful scientific research and testing rather than through the addition of larger boilers and wheels to older types.

In 1902 Pennsylvania president Alexander J. Cassatt toured the railroad between Altoona and Pittsburgh to determine what steps should be taken to alleviate traffic congestion on that route. Atterbury, a member of Cassatt's party, so impressed the president with his knowledge of operating conditions that within the week Cassatt asked him to come to the railroad's headquarters in Philadelphia to become general manager of Lines East. The new position placed Atterbury in the operating department, where prospects for further advancement were brighter than in the mechanical department.

The next upward move came in 1909, when the company's board of directors elected him fifth vice president, the highest post in the operating department. A reorganization two years later left Atterbury still overseeing operations but as fourth vice president. The system of numbering vice presidencies was discontinued in 1912, at which time Atterbury was designated vice president in charge of operations. Thus far, his rise had been nothing less than meteoric by the standards of promotion on the PRR or most other roads. Time and again, Atterbury's performance was such that he was advanced over the heads of many of his more senior contemporaries. His accomplishments as vice president of operations won him recognition throughout the railroad industry; in June 1916 he was elected to a three—year term as president of the American Railway Association, the major trade organization and predecessor of the Association of American Railroads.

The entry of the United States into World War I in April 1917 produced a tremendous surge in traffic on the nation's rail lines. The Pennsylvania was especially hard pressed as a result of its strategic location in America's industrial heartland and its role as a funnel for troops and materiel moving east to mid—Atlantic points of embarkation. In December 1917, with trains on the PRR at a near standstill and congestion prevailing nationwide, President Woodrow Wilson decreed that the federal government, through the new United States Railroad Administration (USRA), would assume operational control of the railroads.

By this time Atterbury had been absent from the domestic rail scene for some months. In the spring of 1917 he had taken a leave of absence from the Pennsylvania to assume the presidency of the American Railway Association on a full—time basis to help put the railroads on a wartime footing. Then in July, Gen. John J. Pershing, commander of the American Expeditionary Force in Europe, wired President Wilson with an urgent request to send him "the best railroad man in the U.S." to oversee that part of the French railway system that had been assigned to the American army for operation and maintenance. Atterbury was given the assignment, and he arrived in France in August.

Atterbury's "personality, his force, his grasp of the difficulties of the task and his willingness to understand it appealed to me at once," Pershing said in his memoirs. He appointed Atterbury director general of transportation and placed him in charge of a badly strained system of 1,500 locomotives and 20,000 cars that was floundering in chaos. Congress made Pershing's action official in October, conferring on Atterbury the rank of brigadier general.

General "Attaboy," as the troops fondly referred to him, soon had the rail lines and connecting port and terminal facilities running smoothly, with men and equipment being shuttled to and from the front on schedule. For this service, which he continued to render until returning to America in May 1919, General Atterbury (as he preferred to be called thenceforth) received awards of merit

from six nations, including the Distinguished Service Medal from the United States.

The railroads remained under USRA control until March 1920. As Atterbury studied the PRR's wartime performance, he saw that Pittsburgh had proven to be a serious bottleneck. After resuming his office as vice president in charge of operations, he pointed out to President Samuel Rea that traffic would flow much more smoothly even in peacetime if that city could be eliminated as an artificial interchange point between Lines East and West. Rea agreed, and in 1921 the railroad was consolidated into a single operating entity.

Among the most serious problems confronting the Pennsylvania after the war was the high cost of labor. The USRA had increased the railroad's labor force by 25 percent and had recognized the shopcraft unions of the American Federation of Labor (AFL). With congressional blessing, it had also given all employees large pay raises. The PRR had long opposed collective bargaining with national shopcraft unions, arguing that each railroad should negotiate separately with its employees. President Rea was determined to rid the PRR of the AFL and what he regarded as its intolerably expensive wage agreements. He delegated that chore to Atterbury, perhaps realizing that his own reputation as a friend of the workingman could be severely damaged in a confrontation with the unions, but more likely because he knew that Atterbury was equally popular among employees and had more experience in labor relations. Atterbury had risen from the ranks and knew the attitudes and desires of the average workingman. And it was Atterbury who, as Lines East general manager, had signed one of the first written accords between the PRR and its train service employees (an informal recognition of certain employee rights and benefits).

Atterbury also chaired the labor committee of the Association of Railway Executives. That body was instrumental in persuading the United States Railroad Labor Board, created by Congress to oversee the volatile rail labor situation, to permit the Pennsylvania and other railroads to terminate the AFL shopcraft contracts and to form what in effect were company unions. The PRR's union, the Employee Representation Plan, was already functioning by the time the shopcraft unions staged a nationwide strike in July 1922. This plan worked well enough that the Pennsylvania was little affected by the short–lived strike, but the arbitrary manner in which Atterbury had implemented the new labor arrangement and discharged thousands of employees severely damaged what had historically been amicable relations between the company and its workers. In spite of the best efforts of Ivy Lee, the public relations genius Atterbury hired to protect the railroad's image, PRR management gained a reputation for being antilabor and uncaring about employees that was to linger for many years.

In 1924, as Rea neared retirement, Atterbury was named vice president, a newly authorized position that made official his status as Rea's heir apparent. On October 1, 1925, Rea stepped down, and Atterbury was elected the Pennsylvania's tenth president.

The achievement with which the Atterbury administration was most closely identified was the electrification of the 245–mile multitrack main line between New York and Washington, D.C. Rea had deftly guided a steady recovery from the financial shakiness bequeathed the PRR by the USRA, and by the time Atterbury took over, the PRR was on the verge of record prosperity: it would experience an all–time peak of $101 million in net income in 1929. This money was needed, for the electrification work Atterbury outlined in 1928 carried a price tag of more than $250 million, making it the largest capital improvement program undertaken to that date by an American railroad. The Rea administration had done some of the preliminary planning on the project, but it was Atterbury and his vice presidents, Elisha Lee and Martin W. Clement, who made the final decision to convert from steam to the more efficient electric traction, and it was they who oversaw implementation of the program, which was expected to save the PRR more than $8 million annually in operating costs alone.

Less than a year after electrification work got under way, the nation plunged into economic depression. Railroads from coast to coast reeled under the shock and many entered receivership. But Atterbury pushed ahead unflinchingly with the conversion to electric traction and related terminal improvements, shrewdly taking advantage of the artificially low cost of labor and materials and the reduction in traffic that allowed work to proceed with less interference from passing trains. When even the formidable coffers of the PRR neared exhaustion, Atterbury swallowed his distaste for the New Deal and bor-

rowed money from the federal government to keep construction on schedule. At his insistence, as much of the work force as possible was drawn from the ranks of furloughed PRR employees rather than from the contractors' own labor forces. The project was finally completed in February 1935, and an extension west to Harrisburg was added a few years later. Although a specific accounting of savings and increased business brought about by electrification was never made, history has shown it to be one of the wisest investments undertaken by any railroad.

Perhaps only one project captured Atterbury's personal fancy more than electrification, and that was the development of the M1 class 4–8–2 type (a four–wheel leading truck, eight driving wheels, and a two–wheel trailing truck) steam locomotive for heavy passenger and fast freight service. The first experimental M1 was outshopped at Altoona in 1923. Atterbury himself had a hand in its creation and–on the basis of the legend that the operating vice president put some of his own money into the design when certain technological innovations were resisted by the road's more conservative mechanical engineering staff–it and 300 sisters that were to follow by 1930 came to be known as "Atterbury's engines."

Early in his presidency Atterbury became involved in the complex subject of railroad consolidation. The Transportation Act of 1920 had directed the Interstate Commerce Commission (ICC) to formulate a plan to merge the multitude of trunk lines into a handful of large regional carriers. While the ICC was engaged in this work, the larger railroads began to devise their own schemes to rationalize the nation's overbuilt rail network, fearing that any government–mandated consolidation would not be in their best interests. Atterbury's plan called for seven large regional rail lines to be created through mergers, with two–built around the Pennsylvania and its rival, the New York Central–reigning supreme in the Northeast. The plan did not win much favor but did offer a remarkably accurate picture of what American railroading would be like a half–century later.

Before realizing that consolidation was doomed to failure, at least for the immediate future, Atterbury led the PRR in acquiring large amounts of stock in the Wabash and the Lehigh Valley railroads (two lines deemed crucial in any consolidation plan) and fortifying its already sizable interest in the New Haven, the Detroit, Toledo & Iron-ton, and other roads. Many of these investments were made through the Pennroad Corporation, a holding company Atterbury and the PRR directors had established to circumvent government antitrust restrictions. Their ultimate worth turned out to be a fraction of their purchase price ($106 million for the Wabash and Lehigh Valley stock alone) owing to the subsequent onset of the Great Depression and the loss of interest in mergers.

While Atterbury could not escape some stock-holder wrath over these investments, criticism of his administration was considerably muted by his as-tute handling of the railroad during the bleak years of the early 1930s. Implementation of a carefully planned program that blended increased efficiency with austerity enabled the Pennsylvania to record a net income in every year of the Depression and to maintain a record of dividends (albeit modest in some years) that remained unbroken since the com-pany's founding in 1846.

But Atterbury was looking beyond the hard times to an era when the PRR and other railroads would have to adopt new marketing concepts and technologies. Rather than have it compete with other modes of transport, Atterbury wanted the Pennsylvania to become a total transportation com-pany, offering shippers and the traveling public the kind of service best suited to their needs. Accord-ingly, the PRR invested in Greyhound Bus Lines, Trans World Airlines, and several trucking firms. It experimented with the use of boxes or containers that could be filled with a variety of goods and placed on ordinary flatcars or flatbed trucks to ob-tain greater service flexibility and to lower the cost of less–than–carload shipments.

While these innovations brought Atterbury rec-ognition within the railroad industry, he was equally well known in Pennsylvania for his role in the Republican party. He sided with the party's con-servative wing and was a delegate to the 1920 na-tional convention that nominated Warren G. Har-ding for president. After Harding's election, Atterbury was mentioned as a candidate for secre-tary of war, although there is no evidence that Har-ding ever offered him the post. Within Pennsylva-nia, Atterbury allied himself with the Philadelphia political organization of Edwin and William S. Vare to fend off the party's liberal wing headed by Gifford Pinchot. In his successful campaigns for gov-ernor in 1922 and 1930, Pinchot portrayed Atter-bury and the PRR as part of a sinister conspiracy of back–room bosses and corporate moguls deter-mined to thwart the will of the people. When Pin-chot became the Republican gubernatorial standard–bearer in 1930, Atterbury resigned his post as national committeeman rather than support a candi-date who used big business as a political whipping boy and who stood resolutely in favor of Prohibi-tion. (The PRR president was an ardent "wet.")

In July 1934, eighteen months away from man-datory retirement at age seventy, Atterbury entered the hospital for the removal of gallstones. In the fall, he took his yacht (sailing was one of his few di-versions) on a journey of recuperation to Miami. The trip did not have its desired effect. He returned to Philadelphia in time to announce at the April 1935 meeting of the Pennsylvania's board of direc-tors that he would not accept reelection to a final year in office. He recommended that vice president Clement, who was already presiding over the rail-road in Atterbury's absence, be his successor, and the board concurred.

Atterbury then retired to his Boudinot Farms home in suburban Radnor. He died of a stroke on September 20, 1935. Surviving were his second wife, the former Arminia Rosengarten MacLeod of St. Davids, Pennsylvania, whom he had married in 1915, and four children. Atterbury had had no chil-dren by his first wife, Matilda Hoffman of Fort Wayne, Indiana, who had died in 1910 after fifteen years of marriage. After his marriage to Mrs. Mac-Leod, a widow, Atterbury had adopted her sons, George R. and Malcolm W., and her daughter, Eliza-beth; the couple had one child of their own, Wil-liam Wallace, Jr.

Atterbury had simple tastes, in spite of his $150,000 annual salary. He liked to boast that there was not a single piece of furniture at his home that he could not rest his feet on, and his Broad Street office was equally informal in its fur-nishings. His only indulgences were fully equipped machine shops, one at Boudinot Farms and the other aboard his yacht. A shy man who valued his privacy, Atterbury also detested giving public ad-dresses and rarely granted interviews.

Perhaps his avoidance of the public spotlight explains, at least in part, why even standard histo-ries of the American railroad industry fail to accord him significant mention, if indeed he is cited at all.

Yet W. W. Atterbury was among the most powerful and influential figures in railroading in his own or any other era and in many respects ranks as the most able and successful of all the Pennsylvania Railroad's distinguished chief executives.

References:

"Atterbury Elected President of PRR," *New York Times,* October 1, 1925, p. 29;

"Atterbury Elected PRR President," *Railway Age,* 79 (October 3, 1925): 625-627;

"Atterbury Resigns as PRR President," *New York Times,* April 25, 1935, p. 31;

"Atterbury Resigns; Clement Elected President of Pennsylvania," *Railway Age,* 98 (April 27, 1935): 651-653;

Michael Bezilla, *Electric Traction on the Pennsylvania Railroad, 1895-1968* (University Park: Pennsylvania State University Press, 1980);

George H. Burgess and Miles C. Kennedy, *Centennial History of the Pennsylvania Railroad* (Philadelphia: Pennsylvania Railroad, 1949);

"Clement for Atterbury," *Time,* 25 (May 6, 1935): 65-66;

B. C. Forbes, "Give a Good Man Authority–," *American Magazine,* 89 (March 1920): 36-37, 105-124;

"General Atterbury, Rail Leader, Dies," *New York Times,* September 21, 1935, pp. 1-2;

"A Railroad Chief Envisions the Future," *New York Times,* December 22, 1929, IX: 6;

William J. Wilgus, *Transporting the A.E.F. in Western Europe* (New York: Columbia University Press, 1931);

"William Wallace Atterbury," *Transactions of the American Society of Civil Engineers,* 101 (1936): 1518-1524.

Gale B. Aydelott

(July 22, 1914-)

by Don L. Hofsommer

Augustana College

CAREER: Welder's helper and extra gang laborer (1936-1937), assistant trainmaster, trainmaster, assistant to chief train inspector, engineering assistant, roadmaster (1937-1943), mechanical officer (1913-1948), superintendent (1948-1954), vice president and general manager (1954-1955), executive vice president (1955-1956), president and chairman (1956-1980), Denver & Rio Grande Western Railroad.

Gale Benton "Gus" Aydelott was born at La Grange, Illinois, in 1914 to James H. and Pearl B. Aydelott. Aydelott's father was a senior operating officer for the Burlington system and frequently took the boy on business car trips, where he learned much of railroading and where he met many luminaries of the industry. A career in railroading seemed foreordained. He earned a degree in transportation from the University of Illinois in 1936, and then took a job as a welder's helper in track service for the Denver & Rio Grande Western (Rio Grande). Before he retired, Aydelott was president and chairman of the company and one of the industry's most respected leaders.

Aydelott's on-the-job preparation included long stints in the basics–track work, mechanical services, and operations. In a sense, he was at the right spot at the right time: the Rio Grande was plunged into bankruptcy during 1935, not to emerge until 1947; during those difficult years, leadership was vested in the talented Wilson J. McCarthy, who devoted himself to revitalizing the railroad. Aydelott rose through the ranks at this time, learning the necessity of continually maintaining and upgrading railroad properties. He never forgot that invaluable lesson.

At the age of forty-one–a mere youngster among railroaders of the time–Aydelott became president of the Rio Grande at McCarthy's death in 1956. Aydelott followed the progressive philosophy of McCarthy, adding his own stamp. He completed dieselization, ordered more rolling stock, and insisted on new and heavier rail for the main routes. All of these improvements were necessary, Aydelott insisted, to prepare the road for "the increased potential confidently anticipated."

At the same time, Aydelott energetically sought to guard the company's frontiers–a difficult

Gale B. Aydelott in 1956 (Denver & Rio Grande Western Railroad Archives, Denver)

task given the strong railroads bracketing the Rio Grande on the east and west, including the awesome Union Pacific. "We would prefer to remain independent," said Aydelott in 1963. "We are proud of what we have done as a separate road, and we think we can continue to do a better job for ourselves and our territory by staying that way."

To remain independent, Aydelott knew, required that the Rio Grande pay special attention to the needs of customers who had a choice not only among rail carriers but, more importantly, also among the various modes of transportation. Aydelott urged the Rio Grande's sales force to constantly review rates and to pledge adequate and proper equipment, and he demanded that the operating department expedite lading by means of short, preblocked (that is, cars bound for the same destina-

tion placed together) trains. The Rio Grande, as he predicted, gained a favorable reputation among shippers by following this path.

Aydelott did not relish taking unpopular or difficult stands, but neither did he shrink from them. An example was the "passenger problem" or, more correctly, the problem of growing deficits deriving from offering passenger service. The Rio Grande's position was particularly delicate because it was a partner in operation of the California Zephyr, an extremely popular train that passed through some of the most spectacular scenery in North America. "We might as well face up to the fact that, as a public services corporation, we have to take some of the bitter along with sweet," said Aydelott, adding, "if we can't make money, at least we can make friends." Nevertheless, he saw to the gradual whittling of Rio Grande's unprofitable service. The same was true of the company's romantic but archaic narrow (three-foot) gauge operations. Against much nostalgia and extremely explosive emotion Aydelott succeeded in abandoning all except the line in southwestern Colorado between Durango and Silverton, which was sold to a responsible party who agreed to maintain the popular tourist attraction. Finally, Aydelott attempted to gain more lucrative overhead (through) freight by attacking government provisions that favored the Union Pacific by virtually locking the Rio Grande out of the Ogden Gateway. Aydelott won at least a partial victory in that campaign.

On another front he was the clear victor. When the Rio Grande was reorganized in 1947, the company carried a mortgage debt of $83.2 million, but that was cut to $3.1 million by the end of 1980. A little over two years later the remainder was extinguished, and the sole remaining debt consisted of equipment obligations. This debt reduction was notable in itself, but it was accomplished while Aydelott insisted on maintenance and service levels that were the envy of the industry.

Among Aydelott's many gifts were humility and a sense of humor—traits that he employed most skillfully in meeting the public, in dealing with subordinates, and in marshaling support for his policies. He was known for his ability to inspire confidence, his keen sense of fair play, his ability to make decisions, and his capacity to wrestle with issues. He believed in teamwork and in giving credit where it was due; small wonder that he was respected and liked by those he directed. One associate said: "You don't lose any points by disagreeing with him— he'll always listen"; said another: "You feel you're working with him, not for him"; "This is not a one- man operation," said still another subordinate.

Aydelott yielded the presidency of the Rio Grande in 1978 and the chairmanship in 1980, al- though he stayed on as an executive consultant through 1983.

Reference:
Robert G. Athearn, *Rebel of the Rockies: A History of the Denver and Rio Grande Western Railroad* (New Haven: Yale University Press, 1966).

Archives:
There are no archives of Gale B. Aydelott's papers.

Baltimore & Ohio Railroad

by John F. Stover

Purdue University

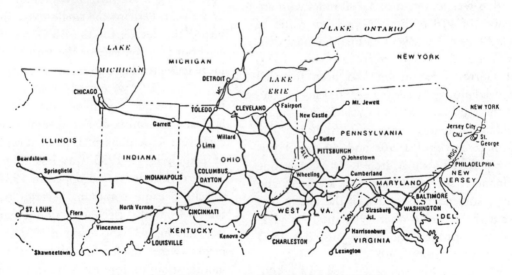

Map of the Baltimore & Ohio Railroad (1938)

Granted a charter in 1827, the Baltimore & Ohio Railroad (B&O) was the first railway projected west- ward over the Allegheny Mountains to the Ohio Val- ley. It was Baltimore's answer to the Erie Canal, which promised to expand the western trade of New York City. The engineering problems faced were so varied and unique that progress was slow. A line to Frederick, Maryland, was opened by 1832 and one to Washington, D.C., in 1835. The 178-mile line to Cumberland, Maryland, was fin- ished in 1842, and Wheeling, Virginia (now West Vir-

ginia), on the upper Ohio, was reached late in 1852. A second line to Parkersburg, Virginia (now West Virginia), was completed in 1857. By 1860 the 515-mile B&O had annual revenues of over $4 million and in good years was paying modest divi- dends. Baltimore had prospered with the building of the road and had a population of 212,000 on the eve of the Civil War. During the war the B&O was clearly the most vulnerable to Confederate at- tack of the several trunk lines serving the mid- Atlantic states; several of its bridges were blown up and Stonewall Jackson destroyed forty-two of its locomotives in a raid on Martinsburg, West Virginia.

John W. Garrett, president of the B&O from 1858 to 1884, greatly expanded the railroad after the Civil War. The B&O leased roads in Ohio in the late 1860s which gave it service to Sandusky on Lake Erie. A line from Cumberland to Pittsburgh was opened in 1871, and by 1874 the B&O had built a line from northern Ohio into Chicago. By 1883 a southern branch was completed to Lexington, Virginia, and in Garrett's last years he was planning an extension to Philadelphia and New York City.

During the 1870s and early 1880s Garrett's line was engaged in endless rate wars with the Pennsylvania and the New York Central. Serious labor trouble came to the B&O in the summer of 1877 when Garrett cut all wages; the strike spread across the nation until peace was restored by state militia and regular army units.

At the time of Garrett's death in 1884, the Baltimore & Ohio was a system of 1,700 miles with annual revenues of $19 million and a labor roster of more than 20,000. The B&O had paid annual dividends of from $6 to $10 every year since 1859. Much of Garrett's expansion had been financed with borrowed money rather than capital stock, however, and the Baltimore & Ohio was soon in financial trouble. Dividends were rare from the late 1880s through the mid 1890s and the B&O was placed in receivership on March 1, 1896. A strong plan of financial reorganization was accepted, and the receivers surrendered control of the line in mid 1899. For a short period after 1900 the Pennsylvania Railroad controlled the B&O, but the B&O was independent again by 1908.

In 1910 the Baltimore & Ohio was a 4,400-mile system with annual revenues of $70 million and was paying dividends of $6 on its common stock. Much of its expanded mileage was the result of adding the Baltimore, Ohio & Southwestern, a 922-mile line in southern Ohio, Indiana, and Illinois, in 1900; but the B&O would always remain in third place behind the two stronger trunk lines, the Pennsylvania and the New York Central.

In 1910 Daniel Willard became president of the Baltimore & Ohio, a position he would hold until 1941. At once Willard embarked upon a major program of improvement of the line, the motive power, and the rolling stock. Bridges were re-

placed, grades lowered, and much single track made into double track; heavier engines, new steel passenger cars, and thousands of freight cars were added. When the United States entered World War I in 1917 the B&O was well prepared for the expanded freight and passenger traffic which soon appeared. During the wartime federal operation of the nation's railroads, which began in December 1917, the B&O's annual revenues increased from $140 million in 1917 to $182 million in 1919; but the firm's operating ratio climbed from 77 to 93 in the same years.

With private management regained on March 1, 1920, the B&O officials worked to make their road profitable. The combination of a reduction in both wages and the labor force plus modest increases in rates and fares pushed the operating ratio down to 82 in 1922 and 78 in 1923. Dividends were resumed at 2½ percent in 1923, and rose to 6 percent by 1926. Between 1923 and 1929 B&O revenues averaged between $240 million and $245 million a year. Perhaps the single most important event during the decade for the B&O was its centennial, celebrated by the Fair of the Iron Horse near Baltimore in September and October 1927.

The 1920s were prosperous for the B&O, but the next decade was filled with problems for Willard and his railroad. For several years after 1929 each year saw a sharp drop in revenue; the roster of employees in 1933 was less than half that of 1927; dividends were dropped in 1932, and annual deficits became common. Several loans were obtained from the Reconstruction Finance Corporation, and in 1933 and again in 1938 special arrangements were made for the postponement and modification of interest payments on the funded debt. The B&O came close to receivership during the 1930s, but revenues increased substantially in 1939 and 1940.

The war in Europe brought an upswing in the American economy and also in rail traffic. During the war years, 1942 to 1945, B&O revenues averaged better than $350 million a year. Revenues during the 1940s were high enough to permit a reduction of $90 million in the long-term funded debt between 1941 and 1953. Preferred stock dividends were resumed in 1949 and 1950, and in 1952 the common stockholders received 75 cents per share, the first dividend in twenty years.

Since the B&O was a major carrier of soft coal, it did not shift to diesel power as rapidly as many lines. By 1953, however, the B&O had more diesel units than steam locomotives, and in that year diesel power was providing three-quarters of the freight service and two-thirds of the passenger service and switching. The B&O was completely dieselized by 1958.

In the late 1950s the B&O suffered a marked decline in operating revenue. The operating ratio increased each year, and in 1961 the firm had a large deficit. In 1962 the Baltimore & Ohio agreed to be taken over by the smaller but more prosperous Chesapeake & Ohio. The Baltimore & Ohio remained a major portion of the Chessie/CSX system in 1987.

References:

Carrol Bateman, *The Baltimore and Ohio: The Story of the Railroad That Grew Up With the United States* (Baltimore, 1951);

Edward Hungerford, *The Story of the Baltimore & Ohio Railroad: 1827-1927* (New York: Putnam's, 1928);

John F. Stover, *History of the Baltimore and Ohio Railroad* (West Lafayette, Ind.: Purdue University Press, 1987);

Festus P. Summers, *The Baltimore and Ohio in the Civil War* (New York: Putnam's, 1939).

Archives:

The corporate records of the Baltimore & Ohio Railroad are at the B&O Museum in Baltimore and at the CSX offices in Cleveland.

Bangor & Aroostook Railroad

by David H. Hickcox

Ohio Wesleyan University

The Bangor & Aroostook Railroad (BAR) was incorporated on February 13, 1891, to construct a railroad from Brownsville, Maine, north to Fort Fairfield, Ashland, and Van Buren. At the time of incorporation, Aroostook County, in extreme northeastern Maine, was one of the most isolated regions in New England. The Bangor & Aroostook's purpose was to provide northern Maine with a rail connection to the rest of the country. Through building its own lines and purchase or lease of other railroads the BAR expanded to 630 miles by 1916.

Aroostook County is one of the country's primary potato producing regions, and potatoes were long the Bangor & Aroostook's mainstay. Potatoes were first shipped in 1895 and reached an all-time high of 899,300 tons in 1930; by the latter year the BAR's fleet of refrigerator cars was second only to the Atchison, Topeka & Santa Fe's. During the 1950s the Bangor & Aroostook's red, white, and blue "State of Maine Products" boxcars were a familiar sight throughout the country. Trucks made serious inroads into the BAR's potato traffic, however, and the completion of Interstate 95 to Houlton in 1968 and poor service west of Boston by the Penn

Central sealed the fate of the potato traffic. By 1979 potatoes were only a memory on the ledger, and the refrigerator cars were retired.

As the potato traffic declined the Bangor & Aroostook became dependent upon forest products. Paper mills at Millinockett, East Millinockett, and Madawaska require a constant flow of inbound pulpwood, petroleum, and chemicals and originate outbound paper products. Passenger service ended in 1961, but the railroad continued to operate a bus service until 1983.

On October 2, 1969, the Amoskeag Company, a holding company based in Boston, purchased the Bangor & Aroostook. A number of branch lines were abandoned, trimming the BAR to 477 miles. Headquarters are located five miles west of Bangor at North Maine Junction.

References:

Jerry Angier and Herb Cleaves, *Bangor & Aroostook Railroad* (Littleton, Mass.: Flying Yankee Enterprises, 1986);

Ron Johnson, *Bangor & Aroostook Railroad* (Portland, Maine: Portland Litho, 1983).

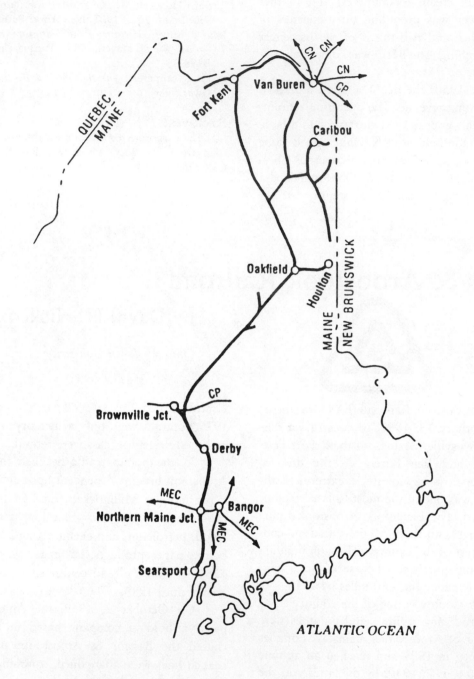

Map of the Bangor & Aroostook Railroad (1983)

John W. Barriger III

(December 3, 1899-December 9, 1976)

by George W. Hilton

University of California, Los Angeles

CAREER: Engineering positions, Pennsylvania Railroad (1917-1927); financial analyst, Kuhn, Loeb & Co. (1927-1929); vice president, International Carriers, Ltd. (1929-1933); chief, railroad division, Reconstruction Finance Corporation (1934-1941); associate director, Division of Railway Transport, Office of Defense Transportation (1942-1943); vice president, Union Stockyards & Transit Company (1943-1976); manager, Diesel Locomotive Division, Fairbanks Morse Corporation (1944-1946); president, Chicago, Indianapolis & Louisville Railway (1946-1952); vice president, New York, New Haven & Hartford Railroad (1953); vice president, Chicago, Rock Island & Pacific Railway (1953-1956); president, Pittsburgh & Lake Erie Railroad (1956-1964); president, Missouri-Kansas-Texas Railroad (1965-1970); chief executive officer, Boston & Maine Railroad (1970-1973).

As railroad president, civil servant, and author, John Walker Barriger III was one of the most conspicuous figures in railroading in the mid twentieth century. He was born in Dallas, Texas, in 1899, the son of a civil engineer who practiced in the railroad industry. The young Barriger spent his school years in St. Louis, where he frequented Union Station and became a railroad enthusiast. In 1917 he entered the Massachusetts Institute of Technology and undertook summer employments with the Pennsylvania Railroad. On graduating in 1921 he continued in the Pennsylvania's program of executive training. In 1926 he wrote an extensive report on ways to make the Pennsylvania's passenger trains more competitive with the New York Central's expresses. In 1927 he served as assistant yardmaster at Altoona. He then left the Pennsylvania to join Kuhn, Loeb and Company, the railroad's traditional financier, as a financial analyst. This move was a crucial one

in Barriger's life, for it led him into a career of relatively short appointments, largely on weaker railroads, instead of a progression through the ranks at the Pennsylvania that would almost assuredly have taken him to a vice presidency and quite possibly to the presidency of the railroad. His resignation was apparently considered by the Pennsylvania an act of disloyalty, and he never returned to the company.

In 1929 Barriger left Kuhn, Loeb to become vice president of International Carriers, Ltd., an investment trust organized by the financial firm Calvin Bullock and Company. While in that capacity, Barriger became associated with F. H. Prince, a Boston financier from whom the newly elected President Franklin D. Roosevelt solicited a plan for railroad consolidation and retrenchment. Barriger in May 1933 brought forth the Prince Plan, a proposal for seven or eight regional systems based on the major existing carriers and accepting the geographical separation of American railroads into eastern, southern, and western. Although the plan was not implemented, it made Barriger at thirty-three a prominent figure in railroading and led to his choice as chief of the railroad division of the Reconstruction Finance Corporation in 1934. In the course of his duties, which mainly entailed ascertaining suitability of applicants for loans, Barriger traveled widely—traveling more extensively by train, it is thought, than anyone had ever done previously—and in the process developed an acquaintance with the managerial practices and the physical plant of the American railroad system that was unequaled. His breadth of reading about the industry was also probably the most extensive in history. He served as the reorganization manager of the Chicago & Eastern Illinois (C&EI) in 1940 and as a member of its executive committee in 1941-1942.

With the coming of World War II he became associate director of the Division of Railway Transport in the Office of Defense Transportation (ODT). Under the ODT he was appointed federal manager of the Toledo, Peoria & Western Railroad, which had been seized because of an intractable strike. Upon leaving government service in 1943 he became vice president of the Union Stockyards & Transit Company of Chicago, a position that he held until his death. In May 1944 he became manager of the railroad division of Fairbanks, Morse and Company, which was entering the diesel-electric locomotive industry.

By this time in his career Barriger had developed a consistent philosophy of railroading, which he exposited in an article, "Super-Railroading," in *Trains* magazine of December 1943 and more fully in a book, *Super-Railroads for a Dynamic American Economy* (1956). Barriger believed that if railroads were to maintain superiority to rival forms of transport, grades should be reduced to 0.3 percent (about sixteen feet per mile), or as a practical alternative to 0.5 percent, except in mountainous country. Similarly, curves should be reduced to two or three degrees. His conception of the super-railroad was very similar to the "Sam Rea Line," a proposal for a shorter, lower-grade route from Fort Wayne, Indiana, to Lewistown, Pennsylvania, developed during or immediately before Barriger's years with the Pennsylvania. This line, which would have bypassed Pittsburgh to the north, was projected with gradients of 0.3 percent eastbound and 0.6 percent westbound on the ascent of Allegheny Mountain north of Altoona (railroad grades are determined as against the direction of the traffic). Barriger is not known to have participated in formation of this plan, but it represents his view that existing main lines should be upgraded, even in difficult country, to something of the character of the Union Pacific main line across the West.

Barriger's concept of super-railroading required replacement of the steam locomotive with a machine capable of continuous torque, higher speeds around curves, and cheaper maintenance. He was among the earliest advocates of dieselization, but when that conversion neared completion in the late 1950s, he concluded that the full benefits of continuous-torque power could not be realized short of electrification of main lines. To generate the traffic on a reduced network of main lines

for the capital-intensive development that he envisioned, he advocated regional mergers of parallel railroads along the lines of his Prince Plan.

From the outset, Barriger advocated vigorous freight solicitation as part of his super-railroading idea: the freight agent was to rank with the civil engineer. The higher standards of physical plants were to allow improved speed and assurance of arrival time, benefits that could be aggressively marketed.

Finally, Barriger sought to have the industry deregulated, though not in the sense of allowing free competition. He accepted the cartelized economic organization of the industry in which the firms are simultaneously rivals and joint venturers, pricing collusively through rate bureaus. He also accepted the regional geographical pattern and the industry's maxim that a railroad should not invade the territory of a friendly connection. He argued for abolition of the Interstate Commerce Commission (ICC) out of a belief that the ICC was a counterproductive element in the industry's traditional organization. He considered the commissioners poorly trained for their function and perverse in many of their actions. He particularly objected to the Hepburn Act of 1906, which, by allowing the ICC to set maximum rates, contributed in his view to the capital starvation from which the industry was suffering.

Barriger's first opportunity to implement his ideas was as president of the Chicago, Indianapolis & Louisville Railway (Monon Route), a post to which he was appointed when the railroad emerged from receivership in 1946. The Monon was hardly well suited to his philosophy, for its physical plant was poor even by the standards of the pre-Civil War period when most of it was constructed. It was built partly on an old highway grade, it had street-running (that is, the line ran down the middle of the street) at several points, and the southern half of its main line had a sawtoothed profile such that no one grade-elimination would much improve the property. He immediately began improving the track, dealing with deferred maintenance dating back nearly twenty years. He completely dieselized the railroad in three years. The experience of the Chicago-Twin Cities streamliners run by other roads had convinced him that passenger service could be profitable even through lightly populated intermediate territory, and he replaced the railroad's passenger cars with modern, streamlined equipment

John W. Barriger in 1962

non. Second, Barriger's experience on the Monon demonstrated that he was an excellent traditional railroad man, an obvious choice to minister to a sick railroad.

In 1952 Barriger's friend Frederic C. Dumaine offered him the vice presidency of the New York, New Haven & Hartford Railroad. Believing that he could accomplish little more with the Monon, he resigned the presidency effective at the end of the year and in 1953 undertook his new duties. Apparently recognizing the carrier's poor prospects, he stayed at the New Haven for only five months before moving to the vice presidency of the Chicago, Rock Island & Pacific Railway. This big, lightly-trafficked carrier also had a bleak future, but it was in the 1950s no worse than a weak sister among the Grangers. By the industry's standards, Barriger had achieved his highest position thus far; and he used it tirelessly to expound his doctrine, publishing his *Super-Railroads for a Dynamic American Economy* toward the end of his tenure with the company.

In 1956 Barriger was offered the presidency of the Pittsburgh & Lake Erie Railroad (P&LE), a semi-autonomous subsidiary of the New York Central, by the Central's chairman of the board, Alfred E. Perlman, a friend and associate of Barriger's since the 1930s. Presidency of the P&LE was Barriger's closest approximation to leadership of a super-railroad. The company had only 273 miles of route, but the main line of 65 miles between Pittsburgh and Youngstown was flat and multitracked, and was usually the most heavily trafficked part of the entire New York Central system. Barriger used his position to become prominent in civic affairs in Pittsburgh and in the railroad industry generally. He made speeches continually and practiced vigorously the traffic solicitation to which he was committed. His position put him in the high councils of the New York Central, which was probably the eastern railroad that most closely approximated his ideal both in physical plant and quality of freight service.

Although Perlman found Barriger a valuable associate, he was unyielding concerning the Central's policy of compulsory retirement at sixty-five. Barriger, a man with few interests outside of railroading, looked upon retirement not with reluctance but with terror. Upon retiring in December 1964, he returned to St. Louis and served briefly as consultant to the St. Louis-San Francisco Railway (Frisco). On

fabricated out of war surplus hospital cars. He even restored a Chicago-Indianapolis express discontinued by the previous management. He increased freight solicitation and made the railroad more competitive with the Chicago & Eastern Illinois, which he considered a stronger property, for movements from the South to Chicago. He made two major improvements in the Monon's physical plant, bypassing a bog on the main line near Cedar Lake and replacing a bridge over the Wabash River at Delphi. Neither project, however, reduced grades or curves as called for by his philosophy.

Barriger's presidency of the Monon demonstrated two things, both of which were to be important to his later career. First, his basic philosophy was not easy to implement. A strong railroad already in possession of a good physical plant, such as the Union Pacific, might make the grade reductions and easing of curves he recommended, but a weak railroad such as the Monon was very unlikely to do so; and neither the C&EI nor any other railroad in the area proved eager to merge with the Mo-

March 11, 1965, he was elected chairman of the board and chief executive officer of the Missouri-Kansas-Texas Railroad (MKT). The position gave him some of the same challenges he had faced on the Monon, but his options were considerably fewer. The MKT had been struggling with a heavy debt as a consequence of having avoided bankruptcy during the Great Depression. The management had dealt with the problem by thoroughly neglecting maintenance; the track was so bad that, as Barriger pointed out, a standing train could derail. He had little choice but to put such funds as he had at his disposal into improving the main line between Kansas City and Dallas. He instituted three daily freights and soon could offer reasonably punctual service. He expanded the car supply with equipment trusts and began replacing the railroad's early diesel locomotives with second-generation units. His efforts were impressive enough that the trade journal *Modern Railroads* made him its Man of the Year for 1968.

Barriger left the MKT in 1970, and proceeded to what was doubtless his least satisfying presidency, the position of chief executive officer of the Boston & Maine Railroad (B&M). The railroad was bankrupt and highly deteriorated, and had exceedingly bleak prospects. The Boston area, though it might be flourishing in higher education and high technology, was becoming a virtual traffic vacuum for a railroad. The B&M had some important originations on its Connecticut River line and in the New Hampshire industrial cities; but it could not be much upgraded physically, and traffic solicitation was unlikely to be much help. Barriger could merely keep it going while reorganization proceeded.

Upon winding up his duties with the Boston & Maine Barriger remained unwilling to retire, and 1973 accepted appointment as special assistant to Federal Railroad Administrator John W. Ingram. Ingram left the Federal Railroad Administration in 1974 to become head of the Chicago, Rock Island & Pacific, which by the 1970s was awaiting merger, dismemberment, or abandonment. In April 1976 Ingram appointed Barriger senior traveling freight agent of the Rock Island—a title of Barriger's own choosing—based at his home in St. Louis. Barriger was also active in 1976 as an expert witness for the railroads in their successful effort in federal tax courts to depreciate their rights-of-way. The railroads argued that the growth of the economy would generate traffic increases which would render existing rights-of-way obsolete and require replacement with something in the nature of Barriger's super-railroads. Thus, at the time of his death in St. Louis on December 9, 1976, less than a week after his seventy-seventh birthday, Barriger remained active in the industry; as he wished, he never reached retirement.

Barriger's administrative ability remains impressive; his philosophy, however, has not stood the test of time. The railroad's quality of service is so low relative to trucking that the industry is characterized by substandard rates of return and net outflow of resources. The capital markets will invest in the kinds of cost-saving improvements Barriger was able to make on the Monon and elsewhere, but not in the major renovations that he advocated. He considered the comprehensive containerization of cargo advocated by John G. Kneiling impractical, as requiring excessive revision in the way railroads operated. Railroading today, however, is in a fairly rapid conversion toward containerization and articulation. Neither massive improvement in rights-of-way nor electrification is making progress. Similarly, the intraregional mergers of parallel railroads that Barriger advocated have proved at best mildly effective in cost-saving, as in the case of the Seaboard Coast Line, but at worst counterproductive, as in the instance of the Penn Central.

Barriger had married Elizabeth Thatcher on September 25, 1926. They had four children, of whom the two sons also pursued railroad careers, John Walker Barriger IV rising to assistant to the president of the Atchison, Topeka & Santa Fe and Stanley Barriger becoming a consultant to the industry.

Publications:
"Super-Railroads," *Trains,* 4 (December 1943): 4-11;
"The Monon is a Guinea Pig," *Trains,* 7 (July 1947): 15-19;
Super-Railroads for a Dynamic American Economy (New York: Simmons-Boardman, 1956).

References:
George W. Hilton, *Monon Route* (Berkeley: Howell-North Books, 1978);
Harold H. McLean, *Pittsburgh & Lake Erie R.R.* (San Marino, Cal.: Golden West Books, 1980).

Archives:
Barriger's personal library—twenty-six tons of materials—is at the Mercantile Library of St. Louis.

Bessemer & Lake Erie Railroad

by Michael Bezilla

Pennsylvania State University

Incorporated in 1900, the Bessemer & Lake Erie Railroad (B&LE) united several smaller lines over which Andrew Carnegie had gained control in order to connect the Lake Erie iron ore docks with his steel operations in the Pittsburgh area. When Carnegie sold his steel interests in 1901, the B&LE was included as part of the transaction and became the property of the newly formed United States Steel Corporation (USS). Approximately three-quarters of the Bessemer's trackage, which held steady through the years at about 220 route miles, was main line, linking the lake ports of Conneaut, Ohio, and (via New York, Chicago & St. Louis [Nickel Plate] trackage rights) Erie, Pennsylvania, with North Bessemer (Pittsburgh). There interchange was made with another USS property, the Union Railroad, which in turn served the company's steel mills in Pittsburgh and the Monongahela Valley.

The railroad hauled iron ore and limestone south, steel products north, and coal and coke in both directions. Consequently it was able to post annual tonnage figures far in excess of larger roads, reaching a high of 2.3 billion ton-miles in the mid 1920s. It was consistently profitable, thanks to efficient management, the absence of numerous branch lines, and the relative security of guaranteed traffic from parent United States Steel even in times of recession. Indeed, during the Great Depression, the Bessemer recorded a net operating loss only in 1932. Throughout its history, the B&LE regularly achieved an operating ratio well below 80.

When the severe economic downturn of the early 1980s nearly wiped out the Pittsburgh area's mostly obsolete steel-making facilities, the B&LE un-

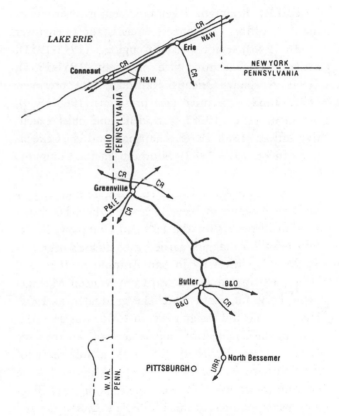

Map of the Bessemer & Lake Erie Railroad (1983)

derwent drastic retrenchments. In 1982 carloadings were barely half those of the previous year, and thirty-one units of the road's sixty-three-unit diesel locomotive fleet were in long-term storage. With the kind of prosperity the Bessemer had traditionally enjoyed unlikely to return, the railroad's sale by USX Corporation, as United States Steel is now known, was the subject of widespread industry speculation in 1987.

References:
Roy C. Beaver, *The Bessemer and Lake Erie Railroad, 1869-1969* (San Marino, Cal.: Golden West Books, 1969);

Gus Welty, "Assembly Line Railroading," *Trains*, 17 (September 1957): 16-25

Benjamin F. Biaggini

(April 15, 1916-   )

by Don L. Hofsommer

Augustana College

CAREER: Rodman, levelman, senior instrument-man, office engineer, assistant engineer (1936-1948), senior assistant engineer (1948-1951), assistant to executive vice president (1951-1955), Texas & New Orleans Railroad; vice president (1955-1963), executive vice president (1963-1964), president (1964-1968), president and chief executive officer (1968-1976), chairman and chief executive officer (1976-1983), Southern Pacific Company.

Born on April 15, 1916, to B. F. and Maggie Switzer Biaggini in New Orleans, where his father was an inspector for the Pullman Company, Benjamin Franklin Biaggini earned a bachelor's degree at St. Mary's University in San Antonio in 1936 and later participated in Harvard's Advanced Management Program, from which he graduated in 1955. His first railroad assignment, in 1936, was as a rodman in the engineering department of the Texas & New Orleans Railroad (T&NO), a subsidiary of the Southern Pacific (SP). In 1937 he married Anne Payton; the couple had two daughters. In 1951 Biaggini was appointed to the T&NO's executive department at Houston. He was named president of the Southern Pacific in 1964 and four years later assumed additional duties as chief executive officer. Few doubted his ability. The president of a connecting railroad said: "He is smart, knows the business, and has a good overview." Another railroad president, who once had worked for him, especially admired Biaggini's talent as a speaker.

Because of his geniality and his capacity for oratory, Biaggini frequently found himself on the speaker's circuit. His themes varied little: the importance of railroads in the opening and prosperity of the

Benjamin F. Biaggini (Courtesy Southern Pacific Company)

West; the pressing need to deregulate the railroads; the value of free enterprise "as a bulwark of the American system"; the obsolescence of the intercity passenger train; and optimism regarding the future of railroading.

Of these topics, Biaggini perhaps felt most strongly about deregulation. "The industry's greatest problem has been its inability to earn an adequate rate of return on its investment," he said in a 1970 address before the National Press Club in Washington. This inability, he maintained, "has been the result of strict economic regulation and of a national policy that has actively promoted and financed the growth of other forms of transportation . . . ." Additionally, he fumed, railroads were subject to difficulties in changing "rates, service and plant" because they were treated as "pure public utilities enjoying protected monopoly status while in fact they fight to stave off government-subsidized transportation at every turn." By the 1970s this combination of counterproductive measures had resulted in the Penn Central debacle, left several major roads with severe liquidity problems because of decreased working capital, and spawned a potential crisis in the Middle West. The SP's railroads were doing well by comparison, but their fate depended in part on that of others. "Even though we are many different companies, we are also an integrated rail system. The failures or disabilities of any part of this system affect the health of the whole," warned Biaggini.

On May 17, 1972, Donald J. Russell retired as SP chairman and the board handed Biaggini the reins. Biaggini's position was at once enviable and frightening. In the first place, the company which he now would lead was in good condition and well respected, but clearly in a period of unpredictable evolution. SP's "Golden Empire" service area and the generous traffic mix it offered had allowed the firm's railroads to prosper in the years following the Great Depression, but the future was uncertain; the very fabric of American railroading was in flux. In the second place, SP's success in becoming a leader of the rail industry in the 1950s and 1960s had bred a sense of pride and confidence which permeated the corporate culture; that pride and confidence, however, sometimes bordered on aloofness and arrogance, which annoyed fellow railroaders and, in some cases—particularly in California—the public at large. Finally, Russell's performance would be hard to follow.

Biaggini set about plotting a course for the SP and for the industry at large. He and most other rail executives were pleased as public sentiment gradually changed in favor of unshackling the carriers. This new sentiment took substantive form with passage of the Regional Rail Reorganization Act of 1973 to restructure the bankrupt railroads of the Northeast and the Railroad Revitalization and Regulatory Reform Act of 1976, which included provisions for flexibility in ratemaking and encouraged Biaggini and others to plead for equal treatment for all modes of transport. In 1978 BIAGGINI called attention to the "agricultural exemption" that allowed truckers to engage in interstate carriage of fresh fruits and vegetables without any rate regulation, and asked the Interstate Commerce Commission (ICC) for the same exemption. The timing was propitious; both Congress and the Carter administration were receptive to the notion of deregulation, and the ICC agreed to the SP's request. The decision, according to Biaggini, had come none too soon: "We have reached the absolute point of choice between either letting the railroads earn a fair return or else putting the whole country on notice to be prepared to pay the staggering bill for nationalization."

Meanwhile, Biaggini labored to better the SP's competitive position. An important part of this effort was the construction of the 560-acre, 5.7-mile–long, $39 million West Colton Classification Yard some 50 miles east of Los Angeles. The West Colton facility, which Biaggini touted as "the most technologically advanced rail terminal in the world," had capacity for 7,100 freight cars. Sophisticated computer and electronic equipment typified the operation, which was placed in service on July 19, 1973.

The West Colton Yard, noted Biaggini, would assume even greater importance once the SP acquired the southern portion of the Chicago, Rock Island & Pacific Railroad. That case, before the Interstate Commerce Commission since the mid 1960s, eventually ended miserably because the regulatory agency tarried while the Rock Island deteriorated. The Rock Island ended up in bankruptcy and sold off many of its railroad assets, including the strategic "Golden State Route," which the SP's St. Louis Southwestern subsidiary acquired to gain the important gateway at Kansas City and to shorten its route from the Los Angeles Basin.

The Rock Island debacle was only one element in the growing problems of the railroad industry as more and more intercity ton miles moved by other modes. These problems notwithstanding, Biaggini remained confident in the rail industry and the place of the SP's railroads in it. Merger, he concluded, was the proper medicine, and he vigorously pursued creation of the nation's first truly transcontinental system. During the early 1970s Biaggini had held informal discussions with W. Thomas Rice and Prime F. Osborn of the Seaboard Coast Line Railroad (SCL) and Hays T. Watkins of the Chesapeake & Ohio Railway (C&O) to see if a three-way partnership might be arranged–replicating, in a sense, the nineteenth century dream of Collis P. Huntington. The C&O eventually dropped out; but in the summer of 1977 the SP and the SCL each authorized initial studies, followed by a more formal agreement a few months later.

The SP/SCL would link the Pacific coast with the Atlantic by way of a 30,000-mile railway serving more than half of the nation's states. But there were problems: long–haul advantages would accrue for transcontinental traffic, but, because of the end-to-end nature of this merger, opportunities for savings by closing redundant facilities would be few. Many at the SCL felt that the SP's proposal offered little financial incentive and that Biaggini interpreted the word *merger* as *takeover*. Others at Seaboard were put off by Biaggini's "domineering style." The SCL's board of directors rejected the SP's offer on May 18, 1978. Biaggini attempted to change opinions at SCL but the Seaboard and the C&O soon announced their own plans for merger. Biaggini was philosophical: had the merger been consummated, he noted, it not only would have created the first transcontinental but also "would have initiated the ultimate wave of them."

Other mergers were coming, however, and Biaggini could not afford to be philosophical about them. The combination of the Union Pacific (UP) and the Missouri Pacific and acquisition of the Western Pacific by the UP created a colossus that could not be ignored by either the SP or its traditional competitor, the Atchison, Topeka & Santa Fe Railway (Santa Fe). Biaggini announced in 1980 that the SP and the Santa Fe were studying the possibility of merger, but again the attempt was abortive; and Biaggini's style was again at issue. While he was characterized by one writer as "an imperial presence, a towering monolith of a man," he was also called "unyielding," "aloof," "rigid," and "uncompromising." Objections were raised to Biaggini's unpredictable and explosive personality, his age (he was sixty-six in 1982), his salary ($699,200 in 1981), his unwillingness to decentralize authority, his active political involvement with wealthy conservative Republicans, and ultimately the very course he had set for the SP.

Those who thought that Biaggini or the company he headed would roll over and play dead were naive in the extreme. Again Biaggini announced merger negotiations with the Santa Fe, and on December 23, 1983, a new holding company, Santa Fe Southern Pacific Corporation, was launched. The fate of its rail assets–the Santa Fe Railway and the Southern Pacific Transportation Company and their various subsidiaries–was placed before the Interstate Commerce Commission in an application for merger. Biaginni retired in 1983.

Reference:

Don L. Hofsommer, *The Southern Pacific, 1901-1985* (College Station: Texas A&M University Press, 1986).

Boston & Maine Railroad

by David H. Hickcox

Ohio Wesleyan University

Map of the Boston & Maine Railroad (1983)

The origin of the Boston & Maine Railroad (B&M) can be traced to 1833, when the Andover & Wilmington Rail Road was incorporated to provide Andover, Massachussetts, with a connection to the Boston & Lowell, eight miles distant. The next year the directors expanded their horizons, declaring that the railroad's goal was to connect Boston with Portland, Maine. In 1835 the Boston & Maine Railroad was incorporated in New Hampshire and soon was consolidated with numerous other lines. The line to Boston was completed in 1845, and Portland was reached in 1873. In 1884 the Boston & Maine took control of its chief competitor, the Eastern Railroad. North Station in Boston, which was still in use in 1987, was completed in 1894 as a hub for both the B&M's commuter and long-distance passenger trains.

The Boston & Maine grew by consolidating neighboring railroads and in 1887 acquired an extension into southern Quebec. Many branch lines were constructed or acquired to tap the vast forests of the North Country as well as to link New England's farm communities with Boston, the region's primary market. Between 1883 and 1922 the B&M expanded from 207 to 2,248 miles.

The Boston & Maine evolved into a bridge line (a line that carries traffic between other railroads) connecting with the Maine Central at Portland and the Delaware & Hudson (D&H) at Mechanicville, New York, north of Albany. Its route through the Berkshires necessitated the 4.7-mile Hoosac Tunnel, the longest tunnel east of the Rocky Mountains, which was opened in 1876. The B&M also handled a considerable amount of traffic to and from Canada, with interchanges with the Central Vermont at White River Junction, Vermont, and with the Canadian Pacific at Wells River, Vermont. The Boston & Maine controlled the Maine

Central from 1933 to 1955; at that time it reached its maximum extent, owning or controlling almost 3,000 miles of track.

The Boston & Maine shrank to about 1,300 miles by abandoning branch lines and selling its line to Canada north of Wells River in 1946 to the Canadian Pacific. A true bridge line, the B&M originates less than 20 percent of its traffic. Paper products account for about 30 percent of the B&M's revenues, and the remainder is primarily chemicals and food products.

In 1970 the Boston & Maine declared bankruptcy. As part of its reorganization, the B&M sold its 279 miles of commuter lines to the Massachusetts Bay Transportation Authority in 1977. In 1982 the B&M acquired from Conrail several former lines of the New York, New Haven & Hartford Railroad, most notably from Springfield, Massachusetts, to Hartford, New Haven, and Waterbury, Connecticut.

Also in 1982 the Boston & Maine was acquired by Timothy Mellon's Guilford Transportation Industries, becoming part of a new regional railroad. Although the Boston & Maine retained its corporate identity, operations were merged with the Maine Central and the Delaware & Hudson and a common paint scheme was adopted. The Guilford

System diverted Canadian traffic from the Connecticut River line to the D&H, emphasizing the bridge line from Mechanicville to Portland. Headquarters are located at North Billerica, Massachusetts.

References:
Francis B. C. Bradlee, *The Boston and Maine Railroad* (Salem, Mass.: Essex Institute, 1921);

Robert M. Neal, *High Green and the Bark Peelers: The Story of Engineman Henry A. Beaulieu and His Boston and Maine Railroad* (New York: Duell, Sloan & Pearce, 1950);

Tom Nelligan and Scott Hartley, *Route of the Minute Man* (New York: Quadrant Press, 1980).

Robert J. Bowman

(April 15, 1891-January 2, 1958)

by Charles V. Bias

Marshall University

CAREER: Clerk (1907-1910), chief clerk (1910-1914), clerk and dispatcher in the superintendent's office (1914-1918), assistant chief clerk to the superintendent of freight transportation (1918-1920), chief clerk to the president (1920-1927), New York, Chicago & St. Louis Railway Company; assistant to the president (1927-1928), assistant vice president (1928-1929), Erie Railroad; vice president (1929-1942), president (1942-1946), Pere Marquette Railroad; president (1946-1948), chairman of the executive committee (1948-1957), Chesapeake & Ohio Railway Company; director, National Bank of Detroit and Detroit Fire and Marine Insurance Company (1957-1958).

Robert J. Bowman served in a supervisory capacity for three different railroad companies from 1928 to 1948. Born in Fostoria, Ohio, on April 15, 1891, Robert Jay Bowman was the son of Hiram Ellsworth and Nora Sarah Trone Bowman. He attended public schools in Fostoria and Findlay, Ohio.

Bowman began his career on the New York, Chicago & St. Louis Railroad (Nickel Plate) as a freight clerk in Mortimer, Ohio, in 1907. Attracted to a career as a telegrapher, he studied at night

until he mastered the Morse code. In 1910 he was made agent-operator and chief clerk for the Nickel Plate in Millers City, Ohio.

Soon his superiors realized that Bowman was able to master quickly the details of railroad operations and to adjust to new and unfamiliar situations. The company began using him as a troubleshooter, moving him from point to point on the line to untangle difficult problems and restore traffic to normal conditions. In pursuing these varied tasks, he acquired a wealth of experience. Meanwhile, he taught himself mathematics and the economics of railroading.

Bowman served in the dispatcher's office and in the superintendent's office of the Nickel Plate in Fort Wayne, Indiana, from 1914 to 1918, and as assistant chief clerk to the superintendent of freight transportation from 1918 to 1920. He received an appointment as chief clerk to the president in 1920. When J. J. Bernet became president of the Nickel Plate in 1923, he implemented an extensive program of rehabilitation and improvement; Bowman was one of the men whose services Bernet utilized.

Bowman moved to the Erie Railroad as assistant to the president in 1927 and became assistant vice president in 1928. In 1929 the Pere Marquette

Robert J. Bowman

appointed Bowman vice president in charge of operations and maintenance. In 1937 Robert R. Young and Allan P. Kirby acquired control of the Alleghany Corporation, which operated the Pere Marquette, the Nickel Plate, and the Chesapeake & Ohio (C&O) railroads. Bowman became one of their key men and received an appointment to the presidency of the Pere Marquette in 1942. He revitalized the railroad through the efficiency he introduced into his operations.

On April 23, 1946, Bowman succeeded Carl E. Newton as president of the Chesapeake & Ohio

Railway Company. During his two-year tenure Bowman continued the policies of his predecessors. Aided by the post-World War II prosperity in the United States and the heavy demands for the bituminous coal produced in areas served by the Chesapeake & Ohio, the line enjoyed great prosperity. The consolidation of the Pere Marquette and the Chesapeake & Ohio was completed during Bowman's presidency, but the C&O had held controlling interest in the Pere Marquette since 1929, and the details of the merger had been completed before Bowman became president. The approval of the Interstate Commerce Commission in 1947 completed the consolidation.

In October 1948 Walter J. Tuohy replaced Bowman as president of the C&O. The C&O reported that Bowman resigned as a result of ill health, but he remained active until his death on January 2, 1958. From 1948 to 1957 he served as chairman of the executive committee of the Chesapeake & Ohio; after resigning from this position, he became a director of the National Bank of Detroit and the Detroit Fire and Marine Insurance Company.

A Methodist and a Mason, Bowman was a self-made man: without the benefit of a college education he rose from the position of clerk with the Nickel Plate to the presidency of the seventh largest railroad in the nation, the Chesapeake & Ohio.

References:

Charles V. Bias, "A History of the Chesapeake and Ohio Railway Company, 1836-1977," Ph.D. dissertation, West Virginia University, 1979;

"Bowman To Head Merged P.M.-C&O," *Railway Age,* 120 (February 23, 1946): 409;

"Walter J. Tuohy New C&O President: Road's First Vice President, A Coal Traffic Specialist, Succeeds Robert J. Bowman, President Since 1946," *Railway Age,* 125 (November 6, 1948): 860.

Alan S. Boyd

(July 20, 1922-   )

by Richard W. Barsness

Lehigh University

Alan S. Boyd (Courtesy Airbus Industrie of North America)

CAREER: Private law practice (1948-1957); general counsel, Florida Turnpike Authority (1955); member (1955-1959), chairman (1957-1958), Florida Railroad and Public Utilities Commission; member (1959-1965), chairman (1961-1965), Civil Aeronautics Board; under secretary of commerce for transportation (1965-1967); secretary of transportation (1967-1969); president, Illinois Central Railroad (1969-1972); president and chief executive officer, Illinois Central Gulf Railroad (1972-1976);

head, United States delegation for United States-United Kingdom civil aviation negotiations (1977); president and chief executive officer, Amtrak (1978-1982); chairman, American High Speed Rail Corporation (1982-1985); chairman and president, Airbus Industrie of North America (1982 to present).

Alan S. Boyd is one of the nation's most versatile and successful transportation executives of the period following World War II. The range of leadership positions he has held in both the public and private sectors, and in different modes of transportation, is unmatched by any other individual. In the public sector his most notable accomplishments were effective leadership of the Civil Aeronautics Board (CAB) and the new United States Department of Transportation (DOT) during the 1960s, and the National Railroad Passenger Corporation (Amtrak) during the late 1970s. His most significant role in the private sector occurred in the early 1970s when he served as president of the Illinois Central Gulf Railroad (ICG).

Alan Stephenson Boyd was born on July 20, 1922, in Jacksonville, Florida, one of two children of Clarence Boyd, a civil engineer, and Elizabeth Stephenson Boyd. The family lived in Macclenny, a small town just west of Jacksonville. Boyd attended elementary school in Macclenny and received his high school diploma from Gordon Military Institute in Georgia in 1939. After completing two years of study at the University of Florida at Gainesville, he enlisted as an aviation cadet in the United States Army on December 8, 1941. After earning his wings, Boyd spent the balance of the war as a pilot in the Troop Carrier Command in the European theater. In 1943 he married Flavil Juanita Townsend. They became parents of one son, Mark Townsend.

Following military service, where he attained the rank of captain, Boyd resumed his formal education at the University of Virginia. He received his LL.B. in 1948, having already been admitted to the Virginia bar the previous year. He was admitted to the Florida bar in 1948 and entered private practice in Miami. He was called back to the military in March 1951 and served as a transport pilot in the Korean War. At the completion of his service, Boyd, who had been promoted to major, returned to his law practice in Miami.

Boyd's aviation experience, legal ability, and interest in politics prompted Governor Leroy Collins in 1954 to appoint him chairman of a civilian committee for the development of aviation in Florida. In 1955 he served as general counsel for the Florida Turnpike Authority until he was appointed to a short-term vacancy on the Florida Railroad and Public Utilities Commission. The next year, in his only bid for elective office, Boyd conducted a successful statewide campaign for a full term. Boyd served as chairman of the commission in 1957 and 1958.

Boyd's regulatory experience, familiarity with aviation law, and close ties with Senators Spessard Holland and George Smathers led in late 1959 to his appointment to the five-member Civil Aeronautics Board in Washington. Under the Federal Aviation Act of 1958, which superseded legislation adopted in 1938, economic regulation remained with the CAB while airway, airport, and most safety responsibilities were consolidated in the newly formed Federal Aviation Agency.

The airline industry in 1959 was in the early stages of the transition from piston-engine aircraft to jets, a technological revolution which brought enormous increases in aircraft size, speed, and range, and dramatic changes in productivity and route possibilities. Many carriers faced severe financial problems because they needed to reequip their fleets for competitive reasons despite excess capacity in the industry generally.

Against this background the CAB was confronted with critical decisions regarding appropriate fare levels, changing competitive relationships among domestic carriers, and international competition between American and foreign flag carriers. The agency's objective was to balance the interests of the traveling and shipping public on the one hand with the financial requirements of the carriers and their employees, stockholders, and creditors on the other. Boyd urged the airlines to broaden their market by lowering fares, to improve load factors by reducing the number of half-filled flights on major multicarrier routes, and, where necessary, to merge. Boyd's sensitivity to industry needs in this period of unusual stress helped the carriers to meet the burden of acquiring jets and to regain a sound financial footing.

Boyd's opportunity to influence policy increased significantly in February 1961 when President John F. Kennedy named him chairman of the CAB. On January 1, 1963, Kennedy reappointed Boyd to a full six-year term as a member. Kennedy and his successor Lyndon B. Johnson recognized Boyd's outstanding leadership of the agency by naming him to five consecutive one-year terms as chairman, a tenure exceeded by only one other individual in the agency's history.

To sharpen the focus of the agency's policies and bring greater efficiency to its operations, Boyd persuaded Kennedy in 1961 to approve a management reorganization plan which gave the chairman direct authority over the CAB staff and its workload. A major overhaul of staff assignments followed, allowing Boyd to promote especially talented individuals to key positions. Boyd also sought to have the board place more emphasis on its responsibility to encourage and promote air transportation, not just regulate it. One authority on the agency's history called Boyd "perhaps the most promotional-minded member the CAB had ever had." Promotional studies and projects included the Supersonic Transport, changing problems of international air transportation, the appropriate balance between various categories of domestic carriers, special transportation needs of Hawaii and Alaska, the relationship of the civil air transport system to national defense, and the needs of local service carriers. Boyd was especially proud of his role in establishing a class rate formula for the continued subsidization of the local service segment of the industry.

Boyd's service on the Civil Aeronautics Board proved to be the turning point in his career. Prior to his appointment he was an able but relatively unknown state official. Membership and then leadership of the CAB at a time of fundamental change in the airline industry gave Boyd both national visibility and an opportunity to make full use of his talents and expertise. Moreover, during this period the national political scene changed to his advantage. Boyd was not part of the "Eastern Establishment," but he was a Democrat and his performance at the CAB earned the respect of the Kennedy and Johnson administrations as well as the aviation industry. He had clearly become a promising candidate for other responsibilities.

In the spring of 1965 Boyd was appointed assistant secretary of commerce for transportation. In this position he was well placed to continue efforts by the Johnson administration to establish a cabinet-level Department of Transportation. Congress also had been gradually moving in the direction of consolidating transportation safety and promotional programs in a single agency, and in 1966 legislation was passed creating a unified DOT the following year. Some units which properly belonged in DOT, however, were omitted; for example, the Maritime Administration remained a separate agency because vested interests in the industry were strongly opposed to Boyd's views on maritime subsidies.

Boyd was the logical choice to head the new department, but he was kept in suspense for a time by President Johnson, who had a penchant for last-minute appointment surprises. In the end, logic prevailed and Boyd was appointed secretary of transportation in 1967. His responsibilities included a vast array of safety and promotional programs and some 100,000 employees.

The Department of Transportation sought to coordinate federal programs within the transportation industry with each other and with other economic and social programs. It also tried to view the various modes as components of a national transportation system which would respond to the needs of its users, rather than as individual industries which forced the users to conform to their requirements. DOT's goals were timely and appropriate, but Boyd recognized that progress would occur slowly, primarily through new programs and incremental funding opportunities. The Office of the Secretary would play a critical role, for this unit was unencumbered by traditional ties to specific segments of the transportation industry and was prepared to think in system terms. Boyd assembled an excellent staff and gave the Department of Transportation a solid start during its first two years.

In 1969, after a decade in Washington, Boyd was ready for new challenges. He accepted an offer to become the eighteenth president of the Illinois

Central Railroad (IC), the principal subsidiary of Illinois Central Industries. Some observers were surprised that Boyd chose to join the railroad industry, but he was interested in the challenges facing the railroads and felt that he could make some useful contributions. Boyd brought a fresh perspective to fundamental problems plaguing the industry—marketing strategy, labor relations, and government regulation. At DOT he had played an active role in the development of high-speed rail passenger service in the nation's northeast corridor and in the promotion of intermodal transportation services.

The principal axis of the IC's 6,760-mile system linked Chicago, St. Louis, Memphis, and New Orleans. Except for its reasonable level of debt, the company faced the same difficulties as the rail industry generally. Boyd's strategy in addressing these problems was developed in conjunction with the Illinois Central's chairman, William B. Johnson, and other senior managers. One particularly urgent problem was the growing magnitude of losses from both intercity and commuter passenger services. Since it was clear that this situation could not be reversed by corporate measures, Boyd argued that the government should determine which services were essential and should cover the resulting losses. Financial and managerial responsibility for intercity passenger service did eventually shift to Amtrak, and the IC's Chicago area commuter operations were ultimately incorporated into a mass transit district.

To increase freight revenues the IC tried innovative services such as Rent-a-Train and the Mini-Train, expanded intermodal service, and aggressively promoted the development of new industries in its territory. On the cost side of the ledger, Boyd and his colleagues made valiant efforts to reduce total labor expenses and to increase productivity. The company also participated in the industry's merger movement. In 1972 the IC merged with the largely parallel Gulf, Mobile & Ohio (G&MO) to form the Illinois Central Gulf Railroad. Boyd was named president of the combined 9,494-mile system, and subsequently chief executive officer as well.

In the end, neither the GM&O merger nor the other measures undertaken by Boyd and his staff were sufficient to produce an upswing in the ICG's fortunes. Fresh ideas and initiatives could not overcome the institutional barriers to change which permeated the industry in management, in labor relations, and in government regulation. Boyd's seven-year presidency proved to be principally an extended holding action which left him disappointed and frustrated. In the context of the severe decline of the railroad industry during the 1970s, however, his record at the ICG was no small achievement.

In 1976 Boyd resigned from the Illinois Central Gulf to concentrate on other directorships he held and to try to do some writing. This interlude did not last long, for in 1977 President Jimmy Carter asked him to take charge of the United States delegation negotiating a new bilateral air services agreement (Bermuda II) with the United Kingdom. Boyd's appointment carried the rank of ambassador. The American objective in the lengthy and difficult negotiations, which were held in London and Washington, was to liberalize the competitive policies governing air service between the two countries. In contrast, the British held that sovereignty took precedence over free competition and insisted that the benefits of the market be split evenly. In the end, a compromise was achieved. The results, however, were not popular in some quarters in the United States.

In 1978 the Carter administration asked Boyd to tackle an even more difficult assignment: leadership of Amtrak, the corporation established by Congress in 1971 to operate most of the nation's remaining intercity passenger trains. The persistent operating losses and lack of new investment that characterized rail passenger service during the 1950s and 1960s had left this once dominant mode of transportation in woeful condition by the early 1970s, a situation which Amtrak could not quickly reverse.

In fact, when Boyd became president and chief executive officer in 1978, there was serious risk that Amtrak itself might sink under the combined weight of the legacy it inherited and its own operating deficiencies. Hopes for the future rested primarily on large quantities of new equipment which had been ordered. But many fundamental issues remained unresolved, including labor costs and productivity, the scope and character of Amtrak operations in the long run, and whether federal budgetary support for these operations would be forthcoming. The issue of budgetary support became even more urgent following the election of President Ronald Reagan in 1980. Amtrak's passenger revenues covered only one-half of its $1.3 billion annual operating costs and none of its capital costs,

making the corporation a prime target of White House efforts to cut the growing federal budget deficit.

Boyd's administrative and political skills proved equal to the challenge. He made realistic cuts in marginal long-distance trains in order to preserve the concept of a national coast-to-coast system, and he cut employment throughout the corporation to bring costs under control. Both in Congress and in the administration he established credibility for Amtrak as a permanent entity. This credibility in turn enabled the corporation to win agreements from its rail labor unions to reform contracts and enhance productivity.

Boyd also pushed hard to improve train operations. The new equipment significantly increased the quality and reliability of service. In addition, Boyd strengthened Amtrak's performance by reorienting operations to serve marketing objectives and by improving relationships with the freight railroads which operated Amtrak trains outside the northeast corridor.

While Boyd was able to build a consensus between Congress, the administration, and other political interests regarding Amtrak's long-term role (and win over some vocal critics in the process), he was not equally successful in his efforts to stabilize the corporation's long-term funding. Boyd pointed out that in the absence of reasonably stable funding, the efficiency and quality of Amtrak's operations were bound to suffer: "We can't run this business like a yo-yo. You've got to be able to do some planning." But neither the administration nor Congress was inclined to provide for Amtrak's capital needs, especially in the face of large federal budget deficits.

When Boyd left the presidency of Amtrak in mid 1982, his accomplishments were widely acclaimed. Even the Reagan administration, which at one time had been less than enthusiastic about his views, had come to appreciate his managerial and political skills and his achievement in setting Amtrak on a steady course. Boyd retained one tie with the railroad industry by continuing as chairman of the American High Speed Rail Corporation, a joint effort by Amtrak and a group of private investors to promote "bullet train" service in California (especially the Los Angeles-San Diego corridor), and possibly Florida, Texas, and the Midwest as well. This promotional effort ran out of funds and died in early 1985.

Boyd's principal new role brought him back to the aviation industry. In 1982 he became chairman and president of Airbus Industrie of North America, a marketing organization for a European consortium producing large, efficient commercial jet aircraft. Airbus Industrie, which is headquartered in Toulouse, France, competes with Boeing and McDonnell Douglas for sales to major airlines throughout the world. Boyd's office is in New York.

Alan S. Boyd's long and impressive career in transportation spanned many different modes and organizations. In both the public and private sectors he demonstrated a sound grasp of strategic issues and a high level of administrative ability, political skill, and integrity. His range of experience was unmatched by any other individual in the post-World War II transportation industry, and because his leadership roles occurred at important junctures in the organizations he served, his impact on the progress of the industry was significant.

Publication:
"Amtrak: A World-Class Railroad," *Railway Age,* 183 (May 31, 1982) 37-40.

References:
Robert Burkhardt, *CAB—The Civil Aeronautics Board* (Dulles International Airport, Va.: Green Hills, 1974);

Dan Cupper, "Drawing a Bead on Boyd," *Passenger Train Journal,* 14 (August 1982): 11-13;

John F. Stover, *History of the Illinois Central Railroad* (New York: Macmillan, 1975);

U.S., Congress, Senate, Committee on Commerce, *Hearing on Nomination of Alan S. Boyd to Be Secretary of Transportation,* 90th Congress, 1st sess., January 11, 1967, serial no. 90-2.

D. William Brosnan

(April 14, 1903-June 14, 1985)

by Charles O. Morgret

D. William Brosnan (Courtesy Chase, Ltd. Photo)

CAREER: Resident engineer, Georgia State Highway Department (1923-1926); student apprentice assistant engineer (1926-1931), assistant engineer (1931-1936), Georgia, Southern & Florida Railway; trainmaster (1936-1938), superintendent (1938-1940), Cincinnati, New Orleans & Texas Pacific Railroad; superintendent, Georgia, Southern & Florida Railway (1940-1946); chief engineer, Western Lines (1946-1947); general manager, Central

Lines (1947-1952), vice president, operation (1952-1960), executive vice president (1960-1962), president (1962-1967), chairman and chief executive officer (1967), Southern Railway Company; consultant, Iron Ore Company of Canada (1970-1980).

To D. William (Bill) Brosnan belongs much of the credit for keeping the railroads of the United States under the free enterprise banner when, in the late 1950s and early 1960s, they seemed about to follow most other railroads of the world into government ownership. By leading the heavily labor-intensive railroad industry in embracing modern methods and technologies and controlling the worst abuses of labor unions, he helped it achieve a survivable, if still not ideal, balance of capital and labor. He was instrumental in removing from railroads the shackles of outmoded and oppressive government regulation, while at the same time arousing long-dormant competitive instincts in some of their managers with provocative and innovative marketing strategies designed to exploit their newly acquired freedom to compete. Robert B. Claytor, who retired as chairman and chief executive officer of Norfolk Southern Corporation in 1987, said of his erstwhile competitor: "Bill Brosnan was a most unique man . . . who literally dragged the railroad industry kicking and screaming into the twentieth century . . . some 50-odd years late. If the industry hadn't adopted the Brosnan approach to railroad operations, I think we would now all be part of a nationalized system."

A tough, always-in-charge, taskmaster–*Newsweek* magazine said that his "blunt, commanding personality dominates any gathering"–Brosnan was known for his demanding and autocratic style; being liked was not high among his priorities. But criticism of Brosnan's personality comes mostly from former subordinates, still smarting from his sharp sting. The broader consensus is that a more easygoing approach probably would have fallen short of reversing the "deteriorating railroad situation" that confronted President John F. Kennedy on taking office in 1961. "If Brosnan's style seems a throwback to the days of pioneering railroad barons," said *Newsweek,* "his line is the most modern in the country. The Southern has developed new concepts and new equipment, changed the economy of the South and led the lethargic railroad industry in adopting modern methods."

Born in Albany, Georgia, in 1903, Dennis William Brosnan was the eldest of the three boys and two girls of Dennis William and Sarah Elizabeth Wimbish Brosnan. He later traced the Brosnan clan in America to a great-great-grandfather who was said to have fled Ireland in 1810 rather than suffer the penalty of losing a thumb for a killing a stag out of season. Brosnan's father, however, who gained international renown as Albany's remarkably successful fire chief, and who died in 1966, stated that it was Brosnan's grandfather, Dennis Brosnan—not his great-great-grandfather—who immigrated to the United States, and that the year was 1860, not 1810. Moreover, he said that Dennis Brosnan's reason for leaving Ireland was not for shooting a stag illegally but for taking a salmon from the River Shannon, fishing in which was reserved for the lords and dukes of England. Other compelling evidence supports this version.

Brosnan graduated with honors from Albany High School in 1918 at age fifteen. Like many southern schools, Albany suffered from a shortage of math teachers and required only eleven total years of schooling for graduation. Brosnan's acceptance at Georgia Tech in Atlanta was, therefore, conditioned on his completing entry-level math, which he did the following summer. He graduated with a degree in civil engineering in 1923.

His first job was with the Georgia State Highway Department as resident engineer at Macon. He stayed there less than three years before finding the environment "too political" for his taste. Accepting a lower-paying job, he went to work for the Georgia, Southern & Florida Railway, a subsidiary of the Southern Railway, as a student apprentice assistant engineer, also at Macon. There he met Louise Geeslin, a clerk in the office of her father, the chief clerk to the Southern's superintendent of transportation. Brosnan had been brought up Roman Catholic, but after their marriage in November 1927 he joined Louise's church, the Southern Baptist, of which he remained a loyal member until his death. The direct opposite of Brosnan in temperament and personality, Louise was friendly and outgoing, yet low-key, the perfect counterbalance to his sometimes volatile behavior. The often-heard observation that he probably could not have achieved what he did without her is almost never disputed.

The stock market crash of 1929 and the Great Depression sent railroad traffic, along with the entire economy, into a tailspin. Many railroads were forced into bankruptcy, others teetered on the brink, and still others, the Southern included, had to stagger employment, two weeks on and two weeks off, to spread the work. The Brosnans were forced to fall back on farming, which Bill had learned as a boy, to make ends meet. Customers were found for the farm's produce, mainly milk and eggs, which Louise assisted in delivering each morning from a makeshift truck.

In October 1931 Brosnan was made assistant engineer in Chattanooga, Tennessee. In February 1936 he moved out of engineering and into train operations, a change he had sought, when he was named trainmaster on the Southern's Cincinnati, New Orleans & Texas Pacific Railroad subsidiary, with headquarters at Oakdale, Tennessee.

First to get his attention as trainmaster was a problem of drunkenness on the job among train and yard crews. Catching the yardmaster drinking on duty, Brosnan took him out of service. After thirty days off the job the officer, accompanied by his wife, came to Brosnan pleading for another chance. Brosnan acquiesced, on the condition that if he ever again caught anyone at Oakdale Yard drinking on the job, the yardmaster himself would be the first to go—permanently. The officer was required to sign a statement to that effect. Having thus secured a strongly motivated ally in his battle against drunkenness, Brosnan went on to bring the problem largely under control, not only at Oakdale but throughout his territory. Finding key people who could help him, and then giving them incentive to do so, was a strategy Brosnan would use often and to good advantage throughout his career.

In October 1938 Brosnan's aggressiveness and performance earned him the superintendent's job at Selma, Alabama. In May 1940 he returned to Macon as superintendent of the division on which he began.

Pearl Harbor was then a little more than a year and a half away, but war was already raging in Europe, and the nation's military was feverishly preparing for possible American involvement. Ever alert to opportunities to gain more business for the Southern, Brosnan and one of the Southern's traffic officers, Hamilton Brown, spotted such an opportunity at Camp Blanding, Florida, which was expanding to handle an expected influx of army trainees. For the Southern to serve it would require building a seven-mile line to the camp from Starke, Florida. Despite opposition from his general manager, who was overruled by management in Washington, D.C., Brosnan built the line in time for the Southern to share in the heavy traffic of the war period. To his superiors in Washington, the incident demonstrated that Bill Brosnan was a "comer" with rare potential.

In 1946 Brosnan reluctantly accepted a one-year appointment as chief engineer, Western Lines. Fearing that he would never get back to operations if he took the engineering job, Brosnan at first rejected the transfer, telling Harry A. DeButts, vice president (operation) that if ordered to take it he would be forced to quit. Only when DeButts promised that he would be returned to operations and shook hands to seal the deal did he accede. True to his promise, DeButts named Brosnan general manager a year later, when O. B. Keister retired.

Earlier than most, Brosnan sensed that in an age of increasing competition railroads would not be able to survive, much less prosper, with primitive tools and backward thinking. Long before others were even talking about the problem, he could see that railroads relied too heavily on human labor—which he often called "the costliest resource"—and far too little on technology. The timeworn practice of using large gangs of laborers with hand tools to build and maintain track was one of the first areas to receive his attention as general manager. It was a practice that had appalled him as a student apprentice in 1926, and nothing basically had changed in the next twenty-odd years of depression and war. With only a few exceptions, the machines to replace these gangs of laborers did not exist; they had to be invented and built. It was to this pioneering work that Brosnan, aided by a few skilled technicians, mainly at the Southern's Roadway Shops in Charlotte, North Carolina, first directed a major effort. Out of this early work came prototypes for

doing mechanically nearly every track and roadway job formerly performed by hand. A machine for pulling and replacing crossties was one of the first to be patented in Brosnan's name. Many others, most of them of a highly technical nature, contributed to his goal of enhancing efficiency and cutting costs by substituting machines for human labor.

Brosnan also started construction at Knoxville of an electronic automated hump freight classification yard, which was the first in the South and only the second in the United States. When the yard was completed in 1952, Brosnan was moving to Washington, D.C., to take over as vice president (operation) from DeButts, who moved up to president, succeeding Ernest Eden Norris. The Knoxville Yard was quickly followed by one at Birmingham, Alabama, which was named for Norris. Dozens of others were soon built nationwide, ending the need for thousands of switching locomotives and for the yard and shop crews who manned and maintained them.

In 1960 Brosnan was promoted to executive vice president, a newly created position giving him responsibility over sales (then called traffic). Long believing that railroads needed to tailor their service to the customer's needs, Brosnan was now in position to put his marketing ideas to the test. To head up an entirely new (for railroads) marketing approach, he brought back Robert S. Hamilton, an industrial engineer who had earlier gained his confidence by modernizing the Southern's car and locomotive shops and who had left the Southern in 1958 for what seemed to be a more promising future with the New York Central System. In his two-year absence, Brosnan had come to the shocking realization that a mainstay of railroad traffic—coal—was about to be lost to emerging technologies. One threat was an experimental pipeline for moving coal slurry (a mixture of powdered coal and water): a coal—fired electric generating plant was being built by Alabama Power Company at Wilsonville, Alabama, with the coal to be supplied by the company's own mines near Jasper, Alabama, with some 135 miles distant. Unwilling to pay the going rail rate of $3.30 per ton, Alabama Power was on the verge of building a coal-slurry pipeline to move its coal. The Southern's answer, supplied by Hamilton's marketing team, assisted by L. Stanley Crane, assistant chief mechanical officer, was a new lightweight, mostly aluminum car of 100-ton capacity, named "Silversides" for its shining aluminum exterior, to be operated in unit trains shuttling between the Jasper mines and the Wilsonville plant. Unit trains were to become another Brosnan and Southern Railway "first," inaugurating a nationwide revolution in transporting coal at sharply lower cost.

An even more famous car built for the Southern at Brosnan's instigation and under the direction of the Hamilton-Crane marketing team was the key to regaining for railroads another major bulk commodity—grain—which they had already lost, mainly to unregulated trucks. Called "Big John," it too was of lightweight construction and 100-ton capacity (later models carried 110 tons). So efficient was the car compared to boxcars formerly used to haul grain that it enabled Brosnan to slash the Southern's rates on grain in five-car lots by 65 percent. Yet, for five years, he was prevented from doing so by the Interstate Commerce Commission, (ICC)—the same government agency, ironically, that Congress had established in 1887 to assure low freight rates.

Only after two trips to the United States Supreme Court did Brosnan, who became president of the Southern in 1962, finally win the right to lower grain rates by the full amount. In essence, the Court upheld Brosnan's contention that a railroad may not be forced to forego a rate advantage merely because a competitor cannot, or will not, meet the lower rail rate. Bowing to the Court's decision, the ICC approved the full rate reduction in September 1965. His historic victory thus reversed nearly a century of the nation's regulatory philosophy, restoring to consumers the benefits of fair pricing competition in the transportation marketplace. Moreover, it set the stage for the passage of the Staggers Act of 1980, which effectively deregulated railroads and freed them to compete on equal terms.

As a junior officer, Brosnan had strongly supported dieselization, a key technology that had helped to bring the railroad's labor-capital ratio into better balance. But neither the Southern nor any other railroad was yet getting from the diesel its full potential for cutting costs by eliminating the fireman, whose job it had rendered redundant. When that burden was finally lifted in the mid 1960s, it was Brosnan who led the way. After a federal court denied him the right to eliminate unneeded firemen by attrition, he filled most of the va-

cant firemen's jobs with black males, sixty-five years of age and older, who, he said, were otherwise unemployable. This master stroke made his point about not needing firemen and made it possible to end the long-running controversy with unions over the fireman issue.

Brosnan had broken the industry's otherwise solid, if largely ineffectual, front to go it alone on the fireman issue. Such departures from industry solidarity had earned him a reputation early on as a maverick. In 1957, while still operating vice president, he had persuaded President DeButts to break with the industry in seeking an across-the-board freight rate increase. "We've all got pencils around here," he later told *Fortune* magazine, "and we can figure. When you increase rates 5 percent and you don't get a 5 percent increase in earnings, or when you increase 5 percent and you get a *decrease* in earnings—that's a real red flag."

An early advocate of the computer, Brosnan looked beyond its obvious potential for trimming the vast army of workers in the accounting department to the promise it held for solving many traditional operating problems and improving service. As vice president, he had helped persuade President DeButts and the board to install the industry's first computer, an IBM 705, Model 2, in December 1956, when computerization was still in its infancy. To accomplish the broader goals Brosnan had in mind would require tying the whole railroad into a central computer by a communications system capable of transmitting voluminous amounts of data, such as information on the freight waybills which accompany each freight car from origin to destination. After several false starts, Brosnan finally found the answer in microwave, another emerging technology. As the system came on line and was perfected, age-old problems of railroads disappeared or diminished in importance. Among these were "lost" cars, which had become separated from their waybills and were unidentifiable as to shipper or destination. Other vintage problems, such as detecting "hot boxes" (overheated axles or journals) were largely solved by tying still other new technologies to the microwave and computer networks. Trackside infrared detectors were installed to measure the temperatures of each passing car and locomotive wheel and convey the information automatically via microwave to a central read-out office in Atlanta for appropriate action.

The use of radio-controlled locomotives to increase the amount of tonnage handled in a single train was begun by Brosnan at about the time he became president and was brought substantially to perfection under his prodding over a five-year period. Usually placed midway in trains but controlled from the head end, such unmanned helper locomotives meant not only fewer train crews but also fewer broken couplers and drawbars caused by pulling too-heavy loads.

An area in which all railroads, the Southern included, had lagged far behind other industries was personnel management. Aware that something needed to be done without knowing exactly what, Brosnan early in 1964 hired George S. Paul, a former professor of industrial relations who was then director of personnel for the J. M. Ney Company. Together, they gave the Southern the first full-fledged personnel department in the industry. The new department centralized hiring and began seeking out the most capable people, including bright young college graduates, and training them in management or other needed skills. Performance was evaluated on a uniform and continuing basis, with promotions and salary advances following according to ability and performance. The rest of the industry soon followed suit.

One unique personnel initiative on which the industry did not follow Brosnan's lead was a practice he had begun as general manager of assembling key operations officers at Almond, North Carolina, to discuss problems and seek solutions. As executive vice president, he had expanded the list of those required to attend these annual gatherings to the sales department, and still later, as president, to all departments. Held at first in October, later in November, the Almond meetings were attended by some 1,500 officers each year from all over the system. Accomodations were sparse and basic, with sessions held in circus-style tents and meals served in a giant mess tent. Despite the austere conditions, many credit the Almond meetings with getting nearly everyone on the Southern Railway pulling in the same direction and, hence, for much of the company's growth and financial success. Although the heads of several other railroads expressed interest in the Almond approach and some even sent representatives to observe and report on it, no other railroad is known to have adopted a similar practice, despite its demonstrable success at the Southern.

Perhaps no railroad has served as the training ground for more presidents of other railroads than the Southern under Brosnan. L. Stanley Crane, who as chairman and chief executive officer is credited with near miracles in restoring Conrail to solvency, is but one of many from the Brosnan "school" who went on to top posts with other railroads.

Not even the Southern's law department survived Brosnan's tenure with its policies and procedures intact. That Brosnan profoundly disliked lawyers was well known, for he made no attempt to hide the fact. As president, he made it clear that he did not want lawyers telling him what he could and could not do; he wanted them only to tell him how he could do, legally, what he knew had to be done. Only those lawyers who understood that distinction were welcome on his team. Despite serious differences with Brosnan on important issues, W. Graham Claytor, Jr., demonstrated remarkable staying power by heading the Southern's law department throughout Brosnan's tenure as president. Perhaps even more remarkable, Claytor, though a lawyer, was Brosnan's choice to be the Southern's president when he retired.

In 1966 Brosnan unofficially transferred his office from the Southern's headquarters in Washington, D.C., to Asheville, North Carolina, where he had bought a house to be near his son and his son's family. Having to deal with him from that distance made it difficult for his associates and staff to give timely handling to matters requiring his attention. Although he was not due to retire until he reached the age of sixty-five in April 1968, Brosnan decided—for tax reasons and out of concern for his wife's heart condition—to take early retirement on November 28, 1967.

In 1970 Brosnan was asked by the Iron Ore Company of Canada to help increase the capacity of its 360-mile-long railroad connecting its Labrador mines with the port of Sept Iles. Expressing no interest at first, Brosnan was finally persuaded to fly to Labrador "just to have a look." To his practiced eye, the opportunities for improvement were readily apparent, and the challenge proved irresistible. He agreed to serve as a consultant, a post he filled with distinction for ten years. The opportunity could not have been more timely, for having important work to do helped Brosnan, devastated in July 1973 by the loss of his wife of forty-six years, to adjust to life without her. With the assistance of specialists made available by the Southern, Brosnan first doubled, then nearly tripled, the railroad's capacity to move ore to the port; the lack of such capacity had limited the company's participation in the world ore market. Brosnan's work in retirement was thus far more than a postscript to his profoundly significant career with the Southern; it amounted indeed to a career in itself.

B. M. (Mike) Monaghan, the company's general manager of operations at Sept Iles, worked closely with Brosnan throughout his years as a consultant. Monaghan journeyed to Asheville in June 1985 to pay his last respects at Brosnan's funeral. "Bill Brosnan," he said, "was one of the world's great industrial leaders, and I am proud to have counted him amongst my friends."

Brosnan was accorded many honors during his illustrious career, including honorary doctorates from Clemson University, Mercer University, and the University of Chattanooga. In 1963 readers of *Modern Railroads* voted him Railroad Man of the Year, and the Sales and Marketing Executives International named him National Salesman of the Year. In 1965 the Freedoms Foundation at Valley Forge awarded him its George Washington Medal of Honor, and he was named president of the prestigious Defense Orientation Conference Association, sponsored by the United States Department of Defense.

On his retirement, Brosnan's fellow directors found other ways to express their appreciation. Claytor, in one of his first acts as president, proposed naming a 15,000-acre forest preserve which the Southern owns south of Charleston, South Carolina, in his honor, and the board unanimously approved. A lifelong aficionado of the outdoors, especially hunting and fishing, Brosnan had called on his engineering expertise to drain a tract of useless swampland into several lakes, which he stocked with fish appropriate to the area. He had added facilities for hunting; spacious, well-equipped cabins for guests; and a main lodge complete with swimming pool and a pitch—and—putt golf course. An enduring monument to his vision and initiative, Brosnan Forest was once called by one of its many notable guests "the finest thing of its kind in the world." Its use for the entertainment of government officials and the Southern's customers was, however, discontinued several years after Brosnan's retirement when such use came under the scrutiny of the Inter-

state Commerce Commission and United States Department of Justice. Since then, Brosnan Forest has become a favorite vacation facility for employees, while also serving as a useful demonstration forest preserve.

The last automated freight yard built by the Southern before Brosnan's retirement was at Macon. Over his objection that memorials should not be erected to the living, the ultramodern $13 million facility was officially named Brosnan Yard and dedicated in his honor in 1968.

Finally, the Southern's board, again at Claytor's initiative, established a $250,000 scholarship in his honor at Georgia Tech. A living memorial, the D. William Brosnan scholarship is helping to educate other young "Ramblin' Wrecks," some of whom just might turn out to be other Bill Brosnans. That would be the most fitting legacy of all for a man who made a career of bringing out the best in people while ever looking forward to and building for the future.

Unpublished Documents:
"Coming Trends in Railroad Technology," speech to the Railroad Public Relations Association, Sea Island, Georgia, June 6, 1960 (Southern Railway Company Archives, Atlanta, Georgia);

"The Choice Is Yours," commencement address, Georgia Institute of Technology, June 13, 1964 (Southern Railway Company Archives, Atlanta, Georgia);

"When Tradition Has No Answers," speech to the National Association of Shippers Advisory Boards, Washington, D.C., October 15, 1964 (Southern Railway Company Archives, Atlanta, Georgia);

"Push-Button Yards," speech to the New York Railroad Club, New York City, November 23, 1964 (Southern Railway Company Archives, Atlanta, Georgia);

"Business and Education—A Partnership," speech at Gardner-Webb College, Boiling Springs, North Carolina, March 22, 1965 (Southern Railway Company Archives, Atlanta, Georgia);

"The Goals We Seek," speech at the University of Tennessee, Knoxville, March 26, 1965 (Southern Railway Company Archives, Atlanta, Georgia);

"The Future Belongs to Those Who Prepare for It," speech to the New York Society of Security Analysts, New York City, September 17, 1965 (Southern Railway Company Archives, Atlanta, Georgia).

References:
Robert E. Bedingfield, "Personality: Traveling Chief of Southern," *New York Times*, November 29, 1964, p. 3:3;

"Boxcars Go to Battle for Southern," *Business Week* (June 8, 1963): 76-80;

"Can a Railroad Win Back Lost Traffic?," *Forbes,* 89 (March 15, 1962): 20-23;

Frank L. Church, "Man of the Year—Southern Railway's Bill Brosnan," *Modern Metals,* (January 1963);

Burke Davis, *The Southern Railway: Road of the Innovators* (Chapel Hill: University of North Carolina Press, 1985);

"How to Run a Railroad," *Forbes,* 94 (December 15, 1964): 38;

Harold B. Meyers, "A Hell of a Different Way to Run a Railroad," *Fortune,* 68 (September 1963): 100-109;

"One Way to Run a Railroad: 'Go to It!'" *Newsweek,* 66 (October 18, 1965): 89-90;

"A Railroad Giant Is Lost," *Traffic World,* 203 (August 5, 1985): 4.

Archives:

D. William Brosnan's papers are in the Southern Railway Company Archives, Atlanta, Georgia, and in the author's custody.

William C. Brown

(July 29, 1853-December 6, 1924)

by Keith L. Bryant, Jr.

Texas A&M University

William C. Brown

CAREER: Section laborer and fireman (1869-1870), telegraph operator, night train dispatcher (1871-1872), Chicago, Milwaukee & St. Paul Railway; train dispatcher, Illinois Central Railroad (1872-1875); train dispatcher, Chicago, Rock Island & Pacific Railway (1875-1876); train dis-

patcher (1876-1880), chief train dispatcher (1880-1881), trainmaster (1881-1884), assistant superintendent (1884-1887), superintendent (1887-1890), Chicago, Burlington & Quincy Railroad; general manager, Hannibal & St. Joseph Railroad and Kansas City, St. Joseph & Council Bluffs Railroad (1890-1896); general manager, Chicago, Burlington & Quincy Railroad (1896-1901); vice president and general manager, Lake Shore & Michigan Southern Railway (1901-1902); senior vice president, New York Central & Hudson River Railroad (1902-1905); senior vice president (1905-1909), president (1909-1914), New York Central System.

For over forty-five years William C. Brown labored in the nation's rail industry, rising from woodcutter and tender loader to the presidency of a premier eastern carrier. Lacking formal schooling, Brown took upon himself the job of education, and he became a leading spokesman for the industry. An inveterate speaker, Brown worked to create a more favorable public image of the railways during the Progressive Era. Before his retirement he represented a quiet, positive voice seeking to bring harmony between the leaders of railroading and the Interstate Commerce Commission (ICC), which had obtained the power necessary to regulate the industry.

William Carlos Brown was born in 1853 in Norway, Herkimer County, New York, where his father, the Reverend Charles E. Brown, served as a Baptist clergyman. The family moved to Vernon Springs, Iowa, in 1857, and Brown received his early education from his mother, Frances Lyon Brown. After attending public schools for a few years, the boy found employment in 1869 on a section gang with the Chicago, Milwaukee & St. Paul Railway (St. Paul Road) in Thompson, Illinois, loading wood on the tenders of locomotives. Soon promoted to locomotive fireman, the ambitious youngster decided to teach himself telegraphy at night in order to advance to a better job. His superiors found him a hard and willing worker, and with their support he secured a telegrapher's position at Charles City, Iowa, in 1871. His skill led to promotions on the St. Paul and then to employment on the Chicago, Rock Island & Pacific in 1875 and the Chicago, Burlington & Quincy (CB&Q) in 1876.

During the next twenty-five years Brown moved up through the ranks of the Burlington, a carrier that proved to be the training school for a number of men who later found executive positions with other firms. Brown demonstrated his willingness to do much more than was required of him, on one occasion helping to unload cattle cars in a blizzard after completing his trick in the telegrapher's office. He seemed always determined to find better ways to get work accomplished, and his superiors allowed him opportunities to demonstrate his ideas. Brown worked the Iowa division on the "Q," rising from telegrapher to chief train dispatcher and trainmaster. During the "Great Burlington Strike" of 1888 Brown replaced a striking engineer in the cab of a mail train and took the consist to Chicago safely and on schedule. In dealing with strikes and labor disputes he became known as "the little man unafraid." After serving as superintendent on the Iowa line from 1887 to 1890, Brown was made general manager of two Burlington subsidiaries. In 1896 he returned to the CB&Q as general manager. For the next five years he contributed to the rising efficiency and profitability of the carrier and also attracted the attention of executives of other railroads.

W. H. Newman, president of the Lake Shore & Michigan Southern Railway (LS&MS), decided that Brown would be a good addition to the management of that line, which was about to become a sub-sidiary of the New York Central (NYC). When Newman became president of the NYC in 1901 he offered the energetic Brown the position of vice president and general manager of the LS&MS, and Brown entered the world of the New York Central. There followed a rapid movement through the management of that huge carrier as Newman gave him ever-increasing responsibilities. In 1902 he moved to New York as senior vice president of the New York Central & Hudson River Railroad, and in 1905 he was named vice president of the other New York Central affiliates. Newman retired in 1909, and on February 1, Brown assumed the presidency of the NYC. His work had obviously pleased the board of directors, which promoted him above many long-time executives of the company.

Throughout his railroad career Brown devoted himself to education to make up for his limited formal training. He read widely in finance, government, and economics. While general manager of the Burlington he had asked his secretary to help him learn proper grammar. After he joined the New York Central his world broadened markedly, and his reading reflected those expanding horizons. Brown became convinced that the railroads had to explain to the public how they operated, why they needed capital, and the negative impact of demands for strict—even harsh—regulation of the carriers.

As Brown was moving up in the management of the NYC, the cries of consumers, small business leaders, farmers, and other interest groups had grown louder in demanding lower rates on the nation's railroads. More than just an end to free passes, rebates, and long haul—short haul discrimination, they wanted the federal government to empower the Interstate Commerce Commission to set maximum rates—that is, much lower rates. Brown and a few other executives saw regulation as inevitable and sought to accommodate it by seeking "fair" rates that would not preclude profits and the raising of capital for modernization through security issues. If investors came to believe that the ICC would set rates so low that profits could not be earned, then stocks and bonds could not be sold and the nation's rail system would deteriorate.

Like most other railways after 1900, the New York Central and its affiliates needed vast sums for modernization. Brown wanted more efficient locomotives, steel passenger cars, freight cars with larger capacities, expanded signaling systems, more lines with double track, and new yards and freight facilities. Also, the NYC had been ordered by the City of New York to electrify its trackage in the city to end pollution, reduce noise, and increase safety. Complying would require huge expenditures for equipment, trackage realignment, and the rebuilding of Grand Central Terminal on Forty-second Street. As senior vice president, Brown had had a 200-page booklet entitled *Freight Rate Premier* printed and widely distributed. The booklet argued that a 10 percent increase in rates would be hardly noticed by consumers; but shippers and the public thought that they would bear the burden, and few listened to the logic of Brown's case. President Theodore Roosevelt told Brown in 1908 that an election year was a poor time to try to raise railroad rates. Brown persevered, however, writing to politicians, shippers, and others trying to present the "facts" about railway finance and pleading for fairness and accuracy in the debates.

As president of a major railroad Brown commanded attention from the press, and as a spokesman for the industry he had the ear of the president of the United States. He and other railway leaders met with President William Howard Taft in 1910 and, "hats in hand," begged for relief from oppressive regulatory legislation pending in congress. But Taft ignored their pleas. In the face of presidential support for extending the powers of the ICC in reducing rates, for ending "communities of interest" through stock ownership, and for placing the carriers under the antitrust laws, Brown saw the need for an immediate public relations effort. He vehemently denied that the NYC was threatening to end or reduce betterment programs if rates were not increased. He and other executives met again with President Taft and, in an effort at conciliation, told him that they would withdraw requests for rate hikes and continue the raises granted to workers. The Progressives in Congress were as unyielding as the president, however, and the Mann-Elkins Act became law.

The authority granted the ICC forced Brown and other railroad leaders to devote considerable attention to the commission in their quest for "adequate" rates. In 1910 Brown tried to show the commissioners the consequences of declining revenues on betterments. A small man with a pleasant voice, Brown spoke quietly, in measured tones. The New York Central and its affiliates, he pointed out, were

in the midst of a $230 million improvement program. Freight and passenger lines into New York City were being rebuilt with no prospect that they would generate additional revenue. A bond issue for improvements on the Michigan Central had brought a bid of only 87 cents on the dollar. The NYC was putting a quarter of its profits into improvements and paying dividends of only 4.7 percent while trying to reduce the system debt of over $254 million. Fixed charges were extraordinary, even though the interest rates on the debt were low. There was no watered stock on the New York Central; it was worth twice its book value, Brown declared. In reply, Progressive attorney Louis Brandeis told the railway president that he should cut dividends; besides, all the problems could be solved, he said, with greater efficiency. Brown assured Brandeis that efficiency experts who could solve the problems of the NYC could find immediate employment there.

Having met with intransigence from the ICC, Brown stepped up his public relations efforts. He appeared before chambers of commerce, trade associations, and press organizations and wrote articles for magazines, newspapers, and trade journals. Brown showed how the railroads themselves had lowered rates through the reclassification of goods in the interest of traffic solicitation. The rising cost of fuel, equipment, and construction, as well as wage increases, while rates fell had deprived the carriers of financial growth and the nation's rail system was suffering badly. The self-educated Brown toured the Northeast speaking to civic and commercial groups, describing the advances being made in improving the New York Central, on the one hand, and missed opportunities because of a lack of capital, on the other.

In 1910 the Executive Committee of Six, made up of Brown and five other leaders, formed the Bureau of Railway Economics, which was supported by contributions from the railroads. Employees of the bureau, including trained economists, worked with the executives to reduce public hostility toward the railroads. Armed with data produced by the bureau, Brown argued in 1913 that no railway president wished to see the ICC abolished; they only wanted the commissioners to see that the assumptions of 1887 were no longer valid. While praising the commission for ending rebates and free passes, Brown urged reconsideration of its position on rates.

The constant fight over rates and the substantial public relations campaign had to be waged while Brown managed the New York Central. After turning over some operational responsibilities to Alfred H. Smith, who had followed him to the Central from the Lake Shore, Brown carried through major engineering works such as the new west side freight terminals in Manhattan, Grand Central Terminal, and the electrification of lines into the city. Brown's capacity for organization was sorely taxed on the Central, but he was clear-headed, possessed an excellent memory, and judged men with accuracy. He also proved adept at keeping the various units of the railroad working harmoniously. Under Brown revenues and traffic doubled in volume, and 75,000 employees, 3,700 locomotives, 147,000 cars and 14,000 miles of track received his constant attention. But while wages rose 21 percent from 1910 to 1914, revenues climbed only 14 percent. Efficiency did improve, as Brandeis had maintained it should, but not to the point of making the Central, or American railroads in general, attractive investments. Over $78 million in capital outlays were made between 1910 and 1914, but much of that expenditure did not produce any new revenues and many betterment needs had to be postponed.

By 1914 Brown showed increasing signs of deafness. His loss of hearing led him to retire as president of the railroad on January 1 of that year. He had married Mary Ella Hewitt at Lime Springs, Iowa, in 1874, and upon his retirement they moved to a farm near that community. The Browns had three daughters, and it was to his family and the promotion of agriculture that he devoted himself after 1914. He actively campaigned for soil conservation and the creation of experimental farms. Brown and his wife lived in Pasadena, California, in the winter, and he was in residence there at the time of his death in December 1924.

Publications:

Freight Rates and Railway Conditions: Addresses and Correspondence (New York: New York Central, 1909);

"The Remedy for the High Cost of Living," *Independent,* 68 (June 30, 1910); 1424-1428;

"Relations of the Railroads to the Public—Co-operative, Not Antagonistic," *Scientific American,* 104 (June 17, 1911): 587, 607-608.

References:

"A Back-To-The–Lander's Vision," *Literary Digest,* 47 (December 13, 1913): 1192-1193;

"The Footprints of William C. Brown," *Current Literature,* 51 (December 1911): 618-620;

Albro Martin, *Enterprise Denied: Origins of the Decline of American Railroads, 1897-1917* (New York: Columbia University Press, 1971);

John Kimberly Mumford, "This Land of Opportunity: The Story of a Man Who Stayed 'On His Job,' " *Harper's Weekly,* 52 (June 20, 1908): 11-14.

John M. Budd

(November 2, 1907-October 25, 1979)

By W. Thomas White

James Jerome Hill Reference Library

John M. Budd

CAREER: Assistant chairman (1926), assistant to electrical engineer (1930-1931), assistant trainmaster (1933-1934), trainmaster (1934-1940), divisional superintendent, Great Northern Railway Company (1940-1942); major, lieutenant colonel, Military Railway Service, United States Army (1942-1945); assistant general manager, lines east of Williston, North Dakota, Great Northern Railway Company (1945-1947); president, Chicago & Eastern Illinois Railroad Company (1947-1949); vice president-operating (1949-1951), president (1951-1970), Great Northern Railway Company;

chairman and chief executive officer (1970-1971), finance committee chairman (1971-1972), director (1970-1977), Burlington Northern, Incorporated.

John M. Budd was one of the great consolidators and modernizers of the railroad industry in the twentieth century. Like his father, he served as president of the Great Northern Railway (GN), on which he introduced a number of important technological and managemental innovations. Largely as a result of his efforts, the GN entered into a "mega-merger" with three other railroads in 1970 to form Burlington Northern, Inc. (BN). This merger was the direct descendant of the Northern Securities Company, which had been set up by James J. Hill and Edward H. Harriman in 1901 and was broken up by the United States Supreme Court in 1904 in one of the most spectacular cases of the Progressive Era.

John Marshall Budd was born in 1907 in Des Moines, Iowa, to Ralph and Georgia Anna Marshall Budd. The senior Budd was then serving as chief engineer for the Panama Railroad at Colon, Panama. Subsequently, he served as president of the Great Northern Railway, the Chicago, Burlington & Quincy, the Colorado & Southern, and the Burlington–Rock Island, as well as a term as chairman of the Chicago Transit Authority.

John Budd often accompanied his father on inspection trips throughout the nation, gaining a solid sense of America's geographical diversity. After attending the prestigious Saint Paul Academy in Minnesota and Phillips Exeter Academy in New Hampshire, he received a degree in civil engineering from Yale University, followed by graduate study in transportation-related subjects in 1932-1933.

Budd's railroading career began earlier, however. In the summer of 1926 he was a chainman on a Great Northern engineering party working on the construction of the railroad's Cascade Tunnel in Washington State. In subsequent summers during his collegiate career he worked on other parts of the GN line, where he gained valuable practical experience. Upon his graduation from Yale, Budd accompanied his father on a two-and-one-half-month inspection tour of the Russian railway system. Returning home, he again went to work for the Great Northern, serving as an assistant to the railroad's chief electrical engineer until he returned to Yale for his year of graduate work.

In 1933 he was appointed assistant trainmaster for the GN at Willmar, Minnesota. He was promoted to trainmaster the following year and served in that capacity at Sioux City, Iowa, and Wenatchee and Spokane, Washington. He was promoted to superintendent at Klamath Falls, Oregon, in 1940 and two years later was rotated to the same position at Whitefish, Montana.

Although he was thirty-five years old and held a responsible position, Budd volunteered for service in World War II in late 1942. He entered the army with the rank of major in the Military Railway Service and served in Algeria, Italy, France, and Germany. A lieutenant colonel and commander of the 727th Railway Operating Battalion by the end of the war, he was discharged immediately following the end of hostilities. Returning to St. Paul and the Great Northern in late 1945, he was appointed assistant general manager, lines east of Williston, North Dakota.

In 1947 Budd became the youngest president of any Class I railroad in the nation when he accepted an offer to head the Chicago & Eastern Illinois Railroad Company (C&EI). He was credited with substantially increasing the railroad's operating efficiency and, consequently, its net revenues at a time when gross revenues decreased markedly. "Increased efficiency," he insisted, "results from a more profitable output per man and machine, and the continued application of improved methods. Costs are reduced by the elimination of wasteful service and practices. Such economies are the yarn from which profits are woven."

One of his long-term contributions was his aggressive modernization program. "It has been my earnest desire to improve the physical property and provide the road with better tools for efficient operation. Retooling a plant such as the C&EI is not a unique or an inexpensive job," he observed. By the time he left the C&EI over half the railroad's freight and passenger service was diesel powered, and the company was physically and technologically well prepared to meet the challenges of postwar America.

Budd resigned from the C&EI in 1949, returning to the Great Northern as vice president for operations following the death of Thomas F. Dixon. In 1951 he was elected president of the Great Northern, succeeding Francis J. Gavin, who had led the railroad since 1939. At the age of forty-three, he was the youngest president of any major United States railroad.

Budd instituted a number of reforms and programs that made the GN an industry pacesetter. In addition to continuing the long-term program of track improvement that he inherited from the Gavin administration, including the introduction of continuously welded rail, he embraced other important technological advances. By spring 1958 the steam transportation era had ended on the Great Northern with the retirement of its last thirty-six steam engines, making the railroad one of the first in the nation to convert completely to diesel power. Dieselization was a highly controversial innovation because it threatened the jobs of locomotive firemen and others, but it resulted in marked improvements in operating efficiency and savings for the railroad industry.

Other programs developed under Budd's leadership to modernize the GN system included the installation of centralized traffic control, the introduction of a Univac computer system and advanced communications systems (the GN was the first Western railroad to utilize such technologies), and the construction of the state-of-the-art Gavin freight classification yard at Minot, North Dakota. The Great Northern also commenced and rapidly expanded the practice of freight "piggy-backing" to facilitate the loading and unloading of goods. Loaded truck trailers were placed atop flatcars; at their destination they could be reattached to trucks and driven directly from the rail yard. From this technique grew the notion of "rack cars" to transport automobiles from assembly plants to retail and distribution centers.

Under Budd's direction the Great Northern expanded into new areas of endeavor. In 1960 the Great Northern Pipe Line Company was formed to construct a crude oil pipeline in North Dakota between the Newburg, Wiley, and Glenburn fields and tank loading facilities at Minot. Two years later, the subsidiary became part of the 373–mile Portal Pipeline Company, which was owned jointly by the railroad and several oil companies to serve refineries in Minnesota, Wisconsin, and the Toronto-Buffalo market on the Great Lakes.

Conversely, Budd's administration scaled back a number of the GN's traditional activities—most notably, the Glacier Park Company, which had been one of the railroad's wholly-owned subsidiaries since Louis W. Hill created it to stimulate tourism in the national parks. In late 1960 the railroad disposed of its hotel and motel assets in Glacier National Park, Montana, and Waterton Lakes National Park, Alberta, Canada. With the proceeds the GN purchased 175,000 shares of stock in the Western Pacific Railroad Company.

Perhaps the most significant event of Budd's term was the 1970 merger that resulted in the formation of Burlington Northern, Inc., one of the largest railroad systems in the United States. The new corporation combined the properties and assets of the Great Northern, Northern Pacific (NP), Chicago, Burlington & Quincy, and Spokane, Portland & Seattle railways into a network of almost 25,000 miles that dominated the rail transportation industry in most of the Pacific Northwest and much of the upper Midwest. The NP's vast land grant allowed the new entity to diversify and expand further.

Budd was dubbed "Empire Builder II" for his efforts in cooperation with Northern Pacific President Robert S. Macfarlane in creating the merged company. He was following directly in the tradition of the first "Empire Builder" and founder of the GN, James J. Hill. In the wake of a fight with Edward H. Harriman over Northern Pacific stock that rocked Wall Street, Hill and Harriman had formed the BN's predecessor, the Northern Securities Company, in 1901. A holding company for the rival magnates' stock in the Great Northern, Northern Pacific, and Chicago, Burlington & Quincy railways, Northern Securities was the largest corporation of its day. It immediately drew criticism and

the attention of Theodore Roosevelt, who was anxious to distance himself from his predecessor's administration and align himself with the rising tide of progressive reformers. The United States Supreme Court ordered Northern Securities dissolved under the Sherman Antitrust Act in 1904, but the three railroads continued to cooperate closely with one another until their formal merger in 1970.

Budd served as chairman and chief executive officer of the BN in 1970 and 1971, followed by two years as chairman of the corporation's finance committee. He was a member of the board of directors from 1970 to 1977. He had alternated with Macfarlane as president of the Spokane, Portland & Seattle Railway Company prior to the 1970 merger and was also a director of the Chicago, Burlington & Quincy, the Colorado & Southern Railway, Duluth and Superior Bridge Company, St. Paul Fire and Marine Insurance Company, New York Life Insurance Company, First Trust Company of St. Paul, Marshall Field and Company, International Harvester Company, Western Fruit Express Company, and the First National Bank of St. Paul.

Outside his business concerns, Budd was involved in a variety of social, cultural, and educational activities in St. Paul, particularly alcoholic rehabilitation and youth-oriented programs. He was a member of the board of trustees of the James Jerome Hill Reference Library from 1953 to 1974, serving a term as president, and was a trustee for Hamline University. He was active in the Boy Scouts of America and served as a member of that organization's executive board of the National Council. Budd died at the age of seventy-one on October 25, 1979.

References:
"John Budd Goes to G.N.; Roddewig Heads C. & E. I.," *Railway Age*, 126 (May 28, 1949): 41-42;
"John M. Budd, New President of the C. & E. I.," *Railway Age*, 122 (May 24, 1947): 1081.

Archives:
The Burlington Northern, Incorporated, Papers, the Great Northern Railway Company Papers, and the Northern Pacific Railway Company Papers are all at the Minnesota Historical Society, St. Paul.

Ralph Budd

(August 20, 1879-February 2, 1962)

by Albro Martin

Bradley University

Ralph Budd

CAREER: Division engineer, Chicago, Rock Island & Pacific Railway (1903-1906); engineer in charge of rebuilding Panama Railroad (1906-1909); chief engineer, Oregon Trunk Railroad (1909-1912); assistant to president (1912-1918), executive vice president (1918-1919), president (1919-1931), Great Northern Railway; president, Chicago, Burlington & Quincy Railroad (1932-1949); chairman, Chicago Transit Authority (1949-1954).

Ralph Budd is an outstanding example of the entrepreneurial railroad man in the twentieth century, when the era of the great system builders had ended and the railroads' latitude to make business decisions was being increasingly limited by govern-

ment intervention. Despite the discouragements of repressive regulation that strongly favored the rise of competing transportation modes, the growth of labor union power, a decade of economic depression, and the unprecedented demands of total war, Budd repeatedly demonstrated that opportunities for innovation in railroad management were still abundant. Almost alone among railroad leaders, he saw the appeal that high-speed, streamlined trains would have in the face of overwhelming competition from the private automobile, and in deciding to power the first such train with diesel engines he introduced a new and more efficient form of motive power that replaced the steam locomotive in both freight and passenger service in less than a generation.

Budd was born in 1879 to Charles Wesley and Mary Ann Warner Budd on a farm near Washburn, Iowa, about seven miles from Waterloo in the east central part of the state. His ancestors of English, Scottish, Welsh, and German stock had settled in America as early as 1668. Budd had an older brother and sister and a younger brother and two younger sisters. When he was thirteen, the family moved to Des Moines where he flourished in school in mathematics as well as in literature (reading was always his main leisure activity) and was allowed to move ahead at his own pace, completing the high school course and a degree in civil engineering from the local Highland Park College by the time he was nineteen.

Budd early determined to follow the example set by his older brother, John, who became a civil engineer on the Chicago, Rock Island & Pacific and the Chicago, Burlington & Quincy lines. Upon graduation in 1899, he took a draftsman's job with the Chicago Great Western Railway but, preferring the real thing to a drawing board, soon persuaded his superior to put him in charge of a gang that was upgrading a section of the line. Starting at $45 a month, he quickly proved his worth and by the end of the season his pay had been raised to $75. In 1901 he married Georgia Marshall, with whom he had two sons and a daughter. In 1903 he became division engineer of the trackage that the Rock Island was building between St. Louis and Kansas City. The line was never a major contender on this highly competitive route; but it was the springboard for a remarkable career, for it was on the Rock Island that Budd met John F. Stevens, who was then a vice president of the railroad.

As consulting engineer for James J. Hill's Great Northern (GN) during its spectacular leap westward to Seattle in the four years before the onset of the depression in 1893, Stevens had braved incredible hardships to find the Marias Pass through the Rocky Mountains, and later the Stevens Pass through the Cascades. In 1906, upon his blunt recommendation, the United States abandoned its original plan to dig a sea-level canal across the Isthmus of Panama for a conventional canal employing locks. The decision meant that the spoil removed by steam shovels would have to be carried away by rail. The existing Panama Railroad, built in the 1850s to carry across the isthmus men who were willing to risk yellow fever to get to the California gold fields in a hurry, was inadequate to the task. To accomplish this feat of engineering Stevens recruited Budd, who moved to Panama with his family.

Three years later Stevens called Budd to the Pacific Northwest on a mission related to one of the last great railroad building competitions in America. The epic struggle between Hill and Edward H. Harriman for domination of transportation in the Northwest had not ended with Hill's 1901 victory in the fight to control the Burlington Railway, nor did it end with Harriman's death in September 1909. Harriman's Union Pacific (UP) contended effectively for traffic between the Midwest and the Pacific Northwest, while the Hill roads had no rail connection to San Francisco. Hill's gambit was to attack the UP head-on. Southward from a point on his affiliate, the Spokane, Portland & Seattle Railroad (SP&S), which he had recently and expensively completed to free himself from use of Harriman's Columbia River line into Portland, Hill projected the Oregon Trunk Railroad (OT) into

northern California. The Deschutes River Canyon route was a difficult one, and the vast interior to the east had never been explored for railroad possibilities.

Stevens had gone out to Oregon to scout a possible location for the line when Hill's plans were still secret. Finding Budd and his family on their annual vacation trip to the United States in the summer of 1909, he offered Budd the job of surveying the entire area. This was railroad building from the ground up, and Budd jumped at the chance. By 1912 Budd was chief engineer of both the OT and the SP&S. That year he met Hill, who was on an inspection trip to the Oregon Trunk. Impressed with the young man's secure grasp of the transportation scene in the Northwest and the Hill lines' position in it, and above all his awareness that constant reduction of operating costs was the key to survival and growth in the railroad business, Hill took Budd back to St. Paul with him as assistant to the president of the Great Northern.

Hill had "retired" from the presidency of the GN in 1907, assuming the position of chairman of the board, so Budd was nominally assistant to Hill's son Louis W. Hill. But until James J. Hill died in 1916 there was no doubt about who really approved all decisions. Hill undertook almost from the beginning of their association to groom Budd for a leading role in the management of the GN. On long drives around St. Paul on Saturday afternoons, after the offices had closed, he confided to Budd his hopes and dreams for the GN after his death, especially his determination that the line over the Cascade Mountains in Washington should become a first-class, low-gradient route. This plan would require a long and costly new tunnel to replace the old one, but Hill was confident that the tunnel would be built to keep the GN the low-cost carrier in the Pacific Northwest. When Budd convinced Hill that he believed it, too, his future was settled.

By 1918 Budd was executive vice president, but his duties as assistant regional director of the Central Western District of the United States Railroad Administration during the period of federal control meant that he really ran the company. In 1919 he became president of the GN under Louis Hill's chairmanship, thereby replacing James J. Hill as determiner of the GN's fortunes, insofar as anyone could replace Hill. Hill had made it clear to George

Fisher Baker, a prestigious New York banker and longtime adherent of Hill's railroad policies in the West, that he wanted Budd at the helm; and Baker, a large and influential stockholder in the GN, had seen to it that Budd was given the position.

American railroads faced an uncertain, even a grim, future in the early 1920s. First there was the fight to return them to private ownership over the bitter opposition of the labor unions that had fared handsomely under government control. But after that fight was finally won on March 1, 1920, indemnity payments from the government, representing wartime deferrals of maintenance to roadbed, motive power, and rolling stock, hardly covered the real deterioration of the nation's main transportation system. Finally, the Interstate Commerce Commission (ICC), which had repressed all efforts to raise rates even modestly during the inflationary decades before World War I, was given still more powers by the Transportation Act of 1920. It was soon apparent that the ICC was going to determine national transportation regulatory policy by regulating in favor of the growth of "competitive modes" of transportation—that is, the nascent trucking industry. Worst of all, it must have seemed to a new president of a major railroad, the ICC had been given a mandate by the Transportation Act to recast the American railroad network by "consolidation" into a limited number of systems.

Budd managed, in the face of this hostile environment, to make the GN stronger by the time the Great Depression hit in 1930 than he had found it in 1919. His most indelible mark upon the railroad was the new Cascade Tunnel. Construction began in 1926, and the tunnel was opened in 1929 with a pioneering live coast-to-coast broadcast over the fledgling National Broadcasting Company network that featured an address and button-pushing ceremony by President Herbert Hoover from the White House. The 7.79-mile bore, part of a major line relocation program, helped eliminate 9 miles from the route, 10 miles of curvature, and 1,000 feet of rise and fall in elevation. For sixty years the longest tunnel in the western hemisphere, during which it has paid for itself several times over in lower operating costs, the Cascade will be pushed into second place by the 9.1-mile tunnel the Canadian National Railway is digging through the Canadian Rockies.

Completion of the Oregon Trunk to Bieber, California, in 1931 produced an interior route to San Francisco, but the Depression delayed for ten years the rewards that the GN and Western Pacific (WP) expected from it. Meanwhile, Budd forestalled a pointless move by the ICC to split off the Burlington from the GN and NP as the price for allowing the latter two railroads to merge—which would have brought major operating economies—but as a result there would be no merger of the Hill lines for another half-century. Budd turned his attention to the hemorrhaging passenger traffic, ending Hill's long-time contempt for passenger trains by introducing the Empire Builder, one of America's most famous trains, which cut a full business day off the old schedule between Chicago and Seattle. Budd also reduced the costs of freight service most notably by increasing from fifty to seventy tons the net capacity of iron ore cars, of which the GN carried a small mountain from the Mesabi Range to Lake Superior every season.

The nervous prosperity that the railroads enjoyed in the 1920s came to an abrupt end after 1929, when the industry recorded the swiftest and most drastic traffic slump in its history. By 1932 it was beginning to look as though the slump was permanent. The Burlington, whose handsome dividends had been a major source of income for the GN and the NP for thirty years, faced growing difficulties. A carrier of gigantic volumes of agricultural commodities, the Burlington saw farm prices collapse and unmarketable surpluses pile up throughout its region. Gross revenues were diminishing, and it takes only a moderate decline in revenues to wipe out most railroads' net profits. Strong, decisive leadership on the Burlington was crucial; thus it was that Budd found himself in Chicago in January 1932, sitting down at his desk as the new president of the Chicago, Burlington & Quincy Railroad, a post that he would man for the next seventeen years.

The mild-mannered executive quickly revealed the iron fist in the velvet glove as he cut the Burlington's divisions from seventeen to eleven, thus reducing the middle management echelons of the railroad significantly. The "Q," as railroad men have always called it, responded gratifyingly to Budd's belt-tightening policies, and the reassurances he gave Wall Street about this bluest chip among Granger railroads stood the GN and the NP in good stead as they struggled to refinance maturing bond issues in the depressed money market of the 1930s.

Budd next sought to strengthen the Burlington as a through freight route, most notably its route westward to San Francisco. The Burlington's western terminus was Denver, but its westward connection, the Denver & Rio Grande Western Railroad, went south to Colorado Springs and Pueblo before heading west. The Rock Island, which connected at Colorado Springs, and the Missouri Pacific, which came in at Pueblo, had much shorter routes than the Burlington, although all three had to charge the same rates for through business. Budd saw that by building forty miles of new railroad from a branch of the Rio Grande that ran northwestward from Denver, a direct short line would become a reality. But the Missouri Pacific, which jointly owned the Rio Grande with the WP, was naturally happy with things the way they were. Here, the longtime friendship of the James family with James J. Hill and his successors paid off. Arthur Curtiss James, the son of Hill's associate D. Willis James, called the tune at the WP in which he was a major investor. Thus the Dotsero Cutoff was built and the nation acquired an additional short, low-cost transcontinental route that proved a godsend in the war with Japan.

Like most railroad executives in the 1930s, Budd found his struggle with government and labor adding up to little more than treading water until the war brought overwhelming freight and passenger traffic and vastly increased profits. Budd, by 1933 an important spokesman for the industry, supported the railroads' plea for a general rate increase to make up for dwindling traffic. The increase was a major strategic error, however, for it only encouraged growth of the motor freight business, and the trucks—not yet regulated—began to siphon off the lucrative, high-rated merchandise freight that had always accounted for a disproportionate share of railroad profits. The Burlington reacted to the emergence of highway competition by entering both the motor freight and bus businesses but did not thereby solve the problem of a national transportation policy that subsidized the railroads' competitors. Improvement of the system was more successful. The Burlington's route from Kansas City to Chicago and St. Louis was longer than those of its chief competitors, the Santa Fe and the Missouri Pacific, a situation that was corrected by a combination of new construction and a joint trackage arrangement across Missouri with the Gulf, Mobile & Ohio Railroad.

All of Budd's other achievements on the Burlington pale when compared to his key role in one of railroading's great twentieth-century revolutions: the introduction of diesel motive power. By 1933 Budd had decided that the time had come to make a major bid to retain what passenger business the railroad had left. Not from the existing railroad car manufacturers, who knew how to build only great steel behemoths, but from the Edward G. Budd Company (no relation), who manufactured automobile bodies, he ordered a lightweight, three-car stainless steel train to be called the Zephyr (Greek for west wind). But what would power it? Ever since he had installed big, heavy diesel stationary engines as a supplementary source of electric power during the construction of the new Cascade Tunnel, he had admired the diesel's ability to run continuously hour after hour and day after day with a minimum of maintenance and a maximum of efficiency.

Budd knew that those diesels were far too bulky and heavy in relation to horsepower to power a moving vehicle smaller than a ship. The Electro-Motive Corporation, however, was displaying an eight-cylinder diesel at Chicago's Century of Progress Exposition. He challenged Electro-Motive to adapt it to the new train, and by the spring of 1934 the Pioneer Zephyr, which weighed in total no more than a small steam passenger locomotive, was ready.

Revealing a talent for showmanship, Budd sent the train on a public inspection tour during which it was greeted by enthusiastic crowds at every way station. Thus encouraged, he arranged to have the Zephyr make a spectacular daylight run 1,015 miles from Denver to Chicago, at that time a twenty-six-hour trip on the Burlington's timetable. The streamliner left Denver at 5:05 A.M. on May 26, 1934, and at 8:09 P.M. glided onto the stage of the railroad industry's pageant, Wings of the Century, at the Century of Progress Exposition. From then on the streamlined train and diesel motive power were unstoppable. By 1949, when Budd retired from the Burlington, over 80 percent of passenger trains and at least 50 percent of freight trains were being hauled by diesel locomotives, and today the steam locomotive is a museum piece. Although Budd himself always minimized his role in the introduction of diesel power on the railroads, the Zephyr stands as evidence of his essential entrepreneurial drive, which flourished when many railroad leaders had withdrawn into their shells.

As Budd stood out more and more from the crowd, the demands on his time rose accordingly. As early as 1930 he had accepted an invitation to go to the Soviet Union, then floundering in a chaotic transportation situation, to study its problems. He recommended rebuilding the system along American, not European lines. In the critical year before Pearl Harbor, as America frantically undertook a preparedness program, Budd accepted President Roosevelt's invitation to be transportation commissioner on the Advisory Commission to the Council of National Defense. After studying the situation, he advised against setting up a new agency to coordinate railroad affairs, believing that the ICC was already prepared to do the job, given the right man to guide it. The commission found the right man in Joseph B. Eastman, and Budd's recommendation was vindicated. When war came, the new transportation "czar" found the nation's resources—rail and highway—accurately summarized and commented on by Budd and his staff.

Sensationalists would find little to write about the private life of Ralph Budd. He was a devoted family man for sixty years. In the railroading tradition, where he went, his family went, whether it was the Pacific Northwest or Panama or St. Paul or Chicago or Moscow. Both of his sons made careers in transportation, Robert as an executive of the Greyhound Bus Lines and John, the younger, eventually as president of the GN and chief promoter of the merger of all four of the Hill lines in 1970. Budd looked as little like the stereotype of a big business executive as anyone could: quiet, bespectacled, courteous, and democratic in his bearing, he must have struck many fellow passengers during his travels as a clergyman or college professor. He loved history, especially of the West and the American Indian, and had a thorough knowledge of geography. Invited to address the Newcomen Society in 1938, he chose not to relate his own or the Burlington's accomplishments, but instead presented a scholarly

paper, "Railway Routes across the Rocky Mountains," a story of exploration that can still be read with pleasure and profit. He was a valuable supporter of railroad and business history, and saw to it that a substantial part of the Burlington's archives were deposited permanently in the Newberry Library, Chicago.

Even before his retirement had been officially announced, Budd's skills were already being spoken for. He turned down a professorship at Northwestern University because he felt that he was not adequately prepared to teach the subject that he had dealt with for half a century. But Chicago's new mayor in 1949, Martin Kennelly, wanted to give the recently created Chicago Transit Authority a chance to do what no one thought anybody could do: knit together, place on an efficient operating basis, and make solvent the city's tangled public transportation facilities. For six years Budd, as chairman, worked at a task that was as much political as it was economic, and in the end Chicago had an integrated system capable of making full use of the expensive new subway that lay at the heart of it. In 1954 he retired to Santa Barbara, California, but his remaining years underscored his standing as the leading elder statesman of the railroad industry, and he continued to serve on numerous boards of directors of corporations and foundations until his death in 1962.

Publication:

"Railway Routes across the Rocky Mountains," *Transactions of the Newcomen Society,* 18 (1938).

References:

Ralph W. Hidy, Muriel E. Hidy, and Don Hofsommer, *A History of the Great Northern Railway,* forthcoming (Cambridge: Harvard Business School Press, 1988);
Richard C. Overton, *Burlington Route: A History of the Burlington Lines* (New York: Knopf, 1965);
Overton, "Ralph Budd: Railroad Entrepreneur," *Palimpsest,* 36 (November 1955): 421-484.

Archives:

The archives of the Chicago, Burlington & Quincy Railroad are at the Newberry Library, Chicago; the archives of the Great Northern Railway are at the Minnesota Historical Society, St. Paul.

Central of Georgia Railroad

by James A. Ward

University of Tennessee at Chattanooga

Map of the Central of Georgia Railway (1930)

The Central of Georgia Railway was in many respects a quintessential southern railway. Chartered in 1835 to connect Savannah with the Georgia up-country, the road survived the 1837 panic, was completed to Macon in the depression year 1843, and three years later reached Atlanta. The Central was built primarily with local money; planters subscribed liberally and Savannah took 5,000 shares of the company's stock. The state aided the road with banking privileges that enabled the combined railroad and banking company to pay dividends as high as 10 percent in the pre-Civil War years.

Gen. William T. Sherman's forces devastated the road during their Civil War march through Georgia, twisting hundreds of miles of its rails around

trees; a year after the conflict the road still had a hundred-mile gap east of Macon. Despite its troubles the company's bank bills (bills the railroad issued under its charter, which allowed it to provide banking functions) at the end of the war commanded exchange rates (discount rates against United States currency) in the nineties. Unlike many postwar southern roads, the Central remained locally owned and under the presidency of William Wadley rebuilt its business and avoided receivership in the 1873 depression. Wadley reconstructed the property, continued the line's tradition of high dividends, and expanded the company's mileage. In 1881 the company leased the Georgia Railroad in conjunction with the Louisville & Nashville. By

1890 the line owned and controlled 2,296 miles of road.

Postwar southern railroads were prime targets for northern railway men constructing national systems, and a property of the Central's size and location was an especially tempting victim. In 1888 the Richmond & West Point Terminal Company acquired the Central and in 1891 transferred it to the Terminal's Richmond & Danville. Northern capitalists were unpopular in the South, however, and a minority Central stockholder sued in state courts claiming the Terminal's takeover was illegal under Georgia's constitution. The court agreed and in 1892 placed the road in default; the Terminal followed suit in the 1893 depression.

When J. P. Morgan engineered the rebirth of the Richmond & West Point Terminal as the Southern Railway in 1895, the new system excluded the Central due to its legal difficulties, but the Georgia road retained its loose identification with the Southern's interests and operated in harmony with it. The Illinois Central gained a controlling interest in the Central of Georgia in 1909 and held it until the end of World War II; throughout the period the Central of Georgia remained a separate operating unit.

Independent after the war, the Central limped along until the 1950s, when it had trouble raising capital for improvements. Faced with increased competition from the proposed merger of the Atlantic Coast Line and the Seaboard Air Line to form the Seaboard Coast Line, the Central sought protection in the Southern's fold, and the Southern applied to the Interstate Commerce Commission in 1960 for permission to take control of the Georgia company. The Southern's 1963 takeover of the Central cost the latter 1,500 jobs as the price of corporate security. In June 1971 the Central of Georgia Railway was merged with the Georgia & Florida, the Wrightsville & Tennville, and the Savannah & Atlanta and became the Central of Georgia Railroad. The Central of Georgia became a constituent part of the Norfolk Southern when the latter was created in 1982 by the merger of the Southern with the Norfolk & Western.

References:

Ulrich B. Phillips, *A History of Transportation in the Eastern Cotton Belt to 1860* (New York: Columbia University Press, 1908), pp. 252-302, 306-307;

Richard Saunders, *The Railroad Mergers and the Coming of Conrail* (Westport, Conn.: Greenwood Press, 1978), pp. 85-87, 209-214, 218-219;

John S. Stover, *The Railroads of the South: A Study in Finance and Control* (Chapel Hill: University of North Carolina Press, 1955), pp. 149-150, 205-206, 247-252, 260-261.

Archives:

The Central of Georgia Railroad papers are at the Georgia Historical Society, Atlanta.

Central Railroad of New Jersey

by James N. J. Henwood

East Stroudsburg University

Map of the Central Railroad of New Jersey (1930)

The first step in the formation of the Central Railroad of New Jersey (CNJ) was the chartering of the Elizabethtown & Somerville Railroad in 1831. Somerville was reached in 1842, and a new company, the Somerville & Easton, was formed in 1847 to complete a line to the Delaware River, where it might tap the coal traffic flowing from Pennsylvania's anthracite fields. The new company purchased the old one and adopted the name Central Railroad of New Jersey in 1849. Phillipsburg was reached in 1852. In 1856 connections were made with the Lehigh Valley and Lackawanna railroads, and thereafter coal accounted for a major por-

tion of the firm's revenues. A number of branches were constructed, including a line to Jersey City, where an extensive terminal was developed.

In 1871 the CNJ leased the Lehigh & Susquehanna Railroad, which extended from Easton, Pennsylvania, to Wilkes-Barre and provided direct access to the coalfields. This advantage was offset by the loss of the Lehigh Valley's and the Lackawanna's traffic as these carriers built their own lines to New York Harbor. The heavy debt incurred by expansion pushed the CNJ into receivership in 1877. Following reorganization, in 1879 the CNJ acquired the New Jersey Southern, which ran through the center of the state to the Delaware Bay, and a half interest in the New York & Long Branch, linking Perth Amboy with seashore resorts. A connection at Bound Brook with a line from Philadelphia, controlled by the Reading, made the CNJ part of a new, short route to the Quaker City. From 1883 to 1887 the CNJ was leased by the Reading, and in 1901 the Reading acquired control through stock ownership. Baltimore & Ohio control of the Reading, acquired the same year, made the CNJ part of the B&O's route to New York.

The CNJ prospered as a freight and passenger carrier through the 1920s, but the Depression, the automobile and the truck, the decline of anthracite, the industrial exodus from the Northeast, excessive state taxes, unprofitable commuter trains, and high terminal expenses caused the line to declare bankruptcy in 1939 and again in 1967. Operations in Pennsylvania ceased in 1972 and the CNJ limped along, aided by state subsidies, until it was taken over by Conrail in 1976. New Jersey Transit now operates the road's commuter service, but much of the property has been abandoned.

References:
Elaine Anderson, *The Central Railroad of New Jersey's First 100 Years, 1849-1949: A Historical Survey* (Easton, Pa.: Center for Canal History and Technology, 1984);

Jules I. Bogen, *The Anthracite Railroads* (New York: Ronald Press, 1927), pp. 145-183;
Carl Condit, *The Port of New York*, 2 volumes (Chicago: University of Chicago Press, 1980-1981), I: 64-67, 141-152; II: 101-151, 202-208;
George H. Drury, *The Historical Guide to North American Railroads* (Milwaukee: Kalmbach, 1985), pp. 56-59.

Central Vermont Railway

by David H. Hickcox

Ohio Wesleyan University

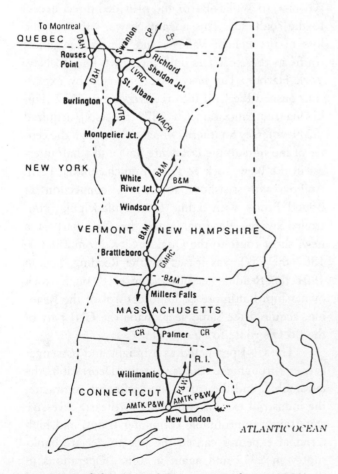

Map of the Central Vermont Railway (1983)

The Central Vermont Railway developed in the latter part of the nineteenth century as a bridge line (a line connecting other railroads) to southern New England from Canada and the Great Lakes. Its predecessor, the Vermont Central Railroad, was chartered on October 31, 1843 to build a line from Windsor, Vermont, on the Connecticut River northwest to Burlington on Lake Champlain. Several other roads were leased or purchased, and by 1871 the Vermont Central controlled lines from Ogdensburg, New York, on the St. Lawrence River to New London, Connecticut, on Long Island Sound. In 1898 the Vermont Central was reorganized as the Central Vermont Railway under control of the Grand Trunk Railway, a wholly owned subsidiary of the Canadian National Railway.

Headquartered in St. Albans, Vermont, in 1987 the Central Vermont operated 377 miles of track extending from East Alburg, Vermont, near the Canadian border south to New London. Newsprint and forest products from Canada as well as grain and other agricultural products destined for New York and for Boston and other southern New England points constituted most of the southbound traffic; manufactured goods routed through Canada accounted for most northbound traffic.

The Central Vermont was put at a competitive disadvantage by the formation of Guilford Transportation Industries in 1981, causing the Canadian National to put the railroad up for sale. There were no buyers, however, and the Central Vermont continued operations as a bridge line, providing an alternative to the Guilford system.

Reference:
Edward H. Beaudette, *Central Vermont Railway* (Newton, N.J.: Carstens, 1983).

Chesapeake & Ohio Railway

by John F. Stover

Purdue University

Map of the Chesapeake & Ohio Railway (1930)

The Chesapeake & Ohio Railway (C&O) was the result of a consolidation in 1868 of the Virginia Central Railroad and the Covington & Ohio Railroad. The Virginia Central had been formed in 1850 from the earlier Louisa Railroad, a short line north of Richmond. By the time of the Civil War the Vir-

ginia Central was a 189-mile line from Richmond via Charlottesville and Staunton to the Jackson River. The Covington & Ohio had been chartered in 1853 to extend the Virginia Central to the Ohio River, but no line had been built prior to the Civil War. The first president of the new C&O was Gen.

William C. Wickham, an ex-Confederate cavalry officer.

When Wickham could find no financial support in Europe for the extension to the Ohio he turned to New York, where he found Collis P. Huntington and northern money. Huntington replaced Wickham as president in 1869 and proposed to build and equip the 200-mile extension for $15 million. The 428-mile through line from Richmond to the new town of Huntington, West Virginia, on the Ohio River was completed in January 1873. The cost of the extension had increased the capital structure of the C&O fivefold to $38 million, but huge new deposits of coal had been discovered along the route.

The C&O defaulted on bonds in 1873 and went into receivership in 1875. The line was reorganized in 1878, retaining Huntington as president. By 1881 the C&O was building an extension from Richmond to Newport News and had annual revenues of more than $3 million. The reorganized C&O did not prosper, however, and Drexel, Morgan and Company reorganized it again in 1888, with Melville E. Ingalls succeeding Huntington as president. In 1889 Ingalls obtained the 230-mile Richmond & Allegheny in Virginia and built the 143-mile Maysville & Big Sandy in Kentucky, giving the C&O a line to Cincinnati. Other mileage was also acquired in Kentucky, and by 1900 the C&O was operating 1,425 miles of line with annual revenues of $13 million. The C&O was a major coal hauler and was finding that the Midwest was a better market for coal than the East. The years under Ingalls were relatively prosperous.

Early in 1900 both the Pennsylvania and the New York Central railroads started to make large purchases of the common stock of several major northeastern lines for the purpose of maintaining coal freight rates in the region. The Pennsylvania had a controlling interest in the Chesapeake & Ohio from 1900 to about 1909. During these years the C&O acquired new mileage in Ohio and Indiana which gave service to Columbus, Toledo, and Chicago. White Sulpher Springs, Incorporated, which operated the Greenbrier resort hotel, was acquired in 1918.

The Chesapeake & Ohio was a prosperous road during the first two decades of the twentieth century and paid modest but regular dividends every year except 1915. Dividends continued to be paid during the years of federal operation in World War I, even though the operating ratio increased to 88 in 1920. By that year the Chesapeake & Ohio was operating 2,544 miles in six states and had revenues of $90 million; 77 percent of its freight tonnage was mine products.

In the early 1920s Oris P. Van Sweringen and his brother Mantis J. Van Sweringen, real estate developers in Cleveland, acquired 30 percent of the C&O stock and sought to merge the C&O with the Nickel Plate, the Erie, and the Pere Marquette into a major eastern trunk line. Their efforts failed, but one result was a growing exchange of traffic between the C&O and the Pere Marquette, which connected with the C&O at Chicago and Toledo.

The C&O suffered revenue losses in the 1930s but seemed to survive the Depression with less stress than some of its competitors. The C&O's coal traffic increased between 1920 and 1940, while some other carriers saw declines in this traffic. The C&O managed to pay modest dividends throughout the 1930s. In 1934 the C&O introduced "Chessie," the sleeping kitten, to the American public in its advertising. In 1937 Robert R. Young, a financier who had left General Motors for a successful career in the stock market, purchased 43 percent of the stock of the Alleghany Corporation, which indirectly controlled the Chesapeake & Ohio. By 1942 Young was chairman of the board of the C&O.

In 1947 the C&O officially merged with the 1,900-mile Pere Marquette, with the C&O as the dominant partner. By 1950 the Chesapeake & Ohio was a 5,100-mile road located in eight states with an annual revenue of $319 million, a capital structure of $862 million, and 35,000 employees. At mid century the C&O was originating more coal traffic than any other American railroad, but the Pere Marquette merger brought in much new noncoal traffic.

In 1954 Young sold his C&O securities to Cyrus S. Eaton, a Cleveland investment banker. Eaton was impressed by Walter J. Tuohy, who had been the C&O's president since 1948, and gave him a free hand concerning the future of the railroad. Under Tuohy, the C&O became one of the first of the major coal carriers to shift completely from steam to diesel power. Tuohy was also tough-minded about railroad mergers. When the New York Central sought to merge with the C&O in

1959, Tuohy quickly pointed out that his road was financially strong, while the New York Central was quite weak. Later both the C&O and the New York Central sought to merge with the Baltimore & Ohio (B&O), but Tuohy easily won the contest and by 1961 held 61 percent of the B&O stock. The merger of the C&O and the B&O was completed in 1962. The two roads continued to be operated as separate lines, thus avoiding many of the errors in the merger of the Pennsylvania and New York Central into Penn Central in 1968.

In 1973 Chessie System was adopted as the name for the C&O, the B&O, and the Western Maryland, which had been acquired in 1968. In 1980 the Interstate Commerce Commission approved the merger of the Chessie System with Seaboard Coast Line Industries into a new holding company, the CSX Corporation. Seaboard Coast Line Industries had resulted from the merger of Sea-

board Air Line, the Atlantic Coast Line, and the Louisville & Nashville. The new CSX had 27,000 miles of line in twenty-two states, 70,000 employees, revenues of nearly $5 billion, and assets in excess of $7.5 billion.

References:

James P. Nelson, *The Chesapeake and Ohio Railway* (Richmond, Va., 1927);

John F. Stover, *The Railroads of the South, 1865-1900: A Study in Finance and Control* (Chapel Hill: University of North Carolina Press, 1955), pp. 126-128, 203-204;

Charles W. Turner, *Chessie's Road* (Richmond, Va.: Garrett & Massie, 1956).

Archives:

There appear to be no archives of the corporate papers of the Chesapeake & Ohio Railway.

Chicago & Eastern Illinois Railroad

by Douglas C. Munski

University of North Dakota

Map of the Chicago & Eastern Illinois Railroad (1930)

The Chicago & Eastern Illinois Railroad (C&EI) was a small but strategic bridge line—that is, a railroad that transfers more traffic between other railroads than it originates or terminates on its own line. The C&EI evolved from several nineteenth-century railroad mergers in the lower Middle West. Its oldest component was the Evansville & Illinois Rail Road, founded in 1849, which became the Evansville & Crawfordsville Railroad in 1853 and the Evansville & Terre Haute Railroad in 1877. The Evansville & Terre Haute's subsidiary, the Evansville, Terre Haute & Chicago formed in 1869, helped it operate from Evansville, Indiana, to Danville, Illinois. The name Chicago & Eastern Illinois

came from the 1877 successor to the Chicago, Danville & Vincennes Railroad founded in 1865 and running from Dolton, Illinois, to Danville. The C&EI cosponsored the Chicago & Western Indiana Railroad in 1879 and used this Chicago entry as leverage when acquiring control of the Evansville, Terre Haute & Chicago in 1880. The C&EI constructed tracks from Danville to Altamont, Illinois, between 1887 and 1896; acquired the Chicago, Paducah & Memphis Railroad from Altamont to Marion, Illinois, in 1896; and opened southern Illinois's Thebes Gateway in 1900.

Under the control of the St. Louis & San Francisco Railway (Frisco) from 1902 to 1913, the C&EI expanded. It operated in two regions from its main line between Chicago and Woodland Junction, Illinois: Southeast traffic used the Evansville Gateway while Southwest traffic used the Thebes Gateway. Furthermore, a secondary line, the Chicago & Indiana Coal Railroad and the Evansville & Indianapolis Railroad, ran from La Crosse, Indiana, into Evansville, and another southern Illinois gateway was opened at Joppa in 1903. Starting in 1905, trackage rights over the Cleveland, Cincinnati, Chicago & St. Louis Railroad west of Pana, Illinois, gave the C&EI St. Louis access. The C&EI absorbed the Evansville & Terre Haute in 1911. The Frisco's 1913 bankruptcy also put the C&EI into receivership.

Between 1913 and 1959 the C&EI survived precariously. During its receivership from 1913 to 1921 it dropped redundant trackage. From 1930 to 1940 the C&EI connected the Van Sweringens' Chesapeake & Ohio and Missouri Pacific (MoPac) systems. From 1940 until 1959 the C&EI engaged in unsuccessful merger bids. When MoPac started purchasing C&EI stock in 1959, the Louisville & Nashville (L&N), the C&EI's main southeastern traffic partner, protested.

A 1963 Interstate Commerce Commission ruling permitted MoPac control of the Thebes and Joppa gateways, with the L&N to purchase the Evansville Gateway; jointly, MoPac and the L&N were to control the Woodland Junction to Chicago line. MoPac acquired part of the C&EI in 1967, and the L&N received the Evansville route in 1969. The remnant C&EI continued until joining MoPac in 1976.

References:

Will H. Lyford, *History of the Chicago and Eastern Illinois Railroad Company to June 30, 1913* (Chicago, 1913);

Douglas C. Munski, "The Frisco Period of the Chicago and Eastern Illinois Railroad: A Study in Early Twentieth Century Railway Geography," *North Dakota Quarterly,* 48 (Winter 1980): 69-80;

Munski, "Modeling the Historical Geography of the Chicago & Eastern Illinois Railroad, 1849-1969," Ph.D. dissertation, University of Illinois, 1978;

William H. Wallace, "The Bridge Line: A Distinctive Type of Anglo-American Railroad," *Economic Geography,* 41 (January 1965): 1-38.

Chicago & North Western Railway

by H. Roger Grant

University of Akron

The Chicago & North Western Railway (C&NW) can truly claim to be Chicago's oldest surviving railroad. A predecessor, the Galena & Chicago Union (G&CU), introduced railroading to the Windy City on October 25, 1848, when a tiny steam locomotive, the Pioneer, pulled a freight car over the G&CU's five miles of line to the west of the city. By 1864 the G&CU operated a 294-mile system with main lines connecting Chicago with Clinton, Iowa, and Turner Junction (now West Chicago), Illinois, with Madison, Wisconsin (the company never reached Galena, Illinois). That year saw the merger of the G&CU with the C&NW, a 315-mile road that linked Chicago with Green Bay, Wisconsin, and Kenosha, Wisconsin, with Rockford, Illinois. This firm had grown out of several short-line projects that had materialized in the 1850s and had been reorganized as the Chicago & North Western in 1859. Following the Civil War, the C&NW embarked on a massive program of expansion. One

milestone was the road's entry into the Omaha Gateway on January 22, 1867; it reached this strategic center ahead of both the Rock Island and the Burlington. Thus the C&NW helped to forge the famed "Overland Route" by linking Chicago and the East with the Union Pacific-Central Pacific and the West.

The individual most responsible for making the Chicago & North Western into a major carrier was Marvin Hughitt. When he joined the company in 1872, mileage stood at 1,382, and when he resigned from the presidency in 1910, mileage had soared to 9,761. It was Hughitt who recognized the value of railroad service on the Great Plains, and by the early twentieth century the C&NW laced Nebraska and South Dakota with a web of tracks. The company's modest efforts to reach the Pacific failed; the road never got beyond Lander, Wyoming, 1,275 miles west of Chicago. Still, it connected the key gateways of Chicago, Milwaukee,

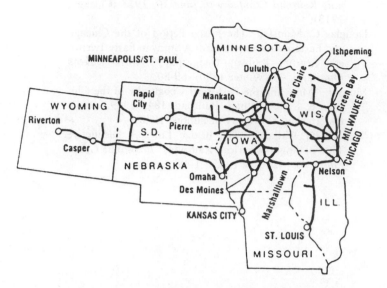

Map of the Chicago & North Western Railway (1983)

Minneapolis-St. Paul, Duluth, Des Moines, Omaha, and St. Louis.

During the Gilded Age the Chicago & North Western made attempts at ending disruptive rate slashing in its ever more competitive environment. Along with the Rock Island and the Burlington, the company was a charter member of the Iowa Pool, which lasted from 1870 to 1884, although it eventually ignored this gentlemen's agreement. The C&NW drew closely toward the Union Pacific, with which it connected at Omaha; the relationship continued into the 1980s.

After the turn of the century, the C&NW mostly ceased breaking with precedent, ending an earlier tradition that had involved some memorable "firsts": the first railroad to operate Pullman sleeping cars west of Chicago (1858); the first to build and operate a modern railway post office car (1864); and the first to offer patrons an all-Pullman train in the West, the Overland Limited, operated in conjunction with the Union Pacific (1901). Yet the company gained considerable fame for its crack "400" passenger trains, the first of which began running between Chicago and the Twin Cities on January 2, 1935. And from the mid 1930s to the mid 1950s the C&NW, in cooperation with the Union Pacific and the Southern Pacific, operated the "city" streamliners on their Overland Route jour-

neys between Chicago and Omaha.

The year 1956 proved to be a watershed time for the Chicago & North Western. In January the brilliant and hard-driving Ben W. Heineman took control and decades of ossification came to an end. The Heineman administration brought about myriad changes: overnight and complete dieselization, ultramodern and innovative Chicago suburban commuter equipment, and a drastic and much needed paring of money-losing passenger trains, branch lines, and terminal facilities.

The Heineman renaissance also included an ambitious program of acquisitions. In 1957 the C&NW officially leased the 1,700-mile Chicago, St. Paul, Minneapolis & Omaha, a property that it had controlled since 1882, and in 1960 it purchased the 1,600-mile Minneapolis & St. Louis. Eight years later the C&NW added another medium-sized Class I carrier, the 1,500-mile Chicago Great Western. The C&NW also purchased several strategic midwestern short lines, including the Litchfield & Madison in 1958; the Fort Dodge, Des Moines & Southern in 1968; and the Des Moines & Central Iowa in 1968. Following the collapse of the Chicago, Rock Island & Pacific in 1980, the C&NW acquired several segments, the most important being the "Spine Line" from the Twin Cities to Kansas City.

The C&NW gained national attention in the 1970s when it became "employee owned." President Larry Provo suggested to Heineman, head of Northwest Industries, the parent holding company formed in 1967, that the railroad's employees be allowed to buy the property. Heineman agreed and the sale took place in 1972. As the board of directors said at the time of Provo's sudden death in 1976, "He conceived the employee-owned company, played the major role in bringing about its reality and guided it through its first and most torturous years." Since 1976 James R. Wolfe has led the carrier; his administration has been characterized by "line rationalization," abandoning of branches and duplicate trackage and spinning off lines to short-line operators. Also, the Chicago & North Western Transportation Company—the railroad's name since employee ownership—has, through its subsidiary Western Railroad Properties, Incorporated, built approximately 100 miles of new track in Nebraska and Wyoming to tap the lucrative coal traffic market from the South Powder River Basin to utilities in the Midwest and South. The railroad today is "streamlined"; main lines rather than branches dominate its route structure.

References:

Robert J. Casey and W. A. S. Douglas, *Pioneer Railroad: The Story of the Chicago and North Western System* (New York: Whittlesey House, 1948);

W. H. Stennett, compiler, *Yesterday and To-day: A History of the Chicago & North Western Railway System,* third edition (Chicago: Rand McNally, 1910).

Archives:

The corporate records of the Chicago & North Western Railway are held by the C&NW Transportation Company, Chicago, and by Northern Illinois University, De Kalb.

Chicago, Burlington & Quincy Railroad

by George H. Drury

Trains *Magazine*

The Chicago, Burlington & Quincy (CB&Q), generally known as the Burlington, was the strongest of the Granger railroads, the railroads that lay between the Great Lakes and the Rockies and depended on agricultural commodities for the bulk of their traffic. One of the principal reasons for the Burlington's strength was the joint control–indeed, all but joint ownership–of the road by the Great Northern (GN) and the Northern Pacific (NP) that dated from 1901.

The existence of the Burlington began with the chartering of the Aurora Branch Railroad on February 12, 1849 to build a connection from the Galena & Chicago Union (later part of the Chicago & North Western) at Turner Junction (now West Chicago) to Aurora, Illinois. In 1852 the thirteen-mile railroad was renamed the Chicago & Aurora Railroad and was authorized to construct an extension to a connection with the Illinois Central at Mendota, forty-five miles west-southwest of Aurora. The road became the Chicago, Burlington & Quincy Railroad on February 14, 1855.

Within two years there existed a string of railroads from Chicago through Aurora, Mendota, and Galesburg to the Mississippi River, both at Quincy and at a point opposite Burlington, Iowa. By 1865 the CB&Q owned all these lines plus a branch from Galesburg to Peoria; it had also built its own line from Aurora thirty-eight miles east to Chicago, parallel to the Galena & Chicago Union line and about five miles south of it.

The Burlington undertook expansion beyond the Mississippi by financing a series of subsidiary railroads. In 1859 the Hannibal & St. Joseph (H&StJ) began operating in Missouri between the cities of its name. A short spur from Hannibal to a point opposite Quincy and a connecting steamboat created the first rail route from Chicago to the Missouri River. In 1855 the Burlington & Missouri River Railroad (B&MR) began building a line west across Iowa from Burlington. It reached the Missouri River opposite Plattsmouth, Nebraska, fourteen years later, not long after the CB&Q had bridged the Mississippi at both Burlington and

Map of the Chicago, Burlington & Quincy Railroad (1930)

Quincy and had built a line from Cameron, Missouri, to Kansas City; the latter line, on completion, was turned over to the H&StJ to operate. The B&MR line was extended to Lincoln, Nebraska, in 1870 by the Burlington & Missouri River Rail Road in Nebraska (B&MRinN).

Although the H&StJ and both B&MR companies were backed by the CB&Q and shared some officers, they were not strictly under CB&Q control. They did not always agree with the CB&Q in such matters as the routing of traffic, and the H&StJ and the B&MR often competed for the same traffic. To stabilize the situation the CB&Q leased the B&MR in 1872 and merged with it in 1875.

Jay Gould had secured control of the H&StJ in 1871. He soon also gained control of the Union Pacific, the Kansas Pacific, the Wabash, and the Missouri Pacific, effectively surrounding the Burlington's Nebraska lines. To protect its interest the CB&Q consolidated with the B&MRinN in 1880; acquired a line from Kansas City to Council Bluffs, Iowa; bridged the Missouri River at Plattsmouth; and built an extension to Denver, which was opened in May 1882. A year later the CB&Q regained control of the Hannibal & St. Joseph.

About that same time the Chicago, Burlington & Northern (CB&N), which was one-third owned by the CB&Q, began construction of a line along the Mississippi River to St. Paul, Minnesota. As with the Iowa and Nebraska lines there was friction between the parent and the subsidiary; CB&Q increased its interest in the CB&N and absorbed it in 1899. The Burlington extended one long tentacle out from its home area, a line from Lincoln, Nebraska, northwest through Alliance to Billings, Montana.

At the turn of the century James J. Hill, builder of the Great Northern, wanted a connection to Chicago for the GN. At the same time Edward H. Harriman sought the Burlington to form an Omaha-Chicago connection for the Union Pacific. The battle of the magnates was brief; Hill won, and on July 1, 1901, nearly 98 percent of CB&Q's stock was purchased jointly by the Great Northern and the Northern Pacific. A year later Hill acquired control of the Northern Pacific.

In 1908 the Burlington acquired control of the Colorado & Southern Railway (C&S), which with its subsidiaries formed a route from central Wyoming south through Denver and Fort Worth to the Gulf of Mexico at Galveston, Texas. In 1914 the Burlington opened a line from Billings south to a connection with the C&S. The other major extension of that period was a line into the coalfields of southern Illinois (to ensure a supply of high-quality coal for the firm's locomotives) and across the Ohio River to Paducah, Kentucky, partly by purchase of existing railroads and partly by new construction.

The only major construction after 1920 was a line across Missouri opened in late 1952, shortening the Chicago-Kansas City distance by twenty-two miles.

Over the years the Burlington considered extensions to the Pacific and mergers with nearly every railroad it connected with. But conservative management, particularly the administrations of Charles Elliott Perkins from 1881 to 1901 and Ralph Budd from 1931 to 1949, kept the Burlington a midwestern railroad–and a healthy, well-run one.

The Burlington was one of the pioneers in railroad dieselization. The streamlined Zephyr of 1934 was the first successful high-speed diesel passenger train, and it was soon followed by a fleet of Zephyrs that covered most of the main lines of the Burlington system. By mid 1947 virtually all through freight trains on the lines from Chicago to the Twin Cities and to Denver were powered by diesels, as were nearly all the named passenger trains. Chicago-Aurora commuter service was dieselized by 1952, not with units bought specifically for those trains but by combining commuter and long-distance assignments in a single passenger diesel pool and purchasing enough main-line passenger diesel units to cover all the duties. The commuter service is also noteworthy for the air-conditioned double-deck coaches that Burlington pioneered in 1950. By 1955 steam power was used only to cover the extra trains required by the grain harvest, and even that was soon gone.

In 1970 the GN, the NP, the CB&Q, and the Spokane, Portland & Seattle merged to form the Burlington Northern, the largest railroad in the United States.

References:

George H. Drury, *The Historical Guide to North American Railroads* (Milwaukee: Kalmbach, 1985), pp. 71-74;

David P. Morgan, *Diesels West* (Milwaukee: Kalmbach, 1963);

Richard C. Overton, *Burlington Route: A History of the Burlington Lines* (New York: Knopf, 1965);

Overton, *Perkins-Budd: Railway Statesmen of the Burlington* (Westport, Conn.: Greenwood Press, 1982).

Archives:

Burlington archives from the early years are at the Newberry Library in Chicago.

Chicago Great Western Railroad

by H. Roger Grant

University of Akron

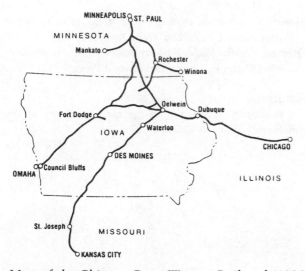

Map of the Chicago Great Western Railroad (1930)

One of America's most innovative railroads was the Chicago Great Western Railroad (CGW). Its history supports the thesis that the smaller, less-entrenched carriers often contributed mightily to the industry. These roads probably had little choice; they either responded to competitive challenges or they failed. The Chicago Great Western started life rather late for a Midwestern carrier. Its founder, the hard-driving A. B. Stickney, pushed what had formerly been a "paper" railroad, the Minnesota & Northwestern, from St. Paul, Minnesota, to Dubuque, Iowa, between 1884 and 1886. By March 1888 he controlled a through route from the Twin Cities to Chicago. Stickney quickly reorganized his expanding property as the Chicago, St. Paul & Kansas City and struck out for St. Joseph, Missouri, and then Kansas City. He completed his "Maple Leaf" system, renamed the Chicago Great Western Rail-

way in 1892, by purchasing and leasing connecting trackage and by constructing the "Omaha Extension" between the Iowa communities of Fort Dodge and Council Bluffs early in the twentieth century. Stickney's efforts to build to Sioux City, Iowa, however, failed, as did a scheme to reach Denver and a west coast connection. When Stickney retired in 1908, the 1,500-mile CGW had been virtually completed.

In the twentieth century the Chicago Great Western benefited from management that ranged from competent to brilliant. In 1909 the "doctor of sick railroads," Samuel M. Felton, Jr., assumed control under the auspices of J. P. Morgan and Company, which had just reorganized the property as the Chicago Great Western Railroad; Felton served as president until 1925 and chairman from 1925 to 1929. Except for one intermission in the 1930s when a holding company, the Bremo Corporation, milked the CGW and threw it into a short receivership, the self-proclaimed "Corn Belt Route" continued to have able leaders. In 1948 a group of Kansas City investors won control and soon placed William N. Deramus III in the presidency, which he held until 1957. His no-nonsense approach to railroading made the CGW a remarkably profitable enterprise, in part because the road returned to its long-established tradition of innovation.

The Chicago Great Western's most significant innovations centered in the area of train operations. The CGW was first "Class I" steam road to offer "piggyback" service—truck trailers atop flatcars—on a regular basis. The company had launched such movements on July 7, 1936, between Chicago and

1912 Baldwin 2-8-2 locomotive in the Oelwein, Iowa, yards of the Chicago Great Western Railroad, circa 1947 (courtesy Roger Grant)

St. Paul, and its "trailer trains" had soon appeared on other parts of the system. Although lacking the national impact of the piggyback triumph, the CGW's early use of diesel-electric passenger and maintenance-of-way equipment also earned recognition. The firm dieselized swiftly; its last steam locomotives disappeared in 1950. The company furthermore led in the use of welded rail, radio and carrier telephone communications, and long and unit freight trains.

Yet being innovative could not guarantee financial success. The consolidation mania that engulfed the railroad industry after 1960 forced the CGW to find a suitable partner. After a near marriage to the Soo Line in 1962, the CGW tied the knot with its old competitor, the Chicago & North Western, and disappeared from the railroad ranks on July 1, 1968.

References:

Frank P. Donovan, Jr., "The Chicago Great Western Railway," *Palimpsest,* 34 (June 1953): 257-288;

H. Roger Grant, *The Corn Belt Route: A History of the Chicago Great Western Railroad Company* (De Kalb: Northern Illinois University Press, 1984).

Archives:

The corporate papers of the Chicago Great Western Railroad are not available for study.

Chicago, Milwaukee, St. Paul & Pacific Railroad

by Carlos A. Schwantes

University of Idaho

Map of the Chicago, Milwaukee, St. Paul & Pacific Railroad (1976)

The twentieth century has not been kind to the Chicago, Milwaukee, St. Paul & Pacific Railroad. In 1901 its predecessor, the Chicago, Milwaukee & St. Paul, was an exceedingly prosperous midwestern carrier, and within the decade had added a line to the Pacific coast. At its peak in the early 1920s it formed a 10,000-mile system extending from Chicago into the coalfields of southern Indiana, the timber and mineral country of northern Wisconsin, Minnesota, and Michigan, the grain belt of Iowa, Minnesota, and South Dakota, and west to the coast of Washington. But neither its past prosperity nor its impressive mileage saved the company from the ruinous consequences of a series of unwise management decisions and changing patterns of competition.

The history of the Milwaukee Road (a nickname that came into general use in the late 1920s) evolved in four phases. The pioneer phase began in 1847 with the incorporation of the Milwaukee & Waukesha Rail Road Company, which was renamed the Milwaukee & Mississippi Rail Road Company in 1850. President Byron Kilbourn pushed its rails west from Milwaukee to Prairie du Chien on the Mississippi River in 1857, but only a short time later the struggling company plunged into bankruptcy. Eastern capital rescued it in 1860.

The second phase, which occurred over the next half-century, was a time of steady and orderly expansion; the road grew up with the country it served and became exceedingly prosperous. The company was renamed the Milwaukee & St. Paul Railway in 1867. In 1874 the growing collection of lines and companies became the Chicago, Milwaukee & St. Paul. Under the direction of Alexander Mitchell, a Milwaukee banker, its rails reached Aberdeen, South Dakota, in 1881; Council Bluffs, Iowa, in 1882; and Kansas City in 1887. By 1900 the railroad operated 6,500 miles of line and was widely respected for its sound finances and capable management. Among its major stockholders were Philip D. Armour and William Rockefeller.

The third phase of Milwaukee Road history, a time of rapid and costly expansion to the Pacific, began in late 1905 when the railroad's board of directors authorized building a line from the Missouri

A Milwaukee Road Sprint *piggyback train on the main line between Chicago and Minneapolis-St. Paul*

River in South Dakota to Puget Sound in the state of Washington, a distance of 1,489 miles. Under President Albert J. Earling, construction of the Pacific extension commenced in 1906 and continued until the driving of a final spike near Garrison, Montana, on May 14, 1909.

The Chicago, Milwaukee & Puget Sound, a subsidiary absorbed by the parent company in 1912, began through freight service on July 4, 1909, and through passenger service on July 10, 1910. The famous Olympian and Columbian trains commenced their first trips between Chicago and Puget Sound on May 28, 1911. The company, however, was not content to stop at the eastern edge of the sound. During the next two decades it built or acquired lines that took its trains to the shore of the Pacific Ocean and deep into the timber country surrounding Puget Sound.

Hoping to achieve more economical and efficient operation on its numerous mountain grades, the Milwaukee Road electrified 656 miles of its Pacific extension and became the longest electric railway in the world. The portion from Harlowton, Montana, to Avery, Idaho, began regular operation in November 1916; that from Othello, Washington, to Tacoma in March 1920; and that from Black River Junction to Seattle in July 1927. Powering trains with the "white coal" of hydroelectric power saved millions of dollars in operating costs and captured the popular fancy. The electric line served as a prototype for similar systems around the world.

The well-engineered right-of-way of the Pacific extension crossed five mountain ranges. It served a country as rich in scenery as it was devoid of inhabitants. The low population density forced the railroad to become deeply involved in the promotion and settlement of the western lands it served; in 1913 the Milwaukee Land Company promoted twenty new towns in Montana alone.

The Chicago, Milwaukee & St. Paul had expanded to the Pacific in an effort to remain competitive in the rapidly changing world of transcontinental giants and because of the prevailing belief that the fast-growing Pacific Northwest would generate enough freight and passenger traffic for all. Unforeseen, however, were the blows dealt the northern transcontinental lines by the economic slump that overtook the Pacific Northwest in 1912 and lasted until 1917, the diversion of traffic through the Panama Canal after 1914, and the rapid expansion of a publicly subsidized network of all-weather paved highways between 1916 and 1926.

In addition, the total expense of the Pacific extension and its electrification proved far greater than originally anticipated, even with savings gained in operating costs. Construction costs alone exceeded by more than 400 percent the original estimate of $45 million. As a result of these troubles, in 1918 the company failed to pay a dividend on its common stock for the first time since 1892.

In 1921 and 1922 the railroad leased two lines that enabled it to reach from Chicago into the coalfields of southern Indiana, but these proved so ramshackle and debt-encumbered that they only added to the company's intolerable financial burden. Common stock that sold for as much as $200 a share in 1905 dropped to less than $4 a share when the railroad slipped into bankruptcy on March 18, 1925. This event marked the beginning of the fourth and final phase of the Milwaukee Road's history.

The Milwaukee Road emerged from bankruptcy on January 14, 1928, as the Chicago, Milwaukee, St. Paul & Pacific Railroad. After two relatively prosperous years, hard times returned in 1930 with the onset of the Great Depression. Five years of declining freight and passenger revenues forced the railroad to declare bankruptcy again on June 29, 1935; it did not emerge from this reorganization until December 1, 1945.

The 1970 merger of the rival Great Northern, Northern Pacific, and Chicago, Burlington & Quincy lines as the Burlington Northern Railroad proved a fatal blow despite the Milwaukee Road's acquisition of trackage rights in 1973 that extended its own lines to Portland, Oregon. The Milwaukee Road never was able to capitalize on this arrangement by developing long-haul traffic to and from the Pacific Coast. The electrification of the Pacific extension was phased out during the early 1970s. The company's final bankruptcy occurred on December 19, 1977, following three years of heavy losses. Many lines across the Midwest and Far West were abandoned in 1980.

Despite its frequent financial difficulties after 1925, the Milwaukee Road retained some of the innovative spirit that had earlier been manifested not only in its electrified line across the Rockies and Cascades but also in the development of a refrigerator car in 1874. A high-speed streamliner, the Hiawatha, commenced service between Chicago and the Twin Cities on May 29, 1935. For two decades after World War II a fleet of Hiawathas provided fast, deluxe passenger service between Chicago and Omaha, northern Wisconsin and Michigan, and the Twin Cities and Puget Sound. The Milwaukee Road was also a pioneer in the manufacture of its own locomotives and rolling stock, including the cars used for its streamliners.

In 1985, having endured three episodes of bankruptcy and the abandonment of more than 7,000 miles of line, what remained of the Milwaukee Road was acquired by the Soo Line Railroad. On January 1, 1986, the Milwaukee Road was officially merged into the Soo Line.

References:

John W. Cary, *The Organization and History of the Chicago, Milwaukee & St. Paul Railway Company* (Milwaukee, 1892);

August Derleth, *The Milwaukee Road: Its First Hundred Years* (New York: Creative Age Press, 1948);

Max Lowenthal, *The Investor Pays* (New York: Knopf, 1933);

Carlos A. Schwantes, "The Milwaukee Road's Pacific Extension, 1902-1929," *Pacific Northwest Quarterly*, 72 (January 1981): 30-40;

Richard Steinheimer, *The Electric Way Across the Mountains: Stories of the Milwaukee Road Electrification* (Tiburon, Cal.: Carbarn Press, 1980).

Chicago, Rock Island & Pacific Railway

by H. Roger Grant

University of Akron

Map of the Chicago, Rock Island & Pacific Railway (1930)

A once dominant Midwestern trunk carrier was the Chicago, Rock Island & Pacific Railway. The Rock Island emerged shortly before the Civil War as a modest operation. In 1847 local promoters won a state charter for construction of the Rock Island & La Salle Rail Road between the Illinois communities of its corporate name; they were hoping to link the Illinois and Michigan Canal with the Mississippi River. On April 8, 1851, the property became the Chicago & Rock Island. Soon this line connected Chicago, Rock Island, and Peoria, Illinois, and in 1856 it became the first railroad to bridge the Mississippi River. A subsequent acquisition, the Mississippi & Missouri, pushed west into Iowa in the late 1850s. The two firms united in August 1866 to form the Chicago, Rock Island & Pacific.

The importance of the Rock Island to the Midwest and the nation increased dramatically in 1869. On May 11 the road reached Council Bluffs, Iowa, forging a strategic connection with the newly completed Union Pacific-Central Pacific system. But the Rock Island did not enjoy a monopoly to the East; the Chicago & North Western had arrived at the Omaha Gateway on January 22, 1867, and the Burlington & Missouri River (a subsidiary of the Chicago, Burlington & Quincy) would appear in January 1870. To prevent rate wars, the three carriers in 1870 formed the prototype "gentlemen's agreement," the Iowa Pool. Although this arrangement initially met with moderate success, it collapsed in the early 1880s. The Rock Island subsequently entered the "Tripartite" traffic pool with the Chicago, Milwaukee & St. Paul and the Union Pacific, but aggressiveness on the part of other roads led to that pool's demise. As became commonplace for carriers in the 1880s, the Rock Island, spearheaded by its energetic and at times unpredictable president and general manager, Ransome R. Cable, decided that to insure control of business it needed to push its lines into various traffic centers; a needless paralleling of existing systems thereby occurred. By 1898 the Rock Island controlled a web of rails that stretched from Illinois to Colorado and Texas; but of the 3,568 miles operated only 2,877 were owned. The Cable administration preferred leases and trackage-rights agreements to actual building.

A sad chapter in the saga of the Rock Island began in 1901 when the property fell into the hands of the Reid-Moore Syndicate. Led by stock plungers and trust makers Daniel G. Reid, brothers William H. and James Hobart Moore, William B.

Leeds, and, in time, B. F. Yoakum, these men sought to turn their new possession into a money-making machine. The syndicate's years marked a time of reckless expansion. By June 1909 the road's mileage had soared to 8,026, and its level of debt had soared as well. But in 1909 Yoakum turned against the syndicate and forced it to sell him its considerable stock in the St. Louis-San Francisco Railway (Frisco) and related holdings. The Rock Island faced enormous financial problems, and by 1914 it was in the hands of court-appointed receivers. A reorganized Rock Island emerged three years later. The company limped through the era of the United States Railroad Administration and the 1920s, but in 1933 the deepening national depression, along with inept management, threw the road back into bankruptcy.

In 1936 John Dow Farrington, a man of great drive and fierce determination, left the management of the Fort Worth & Denver City Railway for the Rock Island. As the company's chief operating officer he brought about a remarkable renaissance, which included state-of-the-art diesel-powered passenger trains, the Rocket streamliners. Wartime profits and generally good, albeit not so imaginative, management led to an official reorganization out of bankruptcy on January 1, 1948.

The company entered the 1950s with optimism, yet it faced keen competition from both stronger railroads and other transportation forms. And there were signs of serious trouble. The road,

for example, reduced its tie replacement program; 1952 was the last year that it installed a million or more new ties. Profits decreased, although red ink did not come in large quantities until the mid 1960s. A proposed merger with the Union Pacific failed to occur, even though the Interstate Commerce Commission finally gave its approval on December 3, 1974, after nearly eight years of deliberation. In 1975 the company entered its third and final bankruptcy. Industrialist Henry Crown, who had been speculating in Rock Island securities since 1946, decided that the road was worth more dead than alive. His considerable influence led to the railroad's shutdown on March 31, 1980, and to its subsequent and profitable liquidation. The shell of the Chicago, Rock Island & Pacific remains as the Chicago-Pacific Corporation, a nontransportation firm that controls the Hoover Company.

References:
William Edward Hayes, *Iron Road to Empire: The History of 100 Years of the Progress and Achievements of the Rock Island Lines* (New York: Simmons-Boardman, 1953);

Dan Rottenberg, "The Last Run of the Rock Island Line," *Chicago Magazine* (September 1984): 197-201, 234-237.

Archives:
The major body of the corporate records of the Chicago, Rock Island & Pacific Railway is held by the University of Oklahoma, Norman.

Chicago South Shore & South Bend Railroad

by John F. Due

University of Illinois

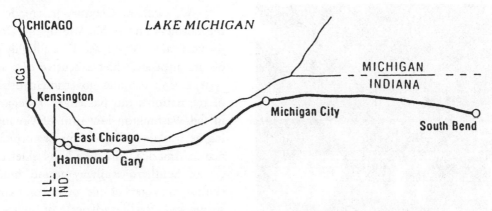

Map of the Chicago South Shore & South Bend Railroad (1983)

Built relatively late in the era of the interurban electric railways, the Chicago South Shore & South Bend ultimately proved to be the most successful such road. The line was opened in 1909 from South Bend, Indiana, to Kensington, Illinois, where connections were made to the Illinois Central suburban trains. The road lacked a good entrance into Chicago, however, and used unsatisfactory AC operation; the company went into bankruptcy in 1925 and was nearly sold for junk. In that year it was purchased by Samuel Insull, who completely rebuilt the road and negotiated with the Illinois Central for direct access to downtown Chicago. Traffic increased greatly and the road became profitable, but the collapse of the Insull empire and the Depression brought the company into receivership again. It was reorganized in 1938 and was sold to the Chesapeake & Ohio Railway in 1967.

The ninety-mile road continued to operate interurban passenger trains through to South Bend, although most of the passenger traffic was commuter in nature. The road developed a substantial freight business, coal being the most important commodity carried. In 1985 the Chessie System sold the line to the Venango River Corporation formed by a group of Chicago area middle-level railway management personnel. New passenger equipment was acquired in the mid 1980s through a transit district formed in the area. The passenger service was subsidized from state and local taxes.

Reference:
William D. Middleton, *South Shore: The Last Interurban* (San Marino, Cal.: Golden West Books, 1978).

Archives:
The corporate records of the Chicago South Shore & South Bend Railroad are at the company's offices in Chicago.

W. Graham Claytor, Jr.

(March 14, 1912-   )

by Albert S. Eggerton, Jr.

Southern Railway (retired)

W. Graham Claytor, Jr. (courtesy of Amtrak)

CAREER: Associate, later partner, Covington & Burling (1938-1967); vice president, law (1963-1967); president and chief executive officer (1967-1976); chairman and chief executive officer (1976-1977), Southern Railway Company; secretary of the navy (1977-1979); acting secretary of transportation (1979); deputy secretary of defense (1979-1981); counsel, Covington & Burling (1981-1982); chairman and president, National Railroad Passenger Corporation (Amtrak) (1982-   ).

W. Graham Claytor, Jr., made his mark on the business and public life of the United States in the years after World War II as a highly respected corporate attorney, chief executive of a major railway system, United States government officer, and head of the nation's rail passenger system. As a partner in the Washington law firm of Covington & Burling he was near the summit of corporate law practice in America. His decade as chief executive officer of Southern Railway found him not only a skillful manager of his own company but also a strong and effective advocate of the trend toward intermodal ownership that began to be realized years later. As secretary of the navy and later deputy secretary of defense in the administration of President Jimmy Carter, Claytor advocated to Congress and to the public a strong but cost-effective defense. His successful stewardship as chief executive of the National Railroad Passenger Corporation was characterized by improved service, increased revenues, and effective cost control.

William Graham Claytor, Jr., was born in Roanoke, Virginia, on March 14, 1912. His father was an electrical engineer who retired as executive vice president of American Gas and Electric Company (now American Electric Power Company). His mother, Gertrude Boatwright Claytor, came from a family with roots in the railroad business reaching back to the earliest days of railroading in America.

After early studies at the Haverford School in Pennsylvania and the Riverdale Country School in New York City, Claytor became a Phi Beta Kappa student at the University of Virginia. He specialized in mathematics and physics and had his eye on a career in electrical engineering, but the Depression year of 1933, when he received his B.A. degree, held out few opportunities in his chosen field, and most of those were out of the country. Claytor decided to enroll for graduate work at the Harvard Law School, with general agreement in the family that if law proved not to his liking he could transfer to the nearby Massachusetts Institute of Technology. But once launched on the study of law, he never looked back. He received his LL.B. degree *summa cum laude* in 1936 after serving as president of the *Harvard Law Review* and achieving one of the finest academic records in the history of the school. For the next two years he worked as a law clerk with two of the most brilliant men in American jurisprudence: in 1936 and 1937 with Judge Learned Hand of the United States Court of Appeals for the Second Circuit, and in 1937 and 1938 with Supreme Court Justice Louis D. Brandeis.

Admitted to the New York bar in 1937 and to the District of Columbia bar in 1938, he began the private practice of law in the latter year as an associate with the Washington law firm of Covington, Burling, Rublee, Acheson and Shorb. His career was interrupted by military service in World War II. Taking a leave of absence from the law firm, he was commissioned an ensign in the Navy in September 1940 and went on active duty the following January. During the war he advanced from ensign to lieutenant commander on assignments that took him from the Washington Navy Yard to the coastal patrol yacht U.S.S. *Opal* and then to commands of a submarine chaser, the U.S.S. *SC-516,* and two destroyer escorts; the U.S.S. *Lee Fox* in 1943 and 1944 and the U.S.S. *Cecil J. Doyle* in 1944 and 1945.

An incident while he was skipper of the *Doyle* highlighted the decisiveness that characterized all of Claytor's career. Cruising near Peleliu Island in the Pacific on routine patrol in July 1945, Lt. Cmdr. Claytor made radio contact with the pilot of a passing navy patrol aircraft. He learned that the plane was en route to a location some 300 miles to the north where large numbers of men had been sighted adrift in shark-infested waters. Claytor immediately changed course and headed north at full speed, an hour and a half ahead of the official orders to take part in the rescue. The first ship to arrive on the scene, the *Doyle* was able to pick up almost 100 survivors of the sinking of the heavy cruiser U.S.S. *Indianapolis* four days earlier.

After the war, Claytor returned to his law firm, which had become Covington & Burling, and in 1947 he was made a partner. On August 14, 1948 he married Frances Murray Hammond of Roanoke, who, like Claytor, was a lieutenant commander in the Naval Reserve. For almost two decades Claytor earned a growing reputation in corporate law while he maintained his enthusiasm for the railroads and trains that had fascinated him since boyhood. The two interests began to coalesce in 1963 when D. William Brosnan, president of the Southern Railway Company, offered him the post of vice president and head of the law department at the Southern's Washington headquarters. Reluctant to give up the private practice of law, Claytor accepted on condition that he could divide his time between the Southern and Covington & Burling.

By the time the Southern Railway's board of directors elected him president of the company in 1967, Claytor was ready to leave his law firm for a new challenge. He was about to shape a new management style for a strong, successful railway still dominated by its operating department and still carrying the mark of Brosnan, one of the rail industry's great innovators and personal managers.

Claytor's style of management involved a team approach. He wanted open communications in all directions, constructive input to the decision-making process from people at every level who had experience and ideas to contribute, and a basic streamlining of the management structure itself. The number of officers who normally reported directly to the president was reduced from between twenty and twenty-five to four executive vice presidents who, with Claytor, made up the management committee. This arrangement was not, by any means, management *by* committee. Discussion flowed freely in the frequent meetings of the group; recommendations and ideas were exchanged and carefully considered. But when it came to a decision, there was only one vote and Claytor cast it. Usually, though not always, it reflected the consensus of the committee.

The new management team made a major contribution to the Southern by establishing a systematic planning and budgeting process for the railway, something that the Southern had never had in the past. The Southern had always worked on the "appropriation" basis, with the chief executive allotting operating funds to the various departments. The new president and his team developed both short-range and long-range plans for the railway and a new kind of budgeting system. Given what the railway expected to accomplish in a particular year, and the revenues likely to be produced, lower level supervisors had to develop their own goals and budgets. Then they were required to defend them to their supervisors in competition with others for the dollars available. Higher level supervisors in turn had to defend a number of such budgets to the budget committee, made up of the four executive vice presidents and the comptroller. In the give-and-take of budget committee sessions, people began thinking in terms of the goals of the company rather than those of individual departments. It took time for this system to be accepted, but it worked.

Claytor's approach to management helped heal much of the estrangement between management and unions that lingered as a result of the labor-saving aspects of modernization during the Brosnan years. Other personnel-related actions of the management team included an annual review of managers' performance, a salary review and bonus system for officers based on overall company profitability rather than individual department performance, and a merit system of pay increases for nonunion employees designed to reward the most productive people.

Claytor instituted an employee safety program that led to the Southern's first Harriman Gold Medal in his final year at the helm. He also presided over the start of the Southern's "Operation Lifesaver" program to promote greater safety at rail-highway grade crossings.

He continued and intensified the railway's accent on marketing and its concentration on customer needs as the basis for operations planning. The industry's customary across-the-board price increases were often rejected in favor of selective rate adjustments, up or down, based on market conditions and the probable effect on profitability. Claytor took the same pragmatic approach to the merger trend that gained strength during his years as the Southern's chief executive. A rail combination had no appeal for him unless it involved benefits for the company in the areas of greater productivity and wider markets.

Diversification, another trend of the times, proved more to his liking but only if it involved moving into transportation-related fields where he felt that the Southern's skills and experience could have the most productive effect. Claytor perceived sooner than most, and advocated publicly and often

throughout his time at the Southern, the value of creating total transportation companies. He characterized the combination of different modes of transportation under one corporate banner as "an opportunity such as we have never had in this country to work hard and effectively to strengthen our whole transportation system."

His experience as a lawyer in focusing on the essentials of a problem and addressing them in orderly fashion helped him in the task of simplifying the railway's complex corporate structure. The Southern's development from the combination of more than a hundred separate companies had left a tangled web of financial transactions among the remaining subsidiaries that needed to be unravelled.

Claytor's regard for open communications in all directions extended also to the Southern's relationship with the financial community. He began meeting each quarter with stock analysts and other financial leaders to discuss the Southern's results in the period just ended and to look at the prospects for the immediate future. The meetings were held in New York, with additional ones later in Chicago, Boston, Philadelphia, and other business centers.

In 1976, as he approached sixty-five, the Southern's mandatory retirement age for senior officers, Claytor was named chairman and chief executive officer and L. Stanley Crane was elected to the presidency. In February 1977 Claytor retired as chairman to accept the post of secretary of the navy in the cabinet of President Carter.

Although reflecting to a considerable extent the inflation of the mid 1970s, the statistical measure of Claytor's stewardship of the Southern Railway is nonetheless impressive. When he took over as head of the railway in 1967, operating revenues were about $470 million, net income was just over $35 million, and capital improvement spending for the year stood at a little more than $91 million. In 1976, his last full year at the head of the company, the Southern recorded its first billion-dollar year in operating revenues; brought more than $89 million to the bottom line; and invested $152 million in capital improvements, part of an improvement program that totaled well over a billion dollars during Claytor's term as chief executive. On his retirement, the Southern's board of directors acknowledged Claytor's contribution:

It is no coincidence that during the tenure of W. Graham Claytor, Jr., as chief executive of the Company, Southern Railway was singled out by *Dun's Review* as one of the five best-managed companies in the United States.

An astute lawyer, a perceptive planner and an able executive, he brought all these qualities to bear in strengthening the Company and in working to advance the industry as a whole.

His enlightened approach to management included both an openness to the ideas and suggestions of others and a personal decisiveness when the facts were in. The combination helped keep Southern strong, growing, profitable and readily responsive to the changing needs of the territory it serves.

When he moved across the Potomac to the Pentagon to become the head of the United States Navy, this tall, rangy Virginian brought an unusual array of qualifications to his new post. Here was a civilian executive with line and combat experience as a navy officer and management skills sharpened by a decade at the head of one of America's major rail systems. These skills he soon put to work in helping shape the modern navy.

Claytor resisted what he considered overly deep cuts in the navy's budget by cost-conscious defense planners just as strongly as he opposed the idea of limiting the navy's role to keeping the sea lanes open to Europe. He argued the importance of the fleet also in the protection of America's interests in the Pacific. His vision of sea power encompassed a strong and versatile navy, with available funds spread over a number of ships, both conventionally and nuclear powered, rather than concentrated on a few huge nuclear-powered vessels. He was concerned that America not pin its security hopes on a naval "Maginot Line." But the new secretary did not lack concern for the necessity of keeping costs in line. In 1978 at the conclusion of negotiations General Dynamics Corporation and Litton Industries absorbed more than a half-billion dollars as their share of cost overruns in the construction of eighteen nuclear-powered attack submarines, five assault ships, and thirty destroyers.

Claytor's railroad experience proved valuable to the Carter administration in 1979 when he was asked to take on the job of acting secretary of transportation. He returned to the Defense Department as deputy secretary later in 1979. With the change of administrations in 1981 his government service came to an end, and he returned to Covington & Burling. His absence from the public scene lasted little more than a year; in July 1982 he was elected chairman and president of the National Railroad Passenger Corporation (Amtrak), the corporation created by Congress in 1971 to revitalize America's slumping rail passenger service.

Progress had been made since the early days when Amtrak inherited the aging equipment and operating deficits of the service formerly provided by private railroads. Still largely a contractor for passenger service with those same railroads, Amtrak had started to become a true railroad when Congress made it the owner and the operator of the Northeast Corridor track in 1976 and granted funds for the wholesale replacement or rebuilding of outdated equipment. Claytor's job has been to make this improving passenger rail network deliver quality service and yet come as close as possible to covering its costs of doing business, and he has made real progress toward these goals. Amtrak reached in 1982 the financial goal Congress had set for 1984: to have the corporation cover out of revenues at least one-half of its costs. That revenue-to-expense ratio went from 53 percent in 1982 to 54 percent in 1983, 56 percent in 1984, 58 percent in 1985, and over 60 percent in 1986.

Claytor has been active in a number of business, professional, and civic organizations throughout his many-faceted career. His business directorships, besides the Southern Railway Company and its subsidiary lines, have included the Florida East Coast Railway Company, the Richmond, Fredericksburg & Potomac Railroad Company, the Association of American Railroads, J. P. Morgan and Company, the Morgan Guaranty Trust Company, and the Penn Virginia Corporation. He has been a member of the American Bar Association, the American Judicature Society, the American Law Institute, the American Society of Corporate Executives, the National Railway Historical Society, and the Protestant Episcopal Foundation of the District of Columbia, and was a trustee of the Episcopal Home for Children in Washington from 1960 to 1965.

Claytor's son, William Graham Claytor III, has kept up the family railroad tradition as an operating officer with the Norfolk Southern; the Claytors also have a daughter, Dr. Frances Murray Claytor. Claytor's younger brother, Robert B. Claytor, has also had an outstanding law and railroad career as a vice president and later president of Norfolk & Western Railway Company, and as the first chairman and chief executive officer of the newly created Norfolk Southern Corporation in 1982. A third brother, Richard A. Claytor, is president of Burns & Roe Pacific, an important engineering consulting firm in Los Angeles.

Claytor's leisure interests include hunting, fishing and sailing, but his favorite hobbies have always involved railroads: photographing and recording trains in motion, collecting antique toy trains, and for a time maintaining a large-scale model railroad in the back garden of his Georgetown home.

References:

"Amtrak Gains Respect," *Modern Railroads,* 39 (May 1984): 27-31;

"Back at the Throttle," *Industry Week,* 221 (April 16, 1984): 59-61;

Burke Davis, *The Southern Railway, Road of the Innovators* (Chapel Hill: University of North Carolina Press, 1985), pp. 250-266;

"Succeeding Where Others Flounder," *Nation's Business,* 64 (October 1976): 29-34;

Daryl Wycoff, *Railroad Management* (Lexington, Mass.: Lexington Books, 1976), pp. 152–169.

Archives:

A complete file of W. Graham Claytor, Jr.'s speeches as the Southern Railway's chief executive, both published and unpublished, is in the library of the Public Relations Department, Norfolk Southern Corporation, Roanoke, Virginia.

Martin W. Clement

(December 5, 1881-August 30, 1966)

by Michael Bezilla

Pennsylvania State University

Martin W. Clement (Pennsylvania State Archives)

CAREER: Surveyor's assistant, United New Jersey Railroad (1901-1910); track supervisor, Pennsylvania Railroad (1910-1914); division engineer, New York, Philadelphia & Norfolk Railroad (1914-1916); division engineer, Pennsylvania Railroad (1916); superintendent, New York, Philadelphia & Norfolk Railroad (1917-1918); superintendent, freight and passenger transportation, Lines East (1918-1920); superintendent, Lake division (1920-1923); general manager, Central Region (1923-1925); assistant vice president in charge of operations (1925-1926); vice president in charge of operations (1926-1933); vice president (1933-1935);

president (1935-1949); chairman of the board (1949-1951), Pennsylvania Railroad.

Martin W. Clement's fourteen-year presidency of the Pennsylvania Railroad (PRR) spanned an era of profound technological change. Clement was personally involved with nearly all aspects of the railroad; in his motive power strategies alone, he left an imprint that lasted to the end of the PRR's corporate life in 1968, and beyond to its successors Penn Central, Amtrak, and Conrail.

Born on December 5, 1881, in the central Pennsylvania town of Sunbury, Martin Withington Clement was a son of Charles M. and Alice Withington Clement. Charles Clement, a distinguished attorney, was an officer in the Pennsylvania National Guard and would have initial command of the guard's famed Twenty-eighth Division in World War I.

After graduating with a bachelor's degree from Trinity College in Hartford, Connecticut, in 1901, Clement took a job as a surveyor's assistant with the United New Jersey Railroad and Canal Company, a Pennsylvania Railroad subsidiary. For the next nine years he was involved in various civil engineering tasks related to the construction of the PRR's New York tunnel extension project, which the road had launched at the turn of the century to provide a direct rail link between its old terminus at Jersey City and its magnificent new Pennsylvania Station in lower Manhattan. Featuring twin tunnels under the Hudson River and electrically propelled trains, its was the greatest railroad improvement project of its day.

With the completion of the tunnel extension work in 1910, Clement was promoted to track supervisor and transferred to the general manager's office at the PRR's Philadelphia headquarters. While performing fieldwork on the Philadelphia division, he designed a new type of lantern that was more convenient for trackmen to carry yet safer, since its light was visible at greater distances. The design soon became the standard on the PRR and eventually was imitated by railroads throughout the nation.

Beginning in 1913 and continuing for the next thirteen years, Clement rose rapidly through a series of posts of increasing responsibility, necessitating changes of residence that were frequent even when compared to the careers of his most well-traveled PRR contemporaries. First, he returned to the New York area as track supervisor on the Manhattan division. He served for only a few months before being assigned a similar task on the Pittsburgh division. In 1914 his civil engineering duties were broadened to include bridges and structures when he was made division engineer of the New York, Philadelphia & Norfolk Railroad (NYP&N), a PRR subsidiary that ran nearly the length of the Delmarva Peninsula, giving the Pennsylvania access to Norfolk, Virginia, by means of a ferry across the mouth of the Chesapeake Bay. After a brief stint as division engineer on the New Jersey division of the PRR in 1916, Clement returned to the NYP&N as superintendent, the chief operating officer of the line, in June 1917. This position gave him his first nonengineering railroad experience.

While Clement was in this post, an incident occurred that was often cited later as evidence of his utter lack of pretension and his dedication to the service of his company. Crossing the Chesapeake on the ferry one evening, Clement learned that the dining room was overflowing with patrons while the serving staff was shorthanded. He immediately donned a waiter's jacket, directed the ship's captain to do likewise, and proceeded to wait on tables for the duration of the voyage.

In December 1917, eight months after the United States entered World War I, the federal government formed the United States Railroad Administration (USRA) to operate the nation's rail lines. The railroads could not cope with the avalanche of war-related freight and passenger business, and on some routes trains came to a standstill for lack of motive power or space to put them in clogged yards. Under USRA supervision, Clement became superintendent of freight transportation for Pennsylvania Railroad Lines East of Pittsburgh—territory that included the Pittsburgh-Philadelphia main line, scene of some of the worst congestion anywhere. Why he was selected by the USRA for this position is not clear. Normal channels of promotion did not prevail during the war, of course, and Clement did enjoy the friendship of the man whom he would one day succeed in the PRR presidency, William Wallace Atterbury, who was already in government service and had highly placed connections. (Formerly the PRR's vice president in charge of operations, Atterbury had become director general of transportation for the American Expeditionary Forces in August 1917.) Clement was handed even greater responsibilities in 1919 when he was named acting director of passenger transportation for Lines East.

In March 1920, when Congress finally returned operation of the railroads to their private owners, Clement was appointed superintendent of the Lake division, with headquarters in Cleveland. Under the Pennsylvania's decentralized managerial system, division superintendents reigned as demigods as far as operations in their territories were concerned, and Clement continued to display a singular flair for this aspect of railroading. Consequently in 1923 he was sent to Pittsburgh as general manager of the Central Region, which included the Lake division and all other divisions between Altoona, Pennsylvania, and Crestline, Ohio.

His ascendency through the upper managerial ranks notwithstanding, Clement spent much of his time in the field, asserting that there he could come face-to-face with problems and could stay in touch with rank-and-file employees. While conducting inspection trips, he was known to stop more than once to assist a heavily pressed track gang or lend a hand at a ticket window besieged with prospective passsengers.

In October 1925, the month that the PRR's directors named Atterbury to succeed the retiring Samuel Rea as the company's president, Clement was brought to Philadelphia to become assistant vice president in charge of operations. A year later he moved up to vice president in charge of operations, succeeding Elisha Lee, who as vice president became the road's second-ranking executive and Atterbury's heir apparent.

In 1929 Clement's wife of nineteen years, Irene Higbie Clement, died, leaving three children: Harrison H., James H., and Alice W. Clement. In 1931 Clement married Elizabeth Wallace. That marriage did not result in children.

As vice president in charge of operations, Clement had systemwide responsibilities for making certain that the PRR's trains ran in the most efficient manner. President Atterbury delegated to him another important task: to oversee the implementation of the electrification of the 245-mile New York-Washington main line, a $250 million project begun late in 1928. It represented the largest single installation of electric traction on an American steam railroad and the largest capital improvement program undertaken by the railroad industry. The switch from steam to electrically powered trains was part of Atterbury's grand vision for electrifying the Pennsylvania's entire main route east of Pittsburgh. By the late 1920s Atterbury had become increasingly involved in questions of railroad consolidation—then a topic of prime interest among rail executives—so the day-to-day direction of electrification devolved on Clement. After the onset of the Great Depression, with Atterbury and Vice President Lee both devoting more time to financial affairs, Clement shouldered ever-increasing authority for electrification and general operations.

When Lee succumbed to a heart attack in October 1933, Atterbury immediately moved Clement up to the vice presidency. That office involved him in broad questions of policy and business strategy as well as operations. His role as Atterbury's heir apparent became official in July 1934 when he was named acting president, as ill health forced his superior to relinquish most of his duties. When continuing illness forced Atterbury to take early retirement in April 1935, the board of directors elected Clement his permanent successor. At age fifty-three he was among the youngest chief executives the PRR had had since its incorporation in 1846. He also carried the imprimatur of his mentor. "Unquestionably one of the ablest railroad executives in the country," was how Atterbury described Clement to newspaper reporters soon after the board announced its decision.

In his two previous positions, Clement had performed ably in reducing operating costs and eliminating waste. The Pennsylvania was one of relatively few railroads to remain even modestly profitable through the worst of the Depression. Electrification and the economies it wrought through lower operating and maintenance costs and higher train speeds had been implemented on schedule, with the New York-Washington corridor opened for electrified ser-

vice over its entire length by February 1935. Clement had advocated extending electrification west from Philadelphia to Harrisburg and, as president, oversaw the accomplishment of this goal in 1937. Electric traction and the other efficiency measures that Clement had introduced in the early 1930s brought the PRR's operating ratio (the ratio of operating expenses to revenues) down to 71.2 percent, the lowest in the company's history, by 1939.

Other than approving additional expenditures for electrification, however, Clement followed the PRR's traditional conservative financial course. The initial years of his administration, like the tenure of an earlier president, James McCrea, who had served from 1907 to 1912, were a time for the company to catch its breath before moving on to additional spending programs. Between 1937 and 1945 Clement presided over a 15 percent reduction of the Pennsylvania's funded debt, bringing it down to $946 million. (That a near billion-dollar debt could be considered manageable testifies to the gargantuan dimensions of the PRR.)

Lean and efficient, the railroad shouldered the increased traffic of World War II with little noticeable strain. During the period 1939 to 1943 ton-miles doubled and passenger-miles rose nearly fourfold; yet there was little sign of the kind of congestion that had plagued the line in World War I.

Ironically, while World War II was in some ways the finest hour for both the Pennsylvania Railroad and Clement, it also marked a downturn in the road's economic well-being. The PRR recorded its first annual net loss—about $8.5 million—in its centennial year of 1946. From then until the end of its corporate life twenty-two years later, the Pennsylvania would never enjoy the consistent prosperity that had characterized virtually all of its earlier history.

The reversals suffered by the road stemmed in large part from circumstances beyond President Clement's control. In the immediate aftermath of the costly electrification program, he had no alternative but to postpone further large capital projects until the nation had recovered from the Great Depression. But that recovery did not occur until—and indeed was spurred on by—the outbreak of World War II. The railroad earned hefty returns during the war, but the adoption of further improvements on a large scale was impossible. Moreover, Congress in 1943 enacted a sizeable excess profits tax. Clement bitterly opposed the legislation, and in his report to stockholders that year he warned that the tax prevented the PRR and other railroads from putting away monetary reserves "for future expenditures which are being made inevitable by wartime conditions and the pressure of wartime traffic. Thus deferred maintenance is mounting at an ever increasing rate."

Consequently, in the first full peacetime year of 1946, the railroad found itself burdened by a physical plant that was seriously obsolete and worn out. Timely renewal had been delayed first by the constraints of the Great Depression, then by the siphoning off of funds for electrification, and finally by war. Modernization of the physical plant and rolling stock was imperative. Nowhere was upgrading more urgently needed than in motive power: fully 80 percent of the railroad's 4,500 steam engines were more than twenty years old. Should more efficient coal-burning steam locomotives be developed, or should electrification be extended, or should diesel-electric locomotives–then being introduced in large quantities on other roads–be acquired to replace steam? Clement wavered in making that decision, the most consequential of his administration, as he considered the PRR's close ties to the coal industry and the massive cost of each of the courses of action before him. Finally, in 1947, the railroad opted for the gradual dieselization of all nonelectrified lines; diesels offered many of the same advantages over steam electric locomotives but required a smaller initial investment. The process was not completed until 1957; in the interim, the use of outmoded steam power and attendant facilities continued to sap the Pennsylvania's vitality.

The PRR faced many other problems in the postwar period. Two of the most ominous were increased competition from government-subsidized highway and air carriers and the gradual decline of the industrial base (especially coal and steel) of the Northeast. The proportions of these difficulties were not fully realized, however, when Clement retired from the presidency effective June 16, 1949. He was succeeded by Walter S. Franklin.

Clement retained control over the railroad by installing himself in the newly created position of chairman of the board. As president, he had found that he was being called upon more frequently to address government bodies and Wall Street on issues of public policy and finance, leaving less time to attend to routine corporate business. Henceforth the

board chairman would be a spokesman for the Pennsylvania and the railroad industry as a whole on what Clement termed "extra-curricular matters," and the president—now the second-ranking executive—would actually run the railroad. It was an arrangement that with a few years' exception lasted through the remainder of the PRR's life and was continued by Penn Central and Conrail.

To be sure, Clement was not a politically oriented executive in the manner of an Atterbury. He had hardly moved into the president's office in 1935 before he had put an end to the PRR's long-standing intimacy with Pennsylvania's Republican party organization (although he remained a lifelong Republican), a relationship that his predecessor had vigorously cultivated. Nor did Clement win any prominence nationally, other than that ordinarily accorded to any president of the PRR, in speaking for American railroads.

Clement was too wedded to the Pennsylvania, too much of an operations man, to have a gift for politics or public relations. He maintained tight personal control over his company and brooked no interference with or questioning of his decisions by subordinates. Rare was the young manager who at one time or another had not become the target of the president's "forthright vocabulary," as one associate called it. *Fortune* magazine in 1936 described him as a man "whose brain works so much faster than other men's that his chronic mood is one of profane impatience with the world's inefficiency." An article in the same publication twelve years later labeled him "an old school operating man who rules his railroad with an unvelveted hand." Clement scoffed at modern managerial and accounting techniques and had no use for the collection and interpretation of satistical data, yet he ran the railroad successfully because he knew it so intimately.

Clement stepped down from the chairmanship at the end of December 1951, though he stayed on as a director for six more years. He took pride in the heritage of the PRR and as chairman had begun setting aside a number of steam locomotives and pieces of rolling stock that by the late 1970s became the irreplaceable core of the collection at the state-owned Railroad Museum of Pennsylvania. The only comprehensive history of the PRR, a work that was remarkably detailed, well written, and frank in its assessments, was published under Clement's aegis in 1949.

Elizabeth Clement died in May 1966 at Cre-feld, the family estate in Rosemont, suburban Phila-delphia. Clement succumbed on August 30 of the same year. At the hour of his funeral, 3:00 P.M. on September 1, PRR board chairman Stuart Saunders ordered all Pennsylvania Railroad trains halted for one minute in the late president's memory.

Clement was cast in the mold of previous PRR presidents in that he was an up-from-the-ranks executive, following the usual route from the engineering corps through the operating department to the managerial level. This system of advance-ment gave the company leaders who were ac-quainted with the "nuts and bolts" of railroading and who tended to be conservative in their outlook. Up to and including Clement's era, executives with this kind of background served the Pennsylvania well. In later years, threatened by competition from nonrail modes of transportation and the steady de-cline in heavy industry in the Northeast, the rail-road would require (but did not necessarily get) man-agers who knew more than simply how to run trains and who were willing to use innovative meth-ods to retain and build traffic. If Clement was not the last of the old guard on the Pennsylvania, he was the final member of that group to preside over a prosperous railroad.

Publication:
A Railroad President Looks at His Job (Philadelphia: Penn-sylvania Railroad, 1936).

References:
"Atterbury Resigns; Clement Elected President of Pennsyl-vania," *Railway Age,* 98 (April 27, 1935): 651-653;
George H. Burgess and Miles C. Kennedy, *Centennial His-tory of the Pennsylvania Railroad* (Philadelphia: Penn-sylvania Railroad, 1949);
"M. W. Clement Elected Chairman of PRR; Franklin Is President," *Railway Age,* 126 (June 11, 1949): 48-49;
"Pennsylvania Railroad," *Fortune,* 13 (May 1936): 67-77; (June 1936): 89-98;
"Pennsy's Predicament," *Fortune,* 37 (March 1948): 84-93.

Archives:
Some of Martin W. Clement's business papers are in the Pennsylvania Railroad archives, which are divided among several institutions and remain uncatalogued.

Conrail

by Richard Saunders

Clemson University

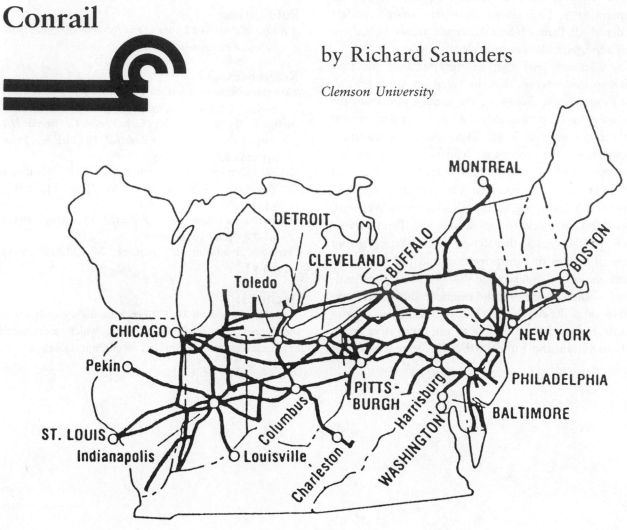

Map of Conrail (1983)

The bankruptcy of the 19,415-mile Penn Central in June 1970 forced national attention on the railroad crisis in the Northeast. The profits of Northeastern railroads had been declining since the mid 1950s due to changing economic conditions within the transportation industry and within the region. Maintenance had been cut back, causing a cumulative deterioration that the Penn Central bankruptcy finally laid bare. Consolidation, the panacea proclaimed both by the industry and by politicians, had failed on the Penn Central, in part because management had lost control of the huge operation but in general because financially strong roads had refused to combine with weaker roads. The three railroads that comprised the Penn Central—the New York Central, the Pennsylvania, and the New Haven—though large and essential to the Northeastern economy, were among the financially weakest.

After bankruptcy, with losses running at about $100 million quarterly, Penn Central trains were kept rolling only by an infusion of government credit. Hundreds of millions of dollars would be necessary before the railroad could be rebuilt enough to be profitable, and such credit was not forthcoming from private sources. Creditors clamored for a settlement, which under bankruptcy law could not be postponed forever, no matter how vital the rail services in question. Judge John

Fullam, presiding over the bankruptcy proceedings, ordered an inquiry into which Penn Central segments, if any, solvent railroads would be willing to acquire. The answer was almost none. Liquidation would, therefore, mean the end of rail service across much of the Northeast. Industries along those lines would be forced to shut down, resulting in lost investment, lost jobs, the collapse of property values, and the crippling of communities and cities. In the prevailing political climate, no one dared advocate outright nationalization. Early in 1973, with the court, private parties, and local authorities at an impasse and with jurisdictional battles erupting between Congress, the executive branch, and the regulatory agencies, Judge Fullam ordered that a meaningful plan of reorganization be drawn up by the end of June; otherwise, he would order liquidation on July 2.

Among those immediately concerned were railroads in other regions of the country that would be unable to forward traffic into the Northeast. The principal author of the plan that was finally adopted was Frank Barnett of the Union Pacific; it was submitted as legislation by Representatives Brock Adams of Washington and Richard Shoup of Montana. The Regional Rail Reorganization (3R) Act of 1973, as modified by the Railroad Revitalization and Regulatory Reform (4R) Act of 1976, called for the creation of a United States Railway Administration, a nonprofit corporation under the Department of Transportation with directors from all interested parties, including labor, creditors, shippers, solvent railroads, and the public. It would issue loans and loan guarantees and plan for a final system based on the ideas advocated by Penn Central trustees for a ruthless elimination of branch lines. When planning was complete, operation of the system would be taken over by the Consolidated Rail Corporation (Conrail), a private, for-profit corporation whose stock would be held by the creditors of the bankrupt roads. As long as more than half of the road's credit was from, or guaranteed by, the government, the government would name a majority of the directors.

Conrail began operation on April 1, 1976, absorbing the operations of the Penn Central and five other bankrupt Northeastern railroads: the Jersey Central, 396 route miles, which had gone bankrupt in 1967; the Lehigh Valley, 954 route miles, bankrupt in 1970; the Reading Company, 1,288 route miles, bankrupt in 1971; the Erie Lackawanna Railway, 2,903 route miles, bankrupt in 1972; and the Lehigh & Hudson River Railroad, 86 route miles, bankrupt in 1972. The Washington-Boston corridor of the former Pennsylvania and New Haven railroads was sold to the National Railroad Passenger Corporation (Amtrak), with Conrail retaining trackage rights for limited freight service. The Penn Central was the core of Conrail: Conrail was head quartered in Philadelphia, like Penn Central and the Pennsylvania Railroad before it, and its operations were basically those of the Penn Central.

Conrail was a failure at first. The elimination of branch lines, regardless of the damage done to local economies, did not make Conrail profitable, as overoptimistic predictions had insisted it would. The decline of "smokestack" (heavy) industry in the Northeast began in earnest after Conrail's creation, reducing traffic volume 18 percent (from 92 billion ton miles in 1977 to 77 billion in 1984). Conrail's management, led by former Southern Pacific executive Richard Spence, seemed as unable to control the railroad as had Penn Central management before it. In 1978, for example, an average of sixty-one trains a day failed to move because of the unavailability of an operable locomotive, and 9,500 miles of poorly maintained track was under slow orders (reduced–speed restrictions), often as low as ten miles per hour.

In final settlements with creditors, the United States government acquired most of Conrail's stock. The Northeast Rail Reorganization Act of 1981 permitted Conrail to drop all passenger service, most of which was taken over by state commuter authorities, and to readjust unproductive agreements with labor. But the fortunes of Conrail really changed with the arrival of L. Stanley Crane from the Southern Railway as chairman and chief executive officer in 1980. Crane continued to radically slim the railroad but did so more effectively than his predecessors had. Maintenance improved remarkably even though employment was reduced dramatically (from 95,000 at the time of Conrail's creation to less than 40,000 in 1986). Care was taken to sever lines that, in some future reorganization, might be extracted to create competition for Conrail in areas where it had a monopoly, notably routes of the former Erie Lackawanna.

In the second quarter of 1981 Conrail posted its first profit, and even in the recession of 1982 and the collapse of smokestack industry across the steel belt it remained profitable every year thereafter, its net income running between $400 million and $500 million a year by the mid 1980s.

The Northeast Rail Services Act of 1981 had set 1984 as a target date for the transfer of Conrail to private ownership, and sale of the system became an active desire of the Reagan Administration. The proceeds would mean a one-time reduction of the federal deficit, but the main reason to sell was ideological: the belief that government should not do what private enterprise could do. One argument against the sale of Conrail was that the government ought to recoup in profits some of the more than $7 billion Conrail, and Penn Central before it, had received in federal advances. Another was that, since Conrail had little rail competition in large parts of its territory, too many vested interests would be at risk if vital transportation were turned over to a strictly profit-seeking entity—especially in an age of deregulation and a time when business morality emphasized short-run paper profits rather than long-run needs and responsibilities. Yet another was that it was not a bad idea for the government to run a profitable railroad as a measure against the claims of other railroads seeking favors or privileges from government.

Of the many parties interested in buying Conrail, the Department of Transportation whittled the list down to three that were thought capable of carrying through with their financial commitments: the Norfolk Southern Corporation; an investor group led by hotelman J. W. Marriott; and Alleghany Corporation, the holding company created by the Van Sweringen Brothers which had controlled the New York Central in the mid 1950s.

Conrail employees, mostly executives led by Crane, mounted an effort to purchase the railroad themselves. Secretary of Transportation Elizabeth Dole selected Norfolk Southern as having the demonstrated ability to run an efficient railroad, although its bid price of $1.2 billion, later raised to $1.9 billion, was ridiculed in some quarters as being a pittance compared to what the railroad was worth and what the government had sunk into it. Under the heat of congressional investigation, opposition from rival CSX Corporation, and the threat of extensive litigation, Norfolk Southern withdrew its offer in August 1986.

On March 26, 1987, Conrail was sold by the government in a public offering of 58.75 million shares priced at $28 a share, the largest single offering in New York Stock Exchange history. Secretary Dole, who had previously opposed the public offering, joined Chairman Crane on the Stock Exchange floor for sale-day festivities. The next day, the price of Conrail stock opened at $31.50 and remained above its original price for some time thereafter.

References:

Richard Saunders, *The Railroad Mergers and the Coming of Conrail* (Westport, Conn.: Greenwood, 1978).

"Federal Rail Officials Expect Shakedown in Conrail Management" *New York Times*. June 25, 1978, p.16.

Archives:

Some records of the component companies of conrail are in the Eleutherian Mills Historical Library, Wilmington, Deleware.

Thomas Conway, Jr.

(August 30, 1882-January 2, 1962)

by John F. Due

University of Illinois

CAREER: Instructor of finance (1905-1908), assistant professor of finance (1908-1914), professor of finance (1914-1929), Wharton School of Finance and Commerce, University of Pennsylvania; president, Chicago, Aurora & Elgin Railroad and Chicago Suburban Power and Light Company, (1922-1926); president, Cincinnati & Lake Erie Railroad (1926-1932); president, Conway Corporation (1926-1962); president, Philadelphia & Western Railway (1930-1946); chairman of the board, Schuylkill Valley Lines (1933-1962); president (1936-1941), member of the executive committee (1936-1962), Transit Research Corporation.

Thomas Conway, Jr., was born in Philadelphia in 1882 to Thomas and Anna Elizabeth Keebler Conway. After graduating from Quaker schools in Philadelphia, he attended the Wharton School of Finance and Commerce of the University of Pennsylvania, earning his bachelors degree in 1904 and his Ph.D. in 1907. He taught at Wharton from 1905 to 1929.

Conway was best known in the transportation field as a reorganizer and rebuilder of electric interurban and suburban railway enterprises as these companies sought to survive in the face of motor vehicle competition. He served as a consultant for a number of transit systems and utilities, and was one of the very few persons to combine an academic career with active financing and management of electric railway and bus systems.

His first major venture in electric railway reorganization began in 1922, when the bondholders of the Chicago, Aurora & Elgin Railroad, most of whom were located in Philadelphia, sent him to Chicago to attempt to solve the problems of the railroad, which was then emerging from bankruptcy.

The rapid transit line operated from downtown Chicago to the western suburbs of Wheaton, St. Charles, Aurora, Elgin, and Geneva, and was primarily dependent on passenger traffic. He reorganized operations, financed the rebuilding of the track, acquired new equipment, and improved service. The reorganized company was sold to the Insull interests in 1925.

In 1926 he was sent by the bondholders to reorganize and modernize the Cincinnati & Dayton Traction Company in southern Ohio, formerly a part of the Ohio Electric system. As with the Chicago line, he succeeded in modernizing the road with new equipment and improved track, and reorganized the company as the Cincinnati, Hamilton & Dayton Railroad. He built up freight service and obtained joint rates from the major railways on LCL (less than carload) traffic. Convinced that there was a future for the interurban on distances of 70 to 200 miles, Conway brought back together the major segments of the old Ohio Electric system under the name Cincinnati & Lake Erie Railroad; he served as president until 1932. The new enterprise had two major lines, 216 miles from Cincinnati to Toledo, with through operations of trains to Detroit and Cleveland on the tracks of other companies; and 45 miles from Springfield to Columbus. As a key element in the improvements he ordered twenty lightweight passenger cars from the Cincinnati Car Company, built to a new design which allowed speeds up to eighty miles an hour and a comfortable ride despite the light track. These cars provided limited service between the major cities served. In a widely publicized event, one of the cars won a race with an airplane of the period.

The modernized road did attract traffic and for several years was successful. But the combined effect of the Depression and the rapid increase in motor vehicle use led to a sharp fall in traffic. While recognizing as early as the mid 1920s that the old style interurban was doomed, Conway was still convinced as late as 1933 that modernized firms could survive and prosper. But the downward trend continued, and the Cincinnati & Lake Erie was abandoned between 1937 and 1939. The company developed an extensive bus system, which took over the routes when the rail lines were abandoned but was eventually sold to Greyhound.

After the mid 1930s, except for widespread consulting, Conway confined his managerial activities to the Philadelphia area, where he headed the Philadelphia & Western, a suburban electric railroad, and affiliated companies from 1930 to 1946. He served as president of the American Transit Association in 1936-1937, was a member of the transit advisory committee of the Office of Defense Transportation during World War II, and was involved in planning a subway system in Shanghai in 1947. He

continued consulting, studying the transit industry, and writing almost to the time of his death in 1962.

Apart from his transit work, Conway was long active in civic affairs. He served as chairman of the Hospital Council of Philadelphia and president and of the board of the Delaware County Memorial Hospital, and worked for hospital expansion. A tall, heavyset man, articulate and highly competent, Conway was a Philadelphian from birth to death, a member of the Union Club, and a devout Republican with an extreme antipathy toward Franklin Roosevelt, whom he blamed in part for the problems of his beloved industry.

Publications:

"The Traffic Problems of Interurban Electric Railways," *Journal of Accountancy*, 7 (January 1909): 214-233;
The Organization of the New Bank Acts, by Conway and Ernest M. Patterson (Philadelphia: Lippincott, 1914).

D. C. Corbin

(October 1, 1832-June 29, 1918)

by John Fahey

Eastern Washington University

D. C. Corbin circa 1890 (Courtesy John Fahey)

CAREER: Surveyor (1852-1862); freight service operator (1862-1865); owner of mercantile business (1865-1871); cashier, First National Bank of Helena, Montana (1871-1876); manager, New York & Manhattan Beach Railway Company (1876-1883); manager, Helena Mining & Reduction Company (1883-1886); president, Spokane Falls & Idaho Railroad and Coeur d'Alene Railway & Navigation Company (1886-1888); manager, Spokane Falls & Northern Railway (1889-1898); president, Spokane Valley Irrigation Company (1899-1901); president, Spokane International Railway

(1905-1917); president, Spokane Land and Water Company (1905-1918); president, Corbin Coal and Coke Company, Ltd. (1908-1918).

D. C. Corbin promoted and built seven feeder railroads from Spokane, Washington, that were pivotal in establishing the city's central position in the inland Pacific Northwest. His roads opened to exploitation the Coeur d'Alene lead-silver mines of northern Idaho, the Kootenay and Rossland copper-gold mines and the Fernie coal fields of British Columbia, and much of the white pine timber of northern Idaho and northeastern Washington. Corbin gave Spokane merchants access to the Canadian Pacific during the city's campaign for terminal freight rates from American railroads.

Daniel Chase Corbin was born on October 1, 1832, in Newport, New Hampshire, the younger of two sons of Austin and Mary Chase Corbin. His father, a farmer and lumberman, was the son of Dr. James Corbin, on whom the family farmland had been conferred for services in the Revolutionary War.

After receiving a public school education, Corbin surveyed lands under government contract in Iowa from 1852 until 1858 and in Nebraska from 1858 to 1862; he also engaged in land speculation in Nebraska. In 1860 he married Louisa Jackson; they had three children. He moved to Denver in 1862 and started a freight business. After seeing a gold display in a Denver window, he moved to Helena, Montana, where he opened a general mercantile business.

Wiry and short, with a beak nose and pointed chin beard, acquisitive and secretive, Corbin associated himself with Montana Governor Samuel T. Hauser, who launched him toward business success. He was cashier of Hauser's First National

Bank of Helena from 1871 to 1876. He moved to New York in 1877 and managed his brother Austin's Manhattan Beach Railway while his wife was in Europe for her health. He returned to Helena in 1883 and managed Hauser's pioneer Helena Mining & Reduction Company until 1886. That year Hauser's cordial relations with the Northern Pacific secured an estimated $1.2 million for Corbin's first railroads, the Spokane Falls & Idaho and the Coeur d'Alene Railway & Navigation company, which, with an intervening line of vessels on Lake Coeur d'Alene, inaugurated large-scale mining in the Coeur d'Alene Mountains. As mining traffic taxed the road's capacity, Corbin leased the railways to the Northern Pacific on October 1, 1888, and sold his stock. Corbin and the Northern Pacific diverted $465,000 in bonds, bankrupting the lines. Unpaid contractor's claims occupied the Northern Pacific for twenty-three years.

Corbin's method was to contract to build a railroad for its bonds at par. He generally constructed the line for less than authorized funding, and then sold the bonds at a premium.

Corbin broke with Hauser in 1889 to organize the Spokane Falls & Northern Railway with associates of his brother Austin. Surveyed to connect Spokane with the Canadian Pacific by way of the Columbia River and Arrow Lakes, the road penetrated mining and timber sections of northeastern Washington. While it was being built, copper and gold were discovered in the Kootenay and Rossland-Trail Creek districts of southern British Columbia. Corbin's political struggles to extend his railroad to Nelson and Rossland, B.C., raised transitory fears in Canada that British Columbia would join itself to the United States.

Austere and demanding, Corbin nonetheless commanded a loyal coterie and was admired at a time when financial achievement was valued more than ethical conduct. He was not above summoning the railroad's chief mechanic from anywhere on the line to repair a faucet in his home. Corbin unwillingly sold the Spokane Falls & Northern system to the Great Northern in 1898. Although he would not disclose his finances, the Great Northern set a value of $9.7 million on the system.

Shortly after the sale of the Spokane Falls & Northern, Corbin introduced irrigation to the gravelly valley of the Spokane River east of Spokane. As the valley blossomed with truck farms and or-

chards, the weathering Corbin Ditch (actually a flume) stood as a landmark. Corbin established a beet factory at Waverly, south of Spokane, but it failed because farmers would not perform the exacting cultivation required for sugar beets.

Corbin's Spokane International Railway, begun in 1905 with a traffic and construction contract with the Canadian Pacific, which held an option on 52 percent of its capital stock, not only gave Spokane merchants access to lower Canadian freight charges but also opened northern Idaho pine forests to associates of the lumberman Frederick Weyerhaeuser. A Corbin pocket notebook (now in the possession of the Eastern Washington State Historical Society) suggests that the costs of constructing and equipping the road were $3.6 million. The Canadian Pacific exercised its option in 1916.

For his role in elevating Spokane above other ambitious inland towns, the Spokane Chamber of Commerce in 1915 elected Corbin its first honorary member at a banquet he did not attend. Corbin also promoted the Corbin Park Addition to Spokane, a sixteen block area of substantial residences around an oval park which had been a racetrack. Corbin gave the park to the city. In 1908 he formed the Corbin Coal and Coke Company to exploit soft coal deposits in Crow's Nest Pass about fifteen miles east of Fernie, British Columbia.

Corbin was not active in politics and professed no religious affiliation. Corbin and his son, Austin Corbin II, erected mansions on hillside Seventh Avenue looking down into Spokane's central business district. Purchased by the city, the D. C. Corbin house is now an art center and its grounds are part of Pioneer Park.

It is indicative of Corbin's manner that in twenty years he never spoke to a bank employee who greeted him every morning on his way to work. His granddaughters were required to visit Corbin for thirty minutes on Saturday. Often they merely sat in silence. At Christmas, he customarily sent each a check for ten dollars signed D. C. Corbin, his business signature.

Louisa Corbin had died in France in 1900. In 1907, at age seventy-five, Corbin scandalized Spokane's upper class by marrying his housekeeper, Anna Larson. He was thereafter ostracized socially, but continued to be sought as a business associate. At his death on June 29, 1918, Corbin was engaged in marketing coal and selling irrigated farm tracts. His estate of $679,564 went to his children; his papers were destroyed. Corbin's widow converted the house to apartments; she deteriorated mentally, at last trudging city streets, an eccentric aspirant to public office. Corbin's memory is preserved in Corbin Park, Corbin Art Center, and the names of hamlets in Washington, Montana, and British Columbia.

Publication:
"Recollections of a Pioneer Railroad Builder," *Washington Historical Quarterly,* 1 (1907): 43-46.

Reference:
John Fahey, *Inland Empire: D.C. Corbin and Spokane* (Seattle: University of Washington Press, 1965).

Archives:
There is no known body of D. C. Corbin's papers, most of which, at his order, were destroyed at his death. There are some Corbin letters scattered in the Samuel T. Hauser papers at the Montana Historical Society; in the right-of-way applications for his railroads in the National Archives in Washington, D.C.; and in pertinent railroad files at the Minnesota Historical Society, St. Paul.

L. Stanley Crane

(September 7, 1915-   )

by Albert S. Eggerton, Jr.

Southern Railway (retired)

CAREER: Laboratory assistant (1937-1938), chemist (1938-1941), assistant chief materials inspector (1941-1943), chief materials inspector (1943-1946), assistant engineer of tests (1946-1948), engineer of tests (1948-1956), mechanical research engineer (1956-1959), assistant chief mechanical officer (1959-1963), Southern Railway Company; director, industrial engineering, Pennsylvania Railroad Company (1963-1965); vice president, engineering and research (1965-1970), vice president, engineering (1970), executive vice president, operations (1970-1976), president (1976-1979), chief executive officer (1977-1980), chairman (1979-1980), Southern Railway Company; chairman and chief executive officer, Consolidated Rail Corporation (Conrail) (1981-   ).

L. Stanley Crane played an active role in the modernization of the Southern Railway system. He has had his greatest impact on American business and transportation as the chief executive who turned Conrail, the government-rescued remains of several bankrupt railroads, into a strong and profitable rail network.

Leo Stanley Crane was born in Cincinnati, Ohio, on September 7, 1915 to Leo Vincent Crane

and Blanche Gottlieb Mitchell Crane. His father was a traffic officer with the Southern Railway who retired as assistant vice president. Crane sampled railroading during vacations from George Washington University in Washington, D.C., first as a track laborer and then as a laboratory assistant in the railway's test laboratory across the Potomac in Alexandria, Virginia.

On graduation in 1938 with a B.S. in engineering, he became a full-time chemist at the laboratory. Crane arrived at a time when the laboratory was taking on an expanding role in helping management evaluate fuel oil, equipment failures, breaks in track, the effectiveness of chemical treatment of wooden crossties, and the performance of different kinds of track ballast.

In 1941 Crane became assistant chief material inspector, then chief inspector, and in 1946 assistant engineer of tests. Among the laboratory's functions, which included the testing of practically everything the Southern bought or used, one of the more important proved to be the frequent sampling of lubricating oil from diesel locomotives. The tests detected contaminants that were early warning signs of engine troubles to come. Such warnings resulted

L. Stanley Crane (Courtesy Conrail)

in timely repairs and maintenance that avoided expensive engine failures on the road.

By the time Crane became engineer of tests in 1948, management tended to rely more and more on the test results obtained at the laboratory, finding them valuable both in operations and in maintenance. Soon Crane caught the eye of D. William Brosnan, Southern's operating vice president, who was in the early stages of transforming the Southern's and the rail industry's concepts of track and equipment maintenance and freight yard operation. Both the test laboratory and the man who headed it were transferred to the mechanical department. Crane became one of the small band of railroaders working closely with Brosnan to reshape the Southern Railway. The field was not new to Crane: he had taken mechanical engineering courses in college and an outside course in metallurgy.

The Southern Railway in the 1950s and 1960s was fertile ground for an innovator, and Crane fit that description. He helped design end-of-car cushioning to protect freight cars against coupling shocks as well as some of the equipment used

in upgrading the Southern's shops and making them models for the industry. He designed cars for hauling and discharging welded rail in quarter-mile lengths to aid the railway's track improvement program. He played a leading part in developing the light aluminum Silversides cars for coal unit trains and Big John cars for bulk grain, and other car innovations that followed. Along the way he was promoted to mechanical research engineer and later to assistant chief mechanical officer.

Challenges were great at the Southern Railway but so were the pressures, so when Crane was offered the opportunity in 1963 to go to the Pennsylvania Railroad as director of industrial engineering, he accepted. In the next two years he learned a great deal about the lines and facilities of the railroad that had once been regarded as the standard of the world. The knowledge was to prove valuable almost two decades later when he set about determining how to remake the road that the United States Railroad Administration had created out of the wreckage of the Penn-Central merger. But his absence from the Southern proved brief: in 1965 Brosnan, who had become president in 1962, brought him back to the railway as vice president in charge of engineering and research.

Crane spent five years as head of the Southern's engineering and research program, including the laboratory where he had once washed test tubes as a student assistant. For the most part, those years marked a continuation of the research and design that had always been the core of his career with the Southern. One major development of this period was the design, construction, and equipping of the R-1 Research Car, used to measure track conditions—including the gauge, evenness, and alignment of the rails—at road speed.

But there were management responsibilities as well, and they increased sharply in 1970 when Brosnan's successor, W. Graham Claytor, Jr., established a new management structure to heighten the Southern's effectiveness. Crane was named vice president, engineering, reporting to the executive vice president, operations, and responsible for all of the railway's track and equipment maintenance, communications, and signals, as well as research activities. Within the year Crane became executive vice president, operations, and had the Southern's whole operating department in his charge.

As a member of Claytor's management team, his broadened responsibilities encompassed trains, yards, shops, offices, agencies—in all, about four-fifths of the railroad. He was part of a style of decision making far removed from the autocratic kind he had known in his early years with the railroad. Communication, interaction, careful budgeting, and planning all appeared as key elements in the Southern's changing management style, and Crane welcomed them. Convinced as he always had been of the need for basic as well as applied research in the railroad industry, he also felt the urgency of more long-range and short-range planning by railroads than they had done in the past.

He recognized, too, that many of the major problems facing railroads were political and economic in nature. One of his valuable legacies from Claytor's approach to management, Crane later acknowledged, was the perception of ways to deal effectively with such problems and the realization that any rail chief executive must establish a relationship of mutual trust and respect with Congress, whose actions so often affected his business.

Crane's six years as executive vice president, operations, saw plant improvements continue and the pace increase, including the installation of more than 2,500 miles of welded rail and the opening of a major new classification yard at Sheffield, Alabama. The Southern during these years took an important part in an in-depth study of railroad service reliability: it not only furnished computer data to the Massachusetts Institute of Technology researchers but put the study results to the test in actual operation and became a leader in the quest for greater service reliability. Crane's interaction with top executives in other departments in Claytor's management committee broadened his experience in marketing, sales, law, finance, and personnel.

In 1976 the board of directors elected Crane president of the Southern Railway to succeed Claytor, who was moving up to the post of chairman and chief executive officer. In the management succession then current at the Southern Railway, it was customary for the new chief executive to be selected a year in advance of the departure of his predecessor and spend the ensuing year helping run the railroad but with the chairman still the chief executive. When Claytor retired as chairman in February 1977 to become secretary of the navy in the new Car-

ter administration, Crane became chief executive officer.

He knew that he was taking over a strong, profitable, and well-maintained rail network; he had devoted almost forty years of his working life to helping shape it. Now his task was to preserve, and where possible improve, that strength and profitability. Certainly he had come to head the company at a challenging time. In Washington, power had passed to a new administration, from which few knew what to expect. Fuel oil prices and general inflation presented continuing problems, but also opportunities inherent in the fuel efficiency of railroads. The Railroad Revitalization and Regulatory Reform Act, passed by Congress in 1975 to create Conrail to streamline and rebuild six bankrupt railroads, also contained promising signs of greater marketing freedom for railroads, and marketing was one of the Southern's strengths.

Crane continued the participative style of management developed under Claytor, the budgeting and cost control that kept the railway on a profitable course, and, of course, the heavy investment in plant and equipment that kept the Southern strong and serviceable. He also carried on the regular meetings with the financial community that Claytor had initiated, as well as the occasional inspection tours of the railway's facilities by financial analysts that the Southern had sponsored for years.

Crane and his management team looked at two possible enlargements of the Southern's system during a time of growing interest in mergers among American railroads. In 1978 they considered the acquisition of the Illinois Central Gulf Railroad lines, but were unable to reach an agreement with IC Industries, the parent company, and broke off the talks early in 1979. In 1979 there were brief negotiations with the Norfolk & Western Railway Company concerning a possible union under common ownership and control, but these talks also ended without an agreement. In 1980, however, the idea was approached again and this time a basis was found for uniting the Southern and the Norfolk & Western. (The consolidation was carried to a conclusion in 1982, after Crane had left the company.)

Late in 1979 Crane was named chairman and chief executive officer for his final year with the Southern, and Harold H. Hall was elected to succeed him as president. From 1977 to 1980, the Southern's operating revenues increased by 50 percent to more than $1.5 billion a year and net income doubled to just over $180 million a year. During the same four-year period more than a billion dollars in capital expenditures was plowed back into the property, including the establishment of a major new classification yard in Linwood, North Carolina. During the five years Crane served as president or chairman, the Southern was never out of the top three finishers in the Harriman Awards employee safety competition, winning two gold medals, two silver medals, and a bronze medal.

Even before he retired as the Southern's chairman on October 1, 1980, Crane was being considered for the top post at Conrail. On January 1, 1981, he took over as chairman and chief executive officer of the troubled northeast rail network. Congress had created the Consolidated Rail Corporation in 1976 to pick up the pieces of the bankrupt railroads in the northeast and midwest and combine them into a profitable rail system. Five years and billions of government dollars later, Conrail was still running in the red at the rate of almost a quarter-billion dollars a year. Crane could see great potential for Conrail but he could also see a number of roadblocks in the way of profitability. He set about persuading Congress to remove them.

With the passage of the Northeast Rail Services Act of 1981, Crane had the freer hand he needed to bring about changes that would help make Conrail profitable. Under the terms of the act he could rid the corporation of commuter passenger services, a consistently losing proposition; phase out thousands of nonessential jobs; and abandon thousands of miles of marginal track. Conrail's labor unions agreed to defer wage increases until economic conditions improved.

Previous management, Crane felt, had done a tremendous job of restoring the property. Now the challenge was to go on making capital improvements, streamline the railway, and make it function at top effectiveness. Crane infused his executives with the confidence that they could turn progress into profitability. Decisiveness, an appetite for risk-taking, and a willingness to share information across departmental lines became features of a management team working diligently for efficiency and cost control. They were also working to develop an innovative marketing strategy to match the changing economy of the northeast. Traditional heavy manufacturing industry in Conrail's service area was

being supplemented and to some extent replaced by lighter manufacturing, high technology businesses, and a consumer-oriented economy. Deregulation allowed railroad marketers to respond to changing conditions with rate and service adjustments and transportation contracts. Conrail took full advantage of all these opportunities.

By the end of Crane's first year, the railway was already slightly in the black and well on the road to greater profitability. From $39 million in 1981, the corporation's net income soared to $500 million in 1984 and held at $442 million during the downturn in traffic in 1985. By 1983 the line was profitable enough to attract a number of potential buyers for the return of Conrail to the private sector, which Congress had mandated in the Northeast Rail Services Act.

Fourteen suitors had appeared by the time the bidding process was closed on June 18, 1984. The three finalists selected by the Department of Transportation were Norfolk Southern Corporation, Alleghany Corporation, and an investor group headed by Washington hotel owner J. Willard Marriott, Jr. Crane, on the other hand, favored a public offering of stock rather than a sale to one party, particularly a competing railroad. A public stock offering, he insisted, would preserve competition, bring in more money for the government, and keep Conrail an independent entity. It would also leave Crane and his management team in control of a railroad which they seemed to be running quite efficiently. Crane and the Conrail board of directors engaged the New York firm of Morgan Stanley and Company to evaluate the various offers for Conrail and explore the alternate possibility of arranging a public offering of stock.

Among the formal bidders for the line, the Department of Transportation selected Norfolk Southern's as the best offer and the sale most likely to preserve Conrail in both good and lean times. Crane opposed the sale, and the unions representing Conrail's employees, who were 15 percent owners of the railway, sided with him. The struggle shifted to Capitol Hill for most of 1985 and a good part of 1986. Early in 1986 legislation authorizing the sale of Conrail to Norfolk Southern Corporation passed the Senate, but the legislation stalled in the House of Representatives and in August Norfolk Southern formally withdrew its offer.

As 1986 drew to a close, a public offering of stock seemed the only alternative to continued government ownership of Conrail. Crane remained firmly in control of the railroad that he had led back to profitability and prominence in the industry when it was sold to the public in March 1987.

Many honors and awards have come to Crane in the course of a railroad career that has spanned half a century. *Progressive Railroading* magazine in 1967 gave him its Research Recognition Award for his work on "developments in larger cars, new concepts in truck design, remotely-controlled locomotives, detection of overheated journal bearings and the continuing search for better rail materials and design." *Modern Railroads* named him Man of the Year in 1974 and again in 1983. *Financial World* magazine singled him out in 1979 as Chief Executive of the Year in the railroad industry. During 1982 he received the Transportation Association of America's Seley Award and the Joseph C. Scheleen Award for Excellence of the American Society of Traffic and Transportation, Incorporated. Recognition reached a peak in 1983 with a half-dozen awards and citations: the second *Modern Railroads* Man of the Year award, the *Industry Week* magazine Award for Excellence in Management, the National Defense Transportation Award, the Penjerdel Council Citizen of the Year Award, the Salzburg Memorial Medallion from Syracuse University, and the St. Louis Railroad Club's Railroad Man of the Year citation. In 1984 Susquehanna University made him an honorary doctor of science, and the American Railway Development Association presented it Distinguished Service Award. The Myasthenia Gravis Foundation recognized him as Transportation Man of the Year in 1985.

In addition to Consolidated Rail Corporation and the Southern Railway Company and its subsidiaries, Crane was director of the Florida East Coast Railway Company, the Richmond, Fredericksburg & Potomac Railroad Company, the Association of American Railroads, the United States Railway Association, American Security and Trust Company, and Woodward and Lothrop, Incorporated, and a trustee of George Washington University. He was a fellow of the American Society of Mechanical Engineers, a fellow and past president of the American Society for Testing and Materials, and a member of the Society of Automotive Engineers, the American Railway Engineering Association, and the Railway Systems and Management Association. He was a member and officer of committees of the Association of American Railroads and its Mechanical Division.

Crane was married on September 3, 1976, to Joan McCoy. He had twin daughters, Penelope Ann and Pamela Blanche Crane, from an earlier marriage.

References:

"Conrail's Future Brightens," *Traffic World,* 190 (April 19, 1982): 92-95; (April 26, 1982): 80-87;

Burke Davis, *The Southern Railway: Road of the Innovators* (Chapel Hill: University of North Carolina Press, 1985), pp. 267-277;

"Excellence in Management Awards," *Industry Week,* 219 (October 17, 1983): 47-55;

Bob Kuttner, "Great Train Robbery," *New Republic,* 191 (July 30, 1984): 21-23;

"Stan Crane: The $283 Million Difference," *Modern Railroads,* 38 (January 1983): 28-31;

Winston Williams, "Turning a Railroad Around," *New York Times Magazine,* January 13, 1985, pp. 32-37, 58, 71, 74.

Archives:

A file of L. Stanley Crane's speeches as a Southern Railway officer and chief executive is in the library of Norfolk Southern Corporation's Public Relations Department office at Roanoke, Virginia. A file of his speeches as Conrail's chairman is in the Public Affairs Department at Conrail's Philadelphia, Pennsylvania, headquarters.

John W. Davin

(March 10, 1892-January 7, 1949)

by Richard Saunders

Clemson University

John W. Davin

CAREER: Check clerk (1910-1911), yard clerk (1911), chief clerk to general yardmaster (1911-1913), night car distributor (1913-1914), car distributor (1914-1916), assistant chief car distributor (1916), chief car distributor (1916-1920), chairman of allotment committee (1920-1923), assistant superintendent of transportation (1923-1931), assistant general superintendent of transportation (1931-1933), assistant to the president (1933-1939), vice president (1939-1942), Chesapeake &

Ohio Railway; president, New York, Chicago & St. Louis Railroad (1942-1949); chairman of the board, Wheeling & Lake Erie Railway (1947-1949).

John Wysor Davin was born to John and Mary Elizabeth Montgomery Davin on March 10, 1892, in Montgomery, West Virginia, a few miles east of Charleston in the coal country and on the mainline of the Chesapeake & Ohio Railway (C&O). He attended public school and spent some time at the New River State School, a division of West Virginia University. Shortly after Christmas in his eighteenth year he hired on as a car checker on the C&O. For the next six years he was stationed at Handley, West Virginia, two miles west of his home, serving as the distribution clerk in the yards where coal hoppers were marshaled for dispatch to the mines on the Cabin Creek and Piney Creek branches. On October 4, 1914, he married Ethel Weathers; they had two daughters.

In March 1916 he was sent to Huntington, West Virginia, where, after a stint as assistant, he became chief of freight car distribution at the road's system car allocation center. In 1920 he was made chairman of the car allocation committee, set up in the wake of Congress's concern over the availability of hopper cars in the coalfields, as reflected in paragraph 12 of the Transportation Act of 1920. In 1922 he was married again, this time to Ruth Ruffing. They had one daughter. In August 1923 he became assistant superintendent of transportation on the C&O system. On December 1, 1933, he was made assistant to the president and on March 14, 1939, vice president of the C&O.

The C&O, the New York, Chicago & St. Louis Railroad (Nickel Plate), and the Père Marquette Railway were all part of the Van Sweringen financial empire. In 1933, with the empire falling on hard times, the three railroads had been put under the common management of John J. Bernet. Bernet and his successors, John Harahan and George D. Brooke, had reversed former president Walter Ross's policy of making the Nickel Plate a competitor in the luxury passenger trade; the Nickel Plate's passenger service would remain adequate but basic, with the railroad's emphasis clearly on freight. They had introduced the Berkshire-type, S-class steam locomotives, designed by the combined roads' Advisory Mechanical Committee, which proved to be the perfect design for the flat terrain and heavy, long-distance freights of the Nickel Plate. And finally, they had reduced outstanding debt by $33.8 million, to $130 million in 1942; fixed charges were down from $7.7 million in 1938 to $5.8 million in 1942. This debt reduction had been accomplished despite the need for emergency short-term borrowing from the Reconstruction Finance Corporation. On December 15, 1942, the common management of the three railroads having been ended, Davin was named president of the Nickel Plate.

Davin's administration began just as the crush of war traffic fell by the Nickel Plate; his first task was to keep the war trains rolling. More Berkshires were bought, and trestles east of Cleveland were rebuilt to permit the engines to operate all the way to Buffalo. Signals were installed on the Clover Leaf District into St. Louis, where more than thirty trains a day were operating. Centralized Traffic Control (CTC) was installed on part of the single-track main line, which was being used by more than sixty trains a day. The Nickel Plate practiced such precision railroading that it could deliver the entire New York Central passenger fleet on time when emergencies forced a detour. Davin was a railroader who inspired other railroaders, although his task was made easier by his able general manager, Gus Ayers. Morale was high on the Nickel Plate, which, in spite of its lean physical plant, had clearly risen to the occasion.

With the railroad's wartime profits Davin doggedly continued his predecessors' policy of placing debt reduction before the payment of dividends. Two major mortgage issues were retired, as were the three-year notes of 1929 which had nearly led to default in the 1930s. Eighty-six million dollars' worth of junior bonds were refinanced at more favorable rates.

Sensing that postwar competition would be intense, Davin plunged ahead with physical improvements. The Berkshire fleet was expanded again. General Motors sent its new F-type diesel units to be tested on the Nickel Plate, but they were sent back and an order went to the Lima Locomotive Works for more Berkshires. Alco passenger diesels were bought for the four Buffalo-Chicago and two Cleveland-St. Louis trains, as the Hudson-type steam locomotives could not pull the expanded postwar consists, frequently running to sixteen cars or more, certainly not at the newly authorized seventy miles per hour speed limit on the main line. Centralized Traffic Control was extended to embrace the entire Buffalo-Chicago line. Kinks and bottlenecks were removed from the St. Louis line so that the Nickel Plate could better take on the Wabash in head-to-head competition for traffic from the Southwest to New York and New England.

Davin made the Nickel Plate into a competitive, physically and financially sound railroad for the first time in its history. Some of its good fortune was the result of its being ideally situated as a bridge carrier, receiving traffic from connections and delivering it to connections, often in solid trains. Its lean physical plant, a product of its earlier poverty, when equipped with CTC, gave it maximum capacity with minimum overhead. But it was Davin who at last had been able to take advantage of these diverse assets and make the Nickel Plate into the jewel railroad of the Northeast.

In September 1945 Robert R. Young, by then in control of the Van Sweringen empire, decided that the time was right to merge the four railroads that remained in the empire. Two of the roads that had traditionally been financially marginal, the Nickel Plate and the Père Marquette, were now up to the physical and financial standards of the two that had traditionally been strong, the C&O and the Wheeling & Lake Erie. Davin was amenable to the Nickel Plate becoming an integral part of a grand consolidation that had been expected for two decades. But a minority group of its preferred stockholders formed a protective committee and swore to fight the merger until their guaranteed dividends, which were in substantial arrears, were paid. Davin's policy of debt reduction before dividends had made serious enemies. Under Ohio law and the Nickel Plate's charter, these stockholders had the power to block the merger. Davin so informed

Young, and less than a month after it had been proposed, the long-awaited merger was quietly aborted.

Young was furious; recalling how the C&O had rescued the Nickel Plate and these ungrateful preferred stockholders from certain bankruptcy during the Great Depression, he said that the C&O would never again "bend its knee to the Nickel Plate Road" and turned his interests to the acquisition of the New York Central. In September 1947 the C&O distributed its Nickel Plate stock to its own stockholders as a handsome bonus. The ownership of the Nickel Plate was thus scattered into thousands of private portfolios, making it a truly independent railroad for the first time in its history.

The price of Nickel Plate stock soon began to rise steadily, as though someone were buying systematically and for a purpose; many guessed that it was the Pennsylvania Railroad. Davin said that he would "stick to his knitting" and serve the stockholders, whoever they turned out to be. Shortly before Christmas, 1947, he received word from William White, president of the Delaware, Lackawanna & Western, that the Lackawanna sought control and eventual merger. Davin was not initially opposed to this plan, for he saw the Lackawanna and the Nickel Plate as each other's best connections and as logical components of a trunk line that would compete with the New York Central and Pennsylvania. But White was clumsy in his approach to the Nickel Plate people, and the same preferred stockholder group that had thwarted Young would thwart him. It is generally believed that Lynne White was brought to the Nickel Plate from the Chicago & North Western as general manager in 1948 by the directors who spoke for the preferred stockholders, and his accession to the presidency upon Davin's death largely sealed the fate of the Lackawanna bid.

Davin was able, however, to strong-arm the minority directors into accepting the Wheeling & Lake Erie into the Nickel Plate system. The Wheeling was a profitable road that, unlike the Nickel Plate, originated most of its own traffic, mostly coal. It was also a participant in the popular "Alphabet" freight route between the Midwest and the Port of Baltimore. The Van Sweringens had bought blocks of its securities in 1929 and 1930 with the intent of consolidating it with the Nickel Plate, but permission was never granted by the Interstate Com-

merce Commission and in 1939, needing quick cash, the Nickel Plate had sold its Wheeling securities to the C&O. Now that its relations with the C&O were ice cold, with the C&O indicating that it no longer cared to hold this stock in a kind of trust for a railroad that had been so unkind to it, Davin felt that the Nickel Plate had to buy it back to keep the Pennsylvania Railroad from getting it. The C&O even asked the Pennsylvania to make a bid. From the Nickel Plate it wanted $5.5 million for the Wheeling stock. The minority preferred stockholders were ready to fight; if the company had $5.5 million to buy an old coal road, it had money to pay their dividends in arrears. Davin summoned his maximum persuasive power, convincing them that not to pay the money would be a disaster for the Nickel Plate. The Wheeling was leased and permission to control it was pending before the ICC at the time of his death.

Davin would leave the Nickel Plate a substantially different, and better, railroad than he had found it. Acquisition of the Wheeling made it less dependent on traffic received from connections and less dependent on connections at Buffalo. Its lean but high-speed, high-capacity line running through the nation's industrial heartland made it perfectly situated to do what railroads could best do in the latter twentieth century—forward heavy freight over long, level distances. In a kind of tribute to the quality of Davin's work, the price of Nickel Plate common stock went from a low of 18 7/8 in 1947 to a high of 236 1/2 in 1951.

Occasionally, Davin liked to order an engine, usually one of the company's old 2-8-0 Consolidations, coupled to his president's car, and he would ride out from Cleveland to Castalia, Ohio, on the Sandusky Division, and there do a little trout fishing by himself. He had been diagnosed as having cancer shortly after coming to the Nickel Plate but had kept his private troubles to himself. He was still president when he died in his sleep on January 7, 1949.

References:

Taylor Hampton, *The Nickel Plate Road: The Story of a Great Railroad* (Cleveland: World, 1947);
John A. Rehor, *The Nickel Plate Story* (Milwaukee: Kalmbach, 1965);
Richard Saunders, *The Railroad Mergers and the Coming of Conrail* (Westport, Conn.: Greenwood, 1978), pp. 66-68.

Frederic A. Delano

(September 10, 1863-March 28, 1953)

by Keith L. Bryant, Jr.

Texas A&M University

Frederic A. Delano

CAREER: Engineering party (1885), apprentice machinist (1885-1886), bureau of rail inspection (1887-1889), assistant to second vice president (1889-1890), superintendent, Chicago freight terminal (1890-1899), superintendent of motive power (1899-1901), general manager at Chicago (1901-1905), Chicago, Burlington & Quincy Railroad; president, Wheeling & Lake Erie Railroad and Wabash-Pittsburgh Terminal Railway (1905-1908); first vice president (1905), president (1905-1911), receiver, (1911-1913), Wabash Railroad; president, Chicago, Indianapolis & Louisville Railway

(1913-1914); member, Federal Reserve Board (1914-1918); deputy director of transportation, United States Army Corps of Engineers (1918-1919); chairman, International Commission, League of Nations on Opium Production in Persia (1925); chairman, National Capital Park and Planning Commission (1924-1942); chairman, National Resources Planning Board (1934-1943).

Frederic A. Delano followed an unusual career path as a railroad executive. He climbed through the ranks of the Chicago, Burlington & Quincy (CB&Q or Burlington), achieving the position of general manager, then moved to a small bridge line, the Wheeling & Lake Erie (W&LE), as president, and subsequently became the president of the Wabash Railroad, another part of the rail empire created by George Gould. When the Wabash entered bankruptcy Delano served as receiver, and then he became president of the Chicago, Indianapolis & Louisville (Monon). After only a few months he resigned to accept appointment to the first Federal Reserve Board. Delano's career subsequently was one of service in the federal government and the League of Nations. But his major interest had become urban planning and land use, and he became a national figure in both areas. Thus Delano left railroading to enter successfully two entirely different fields, a unique career for a man in the rail industry.

Born in Hong Kong in 1863 to Warren and Catherine Robbins Lyman Delano, Frederic Adrian Delano was a member of a wealthy and prominent family of China traders originally from Massachusetts. Sent to the United States as a boy, he was raised at the family home in Newburgh, New York. He was educated at Adams Academy in Quincy, Massachusetts, then at Harvard University, where he received an A.B. degree in 1885. That year he traveled west to enter the railroad business.

Delano joined an engineering party of the Chicago, Burlington & Quincy Railroad in the field in Colorado. Shortly thereafter he transferred to the Burlington's shop facilities at Aurora, Illinois, and then began to move up through the engineering department. He inspected rails in the shops and his diligence was rewarded with promotion to assistant to the second vice president in 1889. After serving from 1890 to 1899 as superintendent of the Chicago freight terminal and two years as superintendent of motive power, Delano became the general manager in Chicago, the Burlington's most important traffic center. His abilities on the railroad and his active role in Chicago civic affairs brought Delano to the attention of George Gould.

The son of Jay Gould, George Gould was in the midst of creating a true transcontinental railroad. Building upon his father's empire—the Missouri Pacific, Wabash, Texas & Pacific, and St. Louis Southwestern—Gould added the Denver & Rio Grande and created the Western Pacific to reach San Francisco Bay. His eastern terminus was to be Baltimore, and he sought to link the Western Maryland to the Wabash by acquiring the Wheeling & Lake Erie, which extended from Toledo, Ohio, to Wheeling, West Virginia, and constructing the Wabash-Pittsburgh Terminal Railway through the city of Pittsburgh. The latter proved to be a massive project, which was fought continuously by the Pennsylvania Railroad. Gould built high bridges and blasted tunnels to reach the heart of the city, but the line was hardly suitable for the extensive freight traffic he envisioned. The system opened in 1904, and Delano accepted the presidency of the Wheeling & Lake Erie and the Wabash-Pittsburgh Terminal Railway the following year.

Delano labored to make the two key segments of Gould's empire profitable, seeking passenger traffic for the elaborate terminal Gould built in the heart of Pittsburgh. But even as Delano was trying to upgrade the Wheeling & Lake Erie and make the Terminal operational, Gould was using funds from the Denver & Rio Grande to build the Western Pacific and money from the Wabash to construct the Western Maryland into Pittsburgh from the east. Delano's burdens were not light as he also served as first vice president of the Wabash in 1905, and then as its president from 1905 to 1911.

Gould's vast projects taxed even his family's fortune, and the companies borrowed heavily. The financial panic of 1907 undermined the scheme, and pieces of the system began to fall into fiscal disarray. Both the W&LE and the Terminal entered receivership, and Delano left his positions there to devote his full time to the Wabash and to civic affairs in Chicago.

Jay and George Gould had developed the Wabash Railway into a significant Midwestern carrier. The railroad extended from Omaha and Kansas City through St. Louis and Chicago to Detroit and Buffalo. Its direct Detroit-Kansas City line and the Chicago-St. Louis service generated considerable traffic. Delano tried to produce profits to cover not only the needs of the Wabash but also the debts George Gould had created in his efforts to reach Baltimore. At the same time Delano worked with civic organizations in Chicago to implement Daniel Burnham's scheme to revitalize the city through a new monumental plan. Burnham's vast enterprise included replacing the many Chicago passenger stations with a great "union station." As president of the Wabash, and because of his interest in rational city planning, Delano served on committees to further the project.

The Gould empire totally collapsed in 1911, and when the Wabash fell into bankruptcy, Delano accepted appointment as a receiver. For almost three years he managed the carrier as it sought to survive the fiscal excesses of the Gould years. As the Wabash moved toward reorganization, Delano agreed to become president of another carrier with a checkered past, the Chicago, Indianapolis & Louisville (Monon). Dominated financially by the Southern Railway and the Louisville & Nashville, the Monon extended north from Louisville to Chicago with a branch to Indianapolis. Delano took over the Monon in December 1913 but resigned in August of the following year to become a member of the first Federal Reserve Board.

This position was not Delano's first government appointment; in 1905 he had left the Chicago, Burlington & Quincy briefly to advise the War Department and the Philippine Commission as a consulting engineer for the Philippine railroads, and President William Howard Taft had appointed him to the Commission on Industrial Relations in 1912. Delano's railroad career and his civic leadership in Chicago, and the fact that he was a progressive Democrat, attracted the attention of President Woodrow Wilson, who named him to a six-year term on the Federal Reserve Board, including two years as vice governor. Delano served with considerable distinction until June 1918, when he resigned to enter the United States Army Corps of Engineers as a major. He was sent to Tours, France, on the staff of Major General William W. Atterbury, director general of transportation for the American Expeditionary Force. Later Delano served as deputy director of transportation in Paris, where he worked with French railways and the Inter-Allied Transportation Council. After the armistice he helped move troops to ports for embarkation and worked to settle claims. Discharged in 1919 as a colonel, he was awarded a Distinguished Service Medal and the French Legion of Honor.

Returning to the United States, Delano held numerous positions in and out of government. The United States Supreme Court appointed him receiver in the Red River Boundary Case between Oklahoma and Texas from 1919 to 1925. The League of Nations named him chairman of a commission to inquire into the production of opium in Persia (Iran) and to seek suitable substitute crops or industries. He toured that country and made an exhaustive report to the League. It was to civic planning, however, that Delano devoted most of his time. He had participated in a citizen's committee that produced the Wacker Plan of 1916 for Chicago. In 1922 Delano organized the Committee of 100 in Washington, D.C., to sponsor the creation of the National Park Commission, which in 1924 became the National Capital Park and Planning Commission. President Calvin Coolidge appointed him to the commission, and he served until 1942. He accepted an appointment as chairman of the Commission on Regional Planning for New York and Environs established by the Russell Sage Foundation in 1927. His nephew, President Franklin Delano Roosevelt, made him chairman of the National Resources Planning Board in 1934, and he continued on that body until 1943. Delano served as president of the Ameri-

can Civic Association from 1925 to 1937; in 1935 he brought that group together with the National Conference on City Planning to form the American Planning and Civic Association, serving as chairman of the new organization. From 1931 to 1936 he chaired the board of the Federal Reserve Bank of Richmond, Virginia.

Despite the obligations of a lengthy list of charitable and civic duties, Delano wrote numerous articles on finance, city planning, transportation, and politics. A trustee, director, or overseer of the Brookings Institute, University of Chicago, Smithsonian Institution, National Botanical Gardens, Russell Sage Foundation, and Harvard College, Delano devoted himself to improving the quality of life in urban America.

He had married Matilda Annis Peasley, the daughter of a Chicago railway executive, in 1888, and they had five daughters. Delano was an active layman in the Unitarian fellowship. Delano died in Washington in 1953. His career had taken him a long distance from Hong Kong and that engineering party in Colorado in 1885.

Publications:
"The Application of a Depreciation Charge in Railway Accounting," *Journal of Political Economy*, 16 (November 1908): 585-601;

"Railway Problems and Railway Rates," *World To-Day*, 20 (February 1911): 159-165;

"The Chicago Plan, with Particular Reference to the Railway Terminal Problem," *Journal of Political Economy*, 21 (November 1913): 819-831;

Regional Plan of New York and Environs (New York: Regional Plan of New York and Environs, 1929);

Joint Committee on Basis of Sound Land Policy: What About the Year 2000? (Harrisburg, Pa.: Mount Pleasant Press, 1929).

References:
Burton J. Hendrick, "A New Federal Tribunal," *World's Work*, 28 (October 1914): 574-575;

Richard C. Overton, *Burlington Route: A History of the Burlington Lines* (New York: Knopf, 1965);

William Swartz, "The Wabash Railroad," *Railroad History*, No. 133 (Fall 1975): 5-30.

Delaware & Hudson Railway

by Richard Saunders

Clemson University

Map of the Delaware & Hudson Railway (1983)

The Delaware & Hudson Canal was conceived in 1823 to connect the Delaware and Hudson river valleys and bring coal to New York City. The canal opened in 1828 from Honesdale, Pennsylvania, to a point on the Hudson near Kingston, New York, with 109 locks in its 108 miles. It carried most of New York City's coal until after the Civil War and re-

mained in use until 1898.

A gravity railroad was built from Carbondale, Pennsylvania, to Honesdale to bring coal from the mines to the canal. A small steam locomotive, the *Stourbridge Lion,* purchased from the George Stephenson Works in England, proved unsuccessful because of the inadequacy of the track; but its experimental run on August 8, 1829, was the first operation of a steam locomotive in the United States and was two months ahead of the "Rainhill Trials" of Stephenson's own Rocket locomotive in England that established the practicality of railroad transportation.

The canal company expanded its rail operations in the anthracite region in the 1850s, acquired an all-rail route to Albany in 1873, and completed a new line to the Quebec border in 1875. These lines were meant as outlets for the anthracite coal from the company's own mines. Its new routes north of Albany reached the popular resort areas of Lake George, Lake Champlain, and Saratoga Springs, turning the Delaware & Hudson Railway (D&H) into a major passenger carrier. The company invested in Lake George and Lake Champlain steamships and in resort hotels, notably the United States Hotel at Saratoga Springs; acquired routes into the Lake Placid and Saranac Lake regions of the Adirondacks; and dabbled in a railroad empire in Quebec and in transit in the city of Albany.

The company was led through its prime years in the early twentieth century by the hard-driving Leonor Loree; he was brought in from the Chicago, Rock Island & Pacific at the urging of E. H. Harriman, who was then on the D&H's board of managers. The line was rich from anthracite. The Montreal Limited operated in multiple sections almost every night of the Prohibition years packed with thirsty Americans heading for a wet weekend in Montreal. Loree wisely discarded the hotel, transit, and steamship operations as their profitability began to wane, and most of the Quebec empire, except for the line from the border into Montreal, was sold. In the federally sponsored consolidation plans under the Transportation Act of 1920, Loree failed to make the D&H the centerpiece of a "fifth" trunkline (as an alternative to the Interstate Commerce Commission's planned four) when he lost a close proxy fight for the Lehigh Valley in 1928. Joseph Nuelle, who succeeded Loree in 1938, recognized that anthracite would go the way of the resorts and the steamships and that the company needed to reequip for the only profitable traffic that would be left to it, "overhead" or bridge traffic between the Pennsylvania, Lehigh Valley, Lackawanna, Erie, and Reading railroads to its south and west and the Boston & Maine, Maine Central, Canadian National, and Canadian Pacific railroads to its north and east.

As the decline of anthracite knocked the props from under the other anthracite roads in the 1950s, the D&H prospered from bridge traffic. The D&H's William White, who was president from 1954 to 1962, conceived of the merger that ultimately resulted in the creation of Erie Lackawanna (EL), but the D&H itself was too wealthy to join; its security holders would never have approved inclusion in such a financially troubled company. The proposed Pennsylvania-New York Central merger, however, would divert the large volume of traffic the D&H received from the Pennsylvania at Wilkes-Barre to an all-Penn Central routing. The Norfolk & Western (N&W) was willing to take the D&H but would have no connection with it unless it also took the Erie Lackawanna, which it did not want. The N&W was eventually required to assume control of the EL and the D&H (through a holding company named Dereco) as a result of the Eastern "inclusion" cases of 1967, but never showed much interest in either. After the Erie Lackawanna's bankruptcy in 1972, the N&W made no further attempt to make the D&H a part of its system.

When Conrail was created in 1976, the D&H was given extensive trackage rights over Conrail lines: westward to Buffalo over former Erie Lackawanna lines, eastward to New York Harbor and Oak Island Terminal over former Lehigh Valley lines, and southward to Potomac Yard in northern Virginia over former Pennsylvania lines. Otherwise, the D&H would have no friendly connection to its west or south. This arrangement was an effort to preserve competition east of Buffalo, but the D&H was not strong enough to instantly double its size and become a regional system. In general, the trackage rights were a burden, not an asset. Interchange traffic fell from 10.7 million tons in 1973 to 6.4 million in 1982. The D&H's operating ratio went above 100 in 1978 and the company posted deficits thereafter. In 1983 the N&W sold the D&H to Timothy Mellon's Guilford Transportation Industries, a holding company that already controlled the Boston & Maine and the Maine Central; the sale was completed on January 4, 1984.

References:

Delaware and Hudson Company, *A Century of Progress: A History of the Delaware and Hudson Company, 1823-1923* (Albany, N.Y., 1925);
Jim Shaughnessy, *Delaware & Hudson* (Berkeley, Cal.: Howell-North, 1967).

Delaware, Lackawanna & Western Railroad

by Richard Saunders

Clemson University

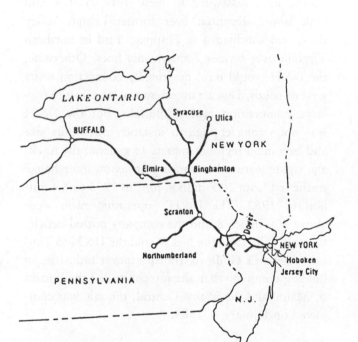

Map of the Delaware, Lackawanna &
Western Railroad (1930)

The Delaware, Lackawanna & Western Railroad (Lackawanna) had its roots in the Liggett's Gap Railroad incorporated in 1832, and the earliest days of anthracite (hard coal) mining in northeastern Pennsylvania. The railroad was renamed the Lackawanna & Western and opened for business on October 20, 1851, from Scranton to Great Bend, Pennsylvania, near Binghamton, New York. It was combined with the Delaware & Cobb's Gap Railroad in 1849 to form the Delaware, Lackawanna & Western. The Scranton family was a principal promoter of the railroad, which was always associated

with their coal and iron operations and the city that bore their name.

Anthracite was the Lackawanna's life's blood, much of it produced by the railroad's own mines (which it was forced to divest in 1909 following a Supreme Court decision on the commodities clause of the Interstate Commerce Act). In 1868 it acquired the Morris & Essex Railroad across northern New Jersey, permitting it to reach New York Harbor over its own rails, and went on to develop extensive pier facilities on the harborfront of Hoboken, New Jersey. It acquired lines northward to Syracuse and Utica, and in 1882, rich from its coal traffic, it built a beautifully engineered double-track line to Buffalo which enabled it to participate in general Great Lakes-to-the-sea traffic.

The Lackawanna's wealth was the salient fact of its history. From the 1880s through 1915 it built and rebuilt its right-of-way—straightening curves, reducing grades, laying heavy rail—until it was one of the most technologically perfect railroads in the nation, even in the mountainous territory around Scranton. The Lackawanna paid good dividends, usually topped off by handsome end-of-the-year bonuses. It played a major role in developing the New Jersey suburbs as bedroom communities in the early years of the twentieth century. In the last of its great engineering triumphs, it pushed the electrification of its commuter lines to completion in 1931 as the Great Depression closed in.

In American folklore, the Lackawanna will be remembered as the Route of Phoebe Snow. To advertise the cleanliness of its anthracite-burning locomotives, it dressed its Miss Snow, of classic Gibson Girl looks, in a white gown.

> Says Phoebe Snow, about to go
> Upon a trip to Buffalo,
> "My gown stays white from morn to night
> Upon the Road of Anthracite."

The advertisements ran from 1900 to 1917. Forever after, Phoebe Snow personified the aristocratic elegance that was the soul of the Lackawanna Railroad.

The Lackawanna never went into receivership, although the depression was a close call and only a voluntary restructuring of its debt by its creditors saved it. After World War II its fortunes declined rapidly. Oil replaced anthracite as the preferred fuel for heating. The St. Lawrence Seaway took the cream of the lakes-to-the-sea traffic. Trucks made early inroads into the Lackawanna's short-distance territory. The once proud commuter trains became insufferable burdens, as did New Jersey's—particularly Hudson County's—extraordinary taxes.

In what were to be the last hours of its financial strength, in 1948 and 1949, it tried to buy control of the New York, Chicago & St. Louis Railroad (Nickel Plate) and make itself into a New York-Chicago trunk line. Certain Nickel Plate stockholders were able to block the move, though the two railroads remained each other's principal connections at Buffalo. In 1955 Hurricane Diane obliterated seventy miles of the mainline. Bethlehem Steel gave the company's order for new rail the emergency designation "rights above everything," and the railroad paid for the damage out of cash on hand. For a short time after the disaster the Lackawanna could still proudly roll its streamliner Phoebe Snow at ninety miles per hour over its supremely engineered right-of-way, but soon its gathering problems overwhelmed it.

It undertook extensive coordination with the Erie in 1958, which permitted it to abandon its own track between Binghamton and Corning, New York. When it merged with the Erie in 1960, the Erie was the surviving corporation. The Lackawanna provided much of the Erie Lackawanna's best management, but all Lackawanna lines west of Binghamton were either abandoned or downgraded to secondary status. Lines east of Scranton came to be used only for passenger trains and overflow freights, with most traffic being concentrated on the former Erie route. The Erie Lackawanna was purchased in 1968 by Dereco, Incorporated, a subsidiary of the Norfolk & Western. The EL entered receivership in 1972 and was conveyed to Conrail in 1976. By the 1980s there was little physical evidence that the Lackawanna had ever existed, except for the commuter zone that was operated by New Jersey Transit and the line between Binghamton and Scranton that was used by the Delaware & Hudson.

References:

Robert J. Casey and W. A. S. Douglas, *The Lackawanna Story* (New York: McGraw-Hill, 1951);

Greg J. McDonnell, "Is There Life After Lackawanna?" *Trains,* 45 (July 1985): 36; (August 1985): 40;

Thomas Taber and Thomas Taber III, *The Delaware, Lackawanna & Western Railroad in the Twentieth Century,* 2 volumes (Muncy, Pa.: Thomas T. Taber III, 1980).

Archives:

The corporate records of the Delaware, Lackawanna & Western Railroad are at the Syracuse University Library, Syracuse, New York and the Eleuthorian Mills Historical Library, Wilmington, Delaware.

Denver & Rio Grande Western Railroad

by Don L. Hofsommer

Augustana College

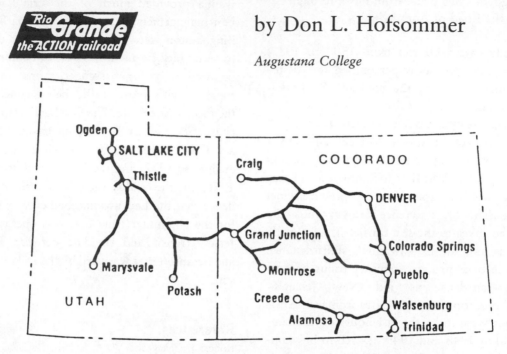

Map of the Denver & Rio Grande Western Railroad (1983)

Perhaps no railroad company in the American West contributed more to the lore of the region than the Denver & Rio Grande Western Railroad (D&RGW) and its predecessor, the Denver & Rio Grande Railway. For example, the wild scramble between the Rio Grande and rival Santa Fe for a route through the Royal Gorge of the Arkansas River near Canon City, Colorado, sparked a Hollywood film, *The Denver & Rio Grande* (1952), that presented a predictable blend of fact and fiction.

The enterprise began on October 27, 1870, as the Denver & Rio Grande Railway, intended to link Denver, in the Territory of Colorado, with El Paso, Texas, on the Rio Grande. Regular service between Denver and Colorado Springs began on January 1, 1872. As construction crews labored on toward Pueblo, surveyors plotted a route in the direction of Santa Fe and a branch was completed to coalfields west of Pueblo. Its aspiration of forging a north-south railroad from the Colorado Rockies to the Rio Grande was crushed when the Atchison, Topeka & Santa Fe preempted Raton Pass; as a consequence, the Rio Grande looked to the west.

The Santa Fe nearly cut off that option, too, in the so-called Royal Gorge War of 1878, but in this case the Rio Grande prevailed. All was not well, however. Financially bereft, it became a short-term captive of the much larger Santa Fe, and then fell to the control of Jay Gould. Expansion followed into the San Luis Valley and across to Durango and Silverton; through the Royal Gorge to Salida; and over Marshall Pass to Montrose, Delta, and Grand Junction. Connection with an associated company provided an indirect route from Denver to Salt Lake City. Later construction from Salida over Tennessee Pass to Grand Junction and the 1906 conversion of many of the Rio Grande's lines from narrow (3 feet) to standard (4 feet 8½ inches) gauge resulted in important economies and made its main route more attractive. Yet it was not until the Moffat Tunnel and Dotsero Cutoff were completed in 1928 and 1934, respectively, and the Rio Grande absorbed the Denver & Salt Lake in 1947 that the Rio Grande's boast–"Through the Rockies, Not Around Them"–made any commercial sense.

Jay Gould sold most of his Rio Grande securities before his death in 1892, but his son George began to acquire the road's stock in 1900 or 1901. A few years later, as George Gould promoted the Western Pacific from Salt Lake City to Oakland, he saddled the Rio Grande with impossible debt—a legacy that would not soon be thrown off. The company was sold in 1920, becoming the Denver & Rio Grande Western Railroad, and was reorganized in 1924 and again in 1947.

During the last proceedings the courts appointed Wilson J. McCarthy as trustee, and in 1947 the D&RGW's board named him president. McCarthy wisely insisted on a constant betterment program—one that was followed by Gale B. Aydelott, who succeeded him in 1956. Between 1947 and 1980 McCarthy and Aydelott whittled the company's mortgage debt from $83 million to $3 million—and did so without damage to mainte-nance levels or service standards, both of which were the envy of the industry.

Late in 1984 the Anschutz Corporation of Denver paid $50 per share, or nearly $500 million, to acquire the 1,800-mile Denver & Rio Grande Western Railroad Company.

References:
Robert G. Athearn, *Rebel of the Rockies: A History of the Denver and Rio Grande Western Railroad* (New Haven: Yale University Press, 1962);

O. Meredith Wilson, *The Denver and Rio Grande Project, 1870-1901: A History of the First Thirty Years of the Denver and Rio Grande Railroad* (Salt Lake City: Howe Brothers, 1982).

Archives:
The archives of the Denver & Rio Grande Western Railroad are in Denver, Colorado.

William N. Deramus III

(December 10, 1915-   )

by H. Roger Grant

University of Akron

William N. Deramus III, circa 1957 (Courtesy Roger Grant)

CAREER: Transportation apprentice, (1939-1941), assistant trainmaster, Wabash Railway (1941-1943); assistant to the general manager, Kansas City Southern Railway (1946-1948); assistant to the president (1948), president, Chicago Great Western Railroad (1949-1957); president, Missouri-Kansas-Texas Railroad (1957-1961); president (1961-1973), chairman, board of directors, Kansas

City Southern Railway (1966-1980).

William N. Deramus III's father, William Neal Deramus, Jr., a native of Coopers, Alabama, lived the life of a Horatio Alger hero. At the age of ten this poor lad started to do odd jobs for the Louisville & Nashville Railroad (L&N) agent in his hometown and in return was taught Morse code and station bookkeeping. He then "hired out" as a telegrapher for the L&N in 1903; thirty-seven years later he assumed the presidency of the strategic Kansas City Southern Railway (KCS). William N. Deramus III was born to Deramus and Lucille Ione Nicholas Deramus on December 10, 1915, in Pittsburg, Kansas, a KCS division point where the elder Deramus worked as a train dispatcher. Unlike his father, the younger Deramus received an excellent postsecondary education, earning a bachelor's degree from the University of Michigan in 1936 and an LL.B. from Harvard Law School three years later.

Rather than hanging out his shingle, Deramus began his career in 1939 as a transportation apprentice with the Wabash Railway. Between 1941 and 1943 Deramus served as an assistant trainmaster on the Wabash's St. Louis Division before joining the U. S. Army Transportation Corps. During his tour of duty with the 726th Operating Battalion he helped to operate a rail line through India and Burma to the famed Ledo Road. After the war Deramus went to work for his father's Kansas City Southern as assistant to the general manager.

In 1948 a group of Kansas City investors, which included Deramus's father, won control over the financially weak Chicago Great Western Railroad (CGW). One of these syndicate members, coal magnate Grant Stauffer, was named president of the CGW and took as his principal assistant the thirty-three-year-old Deramus. Actually, Stauffer functioned only as a figurehead; decisions rested largely with the Deramuses. Indeed, syndicate members from the start saw the younger Deramus as the road's future president. Recalled one associate, "I guess that they figured that [he] . . . was a little bit too young to . . . put him on a job like that. . . ." But just five months after becoming the CGW chief executive, Stauffer died of cancer and William Deramus III assumed the presidency.

Deramus headed the Chicago Great Western for nearly a decade. During his tenure, this 1,500-mile trunk carrier gained considerable strength through the savings brought about by dieselization, passenger train reductions, abandonment of minor lines, and more efficient freight service. Following his father's lead on the KCS, Deramus pushed hard for administrative centralization, long freight trains, state-of-the-art technology (for example, two-way radios, teletypes, and IBM data processing machines), and industrial park development.

Deramus, however, paid a stiff price for his streamlining efforts. Labor-management relations soured, and on January 25, 1953, operating personnel struck the company, shutting down the CGW for six weeks. Deramus knew that railroads needed to reduce labor costs, especially those that involved "featherbedding," and felt that his administration was fighting the battle for all rail managements to retain control over their property. Yet other carriers were reluctant to offer aid or even moral support. "I think the 43-day strike was a perfect example of why the railroads in this country have failed to prosper as they should," he observed in 1982. "During that period of time, I did not receive a single call from the head, or any officer, of any of the railroads of this country."

In January 1957 Deramus stepped down from the CGW presidency to accept a similar position with the Missouri-Kansas-Texas Railway (Katy). Immediately he sought to implement his principal goal: "To get this railroad back on a sound economic footing as soon as possible." His method was straightforward: "Cut all personnel to the lowest possible number that will still permit daily conduct of business." To many, his methods seemed uncaring, even ruthless. Deramus received intensely negative press coverage when he ordered the sudden closing of offices in St. Louis and in Parsons, Kansas. Employees who had enough seniority to hold their jobs had only a few days to relocate to either Dallas or Denison, Texas.

By June 1960 the number of jobs on the Katy stood at 2,817, down from about 8,000 in 1956. Yet trimming the Katy down to a lean operation did not make it profitable. The company's health was directly tied to the quality and volume of the annual wheat crop, and these were years of struggle for Southern plains farmers; the national recession of 1957-1958 hurt the Katy as well. The physical plant looked shabby; indeed, deferred maintenance, part of the Deramus austerity program, led to the road's earning the appellation "transportation slum."

In 1961 Deramus returned to the Kansas City Southern as president and remained in that position until 1973. He was elected chairman of the KCS's board of directors in 1966 and served in that capacity for the next fourteen years.

In 1962 Deramus spearheaded the creation of a holding company, Kansas City Southern Industries (KCSI), which became actively involved outside of the transportation field in broadcasting, manufacturing, real estate, insurance, and data processing. Its most lucrative investment involved the latter: DST Systems, Incorporated, in which KCSI possessed an 80 percent interest by 1986, proved to be a steady money-maker. Income generated by the holding company provided a sound economic foundation for the railroad, broadened the range of managerial support available to the railroad, and even generated new rail business.

When Deramus left the board in 1980, the Kansas City Southern enjoyed good financial health and generally provided shippers with efficient and dependable service. Unlike either the Chicago Great Western or the Katy, the KCS had a high percentage of its traffic originating or terminating on the property; and in the wake of the Arab oil boycott of 1973-1974, the road's many on-line petroleum-related industries boomed.

Deramus did not suffer fools gladly. At least during his stints with the Chicago Great Western and Katy, he seemed often to act arrogantly and to make snap decisions. Both traits proved costly. The former at times weakened morale and the latter, when wrong, wasted financial resources. According to a close financial adviser, "Young Bill was not diplomatic" and "lacked the charm of his father."

Deramus's son, William Neal Deramus IV, took charge of the Kansas City Southern in 1986. He is thus the third generation of Deramuses to do so.

References:

H. Roger Grant, *The Corn Belt Route: A History of the Chicago Great Western Railroad Company* (DeKalb: Northern Illinois University Press, 1984);

Donovan L. Hofsommer, *Katy Northwest: The Story of a Branch Line Railroad* (Boulder: Pruett, 1976).

Detroit, Toledo & Ironton Railroad

by James N. J. Henwood

East Stroudsburg University

Map of the Detroit, Toledo & Ironton Railroad (1930)

The Detroit, Toledo & Ironton Railway (DT&I) was formed in May 1905, by a merger of two smaller railroads. Its lines extended from Detroit through Lima and Springfield, Ohio, to Ironton, a port city on the Ohio River. The DT&I controlled the Ann Arbor Railroad, which gave it access to Toledo, until 1910. The DT&I was reorganized in 1914 as the Detroit, Toledo & Ironton Railroad.

In 1920, Henry Ford purchased the DT&I. Ford was creating the great River Rouge integrated steel and automobile plant at Dearborn, and the railroad would further this aim. Ford management improved the property, electrifying a seventeen-mile section between River Rouge and Carleton, Michigan, and building a forty-six-mile cutoff in southern Michigan. Profits were good, partly because of the traffic to and from the Ford plant.

In 1929, Ford sold the DT&I to the Pennroad Corporation, which was affiliated with the Pennsylvania Railroad (PRR). Most of the DT&I's passenger service ceased in the 1930s. The Pennsylvania Company, a PRR subsidiary, and the Wabash Railroad purchased the line in 1951. The DT&I's last passenger service, between Springfield and Jackson, Ohio, ended in 1955. In 1965, the Wabash sold its interests to the Pennsylvania Company. The DT&I had purchased the Ann Arbor in 1963; that line went bankrupt in 1973, but the DT&I retained access to Toledo by trackage rights over the Ann Arbor from Diann, Michigan.

The Pennsylvania Company became a subsidiary of the Penn Central after New York Central and the Pennsylvania Railroad merged in 1968. Following the formation of Conrail in 1976, the Penn Central offered the DT&I for sale. In 1980, it was purchased by the Grand Trunk Western, a Canadian National subsidiary, and three years later it was merged into the Grand Trunk.

Reference:

George H. Drury, *The Historical Guide to North American Railroads* (Milwaukee: Kalmbach, 1985), pp. 118-119.

Dieselization

Around the turn of the century American railroads began experimenting with internal combustion power. The gasoline engine was considerably more efficient than the steam locomotive in extracting energy from its fuel, and the fuel was much more compact than the coal burned in steam locomotives. Most of the initial experimentation was in self-propelled passenger cars. In the most successful of these experiments, the power was transmitted from a gasoline engine to the wheels electrically rather than through an automotive-type mechanical transmission: the engine drove a generator, which produced current to turn electric motors on two of the four axles. Both the electrical equipment and the construction of the cars themselves, which were generally lighter than standard, drew on the technology of the electric interurban railways, which were competing with the steam roads for passengers and freight.

The gas-electric car was cheaper to operate than a conventional steam train—there was less of it to move, and it required fewer crew members. It was also easier on the track than a steam locomotive, and the railroads soon discovered that such cars were available for service a greater proportion of the time than a steam locomotive. It was a logical step to progress from a motor car with mail, baggage, and passenger compartments to a motor car that was simply a power unit, perhaps with two engines instead of one and motors on all four axles instead of just two.

Most railroad jobs, however, required more power than the gasoline engine could economically produce. The alternative was the diesel engine, which used cheaper, less highly refined fuel. The diesel was much heavier than a gasoline engine of equivalent power, but by the early 1930s lightweight diesel engines had been developed primarily by Winton Engine Company, a subsidiary of General Motors.

In 1924 General Electric and Ingersoll-Rand teamed up to produce a 300-horsepower diesel-electric locomotive, which was demonstrated on several eastern railroads. American Locomotive Company (Alco) then joined the other two companies, and the three jointly offered a standardized line of 300-horsepower and 600-horsepower diesel locomotives. Most eastern railroads bought at least one, usually for some service where smoke from a steam locomotive was considered a nuisance. The diesels were successful and more followed.

The other development of the gas-electric car was the passenger streamliner. In the early 1930s the Union Pacific (UP) and the Chicago, Burlington & Quincy each teamed up with a car builder—Pullman-Standard for the UP and Budd, new to the railroad field, for the Burlington—in the design and production of three-unit articulated streamlined motor trains. The Union Pacific's M-10000 and the Burlington's Zephyr both made their debuts in 1934 and were immediately successful. Both roads ordered more such trains. Within two years streamlined trains were being produced with separable power cars, and by then Electro-Motive Corporation (EMC), a subsidiary of General Motors, which had produced the prime movers for both those

*Atchison, Topeka & Santa Fe Super Chief powered by an early diesel-electric locomotive
(Santa Fe Railway Public Relations Department)*

early streamliners, had built several 1,800-horsepower diesel-electric locomotives designed to pull conventional passenger cars for the Baltimore & Ohio and the Santa Fe.

In 1937 EMC's passenger locomotive evolved to the familiar streamlined configuration, and the company offered a line of standard switchers. The passenger locomotives captured the public's fancy, and the switchers won the admiration of the railroads' motive power departments with their round-the-clock availability.

In 1939 EMC produced a four-unit 5,400-horsepower freight diesel and sent it out on a demonstration trip. It consistently outpulled steam locomotives; it spurned helper locomotives; it passed up water and fuel stops; it could be split into two 2,700-

horsepower locomotives. It changed the face of American railroading.

Until the late 1940s the diesel locomotive existed in two disparate forms: streamlined passenger and freight locomotives, usually comprising two or more separable (but rarely separated) units characterized by a full-width body and a tapered nose, and the lower-horsepower unstreamlined switchers, which had a cab at one end and a narrow hood covering the engine, generator, and other workings. The streamlined locomotive was bidirectional only if it had a unit with a cab at each end. The switcher gave the crew good visibility fore and aft, and servicing was much easier because the hood could be opened or lifted away entirely; the full-width body of the streamlined unit was a load-bearing unit and could not be removed.

The railroads began to recognize the need for a unit that could do several jobs, and the locomotive builders developed the road switcher, an elongated switcher with a short hood housing a steam generator for heating passenger trains and trucks suited to road duties in place of hard-riding switcher trucks. Initially road switchers had a switcher-sized engine, usually 1,000 horsepower; after World War II they were also offered with a 1,500- or 1,600-horsepower engine.

About 1950 the railroads began to consider streamlining and appearance less important than flexibility. Electro-Motive's GP7 had the same machinery as the streamlined F7, but its hood configuration permitted switching and local freight service. By 1952 road switchers—hood units—were outselling streamlined cab units two to one, and the few cab units constructed after 1956 were primarily for passenger service. The bulk of dieselization of American railroads occurred during the ten years following World War II. The last major operator of steam locomotives, the Norfolk & Western, and the last regularly scheduled steam-powered passenger trains, the Grand Trunk Western's Detroit-Pontiac commuter trains, were dieselized early in 1960.

In the late 1960s engines so increased in size that direct current generators able to absorb their output were excessively large and heavy. Locomotive builders began to offer alternators, lighter and smaller and lacking trouble-prone commutators, with solid-state rectifiers to produce the direct current for the traction motors (DC motors being better suited for locomotives than AC motors).

Electro-Motive, which in 1940 became the Electro-Motive Division of General Motors, quickly captured and retained the largest share of the diesel locomotive market. More than any other builder, Electro-Motive stressed standardization. Components were the same across the line; railroads simply bought locomotives "off the shelf." Different railroads had divergent types of steam locomotives, but under the paint their diesels were all the same. A railroad could dieselize with a fleet of a single model, coupling them together or using them singly as needed, rather than having several different sizes and strengths of steam locomotives. Alco and Baldwin divided their loyalties between steam and diesel; Alco marketed a passenger diesel just before World War II, but Baldwin did not offer a road locomotive until after the war.

Fairbanks-Morse entered the locomotive field in 1944 and remained a minority builder. Lima did not produce diesel locomotives until 1949, two years after its merger with Hamilton, a builder of diesel engines; Lima-Hamilton merged with Baldwin in 1950 to form Baldwin-Lima-Hamilton, and the Lima-Hamilton line of locomotives was discontinued with a total production of only 174 units. General Electric supplied electric equipment to Alco, Fairbanks-Morse, and, early on, to Electro-Motive; it produced a line of industrial-size locomotives (generally less than 600 horsepower and 70 tons) through the years and entered the road locomotive field in 1959 with its eyes on the market for replacement of first-generation diesels. Electro-Motive and General Electric were the two principal locomotive builders in 1987.

—George H. Drury

Lawrence A. Downs

(May 9, 1872 - August 10, 1940)

by John F. Stover

Purdue University

Lawrence A. Downs

CAREER: Rodman, Vandalia Railroad (1894-1896); rodman (1896), instrumentman (1896-1897), assistant engineer (1897-1898), division roadmaster (1898-1907), chief engineer, maintenance of way (1907-1910), division superintendent (1910-1914), general superintendent (1914-1919), assistant general manager (1919-1920), Illinois Central Railroad; vice president and general manager (1920-1924), president (1924-1926) Central of Georgia Railway; president (1926-1938), chairman of the board (1938-1940), Illinois Central Railroad.

Lawrence Aloysius Downs was born on May 9, 1872, in Greencastle, Indiana, the youngest of eight children of James and Mary McCarty Downs. His father had moved to Indiana from Ireland in 1851, and was the foreman of a section gang of the Vandalia Railroad. Downs was educated in the public schools and as a youth worked on his father's section gang, saving his money so that he could go to college. He attended Purdue University, where he pursued a course in civil engineering and played guard on a winning varsity football team. Graduating in 1894, he soon found employment as a rodman on a surveying crew of the Vandalia Railroad.

In 1896 Downs joined an Illinois Central (IC) surveying team with an increase in pay to $60 a month. Six months later he was moved from rodman to instrumentman, and in 1897 he was appointed assistant engineer. At the age of twenty-six, in 1898, Downs was promoted to division roadmaster, serving in this capacity for nine years in LaSalle, Illinois; Louisville, Kentucky; and Chicago. On November 27, 1901, he married Ida May Mulligan of Pembroke, Ontario, Canada; they had one daughter.

In 1907 Downs was appointed assistant chief engineer, maintenance of way, for the entire Illinois Central system. Downs, who took as his maxim "Do your job the best you can and always have your eye on the position just ahead," was transferred at his own request from the engineering to the operating department and appointed division superintendent at Fort Dodge, Iowa, in 1910. Later he served in the same position at Dubuque, Iowa, and at Louisville, Kentucky. In 1914 he was appointed general superintendent of the southern lines with headquarters at New Orleans, and in 1916 was transferred to the northern lines with headquarters at Chicago. He became assistant general manager in 1919.

Downs was made vice president and general manager of the Illinois Central-controlled Central of Georgia Railway in 1920 and elected to the presidency of that line in 1924. The IC had had a major interest in the Central of Georgia, with which it connected at Birmingham, Alabama, since 1909. During the six years that Downs was with the Central of Georgia the 1,900-mile line was quite prosperous: between 1921 and 1926 its revenues grew from $22 million to $32 million and in the middle 1920s the Central of Georgia was paying 6 percent annual dividends on its common stock.

In the summer of 1926 Charles H. Markham, who had been president of the Illinois Central since 1919, suffered a physical breakdown and gave up the presidency to become chairman of the board; Downs was quickly elected president, and he moved from Georgia back to Chicago. Downs frequently claimed to be "just an average man," but the enthusiasm he brought to every new position and the great loyalty he gave to his subordinates would suggest that he was really an unusual business executive. As an engineer he was a slide-rule-and-compass man, but his actions as an executive were softened by his belief that success depended upon an understanding of human nature.

During the early 1920s Markham had started a number of major improvement programs-the electrification of suburban service, building the Edgewood Cutoff to speed up freight traffic, and upgrading terminal facilities in Chicago-most of which were completed early in the Downs presidency. As a result the funded debt of the IC had grown from $257 million in 1920 to $359 million in 1930. Instead of growing along with the funded debt, the annual revenues of the IC in the late 1920s stayed at a rather constant average of $180 million a year. With the coming of the Depression, total revenues fell to $148 million in 1930, $117 million in 1931, and $89 million-a figure less than half that of 1929-in 1932. That year interest on the funded debt took almost 18 percent of every revenue dollar. The IC managed to pay its normal $7 dividend in 1930; but dividends were reduced in 1931 and suspended altogether in October of that year. Illinois Central common stock, which had stood at a high of 153½ in 1929, had dropped to a low of 4¾ by 1932.

Downs and his staff in the early 1930s faced up to the financial problems and mounting deficits with a variety of programs, including a drastic cut in operating expenses, wage and salary reductions, aid from the federal government, and efforts to increase traffic. By 1932 Downs could report a reduction of 52 percent in operating expenses. Road maintenance was delayed wherever possible and such costs for the total decade were reduced more than 60 percent. By 1931 the roster of employees had been cut 30 percent, and in 1933 the work force was 55 percent below that of 1929. Early in 1932 Downs was one of seven railroad presidents who, under the leadership of Daniel Willard of the Baltimore & Ohio, obtained from labor a 10 percent reduction in wages across the board, an agreement which saved the IC more than $4 million for 1932. Executive salaries were reduced at the same time and by 1933 Downs had taken a second reduction in his own salary. During the mid 1930s several major loans were obtained from the Reconstruction Finance Corporation, the Railroad Credit Corporation, and the Public Works Administration. Downs continued to push industrial and agricultural promotion programs wherever possible. The Century of Progress Exposition in Chicago, held along the IC track in the summers of 1933 and 1934, modestly increased both suburban and passenger traffic. Even with all these efforts the Illinois Central came close to receivership. In the dark days of 1933 Edward C. Craig, the line's general counsel, drew up the papers necessary for a voluntary trusteeship under the Bankruptcy Act.

Revenues for the Illinois Central in 1933 were down to $88 million, a bit lower than for 1932, but climbed to $91 million in 1935 and to $114 million in 1937. In 1934 wages were partially restored and by the spring of 1935 had returned to the pre-1932 level. The recovery permitted the Illinois Central to offer modest improvements in both passenger and freight service. In May 1936 Downs helped inaugurate the road's first diesel-powered streamliner, the Green Diamond, running between Chicago and St. Louis. Later that year the IC established a fast overnight freight service between Chicago and Memphis.

After nearly a decade of fighting the problems of a major depression, the sixty-six-year-old Downs decided it was time to turn over control to a younger man. On December 14, 1938, he resigned as president and was immediately elected board chairman. Downs held this new position for only a year and a half, dying in Chicago on August 10, 1940.

Lawrence Downs was director of the Association of American Railroads, a charter member and president of the American Railway Engineering Association, a trustee of the Armour Institute of Technology, a director of two Chicago banks, a delegate to the 1922 International Railway Congress in Rome, a member of the Sovereign Military Order of the Knights of Malta, a Republican, and a Catholic. But in his forty-four years with the Illinois Central he was first of all a railroader. In the early 1930s he probably faced more difficult financial problems than any earlier IC president, and was the man most responsible for saving the Illinois Central from receivership in the Depression.

References:

Carlton J. Corliss, *Main Line of Mid-America: The Story of the Illinois Central* (New York: Creative Age Press, 1950);

John F. Stover, *History of the Illinois Central Railroad* (New York: Macmillan, 1975).

Frederic C. Dumaine, Jr.

(September 5, 1902-   )

by George H. Merriam

Fitchburg State College

Frederic C. Dumaine, Jr., in 1979 (Chris Maynard/ Black Star)

CAREER: Director of various companies, including Eastern Steamship Lines, Lehigh Coal and Navigation Company, Boston & Maine Railroad, Maine Central Railroad, New Haven Railroad, Portland Terminal Railroad, Waltham Watch Company (1925-1951); director (1927-   ), treasurer (1939-1967), president (1968-1978), chairman of the executive committee (1979-1986), Amoskeag Company; president, New Haven Railroad (1951-1954); chairman of executive committee and director, Fieldcrest Mills (1953-1985); president, Avis Rent-A-Car System (1957-1962); member of board of managers, Delaware & Hudson Railroad (1963-1968); chairman of the board, Delaware & Hudson Company (1968); president, Delaware & Hudson Railroad (1968); director, Westville Homes Corporation (1978-1986); chairman of the board and chief executive officer (1983), director (1983-1986), Bangor & Aroostook Railroad; chairman of executive committee and director, Fieldcrest Cannon Mills (1986).

Frederic C. Dumaine, Jr., born in Concord, Massachusetts, in 1902, was one of seven children of F. C. Dumaine and Elizabeth Thomas Dumaine, a descendant of Revolutionary War printer Isaiah Thomas. F. C. Dumaine, of French Canadian ancestry, was a self-made millionaire. As a fourteen-year-old officeboy in 1880 he so impressed Thomas Jefferson Coolidge, the head of Boston's Amoskeag Manufacturing Company, that Coolidge sent him to work in Amoskeag's huge Manchester, New Hampshire, mills. In fifteen years Dumaine rose from bobbin boy to purchasing agent and became treasurer (chief executive officer) of the world's leading cotton textile company in 1905.

Frederic Dumaine grew up in relative affluence. He attended Pomfret School in Connecticut, where his aggressive style on the playing fields earned him the nickname Buck. During school vacations he worked in the mills, starting at age twelve as an office boy; was remembered by one of the bosses as a "nice happy-to-lucky kind of fellow." His formal education ended when he graduated from prep school in 1923 and went to work as "Dad's errand boy" for his father, who "taught me all I know."

By 1923 Dumaine's father headed Amoskeag Manufacturing Company and Waltham Watch Company. In 1927 F. C. Dumaine and associates formed two Amoskeag companies: one was a textile manufactory controlled by the other, a hold company with $18 million transferred from Amoskeag Manufacturing Company's $25 million operating surplus. The younger Dumaine worked as a traveling salesman for his father's companies in the 1920s, taking orders for piece goods, speedometers, and watches.

Placed by his father in a variety of directorships, Dumaine served from 1934 to 1948 on the board of directors of the Boston & Maine Railroad. He became treasurer of Amoskeag Company in 1939. By 1948 Dumaine had been a director of ten companies, including Eastern Steamship Lines and the Boston & Maine, Maine Central, and Portland Terminal railroads.

A director of the New York, New Haven & Hartford Railroad for nearly twenty years, F. C. Dumaine remained on the board after the railroad's 1935 bankruptcy. In 1944 he began an involved manipulation of the preferred stock of the Boston Railroad Holding Company, a New Haven subsidiary formed in 1909 which survived the bankruptcy. He was squeezed off the board in 1947, but returned in 1948, gaining control of the just-reorganized New Haven's preferred stock, and Buck Dumaine became a director of the New Haven. F. C. Dumaine was accused by *Business Week,* of failing to main-

tain splendid rehabilitation job" done on the New Haven between 1935 and 1947, but Dumaine has stated that when his father took over the company he (Buck) was sent on an inspection trip over the entire line with the superintendent of maintenance-of-way, and they found a poorly maintained property. F. C. Dumaine tried to increase maintenance while liquidating over 1,300 parcels of real estate owned by the railroad for about $11 million and laying off more than 2,000 employees. After three tumultuous years heading the New Haven, during which he reported profits of $22.5 million, F. C. Dumaine died on May 28, 1951, at age eighty-five.

Within days of his father's death the New Haven's board elected Buck Dumaine president of the railroad. He says that he continued his father's pattern, working hard to restore employee morale and the physical condition of the property. Millions of dollars were poured into maintenance, and passenger service was resumed on the branches to Worcester from Providence and New London. A $5 dividend was paid on preferred stock arrears in 1951, followed by a $9 dividend in 1952. *Business Week* noted on March 14, 1953: "Few will deny that the New Haven is well on the way to becoming one of the nation's most modern and efficient railroad operations." During 1953 Dumaine further increased maintenance by nearly $1.7 million. In 1954 he reported improved commuter services, reduction of the New Haven's debt by $50 million since 1948, elimination of 340 miles of useless branches, purchase of 100 multiple-unit commuter cars and 20 Buddliner self- propelled passenger cars, and an improved right-of-way. In 1954 Amoskeag held 60,000 shares of New Haven preferred stock and 13,172 shares of its common stock.

At that point Patrick B. McGinnis, an experienced railroad raider, used a bare majority of common stock proxies to oust Dumaine's group, taking eleven of twenty directorships on the New Haven's board. Though no longer controlling the New Haven, Amoskeag and Dumaine continued to receive large dividends during McGinnis's twenty-two-month rule, which ended with the railroad's bankruptcy. But Amoskeag was moving into other businesses, among them Fieldcrest Mills, purchased from Marshall Field in 1953.

Dumaine became involved in Massachusetts Republican politics in his post-New Haven years. In April 1963 he was elected chairman of the Republican state organization. Though a Goldwater supporter, during the following year's campaign he tried hard to keep the Massachusetts delegation to the Republican national convention uncommitted.

In 1963 Amoskeag's investments in the Delaware & Hudson Railway (D&H) provided Dumaine a seat on the railroad's board. There he fought a takeover attempt by the Norfolk & Western (N&W). He was elected president of the D&H in 1968 but resigned in less than a year to protest D&H's becoming part of the N&W's Dereco, Incorporated holding company.

Amoskeag bought almost all of the Bangor & Aroostook Railroad's stock in 1969. Dumaine's interests at that time also included Springfield Street Railway Company, Worcester Bus Company, and Fanny Farmer Candy Company. With a view to merging the Bangor & Aroostook with the Maine Central, Amoskeag had begun accumulating Maine Central stock in 1965 and held 35 percent by 1969.

From 1969 through 1977 a battle raged between Dumaine and E. Spencer Miller, long-time president of the Maine Central. Using every legal and regulatory means possible Miller stalemated Dumaine's takeover attempt—only to retire in 1977 and see the Maine Central fall to Timothy Mellon's Guilford Transportation Industries in 1980. Though Dumaine's hopes for a Maine Central- Bangor & Aroostook combination were frustrated, Amoskeag was able to dispose of its Maine Central shares profitably.

Dumaine married Margaret Williams in 1926; they have three children. In 1986 Dumaine was chairman of the executive committee of Amoskeag, a director of the Bangor & Aroostook railroad, chairman of the executive committee of Fieldcrest Cannon Mills, Incorporated (a Southern textile giant formed in 1986), and a director of Westville Homes Corporation. He has offices in Boston's Prudential Center and remains deeply interested in the fortunes of the Bangor & Aroostook railroad.

References:

"Another Collision on the New Haven," *Fortune*, 47 (March 1953): 55;

Robert E. Bedingfield, "Amoskeag Buys 20% Interest in Stock of the Maine Central," *New York Times*, December 27, 1965, p. 39;

Bedingfield, "The Spence and Bucky Show," *New York Times*, October 9, 1977, III: 3, 13;

"By, and For, the New Haven," *Newsweek*, 35 (April 3, 1950): 58;

"Capture of the New Haven," *Fortune*, 39 (April 1949): 86-90, 178, 180, 182, 184, 186;

"Dumaine vs. Stockholders," *Business Week* (April 21, 1951): 128-129;

John H. Fenton, ..New Haven Seen at Brink of Ruin," *New York Times*, April 6, 1961, p. 67;

Tamara Hareven and Randolph Langenbach, *Amoskeag* (New York: Pantheon, 1978), pp. 75-92;

"How to Rebuild a Railroad," *Business Week* (March 14, 1953): 52-54, 56, 58, 61;

"New Boss for New Haven," *Newsweek*, 32 (September 13, 1948): 68-70;

"New Crew [on the New Haven]," *Time*, 52 (July 26, 1948): 76;

"New Haven Switch," *Newsweek*, 42 (January 2, 1950): 42;

"Raid on the New Haven," *Time*, 51 (May 17, 1948): 96-98;

"Union Talks Slowdown to Save Vice President," *Business Week* (March 31, 1951): 21;

John L. Weller, *The New Haven Railroad: Its Rise and Fall* (New York: Hastings House, 1969), pp. 206-216.

Albert J. Earling

(January 19, 1848-November 10, 1925)

by Carlos A. Schwantes

University of Idaho

Albert J. Earling

CAREER: Telegrapher (1866-1871), train dispatcher (1871-1876), St. Paul & Northwestern Railway; assistant superintendent, Milwaukee, Omaha, and Iowa divisions (1876-1882), division superintendent (1882-1884), assistant general superintendent (1884-1888), general superintendent (1888-1890), general manager (1890-1895), second vice president (1895-1899), president (1899-1917), chairman (1917-1919), Chicago, Milwaukee & St. Paul Railway.

Albert J. Earling served as president of the Chicago, Milwaukee & St. Paul Railway during its evolution from a prosperous Granger line (that is, a line serving the states of the upper Midwest) into a transcontinental giant extending from Chicago to the Puget Sound ports of Seattle and Tacoma. The son of German immigrants, Constant Henry and Elizabeth Sauer Earling, Albert John Earling was born in 1848, in Richfield, Wisconsin. In 1866, following a grammar school education, he commenced a career in railroading as a night telegrapher in Prairie du Chien, Wisconsin, for the St. Paul & Northwestern Railway, a predecessor of the Chicago, Milwaukee & St. Paul. He became a train dispatcher in 1871 and remained in that position when the Chicago, Milwaukee & St. Paul Railway was formed in 1874. He continued to rise through the ranks, becoming assistant superintendent of the Milwaukee, Omaha, and Iowa divisions in 1876, division superintendent in charge of construction of a line across Iowa in 1882, assistant general superintendent in 1884, general superintendent in 1888, general manager in 1890, and second vice president in 1895. In 1899 he was elected to succeed Roswell Miller as president of the Chicago, Milwaukee & St. Paul.

Earling, while often described as an austere man with little sense of humor, proved a popular executive. As president he endeavored to keep in close touch with his employees, even spending nights in the yards riding switch engines in order to talk to the men.

Under Earling, the Chicago, Milwaukee & St. Paul extended its lines into several new areas considered likely to generate profitable traffic, and added heavier locomotives and longer cars. During the first decade of Earling's presidency, the railroad was widely praised for its sound finances and excellent management. But Earling's greatest accomplishment (or, according to his critics, his greatest folly) was expansion of the Chicago, Milwaukee & St. Paul to the Pacific and electrification of a major portion of that new route. On June 30, 1901, the road had 6,596 miles of first track (that is, miles of route not including dual or passing tracks), with its westernmost point being Evarts, South Dakota. Fifteen years later it had grown to nearly 10,000 miles, and its line reached the coast of Washington.

Upon the advice of the chairman of the board Roswell Miller, his predecessor as president, Earling in 1901 dispatched an engineer to study the cost of duplicating the Northern Pacific line to the Pacific. The engineer's report confirmed the preliminary estimate of $45 million. After further study, on November 28, 1905, the railroad's board of directors authorized building a line to Seattle and Tacoma, Washington. Construction began four months later.

Earling devoted much time to the Pacific extension. Between the groundbreaking at Mobridge, South Dakota, in 1906 until completion of the line in 1909, he was in constant contact with the project, making frequent inspection trips. When he visited the Pacific Northwest in early 1906 he was greeted with enthusiasm and feted by chambers of commerce, businessmen's associations, and municipal officials. Equally encouraging were newspaper reports that the lines of the Northern Pacific, Great Northern, and Union Pacific were nearly filled to capacity, and these three railroads, in fact, did little to discourage the Chicago, Milwaukee & St. Paul from sharing in the traffic bonanza.

During 1906 construction moved at a rapid pace, although Earling reported that the cost of the Pacific extension would be closer to $60 million than to the original estimate of $45 million. Hardly had the 1,489-mile line been completed in 1909 before Earling began considering electrification of its mountainous portions. The abundance of cheap hydroelectric power in the Pacific Northwest and reduced costs of electrified operation on mountain grades seemed to justify the expense. Moreover, John D. Ryan, the sole Western member of the railroad's board of directors, pushed hard for electrification, though hardly from a disinterested point of view: Ryan had organized the Montana Power Company and was also president of the Anaconda Copper Mining Company, which ultimately sold the railroad 12,000 tons of copper for electric wires.

The project commenced in April 1914, and on November 30, 1915, the first train operated by electricity traveled the 438 miles from Avery, Idaho, to Harlowton, Montana. During the first eight years of operation the company estimated that electrification saved it more than $12 million. But tempering the good news was the fact that construction costs had increased the company's debt in public hands by some $266 million between June 30, 1909, and December 31, 1917. During the same time the company's earnings fell from three times its fixed charges to just one and one-quarter times.

Critics, including the Interstate Commerce Commission, blamed Earling for the decline. He was in reality a cautious man and would not have extended the line to the Pacific had it not made sense in the context of the time. In 1905 it would have been impossible for Earling to foresee the blow the opening of the Panama Canal in 1914 would deal to transcontinental railroad traffic or that the booming Pacific Northwest would enter a five-year slump in 1912. Equally unforeseen during the first decade of the twentieth century was the competitive impact of motorized vehicles and publicly subsidized highways.

Early in 1917 Earling became chairman of the board; succeeding him as president was Harry E. Byram of the Chicago, Burlington & Quincy. As a dollar-a-year man, Earling worked with Charles G. Dawes to trim the expenses of the federal government during the administration of Warren G. Harding. Earling died late in 1925 in Milwaukee.

Earling described himself as a Mason, an Episcopalian, and a Republican. He married Margaret Helen Peebles in 1871; the couple had three children. He listed the study of trees as his special hobby.

References:

August Derleth, *The Milwaukee Road: Its First Hundred Years* (New York: Creative Age Press, 1948);

Max Lowenthal, *The Investor Pays* (New York: Knopf, 1933);

Carlos A. Schwantes, "The Milwaukee Road's Pacific Extension, 1902-1929," *Pacific Northwest Quarterly*, 72 (January 1981): 30-40.

Electric Traction

Both the electric street railway or "trolley" and the electric interurban railroad became possible as the result of major technological developments in the 1880s. The most heralded breakthrough occurred in 1887 when Frank Julian Sprague, a recent graduate of the United States Naval Academy who was intrigued with the commercial possibilities of electricity, succeeded in electrifying the Richmond Union Passenger Railway in Virginia. Sprague's triumph set the pattern for a revolution in intra- and intercity transport, and by the early 1890s additional research demonstrated the feasibility of long-range electric railway construction.

By the turn of the century the electric railway had been largely perfected. Companies generally employed low-voltage (600 or 650 volts) direct current that powered cars by means of simple, light-weight traction motors. They built and operated networks of power stations and substations to supply electricity for themselves and frequently for commercial and residential users, as well.

While virtually every American community of any appreciable size sported an electric streetcar system, interurban lines, too, quickly spread out over the national landscape. Nearly 1,000 route miles of track were operating in 1897; by 1905 there were 8,000. The country's interurban network peaked at slightly over 15,000 miles in 1915. Although Ohio and Indiana emerged as the heartland for these intercity electric carriers, they could be found connecting such remote places as Sheridan and Monarch, Wyoming, and Warren and Bisbee, Arizona.

During most of the first decade of the twentieth century, except for the brief economic downturns of 1903-1904 and 1907-1908, the future of electric intercity transport seemed especially bright. Even projects on the lunatic fringe found enthusiastic supporters. The most ambitious one actually attempted was the Chicago-New York Air Line Railroad. Incorporating in August 1905 under the lax laws of Maine, its backers sought to build a double-track speedway which would make it possible for passengers to travel the 750 miles between its termi-

nals in only ten hours. Financed largely through local investor clubs and energized by the company's slick monthly publication, *Air Line News,* construction began in 1906. Enormous building costs, the panic of 1907, and poor management ended this dream; the road never became more than a twenty-mile pike connecting the Indiana towns of La Porte and Goodrum. When this segment joined the more prosperous Gary Railways, the original Air Line scheme vanished and so did tens of thousands of investors' dollars.

The 1920s saw first a steady and then a rapid decline in the number of electric railways. Marginally profitable roads were extremely vulnerable to auto, bus, and truck competition. By 1920 not only had the production of motor vehicles soared but the condition of the nation's roadways had improved markedly. The best-established interurbans, however, were able to respond to the challenges posed by roadway competitors. After World War I some firms acquired lighter, smoother riding, and faster passenger cars, and many others modernized their older wooden equipment. Those interurbans that could boost freight revenues tried to do so. In Ohio, for example, the largest companies focused on interline freight movements and improved their terminal facilities. In 1928 the Northern Ohio Traction & Light Company, Penn-Ohio Public Service Company, and Lake Shore Electric launched the Electric Railways Freight Company to handle their various freight operations more efficiently. Lake Shore Electric caught the public's eye with the introduction in 1931 of the "Railwagons," six ten-ton truck trailers that could be hauled on specially designed flatcars. This early "piggyback" scheme provided better service for shippers, since their goods did not have to be reloaded from truck to train and back to truck.

But innovations by even the spunkiest interurbans could not save the industry. The depression of the 1930s, together with keen competition from the automobile, bus, and truck, led to the junking of most systems by the end of the decade. The survivors—for instance, the Chicago, South Shore & South Bend, the Illinois Terminal, the Lackawanna & Wyoming Valley, and the Salt Lake & Utah— developed enough freight interchangeable with steam roads to remain in business at least until after World War II. By the 1980s only a few interurbans were still "under wire," and other ex-interurbans operated as diesel-powered shortlines. Only the Chicago, South Shore & South Bend continues to haul passengers.

References:

George W. Hilton and John F. Due, *The Electric Interurban Railways In America* (Stanford: Stanford University Press, 1961);

Fred H. Whipple, *The Electric Railway* (Detroit: William Graham Printing Co., 1889).

—*H. Roger Grant*

Electrification

The first electrification of an American steam railroad (as differentiated from street railways and interurban trolley lines) occurred in 1895, when the Baltimore & Ohio began using electric locomotives to pull trains through a heavily graded 7,000-foot tunnel beneath the city of Baltimore. This operation typified most applications of electric motive power over the next twenty years, with electricity replacing steam over short segments to solve special operating problems caused by long tunnels, steep grades, or newly enacted metropolitan ordinances banning excessive smoke. Tunnel electrifications were introduced on the Great Northern, Boston & Maine, and Norfolk & Western systems, for example, while the New York Central turned to electric traction to haul its trains to and from Manhattan's Grand Central Terminal as a means of complying with smoke abatement laws. The Pennsylvania Railroad (PRR) used electricity to power its trains under the Hudson River between Newark and Manhattan's new Pennsylvania Station, which was completed in 1907. The New York, New Haven & Hartford Railroad in 1906 became the first line to take advantage of the efficiencies inherent in long-distance electrification on seventy-five route miles between New Rochelle, New York and New Haven, Connecticut. Electric locomotives could pull heavier—hence longer—trains at higher speeds than their steam counterparts, in effect increasing track capacity without actually adding more tracks. They were also cheaper to operate and maintain and had longer service lives.

These economies prompted the PRR to embark on what would become North America's most extensive electrified network, 2,200 track miles, beginning with the conversion to electric operation of its Philadelphia-Paoli commuter line in 1913. In 1928, after electrifying nearly all of its Philadelphia suburban service, the PRR began to electrify its densely traveled main line between New York and Washington. This project was completed in 1935, with a westward branch to Harrisburg, Pennsylvania, being added two years later. The only other railroad to opt for long-distance electrification, the Chicago, Milwaukee, St. Paul & Pacific (Milwaukee Road), had the most route miles—about 660—but the installation was for the most part lightly traveled single track. The electrification of the line between Harlowton, Montana, and Seattle was completed in 1927 and was prompted mainly by the availability of cheap hydroelectric power.

By 1920 the battle between the alternating and direct current systems had been resolved in favor of AC, which could be transmitted at low cost over long distances without a drop in voltage. The technological hurdles to electrification had been overcome, but the most formidable obstacle— the tremendously high cost of installation— remained. The PRR's AC electrification of 1928 to 1938 cost $250 million, constituting the largest single railroad capital improvement program undertaken up to that time. The year of its completion was the high tide of electrification; even then only 2 percent of America's 250,000 route miles of steam railway were operated electrically.

The advent of the diesel-electric locomotive after World War II offered many of the advantages of "pure" electrification without the high initial cost. Consequently, diesels replaced steam engines, and most of the short-haul electrifications were phased out. The high cost of modernizing the electrifications of the Milwaukee Road and that portion of the PRR system owned by Conrail led to their demise in 1974 and 1981, respectively; Amtrak, on the other hand, used federal funds to improve its former PRR and New Haven northeast corridor electrifications.

References:
Michael Bezilla, *Electric Traction on the Pennsylvania Railroad, 1895-1968* (University Park: Pennsylvania State University Press, 1980);
William D. Middleton, *When the Steam Railroads Electrified* (Milwaukee: Kalmbach, 1974).

—*Michael Bezilla*

Howard Elliott

(December 6, 1860-July 8, 1928)

by Robert L. Frey

Wilmington College of Ohio

CAREER: Clerk, Chicago, Burlington & Quincy Railroad (1881-1882); auditor and assistant treasurer (1882-1887), general freight and passenger agent (1887-1891), Chicago, Burlington & Kansas City Railroad and St. Louis, Keokuk & Northwestern Railroad (1882-1887); general freight agent, Missouri Lines (1891-1896), general manager (1896-1901), vice president for operations (1901-1903), Chicago, Burlington & Quincy Railroad; president, Northern Pacific Railway (1903-1913); chairman of the board (1913-1914), chairman of the board and president (1914-1917), New York, New Haven & Hartford Railroad; chairman of the board (1917-1918), president (1918-1920), chairman of the board (1920-1928), Northern Pacific Railway.

Howard Elliott did not have the public stature of a James J. Hill or a J. P. Morgan, but for much of his career Elliott was a lieutenant for these "captains of industry and finance." Elliott was typical of many competent railroad executives whose careers were overshadowed by the Hills and the Morgans, but whose day-to-day management skills operated the railroads of the United States. Elliott, in particular, was a reasoned voice arguing for balanced and fair treatment of America's railroads. He also attempted to hear the concerns of the public and to be open and honest with the public. Had his style and attitude been more widespread among railroad men in the late nineteenth century, the history of American railroads might have been different in the twentieth century.

Elliott was born in New York City in 1860 to Charles Wyllys and Mary White Elliott. Although the Elliotts were not wealthy, they were a distinguished New England family. John Eliot, the first American ancestor of Howard Elliott, spent most of his life as a missionary to the Indians and was the first person to translate the Bible into an Indian language—a translation known as "Eliot's Bible." Later generations added an extra *l* and *t* to the family name. Most of Howard Elliott's boyhood was spent in New Haven, Connecticut, and Cambridge, Massachusetts. During the summer before his senior year at the Lawrence Scientific School of Harvard University he worked as a rodman on the Chicago, Burlington & Quincy Railroad (CB&Q) in northwest Missouri.

After receiving his degree in civil engineering in 1881 Elliott worked as a surveyor for a Maryland brick company for three months, then signed on as a clerk for the CB&Q at Burlington, Iowa, at a salary of $40 per month. Probably the major reason Elliott migrated west was because his uncle, Charles Elliott Perkins, had become president of the CB&Q in 1881. Certainly his uncle's position did

Howard Elliott (center) with James J. Hill (left) and Louis W. Hill, Sr., in 1909 (James J. Hill Reference Library)

not hinder Elliott's professional advancement. Frequently President Perkins would direct his special train to proceed over the Burlington at a leisurely pace, stopping each evening in a small town where he could pay a surprise visit to a station agent and play a few hands of poker with local businessmen and farmers. Elliott accompanied his uncle on several of these trips—an unusual assignment for a young freight agent.

Elliott's performance was outstanding, however, and by 1901, the year Hill acquired the CB&Q, he had moved up through positions on the road's subsidiaries to become vice-president in charge of operations, maintenance, and construction of all lines, with headquarters in Chicago. In 1903, when Morgan called Charles S. Mellen from the presidency of Hill's Northern Pacific to that of the New York, New Haven & Hartford Railroad, the board of the former road elected Elliott as Mellen's successor.

Elliott's leadership resulted in what was probably the best decade in the history of the Northern Pacific. New locomotives were purchased, track and

roadbed were improved, the main line was double-tracked where traffic warranted, and one of the first automatic block signaling systems in the country was installed. A decade of excellent agricultural yields, the construction of new factories in some of the towns along the line, and an influx of new residents to the Northwest helped to pay for these improvements. Unlike Mellen, Elliott was a careful and conservative manager. During the decade of his presidency track mileage increased from 7,075 to 9,476 miles, gross income from $47 million to $78 million, net income from $21.8 million to $29 million, and the accumulated surplus from $9.7 million to $83.7 million.

Elliott's achievements did not go unnoticed. In 1913 J. P. Morgan, Jr., whose father had died early in the year, faced a serious problem with the New Haven. Mellen had attempted to create a transportation monopoly in New England by expending huge sums of money to purchase competing railroads (particularly the Boston & Maine), steamboat lines, and trolley companies. The critics of monopoly, led by Louis D. Brandeis, were incensed. A series of collisions and derailments resulted in manslaughter charges against Mellen in addition to investigations into the operation of the company by the Interstate Commerce Commission (ICC) and the Department of Justice. Morgan forced Mellen to resign and Morgan's associates, such as George F. Baker of the First National Bank of New York, a member of the Northern Pacific board, recommended Elliott as Mellen's successor. Elliott was not immediately appointed president of the New Haven, apparently because it was thought that Elliott was not familiar with the New Haven's operating peculiarities—heavy passenger service, numerous terminal facilities, and the predominance of short hauls. Within a year the interim president left, and Elliott became president and chairman of the board.

Newspaper reporters, to whom Mellen refused to give interviews, were amazed when Elliott, on accepting the New Haven's offer, invited them to his hotel room. "The latch of my office is always out to newspaper men," said Elliott. "I am a sort of public official and the people have a right to know what I am doing and thinking about. The only way of finding out the truth is through the newspapers. I have no more right to deny an interview to a reporter than I have to one of the members of my Board of Directors." The press was delighted and the reception Elliott received in New England was positive.

September 1913, however, turned out to be an inauspicious time to assume the leadership of the New Haven. During Elliott's first day on the job a fast-moving passenger express rammed the rear of another crowded passenger train stopped in a dense fog. Twenty-one people died and more than fifty were injured in the wreck. Elliott worked hard to reverse the trend of ill fortune which had befallen the railroad. The speed of passenger trains was slowed immediately, and eventually improved signaling was installed, steel passenger cars replaced wooden cars, and efforts were made to develop mandatory retirement rules for locomotive engineers.

Elliott regularly took his case to the people. In *The World's Work* for December 1913 he wrote: "We of the New Haven Railroad are trying to make it and its associated properties adequate and smooth running; to keep them ready to serve; to operate them safely and economically in harmony with the law and public opinion; and make them

pay a fair return to the stockholder." Elliott also led efforts to break up the New Haven monopoly by placing some of its properties, such as the Boston & Maine, in the hands of trustees appointed by the Department of Justice. These efforts, coupled with his efficient management skills and his elimination of unnecessary expenses, gradually improved the financial picture of the New Haven and laid the foundation for a slow restoration of public confidence. But the exertion required in this leadership effort weakened the health of the five-feet-eight-inch, 205-pound president. On the verge of a nervous breakdown, he was convinced by his doctors to resign his position early in 1917.

In July 1917 Elliott was elected chairman of the board of directors of the Northern Pacific, a position in which his expertise could be utilized without exacting such a heavy physical toll on him. He continued to live in the East and to provide advice to the New Haven. In 1918 he probably saved the company from financial collapse by convincing the United States Railroad Administration (USRA) to cover $44 million of its bonds which had come due. World War I and government control of the railroads found Elliott once again as president of the Northern Pacific. The actual operation of the company under the USRA was in the hands of a federal manager. Elliott's role was to protect the stockholders' investment and to work with the federal manager. As part of a group of railroad executives Elliott took part in the presentations to Congress between 1918 and 1920 which resulted in the Transportation Act of 1920. In 1920 he was appointed chairman of a committee to present the case for higher rates to the ICC; the new rates went into effect in August of that year.

During the last eight years of his life Elliott served as chairman of the board of the Northern Pacific and provided President Charles Donnelly with much helpful advice. The affection and high esteem in which the Northern Pacific held Elliott can be seen in the statement approved by the board of directors on the occasion of his death in 1928: "It would be difficult to measure in words his service. He gave unstintingly of his time and his strength to the problems of the company and no subject affecting its welfare was too small to command his earnest attention and ripe judgment. He was a master of detail and his careful and tireless studies of the company's needs and his wise recommendations were of inestimable value to its officials and employees. He believed in the Northwest and the people of the Northwest trusted and believed in him. He was proud of his company and jealous of its reputation. He labored not from a sense of duty, but with joy in his task and with a deep affection for the property and the men who worked with him. His ever kindly influence permeated the organization for to the men he was not merely an official, but an ever welcome and understanding friend."

Howard Elliott's professional life linked the age of the great railroad builders with the age of government regulation and the beginning of the decline of the American railroad system. Elliott saw the causes of this decline clearly. Some were factors over which railroads had little control, such as the automobile and the airplane. But many causes, including government regulation, Elliott ruefully knew were partially the fault of his colleagues, such as Morgan and Mellen. Elliott did not need to influence legislatures or to buy out the competition; he could "out-manage" most of his contemporaries and proved it many times during his distinguished career.

Elliott was a member of many professional and civic organizations. He married Janet January of St. Louis in 1892; the couple had three children.

Publication:
"What I Am Trying to Do," *The World's Work,* 27 (December 1913): 145-149.

Unpublished Document:
Robert L. Frey and Lorenz P. Schrenk, "The Northern Pacific Railway Company: Age of Standardization, 1900-1925," unpublished manuscript in the hands of the authors.

References:
Robert L. Frey and Lorenz P. Schrenk, *Northern Pacific Railway: Supersteam Era, 1925-1940* (San Marino, Cal.: Golden West Books, 1985);
Richard C. Overton, *Burlington Route: A History of the Burlington Lines* (Lincoln: University of Nebraska Press, 1965);
John L. Weller, *The New Haven Railroad: Its Rise and Fall* (New York: Hastings House, 1969).

Archives:
Letters and memoranda by Howard Elliott can be found in the corporate records of the Northern Pacific at the Minnesota Historical Society in St. Paul, Minnesota.

Emergency Railroad Transportation Act

Signed into law on June 16, 1933, the Emergency Railroad Transportation Act created a temporary coordinator of transportation, to be appointed by the president for a term of two years. The coordinator was to divide railroads into eastern, southern, and western groups, and coordinating committees selected by roads within each group were to eliminate duplication and promote joint use of tracks and terminals, encourage financial reorganization of carriers to cut fixed costs, and study ways to improve transportation. Congress preferred voluntary action by the railroads to eliminate waste and achieve economies, but the coordinator could order action. The act specified that neither the number of employees nor their salaries could be reduced from the level of May 1933 although a 5 percent reduction in the work force by attrition was permitted and labor-management problems were to be adjusted by regional boards established by the coordinator. The Interstate Commerce Commission (ICC) and the courts could reverse or revise orders of the coordinator. The act exempted carriers from the antitrust laws while they were obeying the coordinator's directives. In 1935 Congress extended this experiment in coordination for one year.

Permanent provisions of the Emergency Railroad Transportation Act simplified the work of the ICC's Valuation Bureau in determining the actual value of railroads by repealing the recapture clauses of the Transportation Act of 1920 (an early effort to prevent excess profits) and by no longer requiring the ICC to update all valuations, though it still had to store the data on which revisions could be based. In addition, the act abandoned the 1920 act's ratemaking rule that allowed railroads a fair return on their property value. The new rule required the ICC to determine just and reasonable rates by their effect on traffic, shippers, and carriers. Finally, the 1933 act closed loopholes by giving the ICC authority over all railroad combinations, including holding companies; and, since valuation figures were often not available, it eliminated a rigid capitalization requirement for consolidations.

Coordinator Joseph B. Eastman, a member of the ICC, prepared reports that, if implemented, would have improved service and eliminated waste, but they were ignored by the carriers and no significant coordination of railroad facilities occurred. Eastman also made four reports to Congress, the second of which resulted in the 1935 Motor Carrier Act. Congress allowed his office to lapse on June 16, 1936.

References:

Ari and Olive Hoogenboom, *A History of the ICC: From Panacea to Palliative* (New York: Norton, 1976);

Earl Latham, *The Politics of Railroad Coordination, 1933-1936* (Cambridge: Harvard University Press, 1959).

—Ari Hoogenboom

Erie Railroad

by Richard Saunders

Clemson University

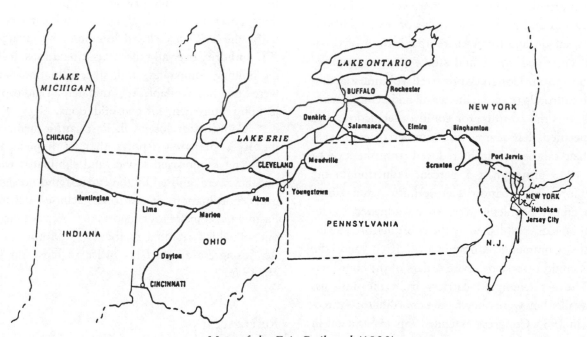

Map of the Erie Railroad (1930)

The original New York & Erie Railway opened in 1851 as a Great Lakes-to-the-sea route across southern New York State. Built to a six-foot gauge and 435 miles long, it was the first trunk line railroad (that is, a carrier extending a significant distance between two major terminals) in the world. Like many pioneer roads, it was underfinanced and plunged into receivership in 1859.

After it was reorganized as the Erie Railway in 1861, control passed into the hands of Daniel Drew, Jim Fisk, and Jay Gould, who became infamous as the Erie Ring. They fought off Cornelius Vanderbilt's effort to make the Erie part of the New York Central monopoly, but did so by watering Erie stock, writing the most sordid chapter of

Wall Street manipulation in an age that was notorious for sordid chapters. At the height of it, Drew, Fisk, and Gould escaped mobs of ruined investors by rowing across the Hudson by night and taking refuge in the railroad's fortress-like terminal in Jersey City, beyond the reach of New York law. The affair gave the Erie the reputation of "the scarlet woman of Wall Street" and left it with a near-worthless stock and hopelessly in debt, which three subsequent reorganizations—in 1874, 1895, and 1941—failed to wring out. The road became the New York, Lake Erie & Western Railroad in 1874 and the Erie Railroad in 1895.

As a railroad, the Erie was well managed and well maintained. It converted to standard gauge in

1880, though its broad-gauge heritage gave it an amazing ability to handle outsized shipments. Its lines were extended to Cleveland, Cincinnati, and Chicago, making it a true Northeastern trunkline, though only a fraction the size of its rival trunklines, the New York Central, the Pennsylvania, and the Baltimore & Ohio. The quality of its management was always good. So many chief executive officers of other railroads began their careers on the Erie that it was known as "the little red schoolhouse for railroad presidents."

During the presidency of Frederick D. Underwood from 1901 to 1927, the Erie was rebuilt to high technical standards and achieved a kind of golden age, even though no dividends were paid after 1907 because of its extraordinary fixed charges. The Van Sweringen brothers purchased huge blocs of Erie stock beginning in 1923 but were refused permission in 1926 and 1928 to bring the Erie under the control of their Chesapeake & Ohio (C&O) and New York, Chicago & St. Louis (Nickel Plate) lines, with eventual merger as the stated intent, because this arrangement did not conform to the Interstate Commerce Commission's plan of consolidation. In 1937 permission was granted for the C&O to control the Erie, but the Erie was forced into receivership the next year, effectively rendering its common stock worthless and hence the question of control moot.

The Erie never competed for the passenger traffic of the eastern cities but provided a gracious service that was proper for the small cities and towns along its line. In freight, it specialized in high-speed merchandise and perishable traffic. It may have been the quintessential American railroad, a railroader's railroad—double track, heavy rail, long trains, and high speed. Through much of its history, it may have enjoyed more genuine affection from the people it served and the people who worked for it than any other American railroad ever has.

But though it skirted the anthracite fields that made rivals like the Delaware, Lackawanna & Western rich, it never shared in much of the coal traffic. It had ominously little on-line freight, leaving it dependent on connections for traffic. It had extensive money-losing commuter operations in New Jersey. And it always had a crushing burden of debt and fixed charges. At its centennial in 1951 it was outwardly prosperous; but trucks were, even then, poised to skim away the merchandise traffic. Termi-

nal expenses, costly lighterage operations (the use of tugboats and car floats to move freight cars) in New York Harbor, New Jersey taxes, the sluggish growth of the northeastern economy, and the relative decline of the Port of New York overwhelmed it before the end of the 1950s.

In a cost-cutting merger with the Lackawanna in 1960 the Erie, renamed the Erie-Lackawanna Railroad, was the surviving corporation. Even as glasses were raised to toast its own merger, the prospect of a Pennsylvania-New York Central merger cast a long shadow. A combined Penn Central could divert traffic, particularly the interchange with the New Haven Railroad over the "Poughkeepsie Bridge Route," which accounted for nearly 20 percent of Erie revenues. The Erie Lackawanna—the hyphen was dropped in 1963—was a perfect complement to the emerging Norfolk & Western (N&W) system, and the N&W might have been interested had it not been for the Erie's nineteenth-century debt. On March 27, 1967, the Supreme Court ordered the N&W to acquire control of the Erie Lackawanna, which it did by merging the Erie Lackawanna Railroad into a new Erie Lackawanna Railway, which in turn was taken over by an N&W holding company, Dereco. But the N&W never wanted the Erie and never integrated it into its system.

Nevertheless, Erie Lackawanna service remained good, enabling it to score traffic coups like the daily high-speed piggyback train it ran for United Parcel Service. As the Penn Central collapsed in ruins, the Erie Lackawanna provided, for a time, the only reliable railroad service in the New York region. But the damage caused by Hurricane Agnes in the summer of 1972 was too much for its fragile financial circumstances. It entered receivership, which gave the N&W an opportunity to get out. Hope that its lines east of Akron might be acquired by the Chessie System collapsed over a failure to reach agreements with labor. In 1976 the property was conveyed to Conrail, which subsequently downgraded to secondary status, or abandoned entirely, nearly all lines west of Hornell, New York.

References:

Charles Francis Adams, *Chapters of Erie* (Ithaca, N.Y.: Cornell University Press, 1956);

Edward Hungerford, *Men of Erie* (New York: Random House, 1946);

Matthew Josephson, *The Robber Barons: The Great American Capitalists, 1861-1901* (New York: Harcourt, Brace & World, 1962);

Richard Saunders, *The Railroad Mergers and the Coming of Conrail* (Westport, Conn.: Greenwood Press, 1978).

Archives:

Papers related to the Erie Railroad are at the Syracuse University Library and at the Eleutherian Mills Historical Library, Wilmington, Delaware.

James H. Evans

(June 26, 1920-   )

by Maury Klein

University of Rhode Island

James H. Evans (courtesy Union Pacific)

CAREER: Loan officer, Harris Trust & Savings Bank, Chicago (1948-1956); secretary-treasurer and general counsel (1956-1957), vice president (1957-1962), Reuben H. Donnelley Corporation; financial vice president and director, Dun and Bradstreet, Incorporated (1962-1965); president (1965- 1968),

president and chairman (1968), Seamen's Bank for Savings; director (1965-   ), chairman (1977-1985), Union Pacific Railroad Company; president (1969-1977), chairman and chief executive officer (1977-1985), Union Pacific Corporation.

James Hurlburt Evans was born in 1920 in Lansing, Michigan, to James L. and Marie Hurlburt Evans. His father was a Baptist minister who moved to Louisville, Kentucky, when Evans was eleven. Although he would later call the change a severe case of culture shock, Evans grew to love Kentucky and attended Male High School in Louisville. A full scholarship gave him the means to attend Centre College of Kentucky, from which he graduated in 1943. He then served three years in the navy and earned the rank of lieutenant.

Evans received a J.D. from the University of Chicago Law School in 1948 but never practiced law. His work as editor of the *University of Chicago Law Review* in 1947-1948 had brought him into a close association with Prof. George Bogert, for whom he also prepared case notes. Bogert, a national authority on trusts and trustees, recommended Evans to the president of the Harris Bank, who wanted to experiment with a lawyer in a line position. A surprised Evans accepted a place as loan officer and found his career headed in new and unexpected directions.

The position at Harris gave Evans a solid background in oil and mineral operations, of which the bank did considerable financing. This experience would later prove invaluable to him. After eight years at Harris he joined the Reuben H. Donnelley

Corporation, which in 1957 promoted him to vice president and moved him to New York in a line management position. This position was, he later admitted, his "baptism of fire" as a corporate manager. When Donnelley merged with Dun and Bradstreet in 1962, Evans was made financial vice president and director of the latter company. Three years later he became president of Seamen's Bank for Savings, adding the title of chairman in 1968.

Although his rise as a corporate manager had been rapid and impressive, nothing in its course hinted at what was to come. Evans had never crossed paths with railroads except to ride them and work briefly as a youth in a mail car. His appointment only a few years later as president of the Union Pacific Corporation (UP) offers a striking illustration of the major changes that were sweeping the industry into a new era of development.

E. Roland Harriman, chairman of the Union Pacific board, got to know Evans through their mutual work with the Red Cross and invited him to become a director in 1965. At forty-five Evans found himself a young man among elders on the board at a time when the company was undergoing a significant reorganization. Like other railroads, the Union Pacific was anxious to free its nonrailroad assets from control by the Interstate Commerce Commission (ICC). To do so it needed both a revised corporate structure and management expertise in such fields as oil, minerals, land, and industrial development.

The company had taken the first step in 1961 by creating three divisions—transportation, natural resources, and land—each with its own chief executive officer. This reorganization removed the nonrail operations from the hands of the railroad president but not from the grip of the ICC. In 1967 the Union Pacific brought in as chairman of the executive committee a brilliant corporation lawyer, Frank Barnett, who was charged with creating a holding company to act as a vehicle for separating these assets. Evans served on the committee that chose Barnett; a little over a year later he found the tables turned when Barnett asked him to become president of the Union Pacific Corporation, which was formed in January 1969.

Barnett recognized that the Union Pacific required a new management structure in which the railroad would not dominate the other assets. The new corporation soon contained four subsidiaries: the railroad, Champlin Oil, Upland (UP land), and Rocky Mountain Energy. Evans played a key role in the acquisition of Champlin from the Celanese Corporation and in recruiting officers from other corporations to staff the nonrail operations. As president and vice chairman of the board, Evans handled the nonrail companies; Barnett had responsibility for the railroad.

A hard-driving but charming and affable executive, Evans was demanding without being imperious; he sized up people well and knew how to use his staff effectively. He was, observed one officer, "wonderful to work for if you did the job," and seemed never to forget the smallest favor. His gracious manner did much to help him implement the grand design perfected by Barnett and Robert A. Lovett, former chairman of the executive committee. In 1977 Evans was made chairman and chief executive officer of the Union Pacific Corporation and chairman of the Union Pacific Railroad. On July 1, 1985, he retired from these offices but retained his seat on the board.

Along with his service as director in several major corporations, Evans served on the boards of the New York Hospital, the Rockefeller Fund, the National Recreation and Park Association, the Red Cross, the Business Roundtable, the Foreign Policy Association, and the Business Council. He also served as trustee for both Centre College of Kentucky and the University of Chicago. The father of three children by a previous marriage, Evans married Mary Johnston Head in 1984.

John D. Farrington

(January 27, 1891-October 14, 1961)

by Dan Butler

Westark Community College

John D. Farrington

CAREER: Timekeeper for track gang (1909-1911), foreman (1911-1912), roadmaster (1912-1916), assistant trainmaster and trainmaster (1916-1917), assistant superintendent (1919-1920), superintendent (1920-1930), general superintendent (1930-1931), Chicago, Burlington & Quincy Railroad; general manager, Fort Worth & Denver City Railway (1931-1936); chief operating officer (1936-1942), chief executive officer (1942-1948), president and director (1948-1955), chairman of the board (1955-1961), president (1961), Chicago, Rock Island & Pacific Railway.

John Dow Farrington was born in St. Paul, Minnesota, on January 27, 1891, to Robert Irving and Caroline Burger Farrington. His father was financial vice president of the Great Northern Railway and a close friend of James J. Hill. Farrington attended St. Paul's Central High School and the St. Paul Academy.

His early life was involved with the Great Northern, where he worked summers with survey crews in Montana and Idaho. Determined to make a railroad career on his own and not rely upon the advantages his father could afford, he began full-time employment in 1909 with the Chicago, Burlington & Quincy (Burlington), where his first job was as timekeeper for a track gang. In 1911 he became a track gang foreman. His promotions came rapidly, and by the time America entered World War I he had advanced to the position of trainmaster.

In 1917 Farrington married Mary Canby, by whom he had three children. The same year he joined the army as a lieutenant and went to Europe with the engineer corps, rising to the rank of major. In 1919 he returned to the Burlington as an assistant superintendent. In 1920 he became superintendent of the railroad's Quincy, Omaha & Kansas City line and in 1922 was transferred to the St. Joseph division with the same title. One year later he was moved to the Aurora division. In 1930 he was made general superintendent of the Missouri district and then the combined Missouri and Iowa district. Farrington's record of increasing efficiency while keeping costs down led him in 1931 to leadership of the Burlington's Texas subsidiary, the Fort Worth & Denver City Railway.

Farrington managed the Fort Worth & Denver City for five years. During that time he rehabilitated much of the mainline between the two cities in the corporate name and built many important branch lines which tapped the area's vast resources. The line was praised for its increase in traffic that followed in the mid 1930s.

Farrington came to the attention of the management of the Chicago, Rock Island, & Pacific Railway because of an extensive study he did for the bond-holders of the Missouri Pacific. The Rock Island was in serious trouble in the middle 1930s. In 1933, after many years of bad management and rising debt, the line had passed into bankruptcy. New leadership was needed and in 1936 the receivers turned to Farrington, who had a reputation for obtaining ultimate service and performance out of each revenue dollar, to be the road's chief operating officer.

The state of Farrington's new employer was deplorable. Maintenance had long been deferred; track and bridges were in horrible condition. The line needed to be revitalized if it was to generate enough traffic to show an increase in earning power. New bonds were issued and the money was used to improve the company's trunk lines and bridges.

One of Farrington's most controversial moves was the introduction of streamlined passenger trains to the company's roster. The railroad had a bad reputation for service in both its freight and passenger operations, and he felt that the new trains would not only serve to increase public awareness of the railroad but also improve employee morale, which was low due to continued reports of possible dismantling of the line. The new trains were called Rockets. The first run, between Chicago and Peoria, had the desired effect: passenger revenue on the line increased. Similar trains were added to other cities, including Colorado Springs and Denver. These trains, plus improved maintenance, resulted in an increase in the company's overall revenues for the first time in several years.

Farrington was next faced with the rehabilitation of the line to the Southwest. The route had great potential but had been poorly planned and contained far too many curves and other obstacles. The most important improvement was the new bridge across the Cimarron River, which greatly increased operating efficiency. Farrington also added more diesel locomotives, making the Rock Island the first Western line to purchase them in large numbers. These expenditures, plus the abandonment of un-

profitable branch lines, further slowed the flow of red ink.

World War II accelerated the move toward profitability that Farrington had started during the previous five years. War traffic made 1941 the first profitable year since 1930, and Farrington was viewed with admiration by the rail industry. As revenues rose talk of ending the receivership increased; but the process would be slow, as various factions juggled for position. Ned Durham, who had been the line's chief executive officer since 1935, retired in 1942, and his position was immediately filled by Farrington. The modernization program continued at a rapid pace.

With the close of the war reorganization was the paramount issue; Farrington was hampered by problems with bondholders and trustees. Infighting between trustee Aaron Cohn and Farrington continued throughout 1946. After lengthy court delays the receivership was ended in December 1947, and Farrington was made president of the railroad.

The newly reorganized company was much healthier than at any time in its recent history: most of the track rehabilitation had been completed, new motive power was rapidly arriving, more than 650 miles of branch lines had been abandoned, and advanced signaling was in place on heavily trafficked routes. Passenger service was further upgraded by the introduction of the Golden State through service to southern California. Farrington continued his plans for construction of the large Armourdale classification yard near Kansas City and started work on a second major classification facility near Moline, Illinois. He actively pursued more industry along the line in order to lessen the company's dependence on agriculture. He issued new bonds to retire the last of the old debts.

Farrington continued to be a leader in innovation. The Rock Island became the first railroad to experiment with microwave transmission on its line across Kansas to Colorado. Later he upgraded service on the Rock Island's commuter routes out of Chicago. In 1949 he purchased the Pullman Railroad, an important switching line on the South Side of Chicago. With this acquisition came a large amount of real estate useful in his plan for further economic development.

In June 1949 switchmen went on strike, demanding increased wages and reduced working hours. The strike, which lasted two weeks, was costly for all concerned. Business lost during the period was hard to get back, and the reduced working time and higher wages further cut into the company's earnings.

The Korean War helped increase revenues but these were in part offset by poor crops in the Midwest and a series of disastrous floods in 1951. Nevertheless, the railroad continued to prosper under Farrington's leadership. In 1952, the centennial year of the company's founding, earnings were up and the system was in good physical shape. But Farrington failed to foresee the adverse impact the changing economy of the region the carrier served would have on his company.

Farrington's first wife died in 1954; the following year he married Doris Cowley Archer, a widow. Also in 1955 Farrington became chairman of the board of the Rock Island. The modernization program he had begun continued, but revenues declined as agriculture, a mainstay of the company's operation, continued to lag throughout the decade. Passenger revenue also dropped despite upgrading

of equipment and curtailment of service. The agriculture depression of the late 1950s further decreased income. In 1961 Farrington again assumed the presidency, which he held until his death in October of that year.

Farrington had revitalized the company and had kept it out of the hands of speculators after World War II, but he was unable to change the fundamental equation of the midwest: too many miles of railroad in a region with a shrinking economic base.

References:

William Edward Hayes, *Iron Road to Empire: The History of The Rock Island Lines* (New York: Simmons-Boardman, 1953);

United States Congress, Senate, *Financial Condition of the Rock Island Railroad* (Washington, D.C.: U.S. Government Printing Office, 1975).

Archives:

Papers relating to John D. Farrington are stored at the University of Oklahoma, Norman, but have not been catalogued.

Samuel M. Felton, Jr.

(February 3, 1853-March 11, 1930)

by H. Roger Grant

University of Akron

Samuel M. Felton, Jr., circa 1915 (Courtesy Roger Grant)

CAREER: Rodman, Chester Creek Railroad (1868); leveler and assistant engineer, Lancaster Railroad (1870-1871); chief engineer, Chester & Delaware River Railroad (1873-1874); general superintendent, Pittsburgh, Cincinnati & St. Louis Railway (1874-1882); general manager, New York & New England Railroad (1882-1884); assistant to the president, Erie Railroad (1884); general manager, New York, Pennsylvania & Ohio Railroad (1884-1885); vice president, Erie Railroad (1885-1890); president, East Tennessee, Virginia & Geor-

gia Railway (1890-1892); president, Louisville Southern Railroad and Alabama Great Southern Railroad (1891-1893); vice president, Memphis & Charleston Railroad and Mobile & Birmingham Railway (1891-1893); vice president, Knoxville & Ohio Railroad (1891-1892); president (1890-1893), receiver (1893-1899), Cincinnati, New Orleans & Texas Pacific Railway receiver, Columbus, Sandusky & Hocking Railway (1893-1899); receiver, Kentucky & Indiana Bridge Company (1893-1900); president, Chicago & Alton Railroad (1899-1907); president, Mexican Central Railway (1907-1909); chairman of board of directors, Tennessee Central Railroad (1909); president, Chicago Great Western Railroad (1909-1925); receiver, Pere Marquette Railroad (1912-1914); director general of military railways (1917-1918); chairman, board of directors, Chicago Great Western Railroad (1925-1929).

In the late nineteenth and early twentieth centuries Samuel M. Felton, Jr., was known as a "doctor of sick railroads." His accomplishments, especially at the Chicago Great Western Railroad Company (CGW) between 1909 and 1925, clearly reveal his vast managerial acumen.

Felton came from old American stock. His ancestors had settled in the Massachusetts Bay Colony in 1633, part of the "Great Migration" of Puritan dissenters. Felton was born in Philadelphia on February 3, 1853. His mother was Maria Low Lippitt Felton; his father headed a Pennsylvania Railroad affiliate, the Philadelphia, Wilmington & Baltimore, during the 1860s. The senior Felton won considerable acclaim throughout the industry for the adoption of a contract system of labor, a cost-cutting concept that his son would later unsuccessfully attempt to employ on the Chicago Great Western.

Felton attended Quaker-sponsored schools in Philadelphia, the nearby Pennsylvania Military Academy, and the Massachusetts Institute of Technology, from which he graduated in 1873 with a degree in civil engineering.

Felton had begun his career in railroading before he entered college. In 1868 he had started work as a rodman for the Chester Creek Railroad, a firm associated with his father's Philadelphia, Wilmington & Baltimore. After leaving MIT, he spent one year as the chief engineer for the Chester & Delaware River Railroad (subsequently part of the Reading system); then, in August 1874, the Pennsylvania Railroad-controlled Pittsburgh, Cincinnati & St. Louis Railway named him general superintendent. In 1880 Felton married Dorothea Hamilton, with whom he had four children. In January 1882 he moved to the New York & New England Railroad as general manager. Between 1884 and 1899 he took a series of assignments, including serving as receiver for the Columbus, Sandusky & Hocking Railway (Hocking Valley). Success with that woebegone company opened an important door. When Edward H. Harriman acquired the ailing Chicago & Alton Railroad in 1899, he knew of Felton's record as a railroad manager and asked this prodigious worker to take over as president. Felton stayed with the Alton for eight years. He then led the Mexican Central Railway from 1907 to 1909 and acted briefly as head of the feeble Tennessee Central Railroad before becoming president of the Chicago Great Western, which was just emerging from receivership in 1909.

There is no doubt that Felton excelled as a railroad leader. His greatest triumph before the Chicago Great Western was with the Alton, which he steadily turned from a dismal property into an efficient and prosperous one. Between 1900 and 1908 the road boosted its tonnage per train mile from 231 to a respectable 406, and net earning soared from $2,964,627 to $4,109,112. When Felton resigned to go to Mexico in 1907, Harriman wrote to him in glowing terms: "Your loyalty & faithfulness has been greatly appreciated & stands as one of the most gratifying results of the . . . Chicago & Alton enterprise."

Eminence as a railroader, however, did not mean human perfection. Apparently Felton's chief weakness was his personality; he did not possess especially likeable qualities. The editor of the Chi-

cago Great Western's house organ, the *Maize*, offered a favorable assessment, yet he hinted at the nature of Felton's temperament: "He is a strict disciplinarian, but eminently just in his rulings; quick to observe merit and equally prompt in rewarding it." Felton customarily showed arrogance, even contempt, toward underlings; he was gruff, humorless, and at times petty. The experience of Walter P. Chrysler, the CGW's superintendent of motive power, supports this assessment. Chrysler's initial impression of Felton was negative and was soon confirmed. Within a year after Felton took charge, he called Chrysler from Oelwein, Iowa, the railroad's operating hub, to the corporate offices in Chicago to ask him about a three-minute delay on the crack passenger train, the Great Western Limited. When questioned about this minor matter, Chrysler replied:

"Mr. Felton, I don't know."

"You don't know? You! The superintendent of motive power?"

"For a week I've been out over the divisions, inspecting the shops. I feel sure my chief clerk will have started an investigation on that delay. . . . As soon as I can get a little time in my office, I'll make a full report on the matter."

"You ought to know now. I shouldn't have to ask for a report."

That exchange proved too much for Chrysler. He quit on the spot, and the company lost a capable and loyal employee.

Felton spearheaded a major rehabilitation of the Chicago Great Western. With the financial backing of J. P. Morgan and Company, the property got hundreds of miles of heavier rails, treated ties, and crushed rock ballast. The 240-mile main line from Chicago to Oelwein received automatic electric block signals and more than 30 miles of double track. Felton thought that one way to increase freight train efficiency on the rugged segment of lines in northwestern Illinois and northeastern Iowa was to employ Mallet-type 2-6-6-2 locomotives. The CGW purchased ten of these giants from the Baldwin Locomotive Works in 1910 and rebuilt three of its own 2-6-2 Prairie types at the Oelwein shops into this unusual design. While these behemoths could pull a 4,000-ton train (the ordinary contemporary engine handled about 1,500 to 2,000 tons), they were slow, damaged the track, and were expensive to maintain. The innovative Felton also made the Chicago Great Western one of the nation's first major carriers to extensively employ internal combustion passenger equipment: in August 1910 the road introduced four gasoline-fueled passenger-mail-express units built by the McKeen Motor Car Company of Omaha to replace much more expensive steam-powered trains on local and branch line runs.

Between 1909 and federalization under the United States Railroad Administration in 1917, the Chicago Great Western experienced a golden period, perhaps the best in its entire history. Total net income amounted to $3,787,048 for 1916, up 45 percent over 1910, and the surplus reached $1,403,458 as compared to $360,536, a 289 percent increase. But government control wrecked the road's positive earnings pattern, and it never seemed to recover fully.

World War I gave Felton another opportunity to show his remarkable abilities as a railroad manager. On July 17, 1917, Secretary of War Newton D. Baker appointed him director general of railways; the name of the position was later changed to director general of military railways so as not to be confused with William Gibbs McAdoo's title as head of the United States Railroad Administration, director general of the railroads. Felton won considerable renown for shipping fully assembled locomotives to France, which experts had thought to be impossible. He also effectively supervised the movements of all American troops to the Atlantic seaboard.

After the war Felton resumed his duties at the Chicago Great Western. While he found the impact of the war and the Transportation Act of 1920 troublesome, he continued to improve the road's operating efficiency. For example, more and newer types of internal combustion-powered equipment appeared on the 1,500-mile property. Yet overall operating ratios did not improve dramatically, surely a disappointment to Felton.

On November 2, 1925, Felton, seventy-two years old and in failing health, stepped down from the presidency of the Chicago Great Western. He remained chairman of the board of directors, and the road was headed by his hand-picked successor, Nathaniel Lamson Howard. But a group of speculators led by Patrick H. Joyce, a railroad car manufacturer, sought an unfriendly takeover of the company, and at the October 7, 1929, meeting of the board of directors the Joyce forces were victorious. Perhaps fortunately for Felton, he did not live to see the decade of scandal and bankruptcy that would engulf the Chicago Great Western; he died in Chicago on March 11, 1930.

References:

Walter P. Chrysler, *Life of an American Workman* (New York: Dodd, Mead, 1950);

H. Roger Grant, *The Corn Belt Route: A History of the Chicago Great Western Railroad Company* (DeKalb: Northern Illinois University Press, 1984);

Norman W. Gregg, "Samuel Morse Felton: A Brief History of the Distinguished President of the Great Western," *Great Western Magazine* (February 1922): 5-6.

Archives:

The few extant papers of Samuel M. Felton, Jr., are at the Baker Library, Harvard University.

William W. Finley

(September 2, 1853-November 25, 1913)

by Keith L. Bryant, Jr.

Texas A&M University

William W. Finley

CAREER: Stenographer for the vice president (1872), assistant general freight agent (1873), New Orleans, Jackson & Great Northern Railway; assistant general freight agent, Chicago, St. Louis & New Orleans Railway (1873-1883); assistant general freight agent (1883-1886), general freight agent (1886-1888), Texas & Pacific Railway; general freight agent, Fort Worth & Denver City Railway, (1888-1890); chairman, Trans-Missouri Traffic Association (1889-1890); chairman, Western Passenger Association (1890-1892); general traffic manager, Great Northern & Montana Central Railroad, (1892-1895); third vice president, Southern Railway (1895-1896); second vice president, Great

Northern Railway (1896); second vice president (1896-1906), president (1906-1913), Southern Railway.

After a successful career as a freight and passenger agent and as a leader of regional traffic associations, William W. Finley joined the newly formed Southern Railway in 1895, and except for a brief period would be an executive of that carrier for seventeen years. Through his energy, tenacity, and strong leadership Finley reduced expenses, built up traffic, and saved the Southern from fiscal disaster.

Born in 1853 in Pass Christian, Mississippi, to Lewis Augustus and Lydia Rebecca Matthews Finley, William Wilson Finley received a public school education before joining the New Orleans, Jackson & Great Northern Railway as a stenographer in 1873. A diligent worker, Finley became an expert on freight rates. He became an assistant general freight agent of the Texas & Pacific Railway in 1883, and with his considerable skills in devising and implementing the intricate system of rate schedules then in use, was promoted to general freight agent three years later. At a time when thousands of rates were employed by the carriers and intense competition meant constant rate changes, Finley's great capacity for detail led to positions in regional traffic associations where his knowledge could be used to prevent, or at least alleviate, some of the frantic rate wars then common in the west and southwest.

By the mid 1890s Finley knew many of the major figures in railroading and had acquired an outstanding reputation as a marketer of transportation. Brought to the Southern Railway as third vice president in 1895 by its president, Samuel Spencer, Finley worked to create a profitable rate structure and to develop traffic for the carrier. He left the Southern for a position as second vice president on the Great Northern Railway in 1896 but returned to the Southern the same year as second vice president of that road. Within a brief period he made the railway's traffic department one of the most progressive in the country. Finley traveled over the system, met with shippers, solicited traffic, and made the Southern competitive in the region. He lobbied state legislatures against fixed rates, arguing that economic forces independent of the influence of railroad management often determined rates. In 1906 he had just launched an attempt to prevent severe rate restrictions by the southern states when Spencer was killed in an accident, and the board of the Southern elevated Finley to the presidency.

A "self-made man" who had achieved the presidency of one of the nation's largest railroads, Finley determined to carry on Spencer's consolidation and modernization programs. But whereas Spencer had been an ardent expansionist, Finley emphasized improvements and increased revenues. To that end he continued to work against excessive regulation and ratemaking by the states. Many progressive southern political leaders, however, such as Braxton Bragg Comer in Alabama, came to power pledged to lower railroad rates. Between 1907 and 1909 average passenger rates fell 11.7 percent; average freight revenues per ton mile also fell, though not as drastically. The carrier's revenues began to decline even as its needs for capital improvements—new equipment and signaling systems, bridge and track rebuilding, and new terminals and yards—dramatically increased. Efforts by North Carolina to reduce passenger fares led to the arrest of ticket agents, and even of Finley himself, and seizure of the railway by state officials before the Southern and the governor of North Carolina reached an agreement resolving the conflict. Finley spent much of his time giving speeches to explain the railway's need for revenues if a modern rail system was to be created.

Traffic growth peaked in October 1907, and the financial panic of that year almost brought the Southern to fiscal ruin. A steep decline in earnings forced Finley to cut expenditures. Employees were laid off, the number of trains was reduced, operating divisions were consolidated, and some capital improvement programs were terminated. Even so, Finley dispatched his assistant, Fairfax Harrison, to New York to obtain short-term loans to meet cash obligations for a few months. Borrowing from

banks and from J. P. Morgan and Company, Finley and Harrison got the company through the crisis, but dividend payments had to be canceled; only in 1912 would dividends on preferred stock be resumed.

Between 1907 and 1913, $49 million was reinvested in facilities and equipment. Hundreds of miles of double track, installation of heavier rail, new freight yards in Chattanooga and Atlanta, new bridges over the Ohio and Kentucky Rivers, and new passenger terminals in New Orleans, Mobile, and Birmingham took vast sums, as did the purchase of oil-burning steam locomotives, steel passenger cars, and freight cars with larger carrying capacities.

As work on the Panama Canal progressed, Finley solicited new business to ports in the south. He saw the canal as a definite gain for the carrier and the region. Finley directed resources to traffic agents along the line and throughout the country. Efforts by the railroad's land and immigration department to expand and diversify the south's agricultural production were intensified. Like Spencer, Finley wanted to end dependence on cotton and tobacco and the sharecropping, crop lien system. The company pushed crop diversification and the adoption of scientific farming methods, hired livestock and dairy agents and sent them throughout the region, and sponsored lectures and demonstrations for farmers. At the same time, the company's industrial department promoted sites for new businesses. Pamphlets and brochures extolling the south were published and distributed. Finley furthered the development of several industries, particularly textiles, lumbering, and manufacturing. The railway even dispatched a "Good Roads Train" to encourage county and state governments to build hard-surfaced roads to aid in economic development.

Finley also worked to establish good public relations for the company, believing that public animosity toward the railroads could be reduced by disseminating information and seeking understanding. He constantly gave speeches showing the importance of well-maintained, honestly administered, and prosperous railroads. While clearly advocating a position favorable to the railway, Finley was perceived as fair and just by his audiences. He traveled over 21,000 miles, addressing chambers of commerce, boards of trade, and civic groups and emphasizing a community of interest between the railroads and the public.

His efforts proved successful. Finley's public relations campaigns, shrewd financial management, and strong modernization program led the *New York American* to name him the third most successful railroad president in the nation in 1913. A group of bankers polled by the newspaper extolled his efforts to build traffic and diversify the region's agriculture and his oratorical skills. But just as his tireless efforts began to achieve the goals he sought, Finley suffered a stroke; he died on November 25, 1913. His widow, Lillie Vidal Finley, whom he had married in 1883, and their son and four daughters were joined by the employees of the railway in mourning Finley's death.

During the seven years Finley led the Southern Railway, gross earnings per mile increased by 40 percent even as a substantial modernization of the physical plant was being carried out. He got the railway through the panic of 1907 intact. The merit system he introduced provided for advancement for employees with a high level of service. A man of modesty and courage, Finley made a significant contribution to the Southern Railway and the south.

Publication:
Addresses and Letters of William Wilson Finley, President of the Southern Railway Company, 2 volumes (Washington, D.C.: Bureau of Railway Economics, 1907-1910, 1911-1913).

References:
Burke Davis, *The Southern Railway: Road of the Innovators* (Chapel Hill: University of North Carolina Press, 1985);

B. C. Forbes, "Here Are The Twelve Greatest Railroad Men in the United States," *New York American*, June 8, 1913.

Archives:
Correspondence, speeches, reports, and other documents by Finley may be found in the corporate records of the Southern Railway, Atlanta. Additional material may be found in a manuscript entitled "History of the Southern Railway System" by Carlton J. Corliss and Keith L. Bryant, Jr., in the same location.

Stuyvesant Fish

(June 24, 1851-April 10, 1923)

by John F. Stover

Purdue University

Stuyvesant Fish

CAREER: Clerk, Illinois Central Railroad (1871-1872); banker, Morton, Bliss and Company (1872-1877); director, Illinois Central Railroad (1877-1908); secretary (1877-1882), vice president (1882-1883), Chicago, St. Louis & New Orleans Railroad; second vice president (1883-1884), first vice president (1884-1887), president (1887-1906), Illinois Central Railroad.

Stuyvesant Fish was born in New York on June 24, 1851, to Hamilton and Julia Kean Fish. One of eight children and the youngest of three sons, Fish was a direct descendant of Peter Stuyvesant, the last Dutch governor of New Amsterdam. His grandfather was Col. Nicholas Fish, a sol-

dier in the Revolutionary War and a friend of Alexander Hamilton. His father had been a New York congressman and governor and later served as a United States senator and as secretary of state in the cabinet of U. S. Grant. After attending the best private schools in the city Fish entered Columbia College at the age of sixteen. He was chairman of the *Columbiad* Committee in his junior year and class president in his senior year. He received an A.B. in 1871 and an M.A. in 1874.

In October 1871 Fish became a clerk in the New York offices of the Illinois Central Railroad (IC), a prosperous and well-run midwestern railroad which had obtained a generous federal land grant in Illinois when it was organized in 1851. Twenty years later it was operating 706 miles of line in Illinois with a mainline from Chicago via Centralia to Cairo at the mouth of the Ohio River, a branch line running north of the Ohio River, and another branch line from Centralia via Bloomington and Freeport to Dubuque, Iowa. West of Dubuque a 400-mile extension ran across northern Iowa via Fort Dodge to Sioux City on the Missouri River. In the early 1870s the Illinois Central was paying a $10 annual dividend on its common stock and had a low operating ratio and a modest funded debt. During 1872 Fish served briefly as secretary to John Newell, president of the Illinois Central.

As the rail mileage of the nation increased from 39,000 to 70,000 between 1867 and 1873 many new brokers and bankers were appearing to meet the investment needs of the railroads. In 1872 Fish joined the New York house of Morton, Bliss and Company, a private bank which had been formed in 1869. Fish started as a managing clerk; later he was made a junior partner and for a short time was a member of the New York Stock Exchange. On June 1, 1876, Fish married Marian

Graves Anthon, the daughter of a New York City lawyer. The couple had four children: Livington, Marian Anthon, Stuyvesant, and Sidney Webster.

In the early 1870s the IC had become interested in two railroads which ran from Cairo to New Orleans and the Gulf. The depression of the mid 1870s forced the two roads into receivership, and during the spring and summer of 1877 the Illinois Central, with financial assistance from Morton, Bliss, acquired both lines and merged them to form the Chicago, St. Louis & New Orleans Railroad. William H. Osborn, a director and former president of the IC and a neighbor of Fish's in Garrison, New York, where Fish had a summer home, was elected president of the new company. In March 1877 Osborn arranged for Fish to be elected a director of the Illinois Central and in November made him secretary of the Chicago, St. Louis & New Orleans. Fish was also appointed treasurer and agent of the purchasing committee of the southern portion of the new line. In 1882 he was elected vice president of the Chicago, St. Louis & New Orleans.

One of Fish's business friends was Edward H. Harriman, who was three years older than Fish and the son of a Long Island Episcopal clergyman. Harriman had become a messenger clerk on Wall Street at the age of fourteen; later he had been a clerk in a broker's office, and at age twenty-two he had purchased his own Stock Exchange seat for $3,000. During the 1870s Harriman had invested in a Hudson River steamer, and later in a short railroad in upstate New York. He had improved the thirty-four mile road and sold it to the Pennsylvania for a good profit. In 1881, when Fish was offering the bankers of New York a major issue of Chicago, St. Louis & New Orleans bonds, Harriman took a large block of them. By 1883 he held as many as 15,000 shares of IC common stock, stock that was paying $8 a year in dividends. With strong support from Fish, Harriman was elected to the Illinois Central board in May 1883.

In 1883 Fish was elected second vice president of the Illinois Central; a year later he was made first vice president. On May 18, 1887, Fish was elected president of the Illinois Central; at thirty-five he was the youngest leader in the railroad's history. Earlier in 1887 Harriman had wrested control of the Dubuque & Sioux City, which the IC had been leasing since the late 1860s, from the rival

Drexel Morgan interests; in recognition of the coup Harriman was elected first vice president of the IC in September. The Harriman-Fish control of the railroad was to last for nearly twenty years. Harriman had far more IC stock than Fish, and in the working relationship between the two men Harriman was clearly the senior partner. Fish's expertise and experience were in fiscal and financial management; since the IC had its financial and transfer offices in New York, Fish continued to live there. Mrs. Fish became a leader in the social life of New York and Newport.

Fish became president of the Illinois Central in the year Congress created the Interstate Commerce Commission. Fish was not happy with the new regulation and in 1888 wrote a fellow IC official: "I do not blame the Commission but the usurpation by Congress of the right to inquire respecting matters not delegated by the states is but the beginning of an Inquisition. . . ."

The Illinois Central in 1887 had 2,355 miles of road in six states, from Sioux City and Chicago to New Orleans. Its equipment roster included 365 locomotives, 9,900 freight cars, and 350 passenger cars. About 8,500 workers earned an average pay of $580 a year. The gross revenue was about $12 million, of which about two-thirds was from freight. The freight tonnage was rather equally divided among farm, mine, and manufactured products. The operating ratio was 59 percent and dividends had been paid since 1861, with those in the 1880s ranging from $6 to $10 a year.

Fish and Harriman were intent on making their line a still better railroad. During the presidency of James C. Clarke from 1883 to 1887 plans had been completed for a bridge over the Ohio River at Cairo to replace the car ferries that had given connecting service with the southern line. The construction of caissons and bridge piers was well underway by the summer of 1887, and the placement of the twelve steel spans was started in June 1888. The four-mile structure (a 4,644-foot bridge plus over three miles of approaches) was completed by the late summer of 1889. The official opening of the $3 million bridge took place on October 29, 1889. Instead of a ribbon-cutting ceremony, an engineering test was to prove the safety of the steel structure. Shortly after 9:00 A.M. nine 75-ton Mogul locomotives coupled in tandem slowly moved out toward the central spans. In the cab of the lead engine behind the regular crew stood President Fish and Vice President Harriman. Lesser officials crowded the cabs and footboards of the engines to the rear. As the test train of nearly 700 tons completed its crossing, locomotive whistles were joined by those in Cairo and on riverboats in celebration of the event.

Improvements were also made in track and equipment. During the 1890s the last of the iron rail was replaced by steel on the principal lines of the system. By 1900 more than 40 percent of the rail on the IC weighed at least seventy-five pounds per yard. At $26 to $27 a ton, new steel rail cost a third less than the lightweight English iron rail laid on the original road in the 1850s. New rolling stock at the turn of the century was available at figures comparable to prices of the 1880s. In 1901-1902 the IC purchased fifteen Mogul freight locomotives at $15,500 per engine and four passenger engines for $16,600 each. Passenger coaches cost $8,500 each, and forty-foot, forty-ton freight cars were priced at only $525. Much new equipment was acquired as the Illinois Central expanded from 2,355 miles in 1887 to 4,400 miles by 1906.

Most of the 2,000 miles of line acquired during the Fish presidency was located in southern states, although minor extensions were made in Indiana and two new routes in Illinois served St. Louis. Considerable mileage was added in western Kentucky, and south of Fulton, Kentucky, a second line ran south via Memphis and Vicksburg to Baton Rouge and New Orleans. Much of the new mileage in Kentucky and Tennessee was acquired from Collis P. Huntington in 1893 after lengthy negotiations between Harriman and Huntington. Both Harriman and Fish believed that it was better to purchase roads than to construct them; in 1887 Fish had written to General Manager Edward T. Jeffery: "As you are well aware, my view is that it is wiser to buy existing roads than to build new ones."

Early in the Fish presidency two very different events in Chicago influenced the Illinois Central Railroad: the Columbian Exposition in 1893 and the Pullman Strike of 1894. As soon as a fair site near Jackson Park, on the South Side near Lake Michigan, had been selected, Fish promised the full support of the Illinois Central in making the fair a success. The location of the fair along the IC tracks assured the railroad of a local traffic to and from the fairground. Two extra tracks were built to the fair entrance to accommodate the crowds, the locomotive and car shops were moved away from the fairground, and a million-dollar combined station and headquarters building was constructed just off Michigan Avenue at the southern edge of Grant Park. During the six months of the fair more than 8 million visitors used the IC local trains, grossing $800,000 in revenue for the railroad. In contrast, the Pullman strike in late June and early July 1894 cost the railroad about $700,000 in destroyed property and lost revenue. When the Pullman Palace Car Company workers went on strike many IC workers either quit work or refused to handle any trains that contained Pullman cars. A train was derailed and forty-eight IC freight cars were burned before federal troops arrived and ended the strike. Without the personal popularity and good services of second vice president James T. Harahan, the Illinois Central might have had even greater trouble with its workers during the strike. The IC men knew that Harahan himself had once worked at the same tasks they were performing.

In the spring of 1901 the board of directors approved a pension plan for all IC workers which was quite generous for the time. Workers were eligible to retire at the age of seventy, or earlier under certain circumstances. The basic payment schedule was to be 1 percent of the worker's average pay for each year of service, with the average pay to be based on the man's last ten years of work. Thus a worker with forty years of service and pay averaging $50 a month during his last ten years would receive a pension of $20 a month. The average pay scale in 1901 ranged from $288 a year for section hands to $1,361 for locomotive engineers. Certainly the retiring IC workers in 1901 were more impressed with their new pension checks than with the bronze fiftieth anniversary medals most of them received that year.

In February 1901 President Fish led his railroad in celebrating the golden anniversary of the charter which founded the Illinois Central. With its more than 4,000-mile network in thirteen states the Illinois Central was among the ten largest railroads in the nation. Its property, including 918 locomotives, 772 passenger cars, and 36,000 freight cars, represented a total capital investment of $195 million with an annual revenue of $32 million. The leaders of the Illinois Central had much to be proud of as they assembled on Saturday evening, February 9, for their golden jubilee banquet. More than 150 government officials, railroad presidents, and top men of the IC listened as Fish reported that at long last financial control of the IC had returned to America, with more than three-fifths of the 600,000 shares of capital stock held in the United States; previously, English and Dutch investors had held a large majority of IC stock. The high point of the evening came when Harriman, a man who rarely spoke in public, rose to speak.

Harriman had given up his IC vice presidency nearly a dozen years before, but he had gained a certain primacy in American railroad affairs with his recent control of the Union Pacific (UP). Harriman gave high praise to the men who made possible the growth of the Illinois Central, concluding with a toast to Fish. Fish replied with a cordial toast for Harriman. In 1901 the two men seemed the best of friends.

During the Fish presidency the gross revenue of the Illinois Central quadrupled to more than $49 million by 1905. All types of freight increased in the period, but mine and forest products increased more rapidly than agricultural products or manufactured goods. By 1900 mine products amounted to a third and forest products to a sixth of the total freight tonnage. Fish was always looking for new types of traffic and in the early 1890s made George C. Power the first industrial commissioner for the Illinois Central. In his first five years Power saw 118 new plants located up and down the railroad. The growth in traffic and revenue made it easy to maintain a good dividend record. Annual dividends, which averaged 7 percent in 1880s, dropped to 5 percent in the depression 1890s but rose to 6 percent in 1901 and 7 percent in 1905. In 1905 the IC had paid annual dividends every year since 1861 and was a first-class line in the eyes of the investing public.

In the spring of 1906 there was evidence of a growing rift between Fish and Harriman. Earlier, from 1903 to 1905, Harriman had supported Fish when several IC directors had come to him with reports that Fish was depositing IC money in a small, weak trust company. About the same time, Harriman had made a personal loan to Fish to help him straighten out his financial affairs. But early in 1906 the IC president had clearly displeased Harriman by calling for a thorough review and investigation of the affairs of the Mutual Life Insurance Company of New York, a firm of which Fish was a trustee and in which Harriman had a substantial investment. When Harriman was not reelected chairman of the finance committee of the Illinois Central board of directors in April 1906, Eastern financial writers saw fresh evidence of a Harriman-Fish split. On April 6 the *Wall Street Journal* referred to Fish as the latest in a long line of "enemies or antagonists of one man, E. H. Harriman."

To be reelected president Fish would need the support of a majority of the board, which consisted of twelve elected members plus the governor of Illinois. Fish knew that Harriman controlled, directly or indirectly, a dominant share of all IC stock and that three members of the board were also directors of Harriman's Union Pacific. Fish himself held only a few hundred shares of IC stock. During the early summer of 1906 Fish quarreled with a pro-Harriman faction of the board over the process of requesting proxies for the election of board members of the annual stockholders' meeting. Fish claimed that if any additional board members were elected from the Union Pacific, the Illinois Central could be dominated by the UP. In midsummer the rival groups were reported to have worked out a compromise on the issue of new board members.

During the late summer and early fall of 1906 the Illinois Central headquarters reflected the tenseness of the Harriman-Fish struggle. Few officials cared to take sides in the controversy. Much of the nation's press seemed to favor Fish; *Railway Age* said: "The sympathy of practical railway officials seems to be with Mr. Fish, while Wall Street sentiment is not altogether favorable to Mr. Harriman."

At the annual meeting of shareholders in Chicago on October 17, 1906, Fish's nominee for a board vacancy defeated the choice of the Harriman group, but the Harriman faction was quick to charge that Fish had violated the "compromise" agreement made in midsummer. The controversy became more bitter, and the press predicted the ouster of Fish at the next meeting of the board of directors. Early in November the *Chicago Tribune* said that Harahan would be the next president of the Illinois Central. Fish desperately sought to crack the phalanx of directors who were supporting Harriman, but on November 7 the board met in New York City and by a vote of eight to four elected Harahan president of the Illinois Central, ousting Fish from the position he had held for nearly nineteen and a half years. Two years later Fish retired as a director of the railroad. The domination of the Illinois Central by the Union Pacific which Fish had predicted had not taken place.

During his last years with the IC Fish had been chairman of the seventh International Railway Congress held in Washington, D.C., in 1905, and president of the American Railway Association from 1904 to 1906. After leaving the Illinois Central Fish was a director of the Missouri Pacific for a time; later he was also a director of the Missouri, Kansas & Texas Railway. Fish had financial interests in several life insurance companies and was a director of the National Park Bank. He also spent much time in the management of two large family estates in Putnam County, New York. He made many speeches for the Association Against the Prohibition Amendment, serving as treasurer of the New York division of that group. Fish had a deep interest in history and served as the vice president of the New York Historical Society. He was a vestryman of Trinity Episcopal Church in New York. Fish died suddenly on April 10, 1923. His wife had died in 1915, and he was survived by a daughter and two sons.

The high point of Fish's railroad career was clearly his years as president of the Illinois Central. He was a popular executive, and his nineteen-year tenure was the second longest presidency in the history of the railroad. The Fish presidency was unique in several ways: his preparation for the post had been quite brief, his apprenticeship had been chiefly limited to the area of railroad finance, and his residency in New York made him almost an absentee leader. Fish was a quite adequate executive, but he was not one of the top men among the score of presidents who have led the Illinois Central since 1851. An assessment of his performance is rather difficult since he was so often working in the shadow of Harriman. Much of the growth and strength achieved by the Illinois Central during its early years must be credited to E. H. Harriman rather than to Stuyvesant Fish.

Publications:

"Nation and the Railways," *Annals of the American Academy of Political and Social Science*, 32 (July 1908): 125-137;

"Prohibition Results," *Current History Magazine of the New York Times*, 16 (June 1922): 377-385.

References:

Thomas C. Cochran, *Railroad Leaders, 1845-1890: The Business Mind in Action* (Cambridge: Harvard University Press, 1953), pp. 317, 320, 323;

Carlton J. Corliss, *Main Line of Mid-America: The Story of the Illinois Central* (New York: Creative Age Press, 1950);

George Kennan, *E. H. Harriman, A Biography* (Boston: Houghton Mifflin, 1922);

John F. Stover, *History of the Illinois Central Railroad* (New York: Macmillan, 1975).

Archives:

Business papers of Stuyvesant Fish are included in the Illinois Central archives at the Newberry Library, Chicago.

John P. Fishwick

(September 29, 1916-   )

by Keith L. Bryant, Jr.

Texas A&M University

John P. Fishwick in 1972 (AP/Wide World Photos)

CAREER: Lawyer, Cravath, Swaine and Moore (1940-1942); assistant to the general solicitor (1945-1947), assistant general solicitor (1947-1951), assistant general counsel (1951-1954), general solicitor (1954-1956), general counsel (1956-1958), vice president and general counsel (1958-1959), vice president, law (1959-1963), senior vice president (1963-1970), president and chief executive officer (1970-1980), chairman and chief executive officer (1980-1981), Norfolk & Western Railway; chairman and chief executive officer, Erie Lack-

awanna Railway (1968-1970); president and chief executive officer, Delaware & Hudson Railway (1968-1970); president, Dereco, Incorporated (1968-1981); lawyer, Windels, Marx, Davies and Ives (1981-1984); private legal practice, Roanoke, Virginia, (1984-   ).

John Fishwick returned to Roanoke, Virginia, in 1945, having been discharged as a lieutenant commander after three years of service in the navy, and joined the legal staff of his town's major industry, the Norfolk & Western Railway. Twenty-five years later he was named president of the company and for the next decade brought the carrier through the throes of mergers, labor disputes, and stringent federal regulation to make it one of the largest and most profitable railroads in the country. By the end of the "Fishwick years," the regional Norfolk & Western had become the dominant partner in the gigantic Norfolk Southern.

William and Nellie Cross Fishwick immigrated to the United States from England a few years after the turn of the century. Their son, John Palmer Fishwick, born in 1916, attended local schools and received a bachelor's degree from Roanoke College in 1937. He graduated from Harvard Law School three years later, having been admitted to the Virginia Bar in 1939. Young lawyers earned little in Roanoke in those days, so Fishwick joined the prestigious firm of Cravath, Swaine and Moore in New York. World War II ended that association. Before entering the navy Fishwick married Blair Wiley, and they eventually had three children. An Episcopalian and a Democrat, the able young attorney cast his lot with railroading, and became a nationally recognized figure in the industry.

For eighteen years the friendly, pleasant Fishwick labored in the vineyards of the N&W, moving through the ranks of the legal department; he shared duties there with Stuart Saunders and Robert B. Claytor, both of whom would also serve as presidents of the company. By 1958, when Saunders became president, the board of directors had reached the conclusion that the future problems of the railway could be solved only by someone outside the area of operations, which had been the traditional avenue to the presidency.

Immediately upon becoming president, Saunders moved to merge with the competing Virginian Railway; the merger was completed in 1959. With the Virginian came substantial coal reserves, more efficient operations over the Virginian's low-grade line, and a reduction in rail competition. As part of the legal team, Fishwick participated in the merger and traveled with the president and other executives to the board meetings in Philadelphia and to the negotiating sessions in New York. The Virginian was but the first step in creating a new Norfolk & Western.

In the 1960s Saunders and Fishwick—who became senior vice president in 1963—planned and carried out mergers with the Wabash and the New York, Chicago & St. Louis (Nickel Plate or NKP) and tried to bring the Norfolk & Western and the Chesapeake & Ohio together. They became key players in the "merger mania" of the nation's railways. The N&W was a profitable carrier, but Saunders and Fishwick saw the need to find new markets for coal north and west of the railroad's terminals at Cincinnati and Columbus. The property entered few cities; it needed independent connections. In 1959 Saunders quietly approached the president of the Nickel Plate about a merger. The stunned NKP president responded that the roads did not even connect, but Saunders was prepared to buy a line to provide a linkage. Even as Saunders acted the C&O began an effort to merge with the Baltimore & Ohio, thus encouraging the N&W to move more rapidly. The Pennsylvania Railroad agreed to sell its large interest in the N&W, but it insisted that the N&W-NKP combination take on another Pennsylvania-dominated property, the Wabash. Saunders and Fishwick suddenly faced the prospect of converting the Ohio-to-Norfolk carrier into a giant reaching Kansas City, Omaha, Chicago, Detroit, St. Louis, and Buffalo. Fishwick conducted the negotiations, and the Wabash was leased as

part of the merger plan, as was the Pittsburgh & West Virginia (P&WV).

For two years the Interstate Commerce Commission (ICC) studied the merger proposal, and in 1964 it agreed to a marriage of the N&W, NKP, and Wabash *if* the Pennsylvania disposed of its N&W stock, and if the new carrier would include in some way three weak eastern "orphans," the Erie Lackawanna (EL), Delaware & Hudson (D&H), and Boston & Maine (B&M). The price was high. The ICC was acting on the assumption that three major carriers would emerge in the East: the N&W, C&O-B&O, and the Pennsylvania-New York Central. Saunders had left the N&W to become president of the Pennsylvania in 1963; the new N&W president, Herman Pevler, formerly of the Wabash, joined Fishwick in carrying through the merger scheme.

In October 1964 the Norfolk & Western began to consolidate its holdings. The leases for the Wabash and P&WV were consummated, as was the acquisition of the Akron, Canton & Youngstown and the Sandusky line of the Pennsylvania to link the N&W to the Nickel Plate. A merger committee labored to work out the details, establish joint operations, and coordinate train movements. Management had demonstrated to the ICC that a merger would enhance service and profits; now all they had to do was prove it operationally. Diesel fleets had to be sorted out and regrouped; yards had to be reoriented for new trains and longer runs; equipment acquisition and use had to be made efficient; traffic solicitation had to be coordinated; and something had to be done about the orphans—the EL, B&M, and D&H.

Acquisition of the Erie Lackawanna would put the new N&W into New York City; the D&H would provide access to Montreal; and the B&M would mean a line into Boston and much of New England. They would also bring serious financial problems, and in the case of the EL, large debts. The merger of the Erie Railroad and the Delaware, Lackawanna & Western (DL&W) to form the EL had not produced a railroad that could compete effectively with the New York Central or the Pennsylvania. The B&M was a chronic loser with high operating costs and taxes in an area of declining industry, and it was plagued with Boston commuter traffic. The D&H was a profitable and well-managed bridge line, but it linked weak and declining connections. Besides, Fishwick hoped to arrange a merger of the N&W and the Chesapeake & Ohio, not the acquisition of three also-rans. Fishwick told Pevler that this brilliant idea had come to him in the middle of the night; he wanted to combine two of the most profitable railroads in the country.

As merger teams from the C&O and the N&W worked quietly under Fishwick on this stunning proposal, a scheme for the orphans was hatched. When the directors of the two railroads announced their merger plan on August 31, 1965, they proposed to create a subsidiary, a holding company called Dereco, Incorporated, to own five companies—the EL, D&H, B&M, and two carriers formerly under the wing of the Baltimore & Ohio, the Reading and the Central Railroad of New Jersey (CNJ). In light of the huge losses of the EL, $100 million since 1958, direct merger was impossible, and without the EL, there was no connection to the D&H or B&M. While it was hoped that the Dereco companies could save money through merger, the proposed C&O-N&W did not wish to acquire them, and their debts, outright. If this scheme gained the approval of the ICC, there would be two systems in the East—the C&O-N&W and the New York Central-Pennsylvania—not three. The N&W-C&O proposal staggered, and angered, the leaders of the proposed Penn Central, which would unite the Pennsylvania and the New York Central—a very upset Saunders could not believe what Fishwick was proposing to do—and the ICC refused to take action because the merger did not directly include the EL, D&H, and B&M. In 1967 the ICC ordered the N&W to take the EL and D&H into Dereco before merging with the C&O; the B&M elected to go its own way, and soon entered receivership.

In April 1968 Dereco absorbed the Erie Lackawanna and Fishwick, as a senior vice president of the N&W and president of Dereco, became chairman of the EL and then president and chief executive officer of the Delaware & Hudson when it entered Dereco in June. Pevler announced Fishwick's new titles and declared, "He is our best man." Fishwick moved to Cleveland to "do the best job I can for Erie Lackawanna and its security holders." He did manage to produce some net revenues, but his managerial skills were sorely tested. Although some thought that Fishwick had been given the

"booby prize" by the N&W, he moved to compete head-on with the Penn Central, trucks, the waterways, and even the parent company, the Norfolk & Western. The EL operated from northern New Jersey, where it had extensive commuter operations, to Chicago; along its entire route the largest city was Akron, Ohio. The old line of the DL&W paralleled the Erie out of New Jersey before breaking north to Buffalo. The EL had lost its coal traffic and the Penn Central was taking its fast merchandise business. The D&H remained profitable, but its on-line business was very limited and its bridge partners on traffic from Montreal to New York and Pennsylvania were being merged into units that no longer used the routing. It was also evident that the sophisticated team from the N&W was seen as condescending by the EL's old management, which had held their carriers together for decades. Fishwick used a low-keyed style and created a more relaxed environment as he sought to reassure the managements in Cleveland and Albany. He met the staffs in the executive departments and began to commute between the two headquarters. Fishwick "picked the brains" of the executives, raised questions about operations, proposed economies, and encouraged employees. He found the EL operating on a shoestring, with little modern equipment such as the N&W had. On the N&W Fishwick had taken for granted that there was plenty of cash available; on the EL he had to make sure that deposits would cover the payroll. But there was pride among the EL's workers, and he tried to capitalize upon that important intangible.

Dereco's subsidiaries had a decent year in 1968 as the EL earned $4.5 million and the D&H $800,000, but then one disaster after another befell the carriers. The Penn Central cut interline traffic and although profits rose slightly in 1969, operating ratios started to climb. Talented and efficient employees were producing meager earnings in a highly competitive climate, but the economy of the Northeast was deteriorating badly. The smokestack industries faced imports of lower cost and higher quality. Steel companies, automakers, machinery industries, and consumer goods manufacturers in the region cut back output and laid off employees, and the railroads suffered massive traffic losses. As the ICC gave preliminary approval to a merger of the N&W and C&O in 1969, Fishwick sought to keep his roads afloat. The Central of New Jersey had gone bankrupt in 1967, and the ICC ordered the N&W and C&O to help the CNJ, Reading, and B&M remain operational as a condition of merger. The next year Pevler retired, and Fishwick returned to the Norfolk & Western as president in this highly volatile atmosphere.

In 1971, after the ICC announced that it planned to reopen the C&O-N&W merger case in light of the 1970 bankruptcy of the Penn Central, the two carriers issued statements that they were abandoning the proposal. The EL began to run up large losses for Dereco that the D&H's small profits could not offset. The Reading and the B&M, meanwhile, joined the CNJ and the Lehigh Valley in bankruptcy. In 1972 Hurricane Agnes swept through the mid-Atlantic states and washed out 135 miles of EL trackage; in June the EL declared bankruptcy. "It grabs my guts to have to vote to do this," Fishwick declared. The N&W had put about $100 million into the EL and D&H, and had lost most of it; only the D&H remained solvent. In a massive rescue of the Eastern carriers, the federal government created the Consolidated Rail Corporation (Conrail), which began pulling the Penn Central, EL, Reading, CNJ, Lehigh & Hudson River, and Lehigh Valley into a single system. The N&W and C&O made it clear that they wanted to acquire nothing east of a line from Albany to Harrisburg—the "firewall," as Fishwick called it. During the next ten years Conrail would rationalize its property, spend billions of federal dollars to rehabilitate its lines, and become a formidable competitor for the Norfolk & Western. But at least the N&W no longer was responsible for the orphans.

With the regional economy worsening and with competitive pressures mounting, especially from trucking, Fishwick initiated a series of economy moves. The dividend rate was cut from $1.50 to $1.25 so that funds could be used to reduce debt. Hiring was frozen and other cost-cutting measures were introduced. Fishwick thought that the appearance of the N&W was poor and he directed a massive one-day clean-up of the entire 7,600-mile system. Labor and management turned out to collect tons of debris. Passenger operations were curtailed, and with the last run of the Pocahontas in 1971, all passenger service on the N&W ended. During their final year the passenger trains lost $4 million. In order to become part of Amtrak, which absorbed national passenger operations, the N&W

paid a fee of $18.5 million. Strikes by longshoremen, miners, and railroad workers continued to disrupt the flow of traffic and reduce earnings. Under Fishwick's constant urging the carrier accelerated its drive for greater efficiency. Automatic car identification systems were installed and the radio communications net was expanded. Roller bearings on more equipment and hot-box detectors reduced burned-out journals on wheels. Additional computers plus a computer training course for personnel introduced savings in management costs. Computers began to be used to locate and allocate freight cars and to get them out of the yards and over the road. The effort to improve productivity paid off: in 1972 the N&W handled 8.1 percent more business with no increase in man-hours.

There was also an aggressive approach to marketing. New ratemaking formulas for grain were applied to trainload rates for phosphates and soybeans. The N&W inaugurated "Mini Land Bridge" trains from Norfolk, New York, and Boston to points in California. With other railroads the N&W operated forty-seven run-through trains that were pre-blocked to destinations without changing engines at connections. The Roanoke shops constructed special freight cars for specific shippers—heavy-duty gondolas for United States Steel, for example. Mobile freight agents in trucks or vans replaced depot agents for greater flexibility and savings. Yet despite these efforts, the deterioration of the national economy caused profits to fall in 1975.

A revival of traffic, and further economies, brought record high earnings the next year and the lowest operating ratio—68.3—since 1966. The upsurge was partially due to rate increases finally granted by the ICC to the beleaguered carriers, but much credit has to be given the management team that Fishwick put together on the N&W. His executives produced an efficient, modern carrier that constantly upgraded plant and equipment. In their quest for savings they reinvested earnings and continued to acquire rail properties. The N&W bought 98 miles of Conrail trackage from Cincinnati to New Castle, Indiana, and cut the east-west route by 130 miles. The line was in a deplorable state and rehabilitation and Centralized Traffic Control (CTC) cost $26 million. Speed limits rose, however, from ten miles per hour to sixty. As net income increased, the board voted to split N&W stock three for one, and the debt retirement program was accelerated. While coal remained the backbone of N&W traffic, merchandise business improved, especially the piggyback trade. To increase efficiency the N&W and the C&O sought jointly to purchase the Detroit, Toledo & Ironton, but the ICC ruled against this effort at route rationalization.

In 1978 Fishwick faced one of his most difficult challenges. With more and more computerization taking place on the railway, the Brotherhood of Railway and Airline Clerks (BRAC) acted to preserve jobs for its members. As a new contract for the union was being negotiated, BRAC demanded that the union have prior approval of technological changes affecting clerk work, that 1,000 jobs not under BRAC rules be shifted to the union, and that BRAC members whose jobs were abolished receive financial or job protection. In July the union struck, and the company immediately initiated emergency plans to keep operating. The carrier had already classified all supervisory personnel according to their operating experience and had given them training sessions and examination. Management and the board were prepared to take the strike. "Service interruption insurance" in the industry generated $800,000 per day during the strike (some $58.4 million was received). When the other N&W unions honored the picket lines, 3,000 nonunion personnel operated the carrier on shifts of twelve hours per day, seven days a week; even Executive Vice President Claytor made numerous runs as an engineer on coal trains from Roanoke to Norfolk, and some old-time male employees learned to respect female supervisors who came aboard locomotives as engineers. By the third month of the strike half the normal trains were operating. Without work rule limitations, productivity soared and safety even improved.

As the strike continued through the summer some union employees came back to work and BRAC acted to broaden the strike. When forty-three railroads were picketed, shutting down freight traffic, President Jimmy Carter used the Railway Labor Act to appoint a fact-finding body. The strike ended in September, but not until the following January was a new contract signed. An exhausted management had kept the trains running and earned record profits, but the price paid in public relations, vandalism, and violence was high. The contract did not include BRAC approval of new technology and only 250 jobs were added to its jurisdic-

tion. The N&W did agree to job protection for up to five years.

The N&W supervisory personnel had learned that they could operate trains with fewer crewmen, that cabooses were unnecessary, and that the work rules seriously limited productivity. The operations had required leasing 227 engines from other carriers, however, as normal maintenance could not be conducted. Bad orders for cars (that is, cars needing repairs) and right-of-way maintenance demands remained heavy for months after the strike ended.

In 1979 the N&W initiated merger talks with the Southern Railway. Fishwick and Claytor looked on in alarm as the Chessie System and the Family Lines System (Seaboard Coast Line and Louisville & Nashville) filed a plan for merger. Continued federal support of Conrail with billions of dollars for rehabilitation, and the shedding of thousands of miles of redundant trackage, had made that carrier far more competitive. The talks with the Southern were broken off in the fall, but reopened in June 1980. By November an agreement had been concluded to form the Norfolk Southern. Fishwick had long contended that there would be four, or possibly six, coast-to-coast systems when the merger era ended, and he was determined that the N&W would be a leader in that development. Having reached age sixty-five, Fishwick retired as president and became chairman and chief operating officer of the N&W; he was succeeded as president by Claytor. But even as he stepped down, Fishwick's aggressive expansion policy continued as the N&W purchased the Illinois Terminal Railroad in central Illinois.

For a decade Fishwick had driven the N&W hard as the carrier expanded and became even more efficient. His impatience with leaders in the industry had become legendary, and his outspoken nature had not made him personally popular with other rail executives. A Wall Street analyst looking over the major portion of the "Fishwick years" said, however, that the N&W was not a railroad but "a money machine." Fishwick could take much of the credit for boosting the annual rate of return from 4.5% to 7.6% and yearly net income from $71.3 million to $232.4 million. He had ignored traditions—traffic gateways were abolished, passenger trains abandoned, new lines were purchased, and merchandise came to rival coal traffic through strong marketing tactics and new ratemaking. The number of employees in 1970, some 30,000, had been cut to 24,000 by 1977. The N&W of William J. Jenks and Robert H. Smith had been a prosperous regional coal-hauler operated by traditional railroad techniques. With Stuart Saunders, Fishwick made the company a national giant yet retained its high level of profitability. He succeeded where the Penn Central failed and where other rail giants continued to struggle. And he refused to retire, becoming a partner in a Washington law firm in 1981; "I wanted to prove I could do something other than run a railroad," he said. In 1984 Fishwick returned to Roanoke and established a private law practice.

Publication:

"N&W Railway Company," *Commercial and Financial Chronicle,* 218 (September 13, 1973): 791.

References:

Jeff Blyskal, "Railroads," *Forbes,* 131 (January 3, 1983): 178-180;

Luther S. Miller, "We Can Handle Adversity," *Railway Age,* 178 (September 26, 1977): 16-20;

Richard Saunders, *The Railroad Mergers and the Coming of Conrail* (Westport, Conn.: Greenwood Press, 1978);

"So Near and Yet So Far . . .," *Forbes,* 120 (July 1, 1977): 49;

"Southern and NW: Strength in Union?," *Railway Age,* 180 (April 30, 1979): 9;

E.F. Pat Striplin, *The Norfolk & Western: A History* (Roanoke: Norfolk & Western, 1981);

"The Way John Fishwick Runs the N&W," *Business Week* (June 10, 1972): 70-72;

Gus Welty, "Zeroing in on Productivity," *Railway Age,* 173 (September 25, 1972): 16-24.

Henry M. Flagler

(January 2, 1830-May 23, 1913)

by Seth H. Bramson

Henry M. Flagler (Collection of Seth Bramson)

CAREER: Oil and shipping commission agent (1853-1865); owner, grain shipping business (1865-1866); partner, Rockefeller, Andrews and Flagler (1867-1870); incorporator, founder and secretary-treasurer (1870-1882), vice president (1882-1908), Standard Oil Company; president, Flagler System, including Florida East Coast Railway, Florida East Coast Hotel Company, Florida East Coast Steamship Company, Model Land Company, and other subsidiaries (1886-1912).

Henry M. Flagler became known to the world upon completion of the Florida East Coast Railway extension to Key West, Florida. "Flagler's Folly," as it was called, was the final and most monumental work in his career as Florida's "Empire Builder."

Henry Morrison Flagler was born on January 2, 1830, in the little town of Hopewell in western New York, the third child of the Reverend Isaac and Elizabeth Morrison Flagler. Flagler engaged in various occupations as he was growing to manhood and eventually became associated with John D. Rockefeller. In 1867 Flagler became a full partner with Rockefeller in the firm of Rockefeller, Andrews and Flagler. That company was the immediate antecedent of the Standard Oil Company, which was incorporated in 1870.

As secretary of Standard Oil, Flagler worked closely with the railroads and was as responsible for Standard's notorious freight rebates as any other individual. Being a major shipper, Standard Oil had an immense amount of leverage and was able to dictate to the railroads, particularly the smaller ones, the terms of freight shipping contracts. As events of the Florida years were to prove, Flagler had a natural sense of industrial power, and he did not hesitate to use this power to the benefit of Standard Oil. Though Flagler was never to retire formally from Standard Oil, he vacated his office in New York in June 1882, and his influence upon the company diminished steadily from that point. The conservative estimate of Flagler's wealth at the time of his "retirement" from Standard Oil was between $10 and $20 million.

Flagler's first wife, Mary Harkness Flagler, whom he had married on November 9, 1853, died in 1881. On June 6, 1883, he married her nurse, Ida Alice Shourds. Their belated honeymoon took place in December of that year, and Flagler decided to vacation in Jacksonville and St. Augustine on Florida's east coast. While impressed with Florida's winter climate, Flagler wondered what St. Augustine might be like if some attention was lavished on the city, whose amenities were far below the standard to which he and his associates were accustomed. Flagler returned to St. Augustine on February 25, 1885, determined to create a resort worthy of himself and his ilk. On December 1 construction began on the Ponce de Leon Hotel.

Flagler, a man of less than average patience, quickly became unhappy with the management and operation of the rickety, narrow-gauge railroad that connected St. Augustine to the south side of the St. John's River in Jacksonville. The Jacksonville, St. Augustine & Halifax River Railway (JStA & HR) was the only direct rail connection with the outside world, and both the equipment and the trackage were in disrepair. Construction delays on the Ponce de Leon were common because supplies and material were constantly being held up somewhere along the line. Entreaties by Flagler to the road's management to improve conditions were met with courtesy, but nothing was done to alleviate the situation. Unable to cope with the dereliction and disinterest any longer, on December 31, 1885,

Flagler purchased the stocks, bonds, assets, properties and good will (such as it was) of the JStA&HR. With this modest investment began the events that would transform Henry M. Flagler into a figure of national interest. Flagler determined to rebuild the line to standard gauge and extend it south along the east coast of Florida. Meanwhile, the Ponce de Leon Hotel was completed on May 30, 1887, and formally opened on January 10, 1888, the beginning of the winter social season.

By 1889 the railroad was in Daytona Beach. Just north of Daytona, in the modest resort of Ormond Beach, stood the Ormond Hotel. In 1890 Flagler purchased the Ormond, retaining John Anderson and Joseph D. Price, the original builders and managers, to operate the property.

By 1894 the railroad had reached West Palm Beach. Palm Beach, across Lake Worth, became the site of two more links in Flagler's growing hotel chain. The Royal Poinciana, for a time the largest wooden building in the world, and the Breakers created a resort industry in northern Dade County. Eventually, Flagler's Florida East Coast Hotel Company would own or operate sixteen hotels—nine of them built while Flagler was still alive—from Atlantic Beach, east of Jacksonville, to Nassau in the Bahamas. The one property still owned by the company in 1987, the Breakers Hotel in Palm Beach, was one of the premier resorts of the world.

In December 1894 and January and February 1895 the worst freezes in history destroyed the citrus crop as far south as West Palm Beach. Sixty miles south of the freeze line an unincorporated area on the May-a-mi (Seminole for "Sweetwater River") had been untouched by the cold, and the produce of the area was healthy and growing. It was because of these freezes that Julia Tuttle, a widow from Cleveland, and William Brickell, a Dade County merchant, were able to demonstrate to Flagler that an extension of the railroad to Biscayne Bay would be a sound commercial venture. Construction of the extension began later in 1895, and in September of that year, the name of the railroad was changed to Florida East Coast Railway (FEC). The road reached Miami on April 15, 1896.

At the same time as the railroad was being extended along the east coast, Flagler was pursuing other commercial and realty ventures. Numerous land companies were incorporated, among them the Perrine Grant Land Company, Ft. Dallas Land Company, Chuluota Land Company, and Model Land Company. Flagler also operated the Florida East Coast Steamship Company, offering passage from Miami to Key West and Nassau, and, following completion of the railroad extension to Key West, from that point to Nassau. The steamship company was later merged with the Plant Steamship line (Henry B. Plant was the leading builder of railroads on Florida's west coast) to become the Peninsular and Occidental Steamship Company. Other Flagler enterprises included the Miami Water Works Company, the *Miami Herald*, the Jacksonville *Florida Times Union*, and a major interest in the Florida Coast Line Canal and Transportation Company, as well as shares in many other businesses along the east coast of Florida.

After Flagler married Ida Shourds, she had begun to show evidence of personality changes. Eventually, she developed what was then referred to as "dementia praecox," or schizophrenia. After a series of highly embarrassing incidents, Flagler determined to divorce her. Already a legend in the state, Flagler was able to convince the legislature to amend the law to make incurable insanity a ground for divorce. Several years later the legislature reversed itself.

On August 21, 1901, seven days after the divorce was final, Flagler became engaged to Mary Lily Kenan, an elegant and refined young woman with an aristocratic North Carolina heritage. On August 24 Flagler was married for the third time at the age of seventy-one. Mary Lily was thirty-four.

The new Mrs. Flagler had always desired to live in a marble palace, and in Palm Beach Flagler built for her what became one of the most treasured landmarks of Florida. "Whitehall" opened in time for the 1902-1903 social season.

In 1904, after having extended the Florida East Coast Railway south of Miami to the "red-lands" growing district of south Dade County, Flagler decided that it would be in the road's best interest to open a deep water port at the nearest point accessible to the Panama Canal. The canal, Flagler was convinced, would create an enormous new market for the FEC. Surveys were conducted, first to Cape Sable on Florida's southwest coast, and then to Key West. The route to Cape Sable, through the Everglades, proved to be totally impassable, and it was decided that the railroad would go to sea. On January 22, 1912, at a cost estimated at between $12 and $20 million, the extension to Key West—"America's Gibraltar"—opened. Flagler, addressing the deliriously happy crowd, said, "Now I can die fulfilled."

On January 15, 1913, at eighty-three, bent with age and nearly blind, Flagler was descending a staircase at Whitehall. He fell on the third step from the bottom, breaking his right hip. At ten o'clock in the morning of May 20, Flagler died peacefully.

Flagler was buried in St. Augustine on May 23. Every train, every machine, and every human being on the Florida East Coast Railway stood in silence for ten minutes.

References:
Seth H. Bramson, *Speedway to Sunshine: The Story of the Florida East Coast Railway* (Erin, Ont.: Boston Mills Press, 1984);
Sidney W. Martin, *Florida's Flagler* (Athens: University of Georgia Press, 1949).

Archives:
Henry M. Flagler's correspondence is in the Flagler Collection, Henry Morrison Flagler Museum, Palm Beach, and the Flagler Letters, Seth H. Bramson Collection, Miami Shores, Florida.

Florida East Coast Railway

by Seth H. Bramson

Map of the Florida East Coast Railway (1983)

The Florida East Coast Railway (FEC) is a 366-mile high-speed freight line, operating, as the name implies, between Jacksonville and Miami on Florida's east coast. The railroad was the result of the amalgamation by Henry M. Flagler of several predecessor railroads and became known as the Florida East Coast in September 1895.

On April 15, 1896, the railroad reached Miami, at that time an unincorporated village of a few hundred hardy souls. The FEC was the driving force behind Miami's growth. Flagler's publicists named Miami "The Magic City" and the east coast of Florida "The American Riviera."

In 1904 the FEC began construction of what has become the ultimate legend in American railroad building: the extension of the railroad across a series of tiny islands to Key West, 126 miles from the mainland. Overcoming the havoc wrought by

hurricanes in 1906, 1909, and 1910, the railroad pressed on to its goal, and on January 22, 1912, the largest gathering of people in Key West's history welcomed Flagler's arrival aboard the first train to reach that city.

Following Flagler's death in 1913, the railroad opened an extension through central Florida to the Lake Okeechobee farm region. During the great Florida boom of the 1920s the FEC double-tracked its main line, built what it called "the most modern railroad repair shops in the South," installed automatic block signaling the length of the railroad, reequipped its freight and passenger car fleet, bought new locomotives, and generally upgraded all facilities.

On September 17 and 18, 1926, the southeast Florida coast was lashed by a storm of monster proportions, killing over 400 people and causing hundreds of millions of dollars in damage to the Miami area. This storm broke the bubble of the boom, and Florida faced a major recession. By 1931 the FEC could no longer meet its fixed charges on equipment mortgages and was placed in receivership.

On September 2, 1935, one of history's worst hurricanes swept the middle Florida Keys, destroying forty miles of the FEC's right-of-way. The FEC filed with the Interstate Commerce Commission for abandonment, and the portion south of the mainland became known as "The Railroad That Died at Sea."

The railroad emerged from bankruptcy on January 1, 1961, as part of the Florida Du Pont interests, under the direction of financier Ed Ball. In 1962 the nonoperating unions demanded substantial wage increases, which the railroad could not meet. The FEC made ten separate proposals to the unions, but on January 23, 1963, the nonoperating employees struck the road, and other unions honored the picket lines.

On February 3, 1963, a train operated by supervisory personnel became the pilot for what would become America's most efficient railroad; the FEC has been a nonunion road ever since. Passenger service, restored briefly in 1965, passed from the scene in 1968, and the railroad has been freight only since that time. The FEC, as of 1987, has the lowest operating ratio (ratio of expenses to revenues), lowest labor cost percentage, and highest profit percentage of any Class I American railroad. It was the first railroad in the United States to eliminate cabooses from main line service.

References:
Seth H. Bramson, *Speedway to Sunshine: The Story of the Florida East Coast Railway* (Erin, Ont.: Boston Mills Press, 1984);
Pat Parks, *The Railroad That Died at Sea* (Brattleboro, Vt.: Stephen Greene Press, 1968);
George Pettengill, *The Story of the Florida Railroads* (Boston: Railway & Locomotive Historical Society, 1952).

Donald V. Fraser

(May 3, 1896-June 9, 1979)

by Don L. Hofsommer

Augustana College

Donald V. Fraser

CAREER: Clerk, American Car and Foundry Company (1912-1916); clerk, Missouri, Kansas & Texas Railway (1916-1918); statistician, United States Railroad Administration (1918-1920), chief clerk—purchasing (1920-1922), assistant to purchasing agent (1922-1925), Missouri, Kansas & Texas Railway; assistant purchasing agent (1925-1931), office manager, executive department (1931-1945), executive assistant (1945), vice president (1945), president (1945-1957), chairman (1957-1961), Missouri-Kansas-Texas Railroad.

Donald Vincent Fraser was among many of his generation of railroaders who rose through the ranks to become head of the company. Born at St. Louis in 1896, Fraser took employment with the American Car & Foundry Company before entering service as a clerk for the Missouri, Kansas & Texas Railway, which became the Missouri-Kansas-Texas Railroad (Katy or M-K-T) in 1923. When Matthew Scott Sloan died in 1945, Katy's board broke with its policy of bringing in outsiders for the top position and promoted Fraser from within.

Katy's plant and its financial condition had been weak before World War II, but with profits resulting from heavy wartime traffic Sloan had worked to make the company more efficient and attractive. These policies were continued by Fraser, who completed dieselization of the road's motive power, streamlined the famous jointly-operated Texas Special passenger train, bought new freight equipment, and improved signaling.

Political observers frequently noted that Warren G. Harding looked the part of a president; the same might have been said of Fraser. He was tall, broad-shouldered, with flowing white hair; his was a commanding presence. He frequently toured the property and was popular with employees. On the other hand, Fraser did not surround himself with especially talented people and his accomplishments at the Katy were limited.

Fraser's long suit was in public relations. He was an excellent front man who sponsored press trains over the Katy to allow important visitors an opportunity to gauge the productive potential of its service area, and who often found himself on the speaker's platform. In 1953 he told the Rotary Club of San Antonio that the country's railroads were a growth industry—"not necessarily in size but rather in the adoption of better and more efficient operating methods, technological improvements, and more realistic thinking on the part of management." Moreover, he noted, railroads recognized "the principle that business success today depends on industry's cooperation in promoting the maximum potentialities of local communities."

Yet the Katy was less and less able to aid in maximizing those potentialities. It fell on hard times shortly after the end of the Korean conflict, the quality of its plant eroding simultaneously with its service and its reputation. Fraser was not altogether at fault for this deterioration, but his leadership proved generally inadequate. In 1957 he was "promoted" to the chairmanship and to obscurity. He retired in 1961 and died on June 19, 1979.

References:

Willard V. Anderson, "Katy Serves the Southwest," *Trains* (April 1949): 16-25;

V. V. Masterson, *The Katy Railroad and the Last Frontier* (Norman: University of Oklahoma Press, 1952).

Francis J. Gavin

(December 15, 1880-April 7, 1962)

by W. Thomas White

James Jerome Hill Reference Library

Francis J. Gavin

CAREER: Office boy (1897-1899), clerk (1899-1905), timekeeper (1905-1906), chief clerk (1906-1911), trainmaster (1911-1916), divisional superintendent, assistant general superintendent, and general superintendent, Western district (1916-1919), general superintendent, assistant general manager, and general manager, Eastern district (1919-1936), assistant to president (1936-1939), executive vice president (1939), president (1939-1951), director (1939-1959), chairman of the board (1951-1959), Great Northern Railway Company.

Francis (Frank) J. Gavin was born in 1880 in Alberton, Prince Edward Island, Canada, to Peter and Anna Ryan Gavin. The family immigrated to the United States in 1888, and Gavin grew up in St. Paul, Minnesota, where he would spend most of his life.

Gavin attended high school but did not receive any formal university instruction. Instead, his was a rather typical "hands on" education in an age when comparatively few, usually economically privileged, individuals were able to attend college. In 1897, when he was sixteen years old, Gavin went to work as an office boy for what became his lifetime employer, the Great Northern Railway (GN). Though a comparatively young transcontinental railroad—it had not completed its line from St. Paul to Seattle until 1893—the GN, led at that time by its founder, James J. Hill, was a sound and fast-growing Victorian enterprise and a promising concern in which to begin a career.

Gavin received a series of rapid promotions during the ensuing decade and a half. From 1899 to 1902 he was a clerk in the GN's car agent office in Spokane, Washington, followed by a similar position for two years at Everett in western Washington. In 1905 he was appointed timekeeper in Spokane and the next year became chief clerk in the divisional superintendent's office there.

In 1911 Gavin was named trainmaster of the Great Northern's Kalispel Division with headquarters in Whitefish, Montana, followed by a 1912-1916 term with similar responsibilities at the important Spokane office. Then, at the comparatively young age of thirty-six, Gavin entered the railroad's major executive ranks. In 1916 he was named divisional superintendent at the vitally strategic Spokane headquarters. The following year he was promoted to assistant general superintendent of all western divisions, and in 1918 he became full superintendent of the Great Northern's western operations, headquartered in Seattle. Gavin's increased responsibilities and service in the Pacific Northwest enabled him to gain valuable administrative experience at a time when the railroad initially found itself in disarray and, subsequently, governed by the United States Railroad Administration during American involvement in World War I.

Immediately after the war Gavin was transferred to Duluth, Minnesota, as superintendent of the GN's Lake Superior district; he was promoted to general manager in 1929. During his time in Duluth he was particularly concerned with increasing the movement of iron ore from northern Minnesota's Mesabi Range to the railroad company's docks at Allouez, Wisconsin, from which it was shipped to steel, automobile, and other manufacturing plants on the Great Lakes. His success in this effort gained Gavin a reputation as an effective, highly efficient operations officer.

In 1936 Gavin moved into the highest echelon of the Great Northern's management hierarchy with his appointment as assistant to the president, W. P. Kenney, at St. Paul. Upon Kenney's death early in 1939, Gavin was named executive vice president and director and acted as interim chief executive officer until a new president was named. The Great Northern directors' first choice to lead the railroad was Duncan J. Kerr, a former GN operations officer then serving as president of the Lehigh Valley Railroad Company. Kerr suddenly contracted an incurable illness, however, and in September the directors elected Gavin the railroad's president.

Gavin's presidency came at a time of momentous change. Buffeted by the Great Depression, the railroad was ill prepared to meet the new economic world that would be ushered in by World War II and the immediate postwar years. In 1939 the GN's locomotive fleet was aged; its freight and passenger cars were also old, often of wooden construction, and too small to handle adequately the demands placed upon them; and track maintenance had declined during the 1930s.

The new president quickly addressed these problems, which were exacerbated by the rapid increase in rail traffic following the German invasion of Poland in September 1939. Most significantly, he committed the GN to dieselization, a program completed by his successor, John M. Budd. At the same time, the railroad upgraded its rolling stock, engaged in a system-wide program to improve its roadbed, and renovated its iron ore loading facilities on Lake Superior.

Gavin also restructured the Great Northern's debt. He was particularly concerned that its bonded indebtedness be reduced, and to that end, the GN did not immediately resume payment of dividends, which had been discontinued with one exception since 1932. The railroad's financial security, coupled with its prosperity during the booming war years that saw an explosion of economic activity in the Upper Midwest and the coastal cities of the Pacific Northwest, left it in an enviably sound position by 1945. Nonetheless, as demobilization began, the GN management remained apprehensive about the course of the immediate postwar world.

Indeed, costs did rise substantially, due in part to higher wages and inflation, while the growth of the rival trucking and airline industries meant increased competition for the railroad industry. At the same time, the GN benefited from its role as a carrier of raw materials and agricultural produce to feed the burgeoning national prosperity. Also, a rapidly growing population and increased industrialization in the Pacific Northwest, fueled in large measure by cheap hydroelectric power, created expanded opportunities for the Great Northern.

Gavin's role as president was basically that of a cautious steward; he did not embark upon bold new departures for the Great Northern. Throughout his career he shunned the limelight, preferring to work quietly and with little publicity. Gavin was completely devoted to the railroad's well-being: commonly described as having no hobby or serious interest outside the GN, he made innumerable inspections throughout the system during his presidency to maximize efficiency in its operations. His principal contributions consisted of general improvements in the GN's traditional operations. Improvements in the railroad's physical plant paralleled those in its locomotive and freight and passenger car fleets, including the streamliner Empire Builder passenger train that made its first run in 1947.

During his long career with the Great Northern, Gavin held a number of other posts, including directorships of the Chicago, Burlington & Quincy Railroad, the Colorado & Southern Railroad, First National Bank of St. Paul, First Trust Company of St. Paul, Mutual Life Insurance Company, and Western Fruit Express Company; he was also president and trustee of the Spokane, Portland & Seattle Railway and president and director of the Great Northern subsidiary, the Glacier Park Company. Gavin relinquished the presidency of the GN in 1951, moving up to chairman of the board. He retired in 1961 and died at the age of eighty-one on April 7, 1962.

References:

"The Great Northern Changes Chiefs: John Budd Succeeds F. J. Gavin," *Railway Age*, 130 (May 28, 1951): 37-38;

Frederick George, "Empire Builder's New Successors," *St. Paul Pioneer Press*, May 13, 1951.

Archives:

Francis J. Gavin's papers are in the Great Northern Railway Company Papers and the Northern Pacific Railway Company Papers, both at the Minnesota Historical Society, St. Paul. Gavin correspondence also is included in the Louis W. Hill Papers, James Jerome Hill Reference Library, St. Paul. The Ralph and Muriel Hidy Papers in the Hill Library include a twenty-three-page transcription of an interview the Hidys conducted with Gavin in August 1953.

George J. Gould

(February 6, 1864-May, 16 1923)

by Maury Klein

University of Rhode Island

George J. Gould (Courtesy Union
Pacific Railroad)

CAREER: Partner, W. E. Connor and Company

(1883-1885); vice president, Texas & Pacific Railway (1888-1893); president, Manhattan Elevated Railway (1888-1913); director, Union Pacific Railroad (1892-1895, 1898-1905); president, Missouri Pacific Railway (1893-1911); president, International & Great Northern Railway (1893-1911); president, Texas & Pacific Railway (1893-1913); vice president, Western Union Telegraph Company (1901-1910); director, Wheeling & Lake Erie Railway (1901-1906); president, St. Louis, Iron Mountain & Southern Railway (1902-1911); director, Western Maryland Railway (1902-1918); chairman, Wabash Railroad (1903-1905); chairman, Wabash Pittsburgh Terminal Railroad (1904-1908); chairman, Missouri Pacific Railway (1911-1917).

George Jay Gould was born in 1864 in New York City, the eldest son of Jay Gould and Helen Miller Gould. As heir apparent of the most notorious financier and railroad manager in the country, George found his destiny fixed in the cradle. At the age of twenty-eight he inherited command of his father's vast business empire; twenty years later, broken and humiliated on the field of combat, he surrendered active management of these once-proud properties and retired to live off his income. Like so many sons of great men, he proved the wrong man to succeed his father.

The Goulds were doting parents who showered their children with every advantage. One driving impulse behind the Gould empire was Jay's burning desire to bequeath it to his children, and from the first George was groomed to succeed his father at its head. As a child he received even more attention than his five brothers and sisters, and grew imperious as only a spoiled regent can be. He learned finance as a clerk for Washington E. Connor, in whose firm he became a partner at nineteen. Two years later he was given a seat on the New York Stock Exchange and his father's power of attorney. Gradually he took on more responsibilities for his father and replaced him on the boards of several companies. "My son represents my interest in these companies," Jay observed. "I can rely upon him. He has not only proven himself a good pupil but an able man."

Marked differences in style enabled George to escape the stigma of distrust and notoriety cast upon his father. Where Jay was shy and reticent, George grew affable and gregarious. He lacked Jay's keen eye and quick, penetrating intellect; indeed, some thought him rather slow-witted. His temperament was mercurial, subject to rapid swings of mood and hasty, careless decisions. The secretiveness that was Jay's trademark was not characteristic of George. George was slow to conceive a large plan, slower to execute it.

Congeniality served George as ingenuity had his father, with results more telling in society than in business. Where his father was indifferent to dress or display, George wore fine clothes, sported a well-trimmed moustache, and strutted like a dandy. Small and lithe, he loved fast horses, hunting, fishing, yachting, boxing, tennis, and fencing. He became an excellent polo player and did much to establish the game in the United States. His tastes ran to clubs, parties, and the theater.

A visit to the theater in November 1884 brought George his first glimpse of Edith Kingdon. A charming woman famed for her bewitching green eyes and hourglass figure, Edith was no ordinary actress but the daughter of a good family who had turned to the stage to help her impoverished mother. When an enchanted George became engaged to Edith without first telling his parents, he provoked a major crisis in the Gould household.

His mother, reared in the stiffly proper tradition of Murray Hill, nearly collapsed at the prospect of her son marrying an actress. By contrast Jay accepted Edith fully and was always fond of her. The marriage took place on September 14, 1886, at Lyndhurst, the Goulds' country estate, in funereal gloom before a handful of family and servants.

The death of his father in 1892 left George Gould atop a great business empire and catapulted him to the front rank of transportation leaders. Contrary to legend, Jay Gould left the Missouri Pacific in good condition by the standards of Western roads; it was George who let the system deteriorate through a combination of neglect and miscalculation.

The road's president, Silas H. H. Clark, who had been Jay's most trusted operations man for two decades, had for some time tried to handle both the Union Pacific and Missouri Pacific, with dismal results. Although desperately in need of an experienced operations man in St. Louis, Gould let Clark go to the Union Pacific in March 1893 and assumed the presidency of the Missouri Pacific himself. He named W. B. Doddridge as general manager but neglected to make him a vice president, which allowed him to be outranked by C. G. Warner, a capable vice president for accounts but not qualified to oversee operations.

As president Gould made little effort to master the property or understand its needs. He remained in New York instead of moving to St. Louis and relied on Warner to keep him posted. Instead of developing the system, he whittled mercilessly at expenditures to protect the dividend. During the next decade other systems endured the depression of the 1890s and jumped into massive improvements programs to ready themselves for the flood of traffic that poured forth after 1897. Lacking any feel for the road, the region, or the shipping public, Gould was in no position to anticipate this spectacular growth or capitalize on it. Gradually, inexorably, the Missouri Pacific slipped behind most of the other Western systems.

Instead of putting his house in order after 1900, Gould looked to expand the house. The business empire left him by his father embraced three major properties: the "Gould system" of railroads, Western Union Telegraph Company, and the Manhattan Elevated Railway. The rail system included the Missouri Pacific, Texas & Pacific, International & Great Northern, and Wabash, as well as a large interest in the Union Pacific. Under the management of E. H. Harriman, the true successor to Jay Gould, the Union Pacific was transformed into the strongest and most efficient road in the West. George served on its board, and his friendship with the ambitious, hard-driving Harriman may have helped kindle his own sudden desire to expand in all directions.

In February 1901 Harriman acquired the Southern Pacific, giving him a dominant position in transcontinental traffic. Gould asked him to give the Missouri Pacific a half interest in the purchase; Harriman refused but did put Gould on the Southern Pacific board. That same month Gould bought control of the Denver & Rio Grande, which in turn gained control of the Denver & Rio Grande Western in June 1902, giving him the only line to Ogden, Utah, other than the Union Pacific. Harriman demanded a half interest in the Rio Grande but was rebuffed by Gould, who offered him a seat on the board. A clash over the Colorado Fuel and Iron Company also created friction between the two men.

To the public Gould and Harriman seemed close allies wedded to the principle of harmony among railroads through what was called a "community of interest." In reality they were maneuvering for position, hoping to avoid the open fight that would surely follow if Gould did not submit to Harriman's lead. "He aims to dominate," Gould once said of Harriman's ambitions, "and if he don't like us he'll throw us out."

In his ingenuous way Gould believed that his presence on the boards of Harriman roads would check any hostile move or sneak attack. Meanwhile, his own ambitions soared to dimensions more suited to his father's abilities. Among the major systems Gould's was the only one with lines on both sides of the Mississippi River. Perhaps this configuration, coupled with resentment toward Harriman and the pace he set, inspired in Gould the notion of putting together a transcontinental system under one ownership. Only Tom Scott and Collis P. Huntington before him had even made the attempt; Jay Gould had long dreamed of such a scheme but died before he could accomplish it.

East of the river Gould controlled the Wabash, which connected St. Louis to Detroit and Toledo. In 1901 he acquired the Wheeling & Lake Erie, which ran from Toledo to Wheeling, West Virginia, and announced plans for a sixty-mile exten-

sion of the line from Jouett, Ohio, to Pittsburgh. A year later Gould picked up the Western Maryland, giving him a road from Baltimore to Connellsville, Pennsylvania, some forty miles southeast of Pittsburgh. A new company, the Wabash Pittsburgh Terminal Railway, was formed to build from Pittsburgh to Connellsville. Closing this gap would create a through line from the Atlantic to Ogden.

In the West Gould flirted briefly with W. A. Clark's new line from Salt Lake City to Los Angeles, only to have Harriman snatch it away. He talked of building an improved road between New Orleans and Houston to better compete with the Southern Pacific but abandoned the idea. The Rio Grande desperately needed improvements to handle an enlarged flow of traffic, but this sort of work seldom appealed to Gould, even though he paid lip service to it. Instead he let himself be wooed into constructing the great missing link in his transcontinental scheme: the Western Pacific, a 927-mile line from Salt Lake City to Oakland that would free him from all dependence on Harriman's roads.

Gould could not have picked more rugged challenges. His plans pitted him against the strongest rivals he could find on both sides of the Mississippi River. The mighty Pennsylvania Railroad under A. J. Cassatt controlled every line into Pittsburgh and had no intention of yielding its monopoly without using every trick in its book. Nor was Harriman about to let Gould build the proposed Western Pacific without a stiff fight. "If you build that railroad," he reputedly shouted at Gould on one occasion, "I'll kill you!"

The physical obstacles were as formidable as the opposition in both cases. Huge amounts of capital had to be mobilized and engineering problems had to be solved in brilliant fashion. For a time Gould tried to keep his connection with the Western Pacific secret, but he had a way of rowing to his object with splashing oars. When his role could no longer be concealed, in 1905, Harriman severed relations with him. Each man resigned from the boards of the other's companies, and the war began in earnest.

This two-front campaign would have taxed the resources of Jay Gould, whose nose seldom strayed from the grindstone. George Gould lacked both the brain power and the staying power of his father. He preferred hosting lavish entertainments at the huge mansion he and Edith had erected in Lakewood, New Jersey, and enjoying prolonged sojourns abroad. Despite the enormity of his undertaking, he thought nothing of leaving his officers in the lurch at key moments to go traveling. He would not allow decisions to be made without him, but he was not there to make them. His indecision was notorious, and he developed a reputation for heeding the last person to catch his ear. Possession of the Rio Grande, however, did bring him an able executive in E. T. Jeffery, the road's president, who became a sort of eminence grise for Gould.

"The last four or five years of George J. Gould's career in railroad finances," wrote a *New York Times* reporter in October 1905, "have been so crowded with contradictions, and 'Gould policy' has become so inscrutable to Wall Street, that members of the financial community refer nowadays to the Gould situation only in terms of bewilderment." Friends were deserting; the old Gould following in the market was fast disappearing; few trusted his plans anymore, so many having been burned too often in the past.

Both railroad-building campaigns turned into disasters. The Pennsylvania fought the Pittsburgh extension with savage ferocity. In May 1903 Cassatt, after the court granted him relief from his contract with Gould's Western Union, sent his crews to demolish 60,000 poles and 1,500 miles of wire along the Pennsylvania route. Beyond this bit of barbarism and other Pennsylvania tricks, the extension suffered from costly blunders, accidents, floods, landslides, strikes, and even an outbreak of smallpox among the workers. Poor planning and incredible shortsightedness resulted in an expensive white elephant reaching the poorest part of Pittsburgh on a single track over an elevated route. The sixty-mile line required twenty bridges and nearly sixty tunnels. "Such a jumble of viaducts, tunnels, bridges, cuts, fills, arches, trestles, and culverts civilization had never before seen," observed one critic.

The Western Pacific fared no better. Harriman threw every possible obstacle in its path, much as Cassatt had done to the Pittsburgh extension. The Rio Grande had to bear the immense cost, and Jeffery became head of the Western Pacific as well. Despite all difficulties, the road was well built and possessed what many deemed the finest route across the mountains. But it did not open until August 1910, and the final price tag neared a stagger-

ing $80 million. Moreover, its capacity for traffic was not matched by the Rio Grande, which had never been modernized and was not capable of serving as an efficient connector. And since the road crossed mostly desert and rough country, it lacked productive feeder branches and had to rely on through traffic carried at low rates.

The financial house of cards created by these projects shook violently during the panic of 1907, and then collapsed. In 1908 the Wheeling & Lake Erie and the Wabash Pittsburgh Terminal both went into receivership, followed later by the Wabash and the Western Maryland. The Rio Grande staggered under the burden of the Western Pacific until both fell into bankruptcy. The Missouri Pacific was also in trouble, its lines ravaged by neglect despite the efforts of some energetic officers to overcome Gould's inertia and policy of starvation.

By 1911 Gould could no longer avoid the final humiliation of surrendering control of the Missouri Pacific and the other lines in the "Gould system" to a syndicate headed by Harriman's ally, the banking house of Kuhn, Loeb and Company. Tired and discouraged, Gould also sold out the family trust's interests in his father's other great properties, Western Union and Manhattan Elevated. The money was put into conservative investments, and Gould gradually retired from active business to live off the proceeds.

Thus did the once promising crown prince, at the age of forty-eight, watch his empire crash in ruins, largely through his own ineptness. Trouble dogged his private affairs no less than his business interests. Two of his brothers and one sister made unfortunate marriages that proved a heavy drain on the family coffers. His other sister, the deeply religious and insufferably prim Helen Gould, never forgave George for wrecking the business empire put together by the father she adored. A bitter squabble among the children over the estate led to a suit in 1916 charging George with mismanagement. Three years later George was removed as chief executor and the estate was divided into six separate trust funds. Nevertheless, the suits dragged on until 1927, smearing the Gould name across the headlines and enriching whole battalions of lawyers in what was called the most expensive private litigation ever conducted. In his remarkable will Jay Gould had sought to keep the children united as trustees of his fortune under George's lead; instead, the bickering and legal infighting drove wedges between them that were never removed.

Amid all his tribulations, Gould looked elsewhere for consolation. The passing years, seven children, and a weakness for chocolates had ravaged Edith's figure. As early as 1887 a reporter had observed snidely that she "now weighs probably more pounds than her husband." During the winter of 1913-1914 Gould took up with a showgirl named Guinevere Jeanne Sinclair, whom he installed first in an apartment in New York and then in a house in Rye. Guinevere bore him three children that became known mordantly in the family as "George's bastards." Despite this liaison, Gould continued to live with Edith until her death from a heart attack on November 13, 1921. The following May 1 he married Guinevere and took her to Europe.

Gould may have planned to reside there permanently, but his own health was failing. For some time he had suffered from heart trouble and high blood pressure. After a visit to the newly opened tomb of King Tutankhamen in Egypt, Gould fell ill; he died of pneumonia at Mentone, France, on May 16, 1923.

Some claimed he was but one more victim of the curse of King Tut, and he may indeed have contracted an infection from the tomb. Even so, Gould had no need of outside curses; he had lived all his life under the curse of too great expectations. For all his ineptness and profligacy, he was in his own way a doting parent and reasonably competent businessman who might have done well in some more modest role. It was his ruinous fate to be the mediocre son of an extraordinary father, and to inherit a mantle that would have swallowed men far more talented than he. He proved to be the only one of Jay Gould's sons who did not amass a fortune by his own hand outside the family trust.

Unpublished Document:

W. L. Burton, "History of the Missouri Pacific," Union Pacific System archives, St. Louis.

References:

Burton J. Hendrick, "The Passing of a Great Railroad Dynasty," *McClure's Magazine*, 38 (March 1912): 483-501;

Ernest Howard, *Wall Street Fifty Years after Erie* (Boston: Stratford, 1923);

Edwin P. Hoyt, *The Goulds: A Social History,* (New York: Weybright & Talley, 1969);

Maury Klein, *The Life and Legend of Jay Gould* (Baltimore: Johns Hopkins University Press, 1986).

Grand Trunk Western Railroad

by James N. J. Henwood

East Stroudsburg University

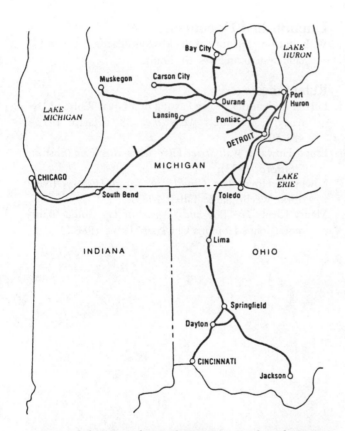

Map of the Grand Trunk Western Railroad (1983)

The Grand Trunk Western Railroad (GTW), was incorporated in 1928 to consolidate various Canadian National-owned lines in Michigan, Indiana, and Ohio. The name Grand Trunk goes back to 1852, when the Grand Trunk Railway was formed in Canada to build a line between Montreal and Toronto. An extension to Portland, Maine, was added in 1853; and a line from Port Huron, Michigan–opposite Sarnia, Ontario–to Detroit was opened in 1859.

The lines in the United States were assembled from the acquisition and consolidation of smaller roads, such as the Detroit & Pontiac, which had been completed in 1844. By 1870, a line reached from Detroit to Grand Haven, on Lake Michigan, where steamers connected with Milwaukee.

What would become the main line of the GTW, between Port Huron and Chicago, was constructed by several companies between 1871 and 1877. The properties were merged in 1880 to form the Chicago & Grand Trunk Railway. After a battle with William H. Vanderbilt, the Grand Trunk Railway of Canada purchased control in 1879. Emerging from bankruptcy in 1900, the Chicago & Grand Trunk was renamed the Grand Trunk Western Railway. Other acquisitions gave the GTW access to Toledo, Ohio, and Jackson, Muskegon, Bay City, and Caseville, Michigan. A tunnel under the St. Clair River between Port Huron and Sarnia opened in 1891.

The Canadian government created the Canadian National Railway (CN) in 1918 and in 1923 that corporation took over the Grand Trunk Railway of Canada, including its American properties. Ten American lines, including the Grand Trunk Western Railway, were consolidated by the CN in 1928 into the Grand Trunk Western Railroad.

Like its counterparts everywhere, the GTW experienced declines in traffic during the Great Depression and an upsurge during World War II. Major commodities carried included automobiles and auto parts, chemicals, and fuel. An extensive passenger service was offered between Chicago and Detroit, Port Huron, and Toronto.

In 1980, the GTW purchased the Detroit, Toledo & Ironton Railroad from Penn Central, which strengthened its position in the Detroit area. The following year the GTW purchased the Norfolk & Western's half-interest in the Detroit & Toledo Shore Line, giving the GTW sole control of that operation. Backed by the CN, the GTW remained a strong carrier in its region in the late 1980s.

References:

Patrick C. Dorin, *The Grand Trunk Western Railroad* (Seattle: Superior, 1977);

George H. Drury, *The Train-Watcher's Guide to North American Railroads* (Milwaukee: Kalmbach, 1984), pp. 86-88;

Charles R. Foss, *Evening before the Diesel* (Boulder, Col.: Pruett, 1980).

Carl R. Gray

(September 28, 1867-May 9, 1939)

by Maury Klein

University of Rhode Island

Carl R. Gray (Courtesy Union Pacific Railroad)

CAREER: Telegraph operator (1883), station agent and operator (1883-1886), chief clerk, traffic office (1886-1897), division superintendent, superintendent of transportation, general manager, second vice president (1897-1909), senior vice president (1909-1911), St. Louis-San Francisco Railroad; president, Spokane, Portland & Seattle Railway (1911); president, Great Northern Railway Company (1912-1914); president, Western Maryland Railway Company (1914-1919); chairman, Wheeling & Lake Erie Railway Company (1917-1919); director, division of operations under director general of railways, United States Railroad Administration (1918-1919); president, Union Pacific System (1920-1937); vice chairman, Union Pacific Railroad Company (1937-1939).

Carl Raymond Gray was a Southerner who was a descendant of Puritans. His parents, Col. Oliver Crosby and Virginia Davis Gray, were natives of Maine who had migrated to Princeton, Arkansas, where in 1858 Oliver Gray became head of Monticello Seminary. When the Civil War erupted, Oliver joined the Confederate army and rose to the rank of captain. After the South's defeat he taught school in Princeton, where Carl Gray was born in 1867, before moving to Fayetteville in 1874 to become professor of mathematics at the University of Arkansas. Carl completed the preparatory course there at the age of fifteen and planned to enroll at the university. Some members of the faculty, however, describing him as "six feet tall and thin as two clapboards nailed together," expressed concern about his health and advised him to remain out of school for a time. This proved to be his only flirtation with college.

The Gray home stood near the line of the St. Louis & San Francisco Railroad (Frisco), and Carl developed a fascination for trains. He hung around the depot, where the staff consisted of an agent, a telegrapher, and a helper, until he was put to work doing odd jobs. "I helped the helper," he later recalled. "I cleaned stoves and spittoons, rustled baggage and between times learned telegraphy. My wages were nothing a month, and I paid the telegraph operator to teach me what he knew."

From this experience Gray was to draw the same moral as many others who rose from humble origins to prominence: "If a young man starts in," he observed, "expecting to get to the top and keeps his eye on the top all the time, he'll never get there. But if he goes in for the love of it and works hard in every position he holds, and keeps his eye on that, he'll get there."

In March 1883 Gray gained a position as telegraph operator for the Frisco and worked at several stations until 1886, when he was made chief clerk in the traffic office at Wichita, Kansas. For nine years he toiled in the traffic department, learning the trade one step at a time. In 1897 he impressed B. F. Yoakum, vice president and general manager of the Frisco, enough to win a position as division superintendent at Neodesha, Kansas. At the age of thirty Gray had mastered the fundamentals of his trade in methodical fashion. During the next dozen years he advanced steadily through the ranks to the position of senior vice president.

Gray took special care to promote agriculture in the area served by the Frisco, hitting upon the novel idea of having the railroad establish scholarships in agriculture at all the state universities in its territory. He worked tirelessly to involve the company in the industrial and civic activities of communities along the route. Gray was the ideal representative for a railroad in an age when transportation companies were the object of dark suspicion and bitterness. A large, affable man without a trace of pretense or arrogance, he inspired confidence with his open, sincere manner. Even his rivals found him impossible to dislike or distrust. But Gray's good nature masked a shrewd mind and a remarkable ability to get things done with a minimum of fuss.

The redoubtable James J. Hill noticed these qualities in Gray and lured him to the presidency of the Spokane, Portland & Seattle Railway in May 1911. In taking charge of this road and a cluster of smaller Hill lines in Oregon, Gray found himself being groomed for a much loftier position. A year later Hill finally carried out the threat he had made so many times to retire from the Great Northern, yielding the chairmanship to his son Louis. Gray replaced Louis Hill as president of the Great Northern and was praised lavishly in the *Railway Age Gazette* for being alert, straightforward, and diplomatic, "especially in his dealings with the Interstate Commerce Commission and with the government."

At forty-five Gray might well have considered himself to have reached the pinnacle of his career. But Louis Hill discovered that he could not work with this most congenial of men and demanded an undated resignation that he put to use in 1914. Gray wasted no time on remorse when a fresh opportunity arose that same year. The Western Maryland had been reorganized into a profitable road from the ashes of its debacle as part of George Gould's ill-fated transcontinental line. Gray was tapped as its president and in 1917 became chairman of its connector, the Wheeling & Lake Erie, as well.

Under Gray's management the Western Maryland realized its potential as a first-class road. Along with his attention to practical issues he also developed a plan for creating under one management the shortest low-grade line between New York and Chicago. Although nothing came of it, the plan revealed a visionary quality in Gray that would one day loom large in his railroad work.

In December 1917 Gray was appointed director of operation and maintenance for the United States Railroad Administration (USRA), the federal agency that took over the nation's railroads during World War I. This position brought Gray into contact with leading railroad men from across the country and became the seedbed for his later career in rail diplomacy. It also enabled him to enter for the first time a larger arena in which to cultivate his views about the industry.

Gray remained in his federal post until January 1919, when he returned to his position with the Western Maryland and its affiliates. A year later he was asked by Judge Robert S. Lovett to take the presidency of the Union Pacific Railroad. Lovett had been chairman of that road's executive committee since the death of E. H. Harriman in 1909 except for wartime service as head of the Division of Capital Expenditures of the USRA, where his experience with Gray convinced him that he had found the right man for the job. Gray assumed the position on January 1, 1920, and remained with the Union Pacific for the rest of his life.

The change in jobs took place on the threshold of a momentous new era in railroad history. For more than half a century the railroads had owned the transportation industry. This dominance subjected them to constant attacks that culminated in strict regulation by state and federal agencies. The war added an ominous wrinkle when the government nationalized the railroads, leading to a spirited debate afterward on what to do with them once the crisis had passed. From this debate emerged the Transportation Act of 1920, which returned the carriers to private ownership but imposed on them even more stringent regulation just at the time they faced formidable new modes of competition. Suddenly the railroads found themselves no longer in command but fighting for their share of business under severe handicaps.

This new era required a different breed of manager, one adept not only at running a railroad but also at diplomacy. Gray was ideally suited to this role. By middle age the "two clapboards" had filled out to generous proportions spread over a large frame topped by a kindly face and a fine mane of prematurely white hair. Gray looked and acted the part of the sincere, benevolent leader who worked with his men and was accessible to them. "He inspires enthusiastic team work," noted one admirer, "by being enthusiastically one of the team; he is not a man who needs to guard his dignity by holding himself aloof." A devout Baptist, he earned from friend and foe alike praise as a fine Christian gentleman whose honesty was above reproach and who could always be relied on to do what he thought right.

The Union Pacific System had undergone major changes in the decade since Harriman's death. It had been forcibly separated from the Southern Pacific by the Supreme Court, which also denied it possession of the Central Pacific. A series of acrimonious rate disputes over the Ogden and Denver gateways had embroiled it with the Interstate Commerce Commission (ICC), and one case had gone to the Supreme Court. The system consisted of four main companies—the Union Pacific, Oregon Short Line, Oregon-Washington Railroad & Navigation Company, and the Los Angeles & Salt Lake Railroad—embracing nearly 8,200 miles of track.

Although still profitable, the system faced serious adjustments to the postwar environment and its new forms of modal competition. At the same time, the railroad's top management was undergoing a transition. The prewar generation of leaders was fast giving way to younger men, and Gray did much to facilitate this transfer of power. When Gray became president in 1920, Judge Lovett still dominated the road as the steward preserving Harriman's policies. By the time Gray retired in 1937 E. H. Harriman's son Averell had donned the mantle of leadership with the help of his brother Roland and Robert A. Lovett, the son of Judge Lovett. Gray's ability to work smoothly with all of these able men ensured for the Union Pacific a rare continuity in its management and traditions for over half a century.

Gray proved a strong and capable manager. Judge Lovett thought enough of him to reorganize the New York office in 1924 in a manner that reduced his own responsibilities while extending Gray's authority over all Western operations. Himself the most careful and exacting of executives, Lovett recognized that Gray possessed not only ability but also a good sense of where the industry was heading. Gray saw how radically the Transportation Act of 1920 had changed the ground rules, not only in the realm of rates and regulation but in the sensitive area of labor as well. The Railroad Labor Board created by the act had shifted the heart of negotiations from the carriers to Washington. Labor contracts were now negotiated at a national level, not by individual roads or regional groups; and the negotiations were now a three-way process, including the government as well as labor and management. Many observers were slow to grasp this fact.

Gray understood early certain crucial aspects of the new era: railroads had to stop fighting each other and join forces against modal competition, and they had to realize that the fulcrum of power was fast moving away from individual roads to Washington. To prosper, the roads had to present a unified front in the political arena. Gray had shown his hand as early as 1922, when a long and bitter strike thrust the railroads into confrontation with both the unions and the government. Once the strike was settled, Gray had helped promote a series of conferences that led to revision of the labor provisions in the Transportation Act.

Although Gray continued his missionary work among his fellow rail managers during the 1920s, the onset of the Great Depression lent a fresh urgency to his efforts. Ralph Budd of the Burlington credited Gray with being "more than any other man . . . responsible for the creation of the Western Association of Railway Executives in December 1932, and its unique plan for composing differences through the medium of a commissioner." Budd joined other rail presidents in urging Gray to become the new commissioner, but Gray did not want to leave the Union Pacific.

Two years later, in 1934, Gray joined several of his peers in forming the Association of American Railroads. The new organization soon emerged as the equivalent of a trade association for large railroads, providing services that ranged from statistical analysis to research to lobbying for or against federal legislation. Gray understood thoroughly the importance of the association to the carriers, and he missed no opportunity to urge its value on other executives. Those in government and industry alike valued his broad sense of vision. Franklin Roosevelt had taken Gray's measure early, having spent a long evening discussing rail policy with him during the campaign summer of 1932. The next year, when Roosevelt was toying with a new railroad program to ease roads through the Depression, Gray was mentioned prominently as a leading candidate to head it.

During Gray's tenure as president of the Union Pacific the old E. H. Harriman policy of aggressive maintenance was pursued vigorously. To hold passenger traffic, the road pioneered in the development of streamliner trains and in 1934 put on the first diesel locomotive built for transcontinental service. New tourist facilities were developed by the subsidiary Utah Parks Company at the Grand Canyon, and an upscale resort, Sun Valley, was constructed in Idaho and provided the company with more publicity than any advertising campaign. A new depot went up in Omaha, and a program of air conditioning for passenger cars was launched in 1932.

In some cases the Union Pacific fought modal competitors by joining them. In 1931 UP Stages Incorporated was formed to provide combined rail and truck service in three states. Bus service was pro-

vided for tourists between Cedar City and the national parks. New technology made freight hauling more efficient, and new locomotives made it faster. Between 1928 and 1935 the time on through mainline freight runs was reduced as much as 55 percent. The Council Bluffs-Ogden run, for example, was slashed from 80½ to 39½ hours thanks to the use of new locomotives capable of hauling heavy payloads at sixty miles an hour. The fleet of rolling stock was expanded and overhauled, as were several of the yards.

Much of this work took place during the Depression, when many roads were collapsing into bankruptcy or cutting maintenance drastically to survive the financial squeeze. Although Union Pacific earnings dropped sharply between 1929 and 1933, the company still turned a profit and paid dividends every year of Gray's presidency. More important, it emerged from the Depression in good physical shape, ready to handle the huge load of traffic thrust upon it by World War II. In 1936 a lease arrangement consolidated the separate lines into one company, enabling Gray to centralize accounting, treasury, and other operations in Omaha. That year also brought a harbinger of future profits when the Union Pacific began drilling for oil near Los Angeles on land owned by the Los Angeles & Salt Lake.

Having reached the mandatory retirement age of seventy, Gray stepped down as president of the Union Pacific on October 1, 1937, and was promptly named vice president of the board. For the next two years he remained active as a spokesman for the rail industry. Early in 1938 Roosevelt asked him to a White House conference on transportation; he was the only railroad man invited. Later that year Roosevelt named him to a committee of six (three from industry and three from labor) charged with submitting recommendations on the transportation situation. These recommendations would strongly influence the Transportation Act of 1940.

Roosevelt also used Gray as an advisor on matters relating to railroads and national defense. At a transportation symposium in February 1939 Gray warned that "utter chaos" loomed unless a coherent national policy was adopted. A week earlier he had told a House committee that "no major war can be successfully waged by this country without a thoroughly efficient system of railroads in high physical condition." He had just completed a joint memorandum with Daniel Willard of the Baltimore & Ohio on the subject of handling rail transportation in the event of war when, on a May morning in 1939, he was found dead of heart disease in his bed at the Mayflower Hotel in Washington.

Gray's sense of family was as strong as his sense of duty. On December 6, 1886, at the age of nineteen, he had married Harriette Flora of Oswego, Kansas, a girl of seventeen. Half a century later the Union Pacific Old Timers sponsored one of the most remarkable tributes ever organized, a sitdown dinner for 1,400 in the Omaha city auditorium to honor the Grays on their golden anniversary. Friends and associates poured in from across the country to attend the affair. Deeply moved, Gray said of his wife, "She's been my inspiration, my helpmate, and my partner at every step of the way." It was precisely the brand of graciousness those who knew Gray expected of him. Two of the couple's three son's followed their father into the railroad business; the third became a surgeon at the Mayo Clinic.

Modesty and humor were not the least of Gray's virtues. Ralph Budd remembered him as a fine companion and "master story teller." Another long-time associate, Eugene McAuliffe of the Union Pacific Coal Company, recalled the time they were together in Gray's business car when the engineer hit the brakes hard at slow speed and tossed his distinguished cargo around. When the conductor came running back gushing apologies, Gray flashed his gentle smile and told him to go forward and tell the engineer about the young soldier who, crossing the parade ground at dusk, overtook a man in uniform and whacked him sharply between the shoulder blades. To his horror the face turning toward him belonged to the colonel of the regiment. The young soldier turned pale and tried to blurt out an apology, certain that the guardhouse awaited him.

"That's all right, my boy," said the colonel. "I don't mind the mistake in the least, but be sure you don't try slapping a second lieutenant."

Reference:

Neil M. Clark, "The Top Is All That Can Stop You if You Keep Going Up," *American Magazine*, 99 (June 1925): 171-175.

Archives:

Many of Gray's business letters are in the records of the Union Pacific Corporation, New York City, and some are in the Union Pacific Museum, Omaha.

Great Northern Railway

by Don L. Hofsommer

Augustana College

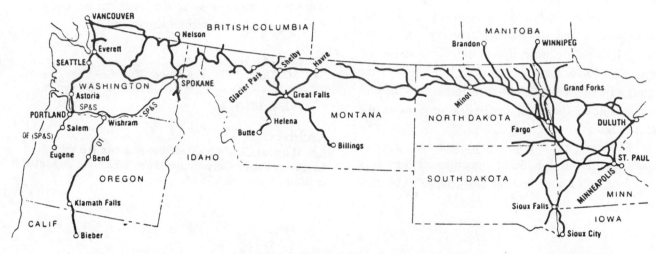

Map of the Great Northern Railway (1940)

The history of the Great Northern Railway (GN) began in 1857 with a charter issued to the Minnesota & Pacific Railroad. In keeping with the traditions of frontier railroads, however, the first train steamed into the record much later and under a different corporate flag. After the Minnesota & Pacific defaulted, the St. Paul & Pacific Railroad took over its charter and gave Minnesota its first rail service—between St. Paul and St. Anthony, ten miles up the Mississippi River from the state capital on the site of present-day Minneapolis—on July 2, 1862.

Again in the tradition of frontier railroads, the St. Paul & Pacific fell on hard times and passed to others. James J. Hill and his associates reorganized the property in 1879 as the St. Paul, Minneapolis & Manitoba Railway. The new company did, in fact, link the Twin Cities with Manitoba, but Hill was looking farther to the west, and in 1889 the more expansive-sounding Great Northern designation was adopted to reflect construction toward Pacific tidewater. In this effort Hill employed John F. Stevens, a locating engineer, to determine the lowest possible grades over the Rockies and Cascades; Stephens was remarkably successful, and when the line was completed to Seattle in 1893, Hill could boast an amazingly easy profile for the GN.

Until he died in 1916, Hill consistently pressed programs to reduce grades and ease curves on principal routes, to increase the volume and quality of agricultural produce in the GN's service area, and to expand the GN's domain through the acquisition of rail lines and the institution of allied nautical operations on the Great Lakes and from Pacific ports.

That Hill's values had been institutionalized to become the hallmark of the GN's corporate culture was reflected in 1929, when the GN completed its famous 7.79-mile Cascade Tunnel in Washington, and in 1931, when it extended operations into California. In all cases, the GN was known for efficiency of operation—a fortunate tradition given the vicissitudes of the Great Depression. The GN survived the hard times of the 1930s as it had earlier survived the panic of 1893.

Prosperity returned during World War II, when new yearly records were set for freight traffic in 1942, 1943, and 1944 and for passenger business in 1944 and 1945. The GN also participated in the postwar prosperity. The company was well served by Hill's tradition of producing transportation at low cost; additionally, it was ably managed by talented and devoted presidents, including Ralph Budd and John M. Budd, who continued to perfect the road's profile and who embraced new data—processing procedures and advanced marketing techniques.

On March 3, 1970, Hill's long dream of greater efficiency through merger was realized when the Great Northern was merged with the Northern Pacific, the Chicago, Burlington & Quincy, and the Spokane, Portland & Seattle to form the Burlington Northern.

References:
James J. Hill, *Highways of Progress* (New York: Doubleday, Page, 1910);

Albro Martin, *James J. Hill and the Opening of the Northwest* (New York: Oxford University Press, 1976);

Charles and Dorothy Wood, *The Great Northern Railway: A Pictorial Study* (Everett, Wash.: Pacific Fast Mail, 1979).

Archives:
The Great Northern Railway Company Records are at the Minnesota Historical Society, St. Paul.

Guilford Transportation Industries

by David H. Hickcox

Ohio Wesleyan University

Guilford Transportation Industries, a holding company formed by Timothy Mellon of Pittsburgh's wealthy Mellon family, was named after the Connecticut town where Mellon resided. In 1981 Mellon purchased the Maine Central Railroad from U.S. Filter Corporation and in 1982 he completed acquisition of the bankrupt Boston & Maine Railroad. Purchase of the Delaware & Hudson in 1984 from Dereco, Incorporated, a subsidiary of the Norfolk & Western Railway, expanded Guilford's trackage to approximately 4,000 miles, extending from Calais, Maine, west to Buffalo, New York, and from Washington, D.C., north to Montreal.

Mellon's goal was to develop the first truly regional railroad in New England, a railroad which would prosper, he believed, from renewed economic vigor in the area. Although the three railroads retained their separate identities, operations and facilities were consolidated and a common paint scheme was applied to locomotives. Springfield Terminal Railway, a wholly owned short line with lower operating costs, operated most of the Maine Central as well as most of the Boston & Maine's and the Delaware & Hudson's lightly trafficked branch lines.

Guilford's primary traffic base of paper products moving south and west from Maine's numerous paper mills is supplemented by other goods moving to and from New England. Intense competition from the trucking industry, internal problems, and a depressed New England economy have kept Guilford from reaching its potential. Guilford's early years were marked by labor unrest as management attempted to significantly reduce the labor force. A system-wide strike in 1986 resulted in federal intervention and was the primary factor in the Boston & Maine's losing its lucrative contract to operate commuter services to Boston for the Massachusetts Bay Transportation Authority.

As of 1987 Guilford's future was unclear due to depressed levels of traffic, the unresolved labor problem, and uncertainty regarding the future ownership of Conrail, Guilford's primary competition.

Archives:

The corporate records of Guilford Transportation Industries are at the firm's headquarters in North Billerica, Massachusetts.

Gulf, Mobile & Ohio Railroad

by James H. Lemly

Map of the Gulf, Mobile & Ohio Railroad (1950)

The Gulf, Mobile & Ohio Railroad (GM&O) was born out of the travails of the rail industry during the Great Depression. The troubles besetting the properties which merged into the GM&O go back much further, however. A history of early promise collapsed due to the poor engineering, poor management, and excessive stock and bond manipulation which plagued several of the companies that became the GM&O in 1940.

The oldest of the merged properties was the Mobile & Ohio Rail Road (M&O). Started in 1848 in Mobile, Alabama, the line's objective was to replace steamboat service on the Mississippi

River between Mobile and the Ohio River. Local communities helped financially, but the real impetus to build came from the grant of land to the states of Alabama and Mississippi under the first railroad land grant bill, which was passed by Congress in 1850. The M&O stopped at Columbus, Kentucky, thirty miles down the Mississippi River from its confluence with the Ohio at Cairo, Illinois, in April 1861; it did not reach Cairo until 1882. After the Civil War the M&O declined to regional and local status. In 1901 the Southern Railway System acquired control, which it held until the GM&O was created.

The other predecessor companies of the GM&O were the Mobile, Jackson & Kansas City Railroad and the Gulf & Chicago Railroad, begun well after the Civil War and built principally in east Mississippi. Although construction was often haphazard and engineering was almost nonexistent, the lines joined at Decatur, Mississippi, in 1906, with trackage from Mobile to Middleton, Tennessee. The companies went bankrupt that year and were combined and reorganized in 1909 as the New Orleans, Mobile & Chicago Railroad. That company failed in 1913 and was reorganized as the Gulf, Mobile & Northern Railroad (GM&N) in 1917. By 1919 the road had built north to Jackson, Tennessee, where it reached significant connections: the Illinois Central, the Nashville, Chattanooga & St. Louis, and the Mobile & Ohio all had tracks to the north from that point. Success was assured when the GM&N hired Isaac Burton (Ike) Tigrett as president late in 1919. The Tigrett management team and operating style brought about a near miracle, and by 1927 the GM&N profitably operated about 1,000 miles of line instead of the 409 it had had in 1920.

The GM&N had to struggle through the Depression, however. It had several conflicts over its trackage agreements to reach Paducah, Kentucky, for a beneficial interchange point with the Chicago, Burlington & Quincy Railroad. For long-term strength, the GM&N needed a more secure entry to its northern traffic connections. Thus, in the mid 1930s the GM&N began its struggle to acquire the older, longer, but relatively ineffective Mobile & Ohio. After extensive discussions, the Southern Railway agreed to sell its first mortgage M&O bonds for about 93¢ on the dollar if the GM&N could effect a merger.

The Illinois Central strenuously opposed the merger and the Chicago, Burlington & Quincy's attitude was lukewarm at best. Finally, after many compromises had been made with unions and other parties, the Interstate Commerce Commission agreed to the merger on October 13, 1939. All obstacles were slowly removed and on September 13, 1940, the new Gulf, Mobile & Ohio Railroad emerged with about 2,000 miles of line between St. Louis on the north and New Orleans and Mobile on the south.

During World War II the GM&O prospered, but continued to look forward. In 1944 studies were begun to investigate merging the ailing Alton Railroad into the GM&O. With the support of the Burlington, the GM&O developed its plan to acquire the stagnant Alton from its unhappy parent, the Baltimore & Ohio (B&O). The B&O was willing to release the Alton for a nominal sum if the GM&O agreed to protect all existing traffic gateways. With this proviso, the merger was completed in May 1947.

The GM&O management team, largely the group Tigrett put together in the early 1920s, now managed over 2,800 miles of main line stretching from Chicago to Mobile and New Orleans. It was a successful if not rich rail property, and its managers had won the respect and admiration of much of the rail and business world. It also had the confidence and, to a remarkable degree, the affection of the people and customers along its lines.

The Gulf, Mobile & Ohio merged with the Illinois Central Railroad in 1972 to form the Illinois Central Gulf.

References:

James H. Lemly, *The Gulf, Mobile and Ohio: A Railroad That Had to Expand or Expire* (Homewood, Ill.: Irwin, 1953);

Robert P. Olmsted, *GM&O North* (N.p.: Olmsted, 1976).

Archives:

The most significant collection of Gulf, Mobile & Ohio corporate records is held by the library of the University of South Alabama, Mobile.

Fred G. Gurley

(February 20, 1889-July 4, 1976)

by Keith L. Bryant, Jr.

Texas A&M University

Fred G. Gurley (Santa Fe Railway photo)

CAREER: Various clerking positions (1906-1911), junior positions in the operating department (1911-1920), division superintendent (1920-1925), general superintendent (1925-1932), assistant vice president (1932-1939), Chicago, Burlington & Quincy Railroad; vice president (1939-1944), president and chairman of the executive committee (1944-1957), chairman of the board of directors and chief executive officer (1957-1959), Atchison, Topeka & Santa Fe Railway.

Fred G. Gurley spent his career with two of the nation's major railways, the Chicago, Burlington & Quincy (CB&Q) and the Atchison, Topeka & Santa Fe. An expert in motive power development and utilization, Gurley believed in the acceptance and adaptation of new technology and in managerial innovation. An ardent economic and political conservative, Gurley favored right-to-work laws and the elimination of work rule restrictions on management in labor relations. As a fiscal conservative, Gurley reduced the carrier's debts even as he reinvested earnings in equipment and betterment projects. Leading the Santa Fe in a time of general national and regional prosperity, Gurley pursued a course that produced profits and gained for the Santa Fe a reputation for a high level of service.

Gurley was born in Sedalia, Missouri, in 1889 to Horatio Nelson and Mary E. Glasse Gurley; when he was four years old, his father was killed in a railway accident. He attended the public schools in Kansas City and Warrensburg, Missouri, and after graduating from high school he attended an engineering school for a year until his mother moved the family to Sheridan, Wyoming. There his older brother, Hayes, got a job for him in 1906 on the Chicago, Burlington & Quincy as a trainmaster's clerk. During the next thirty years Gurley moved through the ranks of the CB&Q. By 1920 he was a division superintendent, although he was only thirty-one years old, and in 1925 he became a general superintendent. His excellent work brought him to the attention of the Burlington's president, Ralph Budd, who made him assistant vice president in 1932. On the Burlington Gurley became widely recognized for his talents in operations and his enthusiasm for new technology. He strenuously argued the case for diesel locomotives, and in 1934 he rode in the cab and personally supervised the record-breaking run of the Zephyr from Denver to Chicago. His promotion of this new motive power brought him an offer of a vice presidency from the Santa Fe, and Gurley joined that carrier in 1939.

The president of the Santa Fe, Edward J. Engel, immediately put Gurley to work on the introduction and expansion of diesel locomotives in passenger, freight, and yard service. Gurley toured the system, gave speeches on dieselization, and published papers on the use of diesels in high-speed passenger service. He urged the purchase of 5,400-horsepower freight diesels to work the main line in California, Arizona, and New Mexico, where poor water supplies kept steam locomotive operating costs high. After the United States entered World War II the Santa Fe could obtain few new diesels, but those in service proved fuel efficient, had a high level of availability, and were cost effective.

The war taxed the Santa Fe heavily. Gurley and Engel had to meet great traffic demands as troops and munitions were hauled to the West Coast. Farmers in the Santa Fe's territory produced bumper crops that had to be moved to Chicago, California, or Gulf ports. Petroleum products were carried from Texas, Oklahoma, and Kansas to destinations throughout the system. The opening of military bases in the Southwest added to the Santa Fe's burdens. The company lost personnel to the draft and hired women as replacements in virtually all job classifications. Although the war generated profits, it also brought excess profits taxes, but Gurley and Engel used substantial sums to retire debts and to purchase equipment when it was available.

When Engel retired in 1944, the board of directors named Gurley his successor. Since 1939 these two men had spent $200 million on rolling stock, signaling systems, and track improvements. Gross revenues had risen from $160 million in 1939 to $471 million in 1943. Gurley intended to continue this betterment program as soon as the war was over. He determined to pursue every possible innovation to raise efficiency and profit levels. "I've always believed we should stay awake at night," he said, "looking for new technology, new techniques."

Even before the war ended, Gurley predicted that the railroads would be challenged by the airlines for passenger business in the postwar era. To meet that competition and to try to retain the vast increase in passenger traffic generated by the war,

Gurley ordered the acquisition of new stainless steel passenger cars to create a fleet of streamliners for the Santa Fe. The Super Chief and the Chief had been equipped with new passenger cars from E. G. Budd and Pullman-Standard before 1941. After 1945 the Santa Fe obtained additional streamline cars to upgrade trains from Chicago to Kansas City, Oklahoma City, and Los Angeles. New trains to Houston (the Texas Chief) and San Francisco (the San Francisco Chief) were introduced. Gurley's staff worked with the car builders to design "hi-level" equipment, which provided for seating and services at two levels, and placed these cars on trains such as El Capitan. Dome cars, luxury sleeping cars, lounges, and new diners cost tens of millions of dollars, but the Santa Fe acquired a national reputation for quality passenger service and Gurley never gave up hope that the passenger traffic would earn profits.

Gurley refused to accept a subordinate role for the Santa Fe at any level of competition. The carrier served Dallas directly from Houston, but because the Chicago-to-Houston main line was through Fort Worth, freight shipments to and from the north reached Dallas in a circuitous manner. The Missouri Pacific, Missouri-Kansas-Texas, and other competing railroads, as well as trucking firms, had a distinct advantage. In 1955 Gurley directed the construction of forty-nine miles of new line into Dallas, which saved half a day on freight shipments. This line was the longest stretch of new trackage built in the United States in twenty years. The Dallas branch not only gained an advantage for long-distance freight shipments but it also provided access to an area of the city that enjoyed substantial growth and development for the next thirty years.

Under Gurley's leadership the Santa Fe became the second most profitable railroad in the nation. *Time, Fortune,* and *Business Week* extolled the management of the carrier, noting the managerial training program Gurley established at the University of Southern California for Santa Fe executives. Believing that managers needed to know more than just railroading, he arranged for USC to provide six-week programs each summer for Santa Fe "juniors," young people moving up through the ranks. They studied economics, political science, and economic history literally day and night. One employee commented, "Nowadays we really have to keep on our toes. Mr. Gurley asks so many questions and wonders about so many things that we constantly have studies going on or are trying out something new."

Under Gurley the company began to develop additional industrial sites on Santa Fe properties and to purchase land for industrial development. He visited potential investors, urging the location of facilities on the sites, and he worked with chambers of commerce to promote manufacturing in their locales. The industrialization and urbanization of California, Texas, Oklahoma, and Arizona after 1945 created new traffic for the Santa Fe, and the carrier played a major role in fostering economic expansion.

In interviews or meetings the tall, lanky Gurley would begin by saying, "Well, now my philosophy on this is . . . ," and would proceed to analyze the question or issue. Santa Fe executives and staff found him approachable, and he always emphasized teamwork. Morale on the system was high although Gurley staunchly defended management prerogatives on labor questions. An outspoken promoter of state right-to-work laws, Gurley advocated "freedom" and "individual choice." In 1952 he worked for Dwight D. Eisenhower's nomination and election as president, and he often provided his private car to the Eisenhowers on their trips to Palm Springs.

Gurley loved to travel over the Santa Fe, if possible in the cab of a diesel unit. "I'd rather see where I'm going than where I've been," he said. His forward-looking administration of the railway produced profits exceeding those of the New York Central, Pennsylvania, and Southern Pacific, although those roads had larger revenues. Dieselization enhanced profits, as did efficiency gained through Centralized Traffic Control, line rebuilding, and new freight cars. Gurley reduced fixed charges by paying off long-term debts and equipment trusts. As early as 1948 the Santa Fe paid only $6.7 million in fixed charges while the Southern Pacific paid $20 million and the New York Central paid $41 million. Yet, from 1945 to 1955, over $530 million was invested in capital improvements on the Santa Fe. Gurley was not satisfied, however, that the firm earned only 5 percent on its investment, and he constantly expressed concern for the rate of return and the quality of the property.

Ernest S. Marsh replaced Gurley as president of the Santa Fe in 1957, and two years later Gurley stepped down as chairman of the board of directors. He continued to serve on the board and in many civic organizations and to pursue his first great love, hunting. On July 4, 1976, Gurley died in Chicago of a kidney ailment. He had married Margaret Smith in 1913, and they had a daughter. Following his wife's death, Gurley had married Ruth Brown in 1920; they had one son.

References:

"America's New Railroad: The Modern Santa Fe," *Modern Railroads*, 8 (December 1953): 42-46;

Keith L. Bryant, Jr., *History of the Atchison, Topeka & Santa Fe Railway* (New York: Macmillan, 1974);

"President Edward J. Engel Retired," *Santa Fe Magazine*, 38 (August 1944): 9-12;

"Santa Fe: No. 1 Railroad," *Fortune*, 38 (November 1948): 122-127, 162, 164, 169-170, 172, 174;

L. L. Waters, *Steel Trails to Santa Fe* (Lawrence: University of Kansas Press, 1950).

Fairfax Harrison

(March 13, 1869-February 2, 1938)

by Keith L. Bryant, Jr.

Texas A&M University

Fairfax Harrison (Courtesy of Norfolk Southern)

CAREER: Lawyer, Bangs, Stetson, Tracy and MacVeagh, New York City (1892–1896); solicitor (1896–1903), assistant to the president (1903–1906), vice president (1906–1910), Southern Railway; president, Chicago, Indianapolis & Louisville Railway (1910–1913); president, Southern Railway (1913–1937).

One of the first presidents of a major railroad to move up from the legal department rather than from one of the operating departments, Fairfax Har-

rison presided over the Southern Railway for twenty-four years. He led the railway from the Progressive Era to nearly the end of the Great Depression, taking the company through World War I, the 1920s, and the worst years of the 1930s. A "Virginia Gentleman" gifted with scholarship, urbanity, and modesty, Harrison modernized the carrier and prepared it for vastly expanded services in the two decades following his death.

Born in New York City in 1869, the son of Burton Norvell and Constance Cary Harrison was given the first name of Reginald, which he never used. His father, a lawyer, came from an old Virginia family and had served as private secretary to Jefferson Davis during the Civil War. His mother descended from the Fairfax family of Virginia, and became a nationally-known author of romantic fiction. Fairfax Harrison received an excellent education at private schools in Maryland and New York before entering Yale University in 1886. He graduated with an A.B. degree in 1890, and then studied for an A.M. in law and political science at Columbia University. He received his graduate degree in 1891 and gained admittance to the New York bar the following year. From 1892 until 1896 Harrison practiced law with Bangs, Stetson, Tracy and MacVeagh, a leading New York firm. In May 1896 he accepted a position as solicitor for the Southern Railway and embarked on a career with the company that would extend over forty years.

No doubt young Harrison had come to the attention of President Samuel Spencer because of the two years he had spent working on the railway's legal problems at Bangs, Stetson, Tracy and MacVeagh. He had excellent family ties to the south and a dignified, courtly manner; he was a perfectionist; and he wrote a clear but distinguished prose. In 1896 Harrison moved to Washington,

D.C., the headquarters of the railway, taking with him his bride of two years, Hetty Cary of Baltimore. The Harrisons would have three daughters and a son who would reach maturity on the family estate, "Belvoir," in Fauquier County, Virginia. Purchased in 1906, "Belvoir" helped Harrison reestablish his Southern roots and came to be a major aspect of his life. His efforts to revitalize the estate led him to study agricultural sciences, and in 1913 he translated and published the farm management treatises of the Roman writers Cato and Varro, which he had found in a bookstall in Paris. Few railway lawyers and executives translated Latin before breakfast and then edited and published their work. Harrison also read widely in French literature and English history.

As solicitor for the Southern Harrison wrote a legal history of the firm in 1901, and his skills as a writer and lawyer led Spencer to name him assistant to the president in 1903. In that capacity he learned railroading from one of the nation's outstanding railroad executives. Spencer made frequent tours of the line, rebuilt trackage, modernized equipment, acquired branches to St. Louis and in the Carolinas and Georgia, and installed new signaling devices. Harrison participated in Spencer's efforts to create a system out of the group of carriers that had been brought together from the wreckage of the "Great Richmond Terminal" debacle of 1893. Harrison devoted much of his attention to fiscal matters, and in 1906 he was promoted to vice president for financial affairs. No sooner had he taken office than a sharp turndown took place in the stock market and the Southern entered a period of fiscal crisis. Harrison arranged emergency financing in New York that carried the company through a difficult period.

In 1902 the Southern and the Louisville & Nashville had jointly purchased the Chicago, Indianapolis & Louisville Railway (Monon). Never a successful property, the Monon encountered extreme difficulties in 1910 when its president committed suicide amid rumors of malfeasance while with another carrier. The owners of the Monon immediately named Harrison to the presidency with a charge to return stability and revitalize the morale of the workers. Harrison struggled to bring the property up to the standards of its owners, but his work was only well underway when he was elected president of the Southern Railway on December 1,

1913. During his three years with the Monon he had retained his directorship on the Southern and had served as a member of the executive committee. Thoroughly conversant with the company and its structure, the forty-four-year-old Harrison seemed the ideal choice to replace the conservative and sagacious W. W. Finley, who had succeeded Spencer in 1906 and who had died on November 25.

Immediately upon taking office Harrison notified the employees that he intended to follow Finley's policies: "I hope to continue to build the Southern as he built it, by promoting and enhancing its usefulness to, and its cordial relations with, the people of the South." As Harrison assumed responsibility for managing and directing the Southern the nation was enjoying an unprecedented era of prosperity. The railway had established new operating and tonnage records, and the future appeared promising indeed. But within a few months war in Europe shattered that dream and in less than four years the United States prepared to enter the conflagration.

Upon Harrison rested the responsibility of guiding the firm through the war period safely and solvently. The patrician Harrison represented a new breed of railroader: businessmen in the south saw him as a brilliant, if aloof, leader dedicated to a "New South" of cities, industrialization, and prosperity. Harrison responded to the burdens of his new position with a cautious view to the future. He retained Finley's staff and assured stockholders in his first annual report that great loyalty to the firm existed among its employees. Overcoming his essential shyness, Harrison came to know hundreds of the employees, some by their first names. In numerous speeches he described the spirit and unity of purpose that existed among the workers and their commitment to improve the line and the region it served. In 1914 he abolished the executive committee that had acted on behalf of the board of directors so that all directors became involved in policymaking. That same year five new board members were added, and to the surprise and consternation of some stockholders they included Edwin A. Alderman, president of the University of Virginia, and the Reverend John Carlisle Kilgo, bishop of the Methodist Episcopal Church, South. These appointments, Harrison explained, were based upon the policy of recognizing the public interest in railroads and securing public approval of company policy.

Harrison moved to replace directors from the north with residents of the southern states after ending the voting trusteeship with which the company had operated since its formation. The trustees had made the significant fiscal decisions, but now that the railway had attained financial stability and conservative leadership, this safeguard was no longer needed. Harrison would need support from both the public and the new directors during the war years.

The outbreak of war in Europe devastated the southern economy as cotton exports fell drastically. In other areas of the nation, however, ports became clogged as exports to Great Britain, France, and other Allied powers filled docks, yards, and terminals. While Harrison faced declining revenues and reduced or omitted dividends, other carriers could not cope with burgeoning traffic. Harrison sought to redirect traffic to ports in the south served by the Southern. Following the opening of the Panama Canal he solicited Latin American trade and told a foreign trade convention in New Orleans that special services and freight agents had been organized to help capture traffic for southern ports.

Some of these agents had participated in the "Training for Management" program Harrison had organized for recent college graduates. They received special instruction and intensive training in all aspects of the carrier's operations, including manual labor along the tracks. Harrison himself often acted as a counselor to the trainees in the program, which would produce five presidents of the company and hundreds of executives throughout the system. He did not want his managers' oral or written reports embellished; he demanded facts, candor, and perfect frankness, and dealt with his subordinates the same way. He did not hesitate to ask the managers to make sacrifices: in 1914 he cut his own salary by 20 percent, with proportional cuts for virtually all employees, but he devised a promotion policy based on merit and the acquisition of new skills. Baseball teams and apprentice programs created a renewed loyalty to the firm that was thoroughly tested from 1917 to 1920.

On April 11, 1917, five days after Congress declared war on Germany, fifty railroad presidents met in Washington to respond to a call from the Council of National Defense to deal with the horrendous traffic problems. Harrison wrote a resolution passed by the presidents calling for coordination of services to produce maximum efficiency. They agreed to terminate their competitive relationships and act as one giant rail network. Five executives were named to the Railroads' War Board to lead the industry, with Harrison as chairman. Harrison rarely wrote for the general public, but in an article in *Scribner's* in September he explained the goals of the board and the issues facing the carriers. As demands on the railways rose, freight traffic alone increased 44 percent, and the railroads could not break the logjams at eastern ports. In December 1917 President Wilson transferred control of the nation's railroads to the United States Railroad Administration (USRA). Harrison had hoped to avoid federal control and had promoted the work of the board in speeches and articles, but without success.

Under Finley and Harrison over $67 million had been spent on improvements on the Southern. New locomotives, freight cars, yards, and trackage had been added, and the mainline from Washington to Atlanta had received double track and grade reductions. But with the growth of military installations in the south, the railway was taxed to the limit. Harrison and the Southern's management team lost control of the carrier in 1919 when the government ordered separation of the railways from their civilian executives. The operating ratio rose even as the system met higher and higher levels of service: fuel and labor costs soared, but maintenance fell. When federal control ended on February 29, 1920, and Harrison assumed managerial authority again, he faced enormous challenges.

From 1920 to 1929 Harrison sought to overcome the problems created under USRA control, continue the modernization program, and lead the south toward economic growth. Gross operating revenues reached a record $152 million in 1920, a 68 percent increase over 1917, but the operating ratio had risen to 88.95. Harrison moved to reduce rising fuel and labor costs and to obtain rate increases from the Interstate Commerce Commission. Increased traffic and rising revenues allowed Harrison to restore the line's working capital, but still no dividends could be paid on common stocks, and this led to sharp criticism at stockholders' meetings. Harrison believed that he had an obligation to the stockholders, customers, and employees to develop the property before distributing profits to the investors. Finally, in 1924 the directors voted to pay the company's first common stock dividend, and average share prices soared from the 17 1/8 of 1922 to 55. For the first time in the Southern's history, interest and dividends were being paid on all securities.

Harrison's frugal fiscal policies produced revenues that allowed for an expanded advertising campaign—"The Southern Serves the South"—and extensive improvements. Programs for grade and curve reduction, rail and tie replacement, bridge construction, Automatic Train Control installations, and equipment acquisitions accelerated. Under Harrison steam locomotive development on the Southern reached its apogee: modern engines were acquired in substantial numbers, and following a trip to England, where he greatly admired the colorful locomotives of the London & North Eastern, Harrison ordered that the new Ps-4 Pacifics (4-6-2) be painted Virginia green with gold lettering and stripes and a brick red cab roof. These handsome locomotives epitomized the "spit and polish" of the modern engine fleet. To reinforce a sense of pride among the crewmen, locomotives were specifically assigned to crews, and "old heads" among the engineers were allowed to have their names stenciled on the cabs. Harrison also had a new headquarters building erected in Washington in 1928.

These improvements prepared the railway for a substantial traffic increase that would not come for over a decade as the stock market crashed in 1929 and the nation moved inexorably toward the Great Depression. The southern economy sagged quickly because of the overdependence on already depressed agriculture. Gross operating revenues fell from $143 million in 1929 to $73 million in 1932. Yet dividends continued to be paid until 1932, bringing severe criticism of Harrison and the board of directors. Harrison ordered cutbacks in train service, capital expenditures, and operating costs, but to no avail. The railway fell into the red in 1931, and the deficit reached $11 million the next year. Management and labor accepted salary cuts, Harrison slashed his own pay by half, and orders for drastic cost reductions were issued. But common stock that sold for 151 in October 1929 brought only 2½ in 1932. The proud Harrison was forced to borrow $7.5 million from the Reconstruction Finance Corporation to pay the carrier's bills. Additional federal loans of over $14 million prevented bankruptcy, but a bankruptcy petition was kept handy in a desk drawer. The corporate debt of over $300 million in 1932, plus excessive rates of interest, meant that

the carrier's high fixed charges continued to be a crushing burden.

By 1936 the regional economy had improved slightly, and Harrison could announce that the carrier had earned modest profits and that "there are no financial difficulties facing the Southern Railway." The following year he voluntarily requested retirement and on October 21 at age sixty-eight, he relinquished the presidency of the company.

The courtly Virginian hoped to retire to "Belvoir" and continue to write books about his beloved adopted state, his family, and horse breeding. Previously he had published *The Harrisons of Skimino* (1910), *The Virginia Carys* (1919), and *The Devon Carys* (1920). But a few weeks after he retired Harrison entered a Baltimore hospital, and on February 2, 1938, he died there from heart disease. A modest man, Harrison had refused honorary degrees from several institutions, including Yale University, though he had written scholarly works strongly influenced by the historian Frederick Jackson Turner and had aided the research of many others. All along the Southern Railway System employees mourned the loss of the man who had led their company longer than any other.

Unpublished Document:

Carlton J. Corliss and Keith L. Bryant, Jr., "History of the Southern Railway System," manuscript in the records of the Southern Railway Company, Atlanta.

Publications:

A History of the Legal Development of the Railroad System of the Southern Railway Company (Washington: Southern Railway Company, 1901);

Aris Sonis Forisque: Being a Memoir of an American Family, the Harrisons of Skimino, and Particularly of Jesse Burton Harrison and Burton Norvell Harrison, edited by Harrison (N.p., 1910);

Roman Farm Management: The Treatises of Cato and Varro, translated by Harrison under the pseudonym A Virginia Farmer (New York: Macmillan, 1913);

"The Railroads' War Problem," *Scribner's*, 62 (September 1917): 363–369;

The Virginia Carys: An Essay in Genealogy (New York: Privately printed, 1919);

The Devon Carys (New York: Privately printed, 1920);

Virginia Land Grants: A Study of Conveyancing in Relation to Colonial Politics (Richmond: Old Dominion Press, 1925);

A Selection of the Letters of Fairfax Harrison, edited by Francis Burton Harrison (Charlottesville, Va.: Jarman's, 1944).

References:

Burke Davis, *The Southern Railway: Road of the Innovators* (Chapel Hill: University of North Carolina Press, 1985);

Edward Hungerford, "Men Who Are Winning the War: Fairfax Harrison," *Leslie's Weekly,* 125 (December 1, 1917): 758, 766.

Archives:

Correspondence, reports, speeches, and other documents of Fairfax Harrison may be found in the records of the Southern Railway Company, Atlanta, Ga. Personal letters to friends and family can be found in the University of Virginia's Alderman Library and the library of the College of William and Mary.

Edwin Hawley

(?1850?-February 1, 1912)

by Don L. Hofsommer

Augustana College

CAREER: Clerk, New York & Erie Railway (1867-1868); billing clerk, Ohio & Mississippi Railway (1868-1870); clerk and contracting agent, Chicago, Rock Island & Pacific (1870-1874); contracting agent (1874-1875), general eastern agent (1875-1883), California Fast Freight Line; general eastern agent, Southern Pacific Company and subsidiaries (1883-1890); assistant general manager, New York, Southern Pacific (1890-1894); vice president (1894-1896), president (1896-1912), Minneapolis & St. Louis Railway; president, Iowa Central Railway (1900-1912).

Edwin Hawley was born of humble parentage at Chatham, New York, around 1850. As a youth he bought potatoes and eggs from nearby farmers and shipped them to distant markets, but at the age of seventeen he left for New York City to seek his fortune. When he died in 1912, Hawley was in command of a huge railroad empire and had plans for even greater growth.

When Hawley began his railroad career in 1867 as a clerk for the New York & Erie Railway, certain personal traits were already evident. He was in no sense an educated man; rather, he was an extraordinarily persistent worker, slow-moving, careful, and somewhat ponderous, but bright and with a clear vision of what he wanted to attain. A shadowy figure, he talked as little as possible; many years later, when a reporter asked him for an interview, Hawley said that talking was distasteful to him and that he hated any attempt to make him do so. His taciturnity served to make him all the more mysterious.

In 1868 Hawley became a billing clerk with the Ohio & Mississippi Railway. Two years later he moved to the Chicago, Rock Island & Pacific as a clerk and contracting agent. He became a contracting agent for the California Fast Freight Line in 1874, and the following year moved up to general eastern agent for the road.

During his years as an officer with the California Fast Freight Line Hawley attracted the attention of Collis P. Huntington, who in 1883 enticed him into service with the Southern Pacific (SP) as East Coast sales representative for that company and its many subsidiaries. While working for the SP Hawley made important contacts among the moguls of Wall Street.

Huntington helped his subordinate become vice president in 1894 and president in 1896 of the Minneapolis & St. Louis Railway (M&StL). Huntington subsequently served on the M&StL's board of directors, and Hawley found himself a director of the SP. Hawley left his salaried position at the SP following Huntington's death in 1900 and formed a brokerage house with Frank H. Davis, former assistant treasurer of the SP; but he retained impressive influence among Huntington's heirs, which led Edward H. Harriman to seek him out in an attempt to gain control of the SP. A deal was struck with Hawley as mediator, and in 1901 Harriman

tween Oakland, California, and northern Utah. The nadir came in 1908 when "the Hawley crowd" agreed to convey the strategic Colorado & Southern and its important Fort Worth & Denver City subsidiary to the "Hill interests," tweaking Harriman's ego and disadvantaging his Union Pacific in the process.

That move did not mean that Hawley was siding with James J. Hill in the "Empire Builder's" continuous campaign with Harriman for territorial dominion. Hawley was simply playing his own hand in his solitary fashion. As he said late in his career: "I have played a lone hand and stuck to my job. I have simply done two things—I have worked and I have waited."

During the dozen years before his death Hawley gained control of several properties which were known generally as the "Hawley Roads." Included were the Iowa Central, the Toledo, St. Louis & Western (Clover Leaf), and the Chicago & Alton. To these were added the Colorado & Southern, the splendid Chesapeake & Ohio (C&O), and the strategically located Missouri, Kansas & Texas (MK&T). Hawley also claimed the Des Moines & Fort Dodge for the M&StL, the Chicago, Cincinnati & Louisville to give the C&O an independent entry to Chicago, and the Hocking Valley to allow the C&O access to coal-producing regions in central Ohio. This impressive collection of roads reached from Atlantic tidewater to the Missouri River at LeBeau, South Dakota, and from the Great Lakes at Chicago and Toledo to the Gulf of Mexico at Galveston.

After Harriman's death in 1909, observers of the railroad industry speculated that Hawley might become the nation's new "railroad king." Hawley was known as a shrewd financier rather than as a railroad builder, but the press frequently took note of his "comprehensive railroad plans," especially from 1909 through 1911. From his luxurious office on the thirteenth floor of the Broad Exchange Building in the heart of New York's financial district, Hawley directed a series of studies designed to integrate his rail operations in a systematic way. For instance, late in 1911 he made plans to lengthen the M&StL to Winnipeg and the Iowa Central to St. Louis, thereby forging a direct route from Manitoba and the Twin Cities of Minneapolis and St. Paul to the Gulf via the MK&T. At the same time, rumors had Hawley's M&StL completing a branch in

Edwin Hawley (Collection of Donovan L. Hofsommer)

purchased Hawley's stock and that of the Huntington heirs. Hawley continued on the SP board and was elevated to the executive committee.

For some reason, the ardor between Hawley and Harriman cooled. Relations between the two men worsened when Hawley's brokerage firm agreed to purchase shares of the Chicago & Alton Railroad (Alton) for clients hostile to Harriman. In the end, Harriman—who did not own a majority of the Alton but controlled it nevertheless—lost out and accused Hawley of bad faith, and Hawley left the SP board. The division deepened when Hawley aided George J. Gould in fostering the Western Pacific as a rival to Harriman's Southern Pacific be-

western Iowa to Kansas City, thus creating an important new route from the Twin Cities to the Gulf by way of the MK&T. There was even speculation that the M&StL might be extended to the Pacific.

In all cases Hawley followed a predictable path. He was patient and tenacious, lurking in his office while others did his bidding. Work was his chief pleasure, although once or twice a year he left it behind for some sailing and fishing. He amused associates and employees by saving unsealed envelopes that arrived in the mail and carefully salvaging uncanceled and torn stamps. In spite of his parsimony, he was a member of the "Waldorf Crowd," composed of moneyed men such as George Crocker, whose father had earned fame and fortune by pushing the first transcontinental railroad over the Sierra Nevada; L. C. Weir, president of Adams Express Company; James Buchanan ("Diamond Jim") Brady; Charles Sanger Mellen, late of the Northern Pacific and then president of the New York, New Haven & Hartford; a young banker named Bernard M. Baruch; and John W. "Bet a Million" Gates. Hawley's poker face was legendary on Wall Street, and it also served him well in the games of chance that began after lunch each Saturday and ran well into the night. These marathon poker sessions served Hawley as a sounding board for prospective business ventures.

Hawley's grand design for railroad empire came to an abrupt conclusion when he died after a brief illness on February 1, 1912. He had been a dominant figure in high finance and in railroads; *World's Work* noted that there had "hardly been a [railroad] conflict in the last ten years in which Ed Hawley failed to ride with the foremost." At his death he served on the boards of directors of forty-one companies; the *New York Times* estimated his worth at upwards of $60 million. A bachelor, Hawley left no will; as far as is known, his papers have not survived.

References:
Frank P. Donovan, "Edwin Hawley," *Trains & Travel,* 12 (September 1952): 52-53;
Donovan, *Mileposts on the Prairie: The Story of the Minneapolis & St. Louis Railway* (New York: Simmons-Boardman, 1950).

Ben W. Heineman

(February 10, 1914-   )

by Richard W. Barsness

Lehigh University

Ben W. Heineman (Kalmbach Publishing Company)

CAREER: Private law practice, Chicago (1936-1941); assistant general counsel, U.S. Office of Price Administration (1941-1943); U.S. State Department assignments in North Africa (1943); partner, Swiren & Heineman, Chicago (1944-1956); chairman of executive committee, Minneapolis & St. Louis Railway (1954-1956); chairman, Four Wheel Drive Auto Company (1954-1957); chairman of board and chief executive officer, Chicago & North Western Railway (1956-1972); president, chief executive officer and chairman, Northwest Industries, Incorporated (1968-1985).

Ben W. Heineman began his career as an attorney specializing in administrative and corporate law. His efforts on behalf of railroad investors led to the chairmanship of the Chicago & North Western Railway (C&NW). Heineman's impressive and well-publicized revitalization of the tottering C&NW made him a prominent figure in the Chicago business community as well as the railroad industry nationally.

Ben Walter Heineman was born on February 10, 1914, in Wausau, a small city in central Wisconsin, where his grandfather, an immigrant from Germany, had established a lumber business in 1869. His parents, Walter B. and Elsie Deutsch Heineman, also had three daughters. Walter B. Heineman prospered for many years in the family lumber business and was a prominent Republican in Wisconsin during the 1920s.

Ben Heineman graduated from Wausau High School in 1930, the year his father went bankrupt and committed suicide. He gave up plans to attend Yale and entered the University of Michigan. After three years of study he persuaded the Northwestern University School of Law in Chicago to admit him without a bachelor's degree. At Northwestern Heineman participated in legal research projects, and when he received his LL.B. degree in 1936 he ranked among the top ten in his class. A year before graduation he had married Natalie Goldstein. They subsequently became parents of a son and a daughter.

In 1936 Heineman was admitted to the Illinois bar and joined the Chicago firm of Levinson, Becker, Peebles and Swiren, specialists in corporate law. He spent the next five years with the firm, during which he also contributed research papers to the *Illinois Law Review*. Heineman was deferred from military service during World War II because of blindness in one eye. From 1941 to 1943 he served as assistant general counsel with the Office of Price Administration in Washington, and in 1943 he spent several months in Algiers and other locations on legal and economic assistance assignments for the United States State Department.

Heineman declined a State Department assignment in London and returned to Chicago, where in 1944 he and Max Swiren formed a new partnership, Swiren & Heineman, specializing in corporate law. In addition to his private practice, Heineman remained actively involved in legal research as well as important bar association committees at the local, state, and national levels. In 1951 he served Governor Adlai E. Stevenson of Illinois as a special assistant district attorney investigating cigarette tax fraud. A self-described "independent Democrat,"

Heineman also supported Stevenson's first presidential campaign in 1952.

Heineman first attracted attention in the railroad industry in 1950 when he negotiated an out-of-court settlement of dividend claims brought by some shareholders of the Chicago Great Western Railroad; successful dividend cases were a rare occurrence in the industry. Three years later Heineman joined other dissatisfied stockholders of the Minneapolis & St. Louis Railway (M&StL) in gaining seats on the company's board, long controlled by Lucian C. Sprague. A bitter proxy fight ended with Sprague's retirement in May 1954 and Heineman's election as chairman of the newly created executive committee.

Because the previous management of the 1,400-mile M&StL had not kept pace with the times, it was relatively easy for Heineman to improve the company's operations and gain recognition. But his plans to strengthen the company's long-term prospects by acquiring the Toledo, Peoria & Western and the Chicago, Indianapolis & Louisville Railway (Monon Route) were thwarted by major carriers, especially the Pennsylvania and the Santa Fe.

In 1955 Heineman became the leader of Chicago and Cleveland investors who were gaining control of one-third of the stock of the Chicago & North Western Railway, a 9,362-mile system which extended north and west from Chicago. In February 1956, with the company teetering on the edge of bankruptcy and the growing risk of a proxy fight, President Paul E. Feucht agreed to retire. Heineman was named chairman of the board and chief executive officer, effective April 1. In order to devote full attention to the challenge of saving the C&NW, Heineman resigned from the Minneapolis & St. Louis and terminated his law partnership.

The C&NW's problems were numerous and fundamental. They included too many light-traffic branch lines, relatively short freight hauls vulnerable to truck competition, large losses from passenger operations, obsolete rolling stock, widespread deferred maintenance, the highest ratio of wages and salaries to revenue in the industry, and poor management. The company had annual revenues of $225 million but was, as one observer put it, "leaking money from every pore." To help turn the situation around, Heineman appointed a knowledgeable railroad executive, Clyde J. Fitzpatrick of the Illinois

Central, as the new president of the Chicago & North Western.

Heineman and Fitzpatrick promptly embarked on a comprehensive program to rehabilitate and modernize the railroad's plant and equipment, improve service, cut employment costs, increase productivity, and rebuild the carrier's finances. Well over 100 steam locomotives were retired and replaced by more efficient use of the company's diesel locomotives. This action also permitted elimination of many facilities previously needed to support steam operations. Track crews were provided with a host of machines for maintenance and replacement of track, greatly improving their efficiency, and high quality rock ballast was purchased to improve roadway surfacing. New freight cars were ordered, and a modern car rebuilding and repair shop was built at Clinton, Iowa, to replace fourteen obsolete facilities scattered throughout the system. Losses from intercity passenger operations ($23.4 million in 1956) were reduced substantially by discontinuing particularly unproductive trains and improving service on other routes. Accounting operations were modernized with data processing equipment, and management was significantly improved by eliminating excess layers of supervision, delegating authority to the field wherever possible, and bringing in talent from other railroads and other industries.

Heineman believed that the C&NW and the rest of the railroad industry had a promising future, provided that fundamental changes were made in both railroad operations and the structure of the industry. He was appalled by the archaic, expensive work rules which permeated the industry, and weathered several strikes which resulted from his efforts to change prevailing practices. He also was dismayed by the rail fraternity's preoccupation with intra-industry competition rather than the loss of traffic to trucks, barges, and pipelines. Heineman was convinced that many railroad rates were too high and had to be reduced to retain traffic or regain it from other modes. This view challenged longstanding rail industry pricing attitudes as well as state and federal regulatory policies. He felt that the rail industry reflected "sheer economic waste" and was its own worst enemy. As chief executive officer of the C&NW he repeatedly asked subordinates, "Why?" He frequently found the answers unconvincing.

The most striking example of Heineman's willingness to set an independent course was his approach to the railroad's Chicago area commuter operations, which served 40,000 riders daily. Conventional wisdom declared that commuter service was inherently unprofitable and that carriers should simply try to minimize losses; new investment was unthinkable. Heineman's revolutionary view was that with efficient new equipment, improved operating procedures, and effective marketing, commuter service could be made profitable. Between 1958 and 1961 the North Western acquired 200 high capacity double-deck suburban cars to replace 417 old cars; established fast, efficient "push-pull" train operations; closed marginal stations; revamped ticketing; and raised fares sharply.

This daring strategy, which required an investment of $43 million, was a great success. Ridership and productivity increased significantly, and Heineman received widespread favorable publicity as the innovative leader of a new generation of railroad management. Despite competition from new expressways, the C&NW's modernized commuter service was able to break even or turn a profit during most of the 1960s. This success facilitated Heineman's efforts to restructure all of the company's operations.

From the outset of his career in the railroad industry, Heineman was convinced that mergers were essential if Midwestern railroads were to survive. While he acted without delay in 1957 on the C&NW's opportunity to purchase the small Litchfield & Madison Railway with its access to East St. Louis, he was not ready to negotiate immediately with the North Western's natural partner, the Chicago, Milwaukee, St. Paul & Pacific Railroad (Milwaukee Road), which served many of the same markets as the North Western. In order to maximize returns to shareholders, Heineman felt that the North Western must be revitalized before it became involved in major merger proceedings.

Once Heineman was ready to proceed, his interest coincided with a wave of restructuring activity throughout the industry. Some carriers pursued end-to-end mergers to extend their length of haul and reach new markets. Others sought to consolidate with parallel competitors to reduce excess capacity and improve efficiency. Merger proposals which improved prospects for some carriers typically diminished prospects for others and brought vigorous counterattacks within the railroad industry and before the Interstate Commerce Commission (ICC).

Recognizing the inherent market limitations of the C&NW even if fully rehabilitated, Heineman pursued both parallel and end-to-end mergers which would strengthen the system and increase its value to shareholders. The first step occurred in 1960 with the North Western's purchase of the rail assets of Heineman's former company, the Minneapolis & St. Louis, for $20.9 million. Later that year negotiations were reopened between the Milwaukee Road and the North Western. The Milwaukee discussions proceeded slowly over the next several years, with ups and downs caused by other proceedings involving the two carriers and by lack of agreement regarding an appropriate exchange ratio for securities.

In 1965 the Milwaukee and the North Western reached an agreement to form the Chicago, Milwaukee & North Western Transportation Company. By the time the ICC completed its hearings and examiner Henry C. Darmstadter recommended approval in December 1968, however, circumstances had changed sufficiently to cause some Milwaukee interests to consider the original exchange ratio unacceptable. Heineman wanted no part of either further negotiations or ICC proceedings. He was tired of the whole affair, and the merger plan unraveled.

Meanwhile, in 1968 the North Western completed a parallel merger with the 1,411-mile Chicago Great Western Railroad. The C&NW also played a central role in the epic struggle over the Chicago, Rock Island & Pacific Railroad (Rock Island). Starting in 1963, control of the Rock Island was sought first by the powerful Union Pacific Railroad (UP) and then by Heineman's North Western. Because any merger decision involving the Rock Island had profound strategic implications for other midwestern and western railroads, the case generated an unprecedented and complicated series of financial and legal actions by carriers seeking to preserve or enhance their positions.

Heineman felt that his own company's survival was at stake, and during the protracted course of events he turned to one strategy after another to protect the North Western's large interchange traffic at Omaha and other interests. Heineman tried to block a UP-Rock Island merger, merge the North Western and the Rock Island, sell the North Western to the UP, or have the North Western acquire control of the UP. The result was a stalemate before the ICC which was not settled until the Rock Island shut down in 1980, several years after Heineman had severed his ties with the C&NW.

Although the benefits of physical rehabilitation of the North Western were increasingly apparent as the 1960s progressed, and the company was active in the railroad merger arena, Heineman had become convinced by 1963 that no company, no matter how well managed, could achieve a secure future in the railroad industry alone. Profits were limited at best, and the industry seemed incapable of making the fundamental changes needed in labor relations, pricing, and regulatory policies. To offset these limitations and the cyclical nature of the industry Heineman turned to diversification, starting with the C&NW's acquisition in 1965 of Velsicol Chemical Corporation and Michigan Chemical Corporation. Two years later he established Northwest Industries, Incorporated (NWI), to serve as a holding company parent for the railroad, the two chemical companies, and future acquisitions. Heineman was president, chief executive officer, and chairman of the new company.

Northwest Industries offered Heineman a splendid opportunity to turn away from the rail industry's merger morass and the C&NW's erratic profits and pursue more promising ventures. His initial move was a merger in 1968 with the Philadelphia & Reading Corporation, a New York-based holding and management company. Philadelphia & Reading's disparate but profitable subsidiaries included Lone Star Steel (tubular products), Union Underwear, Universal Manufacturing (ballasts), Imperial Reading (clothing), Fruit of the Loom (soft goods), and Acme Boot Company. These firms transformed NWI into a full-fledged conglomerate and also provided a stronger earnings base to support Heineman's ambitions. These ambitions escalated rapidly, but the results were not always successful. Heineman's most damaging failure was a widely publicized tender offer by Northwest in 1968 to gain control of the B. F. Goodrich Company. This attempt brought sharp criticism of Heineman's managerial record and charges of opportunism, and was soundly defeated.

On more than one occasion during the 1960s Heineman tried to extricate his company from the rail merger contest by offering to sell the C&NW's

rail assets to another carrier. Since no company found the opportunity, price, and financing requirements sufficiently advantageous, no deal was struck. It was clear that Heineman had lost his enthusiasm for the industry and, unlike most railroaders, felt no emotional attachment to it. He would welcome an opportunity to divest the C&NW so long as the financial terms were reasonable.

Given the absence of serious interest by other carriers, the C&NW's top management, led by Larry S. Provo, who had become president in 1967, proposed a novel plan under which Northwest Industries would sell the railroad for a modest sum to a new employee-owned corporation. The transaction would free Northwest Industries from the railroad business and provide a $200 million tax loss carryforward which NWI could use to offset profits in other subsidiaries. The C&NW's employees would acquire ownership of the railroad's assets, responsibility for its substantial indebtedness, and presumably a greater incentive to operate the company in the most efficient manner possible. Heineman agreed to the plan and worked to secure approval by NWI shareholders and the Interstate Commerce Commission. In 1972 the C&NW became the first employee-owned railroad in the nation. Approximately 1,000 of the company's 14,000 employees elected to become stockholders.

The balance of Heineman's business career was devoted to running Northwest Industries. He was an active, strong-willed executive who was constantly making deals and watching Northwest Industries stock swing widely. Velsicol Chemical and Michigan Chemical turned out to be particularly difficult challenges for NWI because of serious environmental incidents caused by hazardous chemicals which they produced.

Heineman remained in charge of Northwest Industries until he was seventy-one years old. Having failed to groom a successor as chief executive, he did not wish to retire until he could sell the company to new owners at a favorable price for Northwest shareholders. In 1985 Northwest was purchased for $1.4 billion in a leveraged buyout by Farley Industries, a large privately held industrial corporation.

Ben Heineman's impressive professional career spanned half a century and consisted of three distinct stages. After nearly twenty years as a brilliant attorney specializing in administrative and corporate law, he became a nationally prominent railroad executive. When opportunities lagged in the railroad industry he turned his attention to corporate diversification and spent almost two decades developing and leading a major conglomerate. Heineman also had a broad array of interests beyond business. He was deeply involved in civic, educational, and cultural activities in Chicago and Illinois and served on several important national commissions and foundations. Heineman was a talented, outspoken, often autocratic, and sometimes controversial individual, who enjoyed the limelight and did not shirk difficult decisions. He unquestionably was a major American business leader in the post-World War II era.

Unpublished Document:
"Railroads: A Revolution in the Making," address at the annual meeting of the Illinois State Chamber of Commerce, Chicago, October 17, 1957.

References:
"C & NW's Spectacular Comeback: The Heineman Years," *Railway Age*, 160 (March 21, 1966): 24-31;

"Northwest Industries: The Acid Test for Bill Farley's Offbeat Style," *Business Week* (September 9, 1985): 68-69;

Joseph Poindexter, "The Return of Ben W. Heineman," *Dun's Review*, 99 (March 1972): 33-37, 89;

Richard Saunders, *The Railroad Mergers and the Coming of Conrail* (Westport, Conn.: Greenwood Press, 1978).

Hepburn Act

After the Supreme Court in the *Maximum Freight Rate* decision (1897) declared that the Interstate Commerce Commission (ICC) could not regulate railroad rates, Progressive reformers, abetted by Midwestern shippers and farmers, campaigned to give the ICC that power. Railroads opposed the move, but by early 1906 agitation, orchestrated by President Theodore Roosevelt, had made rate regulation unavoidable. The contest then centered on the question of the extent of judicial review. Narrow judicial review, which the Progressives wanted, would determine the ICC's right to set a rate in a particular case but would not second-guess the rate's reasonableness, thereby converting the ICC into an independent regulatory commission with quasi-legislative, executive, and judicial powers; a broad review of the facts, advocated by railroad officials, would lodge the ratesetting power in the courts. With Roosevelt pressing the Senate, Congress compromised in the Hepburn Act of May 1906. This act gave the ICC the power to set rates but left the extent of judicial review undetermined. ICC ratemaking decisions could be appealed to federal circuit courts, which would themselves determine the breadth of their review. The act permitted the courts to enjoin ICC orders but provided for quick appeal to the Supreme Court.

Even with the judicial review question unresolved, the Hepburn Act increased the ICC's control over rates enormously. Explicitly giving it the power, upon complaint and after a full hearing, to replace an existing rate with a "just and reasonable" maximum rate, the Hepburn Act specified that the ICC's orders were binding on promulgation, that the courts were to compel obedience, and that the railroads must obey or contest the order in court. Widening the ICC's jurisdiction to include express and sleeping car companies, switches, spurs, yards, depots, terminals, and oil pipelines, the act also gave the commission the power to require standardized reports and to inspect railroad accounts. To cope with its new duties, the ICC was empowered to appoint examiners and agents and was increased

from five to seven members, whose terms of office were lengthened to seven years. The Hepburn Act also eliminated charges made by private car lines and industrial railroads for services rendered to common carriers, and required railroads not to discriminate in providing shippers with freight cars and with switches for their sidings. To keep railroads from competing with other producers, the act prohibited railroads after May 1, 1908, from hauling, except for their own use, any product that they produced or mined, except lumber. The act also required a thirty-day notification period before rate changes, restored imprisonment as a punishment for giving or taking rebates, and abolished free passes for those not employed by the railroads.

The Hepburn Act made the ICC, not the courts, the dominant government agency regulating railroads. Despite the vagueness of the act, the hopes of conservatives, and the fears of Progressives, the courts adopted a narrow-review policy. The Supreme Court pronounced that even if it believed that administrative power had not been wisely exercised, it could not usurp administrative functions. "Power to make the order and not the mere expediency or wisdom of having made it," the Court declared, "is the question" (*Interstate Commerce Commission* v. *Ill. Cent. R.R.*, 215 U.S. 452 [1910]).

References:

John Morton Blum, *The Republican Roosevelt* (Cambridge: Harvard University Press, 1954), pp. 73-105;

Ari and Olive Hoogenboom, *A History of the ICC: From Panacea to Palliative* (New York: Norton, 1976), pp. 46-54;

Albro Martin, *Enterprise Denied: Origins of the Decline of American Railroads, 1897-1917* (New York: Columbia University Press, 1971), pp. 111-114;

I. L. Sharfman, *The Interstate Commerce Commission: A Study in Administrative Law and Procedure,* 5 volumes (New York: The Commonwealth Fund, 1931-1937), I: 40-52.

—*Ari Hoogenboom*

Louis W. Hill, Sr.

(May 19, 1872-April 27, 1948)

by Albro Martin

Bradley University

Louis W. Hill, Sr. (James J. Hill Reference Library)

CAREER: Vice president (1903-1907), president (1907-1912), chairman (1912-1929), Great Northern Railway; president, Great Northern Iron Ore Company (1916-1945); chairman, First National Bank of St. Paul (1916-1935).

The career of Louis W. Hill, Sr., is an illuminating study in the transfer of business leadership from the founder and builder of a great enterprise to his son and chosen successor. James J. Hill, with several associates, took over the old St. Paul & Pacific

Railroad in 1879 and in the next thirty years built it into The Great Northern Railway (GN), one of America's largest and strongest railroads, a transcontinental running through the northern tier of states from St. Paul, Minnesota, to Seattle, Washington. The Great Northern; the Chicago, Burlington & Quincy Railroad, of which the Great Northern owned one half and the Northern Pacific (NP) the other; and the Northern Pacific itself, controlled through stock ownership, were known as the "Hill roads" until their consolidation as the Burlington Northern in 1970.

Hill had hoped that the eldest of his three sons, James Norman, would gradually take over management of the railroads after 1900, but the young man proved unequal to the task. The second son, Louis, who had also been expected to play an important role in the properties, then became Hill's heir apparent.

As Roman Catholics in a Protestant community—their mother, Mary Theresa Mehegan Hill, was a Catholic—James Norman and Louis Warren Hill were educated by tutors rather than in the public schools. By 1887 the failure of the tutors was obvious and both boys were packed off to Phillips Exeter Academy. Louis graduated in 1890 but without qualifying in the classics, which Yale University required for admission. The three-year course in Yale's Sheffield Scientific School was the alternative. When Louis received the Bachelor of Philosophy degree in 1893 his father was far out west putting the Great Northern's new Pacific coast extension into operation, and a major depression was just beginning. Louis went immediately to work as assistant to the president.

The years from 1893 to the turn of the century proved to be some of the most productive of Louis's career, for it was in this period that he became convinced of the future value of certain cut-over-timberlands that lay astride the fabulous Mesabi iron range. Sent to Duluth to work on the Great Northern's line from St. Paul to Lake Superior, he found a huge tract which he persuaded his father to buy. During the next several years, while living the lonely life of a bachelor in a dull provincial hotel, he bought up 17,000 more acres. The total investment was $4 million, while royalties received for the ores ultimately reached more than $400 million. The lands were put in trust for all stockholders of the Great Northern, and formed the basis for Louis's own substantial private fortune.

As James Norman retired from active railroad work, his father pushed Louis forward rapidly. After 1900 he sometimes sent Louis west to fire certain deficient GN officers, on the theory that this task was the most exacting form of preparation for leadership. When the United States Supreme Court in 1904 struck down the Northern Securities Company, the holding company into which James J. Hill and J. P. Morgan had placed the securities of both the GN and the NP, Hill despaired of railroading's future appeal to enterprising young men and advised his son, "Louis, be out of the railroad business by the time you are forty." But in 1907, when James J., aged sixty-nine, gave up the GN presidency for the chairmanship, he was content to put the thirty-five-year-old Louis in the presidential post.

The railroad made great strides in the nine years of life remaining to James J. Hill, and as Louis was always quick to point out, they were largely the work of his father and Ralph Budd, who became president when Louis moved up to chairman in 1912. Louis, however, monitored capital improvement plans and their execution, and as chairman headed the management group that had to approve them. He oversaw the expansion of route mileage from 6,489 to 8,387; installation of automatic block signals on the transcontinental passenger route; construction of the Fargo-Surrey cutoff in North Dakota, opened in 1912, that shortened the route significantly; and construction of a new 7.79-mile tunnel through the Cascade Mountains of Washington that vastly improved the GN as a transcontinental route. He was also active in public relations for the railroad.

Louis W. Hill, Sr.'s reputation in the Northwest and among railroad historians lies primarily in his work in establishing and developing Glacier Na-

tional Park in western Montana. In the early years of the twentieth century a slowly growing movement to make this section of the Rocky Mountains into a national park was greatly stimulated by the rising conservation movement and the ascendancy of Theodore Roosevelt, one of its most ardent supporters, to the presidency of the United States.

This awesome land of snow-covered peaks, approaching two miles above sea level in height and interspersed with idyllic valleys and turquoise lakes, lies just north of the GN's main line near the point where the railroad crosses the Continental Divide via the Marias Pass at 5,216 feet, one of the lowest crossings of the Divide in the United States. As the last quarter of the old century waned, prospectors looking (unsuccessfully) for copper and, later, oil and gas, were joined by settlers, notwithstanding the fact that the land was part of the Blackfoot Indian Reservation that extended eastward from the Divide. A potentially embarrassing problem was solved in 1896 by adding the segment between the Divide and the beginning of the plains to the public domain by purchase from the Indians, who were to retain forever their historic rights to hunt and fish. Finally, in 1910, with considerable pushing from Louis W. Hill and the GN, Congress created Glacier National Park.

Whereas his father had considered the Great Northern almost exclusively as an efficient, low-cost transcontinental freight railroad, and more than once had expressed his low regard for passenger trains and Rocky Mountain scenery, Louis Hill enthusiastically threw the GN behind the new park. A national park needs a steady and substantial stream of visitors during its season, and the vital role of the GN was obvious from the outset. Hill approved plans to improve GN passenger service, culminating in the introduction of the Empire Builder, one of America's most famous trains, in 1929. Internal development of the park was vital if tourism was to grow, and Hill did not wait for the government to supply facilities. He saw to the building of several comfortable hotels and lodges, even designing some of them himself, and laid out roads for the automobiles that would ultimately replace the railroad as the chief mode of access to Glacier National Park.

Louis W. Hill, Sr., lived almost all his life in St. Paul, and was one of its leading citizens. He revived the St. Paul Ice Carnival and was active in other civic enterprises. A serious amateur painter, he encouraged other artists to record the life of the Northwestern Indians on canvas. He was married in 1901 to Maud Van Cortlandt Taylor and they had a daughter and three sons, one of whom, Louis, Jr., worked briefly for the Great Northern. Hill retired as chairman of the GN in 1929 at age fifty-seven and pursued other business activities until his death in 1948.

References:

Robert Orr Baker, *One Family* (St. Paul, Minn.: Privately printed, 1986);

Warren L. Hanna, *Montana's Many-Splendored Glacierland* (Seattle: Superior, 1976), pp. 109-116;

Albro Martin, *James J. Hill and the Opening of the Northwest* (New York: Oxford University Press, 1976).

Archives:

The papers of James J. Hill, in the James Jerome Hill Reference Library, St. Paul, Minnesota, are open to scholars, and the letterbooks are available on microfilm. The papers of Louis W. Hill, Sr., are also in the James Jerome Hill Reference Library, but at present admission is by permission only.

Walker D. Hines

(February 2, 1870-January 14, 1934)

by William R. Doezema

Houghton College

CAREER: Secretary to assistant chief attorney (1890-1892), assistant attorney (1893-1897), assistant chief attorney (1897-1901), first vice president (1901-1904), Louisville & Nashville Railroad Company; partner, Humphrey, Hines & Humphrey (1904-1906); attorney, Craveth, Henderson & de Gersdorff (1907-1913); chairman of executive committee (1908-1916), chairman of board of directors (1916-1918), Atchison, Topeka & Sante Fe Railway Company; assistant director general (1918), director general (1919-1920), United States Railroad Administration; arbitrator for Allied Council of Ambassadors (1920-1921); League of Nations shipping investigator (1925); president (1926-1929), chairman of board of directors (1929-1931), Cotton-Textile Institute; member of board of directors, Colorado & Southern Railroad Company (1924-1934); partner, Hines, Rearick, Dorr, Travis & Marshall (1927-1934); member of board of directors, Chicago, Burlington & Quincy Railroad (1930-1934).

Walker D. Hines, railroad lawyer, executive, and public advocate, as well as director general of the United States Railroad Administration (USRA), was born at the very time that the "railroad prob-

lem" emerged as a major issue in American politics, and he devoted most of his professional life to defining and resolving it. Privately and publicly, in court and out, before state legislatures and Congress, and in speeches and writings, Hines was among the most active, articulate, and respected of all railroad advocates. It is a measure of his reputation that many of the most critical regulatory cases taken to the Supreme Court and the Interstate Commerce Commission (ICC) were entrusted by the railroads to Hines, and that during the rail congestion crisis of late 1917 even the government turned to its long-time opponent for assistance. It was his appointment to the USRA, which administered federalization of railroads during and shortly after America's involvement in World War I, that gained Hines national prominence outside of railroad circles. Having strongly resisted for two decades nearly all government efforts to regulate big business, he became America's most powerful government regulator—an experience which changed his mind about regulation so much that he advocated a continuation of federalization for five years after the war as a peace-time experiment. Indeed, Hines came to believe that the way to ameliorate the railroad problem and pre-

Walker D. Hines

serve private ownership of railroads was not by returning to an unregulated economy but by establishing strong, positive regulation. After the war he continued to participate in public life, applying his new ideas to domestic and international problems.

Walker Downer Hines was born in Russellville, Kentucky, on February 2, 1870, to James Madison Hines, a lawyer and journalist, and Mary Walker Downer Hines. His mother raised him after the death of his father. At age fourteen Hines began study at Ogden College in Bowling Green, Kentucky. He also did stenographic work at this time for the law office of James A. Mitchell and John E. Du Bose, and for the Circuit Court of Warren County, Kentucky. After graduating with a B.S. in 1888 Hines engaged in private and court stenography in Trinidad, Colorado, where he lived with his cousin, a county judge.

In 1890 Hines moved to Louisville, where he was taken on as a secretary to Horatio W. Bruce, assistant chief attorney of the Louisville & Nashville Railroad (L&N). After taking a leave of absence in 1892 to earn a University of Virginia law degree—in one-third the normal time yet with "a distinguished

record"—Hines became the L&N's assistant attorney in 1893. A promotion to assistant chief attorney came in 1897. In 1901 he was made first vice president, responsible not just for legal affairs but for many financial and operating matters as well. Hines held the post until 1904, when he was lured away from the L&N by Louisville judge Alexander P. Humphrey to join his firm, which became Humphrey, Hines & Humphrey. In 1906 Hines moved to New York City, where he practiced private law with the firm of Craveth, Henderson & de Gersdorff from 1907 to 1913 and associated himself with the Atchison, Topeka & Sante Fe as general counsel from 1906 to 1918; as chairman of the executive committee from 1908 to 1916; and as chairman of the board of directors from 1916 to 1918.

By any account, Hines was a legal genius. During his early career he built a reputation for being what a lawyer later termed "quiet and serious, scholarly and analytical. . . ." Indeed, "despite his mild and unaggressive nature," wrote the historian of Hines's high-powered New York law firm, "he dominated every matter in which he was retained, and regardless of the number or importance of his colleagues, in the end they looked to him for the organization of the case." Hines was extremely hardworking; he had few diversions, save a dry wit: when an interviewer asked him about his golf game, he replied, "O yes, I play golf sometimes, but I'm always the poorest player on the grounds. I can't play golf and work in the same month." He did find time to marry Alice Clymer Macfarlane on October 24, 1900, and to play with their only child, Helen Macfarlane Hines. But "if you wish to know Walker Hines as he is," a journalist stated, "you must know him at work."

It was during Hines's years with the L&N that he began to apply his considerable abilities to the railroad problem that had surfaced around the time of his birth and had only worsened by the time he joined the road's legal staff. By the late 1860s the railroads had lost much of their mystique and come under substantial attack, particularly in the Midwestern "Granger" states of Illinois, Minnesota, Iowa, and Wisconsin. The sheer magnitude of the nation's first big business, various discriminations (some unfair, others legitimate reflections of railroad economics), the arrogance of many rail executives, and stock manipulation were among the factors that contributed to antipathy toward railways and movements to regulate them. Unable to find relief from high rates in the rate stipulations of rail charters, which placed high ceilings on rate levels, or from discriminatory rates, to which the common law did not speak, discontented Midwesterners turned in the early 1870s to legislative solutions. From the Granger states emerged the Illinois model of the "strong" railroad commission, an independent regulatory agency endowed with the power to fix rates. In the landmark Granger cases later in the 1870s the Supreme Court denied most of the carriers' claims: that the states were improperly regulating interstate traffic; that legislative rate-fixing violated the Fourteenth Amendment if not state railroad charter provisions; that the determination of a rate's reasonableness was a judicial rather than a legislative function; and that singling out railroads as having a special public character, and hence especially needful of regulation, was unwarranted.

The Granger laws were called radical and crude by the railroads, but many of the laws were short-lived and were moderated by the commissions which administered them. The Panic of 1873 and ensuing depression, growing railroad competition in the Midwest, improved rail technology and efficiency, and a long-term deflationary trend beginning in the latter 1870s combined to drive rates downward, take the steam out of much rail criticism, and cause some of the states to repeal or modify their rail regulation.

As the drive for regulation faded in the Midwest, however, it began to gather momentum in the East, partly because the roads were trying to make up for losses (or low profits) on competitive long hauls between the Midwest and the East with high charges on shorter, less competitive hauls within the East itself. A realization that such problems could not be resolved merely through regulation at the state level, especially after the Supreme Court in the *Wabash* case of 1886 ruled that states could not regulate the rates of interstate shipments, helped propel a national drive for regulation, culminating in the Interstate Commerce Act (ICA) of 1887.

Many rail executives, including Hines, were not opposed to regulation in principle; some, for example, called for government restrictions on new rail construction. A number of them also hoped to dampen competition, and thus raise and stabilize rates, by making pool members adhere through legal compulsion to agreements made with other members. While Hines was to realize more than most railroad men that legalizing cartels would not be effective unless all roads in a given area were compelled to join a pool, he concurred with most rail executives in desiring legal prohibitions against rebating. The railroads thus favored the antirebating provisions of the ICA, which they hoped would make railways less captive to large shippers.

On balance, however, they opposed the act, for it prohibited some forms of long-and-short-haul discriminations and made pooling illegal. The nation's first modern regulation was to be guided by the principle of enforced competition, the very principle the railroads sought legislatively to repudiate. Moreover, although many rail managers had no objection to the idea of railroad commissions, they became angered at the ICC's increasing willingness to apply the long-and-short-haul clause and to fix rates, which the ICA had mandated must be "just and reasonable."

By the late 1890s the railroads had successfully challenged the ICC in the courts on the validity of these two rate powers, and they intended to do everything in their power to keep them a dead letter. Government, they believed, was the primary cause of their most serious problem—excessive competition. Overbuilding, deflation, and the 1893-1897 depression all were recognized by rail leaders as contributing to the steady decline in rates and widespread rail bankruptcies and receiverships during the 1880s and 1890s, but government, they contended, had compounded the problem. The antipooling provision seemed particularly obnoxious: not only did it lead to ruinous rate wars and industry instability, it also encouraged the very things which the ICA sought to eliminate—rebates and other discriminations. To make matters worse, the roads' favorite alternate means of diminishing competition short of outright merger, the traffic association, was also declared illegal by the Supreme Court in two cases in 1897 and 1898. It is a measure of how variously the railroad problem was defined by different parties that one rail executive, shortly before passage of the ICA, could speak of "the chaos which some reformers think is competition."

What dramatically, if temporarily, turned things around for the rail industry was the decade-long economic boom following the 1893-1897 depression. Financially, this was the golden period of American railroading. Almost overnight the roads went from being overextended to being underbuilt—despite a massive physical reconstruction to enlarge carrying capacity. The new traffic demands, a rail consolidation movement, a strengthened anti-rebating law in 1903, and rising rates boosted profits and made railroads an attractive investment. Even as the picture brightened, however, clouds began to appear: public opinion tended to associate the rate increases not with postdepression inflation but with the consolidation movement and the weakening of the ICC.

If, as one railroad man phrased it, government ratemaking became "the storm-centre of the railroad problem," Hines was to provide much of the railroads' thunder. Probably no one in rail circles devoted more time to confronting the railroad problem than Walker Hines. Some railroad men spoke to the issue more eloquently; some had more practical experience in running railroads. But none possessed Hines's combination of rail experience, clarity of expression, ability to marshall economic and legal data in support of an argument, and single-mindedness of purpose. By common consent, no one in the industry knew interstate commerce law better, followed its developments more closely, analyzed it more deeply, or fought it so successfully before courts and railroad commissions. It was a tribute to his expertise that even the ICC, against whom Hines argued many important cases for the railroads before the Supreme Court, employed him in one of its cases before that court.

Hines honed his skills with the Louisville & Nashville at the state level, where government rate powers were expanding. In 1887 eighteen of the twenty-six state railroad commissions were only advisory in nature, but by 1903 there were thirty state commissions, twenty of the "strong" variety. Hines fought establishment of government ratemaking in general and its application to the L&N in particular.

But it was his simultaneous public debate with outspoken ICC commissioner Charles Prouty over whether to rearm the ICC with independent rate powers that thrust Hines into national prominence. The two antagonists carried on the debate in all of the contemporary media between 1897 and the passage in 1906 of the Hepburn Act, which en-

dowed the ICC once again with rate-fixing power. In seeking the ratemaking power, Hines argued, the ICC was making "extravagant demands far beyond what Congress intended." Congressional records made it clear that the ICA's framers had meant to create not an independent body whose powers were self-enforcing and virtually exempt from judicial review but an investigatory and advisory agency whose recommendations, if contested, had to go to the courts for final determination. The Supreme Court, noted Hines, had confirmed this original intent by ruling that the ICC had improperly assumed rate powers it did not legally possess. To claim, as did the ICC and its supporters, that the highest court in the land had emasculated the commission of its powers and thereby left the public unprotected from rail abuses was to distort the truth and dishonor the good sense of the Supreme Court.

In constructing the act, contended Hines, Congress had wisely followed the separation of powers principle. Making ICC rate powers "practically conclusive" would violate due process of law. Actually, the Supreme Court neither had nor would explicitly declare it unconstitutional to combine legislative, judicial, and executive powers in one administrative body. Hines and many other railroad men claimed with some justice, however, that acceding to ICC rate powers would involve merging government functions that traditionally had been kept distinct. The ICC should not become, as Hines put it, at one and the same time "a detective, prosecutor, complainant, judge, and jury." The irony, according to Hines, was that even as the ICC sought the ratemaking power, it did not sufficiently use the powers it did legally possess. The ICA, for example, clearly gave the commission power to deal with rebates—in Hines's mind the most serious side of the railroad problem—but the agency had made only half-hearted attempts to eliminate them. In any event, the ICC's powers were adequate to protect the public: where unjust discriminations or exorbitant rates did exist, the commission was available to investigate them and seek redress through the courts.

Hines also opposed government ratemaking on the basis of America's tradition of limited government and free enterprise. In his view, "immutable commercial conditions" ultimately and quite appropriately set rail rates, not the railroads themselves. Why else were America's rail rates the lowest in the world? Placing ratemaking powers in the hands of ICC members, who were typically inexperienced in railroad economics, would artificially disturb the self-regulative market and politicize it—as was being demonstrated in many states where legislatures made rates or delegated such powers to commissions. Inevitably, railroads would be the victims, for the ICC clearly was "the champion of the shipper." The powers desired by the ICC were, in short, "unnecessary, unreasonable, and dangerous."

Whether or where Hines's convictions and rationalizations began and left off is impossible to determine. Surely as a lawyer he was accustomed to taking positions at variance with his personal opinion. Perhaps as an employee of the L&N's president Milton Smith, whose repugnance for regulation was legendary, Hines was merely catering to his employer's biases; later he may have been catering to the similar biases of the general rail community, on which his private practice thrived. On the other hand, Hines might have developed a genuine antiregulatory stance precisely because of the influence of Smith. Ultimately, most rail leaders seem to have resisted most kinds of regulation more for practical than theoretical reasons. While willing to support regulation deemed helpful to the railroads, nearly all railroad men drew the line with governmental ratemaking, for they feared losing control over their own financial destinies. As one rail executive had expressed it in the 1870s, "There is no such thing as separating control and ownership. Control is ownership."

The hard-fought campaign of Hines and others to prevent the revitalization of the ICC and the proliferation of state regulation proved unsuccessful in the end; the swift currents of the Progressive Era swept away all antiregulation arguments. Between 1902 and 1907 fifteen new or remodeled state railroad commissions were created, twenty-two states passed laws fixing passenger fares, and nine states established freight rates by statute. In 1907 alone eleven states reduced freight rates, fourteen lowered passenger fares, and twelve reduced hours of labor. The states also initiated a host of new taxes and regulations related to rail operations and service. At the federal level, the Hepburn Act of 1906 empowered the ICC to set rates upon complaint from shippers. Stronger still was the Mann-Elkins Act of 1910, which restored the validity of the long-and-short-

haul clause and required proposed rate increases to be sanctioned by the ICC before going into effect.

Many factors contributed to the railroad defeat. Some of these were beyond the roads' control; others were of their own doing. An age that did not fully understand the concept of "real" price levels found it easy to identify turn-of-the-century rate increases with railroad greed and consolidation rather than with inflation. However misinterpreted, the rate increases created public resentment, which, in an era when laissez faire was on the defensive, was easily converted into new rail legislation, especially since the railroads were the most visible and hence politically vulnerable of the so-called trusts. But the roads themselves poisoned the political atmosphere. The Hepburn Act, for example, was made all the more inevitable by public disclosures of how rebates had contributed to the consolidation of giants like Standard Oil. The abuses came to touch even the White House: President Theodore Roosevelt's secretary of the navy, Paul Morton, was forced to resign when it was revealed that while he was a vice president with the Santa Fe, his railroad had granted rebates. Such practices were actually more prevalent during the nineteenth century than during the Progressive Era, but the exposure had an immediacy to it that had explosive political results. The roads also evidently engaged in a clandestine campaign via newspapers and other means to stop the drive for ICC rearmament; when divulged, it naturally boomeranged on the roads. The muckrakers did not have to work hard; it was as if the roads were handing them the muck ready made. Even less calculated to win friends in legislative circles was the carriers' attempt to file general rate increases averaging 10 to 15 percent just prior to passage of the Mann-Elkins Act. The roads backed down when President William Howard Taft twisted their arms at a meeting at which Hines was in attendance, but the blunder nonetheless "outraged public opinion," as one scholar states it, "hampered conservatives, and produced . . . a more stringent act."

Such miscalculation, or perhaps outright bungling, was indicative of the rail industry's public relations' growing pains. These relations had begun in the nineteenth century with the remark attributed to the New York Central's William H. Vanderbilt, "The public be damned," and came of age in the early twentieth century when Treasury Secretary William McAdoo suggested that the railroads adopt a new attitude of "the public be praised." Some rail executives had realized the need for favorable publicity long before professional public relations firms surfaced at the turn of the century, but this recognition was neither widespread nor frequently acted upon. One rail leader accurately observed in 1880 that the public misunderstood railroading because even though "the railways represent the most important industrial and financial interest in the land, they have the scantiest literature, and have written little in self-defense. . . ." It was not just the limited quantity of public relations but its uncreative quality that hurt the roads. Again, certain railroad men were their own best critics: "All through the Granger contests," noted one executive, "the railways have weakened the force of their arguments by their misrepresentation of facts and their extravagant prediction of ruin."

When Hines began his antiregulatory campaign in the 1890s, public relations had come a long way from the level of the 1870s, when the best the railroads seemed to be able to do was to argue how proposed regulation would afflict—as one railroad man put it—"minor children" and "widows." Hines appreciated the value of public relations, and on balance his dozens of speeches and writings probably helped the roads' cause. Yet even the normally self-controlled Hines damaged his campaign by occasional intemperate language and personal attacks, thereby polarizing the debate between the ICC and its opponents. He charged, for example, that ever "since the courts have decided against the Commission's cherished views, the Commission has been sulking . . . . It has apparently sought to discourage attempts to enforce the act . . . , apparently with the hope that if it can bring about the complete failure of the present act it can thereby secure the gratification of its ambitious desires."

Given the ICC's use of its official position to advance its point of view, Hines and other railroad men were entitled to some indignation. He was in good scholarly company, moreover, in questioning the constitutionality of commission ratemaking, and his fears about how the ICC would use proposed rate powers were proved legitimate. Yet with much truth a railroad man could say in 1912: "The drastic features of some enactments would have been avoided had railway managers always exercised the spirit of forbearance and compromise."

The roads needed all of the "forbearance" they could muster in the later Progressive years, when the American rail industry began a decline from which it never fully recovered. While regulation was not the sole cause of this decline, scholars see it as a major one. Armed with powers obtained in the Hepburn and Mann-Elkins acts, the ICC generally refused rate advances; given the inflation of the period, it can be argued the ICC actually reduced rates. This policy led to a chain of problems for the roads: profits dropped, investments in the industry sank, and improvements and maintenance were scaled back or abandoned, thus leaving the roads ill equipped to meet growing domestic traffic, much less World War I's shipping needs.

Hines's fortunes, like those of the rail industry, plummeted: as the prime witness in the extensive pre-Hepburn Act hearings, his arguments obviously went unheeded; he was unsuccessful in representing many roads in their joint rate increase requests before the ICC in 1910; and he was unable to convince the Supreme Court that the Adamson Act of 1916, which gave rail workers an eight-hour day, was unconstitutional. Hines claimed publicly that the railroads were "defenceless" before labor, and in 1917, with the war economy booming, he wondered if the roads would "get some crumbs of this prosperity."

One of the few bright spots for the industry during these years was the emergence of a more professional level of public relations. Increasingly after the Hepburn and Mann-Elkins acts, the ability to perform public relations work became an integral part of the rail executive's role. Once rarely seen or heard in public, many managers became highly visible and available for speaking engagements, and their speeches were often printed and mass distributed. Some executives traveled thousands of miles along their lines (Hines did so for the Sante Fe) to learn of and reduce sources of public irritation, to counter the image of absentee management, and ultimately to muster support for more constructive regulatory policies. The roads worked together, too, as evidenced by formation in 1910 of the Bureau of Railway Economics, whose staff of economists and statisticians lent a much more professional air to public relations efforts. The roads' cause was further advanced by their being less negative and alarmist in tone, and acknowledging—publicly at least—the validity of the principle of public regulation.

Perhaps most important of all was the decision of many rail leaders to tie public relations closely to the notions of "scientific management" and efficiency that had become the intellectual rage during the Progressive years. Whereas previously most rail executives had appeared obstructionist and anachronistic in their opposition to regulation, they now appeared more in the vanguard of contemporary "gospel of efficiency" thought. The roads thus began to score points among transportation professors, journalists, and even congressmen by noting how the antipooling clause caused wasteful duplications of facilities and competitive pressures to grant rebates. Hines and others also pointed out the irrationality of having interstate railroads subject to so many different, often conflicting state regulations. Regulation, Hines repeatedly argued, was confused, divided, and out of control; no one in government really was assuming responsibility for it.

Although the railroads began to find the public more sympathetic to their plight in the later Progressive years, it was the war that exposed the shortcomings of the regulatory system and that forced the government to develop a more positive, more rational, and more accountable approach. Suddenly the railroad problem seemed to be the same for everyone; or at least almost everyone could finally agree on what was the most urgent of the several railroad problems. Scientific management became more than just a buzzword: it was crucial to a war based on a full-scale mobilization of economic resources. Most railroad men had been forced to recognize their own blame for the railroad problem; now the government was forced to admit its responsibility as well.

The immediate difficulty was the freight congestion crisis of late 1917. Even a robust rail industry would have been hard-pressed to meet the extraordinary traffic demands. But the ICC rate increase refusals and resulting retrenchments and the antipooling and antitrust laws made the situation worse than it needed to be. The Railroads' War Board privately attempted to cope with the situation but was hamstrung by the laws of enforced competition, by what Hines termed "individual instinct," and by conflicting and excessive government war "priority orders." Given these and other problems, President Woodrow Wilson decided to impose federal control on the roads beginning on December 28, 1917. And so cooperation developed between the national government and the railroads—a

precedent whose significance would stretch far beyond the war years and this single industry.

It is a measure of the urgency of the congestion problem that the railroads were the most federalized of all the industries during the war and that Wilson made his most able cabinet member, treasury secretary McAdoo, director general of the United States Railroad Administration and Hines, a Democrat in addition to his many other qualifications, assistant director. McAdoo and Hines seem to have seen eye to eye on most issues, with Hines handling day-to-day USRA operations because of McAdoo's preoccupation with treasury duties.

Hines's appointment, first as assistant director, and then as director general in mid–January 1919 after McAdoo resigned from the post, met with heavy criticism from some quarters because of the lawyer's close identity with rail interests. It seemed inconceivable to some that one of regulation's most forceful opponents would be made responsible for federal control.

Yet Hines surprised these individuals and perhaps most of all his rail colleagues by how abruptly and extensively he changed his regulatory views. He had "started out," as he stated it to some USRA personnel, "believing that practically no public regulation was necessary." In past years he had always "studied it from the standpoint of the Railroad Companies," but recently he had evaluated it "from the standpoint of the general public." Taking this broader view, he came to conclude that the railroads were in trouble for more than just regulatory reasons, that their survival—especially that of the weaker roads—depended upon acceptance of strong but positive postwar regulation which would protect the railroads, investors, labor, and the public alike. This kind of regulation could best be accomplished, Hines believed, by mandatory regional consolidation comparable to what had been done by the Railroad Administration. Ideally, each regional rail system would be run by a board of directors, some members of which would be public officials appointed by the federal government. Regulation would emanate from a national commission and several regional commissions, with public board members on each of the commissions. Similarly, labor issues would be resolved through boards composed of government, labor, and management personnel. Hines realized these changes would entail a "radical reconstruction" of rail management, but he contended that collective management would help foster "a direct understanding" and "direct sense of responsibility for . . . public service." Financially, according to Hines's scheme, the railroads would be guaranteed a minimum 5 percent income, beyond which two-thirds would return to the federal government. Such permanent changes could mitigate, as was already the case with the Railroad Administration, the older style railroad politics that had been so punctuated with conflict and misunderstanding (he characterized prewar railroading as "largely conducted through a series of law suits").

The change in Hines's views was partly a function of the office remaking the man. But Hines was also a convert to the new scientific management ideas of the time, which were aimed at abating the competition, conflict, decentralization, amateurism, and politicoeconomic irresponsibility of the late nineteenth and early twentieth centuries. Hines's vision stemmed from the larger "search for order," as one scholar has aptly termed it, during a dizzying era of rapid industrial, urban, and technological change. Like many others, he believed that industrial society could be rationalized through careful, centralized organization. These ideas shaped Hines's perception of the director general's role as conciliator between different rail parties. He proved, in fact, to be more astute in handling Railroad Administration politics than the more emotional McAdoo.

Yet for all his gifts of conciliation, and despite the widespread respect that he earned for some of his decongestion and unification efforts, Hines found himself embroiled in controversies with various groups. He felt compelled even during the busy days of running the nation's railroads to take time before Congress and in newspapers and speeches to defend Railroad Administration decisions. A defensive tone is still evident in his *War History of American Railroads* (1928), published a decade after federalization.

Shippers accurately complained that the USRA was much less sympathetic to them than the ICC had been: rate increases were announced in 1918, they noted, with virtually no shipper consultation, thus proving the prorailroad bias of the Railroad Administration. The public frequently voiced its dissatisfaction with the inconveniences of reduced civilian passenger service. The railroads and labor, which received large rate and wage increases under McAdoo, claimed less generous treatment under

Hines's tenure as director general. Even so, the roads claimed that too much had been sacrificed to labor in respect both to wages and to the creation of national work rules, whose excesses plagued rail productivity even after the war. In addition, the roads maintained that Hines's rate increase denials left them in poor shape physically as well as fiscally after the war.

Hines and many contemporary transportation experts countered some of these charges by noting that shippers were given more say during the latter part of the USRA's tenure; that public transportation inconveniences were a function of the primary goal of troop and war-related freight movement; that wage increases and many labor rules were long overdue (railroads, for example, had been losing skilled workers before the war because of higher wages in other industries); that rail undermaintenance claims were frequently inflated; that while rail rates could legitimately have been raised toward the end of federal control due to inflation and a slump in freight traffic after the armistice, such a move—directly paralleled by the 1910 attempts to raise rates before new ICC rate powers went into effect—would be politically inexpedient since it might sour chances of a postwar reconstruction of federal regulatory policy (the ICC, in fact, operating under the Transportation Act of 1920, was to raise rates about 30 percent in 1920); and that, in general, Hines had fairly treated all rail interest groups.

However statesmanlike Hines may have been, it was his misfortune to assume the directorship in early 1919, a year beset, in his words, by "kaleidoscopic changes." During much of the previous year, when the United States was actually at war, patriotism had muted many criticisms. But with the November armistice, older competitive, individual, and political influences resurfaced with new force. The depression of early 1919, moreover, swelled an already existing USRA deficit, and Hines refused to overcome it through rate increases because of White House desires to contain inflation. A refusal by Congress in March 1919 to appropriate additional USRA funds, and then the granting of a smaller than expected appropriation in June, forced Hines to abandon or greatly retrench railroad physical improvements and regulatory innovations. Finally, many of the most competent and experienced USRA officials resigned from the USRA once the war crisis appeared to be over. What had been entered upon enthusiastically as a bold experiment in government management turned into what one historian has termed an "impossible situation," a thankless job of winding down federal control in the face of a public eager to return to private operation and hypercritical of government control.

Sensing that federal control would end soon, railroad interest groups began maneuvering for a favorable restructuring of peacetime regulation. By 1919 it had become clear that Congress was disinclined to return to the prewar regulatory system. The real questions were how extensive regulatory reconstruction would be, by what date Congress could devise new legislation, and whether, in the interim, federal control should be retained.

As he was departing from the USRA in early 1919 McAdoo had announced his belief that federal control should be extended for five years. Federal control during the war, McAdoo reasoned, represented too brief and abnormal a period on the basis of which to judge the merits of federal control as a peacetime phenomenon. By continuing federal control for several years, Congress could observe it under normal conditions and have sufficient time to fashion a new regulatory system with the deliberation it deserved. Hines supported McAdoo in these opinions.

Most interest groups, however, were opposed to all but a very brief extension and began feverishly promoting their own particular regulatory schemes for the postwar period. The USRA became the most available foil: "The atmosphere," noted one transportation expert at the time, "was befogged by propaganda designed to create a favorable public attitude toward each of the many plans advanced for the solution of the railroad problem, and practically all . . . propagandists set out to discredit the record of the Railroad Administration." A favorite target was the USRA's efficiency record. While virtually all parties admitted that some economies had resulted from federal control, many argued that these were more than offset by such specific factors as the increase in rail employees and the sizable deficit.

Again, Hines and some of the more disinterested rail observers addressed many of these charges. It was claimed, for example, that the absolute number of rail employees had gone up not because of inefficiency but because of the shorter rail

workday mandated by the Adamson Act. Nor was the deficit necessarily a reflection of inefficiency; rather it could—perhaps should—be viewed as one of the costs either of inflation-saving rate increase denials or of the war itself, which left many federal agencies in debt. In any event, it was maintained, the USRA's primary mandate of ending congestion and facilitating the movement of troops and war goods at times conflicted with pure efficiency considerations. The unique conditions of war, combined with the haste with which many decisions had to be made, made it unfair to project the efficiency of peacetime federal control on the basis of wartime federal operation.

While some of the attacks on the USRA may have been unfair, some of that criticism was brought on by the USRA itself, which early in its life had raised unrealistic expectations about the potential savings of federal control. Hines was probably less to blame for this situation than McAdoo, but it was Hines who headed the agency when its deficit reached such great proportions ($900 million when federal control ended). Most scholars who have evaluated the USRA's efficiency have concluded that there were overall efficiency gains but that they were, at best, moderate rather than dramatic. It appears that the argument of those who condemned the concept of federal control on the basis of wartime experience was no more valid than the position of those who argued for federal control on the ground that the congestion crisis had proved the inherent defects of private rail management. Management justifiably contended that ICC rate policy and antitrust laws had given it no real opportunity to demonstrate its abilities; World War II did give it a chance, and its performance was such that it was left largely free of federal control.

In the end, Congress continued federal control until passing the Transportation Act of 1920, which returned regulatory power to the ICC and management to private owners. In certain respects, however, "this act expressed," in Hines's words, "a revolution in the attitude of the public toward railroad regulation." He, like most rail leaders, especially liked four features of the new law: allowances for pooling and encouragement of consolidation; delegation to the ICC of power to set minimum as well as maximum rates; establishment of rates on a "fair" valuation of capital investment; and authorization for the ICC to revise intrastate rates in those cases where such rates discriminated against interstate traffic.

Hines thought that the act's greatest weakness was that it made consolidation voluntary rather than mandatory. During the 1920s and 1930s he would advocate consolidation more strongly than any other regulatory measure, believing that the resulting economies would better enable the railroads to compete with automobiles and trucks. He contended that the ICC could design consolidations that would preserve "competition of a salutary character which at the same time would eliminate some purely wasteful duplications of service."

With the Transportation Act marking an end to one regulatory era, Hines seemed to have lost some of his interest in the railroad problem, although he continued to write and speak on regulatory issues. His long and largely successful campaign for a more positive regulatory program left him longing for new challenges, and he resigned from the USRA on May 15, 1920. His experience with public service seems to have whetted his appetite for more of it, and his involvement in the war had awakened him to broader public concerns. It soon became clear that the peace treaties left many international problem unresolved and, in fact, created some new ones. Hines worried, as he stated in a 1923 article in *Foreign Affairs,* about America's reluctance to "do anything to help tranquillize an unfortunate world . . . . The fact is that all the Allies are tarred with the same brush. Each appears to have been utterly devoid of spiritual and unselfish principles since the Armistice," and "so has jeopardized its own welfare."

Hines made a personal contribution to tranquilizing the world when, while vacationing in Europe in June 1920, he accepted President Wilson's invitation to become an arbitrator for the Allied Council of Ambassadors, which was trying to resolve international shipping disputes regarding central European rivers. Most of the problems involved sorting out which countries would get which commercial ships, given the realities of wartime seizures and changes in territorial possessions. "The most intricate problem of all," according to Hines, "was to decide how much of German, Austrian and Hungarian shipping on the Danube would should be turned over to Czechoslovakia, Yugoslavia and Rumania—a sort of six-sided puzzle." He was pleased to report that politicoeconomic problems were less troublesome in

respect to the Rhine because the League of Nations' Transit Section was showing "an amazingly international, well-balanced spirit." Unfortunately, he observed, "In this country we do not adequately realize that the existence of the League has developed an international sentiment . . . ." Successfully completing his work in October 1921 he was awarded honors from three countries: France designated him a Commander of the Legion of Honor; the Kingdom of the Serbs, Croats and Slovenes (Yugoslavia) decorated him with the Order of the White Eagle, First Class; and Czechoslovakia made him a member of the Cross of Grand Officer, Order of White Lion.

Hines returned to the private practice of law in New York that same month but international questions drew him back to Europe in 1925, when the League of Nations asked him to investigate the status of navigation on the Danube River. In his *Report on Danube Navigation* (1925) Hines pointed out that the breakup of Austria-Hungary meant that the Danube was now bordered by many more nations, whose varying shipping rules and protectionist tariffs had reduced the volume of international traffic on the river and hurt a number of industries. The problem must have reminded Hines of the "forty-eight masters" situation in the United States, involving the conflicting and often protectionist railroad regulations of the various states—a problem which had at least been partially addressed by the Transportation Act.

Hines's capacity for analysis, publicity, organization, and mediation, evident in respect to railroad companies, domestic political interest groups, and countries, contributed to his selection in 1926 as the first president of the Cotton Textile Institute in New York. Being part of this new trade association attracted Hines because, in his words, "it constitutes the first effort in the country to establish . . . a single organization representing the cotton textile industry for both the North and the South." The agency was founded in order to limit production, which had greatly expanded during the war; to develop new products and markets; and to generate statistics for better-informed decisions. Hines served in this capacity until 1929, when he became chairman of the institute's board of directors; he resigned from that position in 1931. According to one source, "The soundness of his conclusions became generally recognized," and his "educational work not only laid the foundation for that industry's distinction as the first to adopt a code under the National Industrial Recovery Act, but [the Cotton Textile Institute's] principles were directly reflected in that Code."

Institute duties did not prevent his participation in various other private and public matters. The firm of Hines, Rearick, Dorr, Travis & Marshall was formed in early 1927, and Hines became a member of the board of directors of the Chicago, Burlington & Quincy Railroad in 1930. He also held positions in the Association of the Bar of the City of New York, and for a time he was president of the New York Economic Club. By the 1930s Hines had gained something of a reputation for his economic expertise: President-elect Franklin D. Roosevelt consulted him on how to cut federal expenses, and even considered Hines for director of the budget.

In 1933 the Turkish government asked a team of economic experts, headed by Hines, to visit Turkey to survey its economy and make financial and business development proposals. While on a second trip to Turkey he fell ill in Italy, where he died on January 14, 1934.

Hines had traveled a good distance geographically and intellectually since his boyhood days in Logan County, Kentucky. His loyalties, interests, understanding, and service broadened, while remaining consistently focused on questions of public policy. Whether or not one agrees with all of Hines's ideas and actions, he should be admired for his dedication to the railroads, the nation, and the world. It was not Hines's personality but the sheer competence of this intense, indefatigable, self-effacing man that attracted people to him. He typified the passing of the flamboyant Gilded Age businessman and the arrival of the low-profile, bureaucratic, professionally trained organization man. Yet he was no mere company man. Hines proved himself capable of transcending a one-sided view of regulation. He moved beyond the private concerns of many of his lawyer colleagues and became, in one of the better traditions of the legal profession, a problem-solving, conflict-resolving public servant.

Publications:

"When a Federal Question Is Raised on the Record," *American Law Review*, 35 (July-August 1901): 536-545;

"The Proposals of the Interstate Commerce Commission," *Forum*, 33 (March 1902): 3-14;

"Legislative Regulation of Railroad Rates," *Proceedings of the American Economic Association*, 4 (February 1903): 84-103;

"Unfair Railroad Regulation," *Saturday Evening Post*, 177 (April 22, 1905): 17-19;

"Shall Railway Rates Be Raised?" *Outlook*, 96 (December 10, 1910): 815-821;

"Our Irresponsible State Governments," *Atlantic Monthly*, 115 (May 1915): 637-647;

"The Conflict between State and Federal Regulation of Railroads," *Annals of the American Academy of Political and Social Science*, 63 (January 1916): 191-198;

"The Director-General's Position," *Nation*, 109 (August 16, 1919): 202-203;

"The Relationship of the Burlington-Great Northern-Northern Pacific Group to the Federal Railroad Consolidation Law," *Harvard Business Review*, 1 (October 1922): 398-413;

"Peace Agencies and Politics," *Foreign Affairs*, 2 (December 1923): 244-257;

Report on Danube Navigation (Lausanne: Imp. reunies s.a., 1925);

"International Transit Problems," *Proceedings of the Academy of Political Science*, 12 (July 1926): 445-453;

"Walker D. Hines before Convention of Cotton Interests Discusses Purpose of Cotton Textile Institute," *Commercial & Financial Chronicle*, 124 (May 21, 1927): 2995-2996;

War History of American Railroads (New Haven: Yale University Press, 1928);

"The Public Interest in Railroad Unification and Consolidation," *Proceedings of the Academy of Political Science*, 13 (June 1929): 329-338.

References:

Bernard Axelrod, "Railroad Regulation in Transition, 1897-1905: Walker D. Hines of the Railroads v. Charles A. Prouty of the ICC," Ph.D. dissertation, Washington University, 1975;

William J. Cunningham, *American Railroads: Government Control and Reconstruction Policies* (Chicago: Shaw, 1922);

Frank Haigh Dixon, *Railroads and Government: Their Relations in the United States, 1910-1921* (New York: Scribners, 1922);

William R. Doezema, "Maneuvering within the System: Railroad Responses to State and Federal Regulation, 1870-1916," Ph.D. dissertation, Kent State University, 1978;

Doezema, "Railroad Management and the Interplay of Federal and State Regulation, 1885-1916," *Business History Review*, 50 (Summer 1976): 153-178;

Ari and Olive Hoogenboom, *A History of the ICC: From Panacea to Palliative* (New York: Norton, 1976);

K. Austin Kerr, *American Railroad Politics, 1914-1920: Rates, Wages, and Efficiency* (Pittsburgh: University of Pittsburgh Press, 1968);

Gabriel Kolko, *Railroads and Regulation, 1877-1916* (Princeton: Princeton University Press, 1965);

Albro Martin, *Enterprise Denied: Origins of the Decline of American Railroads, 1897-1917* (New York: Columbia University Press, 1971);

National Archives of the United States, *Records of the United States Railroad Administration* (Record Group 14);

Alan R. Raucher, *Public Relations and Business, 1900-1929* (Baltimore: Johns Hopkins Press, 1968);

Jackson Reynolds and C. H. Hand, Jr., "Memorial of Walker Downer Hines," *Association of the Bar of the City of New York Yearbook* (1934): 324-328;

I. Leo Sharfman, *The American Railroad Problem: A Study in War and Reconstruction* (New York: Century, 1921);

Robert T. Swain, *The Craveth Firm and Its Predecessors, 1819-1948,* 2 volumes (New York: Ad Press, 1946-1948);

Thomas H. Uzzell, "Walker D. Hines," *Nation's Business,* 7 (March 1919): 28-29, 60;

Robert H. Wiebe, *The Search for Order, 1877-1920* (New York: Hill & Wang, 1967).

Archives:

Copies of Walker D. Hines's speeches can be found at the Interstate Commerce Commission Library, the Library of Congress, and the Association of American Railroads Library, all in Washington, D.C., and the Association of the Bar of the City of New York Library in New York. A collection of Hines's materials, much of it published and available elsewhere, is in the John W. Barringer III Railroad Library of the St. Louis Mercantile Library Association. The records of the United States Railroad Administration are in Record Group 14 at the National Archives of the United States, Washington, D.C.

Hale Holden

(August 11, 1869-September 23, 1940)

by Don L. Hofsommer

Augustana College

Hale Holden

CAREER: General attorney (1907-1910), assistant to the president (1910-1912), vice president (1912-1914), president, Chicago, Burlington & Quincy Railroad (1914-1918); regional director, Central Western Region, United States Railroad Administration (1918-1920); president, Chicago, Burlington & Quincy Railroad (1920-1928); chairman of the executive committee (1929-1932), chairman of the board of directors (1932-1939), Southern Pacific Company.

Defying an industry tradition that tended to favor an up-from-the-ranks route to executive quarters, Hale Holden came to railroading with a law degree and quickly found himself in the corner suite. Born at Kansas City, Missouri, in 1869 to Howard Malcolm Holden, a banker, and Mary Oburn Holden, Holden was educated at Williams College and the Harvard Law School. In 1895, while practicing law in Kansas City, he married Ellen Weston; they had three children before her death in 1936. In 1907 Holden became general attorney for the Chicago, Burlington & Quincy Railroad (CB&Q or Burlington).

Holden was a born diplomat who won important legal victories for the Burlington and was rewarded with a vice presidency in 1912. When the company's president, Darius Miller, died suddenly in 1914, Holden was thrust into the presidency of the CB&Q. As American involvement in World War I approached, Holden took an active role in industry plans to deal with expanded traffic, and during the period of government control he served as director of the Central Western Region for the United States Railroad Administration. When private operation returned in 1920, Holden was again named president of the Burlington.

Richard C. Overton, historian of the CB&Q, considered Holden "one of the ablest men ever to occupy the Burlington's presidency." Holden was at his best "in expounding lucidly and forcefully whatever idea he thought important for the company or industry he served." Although he delegated authority, assembling a management team that was strong in both operations and sales, he clearly set the general tenor of managerial style at the Burlington. Thus, for example, his interest in the welfare of employees and their families quickly became a matter of corporate policy.

James J. Hill had gained control of the Burlington in 1901, dividing its ownership between his Great Northern Railway and the Northern Pacific Railway, which he also controlled at that time. The CB&Q was a rich plum indeed; it produced profits with regularity, often providing better margins than the Great Northern and the Northern Pacific. A general harmony existed among the managers of the several roads, but it was clear that the Great Northern and the Northern Pacific were in a position to call the shots. This situation was a source of unease for Holden, whose reputation in the industry was growing at the same time as that of Ralph Budd, another man of great ability, who was Holden's counterpart at the Great Northern. Holden and Budd held somewhat different views as to the general direction the "Hill Lines" should take, and when Holden was offered the position of chairman of the executive committee at the Southern Pacific (SP) in 1928, he accepted. He became chairman of the board in 1932.

Holden's work at the SP took on a rather differ-ent character from his efforts at the CB&Q. His location, unlike that of his years at the Burlington, was off-line—at New York. And, in part because of the hard times of the 1930s, much of his energy was spent on financial matters, especially efforts to keep the company out of the bankruptcy courts. Nevertheless, he also concerned himself with technology, urging the company's officers in San Francisco, for instance, to study the possibility of electrifying the SP's major arteries in California and warning them of the need to keep up with the streamlining fad that was causing such a stir in rail passenger service.

Holden retired in July 1939, and died slightly over a year later following an illness complicated by a heart ailment.

References:

Don L. Hofsommer, *The Southern Pacific, 1901-1985* (College Station: Texas A&M University Press, 1986);

Richard C. Overton, *Burlington Route: A History of the Burlington Lines* (New York: Knopf, 1965).

Marvin Hughitt

(August 9, 1837-January 6, 1928)

by H. Roger Grant

University of Akron

Marvin Hughitt

CAREER: Telegrapher, New York, Albany & Buffalo Telegraph Company (1852-1854); telegrapher, Illinois & Missouri Telegraph Company (1854-1857); trainmaster and superintendent of telegraph, St. Louis, Alton & Chicago Railroad (1857-1862); superintendent, Southern Division (1862-1864), general superintendent (1864-1870), Illinois Central Railroad; assistant general manager, Chi-

cago, Milwaukee & St. Paul Railway (1870-1871); general manager, Pullman Palace Car Company (1871-1872); general superintendent (1872-1876); general manager (1876-1880), vice president and general manager (1880-1887), president (1887-1910), chairman of board of directors (1910-1925), chairman of the finance committee (1925-1928), Chicago & North Western Railway.

In the history of American railroading some individuals have come to be closely identified with certain companies. A leading example is Marvin Hughitt and the Chicago & North Western Railway Company (C&NW). By the 1890s C&NW employees frequently called Hughitt "King Marvin," an unmistakable indication of his standing with the road. Hughitt is thus to the C&NW what James J. Hill is to the Great Northern, Collis P. Huntington is to the Southern Pacific, and Henry M. Flagler is to the Florida East Coast Railway.

Born on August 9, 1837, on a Cayuga County, New York, farm, Hughitt was the son of Amos and Miranda Clark Hughitt. At the age of fifteen and with only modest public-school training, he went to work for the New York, Albany & Buffalo Telegraph Company in its Albany office. Two years later he moved to Chicago, where he was employed by the Illinois & Missouri Telegraph Company. Finally, in 1857, Hughitt entered railroad service in Bloomington, Illinois, as trainmaster and superintendent of telegraph for the St. Louis, Alton & Chicago Railroad, which became the Chicago & Alton in 1861. In 1858 Hughitt married Belle Barrett Hough, with whom he had six children. In 1862 he moved to the Illinois Central Railroad as superintendent of its Southern division. During the Civil War he faced a hectic and unpredictable work load, laboring continuously for long stints at the telegraph keys in the Illinois Central's Centralia office to keep Union army troop and munition trains on the move. Hughitt was promoted to the general superintendency of the Illinois Central in 1864, but left the road in 1870 to become assistant general manager of the Chicago, Milwaukee & St. Paul Railway. In 1871 he assumed the general managership of the Chicago-based Pullman Palace Car Company, but resigned on March 1, 1872, to assume the position of general superintendent with the Chicago & North Western. Hughitt advanced steadily until on June 2, 1887, he became the road's sixth president; he remained in that office until October 20, 1910, then served as chairman of the board of directors until June 30, 1925. He maintained his ties with the road until his death in 1928. Even as chairman of the board, Hughitt remained a powerful force within the C&NW. Recalled a company vice president in the 1940s, "At the time [1910] it was predicted that the change of title would mean little in the way of shelving of responsibility and active management by Mr. Hughitt, and so it turned out to be. The new president [William A. Gardner] was obliged to continue to defer to Mr. Hughitt on questions of policy and details of management."

Hughitt realized that the Chicago & North Western needed to become an aggressive regional carrier. When he arrived in 1872, mileage totaled a respectable 1,382; when he stepped down from the presidency thirty-eight years later, it had increased to an impressive 9,761, making the C&NW one of the largest railroads in the nation. During this period the C&NW absorbed a host of independent companies, including the Milwaukee, Lake Shore & Western, the Toledo & Northwestern, and the Fremont, Elkhorn & Missouri Valley, and it won control over the strategic 1,700-mile Chicago, St. Paul, Minneapolis & Omaha Railway. By 1910, too, the C&NW sported hundreds of miles of double and even triple track. Throughout his presidency Hughitt vigorously embraced a strategy designed to protect his ever-growing system; he repeatedly attacked competitors who dared to build into his domain. Hughitt seemed to be most proud of opening up large sections of the northern plains. On a trip to the eastern Dakota Territory in the late 1870s he concluded that "business follows the rails," and he energetically pushed his company's rails, under the banner of the Dakota Central Railway, from western Minnesota across the mostly empty prairies to the Missouri River. The iron horse reached this terminus, the future South Dakota capital city of Pierre, in 1880. According to Doane Robinson in *A Brief History of South Dakota* (1905), "Within two years [the C&NW] was sending out of Chicago every day on an average of 200 emigrant families, who speedily populated [South Dakota] . . . and confirmed thereby that prediction that business would follow the rails."

In no way did Hughitt fit the "robber baron" stereotype. He attempted to make his railroad a good corporate citizen; in fact, he won the appellation "the shipper's friend." Hughitt and his son, Marvin, Jr., who joined the road in 1881, made every effort to provide customers with efficient, low-cost service. Moreover, the senior Hughitt vigorously boosted the C&NW's service territory by promoting agricultural and industrial development; the company, for example, spearheaded the raising of alfalfa and sugar beets in Nebraska and South Dakota in the early twentieth century. Hughitt also oversaw the rebuilding of the C&NW's plant, and his efforts won high marks from travelers for the speed, comfort, and safety of the road's passenger trains. By 1905 the all-steel cars of the C&NW's crack North Western Limited (Chicago to the Twin Cities) and Overland Limited (Chicago to Omaha) rolled over heavy rails atop treated ties and deep crushed-rock ballast and were protected by miles of electric-block signals.

Hughitt was a hard-driving railroad leader, who, according to long-time C&NW vice president Barret Conway, apparently had only two major interests: "his family and . . . the North Western Railway." Although Hughitt lacked a formal education, he was described as "well-educated" and "highly cultured." He loved to read, especially biography, history, and philosophy. One associate described Hughitt as "dignified, courtly, impressive, not easily approachable, but withal kind, considerate, and a most interesting, well-informed conversationalist." Hughitt dedicated much of his eighty-seven-year life to the Chicago & North Western Railway Company and left an indelible mark on the railroad.

References:
Robert J. Casey and W. A. S. Douglas, *Pioneer Railroad: The Story of the Chicago & North Western System* (New York: McGraw-Hill, 1948);

W. H. Stennett, comp., *Yesterday and To-day: A History of the Chicago & North Western Railway System*, third edition (Chicago: Rand McNally, 1910);

Carlton J. Corliss, *Marvin Hughitt* (Chicago: Privately printed, 1927);

Doane Robinson, *A Brief History of South Dakota* (New York: American Book Co., 1905).

Clark Hungerford

(December 22, 1899-October 18, 1962)

by Dan Butler

Westark Community College

Clark Hungerford (Kalmbach Publishing Company)

CAREER: Transitman (1922), bridge inspector (1922-1924), engineering draftsman (1924), assistant engineer (1924-1925), assistant trainmaster (1925-1926), trainmaster (1926-1927), superintendent (1927-1939), general manager, western lines (1939-1946), Southern Railway Company; vice president, operations and maintenance, Association of American Railroads (1946-1947); president, St. Louis-San Francisco Railway (1947-1962).

Clark Hungerford was born in Jackson, Tennessee, on December 22, 1899, to Homer Leslie and Lizzie Phillips Clark Hungerford. Graduated from Porter Military Academy in Charleston, South Carolina, in 1917, he received a degree in civil engineering from Princeton University in 1922.

He began his railroad career in 1922 as a transitman with the Southern Railway at Charlotte, North Carolina. He became a bridge inspector at Charlotte later that year and in 1924 was advanced to engineering draftsman. Later that year he was transferred to Knoxville, Tennessee, as an assistant engineer. He entered the operating department in 1925 at Ashville, North Carolina, with the position of assistant trainmaster. The following year he was promoted to trainmaster at Macon, Georgia. On November 3, 1926, he married Augusta Cannon; they had three children. In 1927 he was promoted to superintendent of the Mobile Division at Selma, Alabama. Subsequently, he served as superintendent at Macon, Georgia; Alexandria, Virginia; and Birmingham, Alabama. In 1939 Hungerford was made general manager of the Southern's western lines at Cincinnati. In that position he also served as a member of the board of managers of the Cincinnati Union Terminal. In 1946 he was elected vice president of the operations and maintenance department of the Association of American Railroads.

In 1947 the St. Louis–San Francisco Railway (Frisco) ended fourteen years of receivership, and the newly reorganized company elected Hungerford president. He inherited a railroad that had made substantial progress during the previous decade in rehabilitating its property. It had improved its mainline between St. Louis and Oklahoma and had begun large purchases of diesel-electric motive power. It had also installed heavier rails and begun implementation of a Centralized Traffic Control system. As part of the reorganization a limited five-year voting trust was established under Hungerford's leadership, which lasted until 1951. This arrangement greatly increased his control of daily operation.

In December 1948 the Frisco gained control of the Alabama, Tennessee & Northern Railroad, which operated between Reform, Alabama, and Mobile. Before the merger the two lines had interchanged cars at Aliceville, Alabama. This acquisition gave the company its second seaport city in addition to Pensacola, Florida, and stimulated economic development of Southwestern Alabama. Hungerford also increased capital expenditures at Springfield, Missouri, the system operating hub, and installed Centralized Traffic Control on mainline trackage throughout the system.

Dieselization was completed in February 1952. The program had begun in earnest after the reorganization and followed a logical, conventional pattern: the company first converted its switching fleet and then its mainline trains. The Frisco largely relied on the experience of other carriers in determining what to buy and did not possess a wide variety of motive power. Its limited fleet of passenger locomotives was converted to a single model, with the first units being delivered in 1947; the company named its passenger units after famous race horses. The line converted to diesels in record time and with a minimum of different types of equipment.

These factors helped reduce operating and maintenance costs both during and after the changeover.

In 1955 construction began on the Tennessee Yard at Capleville, near Memphis. Total cost of this electronic hump yard facility, which was completed in 1957, was approximately $10 million. (A hump yard is a classification yard with an elevated track from which freight cars are pushed; through the force of gravity they then roll to switches which direct them onto the proper track.) The following year a similar project was undertaken in Tulsa, Oklahoma, with the construction of the $6 million Cherokee Yard.

During the later years of the Hungerford presidency passenger service was curtailed as secondary runs were discontinued or consolidated, and branch line passenger train service was reduced.

Hungerford died on October 18, 1962, and was replaced as president of the St. Louis–San Francisco Railway by Louis Menk. During Menk's administration the line was able to complete its modernization program and serve as a vital component of the midwestern rail network. With its central operating hub at Springfield, the line provided efficient service to its market area until it merged with the Burlington Northern Railroad in 1980.

References:

S. Kip Farrington, *Railroading the Modern Way* (New York: Coward McCann, 1951), pp. 196-204;

"Frisco's New Officers Named," *Railway Age*, 121 (December 1946): 1087-1088;

History of the Frisco (St. Louis: St. Louis–San Francisco Railway Company, 1964);

Louis Marre and John Baskin Harper, *Frisco Diesel Power* (Glendale, Cal.: Interurban Press, 1984).

Henry E. Huntington

(February 27, 1850-May 23, 1927)

Richard W. Barsness

Lehigh University

Henry E. Huntington

CAREER: Manager and subsequent owner of sawmill in St. Albans, West Virginia (1871-1876); superintendent of construction, Chesapeake, Ohio & Southwestern Railroad Company and related lines (1881-1885); superintendent (1884-1886), receiver (1886-1887), vice president and general manager (1887-1890), Kentucky Central Railroad; vice president and general manager, Elizabethtown, Lexington & Big Sandy and Ohio Valley railways (1890-1892); first assistant to president, second vice president, and first vice president, Southern Pacific Company (1892-1904); president, Los Angeles Railway, Pacific Electric Railway, Los Angeles Interurban Railway, Huntington Land & Improvement Company, Los Angeles Land Company, and Pacific Electric Land Company (1900-1910).

Henry E. Huntington spent most of the first three decades of his career as a successful manager of railroads and other business firms associated with his uncle, Collis P. Huntington. When Collis died in 1900, Henry unsuccessfully sought to succeed him as president of the Southern Pacific Company. He then directed his energy to developing the Los Angeles street railway system and the Pacific Electric interurban system. These highly successful ventures, together with related land development activities, played a major role in the development of Southern California and brought Huntington enormous wealth. Much of this wealth was devoted to the acquisition of rare books, manuscripts, and paintings, which Huntington subsequently made available to the public.

Henry Edwards Huntington was born on February 27, 1850, in the village of Oneonta in upstate New York, the fourth of seven children of Solon and Harriet Saunders Huntington. Ancestors of the Huntington family first settled in New England in 1633, and Solon Huntington moved from Connecticut to Oneonta in 1840 seeking opportunity as a merchant. As the village grew, Solon's general store prospered and he admitted his younger brother, Collis P., as a partner. The latter remained only a few years before responding to news of the gold rush in California. The family's ties remained strong, and Collis P. Huntington subsequently played a major role in his nephew's life—as well as in the history of the United States.

Ed Huntington (as he was known to family and friends throughout his life) attended school in Oneonta. He was fascinated with business and in 1870, at age twenty, he set off for New York City to learn the hardware trade. He was committed to making his own way, but progress was slow and his finances were tight. His Uncle Collis, by then one of the "Big Four" of the Central Pacific Railroad, came to New York periodically on business and formed a good opinion of his nephew. After declining initially, in 1871 Huntington accepted Collis's offer to manage a small sawmill cutting railroad ties in St. Albans, West Virginia.

Huntington's efficient management led to partial and then sole ownership. In 1873 he married Mary Alice Prentice of Sacramento, the eldest sister of Clara Prentice, who had been living with Collis and his wife since the death of the girls' father in 1862. The Huntingtons had one son and three daughters.

In 1876 Huntington sold the sawmill and returned to Oneonta to assist in his father's growing business. He remained until 1881, when he accepted employment as superintendent of construction for one of the railroads Collis was forging into the Chesapeake & Ohio (C&O) system. Huntington's energy and managerial talents led to other C&O–related assignments, including the reorganization of the Kentucky Central Railroad. Although he worked principally for companies in which Collis had an interest, by the 1890s he had established an independent reputation as a knowledgeable and effective railroad executive committed to high maintenance standards and development of a loyal, efficient work force. He had become known in the industry as "H.E." (his uncle was "C.P.") and had accumulated some capital in the process.

At Collis's request, Huntington moved to San Francisco in 1892 to represent the Huntington interests on the Pacific Coast and participate in the management of the Southern Pacific Company (SP). His initial title was first assistant to the president. At age forty-two he was a vigorous, impressive man, nearly six feet tall and accustomed to working in the field as well as the office. He traveled widely in the state to grasp its potential, and became convinced that improved transportation would lead to a particularly bright future in southern California. While in San Francisco, Huntington invested in street railways in the city.

Collis P. Huntington died unexpectedly in New York in August 1900, leaving one-third of his huge estate to his favorite nephew. Huntington aspired to succeed Collis as president of the Southern Pacific Company, but financiers holding large blocks of Southern Pacific securities preferred overtures from Edward H. Harriman of the Union Pacific, who was vigorously seeking control of the SP.

In early 1901 Huntington abandoned his goal of becoming president and sold the stock he had inherited. He also withdrew from an active role in the SP's management, although he retained his title as first vice president until 1904 and remained a director until his death. In 1902 he moved his office from San Francisco to Los Angeles, where he had already begun to invest heavily in the city's street railway system and in the formation of a new interurban railway, the Pacific Electric (PE). The PE was designed to connect communities in spacious Los Angeles County with the city and with each other.

Huntington was not interested in electric traction as an end in itself, but rather as a means of stimulating the growth of the city and surrounding area. The Pacific Electric, in particular, was built largely in advance of population and contributed to one of the area's most spectacular periods of development: in 1900 the City of Los Angeles had a population of 102,479; by 1910 it had trebled to 319,198, and by 1920 it had almost doubled again to 576,673. Similar rates of population growth occurred throughout the area. Huntington was an enthusiastic booster of the city, stating, "I am a foresighted man, and I believe Los Angeles is destined to become the most important city in this country if not in the world. It can extend in any direction as far as you like. . . . We will join this whole region into one big family."

The Pacific Electric was a well-constructed standard gauge system which provided freight as well as passenger service. Huntington developed it by consolidating existing short lines and undertaking extensive new construction. Busy routes were double tracked—some were even quadruple tracked—and the company offered frequent, economical, high quality service. The PE's "Big Red Cars" became a symbol of the region and presented a serious competitive challenge to steam railroads in the area. When the Pacific Electric reached its peak in the early 1920s, a decade after Huntington's retirement, it operated over 600 route miles of service; carried approximately 100 million passengers as well as substantial quantities of freight annually; and represented an investment estimated at $100 million, nearly 10 percent of the total interurban investment in the United States.

Huntington's headlong expansion of his traction systems, especially the Pacific Electric, required more capital than he and his minority partners could readily provide. This shortage of funds enabled Harriman's Southern Pacific in 1903 to acquire approximately half of the stock of both the Pacific Electric and the Los Angeles Railway. When Huntington retired from most of his business activities in 1910, he sold his interest in the PE to the Southern Pacific for the latter's Los Angeles Railway stock. The Southern Pacific took complete control of the PE and Huntington turned the Los Angeles Railway operation over to his son Howard.

Huntington's electric railway investments were closely allied with his other development activities in southern California. He owned large tracts of land, as well as substantial interests in gas, water, and electric utilities, all of which benefited significantly from the stimulus of improved transportation. At the same time, he was involved in important business interests outside California as a result of his previous activities and his inheritance. The period from 1904 to 1910 was exceptionally busy. He served on some fifty corporate boards and was particularly active in the Newport News Shipbuilding and Dry Dock Company, in which he held a controlling interest.

As Huntington looked forward to his semiretirement in 1910, he greatly accelerated his activities as a collector. As part of his plan, he selected his San Marino ranch as the site for a palatial home for his growing collection of books and paintings. It also became the site for extensive botanical gardens designed to determine which plants of economic or ornamental value would thrive in southern California.

Huntington's instinctive appreciation of fine books had been evident early in his business career and had grown along with his financial means. To the dismay of other collectors accustomed to more leisurely approaches, he applied systematic business methods to collecting. Huntington engaged the best professional advisers and agents available—principally George D. Smith and Dr. A. S. W. Rosenbach—did not quibble over prices, and purchased collections en bloc whenever possible. His two decades of intensive collecting, which lasted until within a year or two of his death, coincided with the availability in the United States and England of several extraordinary private collections of books and manuscripts as well as many exceptionally valuable individual literary, historical and artistic works. Huntington reacted decisively to these opportunities. After 1913 he was assisted by his second wife, Arabella Duval Yarrington Huntington. She was Collis's second wife and widow, and had also received one-third of C. P.'s estate. Huntington and his first wife had separated in 1900 and had been divorced in 1906; he and Arabella were married in France in 1913. She died in 1924.

Huntington's literary acquisitions ranged from the Middle Ages to the twentieth century and concentrated on the history and literature of the English-speaking peoples. He was primarily interested in first, early, and rare editions as well as manuscripts, and spent so lavishly that some of his collections rivaled those of world-renowned institutions. For example, his English Renaissance materials (circa 1500 to 1641) were exceeded only by the British Museum and the Bodleian Library of Oxford University.

To enable scholars to use and the public to view these treasures, Huntington built a large separate library on his San Marino estate, and in 1919 transferred administration of the collections to a trust. Before his death in 1927 he gave the trust about 175,000 books, at least half of them extremely rare; approximately one million manuscripts; many priceless works of art; and a substantial endowment to support the future operation of the Henry E. Huntington Library and Art Gallery.

Henry E. Huntington's important contributions to the economic development of southern California at the turn of the century reflected foresight, judgment, and determination. His achievement in building the great Huntington Library collection within the span of two decades reflected similar determination and exceptional generosity (estimated at up to $30 million). He clearly regarded the library as his most significant accomplishment, both for the future role it would play and for his own place in history. He was convinced, as he said, "that the ownership of a fine library is the surest and swiftest way to immortality."

References:

Spencer Crump, *Ride the Big Red Cars* (Los Angeles: Crest, 1962);

Robert M. Fogelson, *The Fragmented Metropolis: Los Angeles, 1850-1930* (Cambridge: Harvard University Press, 1967), pp. 89-105, 164-185;

William B. Friedricks, "Henry E. Huntington and Metropolitan Entrepreneurship in Southern California, 1898-1917," Ph.D. dissertation, University of Southern California, 1986;

David Lavender, *The Great Persuader* (Garden City: Doubleday, 1970);

John E. Pomfret, *The Henry E. Huntington Library and Art Gallery* (San Marino: The Huntington Library, 1969);

Robert O. Schad, "Henry Edwards Huntington," *Huntington Library Bulletin*, No. 1 (May 1931).

Archives:

The Henry E. Huntington Biographical File is located in the Henry E. Huntington Library and Art Gallery, San Marino, California.

Illinois Central Railroad

by John F. Stover

Purdue University

The Illinois Central Railroad (IC) was chartered in 1851 to build a railroad from Cairo, Illinois, at the mouth of the Ohio River, north to Dunleith in the northwestern corner of the state, with a branch from the main line to Chicago. The building of the line was aided by the federal land grant act, the first of its kind, sponsored by Stephen A. Douglas and signed by President Millard Fillmore in 1850. With borrowed money secured by the 2.5 million—acre land grant, the 705-mile charter line was completed by 1856. Many observers thought the north-south line was running the "wrong way," since most roads built in the 1850s were headed west toward the expanding frontier. In the late 1850s IC revenues were not much above $2 million a year. The Civil War, however, pushed annual revenue to $7 million, since the road to Cairo was heavily used for the support of General Grant's campaigning in Tennessee. The Illinois Central started to pay dividends in 1861, and continued to do so for the next seventy years.

At the end of the Civil War Illinois Central officials, eager to extend their road into Iowa, leased a short line running west from Dubuque, and by 1870 they were in operational control of 400 miles of line extending west to Sioux City on the Missouri and north to the Minnesota line. By 1870 the Illinois Central had sold about 2 million acres of its land grant in Illinois to new settlers for a total of about $25 million. During the 1870s, largely under the direction of President William H. Osborn, the Illinois Central acquired two southern railroads which gave the IC a line from Cairo to New Orleans. By the time Stuyvesant Fish became president of the Illinois Central in 1887, the IC was a system of 2,300 miles with annual revenues of $12 million and 8,500 employees. As E. H. Harriman acquired a major financial interest in the Illinois Central in the 1880s the system was extended with major new mileage in Illinois, Kentucky, Tennessee, and Mississippi. Both Harriman and Fish believed that it was better to purchase established lines than to build new ones. When the Illinois Central celebrated its golden anniversary in 1901 it was a 4,200-mile road in thirteen states with annual revenues of $32 million and 32,000 employees.

In the first decades of the Illinois Central's existence farm products had made up half or more of

Map of the Illinois Central Railroad (1930)

the total freight tonnage carried by the road. Products of mines and forests became more important after the Civil War. By 1890 products of agriculture, products of mines, and manufactured goods each constituted 27 to 28 percent of the total tonnage of the railroad. In 1910 mine products were nearly twice the agricultural tonnage, and later would amount to nearly half the total IC freight tonnage. Between 1890 and 1910 the total freight tonnage moving over the IC increased more than fivefold while the average freight rate declined from 95 cents to 59 cents per ton-mile. Between 1912 and 1917 the Illinois Central spent millions of dollars on new freight equipment and motive power, increasing both the total tractive power of the engine fleet and total freight car capacity by nearly 25 percent. This improvement program meant that the IC was well prepared for the increase in traffic that came with the defense buildup and World War I. The rail industry at large was not well prepared for the war traffic, and late in 1917 the federal government took over the operation of all the railroads. Under federal control railroad wages and operating costs rose faster than freight rates and passenger fares with the result that the operating ratio for the Illi-

nois Central climbed from 71.5 in 1917 to 84 in 1918, 91.7 in 1919, and 94.4 in 1920. In 1920 the Illinois Central had 4,800 miles of line, about 60,000 employees, and revenues of more that $145 million.

The owners and managers of the Illinois Central were happy to see the return of private control on March 1, 1920. In the early 1920s wages were moderately reduced along with other operating expenses, and after 1922 the operating ratio generally was below 78. During the decade annual revenues averaged about $180 million, and dividends of $7 per share were paid every year. In the mid 1920s the Illinois Central completed several major improvement projects: the building of the Edgewood Cutoff to expedite freight service, the electrification of the Chicago suburban service, and the upgrading of terminal facilities; as a result, the funded debt grew from $257 million to $359 million. By 1930 IC mileage had grown to 6,700, largely because of the acquisition of several branch lines in Mississippi and Louisiana.

With the coming of the Great Depression, IC revenue dropped to $148 million in 1930; in 1932 it was only $89 million, a figure less than half that of 1929. In 1932 interest on the funded debt took nearly 18 percent of every revenue dollar. Dividends were cut in 1931 and suspended in 1932. In 1932 President Lawrence Downs reported that operating expenses had been cut 52 percent. By 1933 the IC labor force was down to 25,350, much less than half of what it had been in 1929. The Illinois Central had deficits in several of the worst years and came very close to receivership in 1933. All wages were cut 10 percent in 1932, and several major loans from the Reconstruction Finance Corporation and Public Works Administration eased the financial problems of the railroad. Annual revenues climbed a bit in the mid 1930s and were up to $114 million by 1937. Downs was the man most responsible for saving the IC from receivership in the mid 1930s.

A major increase in revenues accompanied the war in Europe in 1939 and American involvement in 1941. The increases achieved in operating efficiency in the 1920s and 1930s plus the fact that the war was a two-ocean, two-front war permitted the nation's railroads to avoid federal control during World War II. Illinois Central revenues climbed to $142 million in 1941 and $256 million in 1944, with the operating ratio under 65 in 1944. The war brought prosperity to the Illinois Central and permitted a reduction of $100 million in the funded debt by 1945.

Early in 1945 Wayne Johnston was elected president of the Illinois Central, a position he held until 1966. He continued to reduce the funded debt of the IC in the early postwar years and resumed dividends in 1951. Johnston simplified the capital structure of the line and completed a modernization program that made the IC a showcase railroad. The Illinois Central did not complete its dieselization program until 1961 because Johnston gave first priority to debt reduction and because the IC had an excellent fleet of steam locomotives at the end of the war. Between 1945 and 1966 the roster of employees on the Illinois Central dropped from 41,000 to 21,000. During the same years total operating revenues averaged about $280 million a year. In the 1960s many American railroads either merged or started to diversify by engaging in nonrailroad enterprises. In 1963 the Illinois Central started a diversification program with the creation of a holding company, Illinois Central Industries (ICI).

Illinois Central presidents after Johnston greatly expanded the number of nonrailroad companies controlled by Illinois Central Industries. By 1971 ICI had acquired companies producing soft drinks, pumps, electric motors, and automobile mufflers, and in that year the Illinois Central Railroad produced less than half the annual revenue of ICI. In 1972 the Illinois Central Railroad merged with the 2,700-mile Gulf, Mobile & Ohio to form the Illinois Central Gulf Railroad (ICG), a system of 9,500 miles. Even with a larger line the annual report for 1980 showed railroad revenue to be only a quarter of total ICI revenue. In the early 1980s ICI management started to dispose of less profitable portions of the ICG rail system, and by 1985 the Illinois Central Gulf Railroad had been reduced to 4,679 miles.

References:

Carlton J. Corliss, *Main Line of Mid-America: The Story of the Illinois Central* (New York: Creative Age Press, 1950);

John F. Stover, *History of the Illinois Central Railroad* (New York: Macmillan, 1975).

Illinois Terminal Railroad

by John F. Due

University of Illinois

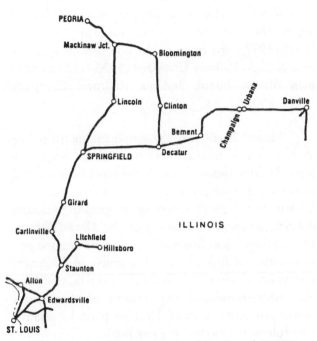

Map of the Illinois Terminal Railroad (1937)

The Illinois Terminal Railroad, with a total of over 400 miles, was the largest electric interurban railway system in the United States outside of the essentially suburban Pacific Electric. It was also one of the most successful, continuing to operate interurban passenger service until the mid 1950s and surviving as a freight road until the mid 1980s. The lines were built between 1901 and 1908, with a major bridge into St. Louis completed in 1910. Originally known as the Illinois Traction Company, the system

was developed by William B. McKinley, a Champaign, Illinois, investment broker, who also developed the Illinois Power Company and street railways in central Illinois cities. The major routes extended from St. Louis via Springfield to Peoria, Springfield to Decatur, Champaign-Urbana, and Danville, and Decatur to Bloomington and Peoria. The railroad was one of the few electric lines to provide sleeping car service and was successful in building up freight traffic in coal, grain, and various manufactured goods.

In 1925 McKinley, by then a United States senator, disposed of the controlling stock to the North American Light and Power Company, then dominated by the Studebaker family of South Bend, Indiana, but later under Samuel Insull control. In 1927 the Illinois Traction Company was renamed the Illinois Terminal Railroad Company. Insull lost control in 1932, and North American, required to dispose of the railroad by the Public Utility Holding Company Act, sold it to a group of St. Louis investors in 1945. With the end of passenger service in the mid 1950s, the freight service was dieselized. In 1954 the property was sold to a group of eleven Midwestern railroads, and in 1982 it was absorbed by the Norfolk Southern Railroad. Some of the track remained in use in 1987.

References:

George W. Hilton and John F. Due, *The Electric Interurban Railways in America* (Stanford, Cal.: Stanford University Press, 1959), pp. 82-88, 144-147, 346-349;
Illinois Traction System, Bulletin of the Central Electric Railfans' Association, no. 98 (Chicago, 1954).

Samuel Insull

(November 11, 1859–July 16, 1938)

by John F. Due

University of Illinois

Samuel Insull

CAREER: Private secretary to Thomas A. Edison (1881–1889); vice president, Edison General Electric Company (1889–1892); vice president, General Electric Company (1892); president, Chicago Edison Company and Commonwealth Electric Company (1892–1907); president (1907–1930), chairman of the board (1930–1932), Commonwealth

Edison Company; chairman of the board, Chicago North Shore & Milwaukee Railway Company (1916–1932); chairman of the board, Chicago South Shore & South Bend Railway Company (1925–1932); chairman of the board, Chicago, Aurora & Elgin Railway Company (1926–1932); chairman of the board, Indiana Railroad Company (1930–1932).

Samuel Insull was the dominant figure in the electric power industry in the United States for three decades and was one of the most brilliant and constructive entrepreneurs the country has ever known, but a combination of misguided financing policies, political mistakes, and the Great Depression destroyed him financially and made him the primary object of attack by a wide segment of the American political scene. It was Insull, more than anyone else, who introduced the concept of the central power generating station. He also played a significant role in the electric railway field.

Insull was born in London in 1859 to lower-middle-class parents, Samuel and Emma Short Insull. His father, who had strong Dissenter religious principles, struggled to make a living as a small dairy farmer and, for a time, as an official of temperance societies. Insull received a good primary and secondary education in private schools but never attended a university. He did not inherit his father's religious tendencies but he became a strong defender of Catholics and much preferred Irish Catholics as key employees.

In 1874 he obtained a job as office boy for a firm of auctioneers and quickly learned office procedures and bookkeeping. Four years later he was fired to make way for a relative of the owners but obtained a position as personal secretary to Col. George E. Gouraud, the London representative of a

New York bank and of Thomas A. Edison. Insull worked closely with Edward Johnson, Edison's chief engineer, who was in England supervising the installation of a telephone system. Johnson was greatly impressed with him, and Insull was invited to come to New York in 1881 to become Edison's private secretary. Edison was also impressed with Insull's diligence and ability, and they worked together closely for a decade. The lack of a university education was a great advantage for Insull in light of Edison's antipathy toward college graduates.

During the 1880s Edison was promoting the central power station system for the distribution of electricity, and Insull was an instant convert. To carry on his various activities, primarily the manufacture of electric equipment, Edison had developed several companies; the corporate structure was chaotic, as Edison had little organizational skill. Insull brought order to the enterprise and aided in the sale of the central power systems. In 1886, when the firm's manufacturing plants were moved to Schenectady, New York, Insull was sent to manage the operations. In the late 1880s the firm benefited greatly from the development of street railways, which became a major user of power, but suffered from the competition of Westinghouse, the prime developer of the use of alternating current, which Edison strongly opposed, and Thomson-Houston, regarded by many as a predatory firm.

In 1889 the Edison General Electric Company was formed from the various Edison companies through the initiative of Henry Villard, who had been primarily a railroad promoter. This step was taken with the reluctant approval of J. P. Morgan, who had backed Edison financially. In order to lessen competition, Villard sought to acquire Thomson-Houston; but under pressure from Morgan the reverse occurred, and in 1892 General Electric was created, with Thomson-Houston executives in command. Insull was named a vice president but left after a few months, unwilling to work with the new management.

Insull wanted to leave New York because of his great dislike of Morgan and accepted the presidency of the two Chicago electric power firms, Commonwealth Electric and Chicago Edison. After that his career centered on Chicago, which he sought to make the electric power capital of the country. With the two companies merged in 1907 and with the acquisition of several smaller companies, he came to dominate the industry in the city completely. His utilities monopoly was further strengthened when he acquired control of Peoples Gas Company in 1919. He stressed and in many instances pioneered several principles with regard to electric utilities. First, he upheld the importance of monopoly in production and distribution of electric power in order to attain economies of mass production. This notion came to be generally accepted; only in recent years has it been questioned. Second, he gave substantial attention to ratemaking, developing the principle of lower rates for off-peak use and, above all, a continual reduction in overall rate levels in order to stimulate use. When he took over the Chicago system, electric power was regarded as a luxury; two decades later it was a household necessity. Third, he introduced the use of alternating current (AC) for transmission, direct current (DC) for distribution; the latter idea was ultimately dropped except for street railways, which functioned best on direct current. Fourth, much of his pioneering work was in utility financing: the use of the open-end mortgage (a mortgage without firm limits); issuance of bonds for long periods, such as forty years; and, ultimately, widespread sale of stock to the public, including customers and employees. His financing was handled through the Chicago investment banking firm of Halsey-Stuart; he refused to deal with New York bankers until he was forced to do so near the end of his career. Fifth, he placed great stress on public relations, giving heavy publicity to rate reductions, for example, and creating good will for the companies and himself. Sixth, he stressed the desirability of providing service to smaller cities and towns, supplied from central stations. His first such venture, Northern Illinois Public Service Company, served the north and northwest suburbs of Chicago; the second, Middle West Utilities, served downstate Illinois. Other systems followed. Seventh, he did not use depreciation accounting, instead following the principle that properly maintained equipment did not depreciate and that replacement would be paid for from earnings. Eighth, Insull was a strong supporter of state regulation of public utilities, primarily because he preferred state to local regulation. He also regarded state regulation as a bulwark against municipal ownership of utilities, for which there was strong support in various periods after 1900. Finally, Insull maintained good labor relations, which was relatively easy in the capital intensive electric power industry. He took a somewhat paternalistic attitude toward his workers.

Without question Insull made great contributions to the development of electric power in the period from 1890 to 1920, and he established Chicago as the financial center of the industry.

Insull's role in transportation was less significant than in the electric power field, but it was by no means negligible. In 1914, in order to save the Chicago elevated railway system (the "el"), Insull advanced substantial sums of money and acquired controlling ownership of the system. For more than twenty years efforts were made to merge the elevated lines with the surface lines owned by four other companies, but this plan did not succeed until a much later date.

Insull's greatest impact in the traction field was upon the three major Chicago suburban carriers. The Chicago-Milwaukee line, completed in 1906, was in receivership by 1908; it was acquired and reorganized by Insull in 1916 as the Chicago North Shore & Milwaukee Railroad (North Shore). Major improvements were made, including gaining direct access to downtown Chicago on the elevated lines and the building of a cutoff in the Skokie area to reduce the amount of slow street running (that is, the running of trains along city streets). The company also pioneered piggyback freight service. The North Shore went into bankruptcy with the collapse of the Insull empire in 1932 but was reorganized and continued to operate until the early 1960s.

In 1926 Insull acquired the Chicago, Aurora & Elgin, with sixty-one miles of line connecting downtown Chicago (via the El tracks) and the west suburbs. The line had been built between 1902 and 1907, had gone into bankruptcy in 1919, and had been reorganized between 1922 and 1924 by Thomas Conway, who effected extensive track and equipment improvements. Operation of the railway changed little during the Insull years. The line went into bankruptcy after the Insull era but was reorganized and operated until the late 1950s.

The Chicago South Shore & South Bend, completed in 1909 and operating ninety miles of line between Chicago and South Bend, Indiana, was almost worthless when it was purchased by Insull in 1925. It was completely rebuilt under the direction of Insull's son Samuel, Jr., and new equipment was acquired. It was the most successful of the three lines, and in time it built up an extensive freight traf-

fic. Following receivership with the collapse of the Insull empire, it was reorganized; as of 1987 it was the only remaining electric interurban railway in the United States.

The Insull system also developed or acquired several smaller electric railways in Illinois, usually in conjunction with local electric power operations. These lines included the Chicago & Interurban Traction Company (Chicago-Kankakee), the Chicago & Joliet Electric Railway (Chicago-Joliet), the Bloomington, Pontiac & Joliet Electric Railway (Pontiac-Dwight), and Central Illinois Traction (Mattoon-Charleston). Most of these roads were subsidiaries of Northern Illinois Public Service or Central Illinois Public Service; all were abandoned in the late 1920s or early 1930s.

While the Chicago area roads had some potential, the network developed by Insull in Indiana had none. In the north, Gary Railways became an Insull property in 1924. Under the auspices of the Insull-owned Midland United Corporation, the extensive interurban network in central Indiana was brought under Insull control, and in 1930, after some weak branches were abandoned, the remaining lines were merged to form the Indiana Railroad. The company's major routes included two lines from Indianapolis to Fort Wayne and lines from Indianapolis to Louisville, Dayton, and Terre Haute. By 1932 several of the lines had been abandoned; the company went into bankruptcy and out of Insull hands. A few lines continued in operation until 1941. The whole venture was a serious mistake; by the time the Indiana Railroad was formed, the handwriting was clearly on the wall. The lightweight, high-speed equipment that the new company bought could not save it from collapse.

There were other Insull lines scattered around the country, all in conjunction with power companies—for example, the Lewiston-Portland line in Maine.

In 1926 Insull was at the peak of his success; his personal wealth was about $5 million, but he controlled an empire of at least $3 billion. During the next several years, with a booming stock market, his known assets reached $150 million. But several events, some initiated by Insull and some of external origin, were to destroy the empire.

The key source of the ultimate difficulty was a series of business errors made by Insull. Most of these errors resulted from his interest in perpetuating a "dynasty"—continued control of the empire by his son and successive heirs. His concern about possible loss of the empire was triggered by large purchases of stock in his companies by Cyrus Eaton, a Cleveland investment banker and industrialist. There is no evidence that Eaton intended to oust Insull from control, but Insull feared that he did. Accordingly, Insull set up two investment trusts—super holding companies—to which he and his associates turned over their stock in the companies in exchange for securities of the trust—the typical holding company pyramid structure. Meanwhile, the 1929 stock market collapse had reduced the values of his holdings; but Insull, optimistic about the future and not believing that a severe depression was under way, substantially expanded his companies' investment in both power and traction in 1930 and 1931. He also bought Eaton's holdings. To finance these investments he turned heavily to debt financing and to loans from New York Banks.

But the continued fall in the stock market in 1931 and 1932 wiped out the value of the stock held as collateral by the lenders, despite strong efforts by Insull to maintain the price. The banks had the accounts of the various firms audited, and reconsideration of depreciation methods showed Middle West Utilities to be insolvent. In the spring of 1932 the banks refused to refinance a $10 million loan coming due and forced Insull's resignation from all of the companies, though the key one, Commonwealth Edison, itself was solvent.

Mistakes of a political nature were made by Insull as well. In 1926 Frank L. Smith, chairman of the Illinois Public Utilities Commission, sought to oust William B. McKinley from his United States Senate seat. Insull had long regarded McKinley as a prime enemy—apparently for no good reason beyond the fact that McKinley, a small-town broker, had built the Illinois Power and Illinois Traction empire across central Illinois, blocking Insull from tapping this territory. Insull was determined to defeat McKinley and gave Smith $125,000. Because of the money spent by wealthy persons to aid Smith, a Senate committee investigated after Smith won the election, and the Senate refused to seat him. The Insull contribution was widely publicized.

The Insull empire came under increasing criticism in the late 1920s and early 1930s. Two distinguished University of Chicago professors, political scientist Charles Merriam and economist (later United States Senator) Paul Douglas, led the attack on holding companies generally and Insull's in particular. As stock prices collapsed, many people who had invested in shares of Insull's companies at his urging lost their savings. As the depression grew worse, attacks on concentration of wealth, public utilities, and holding companies grew in intensity. Holding company pyramiding was a favorite target of Franklin D. Roosevelt's presidential campaign. By 1932 Chicago and Illinois political leaders were deserting Insull, who went to Europe to escape the turmoil. After the collapse of his empire, he and several associates were indicted on charges of fraud, embezzlement, and violation of federal bankruptcy laws. While he had always been careful to avoid any illegal activity, in the first months of his desperate struggle to maintain control he had been involved in some transactions that were at least questionable. He was extradited from Greece in 1934, tried in both state and federal courts, and acquitted of any illegal activity. But he never recovered from the ordeal financially or psychologically and died in 1938 waiting for a train in a Paris subway station.

Insull was a strong innovator; change was essential for him, but so were efficiency and orderly procedure. He enjoyed great loyalty from his associates, his employees, and, until the early 1930s, the public. His few enemies before the 1930s included the New York bankers, particularly the house of J. P. Morgan, and much of Chicago's conservative business community. His most important contributions were the use of central power stations, consolidation of electric utilities into efficient operations, and extension of service to smaller communities. These changes would have come anyway, but Insull played a major role in their implementation. He was an extremely hard worker; a sixteen-hour day was typical. He had interests other than work, such as raising horses on his farm at Libertyville and building Chicago's new opera house. But his work was of paramount importance—an importance perhaps intensified by his rather cool relationship with his wife, Margaret Bird, a beautiful stage star he married in 1899 and with whom he had one son. He received honorary degrees from Union College, Northwestern University, Notre Dame, and Queens (Ontario).

Whether he was in fact guilty of the crimes with which he was charged was long debated, but juries acquitted him of any violation of the law.

The pyramiding structure of holding companies he developed in the later years was criticized for permitting a relatively small amount of capital to control a vast empire and for concentrating earnings in the hands of a few persons, and such practices were outlawed by federal legislation in the 1930s. His power systems in the Chicago area and elsewhere remained intact; the Chicago transit properties passed into public hands in 1947; the remainder of his properties ceased to exist except for the Chicago South Shore & South Bend, which would also have gone out of business had it not been for Insull's modernization.

Publications:

Central Station Electric Service (Chicago: Privately Printed, 1915);

Public Utilities in Modern Life (Chicago: Privately Printed, 1924).

References:

Francis X. Busch, *Guilty or Not Guilty?* (Indianapolis: Bobbs-Merrill, 1952);
Forrest McDonald, *Insull* (Chicago: University of Chicago Press, 1962).

Archives:

Samuel Insull's business and personal papers are held by the University of Chicago Press. Some of his letters are at the Edison Museum, West Orange, New Jersey. His unpublished memoirs were left to his son; their present location is unknown.

Interstate Commerce Act

Beginning in 1832, but especially from 1869 to 1887, various states created commissions to regulate railroads. Many of these commissions, particularly in New England, were advisory and relied on publicity to enforce their decisions; others, concentrated primarily in the Midwest and inspired by farmers and local merchants, had the power to set maximum rates to prevent railroads from favoring major collecting points. The United States Supreme Court in *Munn* v. *Illinois* (1876) recognized that railroads had a public character, that their rates should be reasonable, and that in the absence of federal legislation state legislatures could regulate even interstate railroads. Regulatory policies, however, differed from state to state and were often complex and contradictory.

Many Americans wanted the federal government to regulate railroads. Farmers, manufacturers, and merchants wanted an end to discriminatory rates, especially the "long-and-short-haul abuse" that favored certain cities by making up for losses on competitive long hauls with higher charges for less competitive short hauls and the rebates that benefited certain large-scale shippers. Beginning in 1878, Representative John H. Reagan of Texas regularly introduced, the House of Representatives periodically passed, and the Senate ignored a bill prohibiting rebates, the long-and-short-haul abuse (with a particularly strong clause) and railroad pools, which maintained rates by eliminating competition and dividing traffic. Providing for no commission, the Reagan bill relied on the courts for enforcement.

With the disintegration of pools and the return of cutthroat competition in the early 1880s, many railroad officials came to accept the principle of federal regulation; but they found legislation proposed by Senator Shelby M. Cullom of Illinois less objectionable than Reagan's bill. Both bills outlawed discrimination and rebates and called for reasonable and publicized rates, although neither bill specifically provided for rate regulation. But Cullom's bill did not outlaw pooling, had a more flexible long-and-short-haul clause, and set up a commission, which conceivably could serve as the mechanism to enforce pool agreements. The Senate approved Cullom's bill in 1885, and after the *Wabash* v. *Illinois* decision (1886), in which the Supreme Court held that interstate commerce could only be regulated by the federal government, both the House and Senate again approved their regulation bills by a wide margin. The two houses compromised their differences, leaving everyone dissatisfied. The compromise bill annoyed farmers by accepting Cullom's commission and aroused opposition from railroads by including Reagan's antipooling section and stiffening Cullom's long-and-short-haul clause. Railroad leaders had been prepared to accept the Cullom bill, but they found the compromise bill abhorrent.

The compromise bill passed both houses in January 1887 by comfortable bipartisan majorities. Most congressmen were convinced that "the people," particularly farmers and businessmen in the interior of the nation, were demanding legislation. Those congressmen opposed to the bill were either involved with railroads or represented shippers at terminal points in the Northeast and California. New Englanders, for example, living both at the end of the line and close to unregulated Canadian competition, were convinced that the long-and-short-haul clause, with its requirement of proportional charges, would damage their competitive position. Although independent Pennsylvania oil producers and New York merchants helped originate the Reagan and Cullom bills, respectively, when the chips were down their senators opposed the compromise bill; and in both houses those states, along with New England, provided the only significant pocket of resistance. The Midwest and the South muscled the bill through; the Northeast and the railroads could not block legislation which had been demanded for nearly two decades. During those years more than 150 bills for federal railroad regulation had been introduced in Congress; this time the momentum could not be stopped.

On February 4, 1887, after study and hesitation, President Grover Cleveland signed the bill into law. Creating a five-person Interstate Commerce Commission (ICC), the Interstate Commerce Act (ICA) outlawed pools and rate discrimination—whether by special rates, rebates, drawbacks (rebates paid by railroads to a dominant shipper on freight shipped by weaker competitors), or long-and-short-haul abuses—and demanded that rates be "reasonable and just" and be published. Presidentially appointed commissioners were to serve staggered six-year terms. No more than three commissioners were to belong to the same political party, and none were to have railroad connections. The ICA authorized the ICC to investigate any railroad engaged in interstate commerce and empowered it to compel witnesses to testify and to secure relevant books and papers. The ICC could also require railroads to submit annual reports and to use a uni-

form accounting system. If a railroad ignored the ICC's orders or decisions, the ICC had to petition the appropriate circuit court "to hear and determine the matter."

Some provisions of the ICA were vague. Pooling traffic and earnings was illegal, but collective ratemaking was neither legalized nor outlawed. The ICA outlawed the long-and-short-haul abuse only with the ambiguous qualification "under substantially similar circumstances and conditions." With the value-of-service rate system (based on a railroad manager's guess of what the traffic could afford, rather than on his computation of what the service cost) left undisturbed by the ICA, "reasonable and just" rates were difficult to define.

The ICA and its creation, the ICC, did little to augment the flow of interstate commerce. The ICC was no better than its members, who were political losers more often than transportation experts. From its beginning, the ICC assumed a passive judicial posture rather than an active administrative role. It accepted and perpetuated value-of-service ratemaking and reacted to specific questions, but it did not try to solve major transportation problems. These problems became more complex as competing modes of transportation developed and began to challenge railroads. In 1906, 1920, 1935, 1940, and 1958 Congress amended the ICA, widening the ICC's jurisdiction and increasing its control over rates. Although charged by Congress to fashion "a more rationally conceived, stable, and profitable" transportation industry, the ICC failed to shape a coherent transportation system. Bogged down by minutiae and case-by-case approach, the ICC handed down contradictory decisions. Criticism of ICC regulations during the 1960s and 1970s culminated in 1980 with Congress fostering competition by largely deregulating railroads and motor carriers. By 1987, a hundred years after the ICA, deregulation had eroded the ICC's power and threatened its demise.

References:

Lee Benson, *Merchants, Farmers, & Railroads: Railroad Regulation and New York Politics, 1850–1887* (Cambridge: Harvard University Press, 1955);

Ari and Olive Hoogenboom, *A History of the ICC: From Panacea to Palliative* (New York: Norton, 1976);

Edward C. Kirkland, *Industry Comes of Age: Business, Labor, and Public Policy, 1860–1897* (New York: Holt, Rinehart & Winston, 1961);

George H. Miller, *Railroads and the Granger Laws* (Madison: University of Wisconsin Press, 1971);

Gerald D. Nash, "Origins of the Interstate Commerce Act of 1887," *Pennsylvania History*, 24 (1957): 181–190;

Edward A. Purcell, Jr., "Ideas and Interests: Businessmen and the Interstate Commerce Act," *Journal of American History*, 54 (1967): 561–578;

I. L. Sharfman, *The Interstate Commerce Commission: A Study in Administrative Law and Procedure*, 5 volumes (New York: Commonwealth Fund, 1931–1937).

—Ari Hoogenboom

Arthur Curtiss James

(June 1, 1867–June 4, 1941)

by Arthur L. Lloyd

Amtrak

Arthur Curtiss James celebrating the connection of the Great Northern Railway and the Western Pacific Railroad at Bieber, California, in 1931 (Courtesy Burlington Northern)

CAREER: Partner (1892-1908), director (1908-1941), vice president (1909-1930), Phelps Dodge Corporation; first vice president (1901-1905), president and chairman of the board (1905-1924), El Paso & Southwestern Railway; director, Chicago, Rock Island & Pacific Railway (1906-1924); director, Southern Pacific Company (1924-1926); director, Great Northern Railway (1924-1941); chairman of the board, Western Pacific Railroad Company (1926-1939).

Dubbed the "last of the great railroad barons," Arthur Curtiss James followed in the footsteps of and was the most colorful rail company owner since James J. Hill. James was born in New York City on June 1, 1867, to Daniel Willis and Ellen Stebbins Curtiss James, and matured while his father was closely associated with Hill in the development of the Pacific Northwest. It was probably this early influence that caused him to become interested during the 1920s in the development of the West as an investment for the future rather than for speculation, as had most of his predecessor rail builders.

James attended the private Arnold School in New York. After graduation from Amherst College in 1889 with the A.B. and A.M. degrees, he became associated with the Phelps Dodge Corporation, in which his father held a substantial interest. He married Harriet Eddy Parsons on April 23, 1890; they had no children. James's entrance into the railroad field occurred in 1901 when the railroad properties of Phelps Dodge were merged to form the El Paso & Southwestern Railway (EP&SW), with James as first vice president. This railroad was to be his major interest for the next twenty-three years. Its component railroads had been built to serve the Phelps Dodge copper mines, but as coal traffic to the smelters increased, followed by the development of the surrounding territory, James envisioned a greater vista for the 229-mile road. The EP&SW extended from Deming, New Mexico, to Benson, Arizona, but James dreamed of a transcontinental railroad to California.

This vision approached reality in 1906 when the EP&SW reached Tucumcari, New Mexico, where it connected with the Chicago, Rock Island & Pacific (Rock Island). James joined the Rock Island as a director and member of the executive committee that year. The line was extended west to Tucson, Arizona, but James's intention to continue to California was abandoned in 1924 when the Southern Pacific, in order to keep the EP&SW from reaching Los Angeles, purchased the line for $28 million in Southern Pacific capital stock and $29 million in bonds. This transaction made James the largest individual stockholder in the Southern Pacific, but he sold his shares in 1926. In the meantime, in 1907 he had inherited his father's interests in the Great Northern, Northern Pacific, and Chicago, Burlington & Quincy (Burlington) railroads, the so-called Jim Hill lines.

In 1926 James acquired a substantial interest in the Western Pacific (WP), a 900-mile San Francisco–Salt Lake City carrier, and again undertook the development of a transcontinental line to California. Such a line had been George Gould's aim when the WP was built in 1909. At the time of the purchase James said, "For many years, I have been a holder and believer in the Great Northern, Northern Pacific, Burlington and Southern Pacific, and now have added a holding in Western Pacific to support an independent company, which shall have for its sole objective the building of the territory served by it." On November 10, 1931, he drove the last spike at Bieber, California, linking the 112-mile extension of the Western Pacific north from Keddie, California, with the 88-mile line completed by the Great Northern south from Klamath Falls, Oregon. Thus a line was completed from San Francisco to Bieber via the WP, from Bieber to St. Paul, Minnesota, via the Great Northern, and from St. Paul to Chicago via the Chicago, Burlington & Quincy,

which was owned by the Great Northern and the Northern Pacific.

In 1933 a six-year program of improvement of the Western Pacific mainline between Salt Lake City and Oakland, California, was completed. While the program's principal objective was the development of freight traffic, it also made possible the establishment of competition in passenger service. In the summer of 1939 the Exposition Flyer was placed in operation on a fast schedule between Chicago and San Francisco by the Western Pacific and the Denver & Rio Grande Western to coincide with the Golden Gate International Exposition in San Francisco.

James's success was due in no small measure to his characteristic of giving all credit for accomplishments to his associates. He gained the reputation of selecting men who could perform their duties without his constant supervision and direction.

Another outstanding characteristic of James was his foresightedness. For many years he advocated the speeding up of passenger service, demanding fast, often record runs. He made it his personal goal to travel 50,000 miles per year on his passenger trains. He was an early advocate of lightweight, high-speed trains. In 1933 his vision was expressed in a letter to D. A. Steel, associate editor of *Railway Age*: "It is my personal belief that the Century of Progress Exposition in Chicago will be a splendid eye-opener to some railroad men, particularly along the lines of reducing weights of passenger cars. The trend is already in that direction for the dead weight per passenger on the Royal Scot in England in just about half what it is on first-class American trains. The Pullman Company is evidently alive to this situation and its new light weight car and streamline design is the beginning of a radical change in our ideas in this country." A few months later, the Burlington ordered the first of its nine Zephyrs.

While James had a large financial interest in railroads, his primary motive remained that of developing the West. Even though he predicted the Great Depression, he declined the opportunity to dispose of his holdings in the Western Pacific at a profit in 1930, saying that selling would be directly contrary for his reason for buying the line in the first instance. At that time he was the largest stockholder in the Western Pacific, Southern Pacific, and Great Northern railways.

James proudly called himself a capitalist and refuted the notion that "absentee owners" (his home was always in New York City) were concerned only with dividends. He took a particular interest in his employees and did much to improve working conditions. In addition to his reputation as a financier, he was also recognized as one of the country's outstanding philanthropists. He gave away an estimated $20 million during his life to a variety of institutions, including Union Theological Seminary, Amherst College, and the Metropolitan Museum of Art.

James resigned as chairman of the board and director of the Western Pacific on November 4, 1939, after having served in those capacities for more than thirteen years. He indicated that he wished to lighten his responsibilities, but he did not dispose of any of his investment in the Western Pacific. He remained on the boards of directors of the Great Northern, Chicago, Burlington & Quincy, and Colorado & Southern railroads. The Western Pacific had filed for voluntary reorganization in 1935 and did not come out of the plan until 1944 due to objections by various charitable institutions and trusts that had been set up by James and had inherited his interests in the road.

James died of pneumonia in New York on June 4, 1941, a month after the death of his wife. In their 1941 annual report, the board of directors of the Great Northern eulogized the man who had been a director for seventeen years:

> No man since the passing of James Jerome Hill has exercised a greater influence on the general course of Great Northern which, throughout the years, has been held unwaveringly to those principles which were responsible for its initial success and which have contributed so substantially to the development and welfare of agriculture and industry along the company's rails.

At times the largest shareholder in the Company, Mr. James counseled modest dividends to shareholders and the investment of surpluses in improvements to the property to the end that it continuously became a more efficient instrument of service. He counseled the procurement of new capital for such noteworthy improvements as electrification of the railway in the Cascade mountains and the building of the great Cascade tunnel.

With his support, the Great Northern was extended southward through Oregon into Northern California, and through his investments in Western Pacific, a connection was effected in Northern California which brought into existence a new rail route between the Pacific Northwest and San Francisco. Making an exception to his disinclination for public appearances, Mr. James drove the Golden Spike which marked the completion of this project on November 10, 1931.

Publications:

"Advantages of Hawaiian Annexation," *North American Review*, 165 (December 1897): 758–760;

"A Plea for Our Railroads," by James and Thomas C. McClary, *Saturday Evening Post*, 204 (January 16, 1932): 21, 102–103.

References:

"Arthur Curtiss James Retires," Railway Age, 107 (November 11, 1939): 750–753;

Gilbert H. Kneiss, "Fifty Candles for Western Pacific," *Western Pacific Mileposts*, 4 (March 1953): 1–20, 45–64.

Downing B. Jenks

(August 16, 1915–)

by Craig Miner

Wichita State University

Downing B. Jenks (courtesy Union Pacific)

CAREER: Chainman, Spokane, Portland & Seattle Railway (1934-1935); assistant, engineer corps, Pennsylvania Railroad (1937-1938); roadmaster, division engineer, trainmaster (1938-1947), division superintendent (1947-1948), Great Northern Railway; general manager, Chicago & Eastern Illinois Railroad (1948-1949); vice president and general

manager (1949-1950), assistant vice president for operations (1950-1951), vice president for operations (1951-1953), executive vice president and director (1953-1956), president (1956-1961), Chicago, Rock Island & Pacific Railway; president and director (1961-1972), chief executive officer (1961-1974), chairman (1972-1983), Missouri Pacific Railroad; president (1971-1974), chief executive officer (1971-1983), chairman (1974-1983), Missouri Pacific Corporation; director, Union Pacific Corporation (1983-).

Downing B. Jenks was born to railroading. His father was a prominent railway officer in the Northwest; as a boy, Downing Jenks ran a tight and coordinated operation on his model railway. His background, early experience, vision, and tremendous drive to contribute something substantial to railroad history took him to a Class 1 railroad presidency at age forty and led to his reputation as one of the great innovators and disciplinarians in translating ideas into practice.

The primary object of Jenks's genius was the Missouri Pacific Railroad (MP or MoPac), the 12,000-mile midwestern system which he took from a poorly-maintained also-ran in 1961 to a world-beater and type model when it was absorbed into the Union Pacific system in 1983. Along the way he revolutionized industry ideas about both what was possible and what was desirable in mid twentieth-century railroading by pioneering in such areas as piggybacking, intermodal shipping, and, through the development of the MoPac's remarkable Transportation Control System, shifting of rail computerization from accounting and management information to true real-time operating control.

Jenks's grandfather, Cyrus H. Jenks, was a superintendent on James J. Hill's Great Northern. C.

O. Jenks, Downing's father, was general manager of the Spokane, Portland & Seattle and later vice president of operations for the Great Northern. The maternal grandfather for whom he was named, W. O. Downing, was a state senator of Missouri and an attorney for several railways.

Downing Bland Jenks was born in Portland, Oregon, on August 16, 1915, to Charles O. and Della Downing Jenks. During vacations from Yale in 1934 and 1935 he worked as a chainman on the Spokane, Portland & Seattle. After receiving his B.S. in 1937 he became an assistant in the engineer corps on the Pennsylvania Railroad. He moved to the Great Northern as a roadmaster in 1938, becoming in succession division engineer, trainmaster, and division superintendent. After serving as general manager on the Chicago & Eastern Illinois Railroad in 1948-1949, he joined the Chicago, Rock Island & Pacific as vice president and general manager. He was made assistant vice president for operations in 1950, vice president for operations the following year, executive vice president in 1953, and president in 1956.

Purpose and character mixed with opportunity and accident in just the right way several times in Jenks's rail career. One of those times was when he came to St. Louis in November 1960 to inquire whether the Missouri Pacific might be interested in a merger with the ailing agriculture-based Rock Island. Jenks spent much time with Harvey Johnson, executive vice president of the MoPac and spoke briefly with its chairman, William Marbury. Neither Johnson nor Marbury were interested in a merger with the Rock Island, but they were interested in Jenks, and saw the opportunity in the struggles at Rock Island to lure away one of the brightest young stars in railroading.

Marbury was as direct as Jenks. "Would you like to come here as president?" he asked Jenks when the younger man arrived in his office. Perhaps, Jenks replied, if his merger prospects did not work out, particularly one with the Chicago, Milwaukee, St. Paul & Pacific. They arranged that Jenks would call Marbury on November 14, the day the Rock Island board was to decide on the merger, and accept or reject the MP presidency. On the fourteenth Marbury's phone rang: "I am available," said Jenks.

Running the Missouri Pacific was not as simple as becoming its president, though Jenks approached the job with the same decisive energy. He remembered later that despite all his experience to that point he was apprehensive both about working with Marbury and about turning around such a famous "difficult case" as the Missouri Pacific. Somewhat to his surprise, he received complete trust and support from Marbury. Jenks left Marbury in charge of the boardroom and attacked the line. "The company was a little like a dowager," he said later. "It was already over a hundred years old then, and it acted like it. It was a little down at the heels."

Jenks revamped the motive power and standardized it with General Motors Electro-Motive Division equipment. It appeared that the MP had been a soft touch over the years for motive power salespeople and had "everything but a Maytag washer" running on the line. He took delivery his first year on 1,100 new freight cars at a cost of $12 million with the goal of reducing the bad-order ratio (the percentage of cars out of service for repairs) to 3 percent. He cut passenger service until it was gone, taking off the railroads' first streamliner route—and its most unprofitable one—first. He accelerated the installation of computers, first to operate the new hump yards, then to control inventory in centralized depots, and finally to track the movements of cars and report to customers through service centers. Special teams developed continuous-weld rails and innovated in piggyback and Less-Than-Carload (LTC) marketing. Jenks used automation, standardized yard and yard office design, and streamlined the sales department and executive style. "We'll still have superintendents," he explained, "but they won't have big office forces. They'll spend more time out on the road and less on paperwork." Those who could not stand the pace were first in line for dismissal. Difficult objectives were set, and they were met or Jenks wanted to know the reason why. The "hot shot" freights began to run on time, and the roadbed at the southern end of the line was transformed into something on which trains could run fast.

Almost as soon as Jenks had made some headway operating the Missouri Pacific, he and Marbury acquired the Chicago & Eastern Illinois in 1966 and proceeded to rehabilitate a railroad that made the problems on the MP look mild. Again, Jenks knew exactly what he wanted to do, and his prior experience with the C&EI made him invaluable both in the delicate negotiations to acquire it and in setting strategy for integrating it into the MP system. Jenks poured $4.7 million into the C&EI during the first years and escalated the investment for several years after that. But the operating advantages to the MP of the Thebes gateway in Southern Illinois started paying immediately.

"In the early days," Jenks remembered, "it was easy. The things that needed to be done were so obvious." His right-hand man at both the Rock Island and the MP, John Lloyd, thought that they would not have been so obvious to everyone: "He's an impetuous fellow," said Lloyd of Jenks. "I get madder than hell at him."

Through the turbulent 1960s Jenks was instrumental in encouraging an internal "MIS study group" at the MP to create what became one of the most remarkable computer-control systems in railroading. His earliest idea of the use of computers was, as was most businesspeople's, as an accounting and inventory tool. But Jenks's instinct for people and their potential, and his willingness to trust a "skunk works" type group and give brilliant individuals a little rein, paid large dividends in the creation of the Transportation Control System (TCS). "What would you do," he asked his young ad hoc committee on computerization in 1966, "if you were creating a new railroad using computers?" Although he himself did not know the answer, asking the question in that way was, one of the team remembers, an injection of some powerful management medicine that got the juices flowing.

As Marbury backed him, Jenks backed his computer team as it designed and implemented one stage after another of TCS. He studied and copied the best from elsewhere, and when a brilliant mind was discovered, he did everything he could to lure that mind away from its current employment and put it in the MP mix. In the process, the whole purpose of the computer was changed from providing management with information to providing centralized control. Such control perfectly suited Jenks's management style with its elements of order, speed, standardization, and quantifiable results. The computer could balance abstract policy and daily decision-making without one dominating the other and with each constantly influencing the other, the way Jenks could do it in his own person.

Jenks was dynamic and articulate as a speaker both in public and person-to-person. His comments were always direct, incisive, honest, often had a humorous twist, and were brief and to the point.

He was highly organized and highly disciplined; his nickname was "Mr. Clean." Subordinates said he had a "blotterlike" memory and could absorb complex tables of statistics at a glance. People who came before him with disorganized programs described him as "brisk" or "brusque." Jenks maintained a clean desk through system and proper delegation and always maintained a clean railroad for the same reasons. When he first arrived at the Missouri Pacific and visited some of the shops, he thought he was either at a railroad museum or an archeological dig. Layer by layer he stripped away the nostalgia and sentiment in the physical plant and the management and got down to the bedrock upon which the lean railroads of the era of merger and deregulation would have to depend.

A fastidious person, Jenks disliked long hair on his employees and was genuinely comfortable in a suit and hat. He brooked no moral compromise and subscribed to a personal code much like that of the Boy Scouts, of which he served as national president.

The variety of operating positions he held taught Jenks to spend more time out on the line than in the paneled rooms of corporate headquarters, no matter what his title, to mix with all the classes it took to run a railroad and to keep apprised of the pulse of the company. In his first three months with the MP Jenks traveled more than 30,000 miles exploring the railroad. When there were floods in Texas in 1966, Jenks set up a field camp at the point of the emergency, rolled up his sleeves, and dived into the work, communicating with St. Louis through a field telephone tapped into the lines that were still operative. "You've got to get out and see the property," he said, "see what's going on, talk to people."

Despite his reputation as an operator, Jenks was always much more than a nuts-and-bolts man. He was a true executive in all ways, from public relations to secret negotiations. In that last category, perhaps his greatest triumph was the recapitalization of the Missouri Pacific in 1974, which ended a stock fight between "A" and "B" holders that had been going on acrimoniously since the reorganization of the road in 1956 after a twenty-two-year receivership. Marbury was too volatile and outspoken to be effective in such situations and was always willing to go on to something new if his strategies did not work. Jenks, on the other hand, was deeply committed to the property on which he had staked his chance to make railroad history. Though he was a stubborn negotiator who would not throw away anything important for the sake of peace, and though he knew the value of patience, he had too clear a vision of his goals to start a fight to the death.

Jenks was in rare form during the tense negotiations over the fate of the MP "B" stock, when he was often under scrutiny by determined lawyers and a press looking for irregularities. His wry sense of humor came to his aid on numerous occasions. When asked whether the MP had "gold-plated" the railroad, running up expenses to keep the "B" stockholders from getting any dividends, Jenks responded with his always-ready store of organized statistics, then commented: "If we were gold plating it, we were sure putting a pretty thin coat on." Asked about statements concerning profitability in an article in *Forbes*, Jenks claimed never to have read the article because the picture of him on the cover was a "poor likeness." When attorneys tried to corner Jenks on the question of how much money it really took to run a railroad they were entering the turf of a relaxed and confident master.

From his first public statements as a railroad officer, Jenks argued for regulatory changes that would allow railroads to run truly integrated operations including barge, ship, truck, and air components. Railroads were moving in that direction in the nineteenth century, he was fond of pointing out, until government intervention to regulate the "Robber Barons" during the early twentieth-century Progressive Era. In the 1960s he spoke of container-laden unit trains running from deep water to river ports and turning St. Louis into a port city for the import-export trade. He predicted the creation of five or six large rail systems in the West. There was no excuse, he thought, for "vicious infighting" among common carriers when they had a $44 billion freight transportation market to share; they should join into integrated companies and lobby as a united front. The first steps would have to be deregulation and the elimination of special interest subsidies. "The railroad industry pays its own way," Jenks said in his 1969 annual report, "while fighting for traffic against competitors who receive hundreds of millions of tax dollars in the form of subsi-

dies. At the same time, a mass of antiquated regulations restricts the railroads' abilities to offer more attractive prices and additional services."

Jenks lobbied against restrictive regulations on the truck line, and he tried to get the railroad more heavily into the barge and air freight businesses. He set up offices in Japan and Canada and started an advertising campaign under the theme "MP hauls All" that emphasized the railroad's sixteen transportation and distribution services. His vision of large, integrated, intermodal transportation companies might seem, he told an audience in 1962, "too much like a dream, but you will have to admit that what we are doing now looks too often like a nightmare."

From the perspective of the mid 1980s, it is clear that Jenks was precisely right about the direction the railroad industry would take, and perhaps even he was surprised at the speed with which the industry has moved toward deregulation, merger into a few large systems, and, more slowly, toward the creation of intermodal transportation systems.

Thanks to him, the Missouri Pacific was ready for the revolution. It took advantage of the opportunites that came with the deregulated atmosphere of the 1980s and in 1983 joined with the Union Pacific to form one of the giant Western systems Jenks had envisioned in the 1960s. Now on the board of the Union Pacific corporation, Jenks is where he imagined he could be, and the industry is where he thought it might be. However, it is a good guess that he is not satisfied, but restless still to make one or two more good moves before he passes from the scene.

"The so-called 'railroad problem,' " Jenks once told an audience, "has been the subject of more study but probably less action, than perhaps any other aspect of national industrial life." Descended from generations of railroadmen, it was Jenks's destiny to take some of that too-long-delayed action. He was one of the first railway officers to argue and believe that his industry could grow as fast as others, and he invested in continuing high-level education at Northwestern's University Transportation Center for the bright young people he recruited to make it grow. Asked for the secret of his success, Jenks was, as usual, brief: "I just started early, and knew what I wanted to do."

Jenks had two children by his first wife, Louise Sweeney Jenks, whom he married in 1937. In 1985 he married Helen Stark.

References:
"Magnate of Mid-America," *Forbes*, 91 (June 15, 1963): 20–25;

Craig Miner, *The Rebirth of the Missouri Pacific, 1956-1983* (College Station: Texas A&M University Press, 1983).

William J. Jenks

(March 21, 1870-January 17, 1960)

by Keith L. Bryant, Jr.

Texas A&M University

William J. Jenks

CAREER: Telegrapher, Raleigh & Augusta Railroad (1886); telegraph operator, Richmond & Danville Railroad (1887); agent (1887), operator (1887-

1889), train dispatcher (1889-1899), car distributor (1899-1901), Norfolk & Western Railway; chief dispatcher (1901), trainmaster (1901-1904), superintendent (1904-1908), Seaboard Air Line Railroad; chairman, car allotment commission (1908-1912), superintendent (1912), general superintendent (1912-1918), general manager (1918-1924), vice president, operations (1924-1936), president (1936-1946), chairman of the board (1946-1954), Norfolk & Western Railway.

Born in 1870 on a farm in Wake County, North Carolina, to William S. and Retta Baucom Jenks, William Jackson Jenks was educated in private and public schools. At the age of sixteen he learned telegraphy and found employment with the Raleigh & Augusta Railroad, a predecessor of the Seaboard Air Line Railroad, for ten dollars per month plus board. For the remainder of his life he labored in railroading; most of his career was with the Norfolk & Western (N&W).

The Norfolk & Western served as a major coal hauler transporting "black diamonds" from West Virginia to the piers at Norfolk. The coal traffic required a well-constructed system with large-scale motive power. The N&W took heavily laden hopper cars to the port and returned the empties to the mines. For this trade it competed directly with the Baltimore & Ohio; the Chesapeake & Ohio; the Western Maryland; and the Virginian, which virtually paralleled the N&W. The Norfolk & Western was in receivership from 1895 to 1896, and during the next decade the firm was reorganized financially, and its many branches were rebuilt. New, heavier steel rail was placed on the main line, and extensive purchases of locomotives and cars helped to make the company prosperous for the first time. The Pennsylvania Railroad, a dominant force in eastern railroading, saw the potential of the N&W, and in 1900 purchased over one-third of its stock. Thus the Norfolk & Western entered the "community of interest" of the Pennsylvania.

Jenks worked for the N&W in good times and lean. He joined the carrier in 1887 as it was expanding into the coalfields and moved through the ranks as the company entered and exited the bankruptcy court. His service on the Seaboard Air Line from 1901 to 1908 broadened his experience. As a trainmaster at Savannah and Jacksonville and as superintendent at the latter city, he saw the importance of general merchandise traffic and diversification to balance the flow of freight.

Returning to the N&W in 1908, Jenks found a very different firm from the one he had left. A line had been purchased, extending the carrier west to Cincinnati, and through traffic of general merchandise augmented the shipment of coal. The N&W was becoming an extremely efficient company; its operating ratio of 62 in the early 1900s fell to 56.1 by 1916. Heavy demands for coal during World War I led to the acquisition of larger locomotives and the construction of a new steel pier at Norfolk. As, successively, superintendent, general superintendent, general manager, and vice president for operations, Jenks played a major role in the development of one of the finest physical properties in railroading.

The N&W electrified a portion of its line in West Virginia to cope with heavy grades and throughout the 1920s continued a betterment program to increase operating efficiency. The operating ratio under federal control during and after World War I had soared to 95.9 by 1920 but by 1930 had fallen to 59.3. Even the Great Depression did not have the devastating impact on the N&W that it had on other carriers. The company remained profitable because of its efficiency and the economy measures Jenks employed as vice president for operations.

In 1936 the board of directors named Jenks president of the N&W. He immediately initiated a major program of locomotive development. At its

Roanoke, Virginia, shops, the N&W in 1936 constructed the first of a series of "super power" locomotives. The J-Class 4-8-4s and the Mallets built for service in the mountains proved to be some of the finest steam locomotives ever produced in the United States. Jenks also carried to conclusion the program to relay the main line with 131-pound rail, and he pushed hard for a safety program that won the N&W a Harriman Gold Medal in 1939.

Following the outbreak of war in Europe, the flow of coal over the N&W accelerated at a rapid rate. For the next seven years Jenks coped with rising demands for coal, both for consumption in the Midwest and for export. With fewer locomotives, cars, and employees than it had during World War I, the N&W exceeded all previous records for traffic volume. A new hump yard at Roanoke, additional miles of Centralized Traffic Control, and a few new locomotives and rebuilt freight cars allowed Jenks and his staff to meet the traffic demands. Defense installations along the N&W added to the volume of business and also diversified the tonnage, an important factor after 1945 when coal traffic began to decline. By 1946 the N&W was a lean, prosperous railway producing high levels of profits and huge dividends for the Pennsylvania Railroad. That year Jenks stepped down as president and was named chairman of the board.

Throughout the railway Jenks was known for his closeness with a dollar. Part of his success as president had been his emphasis on reducing costs; Jenks had a horror of "unnecessary" expenditures. His successor, Robert H. Smith, launched a large capital investment program in locomotive facilities and other improvements. Jenks retired as chairman of the board in 1954 after seventy years of railroading.

Jenks married Sallie C. Baldwin in 1891, and they had three children. After Jenks returned to the N&W in 1908 he made his home in Roanoke, where he was an active participant in community life and a member of the Episcopal church. He died in 1960.

Reference:

E. F. Pat Striplin, *The Norfolk & Western: A History* (Roanoke, Va.: Norfolk & Western Railway, 1981).

Archives:

There appear to be no archives of William J. Jenks's personal papers. Corporate records of the Norfolk & Western Railway are at the Atlanta regional office of the Norfolk Southern Corporation.

Wayne A. Johnston

(November 19, 1897-December 5, 1967)

by John F. Stover

Purdue University

Wayne A. Johnston (left), discussing the Illinois Central's 1966 car building plans with Hugh H. Young, superintendent of the railroad's car shops at Centralia, Illinois (Kalmbach Publishing Company)

CAREER: Accountant (1919-1920), chief clerk to superintendent (1920-1921), assistant chief clerk to superintendent of northern lines (1921-1925), correspondence clerk to vice president and general manager (1925-1934), general agent (1934), office manager to vice president (1934-1935), general agent of mail, baggage, express, and merchandise traffic (1935-1938), assistant to vice president and general manager (1938-1940), acting superintendent, Kentucky division (1940-1941), assistant to vice president and general manager (1941-1942), assistant general manager (1942-1944), assistant vice president (1944), general manager (1944-1945), president (1945-1966), chairman of the board (1966-1967), Illinois Central Railroad.

Wayne Andrew Johnston was born on November 19, 1897, in Philo, Illinois, the second of three sons of Harry W. and DeEtta Bird Boomer Johnston. His father, a farmer who also operated a grain elevator. died when Johnston was two years of age, and two months before the birth of his younger brother. To support her family Mrs. Johnston returned to teaching school, first in Philo and later in Champaign, a few miles to the north. Johnston attended grade school in Philo and high school in Champaign. During his high school years Johnston and his brothers increased the family income by delivering newspapers and the *Saturday Evening Post*.

Johnston studied railway business administration in the College of Commercial and Business Administration of the University of Illinois. He paid his way through college by waiting on tables, washing dishes, and serving as a janitor for a sorority house. During summer vacations he was employed as yard clerk and switchman on the Peoria & Eastern Railroad, and one summer worked as a guide in Yellowstone National Park. For two years he was a student assistant in the office of the dean of men. Upon receiving his B.S. degree in 1918, Johnston found that he was disqualified for military service in World War I for physical reasons.

In 1919 Johnston started to work for the Illinois Central Railroad (IC), an employer he would serve for nearly half a century. His first job was as an accountant in the office of the division superintendent at Champaign, a station on the main line of the IC 130 miles south of Chicago. Among his fellow workers in the division office was an attractive young lady named Blanche Lawson. In 1920 he was promoted to chief clerk to the superintendent, and a year later he moved to the company headquarters in Chicago as assistant chief clerk to the general superintendent of northern lines. By this time Johnston had saved $400, and he asked Blanche Lawson to be his wife. They were married on June 17, 1922, and settled in Avalon Park, a residential community within Chicago along the line of the Illinois Central. They had two children.

Chartered in 1851 as the first railroad to receive a federal land grant, the Illinois Central in 1922 had a 4,700-mile network in ten states, from South Dakota, Minnesota, and Wisconsin to Louisiana and Mississippi. Its nearly 65,000 employees operated 1,600 locomotives, 1,600 passenger cars, and 71,000 freight cars, which generated annual revenues of over $150 million in 1922. It had paid good dividends continuously since 1861, even during World War I when federal control had pushed the operating ratio well above 90. The IC also owned much valuable real estate in downtown Chicago.

Johnston had a varied experience as he moved up the ladder in the IC Chicago headquarters. In 1925 he was appointed correspondence clerk in the office of vice president and general manager-a position that gave him an in-depth exposure to all phases of rail operation. In 1934 he transferred to the traffic department, first as a general agent and next as office manager to the vice president. In 1935 he was made general agent of mail, baggage, express, and merchandise traffic. In 1938 Johnston returned to the operating department as assistant to the vice president and general manager. While serving in the traffic and operating departments Johnston sometimes spent 200 days a year on the road. Before long he had covered nearly every mile of the system—which had grown to 6,200 miles in 1924 and to 6,500 by 1940—by train, by motor car, or on foot. In these years he not only developed an extensive acquaintance with the property in all departments but came to know literally thousands of key people all along the line. In 1940 he became acting superintendent of the Kentucky division due to the illness of the division superintendent.

Johnston returned to Chicago in 1941 and was promoted to assistant general manager in 1942. During World War II over 10,000 IC employees—about a quarter of the total work force—entered the armed services, and in the spring of 1943 Johnston was placed in charge of a recruiting and training program for boys too young for the draft. In the last twenty-eight months of the war more than 4,000 sixteen- and seventeen-year-olds completed training at IC transportation schools in Chicago, Carbondale, Louisville, and Memphis and took jobs as firemen, brakemen, or clerks all across the

IC system. A large percentage of these young workers stayed on with the IC once the war emergency had passed. Also during the war Johnston headed a system-wide fuel conservation program in which the IC offered a trophy to the division or terminal with the best record in reducing its use of coal. In April 1944 Johnston was promoted to assistant vice president; in September he was made general manager.

Early in January 1945 the president of the Illinois Central, John L. Beven, died suddenly of a heart attack. The board of directors gave the job of finding a successor to the chairman of their executive committee, Eugene W. Stetson. Stetson visited privately with the six top IC executives—the four vice presidents, the general counsel, and the chief engineer. Stetson asked each of the six who would be the man's first choice for the presidency, if he himself was not selected. Each replied: "Wayne Johnston." As Stetson later explained the selection process: "They recommended, I nominated, and the board elected Wayne Johnston president of the Illinois Central Railroad."

The new president was several years younger than the six men who had recommended him, and at forty-seven was one of the youngest presidents of any major railway in the nation. He was the youngest of the IC presidents except for Stuyvesant Fish, who had been elected in 1887 at the age of thirty-five. Johnston was also the first native of Illinois to be president of the Illinois Central. Johnston believed in team effort and his first concern was the welfare of the "Illinois Central Family." A favorite comment of the new top executive was: "You've got to depend on your organization." During his record tenure of twenty-one years as president Johnston would improve and strengthen the Illinois Central in a variety of ways.

The Great Depression had brought the IC quite close to receivership. Revenues had declined sharply, over half the labor force had been laid off, dividends had been dropped in 1931, and IC common stock had fallen to under $5 a share. This situation had quickly changed with the coming of World War II. Between 1939 and 1944 freight revenue on the IC had more than doubled, passenger traffic had increased fourfold, and annual net income had increased more than sevenfold. The real prosperity of the early war years had permitted President

Beven to reduce the funded debt more than $100 million between 1941 and 1944.

With Stetson's help Johnston was able to continue this debt retirement program in the early postwar years. The funded debt of the Illinois Central declined from $282 million in 1945 to $206 million by the end of 1951. During these years the debt structure was simplified and average interest rates were reduced. The Illinois Central and other major railroads celebrated their postwar optimism and prosperity with the Chicago Railroad Fair in the summers of 1948 and 1949. The fair, which commemorated the centennial of the first railroad service in Chicago, was located on the shore of Lake Michigan, paralleling the IC tracks for a mile south of Twenty-third Street. Illinois Central shareholders also had something to celebrate: in 1948 dividends on the preferred stock were resumed and in 1950 resumed common stock dividends were paid for the first time in nineteen years. Shareholders received a dividend of $3 per share during 1950.

As Johnston neared the end of his sixth year as president he led the railroad's celebration of its centennial. The Illinois Central charter had been signed by Augustine C. French, the governor of Illinois, on February 10, 1851. The centennial committee planned a great variety of events for Chicago and the thirteen divisions of the 6,500-mile system operating in fourteen states. A formal party was held at the Palmer House in Chicago with hundreds of railroad, civic, and business leaders in attendance. As the guests entered the banquet ballroom observers noted that Johnston was able to greet nearly every guest by his first name. After dinner a pageant reviewed major events in the history of the railroad. Each guest received a three-inch bronze centennial medal with the motto "For 100 Years Main Line of Mid-America." During the year a centennial history of the line, *Main Line of Mid-America* by Carlton J. Corliss, a longtime Illinois Central official, was published. Also in 1951 the railroad was completing a much larger centennial project, a new $6 million steel multi-span bridge to replace the sixty-two-year-old bridge over the Ohio River at Cairo, Illinois.

During Johnston's presidency the mileage of the IC increased by only 100 miles. In the same years, however the Illinois Central spent $533 million on capital improvements to strengthen the railroad—$194 million on fixed property and $339 million on equipment. The fixed property improvements included the bridge at Cairo, replacing lighter with heavier rail, and installing welded rail in quarter-mile lengths to reduce wear at rail joints and make for smoother riding. Additional sidings were built to serve new patrons and dozens of depots were rebuilt or replaced. Improved signals were installed, and Centralized Traffic Control (CTC) was established on additional mileage. During the Johnston years millions of dollars were spent in improving the major freight yards on the IC. The Mays Yard at New Orleans was completed and the Nonconnah Yard at Memphis was rebuilt and renamed the Johnston Yard. Improvements were made at the Markham Yard in Chicago and at East St. Louis. Electronic retarders and radio communication systems were added to most of the larger freight yards.

Far more money was spent on new equipment than on fixed property. Shortly after the war the IC paid several million dollars for new streamliners for long-distance runs. By 1946 all passenger equipment on long-distance trains had been air conditioned. Even more was invested in new freight equipment. In the summer of 1946 Johnston proposed that more than $7 million be spent for 1,900 new freight cars. Other large orders were made for gondolas, hopper cars, and covered hoppers. Many new cars were specially built to fit the needs of customers. After the introduction of piggyback service in 1955 new, longer flatcars had to be provided. In the early 1960s the IC acquired many double and triple rack cars for the delivery of new automobiles. Additional funds were required to provide cushioned underframes, roller bearings, and improved lubrication for freight equipment.

By far the largest share of new equipment money went for the dieselization program. Diesel units were expensive, costing from $150,000 to $250,000 per unit, but they provided major advantages in lower crew costs, ease of maintenance, and a much reduced cost of fuel. Most diesels could run thousands of miles without major servicing. The faster starts of diesels permitted improved schedules, and they could haul longer and larger loads at higher speeds. In Johnston's first year as president steam engines had made up 96 percent of the motive power fleet. The IC was far from being a leader in converting from steam to diesel power, but in 1961 Johnston reported that the shift to diesels was complete. There were several reasons for the rather slow adoption of diesel power. Johnston felt that the highest priority should be given to debt retirement and in 1945 the IC had an excellent fleet of steam power. The fact that the IC was a "coal road" (a major carrier of coal) also contributed to the slow rate of diesel purchases. In the spring of 1963 Illinois Central officials figured that the 643 diesel units had cost nearly $100 million.

Other technical advances were introduced during the 1950s and 1960s. New track maintenance equipment, such as powered spike hammers and ballast tampers and cleaners, permitted major cuts in maintenance-of-way personnel. The use of radio and television also increased labor efficiency. New computer technology in the late 1950s and early 1960s saved labor in the accounting, purchasing, stores, and engineering departments. Larger cars, longer trains, and more powerful diesels permitted some reduction in the number of train crews required. Thus, during the Johnston years there was a marked increase in the productivity of the IC labor force. At the same time that the number of workers was declining, the strong railroad unions were obtaining large wage increases—nineteen cents an hour in 1957 and twenty-three cents an hour in 1958, for example. During the Johnston presidency the number of IC workers dropped from 40,915 to 21,523, while the average annual pay increased from $2,457 to $7,038. In those twenty-one years IC pay increased 190 percent, while the cost of living rose only 80 percent. These trends of declining employment and substantial increases in wages were typical of the railroad industry. Early in his presidency Johnston had insisted that the salaries of IC executives should, if possible, match the wage boosts received by the railroad brotherhoods. Johnston's own salary, which was only $40,000 a year at the time of his election in 1945, had been pushed up to $100,000 by the early 1960s.

On the Illinois Central the percentage of revenue going for wages increased from 42 percent in 1945 to 56 percent by the mid 1960s. Johnston and his staff had to continuously find ways to cut other costs to meet the ever growing price of labor. One way, put in effect in 1959, was to cut the divisions on the system from twelve to ten; a generation earlier there had been twenty. In 1955 Johnston told an American Bankers Association meeting in Chicago that the railroads were overregulated:

"The corner grocer can raise or lower prices to reflect the costs of business or the pressures of competition, but railroads can do so only after long and costly delays." Johnston and other railroad presidents in the late 1950s became increasingly unhappy with featherbedding by train crews. In the fall of 1959 Johnston told his employees: "What is featherbedding? It is money paid under old-fashioned, outmoded working rules . . . an engineer can collect a full day's pay for working three hours because the rules say running a train 100 miles is a full day's pay." Johnston was a leader in representing the Association of American Railroads in its struggle to eliminate firemen from freight locomotives. He pointed out that the fireman's shovel was an "expensive antique," since the diesel fireman of 1959 had no coal to shovel and no boiler to tend. The operating unions fought the elimination of yard and freight engine firemen for years, but management won the issue in 1964, after many presidential commissions had struggled with the problem.

During the first decade and a half of Johnston's leadership of the Illinois Central all the railroads were in a desperate fight for traffic with trucks, pipelines, barges, buses, airlines, and private automobiles. The railroads' share of intercity freight declined from 68 percent in 1944 to 44 percent in 1960, while their share of commercial intercity passenger traffic dropped from 74 percent to 27 percent. Between 1945 and 1960 total freight on the IC declined from 20.8 billion ton-miles to 17.2 billion ton-miles, while passenger traffic dropped from 1,971 million passenger miles to 848 million passenger miles. During the same decade and a half the annual operating ratio climbed from 72.4 to 81.1. Dividends on common stock rose from $3 a year in 1950 to $4.50 in 1953 and $3.75 in 1957, but dropped to $2 a year in 1959 and 1960. The rate of return on their property for all American railroads averaged only about 3.5 percent during the 1950s and was down to 2.1 percent in 1960. This rate was far lower than those for other modes of transport and for American industry generally. By the early 1960s many railroads were seeking ways to solve their financial problems. Some lines found a solution in mergers, while others looked to diversification.

In the early 1960s the Illinois Central decided to diversify by moving into clearly nonrailroad enterprises. In his 1962 annual report Johnston wrote:

"As you know, the Illinois Central has been studying . . . diversification to provide a broader earnings base . . . We believe that your best interests will be served by such diversification." Johnston and his board created a holding company, Illinois Central Industries, and asked IC Railroad shareholders to exchange their stock for stock in the new corporation. The exchange of shares was completed in the spring of 1963. Illinois Central Industries managed the railroad and also started to more fully promote and develop the railroad's real estate holdings. The most valuable holdings were certain air rights on the downtown Chicago lakefront, east of Michigan Avenue between Raldolph Street and the Chicago River. The use of these air rights was delayed by litigation, but by 1966 both the state and federal courts had ruled in favor of the Illinois Central. In 1964 Illinois Central Industries purchased the Chandeysson Electric Company of St. Louis, a manufacturer of heavy electric equipment. No other nonrailroad enterprises were acquired prior to Johnston's retirement as president in 1966, but after 1967 the expansion of Illinois Central Industries was quite rapid. By 1970 the Illinois Central Railroad was providing less than half of the annual revenues earned by the parent holding company.

As he neared the mandatory retirement age of seventy, Johnston and his board started to look for a new president for the Illinois Central. As the senior member of the board of the Railway Express Agency, Johnston was well acquainted with its president, William B. Johnson, who had successfully revitalized the agency. Johnston proposed Johnson as his successor, and the IC board agreed. On February 18, 1966, Johnson was elected president of the Illinois Central and Johnston was named chairman of the board. The new president took office on May 2. Johnston retired as chairman on November 30, 1967. At his retirement dinner some 200 railroad, industrial, and political leaders applauded as Governor Otto Kerner proclaimed November 30 "Wayne Johnston Day" in Illinois.

Johnston took part in many nonrailroad activities. Back in Philo his widowed mother had taken her three sons to church every Sunday morning, and when the Wayne Johnstons settled in Avalon Park they were active in the Congregational Avalon Park Community Church, where Wayne served as the superintendent of the Sunday school. While a student at the University of Illinois Johnston had been an assistant scoutmaster, and in Chicago he was active in the Chicago Council and at regional and national levels. During these years he received all the major adult scouting awards–the Silver Beaver in 1939, the Silver Antelope in 1959, and the Silver Buffalo in 1962. In Chicago he took an active interest in the Y.M.C.A., the Child Care Society, and the Old Peoples Home of Chicago. He was a member of the board of trustees of several colleges and universities, including DePauw University, which his daughter attended. He was a trustee of the University of Illinois for seventeen years, and was president of the board at the time of his death. Johnston received honorary doctorates from Middlebury College in 1951, from Louisiana State in 1960, and from Mercer University in 1965. In 1967, after leaving the IC presidency, he received the Distinguished Public Service Award from the Union League of Chicago. One of the awards he prized most highly was the Horatio Alger Award of the American Schools and Colleges Association, which he received in 1963 from the hands of his good friend Norman Vincent Peale.

Johnston died suddenly on December 5, 1967, only a week after retirement. He was survived by his two children, his wife having died two years earlier. Johnston was buried in the Cedar Park Cemetery in Chicago.

Wayne Johnston once told a reporter that he could not remember wanting to be anything but a railroad man. He was a man of Spartan habits, normally arriving at his desk half an hour before office hours began. As president he answered his own phone and insisted that all other officers do the same. Johnston was one of the strongest and most productive presidents in the long history of the Illinois Central. His years as president were years of war and peace, of extensive debt retirement and dieselization, of resumed dividends and the introduction of diversification. The philosophy of Johnston's long and active life was best expressed to an interviewer as he approached retirement: "You've got to put back as much or more than you take out."

References:

Carlton J. Corliss, *Main Line of Mid-America: The Story of the Illinois Central* (New York: Creative Age Press, 1950);

George M. Crowson, *A Lifetime of Service: Wayne Johnston and the Illinois Central Railroad* (Chicago, 1968);

John F. Stover, *History of the Illinois Central Railroad* (New York: Macmillan, 1975).

Morgan Jones

(October 7, 1839-April 11, 1926)

by Vernon Gladden Spence

George Mason University

Morgan Jones

CAREER: Construction foreman, Union Pacific Railroad (1866-1869); construction contractor, Southern Transcontinental Railroad (1869-1876); construction contractor, Texas & Pacific Railway and Gulf, Colorado & Santa Fe Railroad (1876-1882); construction chief, vice president, president, and general manager, Fort Worth & Denver City Railway Company (1883-1893); builder, president, and general manager, Pan Handle Railway (1888-1893) and Wichita Valley Railway (1890-1906); builder and president, Wichita Falls & Oklahoma Railway (1903-1904); builder and president, Abilene &

Northern Railway (1906-1926); builder and president, Abilene & Southern Railway (1908-1926).

Morgan Jones was born to Morgan and Mary Charles Jones on a Welsh farm in 1839 and died in Abilene, Texas, in 1926. In the year of his birth, the Republic of Texas did not have a single mile of railroad track, but in the year of his death the state of Texas contained approximately fifty railroad properties with 16,071 miles of rails. Within Jones's lifetime one-fortieth of the world's total rails were built within the boundaries of a single state. Jones built and operated many of those Texas lines, and he did so with a singleness of purpose unmatched by any other individual in the state's railroad history.

A boyhood fascination with the railroad industry caused Jones to leave the family farm in 1859 to serve a seven-year construction apprenticeship with the Cambrian Railway in Wales. Since railroad construction in all of Great Britain had declined after its peak years in the 1840s, Jones moved to the United States just as the Civil War ended; he had heard correctly that his new skills were in great demand. Gen. Grenville M. Dodge, chief construction engineer of the Union Pacific Railroad, immediately placed him on the line as foreman of a construction crew. Moving westward from Omaha, Jones's crew helped to push the rails toward those of the Central Pacific simultaneously moving eastward from Sacramento. Less than three years later, Jones was among those proud onlookers who celebrated the joining of the rails at Promontory, Utah. Under General Dodge, Jones had learned that railroad building in the United States differed from his European experience in two vital respects: in America the time allotted was shorter and the distances were greater. That exercise in rapid construction over great distances later enabled him to meet seemingly impossible construction deadlines throughout the Southwest.

Upon the completion of the first transcontinental railroad, Jones contracted with Gen. John C. Frémont to build sections of the Southern Transcontinental (predecessor of the Southern Pacific) in east Texas just as that state's postwar boom commenced.

Fort Worth, Texas, was the next area to benefit from his railroad building skills. In 1876 the town's 1,600 residents were frustrated when construction of the Texas & Pacific Railway (T&P) tracks stalled just sixteen miles to the east at Eagle Ford. Eager to reach Fort Worth before the Texas legislature could revoke its charter and withhold its land subsidy, the T&P hired Jones to complete the job. The project suddenly developed into a patriotic crusade to "Bring the Railroad Home" before the legislature adjourned. Gen. Nicholas H. Darnell, representing Tarrant County, entered the legislative hall each day on a stretcher to cast his vote against adjournment. A holiday spirit engulfed the town when, on July 19, Jones's crew reached Fort Worth on time. The contest made the young Welshman a local hero and marked the beginning of a new era of growth for Fort Worth.

During the next five decades Jones built hundreds of miles of Texas railroads. He constructed lengthy sections of the Texas & Pacific and the Gulf, Colorado & Santa Fe. He was almost entirely responsible for the construction of the section of the Fort Worth & Denver City Railroad between Wichita Falls and Union Park, New Mexico, and served that company as vice president, president, and general manager during its first critical decade from 1883 to 1893.

After the major Texas railroads were completed, Jones constructed, operated, and was the major stockholder in numerous short-line roads in the state, including the Pan Handle, the Wichita Falls & Oklahoma, the Wichita Valley, the Abilene & Northern, and the Abilene & Southern. His plans to build short-line railroads in other areas of Texas forced the Atchison, Topeka & Santa Fe and the Texas Central to construct long extensions to their mainlines.

Without federal or state land subsidies, and in the face of severe droughts and financial depressions, Jones built most of his railroads into a semi-arid, largely unoccupied region. He enjoyed nothing more than to journey into west Texas frontier regions, study their economic potential, consider their future transportation needs, offer pioneer settlers a solution to their marketing problems, chart a route, supervise construction of a railroad, and finally to administer its initial services until the railroad and the people it served grew prosperous.

Unlike his friends General Dodge, Jay Gould, and Governor John Evans of Colorado, Jones was neither a promoter, a manipulator, nor a railroad politician. The quiet, unassuming Welshman was cut from a different cloth. He detested trivial interrailroad rivalries, petty jealousies, and political manipulation. He insisted upon orderliness, harmony, and privacy. He never married: "Women," he said, "are too impractical to marry." He reveled in the sights of a new locomotive, steel rails projecting into a frontier land, prosperous farms along a completed railroad, a staked-off townsite at the railhead.

Although he devoted almost every day of his adult living to building railroads, Jones also invested in many industrial, banking, timber, and ranching enterprises throughout the trans-Mississippi West. His faith in frontier development made the former Welsh farm boy a very wealthy man. That faith also opened up unsuspected bounties to thousands of pioneer settlers.

Morgan Jones, whose name rarely appeared in print, who never granted a newspaper interview until his eightieth year, and who never reflected upon his role in history, sought no accolades. He was, said the editor of the *Dallas News* at the time of Jones's death, too busy "knitting Texas closer together."

References:

Katharyn Duff, *Abilene . . . On Catclaw Creek: A Profile of a West Texas Town* (Abilene: Reporter Publishing Company, 1969);

Oliver Knight, *Fort Worth: Outpost on the Trinity* (Norman: University of Oklahoma Press, 1953);

Vernon Gladden Spence, *Colonel Morgan Jones: Grand Old Man of Texas Railroading* (Norman: University of Oklahoma Press, 1971).

Archives:

The Morgan Jones Papers are at Texas Technological University, Lubbock; the Grenville M. Dodge Letters are at the Iowa State Department of History and Archives, Des Moines. Material on Jones can also be found in the Fort Worth & Denver City Railroad Company Papers, Fort Worth Club Building, Fort Worth.

Kansas City Southern Railway

by Keith L. Bryant, Jr.

Texas A&M University

Map of the Kansas City Southern Railway (1983)

Conceived by promoter Arthur E. Stilwell as the shortest route between Kansas City and the Gulf of Mexico and built in the 1890s with capital generated in Philadelphia, New York, and Holland, the Kansas City, Pittsburg & Gulf Railroad (KCP&G) operated a line south from Kansas City through Pittsburg, Kansas; Texarkana, Arkansas; and Shreveport, Louisiana, to Beaumont and Port Arthur, Texas. Stilwell saw the KCP&G as a means of exporting grain and other agricultural commodities from the Midwest efficiently and economically through Port Arthur, a new city he was building on Sabine

Lake. The fortunes of the KCP&G rested upon the development of Port Arthur, a process delayed by the failure to complete a ship channel to the Gulf. Traffic did not meet expectations, and the railroad fell into receivership in 1899.

After being reorganized as the Kansas City Southern Railway (KCS) and chartered in Missouri on March 19, 1900, the company prospered. The ship channel was completed, and the railway also benefited from the discovery of oil at Spindletop, between Beaumont and Port Arthur. Oil refineries and related petroleum activities generated traffic, as did coal deposits in Arkansas and Oklahoma. The KCS was initially controlled financially by John W. Gates and his associates, but within a few years it became part of the rail empire dominated by E. H. Harriman. Under Harriman the line was rebuilt, new yards and facilities were constructed, and equipment was replaced. Harriman's representative on the Kansas City Southern was Leonor F. Loree, who served as chairman of the executive committee from 1906 to 1937. In the 1920s Loree hoped to make the KCS part of a new regional system made up of the Missouri-Kansas-Texas (Katy) and the St. Louis Southwestern (Cotton Belt), but the Interstate Commerce Commission denied the proposed merger.

In the 1930s the KCS did expand when it merged with the Louisiana & Arkansas Railway (L&A). The L&A operated a line from New Orleans to Dallas that intersected with the KCS at Shreveport, and had a major branch from Hope, Arkansas, south to Alexandria, Louisiana. This acquisition gave the KCS access to New Orleans, a major Gulf port, and to Dallas.

The KCS prospered during World War II with several major military installations along its lines, and regional economic growth after 1945 enhanced its profits. Before the war control of the KCS had shifted to a group of investors in Kansas City, and William N. Deramus, Jr., had become president and the dominant figure in the firm. The KCS was dieselized, its mountainous trackage in Oklahoma and Arkansas was improved, industrial sites were developed, and trucking subsidiaries were formed. The Deramus family and their allies continued to control the carrier as W. N. Deramus III became president in 1961, and chairman of the board and chief operating officer in 1966. Discussions in the 1960s of a merger with another Deramus-dominated railway, the Chicago Great Western, were not productive, however.

The KCS remained an independent regional carrier in the midst of the great rail merger movement. It formed Kansas City Southern Industries in 1962 and made the railway one of several subsidiaries. This small conglomerate entered the broadcasting business with radio and television stations, and acquired firms in communications servicing, small vehicle manufacturing, record-keeping services, and real estate, as well as petroleum-related activities. The merger of the Union Pacific and the Missouri Pacific in 1982, however, placed the Kansas City Southern Railway in a difficult competitive position.

Reference:

Keith L. Bryant, Jr., *Arthur E. Stilwell, Promoter with a Hunch* (Nashville: Vanderbilt University Press, 1971).

Archives:

Corporate records of the Kansas City Southern Railway are at the company's offices in Kansas City, Missouri.

John C. Kenefick

(December 26, 1921-   )

by Maury Klein

University of Rhode Island

John C. Kenefick (courtesy Union Pacific)

CAREER: Various positions, Union Pacific Railroad Company (1947-1952); various positions, Denver & Rio Grande Western Railroad Company (1952-1954); various positions, New York Central Railroad Company (1954-1966); vice president of operation, New York Central Railroad Company (1966-1968); vice president of transportation, Penn Central Company (1968); vice president of operation (1968-1969), executive vice president of operation (1969-1970), chief executive officer, transportation division (1970-1971), president (1971-1983), Union Pacific Railroad Company; director, Union Pacific Corporation (1972-   ); president and chair-

man, Union Pacific System (1983-1986); vice chairman, Union Pacific Corporation (1986-   ).

Although John Cooper Kenefick admits to a lifelong interest in railroads, he did not come to it by inheritance. Born in Buffalo in 1921, he was the son of John L. Kenefick, an attorney, and Charlotte Cooper Kenefick. Nothing in his youth foreshadowed a career in railroading. He graduated from Princeton University in 1943 with a major in mechanical engineering and entered the navy, from which he emerged a lieutenant (j.g.). After the war he worked for a few months for the New York Central in Buffalo, but grew restless and headed west, carrying a letter to the mechanical superintendent of the Atchison, Topeka & Santa Fe.

He made it only as far as Omaha, where, deciding that the Union Pacific was a good road to work for, he marched boldly into the vice president of operation's office and asked for a job. This brashness landed him in the drafting room, but he saw no future there and a few months later arranged a transfer to the position of brakeman. He was promoted to assistant train manager at Kansas City, and in 1952 was serving as trainmaster in Salina, Kansas, when restlessness seized him again. Alfred E. Perlman, then vice president of the Denver & Rio Grande Western Railroad (Rio Grande), was making a name for himself as a progressive railroad man. Kenefick arranged to see Perlman during a trip to Denver and came away with a job on the Rio Grande.

Perlman saw promise in young Kenefick and moved him around the Rio Grande during the next two years. In 1954 Perlman went to the New York Central, a railroad in deep trouble, as president and chief executive officer. Lacking capable officers to implement his style of management, he brought

Kenefick along and of necessity pushed him through the ranks with remarkable haste. To Perlman's delight, Kenefick responded to every challenge thrust upon him.

After a brief stint in New York Kenefick went to Chicago as head of the western division. Six months later he was rushed to Toledo in relief of a superintendent who had suffered a nervous breakdown. He arrived there in the midst of a howling snowstorm and a wildcat strike, both of which threatened to close the yard. Through a mixture of sound judgment and sheer tenacity he got the place running smoothly and was then promoted to assistant general manager at Syracuse, which had even more serious problems than Toledo. There, too, he acquitted himself well.

At every stop Kenefick showed an impressive ability to turn a bad situation around. He was advanced to general manager of transportation for the system in 1958 and assistant vice president of operation in 1965. A year later, at the age of forty-five, he was named vice president of operation, having earned a reputation as one of the best and brightest rail officers in the country. When the New York Central merged with the Pennsylvania in February 1968, Kenefick became vice president of transportation.

Three months later Kenefick left the Penn Central to return to the Union Pacific as vice president of operation. The firm was in the midst of reorganizing as a holding company, and its officers wanted Kenefick to head the new transportation division. The Penn Central also wanted him back as president, however, and it was not easy to turn down the top office of the largest rail system in the world. But Kenefick decided to cast his lot with the Union

Pacific, and in 1969 he took charge of the transportation division as executive vice president of operation.

Kenefick's impact on the Union Pacific was decisive and enduring. Although the road was financially strong, it suffered from unimaginative leadership, too much inbreeding and infighting among its officers, and a reverence for traditional means of problem solving that bordered on the hidebound. The presidents were absolute despots, benevolent or otherwise, who used the special agents as their private police force. Kenefick replaced cronyism with promotion by merit and infused the work force at every level with a new spirit of innovation. He instilled modern management techniques, delegated authority to junior officers, and did not hesitate to bring in men from the outside when the ranks lacked the talent or skills he needed. In speaking of past problems and abuses, old—timers today echo a common theme: "All that changed when John Kenefick come on the property."

A tall, imposing figure with piercing blue eyes, Kenefick combined unusual ability with a presence that left no doubt who was in charge. In 1983 he was elevated to chairman and chief executive officer of the new Union Pacific System created by the merger of the Union Pacific, Missouri Pacific, and Western Pacific. By then he long had a reputation as perhaps the foremost railroad operation man in the nation. He was promoted in April 1986 to vice chairman of the parent Union Pacific Corporation. His retirement from active service with the railroad that year marked the end of a major era of transition in its history, one that will long bear his imprint.

Kenefick married Helen Walker Ryan on August 19, 1973, and has one daughter and four stepchildren.

Julius Kruttschnitt

(July 30, 1854-June 15, 1925)

by Don L. Hofsommer

Augustana College

Julius Kruttschnitt (Courtesy Southern Pacific Company)

CAREER: Teacher, MacDonogh School for Boys (1873-1878); engineer (1878-1880), roadmaster (1880-1883) chief engineer and superintendent (1883-1885, Morgan's Louisiana & Texas Railroad & Steamship Company; assistant manager, Atlantic System (1885-1889), general manager, Atlantic System (1889-1895), general manager (1895-1898), fourth vice president (1898-1901), Southern Pacific Company; assistant to the president (1901-1904), vice president and director of maintenance, Southern Pacific, Union Pacific, and subsidiaries (1904-1913); chairman (1913-1925), director (1917-

1925), Southern Pacific Company and subsidiaries; director, Erie Railroad (1917-1925); director, Western Union Company (1918-1925).

Julius Kruttschnitt was born in New Orleans in 1854 to John K. and Penina Benjamin Kruttschnitt. His father was the German consul in New Orleans. Although he taught for five years at the MacDonogh School for Boys at Baltimore after his graduation from Washington and Lee University in 1873, Kruttschnitt chose to be a railroader, entering the service of the Morgan's Louisiana & Texas Railroad and Steamship Company in 1878 as resident engineer in charge of construction of the line at Berwick, Louisiana. He became roadmaster in 1880. In 1882 he married Elise Minna Krock; they had four children. He was made chief engineer and general superintendent in 1883. Two years later he joined the Southern Pacific (SP) as assistant manager of the Atlantic System, becoming general manager of the Atlantic System in 1889, general manager of the railroad in 1895, fourth vice president in 1898, and assistant to the president in 1901.

In 1904, three years after Edward H. Harriman gained control of the Southern Pacific as an integral link in the "Harriman Lines"–the Southern Pacific and Union Pacific (UP) and their affiliates–Kruttschnitt was made director of maintenance for the combined system, as well as vice president and general manager of the SP. Some called Harriman the "Napoleon of Railroading" and Kruttschnitt the "von Moltke of Transportation." They were a superb pair. Harriman's devotion to efficiency led him to insist on common standards, central purchasing, and pooling of equipment, but the temptation to overdo was great. A case in point involved Harriman's desire for uniform classes of locomotives for the Southern Pacific and the Union Pacific. This idea was impractical, said Kruttschnitt, because of dissimilar operating conditions, and would impair rather than increase efficiency. Harriman yielded to Kruttschnitt's better judgment in the matter.

When the federal government forced separation of the Southern Pacific from the Union Pacific in 1913, Kruttschnitt chose to stay with the SP, of which he became chairman. The trauma of divorcement was followed by a decade-long attempt by the federal government and the Union Pacific to strip the SP of its valuable Central Pacific subsidiary—linking the San Francisco Bay area with Ogden and the UP as part of the famous Overland Route—in addition to important terminals and secondary lines. It fell to Kruttschnitt to lead the SP through these difficult proceedings.

The government brought suit in 1914 but World War I postponed vigorous prosecution, and the Union Pacific did not activate a great campaign to gain control of the Central Pacific until 1921. That effort, however, sorely offended Kruttschnitt, who found himself laboring against former friends and associates. Indeed, he was appalled at what he considered UP's heavy-handedness in the affair but vowed that he would not stoop to such levels. Said the plainspoken Kruttschnitt, "I am willing to admit at the outset both our unwillingness and our inability to equal or excel them in their campaign of vilification and misrepresentation." He was deeply hurt by the comments of UP officers who had embraced a campaign devoid of "any consideration of friendship or fair dealing." Yet he would not retaliate in kind: "It would be undignified."

The entire affair tried his patience to the limit. In his zeal to protect and advance the SP's cause, he initiated a campaign designed to prove that his plant was more effectively managed than that of the Union Pacific. What resulted was the distribution of materials that showed each to be a fine company but with such dramatic differences in operating conditions as to make comparison meaningless.

In spite of this error in tactics and the surprising slip in Kruttschnitt's dignified style, the SP prevailed in the Central Pacific case in 1923. In his remaining two years, Kruttschnitt devoted himself to a final fleshing out of the system. His activities during those years also allowed further glimpses into his system of values and ethics. For instance, in the Central Pacific case Kruttschnitt had pledged the

company to build impressive station buildings and an important line segment in southeastern Oregon. During the mid 1920s there were many demands on the SP's resources and his subordinates frankly urged Kruttschnitt to renege on his promises. He would have none of it; at issue was his word, his honor.

Quiet and dignified, Kruttschnitt was totally without bombast. Extreme patience and uniform courtesy characterized his relationships with others; his orders to subordinates were couched as requests. He valued hard work and loyal attention to the company's interests, but he also understood the need for detachment. Kruttschnitt's hobbies included chemistry, astronomy, gardening, and golf. He was an omnivorous reader whose interests ranged from scientific works to fiction.

Making decisions was always easy for Kruttschnitt. Written requests for expenditures presented to him on the road were evaluated and decided on without comment; those he approved were stuffed into the right pocket of his greatcoat, those he rejected into the left pocket. In his huge office at 165 Broadway in New York Kruttschnitt pondered weightier matters in a less hurried fashion.

Kruttschnitt considered the most important duty of a company's chief executive to be the selection of his "official staff." That selection required, he believed, a "fair knowledge of the functions of each department." Kruttschnitt also believed it important to promote from within as much as possible, and during his tenure the company fielded a remarkable array of "homegrown" talent.

Kruttschnitt insisted that candidates for managerial positions have a fundamental understanding of science, the ability "to think logically and quantitatively" and "to write and speak clearly and correctly," an adequate understanding of economic theories, and "an unlimited capacity to learn." Other requirements included "the habit of looking forward" and a "pronounced firmness combined with a high sense of fairness and charity"— essential qualities, said Kruttschnitt in a 1925 speech to the New York Section of the American Society of Civil Engineers, "needed to control men."

Kruttschnitt's definition of a railroad was disarmingly simple: "A railroad is a huge manufacturing plant designed to convert the energy locked up in fuel into work for transporting persons and property on specially designed roadways." Yet the business of managing railroads was not simple; it had become complex in the twentieth century because of rising wages and inadequate increases in rates that put an incredible squeeze on the percentage of net income that "could be turned in to the treasury." The problem of lower net returns required, said Kruttschnitt, "the closest kind of management and the services of very much more highly trained executives to meet all the money requirements." He counseled the sparing of no expense "in establishing an Accounting Department to keep track of earnings and expenses, to record the history of operations, to act as general inspectors to expose poor results . . . and to . . . work up cost data . . . ."

Kruttschnitt expounded often on the importance of besting the competition and seeing to the needs of shippers. "I believe that in meeting competition . . . nothing but cold business conditions should govern, and we should seek by all legitimate means to retain traffic that we have enjoyed, and if we have not enjoyed enough we should endeavor strenuously to get more . . . ," he told a subordinate in 1922. Kruttschnitt entreated the SP's sales force to encourage a shipper "to come to us and to tie him to us with bands of steel." He was not content simply to attract new shippers; once they were "captured" it was necessary, he admonished, to keep them satisfied. Kruttschnitt mixed with customers at every opportunity and encouraged them to air their complaints.

Kruttschnitt similarly understood the need for positive public relations. His attitude toward disclosure of information about accidents is illustrative. Under the chairman's direction, the SP provided the press with detailed information "developed by thoroughgoing investigation." This policy of directness and honesty resulted in a curtailment of what Kruttschnitt called "sensational stories." The SP's chairman appeared frequently in public as an exponent of the industry's interests. He was not a Pollyanna. "If the railway is guilty of acts of omission or commission which are inconsistent with its public duty" the government "should adequately restrain and punish it," he said. On the other hand, "when the railway is doing its best to perform its duty it is obviously contrary to the interests of the public for it to be subjected to unnecessary restraints and penalties." Kruttschnitt was firm in his support of the

Transportation Act of 1920, which he believed would strengthen the credit of the carriers and thereby restore the attractiveness of railroad securities to investors. He was dismayed by those who attacked the new legislation or urged its repeal. He was even more distressed by the Interstate Commerce Commission (ICC), which, in his view, nullified the clear purposes of the act through maladministration. The 6 percent return on investment (later reduced to 5 3/4 percent) permitted under the law had been negated by the regulatory commission's unwillingness to grant adequate rate increases, growled Kruttschnitt. Among its other failings, he thought, the commission simply refused to acknowledge that federal laws regarding the Panama Canal restricted railroads in their ability to compete for transcontinental business and that several states had succeeded in establishing make-work legislation while at the same time forcing a reduction in intrastate rates. Moreover, concluded Kruttschnitt, the ICC was blind to new modal competition in the form of "freight and passenger motors."

At a meeting of the SP's board in April 1925, Kruttschnitt announced his intention to retire at the end of May. Just days before he left the SP, however, Kruttschnitt entered the hospital for elective surgery; complications developed and he died on June 15. In an age that was known for a deepening cynicism, Julius Kruttschnitt was genuinely mourned by his former associates, subordinates, and even the rank and file of Southern Pacific employees. Funeral services were held at St. Paul's Episcopal Church in New Orleans; across the entire system, crews respectfully honored this instruction: "Trains and engines in motion will be stopped at 9 A.M. for one minute."

Unpublished Document:

"The Engineer as a Railroad Executive," an address before the New York Section of the American Society of Civil Engineers, March 18, 1925; copy in the Southern Pacific Executive Department files, San Francisco.

References:

"The Career of Julius Kruttschnitt," *Railway Age*, 78 (June 1925): 1459-1462;

Don L. Hofsommer, *The Southern Pacific, 1901-1985* (College Station: Texas A&M University Press, 1986).

Lehigh Valley Railroad

by Richard Saunders

Clemson University

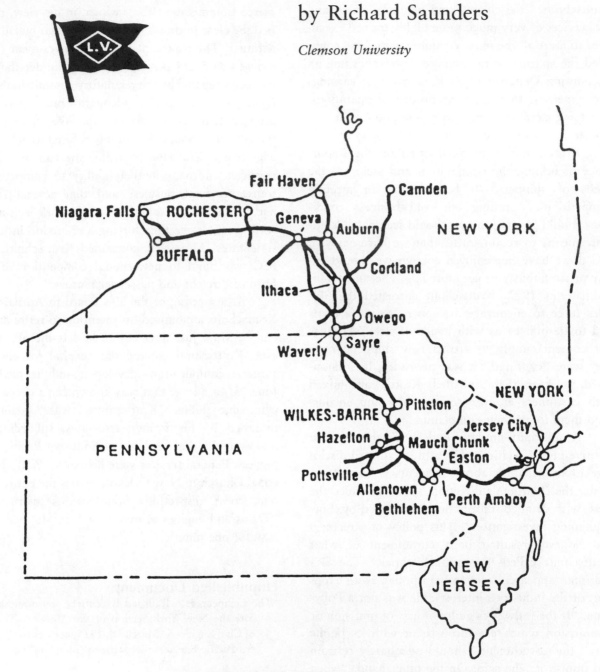

Map of the Lehigh Valley Railroad (1930)

The beginnings of the Lehigh Valley Railroad go back to the canal and inclined-plane schemes of the 1840s to get anthracite coal out of the mountains around the Lehigh River in Pennsylvania. The Dela-

ware, Lehigh, Schuylkill & Susquehanna Railroad was chartered in 1846 to build a line from Easton to Mauch Chunk, Pennsylvania; it was renamed the Lehigh Valley in 1853. The first train did not enter

Bethlehem until 1855. Successful and expansive, the railroad tapped Wyoming Valley coal in the spring of 1867, and that fall it reached Waverly, New York, and a connection with the Erie Railroad for Buffalo. It immediately acquired the Tifft Farm on the Lake Erie shore just south of Buffalo and began building its own terminal and lakefront facilities, twenty-five years before it would enter Buffalo over its own rails. It completed a line across northern New Jersey to New York Harbor in 1875 and built extensive pier facilities on Black Tom Island in Jersey City. Finally, in 1892 it completed its long-expected line to Buffalo. It was the last of the Great Lakes-to-the-sea railroads and the longest, twenty-five miles longer than the New York Central and nearly fifty miles longer than the Delaware, Lackawanna & Western.

The Lehigh Valley overextended its finances with the building of the Buffalo line, and it allowed the Philadelphia & Reading (Reading) to assume control in 1892 in return for guarantees on its debt. The next year the Reading itself was swept into receivership in the Panic of 1893. In the debacle, the Lehigh Valley managed to retain its independence, though it was under the control of the J. P. Morgan interests until 1902.

The Lehigh Valley prospered in the Morgan years and achieved a kind of golden age in the 1920s as a well-engineered, well-maintained railroad, the first in the country to lay its entire double-tracked mainline with 136-pound rail. The railroad was a gritty symbol of the glory days of heavy industry in the Northeast.

But even in its best days, an aura of bad fate hung about the Lehigh Valley. It had serious labor problems in the 1890s and again in the 1920s; both times it used strikebreakers and both times the result was a wave of horrible wrecks. Its Black Tom Terminal, packed with contraband munitions, was blown up in the early morning hours of July 30, 1916, by German saboteurs; the railroad spent years pursuing litigation against successive German governments through the Weimar, Nazi, and post-World War II years, finally winning a hollow settlement in the 1950s. Its passenger service was dowdy, even though it served beautiful resort areas like New York's Finger Lake region and even though it possessed one of the most famous train names in railroad lore, the Black Diamond. Most seriously, its freight service was too slow to compete

for merchandise traffic as successfully as its near-twin, the Lackawanna. The slowness was at least in part its own fault for not investing the money to perfect competitive interchanges with its western connections. Though its yards in Buffalo were less than a half mile from the Nickel Plate's, for example, interchange routinely took five hours, including crossing the New York Central mainline at grade. It remained dangerously dependent on anthracite.

This vital yet vulnerable railroad lived much of its life as a pawn of other railroads' consolidation plans. In Morgan's community-of-interest period, the New York Central, the Pennsylvania, and others owned blocks of its stock. In the 1920s Leonor Loree wanted the Lehigh Valley as the crucial link in his "fifth system" based on his Delaware & Hudson. When he failed to win a close proxy vote in 1928 his stock fell into the hands of the Pennsylvania. In 1941 the New York Central forced the Pennsylvania to put its Lehigh Valley stock in trust out of fear that the Pennsylvania was trying to create a new trunk line of the Lehigh Valley and the Wabash, which it also controlled.

The decline of anthracite probably sealed the Lehigh Valley's fate as early as 1950. The last year it earned a profit was 1956. It used its cash to retire debt, leaving it cash poor when the hard times came, not even able to buy enough freight cars for its customers. In 1958 it became the first railroad that could be classified as a major passenger carrier to petition for total discontinuance of passenger service. The last passenger train it ever operated, the Maple Leaf from Toronto, picked its way through howling blizzards on the night of February 4, 1961, and arrived in Newark eight hours late, the Pennsylvania refusing to accept it for its last lap into Penn Station. It tried to find merger partners, but no one was interested. It finally begged the Pennsylvania to petition to assume full control. That petition was granted in 1962 on the assumption that the Pennsylvania would undertake money-saving coordinations and otherwise pump in money. Whether it could not or did not want to do so is unclear. The Lehigh Valley entered receivership in July 1970, ironically lasting a month longer than its parent, which by then had become part of the Penn Central.

Liquidation was a distinct possibility during the Lehigh Valley's years in bankruptcy court, but the line was preserved as a through route and conveyed to Conrail in 1976. The eastern half of the railroad had some value to Conrail chiefly for the Coxton Yard near Wilkes-Barre and the Oak Island Terminal that became Conrail's principal yard on the New Jersey side of New York Harbor. Nearly the entire line west of Waverly, New York, was abandoned, and by the mid 1980s, where the Black Diamond once rolled there was little physical evidence that the Lehigh Valley Railroad had ever existed.

References:
Robert F. Archer, *A History of the Lehigh Valley Railroad* (Berkeley, Cal.,: Howell-North, 1977);

Jules Bogen, *The Anthracite Railroads: A Study in American Enterprise* (New York: Ronald Press, 1927), pp. 108-144.

Archives:
Some papers relating to the Lehigh Valley Railroad are at the Eleuthesian Mills Historical Library, Wilmington, Delaware.

Long Island Rail Road

by James N. J. Henwood

East Stroudsburg University of Pennsylvania

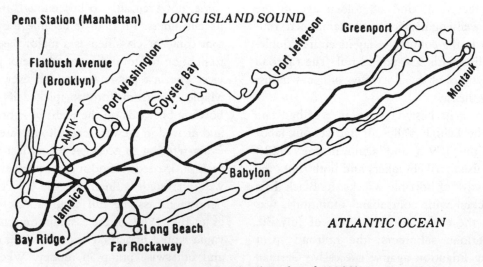

Map of the Long Island Railroad (1983)

The Long Island Rail Road (LIRR) was conceived in 1834 as part of a rail-water route linking New York City and Boston. By 1844, the promoters had constructed a line from Brooklyn through the center of Long Island to Greenport, with steamer connections at each terminal. The line was prosperous, but the completion of an all-rail route to Boston along the Connecticut shoreline in 1850 turned the LIRR into a local and commuter line oriented toward New York City. Gradually, branches were constructed to various towns on the north and south shores of Long Island, and Jamaica became a major transfer and connecting point.

Heavily dependent on passenger traffic, the LIRR suffered hard times until it was revitalized by Austin Corbin, beginning in 1881. In 1900, the Pennsylvania Railroad gained control of the LIRR and provided direct access, via the East River tunnels, to its new Penn Station in Manhattan. A rapid increase in commuter traffic, electrification of some lines, and modernization followed, but profits disappeared in the 1930s as a result of high taxes, artificially low fares, the Great Depression, the automobile, and the nature of the commuter service, which generated heavy capital and labor costs but provided small returns.

Following World War II, the line fell into bankruptcy. In 1966, it was purchased by the state and today is operated by the Metropolitan Transportation Authority. Further modernized and improved, it remains the busiest passenger carrier in the country.

References:

George Drury, *The Train-Watcher's Guide to North American Railroads* (Milwaukee: Kalmbach, 1984), pp. 106-107;
Ron Zeil and George Foster, *Steel Rails to the Sunrise* (New York: Hawthorne Books, 1965).

Leonor F. Loree

(August 23, 1858–September 6, 1940)

by Herbert H. Harwood, Jr.

CSX Transportation (Retired)

CAREER: Assistant in engineer corps, Pennsylvania Railroad (1877-1879); transitman, engineer corps, U.S. Army (1879-1881); transitman and topographer, Mexican National Railway (1881-1883); assistant engineer, Chicago Division (1883-1884), engineer, maintenance of way, Lines West (1884-1889), division superintendent, Lines West (1889-1896), general manager, Lines West (1896-1901), fourth vice president (1901), Pennsylvania Railroad; president, Baltimore & Ohio Railroad (1901-1904); president, Chicago, Rock Island & Pacific Railway, and chairman of executive committee, St. Louis-San Francisco Railroad (1904); chairman of executive committee, Kansas City Southern Railway (1906-1937); president, Delaware & Hudson Company (1907-1938); chairman of the board, Missouri-Kansas-Texas Railroad (1926-1928).

The shaggy, vaguely menacing face which glares out from Leonor F. Loree's formal photographic portrait both reveals and hides the man. Clearly he was commanding, aggressive, and ambitious. Clearly, too, he was no conventional railroader or conformist of any sort. And certainly he was not to be questioned, particularly by some subordinate. But the bearlike visage conceals a wide and restless intellect. He studied history and philosophy; he accumulated three university degrees; he created a multitude of innovative concepts in the railroad business; he wrote and spoke articulately and thoughtfully. He put his individualistic stamp on everything he touched, and he touched many things.

"One of the greatest railroad men of all time," said the trade magazine *Railway Age* when Loree died in 1940. Railroaders of the time had mixed opinions about him, but few disagreed with that summation. Capable, colorful, controversial, and creative, he had made himself a legend. Loree's life also was viewed as symbolizing much of the history of the railroad industry. He lived for eighty-two years, and was an active railroader for sixty-one of them and a chief executive for thirty-seven. He was a part of the peak era of construction and expansion; he suffered through the period of increasing regulation, union power, and dominance by large financial institutions; and his career ended in the early stages of intermodal competition, consolidation, and retrenchment.

Strangely, however, the Loree legend largely evaporated as the people of his era died. From the

Leonor F. Loree

more distant viewpoint of the late twentieth century, assessing his career and contributions is as difficult as reading his portrait.

Most railroad historians know Loree as the absolute ruler who dominated the Delaware & Hudson Company (D&H) for three decades. Beyond that, he is remembered chiefly as the promoter of new eastern and southwestern railroad systems during the 1920s and as the sponsor of a series of spectacular steam locomotive design experiments in the late 1920s and early 1930s. But judging these elements of his career by the end results, one wonders what created the legend. When Loree became president of the D&H in 1907 it was a stolid, medium-sized coal hauler operating in a narrow geographic niche. When he finally retired in 1938 it was physically improved and certainly had been given a distinctive personality, but it was essentially the same kind of railroad serving the same territory. His forays into railroad empire building produced nothing, and his highly publicized steam power experiments were dead ends.

In truth, Loree's life was a conflicting mixture of large accomplishments but even larger frustra-

tions and, ironically, the most lasting accomplishments are less known than the frustrations. Further complicating objective evaluation is his overwhelming personality, which created an awe apart from the importance of his actions. Thus—more so than for many executives—Loree's career must be carefully and critically analyzed to extract the substance from the aura.

Leonor Fresnel Loree was born in Fulton City, Illinois, in 1858 to William Mulford and Sarah Elizabeth Marsh Loree. He grew up to be an active, broad-shouldered six-footer, and was a 200-pound football player at Rutgers, from which he graduated with a B.S. in engineering in 1877. In that era one of the best opportunities for an ambitious, technically-minded young man was in the rapidly expanding railroad business. More ambitious than many, Loree picked the most prestigious railroad—the Pennsylvania (PRR)—and started as an engineering assistant working on construction projects.

After two years on the Pennsylvania he returned to Rutgers for an M.S., simultaneously working as a transitman for the Army Corps of Engineers. Starting in 1881 he spent two years helping locate and build the new Mexican National Railway route from Nuevo Laredo to Saltillo, then returned to the PRR for what he hoped would be a steady climb up its operating management ladder.

He did climb, and quickly. Already the Pennsylvania had established itself as the dominant railroad in the eastern region—and, thereby the most powerful in the country. Now it had to cope with rapidly growing business and increasingly complex traffic patterns. The company was carrying on a wide range of construction and rebuilding projects, and Loree had ample opportunity to demonstrate his talents as a builder and manager. Reentering the railroad as an assistant engineer, he had moved up to general manager for the Lines West of Pittsburgh by age thirty-eight. Helping him get there was his performance in rebuilding the railroad after the 1886 Miami River Valley floods. Using military marshalling techniques, he restored twenty-six iron bridges, two trestles, three stone culverts, and seven miles of track—all in five days. He later helped manage the rapid rebuilding of the vital mainline after the infamous 1889 floods which devastated central Pennsylvania and destroyed Johnstown. Somehow, too, he managed to acquire a civil engineering degree from

Rutgers in 1896. In 1901 Loree, still a young forty-two, was made a PRR vice president.

At that time, many separate railroad companies operated in the territory east of Chicago and St. Louis, but only three comprehensively covered the region -- the Pennsylvania, New York Central (NYC), and Baltimore & Ohio (B&O). While each of the three had different routes and somewhat different markets, they all competed directly at virtually all key cities and interline gateways; together they ruled what was then the country's largest transportation market.

But the overall financial environment was unstable. The late nineteenth century had produced an overbuilt and intensely competitive railroad industry. Such basically strong systems as the Pennsylvania and New York Central were perennially plagued by rate cutting, rebating, and the construction of parallel competing lines; their earnings were depressed and they found it difficult to finance the improvements needed to handle their growing traffic.

In the freehanded days before strong antitrust enforcement, Pennsylvania president A. J. Cassatt developed a bold strategy to stabilize his territory. Cassatt's solution, aided by J. P. Morgan and other large investment bankers, was PRR-NYC "community of interest" control of the weaker lines and potential troublemakers. Starting in 1899, the PRR and the New York Central bought control of various smaller railroads while Morgan and other New York investment banks gradually took over policy-making on many other companies.

The Baltimore & Ohio was the largest of the "troublemakers." Always the weakest of the three large trunk systems, it had resorted to rate cutting to get business. Furthermore, its shaky financial situation made it vulnerable to takeover by some outside empire builder. The B&O's 1896 receivership gave Cassatt his opportunity, and in 1899 he began buying up working control of his big competitor. By 1901 the Pennsylvania's grip was strong enough to dictate policy and install its own president. As one of the Pennsylvania's most promising young officers, Loree was picked by Cassatt to administer the new conquest.

Loree arrived in Baltimore in June and began the most breathtaking reign the B&O would ever experience. His new job brought out all his urges as a builder—and, unfortunately for him, also his strong independent streak.

Loree found the B&O suffering under multiple curses. Its topography was rugged, particularly in the critical sections where heavy coal tonnage moved. In fact, its 2.2 percent Allegheny grades were the steepest of any eastern mainline. In addition, the railroad was struggling with a twisting, cramped main line laid out in the 1830s and 1840s and never substantially rebuilt. Many bridges were of a design that had been obsolete since 1875 and tunnels—of which the B&O had many—generally were built for 1850-era clearances. Finally, although coal was a heavy and growing staple, the company was weak in most of the markets it reached and had poor interline connections to such major areas as the Southeast.

Perhaps sensing that his stay would be short, Loree wasted no time. He quickly put together a twenty-year improvement plan for the railroad and instantly started implementing it. He picked up and accelerated some projects already haltingly begun, added many more of his own, and proceeded to rebuild the railroad Pennsylvania-style. Emulating Cassatt's work with the PRR, Loree built low-grade (that is, nearly level) bypass lines, shortcut routes, stone viaducts, heavy steel bridges, multiple tracks, and new yards. Several long sections of main line were completely relocated, and a program was begun to install heavy locomotives and high-capacity freight cars.

The "community of interest" with the Pennsylvania also enabled Loree's B&O to get a long-sought direct connection with the Southeastern rail network near Washington, D.C., and produced the grandiose joint PRR-B&O Union Station in Washington.

In a different kind of "community of interest" move, Loree and the New York Central bought enough Philadelphia & Reading (Reading) stock to assure joint B&O-NYC control of that strategic system. The Reading and its subsidiary, the Central Railroad of New Jersey, formed the B&O's access to New York and most major markets in eastern Pennsylvania and New Jersey.

But Loree had to find a different solution for the B&O's intractable Allegheny mountain grades. Relocation of these lines was far beyond the company's resources and always would be. Yet hoisting coal trains over them required large numbers of locomotives and workers and consumed vast quantities of fuel. In 1903 Loree promoted an inventive thirty-one-year-old mechanical engineer named John E. Muhlfeld to be his general motive power superintendent. Working with the American Locomotive Company, Loree and Muhlfeld created a milestone in motive power history—the first Mallet compound articulated locomotive in the United States. The design, patented by Anatole Mallet in France in 1874, had originally been intended to allow maximum power on lightly built branch and narrow-guage lines; few could see its application to rugged, heavy-duty North American railroading. The B&O's pioneering 0-6-6-0 (under the Wythe classification scheme for steam locomotives, this designation refers to a locomotive with no leading or trailing trucks of nondriving wheels and two sets of three pairs of drivers), rolled out in 1904, was almost three times heavier than the largest European Mallet. It also carried the first American application of the Belgian-designed Walschaert valve gear, soon almost universally adopted in the United States. After being displayed at the 1904 St. Louis Exposition the B&O monster immediately proved itself as a pusher engine working west from Cumberland, Maryland, and fathered a new breed of locomotive.

But by the time it was delivered, Loree was gone. After only two and a half years on the B&O, he abruptly resigned on January 1, 1904, and the presidency passed to a B&O man, Oscar G. Murray. Loree's departure has never been fully explained, although it was reported that he and Cassatt had quarreled over his too enthusiastic betterment of the B&O. By then the Pennsylvania had found it politically prudent to back away from its direct B&O control, and in 1906 it began liquidating its B&O stock. Whatever the circumstances, apparently there was no spot for Loree back in Philadelphia, and his ambition to be president of the Pennsylvania would never be fulfilled. On the B&O, much of what he started was unfinished when he left, while other planned projects (such as the Magnolia cutoff) were not yet begun. Other men, notably Oscar Murray and Daniel Willard, eventually completed and got credit for what Loree had initiated or planned.

By conventional standards, the B&O marked the peak of Loree's career. Never again would he head as large or important a railroad, nor would he have such an appropriate spot to display his abilities. It also can be argued that Loree's brief reign

marked the B&O's peak. The B&O's best years usually are linked with Willard, who ran the company from 1910 to 1941. Unquestionably, Willard gave the B&O respectability and a unique esprit de corps, but physically it was Loree's railroad. By the late twentieth century the Willard spirit was gone, but Loree's railroad remained.

On his departure day from the B&O, Loree took office as president of the Chicago, Rock Island & Pacific and chairman of the then-affiliated St. Louis & San Francisco (Frisco). The two companies were controlled by the notorious William H. Moore - Daniel G. Reid group, which was primarily interested in creating quick cash for itself by building unneeded branch lines and manipulating securities. Almost instantly Loree realized that this was not the place for someone who wanted to spend money to build a strong, efficient physical plant. His stay on the Rock Island and Frisco lasted ten months. Not naive about his new employers, however, Loree had negotiated a five-year contract at a then-imperial $75,000 per year; his short Chicago sojourn earned him $375,000 in 1904 dollars. Afterward he took a cruise around the world.

But his ultimate deliverance soon came through E. H. Harriman, who had been a B&O director when Loree swept through there. Among his larger interests, Harriman was involved in the Kansas City Southern (KCS) and the Delaware & Hudson. He brought Loree back to railroading in 1906 as chairman of the KCS's executive committee in New York, primarily guiding general policy and finances for the Kansas City-to-Gulf carrier. Completed only nine years earlier by promoter Arthur E. Stilwell, the KCS's single main line ran 790 miles due south from Kansas City to Port Arthur, Texas, which was connected by canal to the Gulf of Mexico. Shortly after Harriman and John W. Gates had squeezed out Stilwell in 1900 the railroad had begun reaping the bonanza of the Texas oil gushers and had become a solid earner; Loree's job was to improve it and keep it on a stable course—which he did for the next thirty-one years.

The primary Harriman gift, however, was the Delaware & Hudson, a compact 910-mile system primarily serving eastern Pennsylvania and upstate New York. Always a prosperous company with its roots in anthracite coal, the D&H was caught in a crisis in early 1907—it had to finance an ambitious acquisition and improvement program in a deteriorating financial market, and its president, David Willcox, was dying. Harriman installed Loree as president and board chairman on April 10, 1907. Knowing that Loree was really nobody's man but his own, Harriman gave him free rein. Loree quickly established himself as the railroad industry's nearest equivalent to a despot—sometimes enlightened, sometimes not.

After the Pennsylvania, the B&O, and even the Rock Island, the D&H was an anticlimax. Undoubtedly Loree saw it as a temporary haven; it was no secret that he hoped that the mantle of Cassatt or Harriman eventually would fall on him. But neither did, and Loree remained in the D&H's ornate New York president's office the remainder of his long working life.

Nonetheless, the D&H supplied some immediate challenges for Loree, and in the long run its financial strength allowed him to indulge his ideas and ambitions in his own style. Small and inconspicuous on a map, the D&H was strategically situated. Not only was it a large distributor of anthracite coal, but also as the years went by its location made it a key segment in the flow of bituminous coal and merchandise into New England and eastern Canada. And, lacking large terminals and a complex route network, it was basically an efficient carrier which Loree could easily make more so.

He first took care of the company's debt problems. Despite the 1907 financial panic he successfully floated a $10 million equipment bond issue and gradually arranged permanent financing for other D&H debts. Afterward there were few significant worries in this area and Loree turned to his other forte: operating efficiency.

Following his own lead from the B&O, between 1910 and 1912 he bought a fleet of ponderous 0-8-8-0 Mallets, the most powerful locomotives of the day. At the same time he built a large central repair shop at Colonie, New York, near Albany, to replace three older shops scattered around the system, plus three new yards. And, always striving for the flattest possible grade profile, he started several relocation projects on the hilly Albany-Binghamton mainline.

Seldom self-effacing himself, Loree determined to give the D&H a grandiose image in the form of a new headquarters building. Begun in 1913 and finished in 1918, the D&H Building's flamboyant Flemish Gothic architecture—with its twelve-story spired

tower and twin five-story flanking wings—made it Albany's most spectacular structure. Outshining the state capitol, it remained a landmark in the 1980s. Loree, however, kept the president's office in New York, close to Wall Street and to "Bowood," his suburban estate in West Orange, New Jersey.

Loree had a particular passion for efficient steam locomotive design, and continually sponsored developments which were at once innovative and primitive. Loree's D&H was essentially a heavy-tonnage railroad, and he was an emphatic believer in heavy, low-speed designs which could churn out maximum tractive power. Ignoring the railroad industry's general movement to faster high-horsepower designs, he stuck with the Consolidation type, a nineteenth-century wheel arrangement which allowed the greatest possible weight on drivers. Over a period of twenty-three years he progressively built ever heavier and more refined versions until he had achieved the ultimate power and efficiency that the type could produce.

On the other hand, Loree constantly experimented with new devices, and throughout the 1920s and early 1930s the D&H dazzled the industry with a succession of both foreign-designed and home-grown mechanical innovations. In 1922—it invented and installed the first tender booster, a small steam-powered geared propulsion unit mounted on a tender truck. In 1926 it introduced the poppet valve—a valve design similar to that used in gasoline and diesel engines—to the United States. After manufacturers told Loree that it was impractical to apply roller bearings to locomotive drive wheels, he had his own mechanical people design the first successful installation in 1930. Subsequently he goaded the bearing manufacturer SKF into developing side rod roller bearings for a D&H engine. In 1937, at the very end of his career, Loree built the first all-welded locomotive boiler. Other sophistications included the one-piece Commonwealth integrally cast locomotive frame and cylinder housing, alloy steel side rods, uniflow cylinders, high-pressure boilers, and smoke lifters. On one of his many trips to England Loree became enchanted with the clean-lined British steam power, and afterward D&H locomotives—particularly for passenger trains—were rebuilt with concealed piping, flush headlights, shrouded domes, capped stacks, and rakish cabs. Engines were also chastely striped and lettered and constantly kept clean. Yet to the end of Loree's reign all D&H locomotives were hand fired; the automatic stoker was apparently considered an expensive frill of value only to the laboring fireman.

Certainly the most memorable of Loree locomotive creations was the quartet of bizarre-looking behemoths turned out between 1924 and 1933. Determined to push beyond the inherent limitations of railroad steam power capabilities, Loree called in his old B&O associate John Muhlfeld, who was then a consulting engineer in New York. Using the inevitable Consolidation wheel arrangement as his base, Muhlfeld developed a design built around high pressure marine-type boilers with water tube fireboxes and cross-compound steam distribution. Steam pressures were gradually raised on each successive prototype, finally reaching an awesome 500 psi. Visually, all four were ponderous, top heavy tangles of piping, which mercifully were shrouded in the later versions. The fourth and final prototype, appropriately named L. F. Loree, used a 4-8-0 wheel arrangement (four front idling wheels, eight driving wheels, no rear idling wheels) and was a four-cylinder triple-expansion engine–the first such nonarticulated example in the world.

The power and cost performance of the four experimentals proved Muhlfeld's and Loree's theories, but none were copied and all were retired by 1935. Aside from the expected teething problems and high maintenance costs, the basic concept of the low-speed, high-tractive-power "drag" engine was obsolete by the 1930s as competition pushed the railroads to move trains faster. Wrote D&H historian Jim Shaughnessy: "Loree's experimentals were twenty years late operationally and twenty years early mechanically."

Something similar could be said about Loree's outspoken and often-quoted views on labor relations and regulation. An adamant advocate of tight, disciplined, and unfettered management, he clearly had no use either for unions or for governmental second-guessing. Labor relations on the D&H and its subsidiaries were notably turbulent in the 1920s, with several bitter strikes against the railroad, its coal mining operations, and its affiliated street railways. In 1931 Loree attempted to take advantage of the Depression and wipe out the costly time-mileage-additive wage formulas for train crews. D&H crewmen were offered a flat monthly wage structure–ostensibly as a voluntary option, although there was little choice. Loree eventually lost–

as he did most of his labor battles–and the old union agreements were reinstated.

He had even less control over the encroachments of regulation and vented his frustrations in thundering speeches. In his keynote address at the D&H's 1923 centennial celebration, for instance, he equated creeping railroad regulation with Russia's "nightmare of Utopian intoxication."

Like his locomotive designs, Loree himself was simultaneously behind and ahead of his peers in the business. He spoke as a late-nineteenth-century manager and entrepreneur in an environment which was becoming increasingly institutionalized. But he also perceptively foretold the railroad industry's critical problems of the 1960s and 1970s.

By the mid 1920s, however, most railroad managers had reluctantly reconciled themselves to the political realities of rail labor's growing power. They were influenced, too, by pressure from financial institutions and large freight customers, who–in a period of prosperity and minor intermodal competition–were anxious to avoid large-scale labor disruptions. Despite the rail industry's erratic fortunes in later years, it did not begin aggressively attacking its wage structure until the 1970s, when it was finally clear to all parties that reform was needed.

The industry's attitude toward regulation was also mixed. Few railroad managers liked the restrictions on their actions or the growing administrative burdens, but they tended to take them as trade-offs for what many saw as protection from price competition and from poaching on their markets. Rate regulation and the industry's cartel-like pricing system particularly worked to the advantage of the large railroads–notably the Pennsylvania–as well as their large established shippers. And as motor carriers became a more serious threat, the railroads pressed to extend regulation to the trucks and buses rather than remove it from themselves.

In 1924 Loree turned sixty-six. He was secure and comfortable in his lifetime niche at the Delaware & Hudson, but the juices of ambition still strongly flowed. He saw his chance to satisfy those ambitions during the railroad consolidation scramble of the 1920s.

Concerns about the still-unsolved problems of the overbuilt railroad system and weak companies had produced a movement to consolidate the multiplicity of separate railroads into large, balanced systems. Such systems, it was hoped, would be strong enough to protect large investments and generate new funds more easily. Thus the 1920 Transportation Act ordered the Interstate Commerce Commission (ICC) to develop an industry-wide consolidation plan. The ICC was, however, both ill-equipped to do genuine economic policy planning and unenthusiastic about its controversial mission. Additionally, it had no power to force consolidations; it could only approve or disapprove voluntary merger proposals based on whether they conformed to its plan. So as the commission hesitantly started its work, the more aggressive forces in the industry quickly began moving on their own to expand or protect their interests before any plan was finished.

By 1924 the silent, swift Van Sweringen brothers of Cleveland—guided by the New York Central's A. H. Smith—had assembled the components of a fourth large eastern trunk system. Using borrowed money and operating through a holding company structure, the two brothers controlled a group of railroads which together roughly paralleled the Pennsylvania, New York Central, and B&O systems. Following this fait accompli, the Van Sweringens, PRR, NYC, and B&O began negotiating among themselves for the remaining "unallocated" Eastern railroads. The D&H was one of those.

Loree was hardly the type to be relegated to the role of an "unallocated" bystander. Aided by the D&H's ample treasury and an odd assortment of allies, he moved to make himself an equal power by forming a fifth eastern system. His staunchest supporter was the Wabash Railroad's board chairman William L. Williams. Williams was a Loree protégé from the PRR and B&O days and had been a close associate since; in fact, Williams concurrently held a vice president's title on the D&H. The Wabash, reaching across the Midwest from Buffalo to Chicago, St. Louis, and Kansas City, had also become a pawn in the consolidation planning process.

Another ally—albeit a wary one—was Loree's old employer, the Pennsylvania. Still the East's largest and strongest system, the PRR had stayed aloof as the Van Sweringens and Smith maneuvered. But by 1924 it found itself encircled by predators as the New York Central, B&O, and Van Sweringens formed a loose alliance to take more railroads for themselves. More interested in protecting his markets and connections than in expanding, the Pennsy's Samuel Rea looked on Loree as a means

of taking key railroads off the market before some big rival did. In the beginning, however, PRR aid was more moral than financial, and there was some justified mutual mistrust.

Already the Van Sweringens had picked off some of the better lines, leaving Loree and Williams with little to choose from. Nonetheless, they designed a system consisting of the D&H, Wabash, Lehigh Valley (LV), Buffalo, Rochester & Pittsburgh (BR&P), Wheeling & Lake Erie, Pittsburgh & West Virginia, and Western Maryland. This somewhat gerrymandered assemblage had some gaps and market weaknesses, but it did create a network extending from New York to Chicago, St. Louis, and Kansas City and reaching Detroit, Pittsburgh, and several large coal-producing regions. And with the Western Maryland, it had the potential of reaching Baltimore, although some new construction would be needed.

Loree's first priority was to get control of the strategic Lehigh Valley, whose New York-Buffalo mainline gave entrée to the New York area and also linked the D&H with the Wabash. At that time the LV was a prosperous company with widely scattered stock, meaning that control would have to be bought in the open market at high prices. Loree quietly began buying in 1924 and gradually built up the D&H's holdings to 25 percent by 1927. In early 1926 the Wabash joined him, and by mid 1927 the two companies together had 44 percent of the LV's stock. (The New York Central also had designs on the LV and started buying, but soon gave up.)

Another major goal was the Buffalo, Rochester & Pittsburgh, which linked Buffalo with Pittsburgh (via some B&O trackage) and reached bituminous coal fields in western Pennsylvania. In 1925 Loree was able to negotiate a long-term lease of the BR&P.

At the same time he astonished almost everyone by proposing to build an entirely new $260 million low-grade freight railroad across Pennsylvania. The project, called the New York, Pittsburgh & Chicago (NYP&C), would extend 283 miles from the LV at Easton, Pennsylvania, to Pittsburgh; linked with other lines, it would provide the shortest rail route between New York and Chicago. Not original with Loree, the NYP&C idea dated to 1903 and Harriman had bought its charter in 1908. In reviving it, Loree actually acted as agent for the Harriman estate, which still held the charter.

Few knew whether to take him seriously. Major new railroad construction in the United States had long since ceased, and the economic justification for still another Eastern mainline seemed dubious. But the mid 1920s was a period of optimism and growing traffic, and trucking was still only a minor threat; Loree, for one, believed that total rail business would double within fourteen years. And, indeed, both the Pennsylvania and B&O had elaborate plans to build new low-grade shortcut routes through Pennsylvania. In any event the NYP&C died a quick death: in mid 1925 Loree applied to the ICC for permission to build the line as one component of his "fifth system" package; the PRR, NYC, B&O, and Erie united to oppose the project and the commission turned it down in 1926.

Soon afterward the Pennsylvania's aggressive new president, W. W. Atterbury, decided to support Loree directly in his efforts to put together the rest of his system. Atterbury shrewdly reasoned that if Loree succeeded, his "fifth system" could become a PRR satellite; if he failed, the Pennsylvania could pick up some of the select pieces for itself. In 1927 the two reached a complex secret agreement which, in effect, exchanged PRR financial aid and trackage rights for what amounted to a lien on Loree's new acquisitions.

Despite Atterbury's sub rosa aid, Loree had many problems. In the face of New York Central and B&O opposition, the ICC turned down his proposed BR&P lease in December 1927. Subsequently the Van Sweringens bought the company and promptly resold it to the B&O. Loree never had a chance to move into the Wheeling & Lake Erie; this link between the Wabash and Pittsburgh was snapped up by the B&O-New York Central-Van Sweringen alliance in early 1927.

Closed off elsewhere, Loree depended for his success on the Lehigh Valley. But despite his 44 percent interest, the LV's management fought a takeover and narrowly won a crucial proxy fight in January 1928. Pushed by the Pennsylvania and with time running out on his financing agreements, Loree bitterly gave up. After more negotiations with Atterbury, Loree finally sold the D&H's interests in the Lehigh Valley and Wabash to the PRR for $62.5 million—making a $21 million profit for the D&H.

All this time Loree had actually been fighting a two-front war, although the second front was far less publicized. In his role as board chairman of the Kansas City Southern, Loree tried to promote a consolidation of three Southwestern companies into a 5,800-mile regional system. Joining forces with Daniel Upthegrove, president of the St. Louis-Southwestern Railway (more popularly and appropriately called the Cotton Belt Route), he conceived a combination of the KCS, Cotton Belt, and the Missouri-Kansas-Texas Railroad (M-K-T); informally known as the Loree Southwestern Lines, it would extend from St. Louis and Kansas City into much of Arkansas, Oklahoma, and Texas. In 1926 he had himself made board chairman of the M-K-T and asked the ICC for permission for the KCS to control the M-K-T and for the M-K-T in turn to control the Cotton Belt. Problems with M-K-T minority stockholders and concern over possible abandonments of redundant lines helped kill this plan, too, and the ICC turned it down in May 1927.

The outcome of his consolidation ventures was an intense blow to Loree. At age seventy in 1928, he had lost his last chance to be a significant power in the railroad world. But Loree the loser turned out to be the winner anyway. Unknowingly, he had sold his LV and Wabash interests at close to the top of the market. The D&H's $21 million profit gave it a much needed fiscal cushion during the Depression, while the Lehigh Valley and the Wabash both developed financial problems. Loree unquestionably had been saved from himself—his fifth Eastern system would have been wobbly at best, and the double blows of depression and motor competition would have made his trans-Pennsylvania line instantly redundant.

Despite defeats and advancing age, Loree was not ready to retire to Bowood and devote himself to the chickens and cattle he raised as a sideline. Nor did he ever give up on his ambitions. In 1929 he proposed to create a North Atlantic Terminal System, which would combine the D&H and most other independent Eastern lines into a 13,500-mile network. And as the Depression deepened he began buying up New York Central stock at bargain prices. By early 1933 the D&H could announce that it owned over 10 percent of the lordly Vanderbilt system, the largest single interest. But by then Loree's own time was running out, and the D&H never made an effort to exploit its Central holdings. Hanging on almost to the end, Loree was finally forced by declining health to retire from the D&H in 1938 at age eighty. He died two years later. He was survived by his wife, Jessie Taber Loree, whom he had married in 1885, and their three children.

Loree's active mind reached into many areas. Among other things, he took credit for inventing the lap passing siding and the upper quadrant semaphore—an early "fail-safe" signaling device. He organized the first railroad police force and developed a disbursement accounting system later adopted by the ICC for all railroads. A wide reader, he baffled railroad employees by quoting from Spengler, Ortega y Gasset, or George Moore. He founded the American branch of the Newcomen Society of England. In 1922 he published *Railroad Freight Transportation*, a wide-ranging text on railroad management covering everything from washing locomotives to theories of human behavior. Written, as one observer noted, "in a style of Gibbonian magnificence," it nonetheless was quoted and excerpted by many railroad managers for decades afterwards.

It is this complexity and individualism which makes Loree so difficult to judge. Variously viewed as an operating genius, a tyrant, a pirate, humane, inhumane, a visionary, and a throwback, he was a bit of all of these. But mostly he was a builder. In his introduction to the D&H's centennial history volume in 1923, Loree quoted Ruskin: "When we build, let us think that we build forever . . . let it be such work that our descendants will thank us for." In everything he did, Loree surely had that goal in mind. Perhaps surprisingly, his most lasting legacy is the Baltimore & Ohio; what he built and planned there has already endured for almost ninety years. It is intriguing to speculate as to what else he might have accomplished if his career had not taken the sudden turn it did in 1904.

Publication:

Railroad Freight Transportation (New York: Appleton, 1922);

References:

Edward Hungerford, *The Story of the Baltimore & Ohio Railroad*, Volume 2 (New York: Putnam's, 1928);

"L. F. Loree Resigns D&H Presidency," *Railway Age*, 104 (April 9, 1938): 659-661;

"L. F. Loree Dies at Age of 82,": *Railway Age*, 109 (Sept. 14, 1940): 369-370;

Dwight MacDonald, "Neanderthal," *New Yorker* (June 3, 1933): 18-21;

Jim Shaughnessy, *Delaware & Hudson* (Berkeley, Cal.: Howell-North, 1967);

U. S. Congress, Senate, Committee on Interstate Commerce, *Railroad Consolidation in the Eastern Region; Investigation of Railroads, Holding Companies, and Affiliated Companies*, Report No. 1182, 76th Congress, 3d sess., 1940.

Louisville & Nashville Railroad

by Maury Klein

University of Rhode Island

Map of the Louisville & Nashville Railroad (1945)

The Louisville & Nashville Railroad (L&N) was incorporated in 1850 but did not complete its 185-mile main line until October 1859. The only road between a Union state (Kentucky) and a Confederate state (Tennessee), the L&N suffered much destruction during the early part of the Civil War as battles were fought along its line. After the war the company embarked on an expansion program that elevated it to the premier system in the Southeast. It was in a unique position to dominate, since most other Southern roads had been crippled by the war. Under the guidance of strategist Albert Fink, the firm's vice president, the L&N secured a line to Memphis and made the fateful decision to extend into Alabama to develop coal and iron resources there. Despite setbacks caused by the depression of the 1870s, this policy led to the creation of the city of Birmingham and the growth of coal, iron, and steel facilities in northern Alabama.

The L&N expanded its mileage from 973 in 1879 to 5,042 in 1916. Late in 1879 it gained control of the 509-mile Nashville, Chattanooga & St. Louis system, a major rival, and in 1890 used it to lease the strategic Western & Atlantic, giving the L&N direct access to Atlanta. More track was acquired in Alabama, development was pushed in Tennessee, and the Cumberland Mountains were breached to open coal lands and a through connection with the Norfolk & Western. The company even penetrated Florida and erected wharves at Pensacola for the export of coal and other commodities. New lines tapped the isolated counties of eastern Kentucky for their treasure of coal.

From 1884 to 1921 Milton H. Smith dominated the policies of the L&N. The gruff, cantankerous Smith did much to rationalize the company's chaotic administrative structure, and his managerial skill ushered the L&N into the complexities of the twentieth century. With savage glee he also fought the road's political battles with state governments and Washington. His wrath against government regulation knew no bounds. Fearful that the railroads would be confiscated by the public, he plunged into politics with a zest that drew a storm of controversy about the company.

In 1902 a freak Wall Street coup delivered a majority of the L&N's stock to the Atlantic Coast Line Company. On paper the company was no longer independent, but in practice little changed. Smith remained president until his death in 1921, just after World War I and the Transportation Act of 1920 had ushered in a new era for L&N. Unlike many roads, the L&N expanded, though only modestly, reaching its peak of 5,266 miles in 1931. Amid sweeping changes in society and the rail industry two presidents, Whitefoord R. Cole and James B. Hill, preserved the vigorous and conservative managerial tradition of Smith. The L&N survived the financial anemia of the Great Depression and sprang to health again with the transfusion of business brought by World War II. This rush of new traffic was not purely transient; between 1940 and 1945 some 701 new firms located along the company's lines.

For twenty-five years after the war the L&N struggled to meet the challenge of modernization that confronted all the roads. Under the leadership of John E. Tilford and William H. Kendall it adjusted to the new competitive and regulatory climate by pushing mechanization, reducing its labor force, embracing new technologies, and devising imaginative new marketing tactics, such as piggyback operations, introduced in 1955. The L&N's heavy reliance on coal traffic made it reluctant to abandon steam for diesel engines; not until 1949 was the decision made to convert the entire locomotive fleet.

Despite its ownership by the Atlantic Coast Line, the L&N remained for over a century a strong, fiercely independent system. That era began closing in 1967 when the Atlantic Coast Line merged with the Seaboard Air Line. Four years later the parent Seaboard Coast Line Industries increased its ownership of L&N stock from 33 to 98 percent. The L&N clung to its separate identity until December 1982, when it was merged with the Seaboard Coast Line to form the Seaboard System Railroad, a subsidiary of CSX Corporation.

References:

Kincaid Herr, The Louisville & Nashville Railroad 1850-1963 (Louisville: Louisville & Nashville Railroad, 1964);

Maury Klein, History of the Louisville & Nashville Railroad (New York: Macmillan, 1972).

Robert A. Lovett

(September 14, 1895-May 7, 1986)

by Maury Klein

University of Rhode Island

Robert A. Lovett (courtesy Union Pacific)

CAREER: Clerk, National Bank of Commerce (1921); runner (1921-1923), manager of foreign department (1923-1926), partner (1926-1931), Brown Brothers; director, Union Pacific Railroad Company (1926-1940); partner, Brown Brothers Harriman & Co. (1931-1940); special assistant to the undersecretary of the army (1940-1941); assistant secretary of war for air (1941-1945); partner, Brown Brothers Harriman & Co. (1945-1947); undersecretary of state (1947-1949); partner, Brown Brothers Harriman & Co. (1949-1950); deputy secretary of de-

fense (1950-1951); secretary of defense (1951-1953); partner, Brown Brothers Harriman & Co. (1953-1986); chairman of the executive committee (1953-1967), director (1953-1969), Union Pacific Railroad Company; director, Union Pacific Corporation (1969-1986).

Robert Abercrombie Lovett was born in Huntsville, Texas, in 1895 to Robert S. and Lavinia Chilton Abercrombie Lovett. His father, known as Judge Lovett after a brief stint filling in for a judge, was a prominent attorney whose firm became the largest in Houston. The Judge, whom Lovett described as "the finest man I ever knew," was a reserved, austere, hardworking lawyer with a dry sense of humor and an insistence on good manners. His stern sense of rectitude and integrity made a deep impression on his only son.

The Judge excelled as a railroad lawyer and did service for Jay Gould's Texas roads before taking on the Southern Pacific as a major client. In 1904 he attracted the attention of E. H. Harriman, who made him the general counsel of the Union Pacific and Southern Pacific systems. Gradually the Judge became Harriman's closest advisor and, on Harriman's death in 1909, succeeded him as president and chairman of the executive committee for both the Union Pacific and the Southern Pacific. Although he had come grudgingly to New York from Texas, the Judge remained associated with the Union Pacific until his death in 1932. The family lived in Locust Valley, Long Island, where Robert Lovett would live for most of his adult life.

Lovett saw little of the Judge except during school holidays, but he saw much of the Union Pacific thanks to hunting and fishing expeditions along the upper lines with old-timers on the railroad. After Harriman's death his sons, Roland and

Averell, drew even closer to the Lovetts, and Robert always considered Roland to be the nearest thing to a brother he ever had. Their careers would remain intertwined throughout their lives.

After preparatory work at the Hamilton Military Institute in New York and the Hill School in Pottstown, Pennsylvania, Lovett entered Yale, but he left during his sophomore year to help organize an Eli squadron to fight in the war threatening with Mexico. Flying appealed early to Lovett, who had been surrounded by it as a boy due to the aviation activity on Long Island during the formative years of flight. Lovett got naval pilot's license number 67 and eventually commanded Naval Squadron Number 1 during World War I. In addition to training work, he flew numerous missions, including night bombing runs against German submarine bases. This duty sparked a lifelong interest in aviation and earned him the Navy Cross in 1919. He was discharged that year with the rank of lieutenant commander.

Lovett finished his degree at Yale in the summer of 1919 and entered Harvard Law School. He expected to become a lawyer like his father, who believed that the mental discipline imposed by the law prepared one well for any line of work. Lovett discovered early, however, that the law did not interest him, and he switched briefly to the Harvard Business School before going to work in 1921 as a clerk for the National Bank of Commerce. On April 19, 1919 Lovett had married a neighbor, Adele Quartley Brown, daughter of the senior partner of Brown Brothers, a private banking firm. The fierce, indomitable James Brown soon brought Lovett into his own firm as a runner.

Lovett managed the foreign department of Brown Brothers in London from 1923 to 1926 and was made a general partner in the latter year. In 1931 the firm merged with Harriman Brothers and Company and W. A. Harriman and Company to become Brown Brothers Harriman & Co., which remains the only private banking company on Wall Street. Like his close friend Roland Harriman, Lovett devoted the rest of his business life to the bank and the Union Pacific Railroad.

In 1926, the same year he became a partner in Brown Brothers, Lovett joined the board of the Union Pacific. It was never the Judge's plan to have Robert follow him into the railroad, but his close association with the Harrimans and the banking firm

made the step a natural one. For the next fourteen years he served on the board, which was dominated by Averell Harriman until the latter was summoned to Washington during the New Deal. As the crisis overseas deepened in the late 1930s, Lovett, too, found himself drawn away from his work. On his own initiative he made a tour of aircraft plants across the country and prepared a report stressing the need to expand the production of military planes. After examining this report in 1940, Under Secretary of the Army Robert Patterson named Lovett his special assistant.

Four months later Secretary of War Henry L. Stimson made Lovett assistant secretary of war for air. In that position Lovett helped the air force gain a position of near autonomy within the army that it maintained throughout World War II. Lovett remained in government service until 1945 and took home from Washington political skills that he would later put to good use. For the next several years he alternated between the private and public sectors, returning to his banking and railroad work only to be summoned again to some new post in Washington.

The first call came in 1947 from Gen. George C. Marshall, who had been named secretary of state and wanted Lovett to be under secretary. A year later Lovett was acting secretary in Marshall's absence when the Berlin blockade began. Gen. Lucius Clay later recalled that "there was a lot of pressure to move American wives and children out of Berlin, but that would have indicated a lack of confidence to the Russians. Bob decided they would stay." Lovett followed Marshall out of office in January 1949, but in October 1950 Marshall returned to Washington as secretary of defense and asked Lovett to serve as deputy secretary.

For the next two years Lovett helped Marshall grapple with the Korean War. In 1951 he advocated mobilization, declaring that "there is no other way. We tried weakness. It didn't work. The oceans that once protected us no longer provide defense. Our task is to get ourselves geared to these realities." That September he succeeded Marshall as secretary of defense, a post he held until President Harry Truman left office in 1953. His policy was to press for arms superiority as a counter to the Soviet Union's larger number of troops. "We don't have to match them man for man," he once quipped. "We aren't going to square-dance with them."

271

In 1953 Lovett returned to private life and was made chairman of the executive committee of the Union Pacific. Roland Harriman, who had served as chairman of the board since 1946, was delighted to have his old friend share responsibility with him through what proved to be a critical period in the company's history. A new era was dawning in which victory would belong to those railroads most adept at modernizing their physical plant, absorbing the latest technologies, and reducing their labor force as rapidly as possible. Competition from other modes of transportation was changing the nature of freight traffic available to the railroads, passenger service was hastening toward extinction, and relations with the government were strained. The railroad map was about to be radically redrawn through mergers and bankruptcies.

Clearly the industry was in the throes of a painful transition, but the Union Pacific was better situated than most roads to survive in the new competitive era. The remnants of its original land grant provided coalfields, other mineral deposits, and land for industrial and commercial development. It also had such attractions as Sun Valley and the Utah parks to draw passenger traffic. In addition, the company had acquired extensive tracts of land rich in oil. The Union Pacific also missed some golden opportunities: Lovett once mourned that the company had passed over a chance to buy for $3 million much of what is now Long Beach, California.

The problem was how to exploit these resources effectively in an age where this most traditional of industries had to innovate constantly to stay afloat. Hamstrung by governmental regulation on every side, the railroads competed poorly against other forms of transportation, which had freer hands and often outright government aid. The first casualty of this struggle was passenger traffic. Although Lovett, with his aviation background, realized that the passenger trade was doomed, he let the Union Pacific fight hard to hold its share before abandoning it to Amtrak. On one occasion he glanced at the losses on dining car service and sighed that it would be cheaper to pay each traveler two dollars not to use the service than to continue providing it.

Elsewhere, Lovett lent his influence to steering the company through an era of rapid change. New technologies such as microwave communications, Complete Operating Information System (COIN),

Centralized Traffic Control (CTC), and computers were adopted early, along with unit trains, piggyback, and a host of other new techniques. Fresh approaches to marketing were developed and new sources of business were cultivated, the most notable being extensive trona mines and refineries in Wyoming. No less a figure than United Mine Workers president John L. Lewis proclaimed coal from the Rock Springs Mines along the UP line in Wyoming to be among the best in the nation. The conversion to diesel locomotives, strongly pushed by Lovett, underscored the growing importance of oil in the national economy, and the Union Pacific organized a subsidiary, Calnev, to build and operate a 248-mile pipeline through California and Nevada.

The Union Pacific was fast becoming a multifaceted company, with large operations in oil and other minerals as well as land development, but it could not maximize its use of these assets. In Lovett's view the gravest problem the company had with the government was its rigid prohibition against the railroad entering other businesses. The company could not sell its coal and oil to customers located off its lines, despite a growing market for them. Nor could it develop them efficiently so long as the management structure funneled major decisions through the president of the railroad, who usually knew little and cared less about the nonrail assets of the company.

Traditionally, the president in Omaha handled all operations matters while the board in New York had charge of financial affairs. Under the Union Pacific's peculiar structure Lovett, as chairman of the executive committee, was in effect the chief operating officer in New York. With the same deft skill he had shown in Washington, he moved quietly to detach nonrail operations from the president's authority and route them into separate divisions reporting directly to him; this plan was carried out in January 1961.

Efforts were also made to secure legislation allowing the railroads to diversify into other areas, and when this campaign succeeded, Lovett steered the Union Pacific toward the same goal being sought eagerly by many railroads: the formation of a holding company in which the railroad would be merely one division. This approach enabled the company to spin off its nonrail assets into separate companies outside the regulatory stranglehold of the Interstate Commerce Commission (ICC). It allowed their full development and also protected them for the stockholders in the event the government should confiscate the railroads—a contingency feared by many veteran rail managers during the turbulent decade or so after World War II.

Once in a position to exploit the company's resources fully, Lovett and Roland Harriman moved to create a managerial structure capable of achieving that objective. The main problem was finding capable managers for the nonrailroad activities. After an international search, Lovett found two key men in his own backyard: Frank Barnett, a top-notch corporation lawyer whose firm had long done work for the Union Pacific, and James H. Evans, president of Seamen's Bank, who served on the Union Pacific board.

With Barnett and Evans as the nucleus of a new management team, Lovett and Harriman created the Union Pacific Corporation in 1969. At first the railroad and nonrail resources continued to be run as separate divisions within the holding company. A year later the corporation acquired Champlain Oil Company, which became the anchor for its oil resources. Two other companies were ultimately formed to join Champlain and the Union Pacific Railroad: Rocky Mountain Energy, which took charge of all mineral development except oil, and Upland Company, which handled real estate development.

This new arrangement enabled Lovett and Harriman to phase themselves out of office with characteristic grace. Lovett had surrendered his chairmanship in 1967; Harriman followed suit two years later. In the new corporation Barnett was made chairman of the board and Evans president. Another Brown Brothers Harriman partner, Elbridge T. Gerry, became chairman of the executive committee. Lovett and Harriman remained on the board and executive committee as senior advisers to a young management team recruited in large part from outside the Union Pacific by the two men they had brought into its higher offices.

In all this work Lovett displayed not only broad vision but a remarkable grasp of detail. Some of his associates thought he possessed a photographic memory because of his insistence on having everything in writing. "You could sit here and tell him something," recalled Gerry, "explain it just as clearly as you could, about a problem. Unless he

saw it in writing, it just wouldn't sink through. Once he read something, he never forgot it."

No individual did more than Lovett to usher the Union Pacific through the ordeal of transition into a new era. While many railroads failed or disappeared through merger, the Union Pacific survived and prospered in large measure because of his foresight and rare ability to accomplish his goals. "Robert Lovett understood power, where it resided, how to exercise it," wrote David Halberstam. "He had exercised it all his life, yet he was curiously little known to the general public. . . . He was the private man in the public society *par excellence*. He did not need to impress people with false images."

Although Lovett's influence was still felt in Washington during the 1960s, he resisted all efforts to lure him back into government. President John Kennedy was said to have offered him a choice of being secretary of state, defense, or treasury, only to be refused on the plea of ill health. Asked by Arthur Krock of the *New York Times* if the reports of the offers were true, Lovett replied in his deferential manner, "Oh, I think he was just trying to make me feel good." He did serve Kennedy as a consultant on government organization and operations and as a member of several advisory committees.

Apart from the Union Pacific, Lovett served as a director for CBS and the Freeport Sulphur Company and as a member of the New York investment committee for Royal-Globe Insurance Companies. He was also a trustee for the Carnegie Institute of Washington, the Carnegie Foundation, and the Rockefeller Foundation. For his record in public life he was awarded the Distinguished Service Medal in 1945, the Grand Cross of the Order of Leopold (Belgium) in 1950, the Presidential Medal of Freedom in 1963, and numerous honorary degrees.

No men in the recent history of the Union Pacific were more esteemed than Lovett and Roland Harriman. They were of opposite and complementary natures, which helped make them a formidable team in a time of change. "He did a magnificent job," declared Gerry. "He was always a very bright guy, quick, had a mind that could analyze a problem like nobody's business. And with it all [he had] the most tremendous sense of humor that anybody ever had. . . . He was the workhorse during the fifties, early sixties."

Although his activities were limited by heart and eye ailments during his later years, Lovett maintained an interest in the affairs of the Union Pacific and Brown Brothers Harriman. His death in May 1986, followed a short time later by that of Averell Harriman, deprived the Union Pacific of its last direct links to the two families that had dominated its affairs for ninety years.

Reference:

David Halberstam, *The Best and the Brightest* (New York: Random House, 1969), pp. 3-10.

Archives:

Some of Robert A. Lovett's papers are in the corporate records of the Union Pacific Corporation, New York.

Maine Central Railroad

by David H. Hickcox

Ohio Wesleyan University

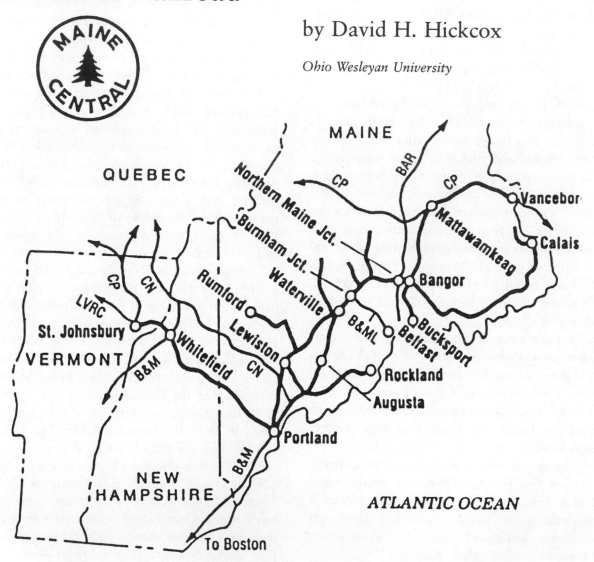

Map of the Maine Central Railroad (1983)

The Maine Central Railroad was incorporated in 1862 with the consolidation of two small unsuccessful 5' 6"–gauge railroads: the Penobscot & Kennebec, which had defaulted on its bonds, and the An-

droscoggin & Kennebec, which had never paid a dividend. The Maine Central at its beginning was a minor railroad with little revenue and no direct connection to Boston. By 1870, however, the line from

Waterville to Bangor had been changed to standard gauge and through trains were running to Boston. The Maine Central continually acquired other railroads, and by 1884 its 524 miles constituted the largest system in New England under one management.

At its greatest extent, in 1924, the Maine Central operated over 1,200 miles of track, extending from Vanceboro on the Atlantic coast southwest to Bangor and Portland. Numerous branches reached out into the hinterlands, the most important of which was the line to St. Johnsbury, Vermont, with its spectacular route through Crawford Notch in the White Mountains. By 1986, however, the Maine Central had abandoned many lines, reducing trackage to about 580 miles.

In 1933 the Maine Central entered into an agreement with the Boston & Maine for joint employment of some personnel, which allowed for merged operations. The Maine Central resumed independent operation in 1952 and was completely independent of the B&M by the end of 1955. In the late 1970s the Amoskeag Company, which owned the Bangor & Aroostook, attempted to acquire the Maine Central. E. Spencer Miller, who was president of the Maine Central from 1952 to 1977, vigorously oppposed the takeover attempt. In 1980 the Maine Central was purchased by the U.S. Filter Corporation. Subsequently, Ashland Oil, which had no interest in owning a railroad, purchased U.S. Filter,

and the Maine Central was put up for sale. On June 16, 1981, the Maine Central was purchased by Guilford Transportation Industries, a company wholly owned by Timothy Mellon. Although the Maine Central remained a separate corporate entity, operations were unified with Guilford's other lines, the Delaware & Hudson and the Boston & Maine, and a common paint scheme was adopted.

The Maine Central's corporate symbol, a Maine pine tree, symbolized the railroad's dependence on forest products. Pulp and paper products from several on-line mills constituted half of the Maine Central's traffic. Outgoing lumber and inbound petroleum products were also important sources of revenue. Interchange with the Bangor & Aroostook provided considerable traffic. A switching line in Portland, the Portland Terminal Company, was owned by the Maine Central.

On June 6, 1867, Guilford Transportation leased virtually all of the Maine Central's trackage to Springfield Terminal Company, a wholly owned subsidiary, to take advantage of Springfield Terminal's lower operating costs. The Maine Central thus essentially ceased to exist.

Reference:

Ron Johnson, *The Best of Maine Railroads* (Portland, Maine: Published by the author, 1985).

Mann-Elkins Act

The Mann-Elkins Act originated in 1908 Republican campaign promises to increase railroad regulation. Attorney General George W. Wickersham constructed a bill that would enable the Interstate Commerce Commission (ICC) not only to supervise railroad securities and to suspend rate advances pending investigation, but also to provide for the legalization of traffic or pool agreements among competing railroads and, at the behest of President William Howard Taft, for a commerce court to review ICC decisions. The provision legalizing pools was especially objectionable to insurgent Progressives, particularly Senator Albert B. Cummins. The bill also failed to please the Democrats, and it perished in the Senate Interstate Commerce Committee after Cummins had tacked on approximately a hundred amendments. The committee then produced a new bill, of which Cummins was the chief architect.

Railroad officials, who were unhappy with the original proposals of Taft and Wickersham, inadvertently strengthened the Progressives' hand by filing for general rate increases in both the West and the East during the last days of the debate. By securing an injunction against the Western advances and threatening to get one against the Eastern proposals, Wickersham postponed rate increases until the ICC could determine their merit under the new legislation. The rate-hike blunder outraged the public, hampered conservative congressional friends of the railroads, and produced a third act that was more stringent than the previous two.

The Mann-Elkins Act was sponsored by James R. Mann, Republican representative from Illinois, who was chair of the House Commerce Committee (and later sponsored the Mann White Slave Traffic Act of 1910), and Stephen B. Elkins, Republican senator from West Virginia, who was also the author of the 1903 Elkins Act that had attacked the railroads' practice of offering rebates to large shippers. The act offered something for everyone and passed by comfortable majorities. It was signed into law on June 18, 1910. Though not legalizing pooling, the act allowed carriers to continue to set rates by concerted action through their traffic associations; but as a check the ICC was empowered to suspend rate changes for up to ten months pending an investigation, and the railroads were made responsible for proving the reasonableness of both proposed increases and original rates. The act also strengthened the long-short-haul clause of the Interstate Commerce Act of 1887 by eliminating ambiguities and requiring that exceptions to the clause be made only by the ICC. In addition, the act extended the ICC's jurisdiction to include telegraph, telephone, and cable lines. The antirailroad insurgent forces did not win everything: ICC supervision of railroad finances was weakened to allow only investigation of their finances; and the act established the Commerce Court Taft wanted. While debate on the Hepburn Act of 1906 had stressed the independent administrative character of the ICC, debate on the Mann-Elkins bill depicted the ICC as an arm of Congress exercising "administrative legislative functions." Congress in 1913 repealed that section of the Mann-Elkins Act which created the Commerce Court.

References:

Robert E. Cushman, *The Independent Regulatory Commissions* (New York: Oxford University Press, 1941);

Winthrop M. Daniels, *American Railroads: Four Phases of Their History* (Princeton: Princeton University Press, 1932);

Ari and Olive Hoogenboom, *A History of the ICC: From Panacea to Palliative* (New York: Norton, 1976);

Gabriel Kolko, *Railroads and Regulation, 1877-1916* (Princeton: Princeton University Press, 1965);

Albro Martin, *Enterprise Denied: Origins of the Decline of American Railroads, 1897-1917* (New York: Columbia University Press, 1971);

I. L. Sharfman, *The Interstate Commerce Commission: A Study in Administrative Law and Procedure,* 5 volumes (New York: The Commonwealth Fund, 1931-1937).

—Ari Hoogenboom

William G. Marbury

(March 31, 1912-July 11, 1971)

by Craig Miner

Wichita State University

William G. Marbury (Photo by Ed Wergeles)

CAREER: Attorney (1937-1939); attorney, Hocker, Gladney and Grand (1939-1945); assistant to the president (1945-1949), president (1949-1956), Mississippi River Fuel Company; chairman of the board, Mississippi River Corporation (1956-1971); chairman of the executive committee, Missouri Pacific Railroad (1960-1971); president, Mississippi River Corporation (1965-1971); chairman of the board, Missouri Pacific Railroad (1967-1971).

During the "urge to merge" crisis of railroading in the 1960s, Bill Marbury was one of the industry's most imaginative, daring, and controversial figures. He had a clear vision of the eventual pattern that would emerge of relatively few large systems in the western United States and the financial and legal acumen that were often more important in implementing consolidation than was rail operating expertise. He was not himself an expert in rail operations, but he had both an outstanding eye for those who were and a remarkable ability to motivate them and to work with them. Perhaps most important, Marbury was a man of extraordinary nerve—or, as some thought, ruthlessness. He was a true "mover and shaker" from the time his relatively tiny pipeline company swallowed up the ailing Missouri Pacific Railroad (MP or MoPac); through his bid to take over the Atchison, Topeka and Santa Fe (Santa Fe) with cash; right up to the moment of his death, when he was close to seeing the recapitalization of the Missouri Pacific, which would position it as the high—stakes player he always imagined that it could be.

It seemed to railway watchers in the late 1950s that William G. Marbury came out of nowhere with his homey drawl, gangling gate, sandy shock of hair, and protestations that he was "just a country lawyer." In fact, he was born in Farmington, Missouri, the youngest of eight children of Benjamin H. Marbury, a country lawyer, and Anne Eversole Marbury. He changed colleges three times due to financial stringency, receiving his law degree from St. Louis University.

Early on, certain characteristics were evident. Marbury was a fighter as well as the possessor of a brilliant analytical intellect. He had the capacity for immense generosity and heartening loyalty toward those he favored, combined with tenacity and toughness—and sometimes rudeness and scorn directed at those who had crossed him or for whom he had no respect. He was a born entrepreneur and risk-taker. He argued with his father over the proper balance between studies, girls, football, and boxing, and boxed so aggressively in college that he lost an eye and afterward wore a glass replacement. In his business career he was given to flights of invective, particularly on the subject of the bureaucratic inanities of government regulators, whose triplicate forms were the antithesis and nemesis of his need for rapid change and innovation. He became so angry in 1951 at the Federal Power Commission (FPC) that, after holding forth on the fact that it had "strangled the pipelines by injecting itself too much into management," he punched an FPC rate divisions chief. This action cost him $6,000 in fines, but it brought him his first national publicity and began the building of a collection of anecdotes retold in boardrooms which became the Marbury legend.

He not only moved fast, but he thought big. "It doesn't pay," he once said, "to play penny ante." Unlike many big thinkers, Marbury was a pragmatist—some would characterize him as an opportunist—whom his close associates remember as a man who was never wedded to any grand scheme for the future if he perceived shifts in the raw materials from which he was going to create or in the legal and financial environment in which he would be forced to create. Marbury was, he said himself, "one of those fellows with a lot of energy."

Marbury's first experience as a corporate leader came with the Mississippi River Fuel Company (MRFC), the operator of a 1,500-mile gas pipeline from Louisiana to St. Louis. Marbury had worked as a night dispatcher for the firm while still in school. After having spent some time in the state auditor's and governor's offices in Missouri, Marbury had gone into private practice in St. Louis, had married Frances Steudle in 1938, and in 1939 had joined the firm of Hocker, Gladney and Grand. One of this firm's clients was MRFC, and Marbury began to handle their business. He so impressed Ben Comfort, the pipeline company's president, that Comfort hired him as an assistant in 1945. When Comfort fell ill in 1949, the board gave Marbury the assignment of finding a replacement. He did such a good job at lining up prospects and preparing reports that the directors decided that he was a better candidate than any of the others. Thus, in his late thirties, Marbury was president of a corporation, a situation that suited him ideally.

Immediately Marbury knew that his goal at the pipeline company was diversification, mainly in order either to get out from under federal regulation or, at least, to have some choice of regulators. He bought several cement plants along the Mississippi River and stayed in the cement business in some form or other throughout his career. He also entered the oilfield supply and chemical businesses. He entertained in flamboyant style in "Selma Hall," his Civil War–era mansion on the Mississippi River north of St. Louis which was called locally "Marbury's Castle" and in general cut a wide swath in St. Louis business circles. But he remained dissatisfied. "We got into some [businesses] that were too small," he told a reporter, "and we realized that we had to go into something big if we wanted to make a real contribution to our stockholders."

The "big" target of opportunity that first appeared was the Missouri Pacific Railroad. A block of 60,000 shares of stock in the MoPac became available in 1959. Marbury had represented this stock interest on the MoPac board since 1958, and a year's experience had convinced him that an investment in the Missouri Pacific would be good for the pipeline company. MRFC bought the stock, and in 1960, with his company's interest in MoPac "A" stock at about 25 percent, Marbury was elected chairman of the board of the railroad.

To an observer an investment by a small pipeline company in such a railroad as the MoPac would hardly have seemed likely. The railroad had been in receivership from 1933 to 1956, and a stock fight between its "A" and "B" shareholders over the true equity had crippled it in the stock trading needed for mergers. In addition, it had a debt load of $500 million. The Pennsylvania Railroad had that much debt, but it was three times the Missouri Pacific's size.

Marbury loved the challenge and perceived enormous advantages if he could overcome the difficulties. He actually liked the debt, not so much because of its size as because of its structure. The earliest maturity on the bonds was 1990, there was much contingent interest debt, and the property had good operating statistics. "That big debt doesn't scare me," Marbury said. "I know it as a technician and it's the most beautiful debt structure I've ever seen." His associate Robert Craft, a banker and one of the few who could completely follow Marbury's financial thinking, thought that some of this confidence was bluff. "Marbury was given to platitudes," Craft noted, "and I didn't pay much attention to what he said most of the time."

Just as important as the debt problem was the stock ownership problem. The "B" stock, created during the receivership at the insistence of the Alleghany Corporation, which was to control the stock, theoretically held the equity in the company though the "A" stock controlled management. Even among the "A" holders Marbury was at first in a minority position and regarded with a good deal of suspicion, while his public contempt for the claims of the "B" holders hardly promised that he would be a good catalyst for a negotiated solution to the struggle between the stock classes.

Russell Dearmont, the MP president, said in introducing Marbury to the stockholders that "we love to ship their pipe . . . and personally I have complete confidence in Mr. Marbury and his associates"; but not everyone in the room, not to mention in conservative St. Louis, shared his confidence. In his address to the stockholders Marbury said that he had invested in the MoPac only to make a little money, not to manipulate the corporation or use it as a pawn in grand schemes. He had to add, though: "Very few people believe it, but it's true." To the St. Louis establishment he was a pariah. His Southern Democrat political views and his bluntness offended many, as did his habit of banking in New York City rather than locally. Socially, his family was either ostracized or received only lukewarm acceptance. "The status quo is very important in St. Louis," Marbury concluded in one of his rare philosophical moods. "People don't like to be moved and I came in from the country and started stirring things up. This is a provincial town and they don't like it."

Marbury's first and maybe his best personal contribution to the MP was to bring in a new management team to replace the aging upper echelon. Those who wanted the jobs did not meet Marbury's standards, and those he wanted were either satisfied where they were or were afraid of the MP's problems. More than a few were afraid of Marbury himself. Downing Jenks, the young president of the Chicago, Rock Island and Pacific (Rock Island) whom Marbury hired as MP president in 1961, remembers being quite apprehensive about meeting Marbury. He was somewhat reassured by meeting a director at a club who assured him that Marbury had no horns and had a wonderful wife and kids. Still, there was trepidation until Jenks actually met the man who was to give him the opportunity of his life and was to support his actions totally until Marbury's death ten years later.

There were many personality differences between Marbury and Jenks. Marbury was careless, outspoken, and dramatic, while Jenks was fastidious, quiet and highly organized. It is to Marbury's credit not only that he realized the deeper commonality of purpose and style that existed between the two, but that he understood perfectly that Jenks was a rail operating man par excellence and that he himself was a financier and negotiator of deals. When Jenks and John Lloyd, whom he had brought with him from the Rock Island, had their first meeting with Marbury concerning new equipment purchases, the chairman accepted their requests to revolutionize motive power without a blink. When they asked how this project could possibly be financed, and whether they could help by making some compromises, Marbury asked what they recommended as the best that could be done to operate the railroad efficiently. Just what they had proposed, they said. "Well then," Marbury told them, "you run the railroad and let me worry about the finances."

Marbury always presented the Jenks and Lloyd requests to the stockholders with pride and confidence, and that pride and confidence drove Jenks and Lloyd to be sure that their plans resulted in success. Also, Marbury lobbied the stockholders to create a generous stock option plan to motivate managers. "You have to do what is the American way," he told the stockholders in 1961, "and that is to make them some money." In explaining manager motivation, he used the example of his protégé Jenks, who was forty-five years old, a graduate of Yale, and had already been the president of two railroads. "It's no small job to get people like that. When you get them, you want to keep them because their continuity of service to this property will be of great value to the stockholders."

While involved in these internal MP matters, Marbury, as president of MRFC, was making bold financial moves to control the railroad completely. Finally, through a tender offer in 1962, MRFC obtained 53 percent of the MP "A" stock, thus putting a pipeline company with assets of $150 million in control of a railroad with assets of $1.1 billion. From that point onward no one snickered when Marbury announced that he intended to do this and that in the world of finance. They might not approve of his personal style, but no one doubted his ability to get things done.

Among the most successful of the astonishing things Marbury got done in the years following was the purchase of and consolidation into the MP of part of the moribund Chicago & Eastern Illinois Railroad (C&EI). While he was unsuccessful in his grand plan of merging both the Texas & Pacific and the C&EI into the MoPac in a way that would "freeze out" the "B" holders and effectively recapitalize the company, by 1965 he had acquired a part of the C&EI (the rest going to the Louisville & Nashville) that was ideally situated to give the MP access to Chicago.

The C&EI purchase, given Jenks's immediate physical revitalization and profitable operation of the well-situated line, was one of the most astute strategic moves in railroading during the 1960s. Yet Marbury did it without any of the usual weapons, crippled as he was by the stock fight and endless objections before the Interstate Commerce Commission (ICC). Even at the lowest point in the hearings Marbury was confident of the eventual result. "We have won the first game by a shutout," he told a newspaper in 1963, "and we expect to sweep the series."

Less successful but more dramatic was Marbury's 1963 bid for the Atchison, Topeka & Sante Fe, which he proposed to buy in order to make the MP into a transcontinental. The Sante Fe had assets of $3.1 billion and was not interested in being sold to anyone. Marbury had been in such situations before. In fact, he was already talking to his attorneys about acquiring an Eastern railroad once the Santa Fe had been purchased in order to form a true coast-to-coast transcontinental.

When talks with the Santa Fe led nowhere in 1964, Marbury showed his spirit. "We're not going to sit around and wait to see what they want to do," he said of the Santa Fe managers. "The Missouri Pacific has other activities and ideas of its own in mind which we are starting to work on."

He was back in 1966 with a proposal to the ICC that the Mississippi River Corporation (the MFRC had been renamed in 1965) purchase the Sante Fe for $340 million in cash. "Tail Has Dog Bite Lion," one headline read. Marbury was not amused: "You can't do the job that needs to be done for the country by thinking in terms of the weak. Overconcern for the weak is a curse of our times." Circumstances, he said, should not control, but leaders should dictate circumstance. "Nobody was dealing us a hand, so we decided to get our own deck to play with." The Sante Fe takeover proposal failed. The MP withdrew from the fight in 1968, concluding that "Marbury's dream" concerning the Santa Fe was a vision out of time.

His direction did not change. Marbury held talks with several railroads in the 1960s, including the MP's eventual merger partner, the Union Pacific (UP), in the hope of implementing his vision. "Only through consolidation into a handful of big systems," he told the *Wall Street Journal*, "can the railroad industry catch up with the times. The scope of railroad operations today is geared to the early part of the 20th century rather than to the mass production transportation needs of the economy today."

The enormously complex recapitalization of the MoPac was always a concern of Marbury's, but its final implementation was to be left to Jenks. Marbury was a "Captain Kidd" type, as one reporter described him, much given to talking off-the-cuff and bluntly to the press about the progress of and his opinion about delicate negotiations with Alleghany Corporation over stock structure. An attorney himself, he was a recapitalization attorney's nightmare. "William Marbury," said one of the Alleghany people years later, was "considered a very strong, very ruthless, very dynamic maverick type guy. He would force a bag of corn down the mouth of a two pound goose if he thought it was good for him." Jenks, on the other hand, never offered more than was asked, had a cutting but subtle and wry sense of humor, and, unlike Marbury, had not alienated the stockholders in New York.

Marbury's bold, abrasive tactics in trying to force out the Alleghany "B" holders through mergers led to embarrassment for the MP in courtrooms all the way to the Supreme Court and unquestionably raised the price of the eventual buyout of the "B" stock considerably. That it was possible at all, even for the $200 million it eventually cost the "A" holders to recapitalize the company in 1974, was probably due to the ill health and death of Marbury in 1971. The MoPac and the UP finally got together in 1983.

Some would say that Marbury was out of place in his own time—that he was a nineteenth-century robber baron in the twentieth century. Marbury was a seemingly shallow man, full of patriotic platitudes, who was not, in the depths of his complex mind and in the inner reaches of his heart, even close to what he appeared to be. He could grill a competitor and give large gifts to beggars on

the street. A fascinating paradox, Marbury contributed much and caused some damage, but his track through the twentieth-century rail industry will remain permanently clear, important, and compelling.

References:

"Magnate of Mid-America," *Forbes*, 91 June 15, 1963) 20-25;

Craig Miner, *The Rebirth of the Missouri Pacific, 1956-1983* (College Station: Texas A&M University Press, 1983).

David O. Mathews

(May 13, 1903-September 3, 1973)

David O. Mathews

CAREER: Attorney, Mathews and Medlin (1925-

by Douglas C. Munski

University of North Dakota

1930); associate, Waldron, Silverman and Newkirk (1930-1934); partner, Waldron, Newkirk and Mathews (1934-1941); counsel, law and enforcement, Interstate Commerce Commission (1941-1942); staff member, office of general counsel, Office of Defense Transportation (1942-1944); special assistant to the United States attorney general (1944-1949); general counsel (1949-1950), vice president (1950-1957), president (1957-1967), Chicago & Eastern Illinois Railroad; partner, Pope, Ballard, Uriell, Kennedy, Shepard and Fowle (1967-1973).

David O. Mathews was president of the Chicago & Eastern Illinois Railroad (C&EI) at a crucial time for that Chicago-Southwest and Chicago-Southeast bridge line. He was instrumental in modernizing the C&EI during the 1950s and 1960s, and he played a major role in the negotiations around the sale of the C&EI to the Missouri Pacific (MoPac), which divided the carrier with the Louisville & Nashville (L&N).

The son of Oscar and Bertha Elizabeth Johnson Mathews, David Oscar Mathews was born on May 13, 1903, into an eastern Nebraska farming family and grew up in the Missouri Valley community of Blair. He went to the University of Nebraska-Lincoln and received the LL.B. in 1925, the same year he was admitted to the Nebraska bar and became a member of the firm of Mathews and Medlin in Omaha. He married Lucile Lawrence Gillette on June 23, 1926. He joined the Omaha firm of Waldron, Silverman and Newkirk in 1930 as an associate member; when that firm was reorganized in 1934 as Waldron, Newkirk and Mathews, he became a partner.

In 1941 Mathews left private law practice to become a counsel in the law and enforcement section of the Bureau of Motor Carriers of the Interstate Commerce Commission (ICC) in Omaha. From 1942 until 1944 he was in Washington, D.C., as a staff member of the general counsel for the Office of Defense Transportation. Mathews continued to live in the nation's capital after becoming a special assistant to the United States attorney general, dealing with antitrust lawsuits and related issues, in 1944.

Mathews reentered the private sector in 1949, joining the C&EI as general counsel. He was named a vice president in 1950 and was elevated to the presidency in 1957. This was a particularly crucial time for the C&EI because it faced territorial incursions by larger railroads.

C&EI control of the Joppa and Thebes gateways in southern Illinois was being undermined in the late 1950s. Both the Chicago, Burlington & Quincy and the New York Central gained access to Tennessee Valley Authority thermal power plants on the Kentucky side of the Joppa gateway in 1958 through an ICC ruling. As a countermove, the C&EI connected with the Missouri-Illinois Railroad, a Missouri Pacific subsidiary, to reduce travel time through the Thebes Gateway between Chicago and the Southwest in order to make up coal traffic losses. But that action prompted MoPac to seek total control of those Chicago-Southwest rail movements.

Starting in 1959, MoPac sought to acquire the C&EI. The C&EI was an attractive property because its equipment was being modernized and its operations improved. From 1957 through 1965 Mathews promoted Centralized Traffic Control, automatic interlocking plants, piggybacking, and consolidations of dispatching, station, and office personnel. Most critically, the C&EI had partial control of the Western Indiana Railroad Company and the Belt Railway Company of Chicago and also had its own wholly owned subsidiary, the Chicago Heights Terminal Transfer Railroad. MoPac wanted this type of access into Chicago—but so did the Louisville & Nashville.

Mathews recognized that the C&EI was a key bridge line (that is, a railroad connecting other railroads) and sought the best deal he could in the railway merger mania of the early 1960s. The C&EI rejected MoPac's 1960 offer and sought the L&N as a partner, but the L&N dropped the negotiations due to the pending merger of the Atlantic Coast Line, its major stockholder, with the Seaboard Air Line Railroad. Mathews was rebuffed when he sought inclusion in the Chesapeake & Ohio-Baltimore & Ohio merger, as he was with efforts to join the Chicago & North Western. He was also unsuccessful in approaches to the Erie-Lackawanna, the Illinois Central, and the Grand Trunk Western.

The L&N turned its attention to the C&EI again in 1961 because MoPac had begun an unfriendly buy-out of the C&EI, a situation that could result in the L&N's loss of its access into Chicago via the C&EI. The L&N first sought complete control of the C&EI but in 1962 changed its request before the ICC to only partial control. The ICC ruled in 1963 that MoPac should own the C&EI's Thebes and Joppa gateways while the L&N was to be able to purchase the Evansville gateway. MoPac and the L&N were to have joint ownership of the C&EI north of Woodland Junction, Illinois, into the Chicago area.

Mathews oversaw an extremely intricate process of financial, administrative, and labor-related activities in the sale of the C&EI to MoPac. The merger was prepared between 1963 and 1965, but a court-ordered delay was arranged on behalf of the Illinois Central, St. Louis Southwestern, and Monon. MoPac won the suit after a two-year struggle and gained operational control over the C&EI on May 12, 1967. Mathews left the C&EI at that time.

Joining the firm of Pope, Ballard, Uriell, Kennedy, Shepard and Fowle in Chicago, Mathews returned to practicing law. Having divorced his first wife in 1965, he married Mary Ann Hurley on December 1, 1967. Commuting from his Evanston home to his Chicago law office, Mathews relaxed by playing golf at the Westmoreland Country Club of Wilmette, socializing at the Chicago Union League, or participating in Shriner activities. He moved to Fort Lauderdale, Florida, upon retiring.

On September 3, 1973, Mathews died in Danville, Illinois, while visiting relatives. Mathews was one of the most important presidents of the C&EI because he oversaw its modernization and eventual direct integration into larger rail systems. Yet, because of the C&EI's strategic position as a railway bridge line, not even his outstanding management was sufficient to maintain the C&EI's independence.

Reference:

Douglas C. Munski, "Modeling the Historical Geography of the Chicago & Eastern Illinois Railroad, 1849-1969," Ph.D. dissertation, University of Illinois at Urban-Champaign, 1978.

William Gibbs McAdoo

(October 31, 1863 - February 1, 1941)

by John J. Broesamle

California State University, Northridge

William Gibbs McAdoo

CAREER: President, Knoxville Street Railway Company (1889-1892); attorney and dealer in securities (*circa* 1892-1901); president, Hudson & Manhattan Railroad Company, as well as preceding and ancillary companies (1901-1913); secretary of the treasury (1913-1918); ex officio chairman of the Federal Reserve Board (1913-1918); director-general of railroads (1917-1919); U.S. senator (1933-1938); president of the board of directors, American President Lines (1938-1941).

William Gibbs McAdoo, originally a railroad promoter, became a promoter in government, a pioneer of certain aspects of the American welfare state, and one of the great secretaries of the treasury. Born near Marietta, Georgia, in 1863 to William Gibbs and Mary Faith Floyd McAdoo, he grew up in a family declassed by the Civil War. McAdoo studied at the University of Tennessee from 1879 to 1882, then moved to Chattanooga, where he read law and gained admittance to the bar in 1885. That same year he married Sarah Houstoun Fleming; they had six children.

In 1889 McAdoo purchased a mule-driven street railway company in Knoxville, intending to electrify it. His first major business venture ended disastrously in receivership. In 1892 McAdoo moved his growing family to New York City, where he practiced law and sold securities.

Always on the lookout for fresh opportunities, in 1901 he purchased a partially completed railway tunnel system beneath the Hudson River which had been begun in 1874 and abandoned twice. With financial backing from Elbert H. Gary of United States Steel and later from J. P. Morgan, work revived in 1902; soon McAdoo's Hudson & Manhattan Railroad Company (H&M) began digging more shafts. In the meantime McAdoo initiated construction of a New York terminal for the

H&M. By 1908 the Hudson & Manhattan had become the largest subaqueous tunnel system in the world; it ultimately comprised four tubes and nineteen miles of track.

McAdoo's "public be pleased" public relations policy gained him fame as a social welfare-oriented capitalist. This reputation enabled him to play a valuable role in the 1912 presidential campaign of Woodrow Wilson, whose New Freedom platform reserved a special place for reform-minded businessmen.

McAdoo was an obvious choice for Wilson's secretary of the treasury; he served in that position from 1913 to 1918, during which time the powers of the Treasury Department grew immensely. Important in the framing and passage of the Federal Reserve Act of 1913, McAdoo became ex officio chairman of the Federal Reserve Board. He strove to maintain an even flow of credit to the South and West and supported the 1916 Federal Farm Loan Act.

McAdoo had clearly stamped himself as the most energetic, capable member of Wilson's cabinet by the time World War I broke out in 1914. Among the ablest figures in early twentieth-century public life, McAdoo was driven by an almost tireless, restless energy. Flexible, self-assured, and a maverick, he had a magnetic personality and a keen sense of salesmanship. Not one to get bogged down in complexities of ideology or detail, he devoted his career in government, as he had in business, to inventive change.

World War I put these strengths to their most grueling test. McAdoo came to see the conflict as a great opportunity for building the nation's economy by capturing foreign trade, especially the markets of Latin America. Toward this end, he spearheaded legislation to expand the United States merchant marine through federally dominated ownership and operation. The Shipping Act of 1916 was denounced at the time as socialistic, but it can more accurately be described as reflecting the promotional drive which McAdoo had brought with him to the Treasury.

Following the American declaration of war, McAdoo, who had urged Wilson to take a hard line against Germany, found himself juggling an extraordinary variety of responsibilities. Most fundamentally, he took charge of financing the war, a $33.5 billion enterprise. Debates broke out over the ratio of taxes to loans and the degree of progressiveness in wartime tax rates, with McAdoo's initial tax program upsetting reformers as too favorable to wealth. The Treasury ran four Liberty Loan campaigns and an additional Victory Loan campaign following the war. McAdoo negotiated economic questions with the Allies, chaired the Federal Reserve and Federal Farm Loan boards as well as the War Finance Corporation, led the Liberty Loan drives, and ran military insurance programs.

An enormous additional burden arrived when the government took over the nation's railroad system in December 1917, with McAdoo as director-general. His directorship proved extremely controversial. McAdoo's overriding priority was uninterrupted transportation efficiency; cost concerns were peripheral. By congressional fiat and administrative practice, the railroads and their workers received generous treatment; users did less well. Sympathetic to labor goals, McAdoo maintained a warm mutual relationship with the heads of the brotherhoods. Wage levels rose under government control, but so, dramatically, did transportation rates. Angry shippers set up a drumfire of criticism against federal management and united against its continuation. McAdoo's introduction of management efficiencies further frustrated shippers accustomed to prewar arrangements. Shipper objections became especially shrill in the South and West. McAdoo urged that federal control continue for five years after the war, with consideration given to permanent nationalization. But in 1920, under the Transportation Act, the lines were returned to private hands.

McAdoo resigned from the Treasury shortly after the war ended. In 1922 he and his second wife, Eleanor—the youngest of Woodrow Wilson's daughters, whom he had married in 1914 following the death of his first wife in 1912 and with whom he had two daughters—moved to California. During the 1920s McAdoo led the dry, rural, small—town wing of the Democratic party against the emergent urban ethnic wets led by Al Smith. In 1924 McAdoo and Smith went head-to-head at the party's national convention, a contest resolved only after 103 ballots and the nomination of neither man (John W. Davis became the Democratic candidate). The 1920s did not bring out the best in McAdoo: he became indirectly sullied by the Teapot Dome scandals and accepted Ku Klux Klan support in the 1924 campaign. Although he was one of the few prominent persons in public life during that decade who were genuinely of presidential caliber, he had attached himself politically to a declining segment of a weakened party.

After playing an important part in nominating Franklin D. Roosevelt at the 1932 Democratic national convention, McAdoo was elected to the Senate from California. He became a consistent New Dealer. Following a divorce in 1934, he married Doris Cross the next year. Defeated in the 1938 primary, he died of a heart attack in 1941 while holding a symbolically suitable position: president of the board of American President shipping lines—run by the federal government.

Publications:
"The Soul of a Corporation," *The World's Work*, 23 (March 1912): 579-592;

Crowded Years; The Reminiscences of William G. McAdoo (Boston: Houghton Mifflin, 1931).

References:
John J. Broesamle, *William Gibbs McAdoo, A Passion for Change; 1863-1917* (Port Washington, N.Y.: Kennikat Press, 1973);

Walter Lippmann, *Men of Destiny* (New York: Macmillan, 1927), pp. 112-119;

Mary Synon, *McAdoo, the Man and His Times; A Panorama in Democracy* (Indianapolis: Bobbs-Merrill, 1924).

Archives:
Collections of McAdoo's papers are the William Gibbs McAdoo Papers, Library of Congress, and the William Gibbs McAdoo Papers, Library of the University of California, Los Angeles.

Wilson J. McCarthy

(July 24, 1884-February 12, 1956)

by David H. Hickcox

Ohio Wesleyan University

CAREER: Attorney (1913); assistant county attorney, Salt Lake County, Utah (1914-1916); district attorney, third judicial district, Utah (1916-1919); district judge, third judicial district, Utah (1919-1920); attorney (1920-1928); Utah state senator (1926-1932); western director, Reconstruction Finance Corporation (1932-1934); president, Denver & Salt Lake Railway (1934-1947); co-trustee (1935-1947), president (1947-1956), Denver & Rio Grande Western Railroad.

Wilson J. McCarthy, who garnered national recognition for his restoration of the bankrupt Denver & Rio Grande Western Railroad (D&RGW or Rio Grande) to profitability, was born in American Fork, Utah, on July 24, 1884, to Charles and Mary McCarthy. The McCarthys moved in 1895 to Alberta, where McCarthy worked on the family cattle ranch for several years. He returned to Salt Lake City to attend Latter-Day Saints University, did two years of Mormon missionary work, and attended Toronto Law College before transferring to Columbia University, which awarded him an LL.B. degree in

1913. He returned to Salt Lake City to practice law. McCarthy became county attorney in 1914 and district attorney in 1916 and was appointed judge of Utah's third judicial district in 1919. Although his tenure as judge was short, he was known as "the judge" for the remainder of his life. In 1926 McCarthy was elected to the Utah State Senate.

In 1932 President Hoover appointed McCarthy one of three Democratic members of the board of directors of the Reconstruction Finance Corporation (RFC). In this capacity he dealt directly with depression-caused problems in the western United States. One of those problems was the Denver & Salt Lake Railway (D&SL), which the RFC had taken over in December 1934 in order to protect its loans to the Denver & Rio Grande Western Railroad, a majority stockholder in the DS&L. This action was the first intervention of the federal government in railroad management since World War I. McCarthy was appointed president of the D&SL in 1934. The following year the Rio Grande, a 2,400-mile railroad with lines throughout Colorado's

(From left) Wilson J. McCarthy, president of the Denver & Rio Grande Western Railroad; Y. Frank Freeman, head of Paramount Pictures; Nat Holt, producer; Robert J. O'Donnell, film exhibitor; and Ed West, D&RGW executive vice president, celebrate the completion of the 1952 film The Denver & Rio Grande
(Kalmbach Publishing Company)

Rocky Mountains and extending into Utah, petitioned for reorganization under Section 77 of the Federal Bankruptcy Act. McCarthy and Henry Swan were appointed trustees of the Rio Grande, with McCarthy having sole responsibility for operations. McCarthy held the position as trustee until 1947, when he was appointed the railroad's president.

Wilson McCarthy's tenure as trustee and president of the Rio Grande is one of the great success stories in modern railroading. McCarthy took over a railroad with a debt of $58 million and referred to locally as the "Dangerous & Rapidly Growing Worse"; twenty-one years later the Rio Grande earned record revenues and profits and was recognized as one of the nation's most progressive railroads.

McCarthy had two goals for the Rio Grande: to keep it financially independent and in the hands of local management, and to build it into a first-class operation. Although neither McCarthy nor Swan were railroad men, both took the position that they had a product to sell and that they could market it. Shortly after taking control of the Rio Grande's operations, McCarthy outlined his philosophy of railroad management in a speech to employees: "The Rio Grande belongs to the people. The people who own it must have a sound property operated at a profit; the people who work for it must be capable and loyal; the people whom it serves must be proud of their railroad and glad to do business with it."

McCarthy's goals were received favorably by Judge J. Foster Symes, who approved McCarthy's requests for expenditures for repairs and new equipment. Rebuilt and developed into a bridge line, the Rio Grande was poised to handle the record levels of traffic that came with World War II. By 1946 the Rio Grande was cited as the best-operated railroad in the country and was ready to emerge from bankruptcy. In that year the United States Supreme Court upheld an Interstate Commerce Commission plan for the D&RGW to return to private ownership, remaining independent and acquiring the Denver & Salt Lake. Accordingly, on April 11, 1947, after twelve years of trusteeship, the Rio Grande emerged from bankruptcy. McCarthy was immediately selected as president, a position he held until his death in 1956.

During his twenty-one-year tenure as trustee and president of the Rio Grande, McCarthy became known as a progressive manager who introduced many innovations aimed at reducing costs and increasing efficiency. McCarthy acquired diesel locomotives, which were much more efficient than steam engines, especially in mountain operations. Centralized Traffic Control (CTC), which allows two-way operation on single track, was installed to the extent that in 1947 the D&RGW was fifth in the United States in miles of CTC track. Off-track maintenance equipment was introduced, greatly reducing maintenance costs. Engine-to-caboose radio communications were utilized. McCarthy developed a company research laboratory which made significant contributions to cost effectiveness and efficiency. He abandoned unprofitable branch lines, most of which were narrow-gauge lines dating back to the gold and silver mining boom of the nineteenth century. He envisioned the air age and made an unsuccessful request to the Civil Aeronautics Board for authority to develop an airline. At the time when the nation was searching for peaceful uses of the atom, McCarthy investigated the feasibility of nuclear-powered locomotives. Concerned with the decline of passenger revenue, McCarthy was instrumental in developing the California Zephyr, a state-of-the-art Chicago-San Francisco streamliner operated in conjunction with the Chi-

cago, Burlington & Quincy and Western Pacific Railroads.

When McCarthy died on February 12, 1956, he had, in the eyes of the railroad industry, performed a miracle: he had made the D&RGW into a competitive railroad, guiding it in the transition from war to peace and from bankruptcy to profitability. The extent of McCarthy's leadership was apparent that year, when the Rio Grande announced record operating revenues and net return.

In addition to his duties as trustee and president of the Rio Grande, McCarthy served two terms as a director of the Association of American Railroads and served on the boards of Mountain States Telephone and Telegraph Company, the First National Bank of Denver, the First Security Corporation of Ogden, Utah, and the Hotel Utah of Salt Lake City. McCarthy was a regent of the University of Utah from 1926 to 1932 and a director of the Denver branch of the Federal Reserve from 1937 to 1942. From 1941 until his death he was president of the Western Live Stock Company of Denver, which sponsored the National Live Stock Show. In 1951 the University of Utah honored him with an Honorary LL.D. degree and in 1955 the University of Colorado named him Man of the Year in Colorado business.

Publication:
General William Jackson Palmer, 1836-1909, and the Denver & Rio Grande Western Railroad (New York: Newcomen Society in North America, 1954).

Reference:
Robert Athearn, *The Denver and Rio Grande Western Railroad* (Lincoln: University of Nebraska Press, 1962).

Archives:
Little of whatever material Wilson McCarthy generated during his tenure with the D&RGW remains. The Rio Grande's corporate archives are located at the Colorado Historical Society in Denver, and some McCarthy materials are included in those holdings.

James McCrea

(May 1, 1848-March 28, 1913)

by Michael Bezilla

Pennsylvania State University

James McCrea (Pennsylvania State Archives)

CAREER: Member of surveying party, Connellsville & Southern Pennsylvania Railroad (1865-1867); assistant engineer, Wilmington & Reading Railroad (1867-1868); assistant engineer, Allegheny Valley Railroad (1868-1871); principal assistant engineer (1871-1875); superintendent of Middle Division (1875-1878); superintendent of New York Division (1878-1882); general manager, Southwest System, Lines West (1882-1885); general manager, Lines West (1885-1887); fourth vice president and general manager, Lines West (1887-1890); second vice president and general manager, Lines West (1890-1891); first vice president and general man-

ager, Lines West (1891-1907); president (1907-1912), Pennsylvania Railroad.

As president of the Pennsylvania Railroad (PRR), the nation's largest by nearly every standard of measure, James McCrea headed one of the most powerful corporations of his day. But his administration came during a period of financial uncertainty for railroads generally and at the close of a period of massive expenditures by the PRR; it is not considered a tenure of noteworthy accomplishments.

McCrea was born in Philadelphia on May 1, 1848 to James A. and Ann Foster McCrea. The family was socially prominent and traced its American roots to 1776, when the first McCreas arrived from Ireland to engage in banking in Philadelphia. McCrea attended the academy of the Reverend John Faris before enrolling at the Polytechnic College of the State of Pennsylvania in his native city. There he took civil engineering courses but left in 1865 before graduating to enter the employ of the Pennsylvania Railroad.

He first went to work as a member of a surveying party for a PRR subsidiary, the Connellsville & Southern Pennsylvania, then building south of Pittsburgh. He returned to the eastern part of the state in 1867 to become an assistant engineer for another subsidiary, the Wilmington & Reading. A year later he accepted a similar assignment with yet a third PRR subsidiary, the Allegheny Valley, for which he supervised the building of the Bennet's Valley Branch in the rugged mountains of north central Pennsylvania. In 1871 McCrea was promoted to principal assistant engineer in the construction department, headquartered in the PRR's general offices in Philadelphia. He married Ada Montgomery of that city, a union that eventually resulted in two sons and a daughter.

The Philadelphia homecoming marked the beginning of a rapid rise through a series of managerial positions of considerable responsibility. In 1875 he was appointed superintendent of the Middle Division, encompassing a segment of busy main line between Harrisburg and Altoona. In 1878 he became superintendent of the even more heavily traveled New York Division between New York City and Philadelphia. After four years in that post he was named general manager of the Southwest System of Pennsylvania Railroad Lines West, with offices in Columbus, Ohio.

The general manager's job gave new direction to McCrea's career. Lines West—or, more formally, the Pennsylvania Company—had been formed in 1871 as a separate PRR subsidiary to operate the Pittsburgh, Fort Wayne & Chicago, the Pittsburgh, Cincinnati & St. Louis (Panhandle), and all other PRR leased lines west of Pittsburgh; the Pennsylvania Railroad as a legal entity extended no farther west than Pittsburgh, Erie, and Buffalo. In 1885 McCrea was elevated to the position of general manager of Lines West. During the next twenty-one years he gained experience in operations, law, real estate, finance, and most other facets of the railroad industry. These years, too, witnessed a continuing series of promotions within the Lines West hierarchy: fourth vice president and general manager in 1887, second vice president and general manager in 1890, and first vice president and general manager in 1891. In this last position he was in effect the chief executive officer of the entire Lines West system. In 1899 he was elected to the PRR's board of directors.

Lines West, especially the Panhandle route between Pittsburgh and St. Louis, was traditionally held in low esteem by the PRR's senior officers. It had repeatedly swallowed large investments without producing commensurate returns; there were railroads in the Midwest whose long-term leases had been acquired by the PRR at great cost but which had never recorded a profit. McCrea began to reverse this situation by instituting more efficient methods of operation, adding new equipment, and showing increased sensitivity to shippers' needs. The Panhandle started to pay dividends for the first time in its history.

These achievements impressed the road's directors, and McCrea was elected to the Pennsylvania's presidency on January 2, 1907, a week after the unexpected death of President Alexander J. Cassatt. He thus became the only Lines West executive ever to hold that office. McCrea's candidacy had been

additionally enhanced by his early and continuing support of Cassatt's massive $100-million improvement program, which included the building of tunnels under the Hudson River and the magnificent new Pennsylvania Station in Manhattan, in spite of the dearth of projects in that program for Lines West. He also enjoyed the influential backing of an old friend, steel magnate Henry Clay Frick, who held a large amount of PRR stock and who was elected a director at the same time McCrea was named president.

Compared to his earlier career, McCrea's tenure as president was uneventful and anticlimactic. Cassatt's expensive improvements were nearly finished; McCrea did not wish to add greater strain to the company's finances and therefore did not undertake notable spending programs of his own. In any case, raising money proved difficult in the wake of the Panic of 1907; the railroad had to turn to the British bond market after finding few takers in America. McCrea preferred to save money rather than spend it. One of his more notable efforts in this regard was to institute policies of strict economy in the utilization of manpower and equipment on branch lines, whose operations systemwide he had long considered a source of inefficiency and waste. McCrea also oversaw badly needed simplification of the corporate structure, as large numbers of subsidiaries—including the Philadelphia & Erie, the Allegheny Valley, and the Bald Eagle Valley, to name a few of the largest—were absorbed by the parent road.

McCrea did not possess the personal dynamism of Cassatt or of the man who was to succeed him, Samuel Rea; he had an imperious manner and few close friends. Yet he commanded the respect of his associates and was a stickler for personal and corporate integrity, going so far as to prohibit shipping clerks from receiving Christmas presents from customers lest the gifts be seen as bribes. During the last years of his presidency he suffered from Bright's disease. Worsening health finally caused his resignation, effective December 31, 1912, and he died of kidney failure at his Narbeth, Pennsylvania home on March 28, 1913.

It would be unjust and unkind to describe McCrea as merely a placeholder in PRR corporate history. The most financially conservative president ever to head the Pennsylvania, he strove to make his administration a period of rejuvenation for the company, and in that he succeeded.

References:

George H. Burgess and Miles C. Kennedy, *Centennial History of the Pennsylvania Railroad* (Philadelphia: Pennsylvania Railroad, 1949);

"James McCrea," *Railway Age Gazette*, 53 (November 22, 1912): 992;

"James McCrea Named Pennsylvania Railroad President," *New York Times*, January 3, 1907, p. 1;

"Life and Career of James McCrea," *New York Times*, March 29, 1913, p. 5;

"*McCrea Is New Pennsylvania Railroad President,*" *Philadelphia Public Ledger*, January 3, 1907;

"McCrea Resigns as President of Pennsylvania Railroad, Samuel Rea to Succeed Him," *New York Times*, November 24, 1912, p. 1;

"Rea Succeeds McCrea as PRR President," *Philadelphia Public Ledger*, November 24, 1912, p. 1;

H. W. Schotter, *The Growth and Development of the Pennsylvania Railroad Company* (Philadelphia: Allen, Lane & Scott, 1927).

Archives:

No family papers of James McCrea appear to have been preserved. The extent of his business papers among Pennsylvania Railroad corporate documents is unknown, as those documents are located at several institutions and have not been catalogued.

Harold J. McKenzie

(October 11, 1904-   )

by Don L. Hofsommer

Augustana College

CAREER: Draftsman, construction inspector (1927-1936), chief draftsman (1936-1939), assistant to chief engineer, assistant chief engineer (1939-1945); chief engineer (1945-1950), Texas & New Orleans Railroad; executive vice president (1951), president (1951-1969), St. Louis Southwestern Railway; vice president, Southern Pacific Company (1967-1969).

Harold Jackson McKenzie was born on October 11, 1904, in Houston, Texas, to Philip Alexander and Alice Julia Hannon McKenzie. His father worked in the car shops of one of the predecessor lines of the Southern Pacific Company (SP). McKenzie's education included a B.S. degree from Texas A&M College, where he was an honor student and letterman on the track and rifle teams, and postgraduate work at the Houston Engineering College and the Harvard University School of Business Administration. He worked for the Texas & New Orleans Railroad (T&NO) during the summer of 1926 and gained permanent employment there a year later, starting as a draftsman. On December 22, 1929, he married Jewel Ina Gatlin; they had a son and a daughter. During McKenzie's years at the T&NO nothing loomed larger than the replace-

ment of the road's spectacular Pecos River bridge in West Texas, and McKenzie was made project engineer for that undertaking. His abilities soon came to the attention of executive officers at the Southern Pacific Company, parent of the T&NO, and in the summer of 1951 McKenzie was named president of the St. Louis Southwestern Railway (Cotton Belt), another SP subsidiary. McKenzie was an excellent choice for the Cotton Belt presidency. He had a fine sense of humor as well as a flair for working with people and getting them to "pull in harness." One subordinate explained his success in turning the Cotton Belt into a most admirable property: "McKenzie knew that he did not know everything. He was not ashamed to learn from anybody, anywhere. He consulted all persons involved, asked for their advice, pondered it, and then made his own decision."

McKenzie's line of command and marching orders were clearly stated; he was to answer only to the chairman of the Cotton Belt board of directors—A. T. Mercier and, after January 1, 1952, Donald J. Russell—and he was to do his utmost to streamline the Cotton Belt and maximize its profits. That process included combining, as quickly as possible, the St. Louis Southwestern Rail-

Harold J. McKenzie

way and the redundant St. Louis Southwestern Railway of Texas. On December 18, 1953, the Interstate Commerce Commission authorized the Cotton Belt to lease and operate all railroad properties of the Texas company, which ceased to exist as an operating property on March 1, 1954.

Since the Cotton Belt had only a small bonded indebtedness and a handsome surplus for dividends, McKenzie was in the enviable position of being able to pay cash for improvements such as Centralized Traffic Control, new rail, a fleet of modern rolling stock, and dieselization of the road's motive power. The improvements were quickly made.

With an excellent physical plant and new power and equipment for his railroad, McKenzie turned to the matter of industrial development. Attractive sites were purchased at North Little Rock, Arkansas; Texarkana, Waco, and Tyler, Texas; and Bossier City, Louisiana. Special attention was given Fort Worth and Dallas, where several valuable tracts were acquired. "We definitely need more indus-

tries to strengthen our company and we are going to do what is necessary to locate them on our line," McKenzie told the Cotton Belt's far-flung sales organization in 1955. He had reason to be concerned about on-line business: more than 60 percent of the Cotton Belt's traffic was overhead (picked up from one railroad to be turned over to another railroad) and there was a clear and steady erosion of certain traditional local traffic.

Even involvement with trailer-on-flatcar (TOFC or piggyback) operations reflected efforts to retain or recapture local business for the railroad. Begun on September 1, 1954, the Cotton Belt's piggyback operations served ramps at thirteen on-line locations. Service was extended through agreements with twenty-one other carriers in 1956, and during the following season the Cotton Belt and the SP joined with others to forge transcontinental TOFC service.

By the mid 1950s shippers acknowledged the Cotton Belt's growing reputation for dependable service, speed, and concentration on the needs of freight traffic. The road consequently increased its market share in its own territory and, in close cooperation with parent SP, in the highly competitive transcontinental business, too. By 1967 Cotton Belt speedsters aggregated nearly as many miles of "fifty mph or over" running as did much larger roads such as the Chicago, Burlington & Quincy and the Union Pacific. Its premier trains included the eastbound Colton Block, the westbound Motor Special, and the westbound Blue Streak Merchandise.

If the Cotton Belt was willing to go head—to—head with all comers in competition for freight traffic, it took quite another approach to its marginal passenger operations. The end came with little remark and no ceremony when the last passenger train completed its run between East St. Louis and Pine Bluff late in 1959.

McKenzie implicitly understood that work habits, levels of productivity, morale, and attitudes regarding safety are inextricably linked. Consequently, he was understandably elated when the SSW earned three gold and two lesser Harriman safety awards during the 1950s and 1960s. He was likewise pleased with news from the auditor's office. In the fifteen years following 1953 the Cotton Belt doubled the tonnage it carried and more than doubled its net income. Furthermore, it did so with only half the number of employees in 1968 that the company had required in 1954. The SSW's operating ratio reflected this reduction in labor force, averaging only 63.74 for the fifteen-year period. There was additional pleasant news: the Cotton Belt had provided a 6.63 percent rate of return on investment for 1954 but the rate stood at an impressive 12.11 percent in 1967.

The Cotton Belt had a policy of mandatory retirement for officers at age sixty-five. Russell, chairman of the Southern Pacific Company, asked him to stay on, but McKenzie felt that he should not be exempt from the rule. "The greatest loss to me," he said on his retirement in 1969, "will be the wonderful associations that I have had with Cotton Belt's fine people." People, after all—getting along with

them, and motivating them to their best effort—were McKenzie's long suit.

Publications:
"Mr. Mac": Keeping on the Right Track (Tyler, Texas: Privately printed, 1985);
The Little Railroad that Could, and Did!: The Cotton Belt (Tyler, Texas: Privately printed, 1986).

Reference:
Don L. Hofsommer, *The Southern Pacific, 1901-1905* (College Station: Texas A&M University Press, 1986).

Louis W. Menk

(April 8, 1918-)

by Robert L. Frey

Wilmington College of Ohio

CAREER: Telegraph messenger, Union Pacific Railroad (1936-1940); telegrapher (1940), train dispatcher (1941-1942), night chief train dispatcher (1943-1944), day chief train dispatcher (1945), assistant superintendent (1945-1949), terminal trainmaster (1949-1950), superintendent (1949-1953), assistant general manager, Western District (1954-1956), general manager (1956-1958), vice president, general manager (1958-1960), vice president, operations (1960-1962), chairman of the board and president (1962-1965), St. Louis-San Francisco Railway; chairman of the board and president, Chicago, Burlington & Quincy Railroad (1965-1966); president, Northern Pacific Railway (1966-1970); president (1970-1978), chairman of the board (1978-1981), Burlington Northern; chief executive officer, International Harvester (1982-1983).

Louis W. Menk was a major force in changing the philosophy of American railroading in the 1960s and 1970s. As competition from trucks, airplanes, and barges drove passenger trains off the rails and reduced the percentage of freight moving by rail to an all-time low in the early 1960s, execu-

tives like Menk formulated strategies to make railroads competitive again. The result was a recovery for most of the railroads willing to realize, as Menk insisted they should, that they were in the transportation and distribution business rather than in the railroad business.

Louis Wilson Menk was born in 1918 to Louis Albert and Daisy Frantz Menk in Englewood, Colorado, a suburb of Denver. His father was a railroad brakeman, and by the time Menk completed high school he had decided to go into the railroad business, too. His father was not enthusiastic about his son's choice of career and warned: "Wilson, I really don't think there's any future in railroading." There was a good reason for the elder Menk's concern: from the end of World War I to the depths of the Great Depression railroad positions had declined drastically. Menk did not heed his father's warning; he signed on as a messenger with the Union Pacific in 1936 for $51 a month.

Menk's ambition was to be a dispatcher, but he also had a desire to earn a college degree. While working for the Union Pacific he enrolled at the University of Denver. Sixty-hour work weeks and col-

Louis W. Menk (UPI)

lege coursework did not go together, so Menk made slow progress toward a degree. In 1940, after the worst unemployment problems of the depression had subsided, Menk was laid off from his job on the Union Pacific, but he was able to get a job as a telegrapher with the St. Louis-San Francisco Railway (Frisco) in Okmulgee, Oklahoma. It was the beginning of a quarter century of good experiences with the Frisco.

Over the next twenty years Menk held many positions with the operating department of the Frisco. He worked night shifts and moved frequently within Oklahoma, Missouri, Tennessee, Mississippi and Arkansas. While in Tulsa, Oklahoma, Menk restarted his college education at the University of Tulsa. Work assignments forced him to take one course at a time, and before he was able to finish the degree another job transfer had taken him too far from the university to continue his course work. While attending classes at Tulsa, Menk met

Martha Jane Swan; they were married on May 30, 1942, and eventually adopted two children.

Not being able to complete a college degree was a disappointment to Menk. He did not stop attempting to increase his knowledge and to improve his managerial skills, however. In 1953 he completed the advanced management program at the Harvard University School of Business, and in 1959 he took the general transportation course at Northwestern University. Eventually Menk received at least three honorary degrees from colleges and universities, including the University of Denver.

Another disappointment took place during World War II when Menk qualified for a commission in the army, only to be ordered back to the railroad by the War Manpower Commission because it was more difficult to get qualified railroad dispatchers than it was to recruit army officers. Despite these disappointments Menk was extremely proud of his rise through the corporate ranks. In a 1980 interview with *Nation's Business* he said: "I don't think too many future executives will come up through the ranks. I mean all the way. These are different times."

In 1960 Menk was named vice president of operations of the Frisco, a relatively high-level position for a person who was only forty-two. Two years later he became the youngest president of a major American railroad on the death of Clark Hungerford. As president of the Frisco, Menk perfected his management style. He was acutely interested in cost-cutting and during his three years as president earnings, revenues, and assets increased. Menk was also interested in overcoming the divisional separations which characterized the operations of almost all railroads; an integrated sales operation, for instance, was mandatory in Menk's mind. He was successful in creating a system-wide rather than a local or divisional view among Frisco executives. Finally, Menk was willing to accept the reality of railway labor unions. Rather than attempting to resist the brotherhoods, Menk used trade-offs and compromises to move toward his goals.

Because of his success on the Frisco, Menk became something of a "boy wonder" in the railroad management field. In 1965 the Chicago, Burlington & Quincy Railroad (CB&Q) elected Menk president to replace the popular Harry Murphy, who was retiring. The Burlington was one of the "flagship" American railroads. It had been a key acquisition of James J. Hill's Northern Pacific and Great Northern railways in 1901 and had operated as a part of the Hill system ever since. During many of the grim years of the Great Depression, when the Northern Pacific and the Great Northern failed to post a profit, it was the "Q" which kept the parent companies in the black. The presidency of the Burlington was a much more visible position on the American business scene than the presidency of the Frisco, and many insiders confidently predicted that Menk would not last a year on the Burlington. Actually, he did not: within a year he was elected president of the Northern Pacific Railway, thus giving him the distinction of being not only the youngest president of an American railroad but also the only one to be president of three railroads in 366 days.

Menk built a splendid performance record in his short stint on the Burlington—a record that gained national attention. In the first half of 1966 the Burlington had a 122 percent increase in earnings and a 7.9 percent increase in revenues. The changes that Menk made on the Burlington did not bring universal acclaim, however. In an effort to reduce inefficiency he laid off 1,200 employees and cut paperwork by the elimination of over 400 forms. Many employees who were not laid off were shifted from one location to another without much consideration for their feelings. Since Menk had quietly endured such location shifts, he did not see why others could not make similar moves.

One of Menk's policies was to run trains of maximum tonnage and move them as rapidly as possible. Careful studies were done of the tonnage on trains, and an effort was made to dispatch trains only when they were fully loaded. Over $6 million was spent on the development of a microwave system to speed the passage of trains and to regulate freight car movements more efficiently. Changes also took place in the management structure of the Burlington. Through retirements and the promotion of a whole group of middle- and upper-level managers Menk built an executive team that was extremely loyal to him because he had enabled them to rise more rapidly than they might otherwise have. When asked why he was so successful as a president of the "Q" Menk replied: "This railroad was just full of good people waiting for someone to say 'let's go.' I was that one and that's all I did." Menk was too modest. He came into the Burlington, a railroad which had experienced success in the 1930s

and had consciously decided to stay with the methods that helped achieve that success, and changed its image and some of its operations. It is true that the Burlington had many good people who were perhaps not utilized effectively under previous management, and it is true that Menk "turned these people loose," but Menk's cost consciousness, his willingness to employ new technologies, and his new philosophy of railroading left an imprint on the Burlington much deeper than his one-year presidency might suggest.

Menk's layoffs and efforts to reduce paperwork were examples of his cost consciousness, as were his efforts to maximize tonnage on freight trains and to reduce money-losing passenger trains. His leasing of an IBM 360 computer, the installation of a microwave system, and the heretical step of buying a turboprop airplane to allow him to move around the system more rapidly were examples of his willingness to use new technologies. And his effort at developing new marketing strategies was the best example of his philosophy of railroading. A new advertising agency was hired soon after Menk's arrival at Burlington headquarters. Probably the most striking advertisement was one which said: "Lou Menk says the Burlington should get out of the railroad business. Who does he think he is? He's the Number One wheel on the Burlington." The ad went on to quote Menk: "We're not in the railroad business, we're in the distribution business." One of the lessons Menk learned at Harvard and Northwestern was that any organization must know what business it is really in, and he believed that the traditional concept of the railroad business was too narrow. The Burlington was supposed to take a product from a producer to a consumer. Whether it did so by rail, by air, or by skateboard did not matter; the point was to get the product there as quickly, as inexpensively, and as safely as possible. This philosophy dominated Burlington advertisements. Menk wanted it to dominate upper-level management ranks, too, but he did not have time to complete the transition in his year as president of the company.

As president of the Northern Pacific, Menk introduced some of the same changes that he had made on the Burlington. Emphasis was placed on operating freight trains at maximum tonnage, and unmanned mid-train diesel helpers were introduced to move the heavier loads. The mid-train units were controlled by the head-end crew through radio signals. The railroad unions opposed this operation because it reduced the need for locomotive crews, and several minor accidents with the units gave the unions ammunition for their opposition to the system. Eventually, more powerful locomotives reduced some of the need for mid-train helpers, but the need for locomotive crews declined as well. A general reduction of employees was experienced on the Northern Pacific as it had been on the Burlington. Total labor costs increased, however, as Menk was not opposed to higher salaries for employees who were putting in a full day's work.

Menk had not been favorably disposed to passenger trains while on the Frisco or the Burlington, although the Burlington did have several long-distance passenger trains which were reasonable money makers and also had heavy commuter traffic into Chicago. The Northern Pacific did not have a similar passenger train situation. Menk chafed extensively about the Northern Pacific's passenger liabilities. He suggested that like the stagecoach, the long-distance passenger train had seen its time and should be allowed to die with dignity. In the Annual Report for 1968 he said: "Northern Pacific's direct losses on passenger train operations in 1968 exceeded $5 million. It is inconceivable that railroads should be required by law to carry the continuing burden of increasing losses." He continued: "Proposed legislation to provide a subsidy to reimburse the railroads for losses incurred by passenger trains considered necessary by the government will be presented to Congress." Such legislation resulted in the creation of Amtrak. To speed up the process Menk reportedly had observation cars removed from trains and reduced services such as washing car windows. There were even reports that the Northern Pacific was deliberately directing passenger inquiries to the Great Northern. The elimination of mail subsidies allowed the company to drop the Mainstreeter, one of its two long-distance passenger trains, but the other, the North Coast Limited, was forced to continue operations until it was taken over by Amtrak in 1970.

The major task facing Menk was the completion of the long-sought merger between the Northern Pacific, the Great Northern, and the Burlington. Since his early days on the Frisco, Menk had been an advocate of combining railroads into larger and more economical units, and he enthusiastically threw himself into the merger efforts. Shortly before Menk's arrival the Interstate Commerce Commission (ICC), in a surprise decision, had blocked the merger of the three railroads plus the Spokane, Portland & Seattle. Menk reviewed the merger proceedings and concluded that opposition from the Milwaukee Road and the unions had not been met with any significant compromise on the part of the merger advocates.

It did not take Menk and his fellow presidents long to work out some concessions and refile for merger before the ICC. The revised plan attempted to meet the Milwaukee Road's concerns by granting it increased trackage rights over certain parts of the combined system and by agreeing to be more flexible on rate and traffic arrangements. To meet union objections the revised plan promised that labor force reductions would be via attrition only. With "fences mended," the renewed merger proposal gained the support of the ICC on November 30, 1967. The original cumbersome name for the new system, The Great Northern Pacific and Burlington Lines, was simplified to Burlington Northern and plans were made for the final merger to occur on May 10, 1968. But at the last minute the Chief Justice of the United States Supreme Court, acting on appeal from the Justice Department, blocked the merger. The Justice Department claimed that the ICC had not adequately contemplated the monopolistic nature of the merger.

Two more years of deliberation were required before the Court rendered a verdict in favor of the merger, and on March 2, 1970, the merger took place. In retrospect the two additional years the Supreme Court gave the four railroads could be seen to have been extremely important in the success of the merger. In 1968, although much planning for the merger had taken place, much had not been accomplished. In the area of motive power, for example, little or no progress had been made on agreements on parts nomenclature, maintenance schedules, lubrication techniques, and traffic communication procedures. Operating department procedures had not been refined, freight train routings were unclear, and yard clerks had not been adequately trained on the new routings. Several weeks before the 1968 merger date lists of new officers had been circulated, and it had become common knowledge that Menk would be president of the merged company. Consequently, during the two years that it took the Supreme Court to render its decision, Menk and the new department heads had taken a more aggressive approach to preparing for the merger than had been the case prior to 1968, when it was not clear who the officers of the new company would be.

By the time the merger took place a good deal of attention was focused on the Burlington Northern. In June 1970 the Penn Central system collapsed. Suddenly the health of the Burlington Northern was extremely critical. Would it go in the same direction as the Penn Central? If it did, the future of railroad mergers might be altered drastically. In this crucial period presidential leadership was critical, and Menk's performance was outstanding. Problems were met with an unusual amount of cooperation and loyalty to the new Burlington Northern rather than retained loyalties to the predecessor roads. The Penn Central merger had been fraught with rivalries between the New York Central executives (the "green hats") and the former Pennsylvania executives (the "red hats"). A similar struggle did not take place on the Burlington Northern. Furthermore, the Burlington Northern had a new source of traffic—coal—and had longer hauls and less terminal congestion than the Penn Central.

By the time Menk became chairman of the board of the Burlington Northern in 1978 it was clear that the merger was a resounding success. The company had revenues of $2.53 billion compared to $1.1 billion in 1970. New branches had been constructed to tap coal mines and unit trains of 10,000 tons or more hauled coal from mines in Wyoming to generating plants in Illinois and Indiana. Coal traffic had increased from 20 million tons in 1970 to 63 million tons in 1978, making the Burlington Northern the number one coal hauler in the nation and eclipsing such coal-hauling giants as the Chesapeake & Ohio and the Norfolk & Western. The Burlington Northern was also the number one hauler of grain, a commodity which had traditionally been a staple of the Northern Pacific, the Great Northern and the Burlington Northern. The motive power fleet was one of the most modern in the nation, and the rolling stock matched the locomotives. Modernized classification yards, high quality track and roadbed, computerized freight car distribution, and aggressive and innovative marketing and sales techniques all paid off in higher revenues. Finally, Menk was instrumental in laying the ground-

work for the merger of the Frisco into the Burlington Northern in 1980.

Throughout his career as a top-level executive, government regulation was a constant concern of Menk's. After one glowing report on the performance of the Burlington Northern he commented: "Railroads could do even better if the government would only let us manage. This industry has gotten whacked by government, by labor, and by just about everybody." He was quoted in a news magazine as saying: "I'm not opposed to regulation. We have to have it in our business because we are, in effect, a public utility." He then went on to argue that the ICC ought to be an advocate for all transportation or it ought to regulate all forms of transportation equally. The ICC drew his criticism on many occasions primarily because of what Menk perceived to be inconsistencies in its decisions. He advocated a smaller commission of about five people drawn from a panel of transportation experts.

When Menk became chairman of the board he moved his office to Billings, Montana, in order to be "out of the way" of the new president. Perhaps another reason for his move was to be closer to his 7,000-acre J-L Ranch near Musselshell, Montana. In 1981 Menk stepped down from his involvement in the Burlington Northern—except as a director from 1982-1986—and retired to his home in Carefree, Arizona, near Phoenix. But retirement did not prove satisfying to Menk, who once said: "I'm one of those people who likes to have a lot of things going on all at once." Thus he surprised the business world in 1982 by accepting appointment as chief executive officer of the International Harvester Company, where he had been a director since 1974. *Business Week* was puzzled as to why the troubled company would choose a retired executive for such a demanding position. Clearly, the board of International Harvester did not believe that Menk's management skills were restricted to railroading nor did it believe that Menk was devoid of the new ideas *Business Week* suggested the company needed. Menk retired from the position in 1983.

Many honors came to Menk during his career. He was named Railroad Man of the Year, A Railroader's Railroader, and Chief Executive Officer of the Year. He received the Seley Award for Outstanding Service to Transportation and the Horatio Alger Award given by the American Schools and Colleges Association. On being given the latter award

Menk was called "living proof that the free enterprise system still offers equal opportunity for all." Menk had a major impact on the American railroad scene for twenty years. In his willingness to try new approaches, his emphasis on the central mission of railroads, and, above all, his wise and innovative management of the Burlington Northern in its first years, he did as much as any other individual to gain public approval of the merger movement in the railroad industry.

References:
"Ailing Harvester Turns to New Doctors," *Business Week* (May 17, 1982): 35;
Wilbur Martin, "For Lou Menk Railroading Has Been a Lifetime Trip," *Nation's Business,* 68 (January 1980): 46-50.

Archives:
Currently there is no collection of Louis W. Menk's papers other than those which are part of the corporate records of the Frisco, the Burlington, the Northern Pacific, and the Burlington Northern.

Microwave Communications

Modern railroads require reliable and abundant communication resources to assure safe and efficient operation. In the past much of a railroad's communication was transmitted by telegraph and telephone circuits installed on telephone poles along the right-of-way. This method of information transfer has limited capacity, is vulnerable to destruction throughout the entire route, and is labor intensive to maintain.

In the early 1960s railroads began installing microwave radio transmission systems which have much greater capacity and higher quality and are less labor intensive than open-wire facilities. Microwave is not vulnerable to destruction throughout its route and is not generally susceptible to adverse weather conditions.

The microwave radio system, which is defined as radio communication using frequencies above one gigahertz, consists of radio transmitters and receivers capable of being modulated by numerous voice channels (12 to 600 in railroad use) simultaneously. This system is frequency modulated by multiplexed single sideband voice channels.

Microwave radio propagation can in many ways be compared to light. The transmission path must be line-of-sight (the transmitting antenna must be able to "see" the receiving antenna) to provide reliable operation over long periods of time. The transmission path distance is normally about thirty miles but is dependent on the terrain between the two sta-

tions. Because of this short transmission path microwave communication networks comprise major terminals with numerous repeater stations between the terminals.

Reliability is extremely important to the railroad communication network as an extended break in communications usually stops train traffic. Railroad microwave networks typically provide a service reliability of 99.9 percent. Redundancy is engineered into the major office equipment, microwave transmission equipment, battery power systems, and antenna systems.

The traffic on a railroad microwave network commonly includes telephone circuits between business offices, VHF radios to provide communication between dispatchers and trains, Centralized Traffic Control (CTC) to operate the signal lamps and switches along the track, data to connect remote terminals to a central computer, and high-speed data to connect computer centers together for the transfer of car and train location information.

Most of the major railroads in the United States have completed their primary microwave networks and are now expanding with lower-density systems to add microwave to the smaller remote locations, thereby eliminating additional open-wire and leased facilities.

In the future, microwave will handle additional circuits to improve voice and telemetry communication to trains, teleconferencing, closed circuit television, and expanded data transmission networks. Some railroads will also use fiber optic transmission systems to supplement their microwave networks, providing additional circuit capacity and

alternative routes for vital circuits in case of catastrophic failure in either transmission system.

—*Roger L. Sullivan*

E. Spencer Miller

(April 23, 1908-   )

by George H. Merriam

Fitchburg State College

E. Spencer Miller in 1952 (Photo by Fabian Bachrach; courtesy Kalmbach Publishing Company)

CAREER: Private law practice, Lowell, Massachusetts (1934-1937); commerce counsel, Boston & Maine Railroad (1937-1940); general attorney (1940-1946), general counsel (1946-1947), first vice president (1947-1952), president (1952-1977), chairman, board of directors (1968-1980), Maine Central Railroad.

E. Spencer Miller, president of the Maine Central Railroad for twenty-five years, was one of the few successful presidents of post-World War II railroad lines in the northeastern United States. During his term in office he ended a thirty-year-old cooperative arrangement under which the Maine Central was managed by the Boston & Maine Railroad (B&M) and brought the Maine Central to complete and profitable independence.

Edward Spencer Miller was born in Springfield, Vermont, in 1908 to Edward Whitney and Grace Agnes Spencer Miller and graduated Phi Beta Kappa from Dartmouth College in 1931. He graduated from Harvard Law School and was admitted to the Massachusetts bar in 1934, the Maine bar in 1940, and the United States Supreme Court bar in 1946. Miller practiced law in Lowell, Massachusetts, from 1934 until 1937, when he joined the Boston & Maine as commerce counsel.

In 1940 he moved to the Maine Central as general attorney. He worked under Edward S. French, for twenty years president of both the Maine Central and the B&M. Miller became the Maine Central's general counsel in 1946 and first vice president in 1947. When French retired from the dual presidency in 1952, Miller became president of the Maine Central.

He ended the cooperative agreement with the B&M within a year. He also faced the task of refunding (refinancing through the issuance of new bonds) over $19 million in maturing bonded debt. Miller's success maintained the Maine Central's unbroken record of meeting its financial obligations. During the early years of his presidency he quickly reduced the burden of fixed charges by buying the remaining leased lines from which the 1,000-mile Maine Central had been built in the previous century. Purchase of the St. Johnsbury & Lake Champlain Railroad and the European & North American Railway at the end of 1955 meant that the Maine Central fully owned almost all of its trackage.

Miller led eastern railroads in the shift to diesel power with complete dieselization of the Maine Central passenger and freight services by 1955. On June 13, 1954, he drove locomotive 470 as it pulled the Maine Central's final steam passenger train, which was met by crowds all along the line.

Between 1955 and 1960 Miller went through the most painful experience of his presidency as he worked to discontinue the Maine Central's passenger service, which lost more than $20 million from 1945 to 1960. In a series of petitions, public hearings, and gradual reductions service was eliminated on the branches by April 1958. After a final series of petitions and public hearings and an appeal to the Maine Supreme Court, the last regularly scheduled passenger run on the Maine Central ended in Portland on September 6, 1960.

Part of Miller's thrust to preserve solvency involved a drive to obtain more freight traffic by improving service to existing shippers (particularly Maine's pulp and paper industry) while attracting new industry along the railroad's right-of-way. This work was carried out in the face of rampant competition from both large regulated trucking companies and individual "gipsy" truckers.

Miller recognized the importance of maintaining and improving track and equipment. He toured the entire system periodically in the Maine Central's business car, frequently stopping to meet with as many of the over 2,000 employees as possible and visiting with shippers over lunch or dinner in the car.

From 1969 through 1977 Miller repulsed Frederic C. Dumaine's attempts to merge the Maine Central with the Bangor & Aroostook Railroad, which was 99 percent owned by Dumaine's Amoskeag holding company. Miller's victory came in part from Interstate Commerce Commission (ICC) orders to the Bangor & Aroostook to stop diverting traffic from the Maine Central to the Canadian Pacific and ICC restraints preventing Amoskeag from voting its 35 percent of Maine Central stock.

In his final year in office Miller arranged the refinancing of $12 million of the railroad's bonded debt which would mature in 1978 and 1980. In 1977 railroad credit nationally was extremely poor, yet confidence in the Maine Central was such that three large insurance companies, several Maine banks, and a college joined in the refinancing.

Miller was courtly, tall, erect, and spare. Married since 1938 to the former Juanita Fownes and with three grown children, Miller was a thirty-third degree Mason and a former member of Kora Shrine in Lewiston, Maine. In 1952 Miller took the Maine Central's Miniature Train—a complete little train mounted on rubber tires with engine, boxcar, and caboose—to New York for the Shriners' Fifth Avenue parade.

Miller represented New England on the board of the Railway Express Agency from 1952 until that company was sold by the railroads. He served many terms as director of the Association of American Railroads and several terms representing the East on the executive committee of the National Railway Labor Conference. He led the formation of the Eastern Railroad Association, acting as chairman and chief executive officer for many years.

Miller wrote extensively on railroad matters, both editorials and short articles for the *Maine Central Messenger* (the railroad's in-house publication) and occasional pieces for Maine newspapers. He wrote a fifty-page history of his years in office for the North American Newcomen Society. In a 1972 article aimed at a national audience he attacked the continuing national railroad crisis. His solution was a consolidation of all American railroads into a single, privately owned American Railroad Corporation. He discussed this proposal in a "Today Show" interview in September 1972. In 1974 he won the national award of the Association of Railroad Editors "for Excellence in the use of Opinion Articles and Editorials."

A Maine weekly in 1973 described Miller as "an unabashed American prototype—a pure, unblemished industrial capitalist." He retired from the presidency of Maine Central Railroad in 1977, leaving it well equipped, well maintained, and profitable. He remained chairman of the board of directors—a position he had held since 1968—until 1980.

Publications:

"A Prescription for Railroad Recovery: How about Running All as One Big Company?," *New York Times*, September 10, 1972, III: 17;

Maine Central Railroad, 1940-1978 (Princeton: Princeton University Press, 1979).

References:

Robert E. Bedingfield, "The Spence and Bucky Show," *New York Times*, October 9, 1977, III: 3, 13;

Frederic C. Dumaine, Letter criticizing Miller's article in September 10 *New York Times, New York Times*, September 17, 1972, III: 9;

E. Spencer Miller: An American Prototype (Portland, Maine: Maine Central Railroad, 1977);

"E. Spencer Miller Retires," *Maine Central Messenger* (Winter 1978): 3-7;

"John F. Gerity Succeeds Miller as President of Maine Central," *New York Times*, December 6, 1977, p. 61;

"Maine Central Head on Aroostook Board," *New York Times*, September 16, 1971, p. 69;

"Maine Central Plans to Continue Its Fight," *New York Times*, December 10, 1977, p. 37;

"Miller Director Assn. American Railroads," *New York Times*, November 17, 1962, p. 35;

"Miller Elected Chief Executive Officer and Chairman of Board," *New York Times*, June 27, 1968, p. 67.

Minneapolis & St. Louis Railroad

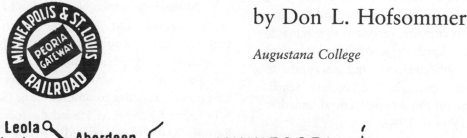

by Don L. Hofsommer

Augustana College

Map of the Minneapolis & St. Louis Railroad (1930)

The Minneapolis & St. Louis Railway (M&StL) was organized in 1870 to provide Minneapolis—especially its milling interests—with a rail service to the South, West, and East. By the end of 1882 the M&StL had completed one line to Angus, a bustling community in a coal-producing region of central Iowa, and another westward through grain-producing country to Watertown, Dakota Territory. Under the leadership of Edwin Hawley, who became president of the M&StL in 1896, additional construction and acquisition extended the road in Minnesota, South Dakota, and Iowa. In 1912 the M&StL acquired the Iowa Central Railway, with which it connected at Albert Lea, Minnesota. With the addition of the Iowa Central's trackage, the M&StL's line linking Minneapolis with Peoria, Illinois, became the railroad's mainline.

The M&StL was the archetypical Granger road, and, as such, frequently suffered the financial reversals of its four-state agricultural service area. The M&StL slumped into receivership in 1923, was placed on the auction block forty-two times before a bidder appeared, and was threatened by dismemberment during the mid 1930s. Survival and even prosperity were assured, however, by traffic resulting from World War II and by the managerial talents of its receiver, Lucian C. Sprague.

Under Sprague's leadership the property was improved, and on December 1, 1943, the road was returned to its owners as the Minneapolis & St. Louis Rail*road*. The M&StL earned plaudits for reliable freight service—especially from the performance of its famous trains 19 and 20, boasting first-class timetable status on the 490-mile route between Minneapolis and Peoria—and for its lack of bonded indebtedness, all of which made it a likely target for a corporate raider. After a bitter fight, in 1954 stock control and thus management passed to a group headed by Ben W. Heineman that in 1960 engineered the sale of the M&StL's assets to the larger Chicago & North Western.

References:

Frank P. Donovan, *Mileposts on the Prairie: The Story of the Minneapolis & St. Louis Railway* (New York: Simmons-Broadman, 1950);

Donovan L. Hofsommer, "A History of the Iowa Central Railway," M.A. thesis, University of Northern Iowa, 1966.

Missouri-Kansas-Texas Railroad

by Don L. Hofsommer

Augustana College

Map of the Missouri-Kansas-Texas Railroad (1983)

The Missouri, Kansas & Texas Railway (Katy) was formed in 1870 as the successor to the Union Pacific Southern Branch, which had been incorporated in 1865 and was not related to the Union Pacific Railroad. In 1870 the Katy became the first railroad to enter Indian Territory (now Oklahoma) and, two years later, the first to enter Texas from the north. The Katy connected with the Houston & Texas Central at Denison, Texas, to open a vast territory from Kansas City and St. Louis in the country's heartland to the Gulf. The new road was the dream

of Judge Levi Parsons and was constructed under the watchful eye of Robert Smith Stevens. A large federal land grant was promised but not delivered, and the Katy fell victim to the Panic of 1873. Jay Gould then came to control the road, expanded it, and melded it with another of his holdings, the Missouri Pacific.

The Gould influence and the relationship with the Missouri Pacific ended in 1888. After a period of uncertainty, the road experienced another period of consolidation and growth early in the twentieth century. By 1915 the Katy was nearly 4,000 miles in length, with a main route from St. Louis and Kansas City to Fort Worth, Dallas, San Antonio, and Houston, and with numerous secondary routes and branches. It was too much growth; interest charges were impossible to meet, and bankruptcy followed again. A trimmer and reorganized Katy, renamed the Missouri-Kansas-Texas Railroad, emerged in 1923; but the hard times of the 1930s followed, and while the company avoided receivership, it probably should have again resorted to the courts. Profits were constant during the hectic years of World War II, and the booming postwar economy implied long-term prosperity; but the Katy suffered from a burdensome capital structure and inadequately maintained and underdeveloped fixed property and equipment. Poor service and retrenchment during the presidencies of Donald Fraser and William Neal Deramus III in the late 1950s and early 1960s cost the company its reputation and many valued customers. Under John W. Barriger III, who served as president from 1965 to 1970, massive abandonments and rehabilitation of remaining properties were undertaken, service levels were restored, and confidence grew. The railroad assets passed to Katy Industries, formed in 1967, and profitability was restored in 1971. Management's search for a merger partner, however, has yet to be rewarded.

References:
Donovan L. Hofsommer, *Katy Northwestern: The Story of a Branch Line Railroad* (Boulder, Col.: Pruett, 1976);
Vincent V. Masterson, *The Katy Railroad and the Last Frontier* (Norman: University of Oklahoma Press, 1952).

Missouri Pacific Railroad

by Craig Miner

Wichita State University

Map of the Missouri Pacific Railroad (1983)

The Missouri Pacific Railroad (MP or MoPac) is one company which deserves the appellation "venerable." Its home base, St. Louis, may have fallen behind Chicago later in the race for a rail network, but the Pacific Railroad, which was reorganized as the Missouri Pacific Railway in 1876, broke ground in 1851 with the transcontinental rhetoric

of Thomas Hart Benton in its founders' ears and the reports of John C. Frémont in their satchels. Its proposed route straight across the Rockies was the least practical of the transcontinental possibilities, and even the second-choice thirty-fifth-parallel route, which the Missouri Pacific tried by leasing the Atlantic & Pacific in the 1870s, was never completed as a continuous line. Still, the MP retained into the twentieth century the aura of a Western pioneer which somehow had miraculously survived into a high-tech age. This reputation turned out to be both an advantage and a disadvantage.

During the initial years of the twentieth century the Missouri Pacific could to some degree rest on its nineteenth-century strengths, which were based not only on its early entry into the field and its connection of the St. Louis hub with the Gulf markets but also on its having been the center of Jay Gould's network and the locus of his considerable managerial ability between 1879 and 1892. Gould's reputation as a "wrecker," if it applied anywhere, did not seem to hold for his "pet" Missouri Pacific. In 1917 the Missouri Pacific Railway and the St. Louis & Iron Mountain were consolidated as the Missouri Pacific Railroad.

In the 1920s the MP was enough of a prize to attract the ambitious Van Sweringen brothers, Oris Paxton and Mantis James, who had risen from modest beginnings in Ohio to control one of the largest rail empires in the United States. The Van

Sweringens formed the Alleghany Corporation in 1929 as a holding company for their diverse purchases, and the next year bought a controlling interest in the MP for $100 million. In the Great Depression the brothers lost control of the MP, then gained it back, only to lose it again through the bankruptcy of the company.

In 1933 the Missouri Pacific was the first major railroad to file under Section 77 of the Bankruptcy Act, and in 1956 it was the last to emerge from the Depression-era rail receiverships. In 1937 a syndicate of Frank Kolbe, Allan Kirby, and Robert Young purchased the Alleghany Corporation and its large block of MP common stock. Kirby and Young insisted that the MP common stock not be wiped out in the reorganization, as was standard procedure in such cases. Partly because of the length of its time with the receivers and partly because of the acrimonious and highly publicized struggles over who was to control the company if and when it did emerge as independent, the MP's reputation by 1956 was as much connected with the slightly disreputable doings of attorneys and bondholders of the 1930s as it was with the fading memory of its Gilded Age glories. Concluded one politician along the way: "It is a very trying picture for the public in general for a great railroad concern to be in receivership 17 years [eventually twenty-three]. People live, die and pass out and don't know whether they have an estate or not. . . . It is tragic. Don't you see that people are completely disgusted with the *modus operandi* of the receivership?"

In fact, the holders of common stock did get something out of the reorganization in the form of an issue of "B" stock, which was to cause the railroad internal and strategic problems for the next twenty years. The "A" stock controlled MP management and took any dividends up to $5, but the claim was that the "B" stock had true control of the equity. Certainly the "B" holders had to agree to any changes in the capitalization or stock distribution, such as would be required in a merger by stock exchange. Alleghany officers were not willing to allow the "B" interests, theoretical as they might seem in the early years of low profits, to be "frozen out" without adequate compensation in a merger exchange; to do so would be to make their 1930s fight meaningless. Therefore, the MP entered the era of mergers in the 1960s somewhat crippled in its flexibility.

That lack of flexibility however, did not stop a remarkable physical revitalization of the Missouri Pacific under the financial management of William Marbury and the operating management of Downing Jenks. Marbury's Mississippi River Fuel Company gained control of the "A" stock in the early 1960s and Marbury became MP chairman. He hired Jenks as president and gave him free rein to make a modern and efficient railway out of the MP.

A start had been made in the late 1950s with the installation of computer-controlled classification yards at North Little Rock and Kansas City and introduction of computers in the accounting department at the railroad's offices in St. Louis. Under Jenks's management, however, the modernization went faster and further. Jenks standardized yard offices and repair facilities all over the system, reduced the bad-order ratio (the percentage of cars needing repairs) dramatically, promoted piggybacking and containerization as a first step to making the railroad an integrated transportation system, eliminated passenger service, and pursued the creation and implementation of the Transportation Control System, one of the pioneer computer control systems in American railroading.

In addition to instituting operating and physical improvements, Marbury and Jenks recruited managerial talent more actively than ever and revamped the MP's training program. Railroading was no longer viewed as a "special" occupation, where it was necessary to start in the yards and work up to the executive suite, but as a thriving modern business which had to compete with other businesses for the best people by providing incentives and opportunities.

Despite the handicap of the stock problem, the MP expanded from 10,000 to 12,000 miles in the 1960s, primarily through the absorption of the Texas & Pacific and the purchase of part of the Chicago & Eastern Illinois. There were also several dramatic corporate simplifications that, in a way that paralleled the elimination of old equipment or outmoded buildings, eliminated the hundreds of separate subsidiaries left over from the MP's long history.

Marbury and Jenks wanted to ally the MP with one of the five or six Western rail systems that they saw dominating a deregulated, lean railway industry future. There was a serious attempt by the MP to dominate the Atchison, Topeka & Santa Fe through stock ownership, which, had it succeeded, would have been more remarkable than the fact that a small pipeline company controlled the MP itself. Talks were held in the 1960s with the Union Pacific, which was to be the eventual partner of the Missouri Pacific. The "B" stock was finally bought back in 1974 at a cost of $200 million.

Despite the revitalization and recapitalization and despite Jenks's continued speechmaking on the desirability of a few large Western rail systems, the announcement in 1980 that the Missouri Pacific, the Union Pacific, and the Western Pacific had agreed on a merger came as a surprise to the financial press. There were some objections that the creation of the new 22,000-mile system was an unacceptable alliance of the strong with the strong, but the merger proposal was quickly approved by the Interstate Commerce Commission. The atmosphere of deregulation was exactly right to bring the dream plans to realization. Late in 1981 approval of the new system was complete, and for the first time in over 130 years there was no independent Missouri Pacific Railroad.

Observers admired the way the Missouri Pacific management had adapted an old company to the mid twentieth century. "Missouri Pacific has the best management group I know of," wrote one analyst. "It is the only company I know about where I don't know of any strategic or tactical mistakes." The most compact statement of the railroad's management philosophy was made by MP president James Gessner in 1975: "I don't believe we can any longer afford the traditional ways and traditional thinking that pervade our industry. Railroading today possesses little or no mystique. It is not an art based upon personal genius or intuition. Railroading is first a business. . . . All of us have a choice. We can fight change and cling to the traditional methods of performing our function. Or, we can welcome change as an opportunity to develop a railroad system the like of which has never been experienced in our industrial society."

References:

Robert E. Caudle, *History of the Missouri Pacific Lines, Gulf Coast Lines and Subsidiaries, International-Great Northern* (Houston: Published by the author, 1949);

Joe G. Collias, *Mopac Power* (LaJolla, Cal.: Howell North, 1980);

John L. Kerr, *The Story of a Western Pioneer . . . the Missouri Pacific: An Outline History* (New York: Railway Research Society, 1928);

Craig Miner, *The Rebirth of the Missouri Pacific, 1956–1983* (College Station: Texas A&M University Press, 1983).

Monon Route

by George W. Hilton

University of California, Los Angeles

Map of the Chicago, Indianapolis & Louisville Railway (Monon Route) (1930)

The Name "Monon Route" encompassed several corporate entities of a railroad between Chicago and Louisville. It was one of several rail connections between Chicago and the Ohio River crossings but the longest and most difficult to operate. The name, first used in 1882, stemmed from the railroad's unusual geographical pattern of an X across western and central Indiana, with the crossing at the country town of Monon (which had been

known as Bradford until 1879). The two lines in the X-pattern were built separately and for disparate purposes.

The north-south line had its origins in the New Albany & Salem Rail Road, founded by James Brooks in 1847 and completed from New Albany to Michigan City in 1854. Brooks believed that railroads would never be able to compete in cost with steamboats and conceived of his railroad mainly as a means of conveying agricultural products to steamers on the Ohio River at New Albany and on Lake Michigan at Michigan City. Between New Albany and Salem he made use of an existing highway grade acquired from the state. The line entailed street-running (tracks running down the middle of streets) in Bedford and Lafayette and was otherwise built to the primitive standards of the time. The railroad failed in 1858 and was reorganized in 1873 as The Louisville, New Albany & Chicago Railway (LNA&C).

The other major element in the railroad's X-pattern was promoted immediately after the Civil War as the Indianapolis, Delphi & Chicago Railway and completed as the Chicago & Indianapolis Air Line Railway in 1882. The Air Line was obviously attractive to the LNA&C, as it promised entries into both Chicago and Indianapolis with the shortest rail connection between the two. The LNA&C acquired the Air Line in 1881 for merger into itself in 1883. The extension entailed satisfactory terminal arrangements on the Chicago & Western Indiana Railroad and the Belt Railway of Chicago, but termination on the Indianapolis Union Railway was expensive and almost devoid of freight traffic potential. After the LNA&C acquired an entry into Louisville in 1882, the main line became Louisville-New Albany-Monon-Chicago, and the Michigan City and Indianapolis lines were reduced to branches of diminishing significance. The main line served a series of college towns which, like Indianapolis, generated substantial passenger traffic but little freight.

To deal with its limited freight origination potential, the railroad's management in the 1880s sought to penetrate the coalfield of eastern Kentucky by a series of leases and guaranties of bonds of three smaller railroads. But at the shareholders' meeting of March 12, 1890, a New Albany banker and physician, Dr. William L. Breyfogle, unseated the management and aborted the incursion. After an adverse decision concerning the validity of the bond guaranties, the LNA&C, which had been profitable, declared bankruptcy. It was reorganized in 1897 as the Chicago, Indianapolis & Louisville Railway (CI&L). The railroad was necessarily highly dependent on its southern connections, the Louisville & Nashville (L&N) and the Southern Railway, and in 1902 came into their hands through joint stock ownership. The two larger railroads were interested mainly in covering the interest on the debt incurred in acquisition of the CI&L, and neither particularly favored the line relative to other routes to Chicago. Fairfax Harrison served as president of the CI&L from 1910 until he became president of the Southern in 1913.

The CI&L stagnated in the 1920s and went bankrupt in 1933. It was reorganized without change of name in 1946, ending the control by the Southern and L&N, with John W. Barriger III as its president. Barriger dieselized the property, re-equipped the passenger trains, bypassed a bog on the main line near Cedar Lake, and replaced the bridge over the Wabash River on the Indianapolis branch. He was unable to finance more extensive improvements and resigned at the end of 1952. His successor, Warren W. Brown, changed the name to Monon Railroad in 1956. Passenger service to Indianapolis was dropped in 1959, and to Louisville in 1967.

The railroad attempted to build facilities for movement of coal from barges on the Ohio River to bulk freighters at Michigan City but was rebuffed by the Interstate Commerce Commission in 1965. The management saw no further prospect of continuing as an independent railroad, and the L&N absorbed the Monon on July 31, 1971. In 1983 the L&N was itself absorbed by the Seaboard System Railroad, a subsidiary of CSX Corporation. The Michigan City and Indianapolis branches were truncated, but the Monon's main line remained in service in 1987 in the network of the CSX Corporation.

References:

Frank F. Hargrave, *A Pioneer Indiana Railroad* (Indianapolis: Burford Printing Co., 1932);

George W. Hilton, *Monon Route* (Berkeley: Howell-North, 1978);

Leland S. VanScoyoc, "Men, Bonds and the Monon," *Register of the Kentucky Historical Society*, 15 (1961): 197–216.

William H. Moore

(October 25, 1848-January 11, 1923)

by Albro Martin

Bradley University

William H. Moore (Photo by Fabian Bachrach; courtesy Kalmbach Publishing Company)

CAREER: Law clerk in firm of Edward A. Small (1872-1874); partner, Small, Burke & Moore, (1874-1882); senior partner, Moore & Moore, (1882-1916); officer or director, Diamond Match Company (1889-1896), New York Biscuit Company (1890-1898), National Biscuit Company (1898), American Tin Plate Company (1899), National Steel Company (1899), American Steel Hoop Company (1899), American Can Company (1899), United States Steel Company (1899), Chicago,

Rock Island & Pacific Railroad Company (1901-1915).

William Henry Moore, in partnership with his brother, James Hobart Moore, led in the restructuring of the American match, cookie, and steel industries at the turn of the twentieth century, and attempted unsuccessfully to do the same for a major railroad, the Chicago, Rock Island & Pacific. William, a brilliant and innovative corporation lawyer, and James, whose close study of corporation law in the early 1880s intrigued his older brother with the opportunities it offered, combined legal astuteness with an understanding of what the fin-de-siècle American manufacturing firm needed in order to adapt to the economic environment of the new century. But at the same time their single-minded use of what looked like legal sharpness and financial legerdemain, combined with a powerful urge to monopolize markets and a talent for promoting their enterprises at the expense of the companies' stockholders, fanned the flames of anti-big-business sentiment in America at just the moment when Populist and Progressive ideas were providing the ideal fuel.

The brothers were born four years apart in Utica, New York, where their father, Nathaniel Moore, was a prominent banker. Their mother, Rachel, was a daughter of George Beckwith, another upstate New York banker. William Moore prepared for college at a "seminary" in Oneida and the Cortland Academy in Homer, New York. Poor health forced him to withdraw from Amherst College in his third year and, following a familiar American pattern, he went west for his health in 1870. In Eau Claire, Wisconsin, then the center of a booming lumber industry, he studied law and was admitted to the bar in 1872, whereupon, his health restored, he moved to Chicago.

Moore entered the law office of Edward A. Small, a leader in the infant specialty of corporation law, as a clerk and rose rapidly to partnership. On October 31, 1878, he married Small's daughter, Ada, with whom he had two sons and a daughter. Small died in 1882 and William formed a new law partnership with his brother, James. From that time on William acted as the leader and only occasionally were the two referred to as "the Moore brothers." William was an ideal leader. Immaculately informed not only on the financial and operating details of a firm but also on the fundamental economic conditions facing the industry of which it was a part, he stood out in negotiations and in courtroom appearances. He has been described as "tall, thick-set, a commanding figure with a sure and confident voice and a genial, self-sufficient smile."

In 1890 almost the only "big business" in America, whether gauged by the amount of capital employed in a firm, the widespread ownership of its stock, or the participation in its management by "outsider" professionals not related to the founders, was the railroads. "Commerce" had generally meant the financing, transportation, and merchandizing of goods, while manufacturing, although it was already becoming highly mechanized, was still considered too risky and individualistic a pursuit for financing through the public placement of securities. But this situation was about to change. Despite financial panics, the size of the domestic American market was growing prodigiously; and a century of scientific discovery was yielding a host of technological advances that would dramatically lower unit costs of production for firms that could command the capital resources required to dominate the mass markets for the flood of cheaper and better goods that would result.

William Moore's interest in the reorganization of industrial companies centered on the profits to be made by merging firms in a given specialty, modernizing production and marketing, reorganizing the financial structure through the capitalization not only of tangible net worth but also of present and even future expected profits ("blue sky," as the enemies of this radical new practice called it), and, finally, selling the now much more valuable and numerous shares to the public. Modernization of an industry usually meant closing down firms which

were obsolete or of an uneconomic size or location and taking over the sales function from the wholesalers to whom the firms had previously sold. This process involved the discharge of many production workers, traveling salesmen, and other supernumeraries of the earlier age, and herein lay much of the resentment that arose against the curse of "monopoly," as these practices were labeled.

The Moores' first important reorganization was the Diamond Match Company, which was in the process of a thoroughgoing mechanization that would make the common kitchen match universally available. The firm's capitalization of $7.5 million, most of it accumulated from profits retained in the business over the years, proved too small by 1889. Reorganization of the firm increased capitalization to $11 million, transformed the industry from over thirty small firms to one giant plant and three smaller ones, and made rich men of the Moores—who, in the process, had also reorganized the automating firms that made the strawboard boxes in which the matches were packaged.

In 1890 the Moores consolidated and reorganized several eastern cracker and cookie manufacturers into the New York Biscuit Company. As the depression began to wane in 1896, William Moore put his talents for promotion to work. Widespread publicity about Diamond Match's prospects for enormous foreign sales contracts and New York Biscuit's wonderful new automatic production equipment produced a rage for the stocks of both companies. Diamond common rose from 120 in January 1896 to 248 in May. For weeks the Chicago stock exchange was dominated by Moore brothers' stocks, but when news leaked out that Diamond's foreign prospects had failed to mature and that the Moores were overextended, these securities collapsed. The Chicago exchange had to be closed for three months while as many ruined brokers as possible were rehabilitated, and the effects were felt on the New York and London exchanges as well. The Moores' personal losses were estimated at $4 million.

Prosperity returned on the William McKinley tide that swept aside William Jennings Bryan's bid for the presidency. Fully recovered by 1898, the Moores hurried to fulfill the promise that New York Biscuit Company gave to bring the industry to maturity. By means of low prices that its western competitors could not possibly match, the company quickly convinced those competitors that amalgamation into a single big, powerful, marketing-wise company was preferable to liquidation by the sheriff. The National Biscuit Company (Nabisco), as it was renamed, captured over 90 percent of the nation's cracker and cookie business and became the model for future reorganizations.

As important as matches, soda crackers, and cookies were to Americans at the turn of the century, that era was in fact the age of heavy industry, with steel leading the way. Steel, it was widely believed, suffered from overproduction due to overexpansion, which seemed to many to bear out Karl Marx's predictions about capitalism. But there was no excess capacity of *efficient* steel production facilities; there *were* far too many small, closely owned, high-cost family firms struggling to survive. Meanwhile, there was a desperate need for intelligent industry-wide management and modernization of a business that had grown by no detectable pattern over a period of nearly forty years. It would help all concerned if some firms could be paid to go out of business. Production of raw steel ingots, almost exclusively by the Bessemer process although the open hearth process was coming in, was concentrated in a few giant firms, of which the Carnegie properties were the acknowledged leaders. But the production of ore and pig iron "upstream" of the big Bessemer converters, and of end products (rails, sheet, plate, tinplate, wire, tubes, nails, and dozens of other items) "downstream," was in the hands of hundreds of small to medium-sized firms, almost all of them dominated by the families of their founders and varying in efficiency from virtually obsolete to up-to-date.

Integration of the various stages by which steel end products were being produced was in the air; some producers of raw steel were threatening to build tube mills, for example, if tube manufacturers who bought their steel ingots did not desist from building their own blast furnaces and Bessemer converters. This integration posed a real threat of excess capacity of *efficient* plants. Control of roughly 60 percent of national steel capacity, under the aegis of J. Pierpont Morgan and in the shape of the biggest corporate enterprise up to that time, was about to be achieved as the new century began. A long series of mergers, amalgamations, and consolidations preceded the final outcome. The Moores and several strong associates who joined them along the way almost succeeded in playing the role later played by Morgan. Why they failed in the main event is almost as interesting as the great success they enjoyed in the preliminaries.

Many consolidations of specialty steel firms within their respective bailiwicks took place near the end of the century, as financial markets recovered and then displayed a buoyancy never felt before. The Moores led in reorganizing small and medium-size manufacturers of tinplate (thin strip steel coated with a thin layer of tin to inhibit rusting, from which were made in increasing numbers the cans to which Americans were becoming reconciled). At the same time, the brothers gained two new and powerful associates, Daniel G. Reid and William B. Leeds, from the tinplate industry. Before 1899 was half spent, this group had gone on to reorganize several small steel mills into the National Steel Company and other firms into American Steel Hoop, American Sheet Steel, and American Can.

The Moores cooperated enthusiastically in the gigantic consolidation that in 1901 became the United States Steel Company, despite Morgan's refusal to allow them to play any policy-making role in the operation. Into the new enterprise they led the earlier consolidations they had created, which made them one of the four distinct interest groups that made up the new company, the other three being Carnegie, the Rockefellers, and Morgan's earlier consolidations. William Moore became a member of the board of directors and Daniel Reid served on the executive committee; but for once they were sellers, not buyers, and now they had almost more money than they knew what to do with.

It was the Moores' last big operation that blew the fuse of public opinion and demonstrated dramatically that what they had learned in reorganizing the vibrant, growing manufacturing sector had little application to the sorely troubled railroad industry. Not that the railroad industry was in any apparent trouble in 1902, when the Moores, having bought its stock in the open market, took control of the Chicago, Rock Island & Pacific Railroad. If the railroads had one obvious problem in 1902 it was how to haul over their nineteenth-century facilities the unprecedented volume of freight and passengers that the brave new century was piling on them. Profits had risen swiftly as employment of plant exceeded 100 percent of efficient capacity after 1898; but the railroads' needs for fresh capital to increase their capacity and avail themselves of the many cost-reducing technological innovations that were being made in railroading were staggering. More than one railroad corporation would have to change its ways and "think anew and act anew" if the challenge was to be met. One of the least prepared to do so was the Rock Island. The situation seemed to be made to order for the Moores.

A closer look at the Rock Island would have disclosed a prosperous "Granger" road—the first to reach and cross the Mississippi River—that had been content to stick to its profitable business of gathering up the farm output of the Midwest and the Great Plains and carrying it to the Chicago gateway for transfer to the eastern trunk lines; and, in reverse, receiving at Chicago the diverse products of the East and delivering them over a network of branches to the farms, towns, and proudly emerging cities of the heartland. Other Granger roads, notably the Chicago, Milwaukee & St. Paul and the Chicago & North Western, were following the same shortsighted policy, while the Chicago, Burlington & Quincy, whose policies were made by more far-seeing men, made common cause with James J. Hill and eventually became one of the Hill lines along with the Great Northern and the Northern Pacific. The future, as Hill had realized in the early 1880s, would belong to through transcontinental freight, not traffic that originated or terminated amid the wheat—and cornfields—although, as Hill also knew, the notion of Atlantic-to-Pacific control of freight by a single railroad was not practical. After 1900, as the Chicago, Milwaukee & St. Paul would prove, it had passed beyond the resources of any one Granger road to build its own extension to the coast. Along with the Chicago & North Western and the Rock Island, the Chicago, Milwaukee & St. Paul might have built a jointly owned line to the Pacific, in which case the history of western railroads would have been dramatically different; but in the heady prosperity of the new century such collaboration between railroads that had been competing so vigorously for a generation was not to be imagined.

Meanwhile, a cloud had appeared on the horizon, and by 1910 it would grow into a heavy pall over the ability of the railroads to meet current obligations, let alone generate new capital for further development. In 1902 almost no one was yet aware of the rising potential for political demagoguery that lay in the idea of giving the Interstate Commerce Commission absolute control over railroad rates, which would remain at 1890s depression levels while prices and wages galloped ahead. In 1910 railroad men would lose the right to price what they had to sell, and by 1916 they would lose as well the freedom to bargain with the newly powerful railroad labor unions. Such an environment was foreign to any the Moores had ever known.

The lack of any real opportunity to do for the Rock Island what they had done for so many manufacturing concerns inevitably gave the Moores' financial manipulations of the railroad the appearance of a looting of its treasury in the best robber-baron tradition. They had acquired a line whose $60 million in outstanding stock had not been increased since the 1880s, and they proceeded to increase it to $75 million. The additional shares were used to acquire such extensions as the Choctaw, Oklahoma & Gulf Railroad, which ran westward from Memphis, Tennessee, through Little Rock, Arkansas, and Amarillo, Texas, to a junction with the Rock Island's mainline at Tucumcari, New Mexico, where the Rock Island joined the Southern Pacific—country so poor that it would not know real prosperity for another forty years. Meanwhile, the Moores undertook to protect their control of the Rock Island by pyramiding their holdings through not one but two holding companies. These entities, one of which carried on no railroading operations at all, authorized an increase in bonded indebtedness to $275 million. By 1914 it had actually reached $288 million, on which the annual interest burden was $12 million compared with $3 million in 1902, on a railroad whose net profitability had hardly increased at all. Acquisition of many other lines that no one else seemed to want, including the St. Louis & San Francisco (Frisco), further drained the strength of the company and further revealed that the Moores and their associates hardly knew what they were doing. The acquisition of the Chicago & Alton (Alton), which Edward H. Harriman lost to them in an unguarded moment, seems to have been not much more than a "lark," an attempt to "put one over" on the seemingly omnipotent Harriman. If, as has been claimed, Harriman was about to merge the Alton, which he had refinanced and thoroughly rebuilt, with the Union Pacific to give the latter its own rails into Chicago, then the Moores' meaningless move did the American railroad industry a real disservice. Likewise, their control of the Lehigh Valley and acquisition of stock interests in various Midwestern railroads came to nothing.

By 1914 the game was up for the Moores and the Rock Island. Profits were disappearing rapidly—the number of Class 1 railroads in bankruptcy had risen alarmingly in the previous three or four years—and although William Moore fought doggedly to retain control, he and his associates were effectively removed from the picture with the appointment of receivers in bankruptcy on April 20, 1915. Just how much money the Moores, Reid, "Tinplate" Leeds, and a few others made or lost in the Rock Island affair is information that apparently died with them. One authority insists that they sold out their interest "at the top market price" just before the receivership was announced, but it seems unlikely that they did so. The Rock Island's troubles, which were not so different from those of a lot of other regulation-ridden railroads by 1915, had been common knowledge for a long time. What personal satisfaction they may have gotten out of the time-consuming operation must have been slight, although they had obviously become fascinated with the romance of railroading and tried, like so many others whose vision failed when applied to unfamiliar fields of endeavor, to make the Rock Island what it could never be and thereby set it on the slow road to extinction. For years after World War II the Rock Island vainly sought the Interstate Commerce Commission's approval to merge with the Union Pacific, but over the dilatory deliberations of the commission there always hung the spectre of the Moores' stewardship, which had become one of the most frequently cited arguments for government control of railroad finance after 1916. The Rock Island was destitute by the mid 1970s and was shut down in 1980 and liquidated. Except for desirable segments that were bought by other railroads, much of it was abandoned.

Scholarly understanding of the vital significance of the massive reorganization of the American industrial establishment at the turn of the century has grown rapidly thanks to the research of modern business historians. But for the Rock Island affair, William H. Moore's reputation might have been rehabilitated as well. With nothing behind him but his brilliant record as a corporation lawyer and virtually unlimited charisma, he won the confidence of bankers and investors in the 1880s and 1890s, and what he did with their money paid hand-

some returns both for them and the public at large. His strategies had to be *sold* to Americans, accustomed as they were to the rolltop-desk practices of Victorian finance. If he capitalized "blue sky," he did so with stock that placed no contractual financial obligation on the firm, and he succeeded in hammering home what every good businessman knows: that the value of an enterprise is its ability to make money, not the nuts and bolts and bricks and mortar of its physical plant. If he used millions of dollars of freshly raised capital for "promotion," his National Biscuit Company nevertheless helped lay the foundation for the modern advertising and public relations which made the giant consumer goods companies possible.

Most important of all was the Moores' contribution to the rationalization of the steel industry, which has been all but lost to view in the massive publicity that has gone to J. P. Morgan and his men as creators of the U. S. Steel Corporation. That giant operated almost entirely as a holding company for its first quarter of a century. That it was able to do so was due in no small measure to the real restructuring of steel that had been achieved in the preliminary round of mergers that men like William H. Moore, Reid, Leeds, J. W. ("Bet-a-Million") Gates, H. H. Porter, and a few others arranged.

In 1916 the Interstate Commerece Commission published a study of the Rock Island reorganization which was a devastating indictment of the motivation and business ethics of the Moore group. The affair may have been the nadir of railroad manipulation in that day, but it was far from typical of the industry and its management. Tragically, however, it helped postpone any real understanding on the part of politicians, publicists, and professors of what the great merger movement of the 1890-1917 era had been about. All of the brilliant vision of a few leaders in the movement, and all that they accomplished in bringing America to first place in the world economy while improving the standard of living of ordinary citizens, were lost to view.

William H. Moore's many assets as a businessman included his ability to ignore the denunciations of men who had their own axes to grind. The Rock Island affair marked the end of his financial activities, and he turned with typical relish to his other great love: horses. In his extensive stables he bred thoroughbreds and trotters, but he loved all breeds and each year he showed everything from Percherons to hackney horses at the New York Horse Show in Madison Square Garden. He went into the ring with them, for he was a superb horseman and a champion driver of four-in-hands. Until his death from heart disease in 1923 he was a newsworthy figure for the rotogravure sections of the newspapers. In contrast with him, his younger brother was virtually invisible, and his career seems to have been almost entirely devoted to a secondary role in William's undertakings. When James H. Moore died in 1916, aged only sixty-four, the *New York Times* took no notice of his passing.

References:
Alfred D. Chandler, Jr., "The Beginnings of 'Big Business' in American Industry," in *Managing Big Business: Essays from the Business History Review*, edited by Richard S. Tedlow and Richard R. John, Jr. (Boston: Harvard Business School Press, 1986), pp. 2–32;
Chandler, *The Visible Hand–The Managerial Revolution in American Business* (Cambridge: Harvard University Press, 1977), pp. 287–314;
William Edward Hayes, *Iron Road to Empire: The History of 100 Years of the Progress and Achievements of the Rock Island Lines* (New York: Simmons-Boardman, 1953), pp. 147–189;
Joseph F. Wall, *Andrew Carnegie* (New York: Oxford University Press, 1970), pp. 714–793.

Harry C. Murphy

(*August 27, 1892-March 4, 1967*)

by Keith L. Bryant, Jr.

Texas A&M University

CAREER: Clerk, rodman, draftsman, transitman, engineer of construction, assistant engineer, engineer in maintenance of way department, assistant superintendent, superintendent, assistant to general manager (1914-1936), assistant to executive vice president (1936-1939), assistant vice president of operating department (1939-1945), vice president, operations (1945-1949), president (1949-1965), Chicago, Burlington & Quincy Railroad.

When Harry C. Murphy retired as president of the Chicago, Burlington & Quincy Railroad, (CB&Q) in July 1965, a coworker commented: "Harry Murphy earned an affection and esteem that perhaps no other president has exceeded and few have equalled . . . He will leave the railroad very much in debt to him." A quiet, modest Irishman, Murphy spent fifty-one years in the railroad business. He implemented many innovations on the CB&Q, and observers often commented on "the remarkable era of Harry C. Murphy."

Born in Canton, Illinois, to Frank E. and Margaret E. Yaco Murphy in 1892, he grew up in "Burlington country," fascinated by the long freight trains strung out across the prairie. When Murphy

was six his family moved to Iowa, where he graduated from Eldora High School. While still a student at Iowa State College majoring in civil and mechanical engineering, Murphy was a telephone lineman and worked on a section gang for the Iowa Central. After graduating from Iowa State in 1915 he joined the Burlington as an accounting clerk. The following year he attended night classes at Armour Institute of Technology in Chicago. His service with the railroad was interrupted when he became a pilot in the Army Air Service, attaining the rank of lieutenant, during World War I. He returned to the "Q" after the war.

Murphy's long career on the Burlington included a variety of positions. He gained experience in construction, maintenance, and operations and held jobs both along the line and in the corporate headquarters in Chicago. The CB&Q produced many managers for itself and for other railroads, and Ralph Budd, the "Q"'s president from 1932 to 1949, prepared Murphy for ever greater responsibilities. For his part, Murphy appreciated Budd's willingness to do things differently; the Burlington leadership not only accepted change but welcomed it. Murphy was serving in the Chicago offices when

Harry C. Murphy testifying at an Interstate Commerce Commission hearing on railway postal rates in December 1950 (AP/Wide World Photos)

Budd introduced diesel-powered locomotives and streamlined passenger trains. Indeed, Murphy often spoke for management to the board of directors, shippers, and employees, advocating technological innovation and new approaches to marketing.

In 1939, as assistant vice president for operations, Murphy told the Western Society of Engineers why the CB&Q had formed a truck subsidiary in 1935 to fight highway competition and how it was being used to retain general merchandise freight. As the supervisor of the highway unit, Murphy coordinated rail and truck movements, especially less-than-carload (LCL) shipments. Common ownership of trucks and trains permitted operating efficiences and faster deliveries, and Murphy prophesied that the railroads would expand their highway operations in the future. In 1940 the CB&Q engaged in a piggyback experiment, hauling truck trailers from Chicago to Kansas City on flatcars. This ex-

periment was simply another way to meet competition head-on. As one Burlington manager said, "We have no non-competitive territory now."

World War II generated a major increase in traffic. The Burlington's delivery of food from the heartland it served to urban markets and military installations placed heavy seasonal demands on the railroad. The lines to Billings, Montana, carried war materials to the connection with the Burlington's owners, the Great Northern and the Northern Pacific, which conveyed the cars on to the Pacific Northwest. Grain moved south over the Denver-Houston line, and petroleum was shipped north to meet industrial demands. Murphy traveled constantly over the system, removing bottlenecks and seeking more efficient use of employees, equipment, and other resources. His accomplishments led to his promotion to vice president of operations in 1945.

For the next four years Murphy helped organize the transition to complete dieselization, upgraded trackage and signaling systems, and replaced equipment and facilities worn out by war traffic. The Burlington was in good fiscal condition, and Budd was able to direct major resources to betterments as well as debt reduction. The CB&Q improved access to St. Louis with trackage rights over a portion of the Gulf, Mobile & Ohio in Missouri, and in 1952 it opened forty-five miles of new construction to complete a shorter and much improved route between Chicago and Kansas City. New freight cars, additional equipment for the "Zephyr" fleet of stainless steel passenger streamliners, and more diesel units improved operating efficiency and increased profits.

When the legendary Budd stepped down from the presidency of the Burlington in 1949, the board named Murphy his successor. The managements of the Great Northern and the Northern Pacific agreed that Murphy had been well groomed for the job. He had observed and participated in many top-level decisions during the Great Depression and the war as well as in the difficult transition period that followed. As president, Murphy acted quickly to rationalize the Burlington's plant. He eliminated facilities that were no longer necessary or profitable and ordered the abandonment of over 340 miles of line between 1950 and 1963. Grades and curves were reduced, bridges and culverts were replaced, and main line trackage was relaid with 131-pound rail. Murphy ordered the expansion of Centralized Traffic Control (CTC) on the Denver-Chicago line as well as the installation of radios in engine cabs and cabooses. New or rebuilt yards speeded the flow of traffic at Lincoln, Nebraska, and in the Cicero Yard at Chicago, and new diesel servicing facilities were constructed as steam locomotives were retired. Murphy made no headway, however, in reducing labor costs. Wages and benefits rose rapidly, and with few work rule changes labor charges grew from 40.6 percent of income in 1950 to 50.1 percent in 1963, excluding payroll taxes. By 1963 hourly wage rates had increased 111.3 percent from 1947-1949 averages, while revenues per ton-mile in the same period had risen only 14.1 percent. It was necessary to find ways to raise additional revenues and cut costs.

Murphy directed the traffic department to seek new sources of freight. The piggyback operation was expanded, and faster schedules were introduced. Multilevel rack cars were added to carry automobiles and trucks and regain traffic lost to the highway haulers. The traffic department solicited new business, especially in manufactured goods and agricultural commodities. Industrial sites were developed to attract new on-line traffic, and the company worked with local developers and chambers of commerce to find additional industries. These efforts did lead to higher traffic volumes, and the CB&Q's subsidiaries in Texas and Colorado gained greater levels of profitability as the economies of those states displayed rapid growth.

The Burlington had made a major commitment to passenger service with huge investments in streamlined equipment such as vista dome cars and slumbercoaches. Its California Zephyr, operated with the Denver & Rio Grande and the Western Pacific, was one of the nation's finest and most famous trains. But losses from passenger service mounted, and Murphy was forced to drop many passenger trains even as he sought greater support from the city of Chicago for the "Q"s suburban services there. The Burlington was a successful railroad by industry standards, but the rate of return on capital investment remained too low, Murphy believed.

In a move dictated by the Great Northern and the Northern Pacific, the Burlington petitioned in 1961 to be part of a new railroad, the Burlington Northern, which would also include the Spokane, Portland & Seattle. Merger of the four components of the old "Hill Lines" would save almost $40 million per year. The Interstate Commerce Commission delayed approval until 1970.

Murphy did not live to see his beloved CB&Q made part of the Burlington Northern. He died in 1967, two years after retiring as president. He was survived by his wife, Gladys Elizabeth Keating Murphy, whom he had married in 1921 and with whom he had three children. A Roman Catholic and a Republican, Murphy had made his home in Aurora, Illinois, for many years.

References:
Richard C. Overton, *Burlington Route: A History of the Burlington Lines* (New York: Knopf, 1965);
Overton, *Perkins/Budd: Railway Statesmen of the Burlington* (Westport, Conn.: Greenwood Press, 1982).

Nashville, Chattanooga & St. Louis Railway

by Maury Klein

University of Rhode Island

Map of the Nashville, Chattanooga & St. Louis Railway (1930)

Chartered in 1845, the Nashville & Chattanooga Railroad opened in February 1854 as a 151-mile line between the cities of its corporate name. The state of Tennessee aided both the Nashville & Chattanooga and the Nashville & Northwestern, a 170-mile line from Nashville to Hickman, Kentucky, that was completed in 1869. When the Nashville & Northwestern defaulted on its interest that year, the Nashville & Chattanooga leased it and then, two years later, purchased it in foreclosure. The two lines were formally consolidated in 1873 as the Nashville, Chattanooga & St. Louis Railway (NC&StL).

In 1869 the company had elected as president Edwin W. "King" Cole, a colorful figure who had worked his way up from bookkeeper. During the

next decade Cole gradually added 133 miles of short branches, and in 1879 he launched a lightning expansion program designed to transform the road into a major system. In short order he acquired the unfinished Owensboro & Nashville and a 161-mile branch of the bankrupt St. Louis & Southeastern Railroad. At the same time he negotiated for leases of the Western & Atlantic Railroad, which connected Chattanooga and Atlanta, and the prosperous 710-mile Central of Georgia system. If his plans had succeeded, Cole would have possessed a system rivaling that of the Louisville & Nashville (L&N) and might have shut that company out of the Southeast.

Amid rumors that the leases had gone through, Cole offered grandly in December 1879 to merge with the L&N on a share-for-share basis. H. Victor Newcomb, who became president of the L&N in March 1880, had no interest in a merger, but he lured Cole into lengthy negotiations while secretly buying up all the Nashville, Chattanooga & St. Louis stock he could find. Learning belatedly that the NC&StL's charter required a two-thirds majority to ratify any provision, Newcomb grudgingly paid premium prices for a pool of 60,000 shares held by some New York brokers and gained control of the railroad.

In 1890 the Nashville, Chattanooga & St. Louis finally succeeded in leasing the Western & Atlantic, thus assuring the L&N's route into Atlanta. The road also added numerous branch and spur lines, many of them for the purpose of reaching coal and ore fields. During the twentieth century two of the NC&StL's presidents rose to the presidency of the parent company: Whitefoord R. Cole, the son of "King" Cole, and James B. Hill.

On August 30, 1957, the L&N absorbed the Nashville, Chattanooga & St. Louis into its system, ending its history as a separate entity. By then the NC&StL had grown into a system with 1,043 miles of track extending from Memphis, Tennessee, and Paducah, Kentucky, through Nashville and Chattanooga to Atlanta.

Reference:

Maury Klein, *History of the Louisville & Nashville Railroad* (New York: Macmillan, 1972).

New York Central System

by George H. Drury

Trains *Magazine*

Between Albany and Schenectady, New York, the Erie Canal, which was opened in 1825, followed the course of the Hudson and Mohawk rivers. The difference in elevation between the two cities was ninety-four feet; in forty miles canal boats had to traverse a number of locks. The overland distance between the two cities was only seventeen miles, fertile territory for stagecoaches and for a railroad. The Mohawk & Hudson was chartered in 1826 and opened in 1831. By 1841 a chain of seven railroads covered the distance from Albany to Buffalo. They were consolidated in 1853, along with five others, to form the New York Central Railroad.

In 1851 the Hudson River Railroad was opened from New York up the east bank of the Hudson to East Albany. It had already acquired the Troy & Greenbush, which had a bridge across the Hudson at Troy. In January 1852 the New York & Harlem Railroad, which had begun in 1831 as a horsecar system along Fourth Avenue in Manhattan, reached Chatham, New York, on the Western Railroad, forming a second New York-Albany rail route.

By 1863 Cornelius Vanderbilt had gained control of the New York & Harlem and a major interest in the Hudson River Railroad. Within four years he also obtained control of the New York Central, which he consolidated with the Hudson River Railroad in 1869 to form the New York Central & Hudson River Railroad (NYC&HR), which became the nucleus of the New York Central System. Major system components north of the Albany-Buffalo line included the Rome, Watertown & Ogdensburg, leased by the NYC&HR in 1893 and merged in 1913, and the St. Lawrence & Adirondack, later renamed the Mohawk & Malone, which was merged in 1911. Since 1853 the New York Central had controlled the Buffalo

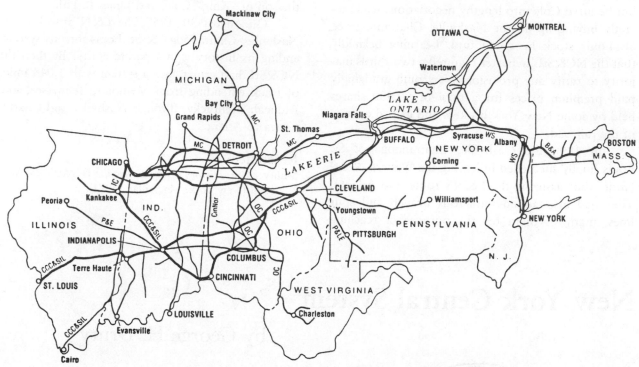

Map of the New York Central System (1930)

& State Line and Erie & North East railroads, which were combined as the Buffalo & Erie in 1867.

The Michigan Southern was built under the auspices of the state of Michigan from the head of navigation on the Raisin River west of Monroe as far west as Hillsdale. Private interests took it over, combined it with the Erie & Kalamazoo—a line from Toledo, Ohio, to Adrian, Michigan—and pushed it west to meet the Northern Indiana. In February 1852 the Northern Indiana reached Chicago. The two railroads were combined as the Michigan Southern & Northern Indiana (MS&NI) in 1855 and included a newer direct line between Toledo and Elkhart, Indiana. A line from Erie to Cleveland had been opened in 1852 by the Cleveland, Painesville & Ashtabula, which took its nickname, Lake Shore, as its official name in 1868. In 1869 the MS&NI was combined with the Lake Shore and the Cleveland & Toledo to form the Lake Shore & Michigan Southern, which soon came under Vanderbilt control. The Lake Shore & Michigan Southern and the New York Central & Hudson River plus several smaller roads were combined

in 1914 to form the second New York Central Railroad (NYC).

The New York, West Shore & Buffalo Railroad, backed by Pennsylvania Railroad interests, opened from Jersey City to Albany and Syracuse in 1883 and all the way to Buffalo in 1884. William Vanderbilt, son of Cornelius, retaliated by starting to build the South Pennsylvania, a short route across Pennsylvania. A truce was eventually negotiated by J. P. Morgan: the NYC&HR got the New York, West Shore & Buffalo and the Pennsylvania got the South Pennsylvania (which consisted of a roadbed and several partially excavated tunnels, which were used decades later for the Pennsylvania Turnpike). The New York, West Shore & Buffalo was reorganized in 1885 as the West Shore Railroad. The NYC merged with the West Shore in 1952; most of its lines west of Albany have been abandoned.

The Boston & Worcester Railroad began operation in 1835, and in 1841 the Western Railroad was completed from Worcester west to Greenbush, New York, across the Hudson from Albany. They were consolidated as the Boston & Albany (B&A)

in 1867. The NYC&HR, the B&A's principal connection, leased the B&A in 1900; the NYC merged with the B&A in 1961.

The Atlantic & Lake Erie was chartered in 1869, and after a receivership and a change of name to Ohio Central it completed a line in 1882 from Columbus to Middleport on the Ohio River. It grew at both ends, northwest to Toledo and southeast into West Virginia's coalfields. It was renamed the Toledo & Ohio Central (T&OC) in 1885. The New York Central & Hudson River acquired control of the T&OC in 1910; the New York Central leased it in 1922 and merged with it in 1952.

The Detroit & St. Joseph Railroad (D&StJ) was chartered in 1832. After Michigan became a state in 1837 it purchased the D&StJ as one of three cross-state railroads. The line reached Kalamazoo and the end of its bankroll in 1846. It was purchased by Boston interests, reorganized as the Michigan Central, and resumed construction, reaching Michigan City, Indiana, in 1849 and Chicago in 1852. The Vanderbilts began acquiring an interest in the Michigan Central in 1869. In 1876 they acquired the Canada Southern, a line from Detroit across Ontario to Buffalo, and leased it to the Michigan Central in 1882. The New York Central leased the Michigan Central in 1930. (Conrail sold the Canada Southern to the Canadian Pacific and the Canadian National in 1985.)

The Cleveland, Columbus & Cincinnati opened a line between Cleveland and Columbus in 1851, after fifteen years of incubation. In 1868 the company reorganized as the Cleveland, Columbus, Cincinnati & Indianapolis (CCC&I); absorbed the "B. Line," an amalgamation of the Indianapolis & Bellefontaine and the Bellefontaine & Indiana; and adopted the nickname "Bee Line." In 1872 it extended its own rails to Cincinnati, since the railroads it had previously used to reach that city had been taken over by Pennsylvania Railroad affiliates. By then the Vanderbilts had a sizable interest in the

CCC&I. In 1882 the CCC&I obtained control of a route from Indianapolis to St. Louis.

Meanwhile, a Cincinnati-Indianapolis-Lafayette-Chicago route had been assembled by the Cincinnati, Indianapolis, St. Louis & Chicago. The Vanderbilts soon had a hand in it and consolidated it with the Bee Line in 1889 as the Cleveland, Cincinnati, Chicago & St. Louis (Big Four). The Big Four soon included a line south to Cairo, Illinois; the Cincinnati Northern, a line that reached from Cincinnati north to Jackson, Michigan; and the Peoria & Eastern, a line from Peoria to Indianapolis. The New York Central leased the Big Four in 1930.

In mileage the New York Central System was the largest of the eastern trunk lines. Its freight tonnage was exceeded only by the coal railroads, and it was in the top rank of passenger carriers. Its problems after World War II stemmed from rising material and labor costs and a passenger-oriented improvement program. The Chesapeake & Ohio became the NYC's largest stockholder in the late 1940s. Robert R. Young became chairman of the NYC in 1954 and put Alfred E. Perlman in charge. Perlman slimmed down the railroad, deemphasized passenger service, and developed a freight marketing department.

In 1957 the New York Central and the Pennsylvania, its longtime rival, began talking about a merger. The two merged as the Penn Central (PC) on February 1, 1968. The PC came apart faster than it went together, declaring bankruptcy on June 21, 1970. Its properties, and those of six other northeastern railroads, were taken over by Conrail in 1976.

References:

George H. Drury, *The Historical Guide to North American Railroads* (Milwaukee: Kalmbach, 1985), pp. 206-217;

Alvin F. Harlow, *The Road of the Century* (New York: Creative Age Press, 1947).

New York, Chicago & St. Louis Railroad

by Richard Saunders

Clemson University

Map of the New York, Chicago & St. Louis Railroad (1930)

The New York, Chicago & St. Louis Railway was conceived in 1881 as a speculative venture by a syndicate headed by New York banker George Seney. It was designed to serve Buffalo, Cleveland, Fort Wayne, and Chicago, an invasion of territory that was dominated by the Vanderbilts' Lake Shore & Michigan Southern—part of their New York Central System—and contested by Jay Gould through his control of the Wabash. It was built to high standards; a satirical reference to the "nickel-plated railroad" first appeared in a Norwalk, Ohio, newspaper in

1881 after that town lost out to Bellevue, Ohio, for the location of the new route, and the line became known as the Nickel Plate Road. On October 21, 1883, two days before the road opened for business, the Vanderbilts acquired control at the promoters' high price. For several years they operated it strictly as a feeder for the Lake Shore & Michigan Southern.

Minority bondholders, with some help from the new Interstate Commerce Act, forced the New York Central to give the Nickel Plate operating autonomy in 1887, but it nevertheless languished under Central control. In 1916, with Gould long dead and the Nickel Plate safely moribund, New York Central president A. H. Smith agreed to sell the line to the Van Sweringen brothers of Cleveland, who wanted to build a rapid transit line on a few miles of its right-of-way between Cleveland and their new housing development, Shaker Heights. Once the brothers became involved in main-line railroading they were fascinated, and in 1923 they arranged one of the few great consolidations of the 1920s: a combination of the Nickel Plate with the Lake Erie & Western and the Toledo, St. Louis & Western (Clover Leaf Route) to form the New York, Chicago & St. Louis Railroad (as opposed to the former Rail*way*). This merger gave the branchless Nickel Plate routes through Ohio and Indiana and into St. Louis. In the heady days of stock manipulation in the 1920s, the Van Sweringens went on to buy control of the Erie, the Pere Marquette, the Wheeling & Lake Erie, and the Chesapeake & Ohio (C&O). The coal-rich C&O replaced the Nickel Plate as the jewel of their empire.

The brothers lost control of their railroads in the Great Depression, but their empire, intact except for the Erie, came under the control of financier Robert Young, who dreamed of merging it into a consolidated line. The Nickel Plate, overcapitalized in the 1930s, was saved from receivership by the C&O; but by 1945, swollen with wartime traffic, it was in prime physical and financial condition. Young's attempt to merge the empire was stymied by a minority of Nickel Plate preferred stockholders. Saying that the C&O would never again "bend its knee to the Nickel Plate Road," the furious Young distributed the C&O's Nickel Plate stock as a very handsome bonus to C&O stockholders in 1947. Out of the wreckage of the Van Sweringen empire, the Nickel Plate gained control of the Wheeling & Lake Erie line, a profitable coal hauler in eastern Ohio and a participant in the complex but reliable freight route between the Midwest and the Port of Baltimore that was popular with customers.

The Delaware, Lackawanna & Western, the Nickel Plate's principal connection at Buffalo, desperately tried to buy control of the Nickel Plate. But the Lackawanna, in 1947, was about to begin its long and painful decline, while the Nickel Plate was on the eve of its most profitable greatness. Nickel Plate preferred stockholders thwarted the Lackawanna just as they had the C&O. The matter went to litigation and the Lackawanna decided to sell its Nickel Plate stock in 1957.

By the late 1940s the Nickel Plate's single-track physical plant, once a disadvantage, made it ideal for Centralized Traffic Control, which turned it into a high-capacity, low-cost fast freight line. It had no commuter losses to drag it down, a minimal passenger service, and none of the passenger-oriented physical plant that burdened its chief competitor, the New York Central. Best of all, it was a bridge line, receiving most of its traffic from connections and delivering most of it, mainly in solid blocks, to connections. It perfected an eleven-minute interchange of solid trains with the Lackawanna at Buffalo that made it competitive with the trunk lines. Its operating ratio was low, its net income high, its fixed charges under control. It was superbly maintained, a winner in the shifting fortunes of eastern railroads in the 1950s, and a coveted prize in the merger schemes of the 1960s.

It chose to join the Norfolk & Western (N&W) system, a merger that was completed in 1964. The N&W combined the Nickel Plate with its old rival, the Wabash. The two roads complemented each other perfectly: the Nickel Plate's strength, its Chicago-Buffalo main line, was the Wabash's weakness; the Wabash's strength, its lines southwestward to St. Louis and Kansas City, was the Nickel Plate's weakness. Under the merger, the old Clover Leaf and Lake Erie & Western routes of the Nickel Plate were turned into secondary lines. In the uncertain railroad structure east of Buffalo following the creation of Conrail in 1976, the Buffalo line declined in importance as well, although it remained a prime piece of freight railroad in the N&W system into the 1980s.

References:

Taylor Hampton, *The Nickel Plate Road: The History of a Great Railroad* (Cleveland: World, 1947);

John A. Rehor, *The Nickel Plate Story* (Milwaukee: Kalmbach, 1965);

Lynne L. White, *The Nickel Plate Road* (New York: Newcomen Society in North America, 1954).

New York, New Haven & Hartford Railroad

by George H. Merriam

Fitchburg State College

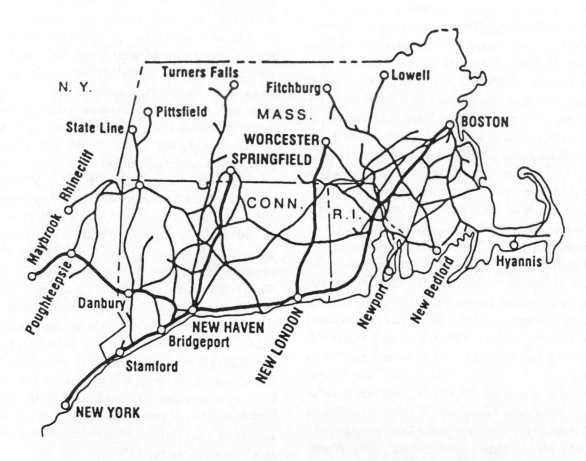

Map of the New York, New Haven & Hartford Railroad (1930)

The New York, New Haven & Hartford Railroad (New Haven) began with an 1870 joint operating agreement between the New York & New Haven Railroad and the Hartford & New Haven, followed by a formal merger in 1872. By 1900 the New Haven had absorbed more than fifty southern and central New England railroads, and by 1912 it oper- ated over 2,037 miles of track. It controlled the Boston & Maine and the Maine Central and shared control of the Rutland and the Boston & Albany with the New York Central. Its trolley empire covered most of southern New England. This transportation giant was managed for J. P. Morgan by Charles S. Mellen.

The New Haven's huge, intricate, monopolistic financial structure was attacked under federal antitrust laws from 1908 to 1914. Morgan died in Rome in March 1913, and in July an indicted Mellen resigned from the presidencies of the Boston & Maine, Maine Central, and New Haven. Major improvements begun under Mellen, including electrification from New York to New Haven and construction of Hell Gate Bridge, were continued by Howard Elliott between 1913 and 1917.

During the 1920s the New Haven operated numerous unproductive branches and aging trolley lines. Its grossly overcapitalized structure and competition from autos and trucks made bankruptcy inevitable in 1935. By 1947 New Haven reorganization was complete, the trolley incubus was gone, many of its branches were closed, and its capitalization had been lowered by $100 million. Its treasury held $45 million in cash and government securities.

In 1948 Frederic C. Dumaine, Sr., seized the restored New Haven. His presidency featured deferred maintenance, sale of $11 million in real estate owned by the railroad, and elimination of over 2,000 employees, including most upper management.

Dumaine died in May 1951 and was replaced by his son, Frederic C. "Buck" Dumaine, Jr., who poured funds into maintenance, equipment, and freight and passenger service. Prospects brightened; but Patrick B. McGinnis, an experienced railroad raider, ousted Dumaine in 1954. In twenty-two months McGinnis reduced maintenance expenses almost $12 million, disastrously invested $5 million in three experimental passenger trains, and paid $9 million to preferred stockholders. He was removed in January 1956, leaving a fatal legacy of financial commitments to him and his allies.

For five years the New Haven steadily weakened. Airline and truck competition, train wrecks on its important and unprofitable commuter service, and legally binding payments to the McGinnis group bankrupted the New Haven in July 1961. There could be no second rebuilding. The receivers' major effort, with assistance from the Interstate Commerce Commission, was to force the New Haven into the pending Penn Central merger. The New Haven finally merged with Penn Central January 1, 1969.

References:

"Another Collision on the New Haven," *Fortune,* 47 (March 1953): 55;

Robert E. Bedingfield, "New Haven's Row Rivals Central's," *New York Times,* March 14, 1954, III: 1, 10;

"Dumaine Takes Over New Haven," *New York Times,* July 15, 1948, p. 33;

"Frederic C. Dumaine, Jr., Succeeds His Late Father As New Haven President and Chairman," *Railway Age,* 130 (June 18, 1951): 49;

"Frederic C. Dumaine, Jr., Takes Over New Haven," *Fortune,* 44 (July 1951): 24;

Barry A. Macey, "Charles Sanger Mellen: Architect of Transportation Monopoly," *Historical New Hampshire,* 26 (Winter 1971): 3-29;

Richard Saunders, *The Railroad Mergers and the Coming of Conrail* (Westport, Conn.: Greenwood Press, 1978);

Robert Sobel, *The Fallen Colossus* (New York: Weybright & Talley, 1977), pp. 250-253;

William L. Taylor, *A Productive Monopoly: The Effect of Railroad Control on New England Coastal Steamship Lines, 1870-1916* (Providence: Brown University Press, 1970);

John L. Weller, *The New Haven Railroad: Its Rise and Fall* (New York: Hastings House, 1969).

Archives:

Minute books and other material of the New York, New Haven & Hartford Railroad can be found at the Office of the Trustee of the New Haven Railroad, New Haven, Connecticut. Additional material can be found at the Conrail Warehouse, New Haven, Connecticut, the Baker Library of the Harvard University Graduate School of Business Administration, Cambridge, Massachusetts, the Wilbur Cross Library of the University of Connecticut, Storrs, Connecticut, and in the G. W. Blunt White Library, Mystic, Connecticut.

Norfolk & Western Railway

by George H. Drury

NW

Trains *Magazine*

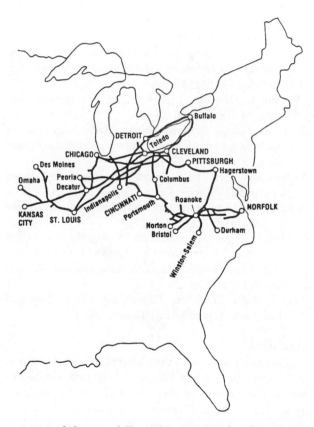

Map of the Norfolk & Western Railway (1983)

The oldest portion of the Norfolk & Western Railway (N&W) was the City Point Railroad, a short line built in 1837 and 1838 from Petersburg, Virginia, to City Point on the James River. It was reorganized as the Appomattox Railroad in 1847. The next oldest piece of the N&W was the Norfolk & Petersburg, which was chartered in 1850 to join its namesake cities. Construction took eight years, in part because of the difficulty of building ten miles of railroad across the Dismal Swamp. The engineering, on the other hand, included a fifty-two-mile

stretch of straight track. Other branches of the N&W family tree were the Southside Railroad, which started service from Petersburg to Lynchburg, Virginia, in 1854, and the Virginia & Tennessee, opened in 1856 from Lynchburg to Bristol on the Virginia-Tennessee boundary.

The Norfolk & Petersburg, the Southside, and the Virginia & Tennessee consolidated in 1867 but kept their identities until 1870, when the combined companies became the Atlantic, Mississippi & Ohio Railroad (AM&O). The AM&O entered receivership in 1876 and was sold at auction in 1881 to Clarence Clark, senior partner of a Philadelphia banking firm, E. W. Clark & Company. The Clark company combined its Shenandoah Valley Railroad with the AM&O to form the Norfolk & Western Railroad. The two roads met at the town of Big Lick, which was renamed Roanoke and was chosen to be the headquarters of the new railroad system.

Under the leadership of Frederick J. Kimball the N&W built northwest from Roanoke into the coalfields and beyond, reaching the Ohio River in 1892. Within a decade the N&W reached Columbus and Cincinnati, Ohio, the latter by the purchase of the Cincinnati, Portsmouth & Virginia. Branches to Durham and Winston-Salem, North Carolina, fleshed out the "old" Norfolk & Western, a coal carrier extending from tidewater to the Ohio River.

William J. Jenks became president of the N&W in late 1936 and saw it through the end of the Depression and World War II. Jenks was succeeded in 1946 by Robert H. Smith, who brought the N&W through the turbulent postwar era of coal, steel, and railroad strikes and began its transition to diesel power.

Indeed, the N&W was the epitome of the coal railroad, remaining with steam power into the late 1950s. The N&W constructed most of its steam locomotives in its shops at Roanoke. It built servicing facilities for its steam power that were as modern and efficient as any diesel house. It experimented with a single steam-turbine-electric locomotive (though with no more success than the Chesapeake & Ohio had with a trio of such machines).

In the late 1950s the railroad situation in the Pocahontas region (Virginia and most of West Virginia, one of the geographical areas used for reporting by the Interstate Commerce Commission [ICC]) included two large competitive railroads, the N&W and the Chesapeake & Ohio, and the smaller Virginian, which more or less paralleled the N&W from the West Virginia coalfields to Norfolk and had valuable coal reserves. In 1959 the Norfolk & Western merged with the Virginian Railway. In 1962 it bought the bankrupt Atlantic & Danville, a line from Norfolk to Danville, Virginia, which had been leased by the Southern Railway from 1899 to 1949. The N&W created a subsidiary, the Norfolk, Franklin & Danville (NF&D), to operate the line.

At the same time, the N&W was working on a merger with the New York, Chicago & St. Louis (Nickel Plate or NKP), prompted in part by the Chesapeake & Ohio's acquisition of control of the Baltimore & Ohio and in part by a desire to carry coal farther into the Midwest. The N&W's original proposal for merger of the Nickel Plate included the Detroit, Toledo & Ironton, another Pennsylvania subsidiary, to connect the N&W with the NKP. (The Pennsylvania Railroad had begun buying N&W stock about the turn of the century, and by 1960 it held, directly and through a subsidiary holding company, approximately a one-third interest in the N&W.) The merger that took effect on October 16, 1964, included purchase of the Pennsylvania's Columbus-Sandusky, Ohio, line to connect the N&W and the NKP, purchase of the Akron, Canton & Youngstown Railroad, and lease of the Pittsburgh & West Virginia and the Wabash Railroad. The last two railroads were both members of the Pennsy family—the Wabash served much of the same territory as the Nickel Plate and Pennsy could see that the already strong Nickel Plate would be a far more formidable competitor when allied with the N&W.

As a condition of the 1964 merger the Interstate Commerce Commission ordered the N&W to take over the Erie Lackawanna (EL)—itself the product of a 1960 merger—and the Delaware & Hudson. The two roads were purchased by Dereco, a holding company that was a subsidiary of the N&W. The EL entered bankruptcy in 1972 as a result of storm damage and became part of Conrail in 1976; the D&H found itself in trouble soon after April 1, 1976, when it became a railroad that primarily connected Conrail with Conrail.

The Norfolk & Western purchased what little was left of the Illinois Terminal Railroad, once an electric railway connecting St. Louis with Peoria and Danville, Illinois, on September 1, 1981. In 1982 the ICC approved acquisition of the Norfolk & Western and the Southern Railway by the newly created Norfolk Southern Corporation. In 1983 the Delaware & Hudson was purchased from Dereco by Guilford Transportation Industries, which had bought the Maine Central in 1981 and the Boston & Maine in 1982. The western portion of the Atlantic & Danville, made redundant by the merger of the N&W and the Southern, was abandoned, and the N&W absorbed the NF&D at the end of 1983. By 1987 the N&W and the Southern were gradually unifying their operations.

References:

George H. Drury, *The Train-Watcher's Guide to North American Railroads* (Milwaukee: Kalmbach, 1984), pp. 139-141;

Joseph T. Lambie, *From Mine To Market* (New York: New York University Press, 1954);

E. F. Pat Striplin, *The Norfolk & Western: A History* (Roanoke, Va.: Norfolk & Western Railway, 1981).

Archives:

Corporate records of the Norfolk & Western Railway are at the firm's general offices in Roanoke, Virginia.

Norfolk Southern Corporation

by Albert S. Eggerton, Jr.

Southern Railway (retired)

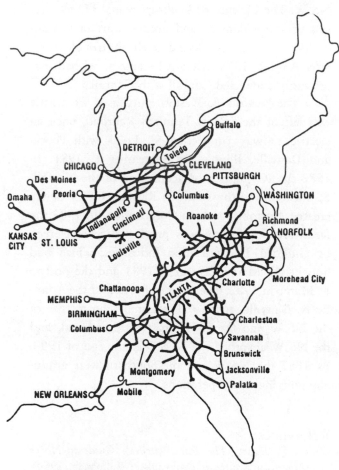

Map of the Norfolk Southern system (1983)

Created in June 1982 in the merger of the Norfolk & Western Railway Company and the Southern Railway Company, Norfolk Southern Corporation was a Virginia-based holding company that owned and managed these two operating railways and a motor carrier, North American Van Lines.

The two railroads formed a single interterritorial system with more than 17,000 miles of road in twenty states, primarily in the Southeast and Midwest, and the province of Ontario, Canada. North American provided household moving, truckload general freight, and specialized freight handling services in the United States and Canada, and also offered certain motor carrier services worldwide.

In 1986 Norfolk Southern, with headquarters in Norfolk, Virginia, had assets of $9.7 billion, about 38,000 employees, annual operating revenues around $4 billion, and annual income in the $500 million range. In a varied traffic mix, coal, coke, and iron ore accounted for more than a quarter of the corporation's revenues, with paper, chemicals, automobiles, intermodal shipments, and motor carrier traffic making up most of the rest.

Norfolk Southern's June 1984 bid to acquire the government-owned Northeast rail network, Conrail, for a price close to $2 billion was approved by the Department of Transportation and by the United States Senate. But it came to grief in the House of Representatives and was withdrawn by the corporation in 1986.

Archives:

Corporate records of Norfolk Southern Corporation, Southern Railway, and Norfolk & Western Railway are for the most part located at Norfolk Southern Corporation's regional office in Atlanta.

Ernest E. Norris

(January 21, 1882-April 23, 1958)

by Keith L. Bryant, Jr.

Texas A&M University

Ernest E. Norris

CAREER: Telegraph operator, Chicago & North Western Railway (1900-1902); car service agent (1902-1904), trainmaster (1904-1906), assistant superintendent (1906-1907), superintendent (1907-1918), assistant to the president (1918-1919), Southern Railway; vice president (1919-1932), receiver (1932-1933), Mobile & Ohio Rail Road; vice president (1933-1937), president (1937-1952), chairman of the board (1952-1958), Southern Railway.

Ernest E. Norris followed the traditional path of executives in the railway industry, moving through the ranks from telegrapher to president in a career of over half a century. The salty, energetic Norris took over the leadership of the Southern Railway in the midst of the Great Depression and led the carrier out of its financial difficulties, through World War II, and into a postwar era of rapid modernization. In 1947 a poll published by *Forbes* named Norris one of the nation's foremost business leaders.

Born in Hoopeston, Illinois, in 1882 to Luther Calvin and Amanda Lightner Norris, Ernest Eden Norris was educated in the public schools. He taught himself telegraphy and at age eighteen found employment with the Chicago & North Western Railway at Arlington Heights, Illinois. In 1902 he joined the Southern Railway as a car service agent at Norfolk, Virginia. Promoted to trainmaster at Norfolk, Norris later moved to Knoxville, Tennessee, where he advanced to superintendent. Transferred to Atlanta as superintendent, he returned to Knoxville as general superintendent. When a wreck occurred in his territory, Norris spent the morning dragging victims out of the wreckage, then went home to have his own broken collarbone set, using a glass of whiskey as an analgesic. His outstanding work on the system attracted the attention of Fairfax Harrison, president of the Southern, who brought him to company headquarters in Washington as assistant to the president in June 1918. Norris never lost his love for the daily routine of railroading; he retained his membership in the Order of Railway Telegraphers throughout his career, often proudly displaying his union card.

In 1919 Harrison gave Norris a tough assignment making him vice president of a Southern subsidiary, the Mobile & Ohio Rail Road (M&O). The problems of the M&O were substantial, and Norris was given the task of attempting to rescue the ailing company. The M&O operated from Mobile, Alabama, to St. Louis but could not compete effectively with the Illinois Central or the Louisville & Nashville. The carrier had been in receivership in the nineteenth century, and despite a growth in traffic in the 1920s, which allowed for the payment of dividends, it went into receivership again in 1932. Norris accepted the thankless job of receiver and held it until he was called back to the Southern as vice president of operations on November 1, 1933.

During the next four years Norris guided the daily operations of the railway as it sought to regain profitability. The employees of the railroad discovered that their new leader could rarely be found in Washington; instead, Norris soon became widely recognized as he toured the lines. His business car could be found parked at shops, terminals, and yards while he made detailed inspections; track gangs also found him along the system checking on tie replacements, bridge rebuilding, or track realignment. When Norris found work lagging, scrap not collected, or equipment without paint or proper maintenance, his volatile temper exploded, and his vocabulary reflected his ire. Energetic, capable, and articulate, Norris was no armchair railway executive; he often spent six months a year traveling over the Southern.

When Harrison announced his retirement in November 1937, the board of directors quickly followed his advice and named Norris his successor. The ever-optimistic Norris knew that the economy of the South remained depressed, or stagnant at best, though the carrier had managed small profits in 1936 and 1937. A recession in 1938 put the company in the red again, and it moved close to bankruptcy. A debt of $24 million to the Reconstruction Finance Corporation (RFC) had to be paid, but there was no reserve, and such a sum could not be raised on Wall Street. Norris urged "courage" among his executives. He renegotiated the debt, and the Southern gave the RFC $80 million in securities as collateral to refinance the note.

The financial crisis had passed, but equipment had to be replaced. The Southern's freight car fleet was woefully outdated and shrinking in size; rental payments to other railroads were enormous. Norris walked over to the office of Jesse H. Jones, head of the RFC, and asked to borrow $20 million more for new cars. The loan would enhance the profitability of the Southern and create many jobs for the car builders, Norris pointed out, promising that the railway would pay back every cent it owed. Jones agreed to take $20 million in equipment trust certificates, and Norris got his new cars. The equipment was soon put to good use as the nation moved toward mobilization for World War II. In November 1939 Norris sent Jones the first payment on the carrier's debts, and on May 15, 1941, a check for $10 million redeemed the securities held by the RFC. The Southern had discharged its indebtedness to the government and escaped the Great Depression without resorting to the bankruptcy courts.

The coming of war in Europe brought a measure of prosperity to the South and the Southern. Norris constantly toured the region, meeting with shippers, promoting industrial sites, and preaching industrial growth. The blue-eyed, ruddy-complexioned Norris, with his lean jaw and high forehead, became a familiar figure throughout the region as he sought to "humanize" the railroad. New defense plants and military installations increased traffic, as did the gradual diversification of the regional economy. After 1941 the volume of war-related traffic soared, and Norris moved to generate greater carrying capacity. Old freight and passenger cars were refurbished, and locomotives designated for scrap were pulled back into the shops and pressed into service. During World War II the Southern carried 69 percent more traffic than in World War I with 29 percent fewer locomotives and 14 percent fewer freight cars. Throughout the war the Southern broke tonnage records as it hauled troops, munitions, and petroleum products in ever-increasing quantities. Solid trains of petroleum moved over the carrier, exceeding a daily quota of 200,000 barrels established by the government.

Norris launched a program of institutional advertising to tell the people of the South and the nation what the railway was contributing to the war effort. The campaign urged civilians *not* to use passenger service unless absolutely necessary and described the activities of the 7,600 employees serving in the armed forces, the efforts of the railway to train four Railway Operations Battalions for the army, and the impact of "excess profits" taxes on the carrier. Norris had great affection for the Southern's 50,000 employees, and he wanted the public to be aware of the sacrifices that they were making both at home and abroad. The campaign featured the slogan "Look Ahead–Look South" as Norris prepared to take the railway into a postwar period that would be characterized by urban growth, industrialization, and economic diversification in the South, and by rapid modernization of the Southern's system. Norris intended to use the national media to market the South as a fertile field for industrial expansion. In addition to his duties on the carrier, he accepted an appointment in 1943 as a colonel in the Army Transportation Corps. He served on active duty and was recalled in 1948 and 1950 when President Truman seized the railroads to halt major strikes.

To prepare the carrier for the postwar period and the traffic growth he believed would develop, Norris committed the Southern to dieselization. In 1939 the board of directors approved a plan by Norris to substitute diesel-powered passenger units for steam locomotives on some branch-line passenger trains. The efficiency of these small locomotives led the company to order six 2,000-horsepower units to pull new streamlined passenger trains in mainline service. The first of these green and light gray passenger diesels entered service early in 1941, and a few months later the first diesel freight locomotive began to operate between Cincinnati and Chattanooga. This 5,400-horsepower unit proved fuel efficient and easy to maintain and had a high level of reliability. Soon the Southern ordered additional units. World War II precluded more rapid dieselization, but by 1951 Norris had purchased 847 diesels at a cost of over $200 million. This rapid acquisition program meant substantial savings, but it also meant new shops and machinery as well as major retraining programs for crewmen and shop forces. The diesels performed more work at less cost and profoundly altered the way the Southern operated. The last steam revenue service ended on June 17, 1953.

After 1945 Norris followed a conservative fiscal policy. He and the other executives remembered the bleak days of the 1930s and were determined to reduce the carrier's funded debt. Although huge sums were invested in diesel locomotives, new streamlined passenger trains, modern freight equipment, line rebuilding, and an expanded Centralized Traffic Control (CTC) system, Norris committed substantial earnings to debt reduction. Fixed charges had taken 24¢ of every dollar earned in 1932, and

Norris determined that that would never happen again. By 1960 fixed charges were reduced to 4.6¢ of each dollar earned as the funded debt fell by almost half from 1930 to 1960. The general mortgage of 1906, which matured in fifty years, was paid in cash from earnings on March 30, 1956, and the prices of Southern Railway securities rose as a result. Bonds selling for 28¢ on the dollar in 1938 brought 120 percent of par by 1945, preferred stock had jumped from $8.50 to $77.00 per share, and, after a ten-year lapse, dividends on common stock had resumed in 1942.

From 1937 to 1951 Norris led the company from fiscal disaster to financial strength. A carrier serving a region of economic weakness became a major railroad whose territory was often to lead the nation in economic growth. Norris toured the system two or three weeks each month calling on shippers and newspaper editors and addressing civic groups, and he sold the South and the Southern at meetings across the nation. With his colorful and flavorful vocabulary, Norris told his audiences that only two things will turn a man's head: one is "a pretty woman, the other is a train." Using his old-school, Southern-gentlemen style, he became a key promoter of regional economic growth. The efforts paid off; from 1941 to 1951, an average of one new industry per day opened its doors along the Southern's 8,000 miles of line.

The modernization efforts on the system began to pay off as well. From 1945 to 1955 some $327 million in capital improvements made the Southern an industry showcase. The main lines received CTC, new sidings were built and old passing tracks were extended, new steel bridges replaced wooden structures, tunnels were removed by "daylighting" (removal of the ceiling and parts of the walls), curve and grade reduction programs accelerated, and average train speeds rose. The operating ratio of 81.02 in 1946 fell to 69.25 by 1952. Ton-miles of freight carried were almost the same in 1951 as in 1946, but freight train miles fell by 40 percent. The recovery of the railway became national news as stories about Norris appeared in *Time, Business Week,* and *Forbes.*

Norris's dream of economic revitalization in the South materialized. The railway's traffic doubled from 1939 to 1951, but it also became far more diversified. Higher-revenue-producing manufactured goods increased and were hauled on scheduled freight trains–the Clipper, Southern Flash, and Jack Pot. Cotton, coal, lumber, pulpwood, and agricultural products remained significant commodities, but as the region industrialized the Southern's traffic reflected the shift. The old pattern of raw materials outbound and manufactured goods inbound altered dramatically, and the railway's revenues increased correspondingly.

Norris reached age seventy and mandatory retirement in 1952. He was succeeded as president by former vice president Harry A. DeButts. The board of directors created the position of chairman of the board for Norris, who held the office until his death; at that time the title was abolished.

Norris had married Kathryn Augusta Callan in Knoxville in 1905, and they had two sons. The Norrises made their home in Washington, where Ernest Norris played an active role in local businesses. A lifelong Republican and Mason, Norris served as a director of the Metropolitan Life Insurance Company, Western Union, and the Riggs National Bank and was a life trustee of the National Geographic Society. A sentimental man who loved

to take long walks, Norris would stop to talk to children, pet a dog, or visit with friends along his route. He died on April 23, 1958, in Washington. He had just attended a board meeting in New York, where he had been his usual gregarious, vigorous self. Workers throughout the system paused in remembrance of "Colonel" Norris.

References:

Burke Davis, *The Southern Railway: Road of the Innovators* (Chapel Hill: University of North Carolina Press, 1985);

Larston Dawn Farrar, "Men of Achievement: Ernest E. Norris," *Forbes,* 60 (July 1, 1947): 16, 18, 41;

"Railroads: The Human Touch," *Time,* 59 (January 14, 1952): 86;

"Resurgent Railroad," *Business Week* (March 31, 1945): 74-78.

Archives:

Correspondence, reports, speeches, and other documents by Norris may be found in the corporate records of the Southern Railway Company, Atlanta. Additional information is contained in a manuscript entitled "History of the Southern Railway System" by Carlton J. Corliss and Keith L. Bryant, Jr., in the same location.

Northern Pacific Railway

by Robert L. Frey

Wilmington College of Ohio

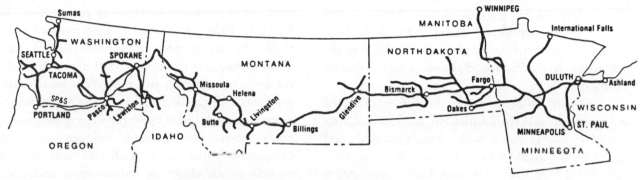

Map of the Northern Pacific Railway (1930)

The Northern Pacific, the nation's second "transcontinental" railroad, was chartered by the Congress of the United States in 1864. The charter authorized the construction of a railroad north of the 45th parallel from Lake Superior to the Puget Sound on the Pacific Coast. For each mile constructed the new company was to receive a land grant more generous than that received by the Union Pacific-Central Pacific, but the Northern Pacific was to receive no cash subsidy. Construction was eventually begun in 1870 near Duluth, Minnesota. Interrupted several times because of financial reverses, the main line was not completed until 1883. By that time the Northern Pacific had gained access to the growing cities of Minneapolis and St. Paul, which became the major eastern terminal of the company. Tacoma became the major western terminal.

The Northern Pacific Railroad of the nineteenth century was characterized by frequent struggles for control of the company and by reckless overexpansion designed to thwart potential competition. The panic of 1893 and the resultant depression drove the unstable company into bankruptcy. It was reorganized in 1896 as the Northern Pacific Railway by J. P. Morgan and associates, some of whom constituted a voting trust until 1901. For many years thereafter "Morgan men" sat on the board of directors of the Northern Pacific, controlling the destiny of the company. These "interlocking directors," such as George F. Baker of the First National Bank of New York and Lewis Cass Ledyard, a lawyer and trustee of Morgan's estate, served on the boards of many corporations, thus extending Morgan's influence and power.

During the early years of the twentieth century the Northern Pacific was a frequent topic in the national news. In 1901 James Jerome Hill, who owned the Great Northern Railway and had a large interest in the Northern Pacific, purchased the Chicago, Burlington & Quincy Railroad from under the nose of E. H. Harriman of the Union Pacific. Harriman retaliated by attempting to purchase enough shares of Northern Pacific stock to gain control of the company. Hill and his associates bought outstanding shares of Northern Pacific stock in order to block Harriman's plan. The price of the stock shot up and the buying spree resulted in the sale of more Northern Pacific stock than existed. A national financial panic was a possibility; it was averted by a last-minute compromise, but many people lost money in "the Northern Pacific stock corner."

Hill's attempt to build a transportation monopoly in the Northwest led to the creation in 1901 of the Northern Securities Company to hold the stock of the Great Northern, the Northern Pacific, and the Chicago, Burlington & Quincy railroads. In 1904 the United States Supreme Court ordered the dissolution of this company after a legal battle which generated much negative public opinion for the Northern Pacific. Despite the adverse publicity the Northern Pacific, under the leadership of Charles S. Mellen, was beginning to stabilize and prosper. Some of Mellen's tactics, however, did not endear him to Hill. Thus, when Morgan called Mellen to the presidency of the New York, New Haven & Hartford Railroad in 1903, Hill was delighted to have a chance to choose a new president for the Northern Pacific.

Howard Elliott of the Burlington was selected to head the Northern Pacific. His efficient and conservative management style was successful and Elliott soon gained Hill's confidence. Between 1903 and World War I the Northern Pacific developed a standardized motive power fleet based on the 4-6-2 Pacific-type locomotive for passenger service, the 2-8-2 Mikado-type locomotive for freight service, and the Mallet compound 2-8-8-2 locomotive for heavy freight service. New long-distance passenger trains were inaugurated and freight train schedules were improved. Upgrading of the main line was a high priority, and many sections were double-tracked and equipped with automatic block signals for greater traffic density, wooden trestles were replaced with steel bridges, heavier rails were installed to support heavier trains, and several line relocations were undertaken to reduce excessive grades and sharply curved track.

On the eve of World War I the Northern Pacific had established itself as a prosperous regional carrier with modern locomotives, rolling stock, and physical plant. Profits were substantial and dividends were regular. With the favorable growth potential of the Northwest, the railroad hoped to capitalize on its careful planning and effective management. World War I was a setback to these plans. Because the Northern Pacific's charter required it to ship government traffic and mail at reduced rates, the United States Railroad Administration channeled such traffic over the Northern Pacific rather than over its rival, the Great Northern. The resultant strain on Northern Pacific mo-

tive power, rolling stock, and physical plant was not balanced by the income from the heavy traffic. When the railroad was returned to private management much rebuilding was required, but there was inadequate capital for the task despite a government payment plan designed to meet the problem.

The 1920s did not bring a return to the prosperity of the prewar era. Costs of labor and materials increased substantially, but government-regulated rates did not increase proportionately. Regulatory agencies forced the company to continue operating branches and local passenger trains that had been rendered unprofitable by highway competition. The Northern Pacific attempted to gain new sources of traffic by encouraging industrial plant location along its line and by opening coal mines. It tried to cut costs by replacing steam-powered local passenger trains with gas-electric cars and by purchasing additional modern steam locomotives to reduce maintenance costs and increase tonnage per train. Cooperation with other railroads was also increased in an effort to reduce costs and utilize freight cars more efficiently. The Northern Pacific reduced the number of its employees during the decade, but improved health benefits, continued to operate hospitals, and introduced a modest pension plan for its remaining workers.

The most severe setback the Northern Pacific faced in the twentieth century, however, was the Great Depression. The nation's industrial slowdown was aggravated in the Northwest by a prolonged agricultural slump caused by a series of bad growing seasons. There were days in the depths of the Depression when one westbound and one eastbound train were adequate to handle the sparse freight traffic. Locomotives and rolling stock were stored or scrapped, layoffs and wage reductions hit labor and management alike, and the grim numbness of "no work and no pay" was a common experience for Northern Pacific families from Duluth to Tacoma. Business began to improve by 1938, but normal traffic did not return until spurred by war preparations in 1940.

If employees wondered if they would work again during the 1930s, they must have wondered if they would get a day off during World War II years. Since key ports for the shipment of men and military supplies to the Pacific theater were located in the state of Washington, the traffic over the Northern Pacific during World War II was more critical than it had been during World War I. The Transportation Act of 1940 relieved the Northern Pacific of excessively low rates for government shipments and, as a result, the company achieved its highest levels of income and traffic in 1943 and 1944. At the conclusion of the war the railroad was in much better physical and financial condition than it had been in 1920.

In the decade following World War II the steam locomotive was gradually replaced by the diesel-electric locomotive. The Northern Pacific had purchased a few diesel locomotives for switching service in large cities before 1940, but it was not until the closing days of the war that the first road freight locomotives were purchased from the Electro-Motive Division of General Motors. The Northern Pacific was reluctant to change to diesels because it had a modern fleet of steam locomotives fueled by relatively low-cost coal from company-owned mines. But improvements in the reliability of diesels, reductions in the cost of diesel fuel, and the disappearance of steam locomotive builders and parts suppliers forced the Northern Pacific to phase out steam operations more rapidly than originally planned. The last commercial steam locomotive operation on the railroad took place in January 1957.

Also in the postwar years the Northern Pacific undertook a major campaign to modernize both its image and its operations. New streamlined passenger equipment with stewardesses and attractive schedules were introduced. Passenger travel was promoted heavily until the late 1960s, when it was obvious that the competition of the interstate highway system, the expansion of airlines, and the end of mail subsidies made long-distance passenger operations unprofitable. New types of freight cars were introduced for the shipment of agricultural and industrial products; automated classification yards were built in several locations for rapid forwarding of freight; Centralized Traffic Control improved the movement of trains over the line, allowing the elimination of miles of double track; and welded rail installations reduced maintenance costs and improved the ride.

Efforts to merge the railroads of the Northwest were renewed several times after Hill's frustration at the hands of the Supreme Court. In the late 1920s a merger effort came to naught when the Interstate Commerce Commission (ICC) made divestment of the Burlington a condition of its approval. In 1970 the long-sought merger was finally consummated after being delayed once by the ICC and once by the Supreme Court, acting on a request from the Justice Department. The merger of the Northern Pacific, the Great Northern, the Chicago, Burlington & Quincy, and the Spokane, Portland & Seattle railroads formally took place on March 2. The resulting Burlington Northern system was the largest railroad in the United States in terms of route mileage. Louis W. Menk, president of the Northern Pacific before the merger, became the first president of the Burlington Northern.

The Northern Pacific was an influential railroad during the first seven decades of the twentieth century. "The Main Street of the Northwest" was a leader in locomotive design and modernization, in signaling systems, in special apprentice programs to train executives, and in adapting to the post-World War II era when competition from highways and airways forced a substantial rethinking of the mission of railroads.

References:

Robert L. Frey, *A Technological History of the Locomotives of the Northern Pacific Railway Company* (Ann Arbor: University Microfilms, 1970);

Frey and Lorenz P. Schrenk, *Northern Pacific Railway: Supersteam Era, 1925-1945* (San Marino, Cal.: Golden West Books, 1985);

Louis T. Renz, *The History of the Northern Pacific Railroad* (Fairfield, Wash.: Ye Galleon Press, 1980).

Archives:

The largest collection of corporate records of the Northern Pacific is located in the Minnesota Historical Society, St. Paul. Permission to use the records must be obtained using a form which will be supplied by the society.

Operating Ratio

Operating ratio is the ratio of operating expenses to revenue from operations, multiplied by 100. An operating ratio of 80 (expenses equal to 80 percent of revenues) used to be considered respectable; anything less than that was good. Beginning on January 1, 1978, the Interstate Commerce Commission added payroll taxes, property taxes, and equipment and joint facility rents to the expenses used in calcu-

lating the ratio, basically increasing the ratio and making it impossible to compare ratios with those of earlier years. An operating ratio over 100 indicates that operating expenses exceed operating revenues—and that the railroad company may soon find itself in financial trouble.

—George H. Drury

Penn Central

by Richard Saunders

Clemson University

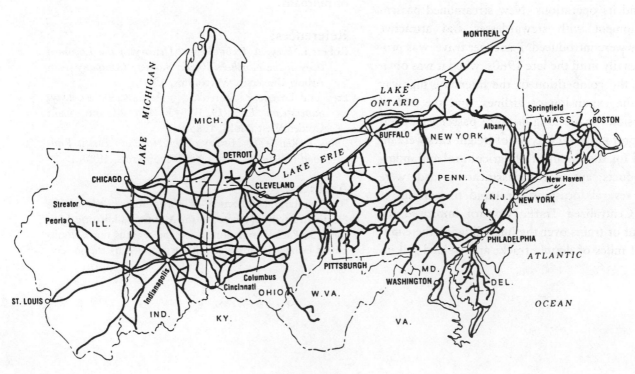

Map of the Penn Central System (1969)

In 1957 the New York Central and Pennsylvania railroads announced plans to merge. The proposed merger was national news, the press dwelling on the superlatives of combining the nation's two largest railroads, which had been for a century the archetype of competitiveness among America's blue-chip giants. The announcement was a shock to the railroad industry, for it had been assumed since the beginning of the century that the northeastern lines would probably sort themselves into one system based on the New York Central and another based on the Pennsylvania. Given the decline of the anthracite roads, a Pennsylvania-New York Central merger would virtually preclude meaningful competition east of Buffalo and Harrisburg and would mortally wound the New Haven, as the traffic it received from the Pennsylvania through the Bay Ridge Yard on Long Island would be rerouted over New York Central lines into New England.

The rationale of the merger was to route all traffic bound for New York and New England over the New York Central's water-level route, marshalling it at Selkirk Yard near Albany, and all traffic bound for Philadelphia and Baltimore over the Pennsylvania, marshalling it at Enola Yard near Harrisburg. Under the leadership of Alfred Perlman the New York Central cooled on the idea of merging with the Pennsylvania, but was rebuffed in its effort to be included in the emerging Chessie System. With the Kennedy administration alerted that the Pennsylvania was trying to create a railroad monopoly in the East, the Interstate Commerce Commission (ICC) forced the Pennsylvania to choose between the savings that might come from merger with the New York Central and the cash dividends that came from its control of the Norfolk & Western. To the surprise of some observers, it chose merger with the New York Central.

Penn Central was created on February 1, 1968, with the Pennsylvania being the surviving corporation. On December 31, 1968, under Interstate Commerce Commission order, Penn Central acquired the assets of the New York, New Haven & Hartford Railroad (New Haven) for an exchange of securities worth $90 million on paper, though only $8 million in cash; this move was thought to be the only way to salvage the essential services of the New Haven short of nationalization. In 1969 a holding company, Penn Central Company, was created to separate the railroad from nonrailroad assets—

notably the property along New York's Park Avenue, which was New York Central right-of-way until the tracks were put underground into Grand Central Station, and development properties in Florida and California. The railroad became the Penn Central Transportation Company.

Though both railroads had paid dividends into the latter 1960s and could still roll their Broadway Limited and Twentieth Century Limited at ninety miles per hour, they were, in fact, cadaverously weak. At the time of the merger it was so important to realize the predicted savings as quickly as possible that the two railroads were thrown together without preparing the necessary physical arrangements and without training clerks and crews. The result was an operating debacle, and the entire railroad became hopelessly snarled. At its nadir, whole trains of "no bills," cars for which the paperwork had become lost and no one had the slightest idea of where they were supposed to go, were dispatched over the line to get them off one yardmaster's back and onto another's. President Stuart Saunders seemed preoccupied with diversification—which, on the whole, was not losing money for the railroad, as some suspected, but was not making much, either, and was distracting management. The former New York Central and Pennsylvania managements had different philosophies of ratemaking and of how to run a railroad. They tended to come from different social backgrounds and just did not like each other very much. Interleaved throughout the management, supervisors tried to bypass their immediate superior from the rival road and reach the friendly ears of someone higher up from their own road. The result was chaos.

By early 1970 the railroad was losing a million dollars a day and its credit was exhausted. At the tumultuous board meeting of June 8, 1970, top management was summarily fired. One of the great mysteries of the disaster was how directors, and bankers who continued to advance the PC credit even weeks before bankruptcy, could have been so deceived about the firm's condition, for all one had to do was look out the window of a Penn Central train to see a dying railroad.

On Sunday, June 21, 1970, the Penn Central declared bankruptcy in the worst business failure in American history to that time. After bankruptcy, no further credit was forthcoming from the private sector. The road's physical condition continued to deteriorate. Solvent railroads showed interest in buying only a few segments. In the impasse, termination of service and liquidation were a possibility, which would have forced the shutdown of industries across the Northeast that depended on rail service. The only alternative seemed to be a government-sponsored corporation: Conrail, which was created in 1976. The Penn Central Company (the holding company) did not enter receivership, retained all the railroad's profitable assets (the "crown jewels,"), and prospered long after the railroad went under.

References:

Joseph R. Daughen and Peter Binzen, *The Wreck of the Penn Central* (Boston: Little, Brown, 1971);

Stephen Salsbury, *No Way to Run a Railroad: The Untold Story of the Penn Central Crisis* (New York: McGraw-Hill, 1982);

Richard Saunders, *The Railroad Mergers and the Coming of Conrail* (Westport, Conn.: Greenwood Press, 1978);

Robert Sobel, *The Fallen Colossus: The Great Crash of the Penn Central and the Crisis of the Corporate Giants* (New York: Weybright & Talley, 1977).

Pennsylvania Railroad

by Michael Bezilla

Pennsylvania State University

The chartering of the Pennsylvania Railroad (PRR) in 1846 represented an effort to preserve the competitive position of Philadelphia, whose importance as a center for trade between the Atlantic Seaboard and the Midwest was threatened by New York City (and the Erie Canal) and Baltimore (and the Baltimore & Ohio Railroad and the Chesapeake & Ohio Canal). Construction began at Harrisburg, which was already connected to Philadelphia in part by a state-owned rail line, and advanced westward. The 245-mile Harrisburg-Pittsburgh segment, which included the famous Horseshoe Curve assault on the east slope of the Alleghenies, was opened for service in 1854. Three years later the PRR purchased the state-owned railroad east to Philadelphia.

From that time through the 1880s the railroad expanded into all parts of Pennsylvania and beyond. Additional main lines radiated from Harrisburg to Erie, Buffalo, and Baltimore. To the east, Jersey City and New York harbor were reached in 1871 over several leased lines. Other leased lines provided a route between Philadelphia, Wilmington, Baltimore, and Washington, D.C. To the west, still more lease agreements gave the PRR control over the Pittsburgh, Fort Wayne & Chicago Railway (Fort Wayne) and access to major midwestern cities. A lease of the Pittsburgh, Cincinnati & St. Louis Railway (Panhandle) extended PRR rails to the Mississippi River. In 1871 the Pennsylvania Company was set up as a PRR subsidiary to manage the Fort Wayne and the Panhandle; it continued as a separate operating entity known as Lines West (that is, lines west of Pittsburgh) until 1921.

The later years of the presidency of George Roberts, who served from 1880 to 1897, witnessed the end of further expansion and the beginning of purchase or consolidation of leased lines and of improvements in service and physical plant. These improvements were pushed vigorously during the presidency of A. J. Cassatt from 1899 to 1906. The heavily traveled main line between Harrisburg and Pittsburgh—the heart of the PRR—was among the busiest in the nation and was expanded to four or

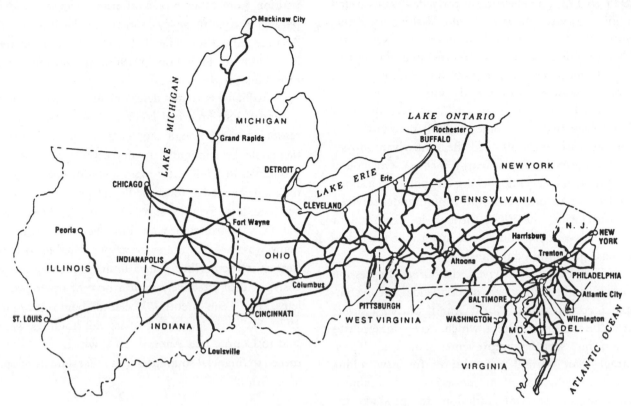

Map of the Pennsylvania Railroad (1930)

more tracks, replete with several new tunnels and a multitude of massive stone arch bridges. The road's premier passenger train, the Pennsylvania Special (renamed the Broadway Limited after the four-track right-of-way), in 1905 began running between New York and Chicago in eighteen hours. Tunnels under the Hudson River were completed in 1907 to allow passenger trains to reach the new Pennsylvania Station in Manhattan, which opened in 1910. Control of the Long Island Rail Road, a commuter line entering Penn Station through tubes beneath the East River, had been secured in 1900. Operating 10,000 route-miles in thirteen states, owning more than 260,000 passenger and freight cars, maintaining 6,600 locomotives, and employing some 215,000 people, the PRR by 1910 was a colossus of American railroading. Proud of the quality of service it offered, it began referring to itself in the Roberts era as "The Standard Railroad of the World."

Under the presidencies of James McCrea from 1907 to 1913 and Samuel Rea from 1913 to 1925, the PRR adhered to the conservative financial course that had become its hallmark. The road was never a popular speculative property, its strength in-

stead depending on the continuity of its relatively modest dividends. The company preferred to reinvest as much of its earnings in improvements as it paid out to shareholders. Another longtime characteristic, standardization of locomotives and rolling stock, reached awesome proportions. Its fleet of lookalike 2-10-0 type steam locomotives, for instance, numbered 598—more than the entire locomotive roster of such lines as the Western Maryland or the Pittsburgh & Lake Erie.

Its approach to technological and marketing innovations was equally prudent but less conservative. In the late nineteenth century it had pioneered in the use of the air brake, steel rails, and automatic block signals. By 1908 it was in the forefront of the adoption of the all-steel passenger car. Within a decade, its 5,100-car all-steel fleet represented half the total of all such cars in America. The railroad was also an early user of electric motive power, first in the New York tunnels and, beginning in 1913, in Philadelphia suburban service. Electrification, which possessed significant economies over steam, reached maturity during the reign of

Rea's successor, W. W. Atterbury, who served from 1925 to 1935, as electrically propelled trains began running between New York and Washington. Along with related terminal modernizations, the New York-Washington electrification represented the largest capital improvement program undertaken to that date by an American railroad. With a westward leg to Harrisburg opened in 1937, it gave the PRR more electrified track miles (2,200) than any other railroad. Atterbury also led the Pennsylvania to secure interests in Trans World Airlines, Greyhound Bus Lines, and several trucking companies in a short-lived effort to offer customers multimodal services. (In the 1950s, the PRR, through its TrucTrain or piggyback service, would once again take the industry lead in multimodal transport.)

The railroad survived the Great Depression with its unbroken string of dividends and net annual incomes intact. World War II placed a severe strain on the entire system, which, except for electrification, had seen few improvements since the 1920s. Larger than normal expenditures for new rolling stock and physical plant modernization combined with severe postwar inflation to produce the company's first annual net loss—in, ironically enough, its centennial year of 1946.

Among the most pressing of the PRR's problems was the need to replace its vast—and mostly obsolete—fleet of steam locomotives. After considerable hesitation, arising in part from its long-standing loyalty to the coal industry, the railroad decided to replace steam with diesel-electric power, which offered many of the economies of "pure" electric traction with less initial cost. Dieselization, a $400 million investment, was finally completed in 1957.

Atterbury's successor, Martin W. Clement, retired in 1951. He was succeeded by Walter Franklin, who served until 1954, and James Symes, who was president until 1963. Both were up-from-the-ranks operating men in the mold of every PRR chief executive since Roberts. Under Symes's leadership the PRR continued to experience a decline in both passenger and freight traffic, the result of competition from other modes of transportation and a parallel decline in heavy industry in the Northeast. Average annual ton-miles fell from 54 billion in the late 1940s to 43 billion in 1960, yet another year of red ink for the railroad.

To halt his road's deterioration, Symes sought a merger with archrival New York Central (NYC), reasoning that enough duplicate routes and facilities could be eliminated to make the new railroad profitable. In 1968, after many years of negotiation, the roads merged to form the Penn Central (PC); Stuart Saunders, Symes's successor on the PRR, was the PC's board chairman. But the NYC was in many ways weaker than its partner. Unable to halt further traffic declines, put a limit on soaring labor costs, or deal effectively with a host of other problems, the Penn Central declared bankruptcy in 1970. Six years later most of its rail holdings were sold to Conrail and Amtrak, after which the PC returned to financial soundness as a real estate development firm.

References:
Michael Bezilla, *Electric Traction on the Pennsylvania Railroad, 1895-1968* (University Park: Pennsylvania State University Press, 1980);

George H. Burgess and Miles C. Kennedy, *Centennial History of the Pennsylvania Railroad* (Philadelphia: Pennsylvania Railroad, 1949);

Stephen Salsbury, *No Way to Run a Railroad* (New York: McGraw-Hill, 1982);

H. W. Schotter, *The Growth and Development of the Pennsylvania Railroad Company* (Philadelphia: Allen, Lane & Scott, 1927);

William B. Wilson, *History of the Pennsylvania Railroad Company* (Philadelphia: Coates, 1899).

Archives:
Corporate records of the Pennsylvania Railroad are scattered among a half-dozen or more institutions in the Northeast, with the core documents at the Pennsylvania Historical and Museum Commission, Harrisburg. These records have not yet been catalogued or opened to researchers.

Pere Marquette Railway

by Charles V. Bias

Marshall University

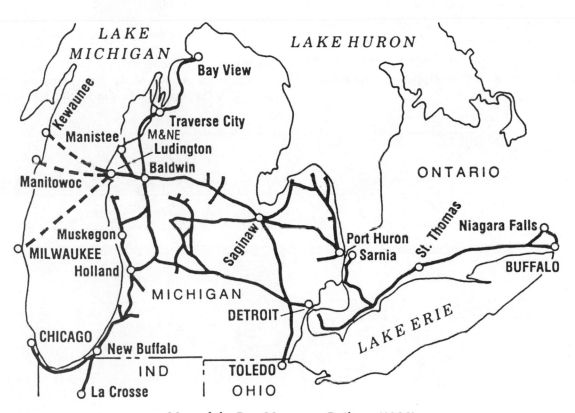

Map of the Pere Marquette Railway (1930)

The merger of the Flint & Pere Marquette Railroad, the Chicago & West Michigan Railway, and the Detroit, Grand Rapids & Western Railroad on November 1, 1899, resulted in the Pere Marquette Railroad Company (PM).

The Pere Marquette provided service to much of Michigan as well as steamboats and ferries across Lake Michigan to Milwaukee and Manitowoc, Wisconsin. Despite serving a thriving industrial region, the Pere Marquette suffered serious financial difficulties throughout its early history. It went into receivership in 1912 and was reorganized in 1917 as the Pere Marquette Railway Company.

In 1929 the Chesapeake & Ohio Railway Company (C&O) purchased controlling stock interest in the road. Still the company had difficulty remaining solvent during the Great Depression from 1929 to 1941. With the entry of the United States into World War II, however, the Pere Marquette had more traffic than it could carry.

On August 21, 1945, the C&O initiated proceedings to merge with the Pere Marquette, the New York, Chicago & St. Louis (Nickel Plate or NKP), and the Wheeling & Lake Erie (W&LE). While the C&O's plans to merge with the NKP and W&LE failed to materialize, the consolidation of the C&O and the PM was completed on June 6, 1947. The merger created a system of 5,122 miles of main-line trackage, embracing lines from Newport News, Virginia, and Washington, D.C., to Toledo, Ohio, and Chicago. Further it provided a line north of Lake Erie from Buffalo, New York, extending throughout Michigan, with a ferry line across Lake Michigan from Ludington, Michigan, to Kewaunee, Manitowoc, and Milwaukee, Wisconsin.

The Pere Marquette served many industrial cities in Michigan, including Detroit, Flint, Lansing, Saginaw, and Grand Rapids, all users of the high-grade bituminous coal brought in by the C&O from mines in southern West Virginia and eastern Kentucky. Many of the products manufactured by Michigan companies were shipped southward and eastward via the C&O.

Robert J. Bowman, who had served with the Pere Marquette since 1929, became president of the C&O in 1946, before the merger had been completed. The Pere Marquette name finally disappeared in 1979.

References:
Charles V. Bias, "A History of the Chesapeake and Ohio Railway Company, 1836-1977," Ph.D. dissertation, West Virginia University, 1979;

Thomas W. Dixon, Jr., and Art Million, *Pere Marquette Power* (Alderson, W.Va.: Chesapeake & Ohio Historical Society, 1984);

Patrick Dorin, *The Chesapeake and Ohio Railway* (Seattle: Superior Publishing Company, 1981).

Archives:
Corporate records of the Pere Marquette Railway are at CSX Corporation offices in Jacksonville, Florida.

Alfred E. Perlman

(November 22, 1902-April 30, 1983)

by Richard Saunders

Clemson University

Alfred E. Perlman in 1974 (Kalmbach Publishing Company)

CAREER: Draftsman (1923-1924), track laborer (1924-1925), inspector of icing facilities (1925-1926), assistant supervisor of bridges and buildings (1926-1927), roadmaster (1927-1934), assistant vice president of operations (1934), Northern Pacific Railway; special consultant to the Railroad Division of the Reconstruction Finance Corporation (1934-1935); engineer in charge of reconstruction, Chicago, Burlington & Quincy Railroad (1935); engineer (1936-1941), chief engineer (1941-1947), general manager (1947-1951), executive vice president (1952-1954), Denver & Rio Grande Western Railroad; president and chief executive officer, New York Central System (1954-1968); president and chief operating officer, Penn Central (1968-1970); president, Western Pacific Railroad (1970-1976).

Alfred E. Perlman was a master railroad engineer who advocated the application of technology to solve railroad problems. He transformed the Denver & Rio Grande Western (D&RGW) from an insolvent, obsolete mountain railroad into a profitable and formidable competitor of the Union Pacific. He will be most remembered for his transformation of the New York Central from a four-track passenger line into a double-track fast freight line, and for the application of new marketing techniques characterized by service tailored to the customers' needs at a price that would be profitable for the railroad. After the Penn Central merger he presided over the operating disaster that brought the firm to chaos in less than three years, although the decision to slam the two railroads together without adequate preparation was not his. He was fired, along with other top Penn Central officers, but was never regarded as the villain of the debacle. At age sixty-eight he began a new career, restoring the profitability of the Western Pacific (WP) and preparing it for inclusion in the Union Pacific.

Alfred Edward Perlman was born in St. Paul, Minnesota, on November 22, 1902, to Louis Perlman, a civil engineer, and Leah Levin Perlman. He grew up in southern California. The family took many transcontinental train trips to visit relatives, and Perlman later suggested that those trips may have been where his love of railroading began. He always regarded railroading as both a profes-

341

sion and a hobby. He studied civil engineering at the Massachusetts Institute of Technology, working summers as a coach cleaner for the Chicago, Milwaukee & St. Paul Railroad in St. Paul. After graduation in 1923 he returned to St. Paul to begin his career as a draftsman for the Northern Pacific (NP).

Eager to learn all he could about railroading, he asked the NP to put him out on the tracks as a laborer. For the next ten years he paid his dues, serving as supervisor of bridges and buildings at Forsyth and Glendive, Montana, and Sandpoint, Idaho, and as roadmaster at Carrington, North Dakota. In 1930 the NP sent him to the Harvard University Graduate School of Business Administration for an accelerated program concentrating on transportation and railroads. Within a year he was back on the NP, a roadmaster at Staples, Minnesota. In 1934, at age thirty-one, he was named assistant vice president of operations.

That year the Reconstruction Finance Corporation (RFC) borrowed him to supervise the preparation of a comprehensive report on the condition of the New York, New Haven & Hartford Railroad (New Haven), a line which had every problem known to railroading. The RFC was so impressed with his report that it asked him to make similar studies of other roads. In 1935 Ralph Budd hired him away from the RFC to supervise the reconstruction of the Chicago, Burlington & Quincy's main line across Nebraska, which had been washed out by floods on the Republican River; 41 miles of line were gone and another 216 were isolated. Perlman experimented with off-track trucks to rebuild the line rather than on-track work trains, a method of track work that he pioneered. The route was reopened in twenty-three days, ahead of schedule. At the reopening celebration, Budd said, "If you want to know who was responsible for this quick job of reconstruction, it was a sparkplug named Al Perlman."

In Denver, Judge Wilson McCarthy was presiding as trustee over the receivership of the Denver & Rio Grande Western Railroad. The D&RGW's operating ratio was almost 95, its main line was ballasted in mud, its single track through the mountains could not carry enough trains for the road to make money, and it still operated a network of nineteenth-century narrow-gauge lines. McCarthy kept creditors at bay to give Perlman a chance to do what could be done.

Perlman rebuilt the main line with off-track equipment, virtually eliminating work trains on the D&RGW. He gave it a profit-making capacity with automatic block signals and Centralized Traffic Control (CTC). He pushed for the early dieselization of standard-gauge operations and for the substitution of bus and truck service for the narrow-gauge operations. He established a laboratory to run controlled tests on various aspects of maintenance and operations; the laboratory was expensive, but was said to have paid for itself in a short time. The most notable experiments, on diesel fuel consumption, were claimed to have produced fuel savings of $1 million a year for the D&RGW. In the midst of all this work, on June 15, 1937, he married Adele Sylvia Emrich of Denver; they had three children.

Perlman became chief engineer on the D&RGW in 1941. He took a leave of absence to work with the Defense Plant Corporation in Las Vegas in the middle of World War II. He became general manager of the D&RGW in 1947. He was credited with reducing the Rio Grande's operating ratio to 64 in spite of its grades, curves, and tunnels. The railroad came out of receivership in 1947 and that year paid its first dividend in seventy-six years. The installation of the California Zephyr streamliner in 1949 brought national attention to what had been a vestige of the Colorado gold rush, now transformed into a modern competitor of the Union Pacific. The public saw only the crown jewel, the Zephyr; but in railroad circles, there was talk that it was all the work of Al Perlman.

In 1949 Perlman was asked by the United States State Department to serve as a consultant for the South Korean railroad system. In 1950 the government of Israel borrowed him as a consultant for the Israeli railways. He became executive vice president of the D&RGW in 1952.

As Robert R. Young's proxy fight for the New York Central headed for its climax in the spring of 1954, the question of whom he would hire to run the railroad became more pressing. The New York Central's management was suggesting publicly that Young, a gadfly, had probably not given the question much thought. In March 1954 Young, speaking at a luncheon of the New York Customs Brokers Association, ticked off a list of railroads he thought were progressive (the New York Central was not among them). One was the Rio Grande. Someone asked whether that was Al Perlman's road; Young said yes, and that Perlman was the kind of progressive railroader he would like to have run the Central. The newspapers garbled Young's statement to imply that Perlman had already been chosen. The *New York Times* contacted Perlman, who said that he had never spoken with Young and had never been offered a job. Henry Sturgis of Citibank, working on behalf of the Central's management and sensing an opportunity to embarrass Young, asked Perlman to say publicly that he would refuse the position if it were offered. Perlman said that Young's remarks had been very complimentary and he had no intention of being ungracious.

Young investigated Perlman rather carefully, inquiring even into his marital happiness; his smoking habits; and his enemies, of which he seemed to have none. Perlman did some checking of his own on Young and was not pleased with Young's preoccupation with flashy passenger trains. Perlman's friends urged him not to get mixed up with a man who was not trusted by the financial community and who had a record of broken friendships and lawsuits by former associates. More telling, as far as Perlman was concerned, was the possibility that the New York Central might be in bankruptcy before he would have a chance to work some technological wonders.

Perlman arrived in New York for his first meeting with Young the evening before the stockholders' meeting that was to be the showdown of the proxy fight. The two men liked each other. Perlman later said that he was surprised at how many railroad issues they agreed on completely. Perlman did warn Young that he thought the future of railroads was in freight and that emphasis on passenger service was foolish. He demanded direct access to Young at all times. He also demanded stock options and a seat on the board of directors. Young hesitated, but agreed. The next day, as they traveled together on the stockholders' special train to the meeting in Albany, Young made a firm offer. Perlman returned to Denver to decide. He knew that taking the job would be the biggest gamble of his career, but he sensed that Young had already become the third great influence on his professional life after Budd and McCarthy. The challenge was too intriguing for him to resist.

Three weeks later, with Young's victory in the proxy fight all but certain, Perlman and his wife step-ped off the Twentieth Century Limited in Grand Central amid popping flashbulbs and reporters' questions. When Young's victory was confirmed, Perlman walked beside Young on the nationally reported triumphal march from Young's Alleghany Corporation headquarters in the Chrysler Building to the New York Central Building on Park Avenue. That day the two men learned that the Central was, in fact, insolvent. "Are you scared, Al?," Young is said to have asked. "No," said Perlman, "but we'd better get to work."

Perlman had always believed that executives should get out on the line and know first-hand what was going on, so the first thing he did was to order up a special train and tour the property. He was heartsick. The Central was more passenger-oriented than he had realized, a disproportionate share of its assets tied up in a service that had no real hope of making money. Two tracks of the four-track main line were for passenger trains only and signaled for eighty miles per hour, making them useless for freight. There were a dozen passenger stations the size of St. Patrick's Cathedral and just as costly to heat. The freight tracks on the main line, in poor repair and signaled for thirty miles per hour, were incapable of providing a competitive freight service. West of Buffalo, along the south shore of Lake Erie where the Central and the New York, Chicago & St. Louis (Nickel Plate) ran side by side, the Nickel Plate's short, fast freights went darting past the Perlman inspection train on their lean, well-signaled single-track line in a dazzling display of technological superiority—an embarrassment made even greater because they were pulled by steam locomotives. Perlman realized that the problems of the sprawling dinosaur that was the New York Central would be more resistant to solution than those of the compact Rio Grande.

Good economic conditions in 1955 and 1956 saved the Central from bankruptcy. During those years Young experimented with low-slung, high-speed, permanently coupled streamliners, supposedly the prototype of the future, that turned out to have the riding quality of a dinghy in a hurricane and were immediate failures. The "travel-tailored timetable" of the fall of 1956, his attempt at an ultimate passenger service, resulted in a $12 million quarterly loss.

Perlman's innovations in freight service were more successful. Centralized Traffic Control with reverse signaling, allowing trains to move in either direction on either track, was installed on the main line between Cleveland and Buffalo in a pioneering application of CTC in high-density, high-speed territory. Two of the four tracks could now be removed and freight trains could roll on the fast passenger tracks. Improvements in service and reductions of maintenance costs were immediate. The Central plunged into container service, Perlman opting for the Flexi-Van system, which did not require the highway trailer's chassis and wheels to be carried aboard the railroad flatcar. The system was superior to the more common form of piggyback in that it reduced tare, lowered center of gravity, did not require expensive state highway licenses on the trailers, and was adaptable to carriage by sea and air. It would be one of Perlman's bitterest disappointments that among other railroads, only the Chicago, Milwaukee, St. Paul & Pacific (Milwaukee Road) adopted the Flexi-Van system, severely restricting the Central's ability to market the service.

All of railroading took a downturn with the onset of recession in 1957. Young was distracted by lawsuits stemming from the proxy fight. Perlman testified before the Smathers Committee hearings on what would become the Transportation Act of 1958 about the industry's need for immediate relief from passenger losses. Young and Perlman seemed to agree that the Central ought to seek a merger partner. Whether they agreed on who that partner should be is not clear, but the matter was Young's to decide. On November 1, 1957, Young and Pennsylvania Railroad chairman James Symes, in separate statements, announced the intent of their companies to merge. The railroad industry was stunned, for it had always been assumed the nation's two largest railroads, and two of the most famous competitors in all of American business, would form the nuclei of separate systems, not join together and freeze everyone else out. Perlman was sent to begin joint operating studies with the Pennsylvania and outwardly appeared enthusiastic. Some thought that Young's willingness to undertake a merger in which the Central, which he had won at such great cost, would be a junior partner was an admission of failure. On January 5, 1958, Young shot himself to death at his home in Palm Beach, Florida.

Perlman, in full command of the Central, began the transformation of the road from a passenger-oriented line built essentially for nineteenth-century purposes into a high-speed, high-capacity freight line with a lean physical plant geared for the needs of the latter twentieth century. Centralized Traffic Control was extended to all main lines. Automatic electronic freight classification yards were built at key marshalling points—Young Yard at Elkhart, Indiana, Big Four Yard at Indianapolis, Collinwood Yard at Cleveland, Gateway Yard at Youngstown, Ohio, Frontier Yard at Buffalo, and Selkirk Yard near Albany. A technical laboratory was built at Cleveland. Secondary lines—the West Shore Railroad west of Albany, for example, and branch lines built mainly to carry vacationers to nineteenth-century resorts in northern New York State—were abandoned. Branch line passenger service was discontinued; main-line service was skeletonized, with a virtual withdrawal of passenger service into St. Louis. Plans were made to aggressively develop the railroad's real estate along Park Avenue in New York City—its right-of-way until the tracks were put underground into Grand Central—including the air rights over Grand Central itself, which resulted in the construction of the Pan Am Building.

Perlman's transformation of the way the Central marketed its services was perhaps his most revolutionary accomplishment. He broke with the traditional practice of offering basic service, mostly in boxcars, at minimum rates to maximize the tonnage that moved over the line. Instead the Central offered to tailor its services precisely to the shipper's needs—even buying special equipment if necessary—in return for a higher rate that would produce a clear profit for the railroad. This philosophy had been the key to motor carrier success: Perlman had watched shippers desert the low-priced railroads for the high-priced trucks because trucks offered service the customer was willing to pay for.

The effect of the marketing revolution was to diversify the Central's traffic base. This diversification made the railroad less dependent on raw materials, whose volume fluctuated wildly in recessions, and gave it a greater share of finished products, which commanded higher rates and whose volume did not fluctuate as much. Making the Central "recession proof" became Perlman's passion. He may not have reached his goal; there were no recessions from 1961 until the Central ceased to exist to really test his success. He could point with pride, however, to the success members of his management team in the heady days of the marketing revolution had after they left the Central: Walter Grant rose high at Consolidated Edison, Wayne Hoffman became chairman of Flying Tiger, John Kenefick became president and later chairman of the Union Pacific, and R. G. "Mike" Flannery became president of the Western Pacific and later of the Missouri Pacific and Union Pacific.

The railroad Perlman built was so much the opposite of Young's dreams of silvery streamliners packed with celebrities that it was hard to imagine that the two men had gotten along well at all. But years after Young's death Perlman told *Trains* editor David Morgan that Young had been like a brother to him. Through Young, Perlman had brushed with celebrities–the Duke and Duchess of Windsor, John and Jackie Kennedy, Richard and Pat Nixon, Nikita and Nina Khrushchev. Had it not been for Young, he never would have come to head the nation's second largest railroad.

After Young's death, Perlman still wore a button on his lapel that said "merge," but his heart never seemed to be in a merger with the Pennsylvania. On the surface it seemed that he just did not want to enter into a relationship in which he would play second fiddle, although perhaps only he understood how different the Pennsylvania's ideas on how to run a railroad were from his own. When the Norfolk & Western (N&W), a rich coal road controlled by the Pennsylvania, announced it would take over the Virginian Railway, the Central's friendly connection into the Pocahontas coalfields, Perlman thought that the PRR had betrayed his trust. He was angry at PRR chairman Symes and N&W president Stuart Saunders, and on January 8, 1959, he broke off merger negotiations, saying, "Before we marry the girl, we want to make sure there is no other heiress around that might fall into our lap." He proposed that all eastern railroads get together and plan a series of rational mergers.

Two weeks after he had broken off negotiations with the Pennsylvania, he paid a call on Walter Tuohy of the Chesapeake & Ohio. Perlman knew Tuohy well: Tuohy was an old associate of Young's whom Young had raised to the presidency of the C&O, and was the man Young had dispatched to Denver in 1954 to convince Perlman to come to the Central. Perlman and Tuohy talked about the possibility of a Central-C&O merger, but no commitments were made. Perlman said that the

Central needed five years to complete its modernization program before it would be ready to merge with anybody. A year later, however, a year in which eastern railroad headquarters had crackled with merger talk, the situation was more urgent. Perlman and Allan Kirby, another Young associate and chairman of Alleghany Corporation, paid a call on Tuohy and his chairman, Cyrus Eaton, also an old Young associate. Combining the Central and the C&O posed a touchy problem: the Central was much larger but the C&O was much richer. It was not clear which company, and which company's officers, would dominate a merged firm. Again no commitments were made.

On March 18, 1960, a few weeks after that meeting, the Norfolk & Western announced that it would seek to merge with the Wabash and the Nickel Plate. Both the N&W and the Wabash were already in the financial sphere of the Pennsylvania, so this move meant that the PRR was making a grab for the Nickel Plate, the last profitable independent in the East and an arch competitor of the Central west of Buffalo. Perlman called Tuohy, who said that he and Howard Simpson of the Baltimore & Ohio (B&O) were having dinner in Washington and that Perlman should join them. Perlman could not make it. It was at that dinner that Tuohy proposed to Simpson terms for the C&O to take control of the B&O. Word of the plan leaked to the press in April, and in the first weeks of May the C&O and B&O made firm commitments to each other. Perlman did have dinner with Tuohy and Simpson on May 18 and learned that the Central had clearly been left out of the C&O's plans. There was near pandemonium at the meeting of the New York Central stockholders the next week in Albany when Perlman told them the news. Perlman, probably with more hope than conviction, assured them that the Central would not be left out in the cold.

The result was the second great railroad proxy fight to pass across the Wall Street stage in less than a decade, and the second in which Perlman and the New York Central played a role. The Central countered the C&O's offer to B&O shareholders with an offer of its own, seeking proxies for a majority of B&O shares. The battle, which raged through the second half of 1960, involved full-page newspaper ads as each side tried to reach B&O shareholders whose stock was in anonymous street names, and jet flights to Switzerland as each side tried to win the endorsement of Swiss bankers who held B&O shares for their clients. The Central's offer was attractive on its face, although there was some question as to whether the road had the financial strength to make good on it. The C&O's offer, backed by its profits from hauling coal, promised more security in the long run. The Swiss bankers opted for the C&O. "I don't know who misled them," Perlman said. In the final frantic days in January 1961, the New York Stock Exchange had to suspend trading in B&O shares twice as offers and counteroffers were made far above market prices for remaining blocks of B&O shares.

When the fight was over the C&O had won, with proxies for about 64 percent of the B&O's shares. The last chance to set up truly competitive rail systems in the East, one based on the Pennsylvania and one on the New York Central, was lost. Perlman flailed briefly, at one point submitting an embarrassing demand to be included in the N&W-Nickel Plate merger. Finally he had to return, hat in hand, to the Pennsylvania.

Planning for the Pennsylvania-New York Central merger went forward. Extensive studies were made on how to combine the operations of the two railroads. In retrospect, it is clear that the studies were neither thorough nor adequate and that neither road made a serious attempt to coordinate with the other while planning was going on. The most famous example of this lack of coordination was their inability to agree on what kind of computer hardware to buy; each bought a system that was incompatible with the other. The failure of people on both sides to discipline their egos and come together on these matters foreshadowed the disaster that lay ahead.

Perlman was never enthusiastic about the merger. He did not like Saunders, who was now the PRR's chairman, and he had no respect for the PRR's management, which he thought was tradition-bound and inefficient. "You run a wooden-wheeled railroad," he said to David Smucker, PRR's vice president for operations. He thought that Saunders's deals with labor for job protection and with trustees of the bankrupt New York, New Haven & Hartford Railroad for inclusion in Penn Central were too generous and would drag the merged company down. The Interstate Commerce Commission (ICC) approved the merger on April 29, 1966, only because there was no other private–enterprise solu-

tion for the New Haven. Derivative lawsuits prevented immediate consummation. In July, at the merger's most politically sensitive moment, Perlman, without consulting his merger partners, filed petitions to end all passenger service on the New York Central. The move brought down on both railroads the instant wrath of the ICC, Congress, and the public. Some thought that it was Perlman's none-too-subtle attempt to derail the merger.

At one minute past midnight on February 1, 1968, the merger was finally consummated. Perlman came to Philadelphia for the press conference and posed for photographers, with a forced smile, beside Saunders. In front of them was a Lionel toy boxcar sporting the new Penn Central (PC) emblem and painted green, the company's new color. Saunders made it icily clear that it was *not* the former New York Central's color of jade green. Perlman did not stay for the champagne toasts but got on his private railroad car and went back to New York.

The decision to merge the two companies' operations at once, without preparation, was probably Saunders's, not Perlman's, because Saunders believed that it was essential to achieve instantly the savings that merger was supposed to produce. Perlman was the man who had to carry out the orders. The urgency was so great that no time was taken to retrain employees or make the necessary physical changes to connect the two railroads properly. The operating breakdown was nearly total and brought the railroad to paralysis by early 1970, with shippers deserting in droves to other railroads or other forms of transportation because the service was so bad. The debacle was worst at two key points—Big Four Yard at Indianapolis, where traffic from all over the Midwest was gathered and cars were preblocked (grouped for common destinations) for dispatch eastward, and at Selkirk Yard near Albany, where trains from the West were broken down for delivery to points on the East Coast. At Big Four, the problem seems to have been largely a failure to instruct crews in the myriad of new routings and new operating procedures they would use. At Selkirk, the failure was in not completing the expansion of the yard before a crush of new traffic fell in on it, making it impossible to either classify the trains or complete the yard.

All over the system, untrained crews mixed up paperwork and sent it to the wrong place. Shipments and paperwork became separated, until whole trains of "no-bills" (cars with no paperwork and thus unknown destinations) were dispatched over the line to get them out of one yardmaster's way and into someone else's. Accountants, equally untrained, failed to bill some customers and continued to dun customers who had paid because the payment had been entered in the wrong account. The latter mistake brought mountains of ill will.

Perlman and the whole New York Central management team—the Green Team—that he had put together felt that they had built a great railroad and that it was the mismanaged Pennsylvania that was dragging them all down. The showdown came at a sales meeting in Tarrytown, New York, at which Perlman delivered a blistering attack on the company's (and former PRR's) vice president for sales, Henry Large, and on the whole Red Team of former PRR people. The Red Team took the attack in stunned silence, but later Smucker detailed the extent of the operating disaster to Saunders and blamed it all on Perlman.

Perlman's critics thought he was preoccupied with electronic classification yards and spent too much money on them. They thought his faith in computers and cybernetics was naive and misplaced. (Cybernetics, the study of replacing human control functions with mechanical or electrical devices, was a lifelong passion of Perlman's; he served as chairman of the World Cybernetics Conference in the 1970s.) A statement by Perlman, quoted in condemnation of Perlman by his enemy David Bevan, the PC's vice president for finance, was equally his own most powerful justification of his stewardship: "I don't care if we lose X dollars this year and X dollars next year. I am building for the future."

In later years, Perlman insisted that the Penn Central could have solved its operating problems, but time and money ran out first. In the fall of 1969 Saunders removed Perlman from operations and kicked him upstairs to the meaningless position of vice chairman until his employment contract ran out in November 1970. There, stripped of power, he whiled away his hours under a kind of house arrest, and the railroad moved inexorably toward breakdown and paralysis. At the tumultuous board meeting of June 8, 1970, Perlman, Saunders, and Bevan were summoned and summarily fired. In the

many investigations and lawsuits that followed, Perlman was never found to have been the party mainly responsible or to have shown incompetence. In the final settlement of damages against the old management, Perlman had to contribute a modest $25,000 to the combined sum of $12.6 million. Saunders's and Bevan's contributions were never disclosed, but they were believed to have been much larger.

After such a humiliation and at age sixty-eight, Perlman could have been expected to enter retirement, but he did not. He accepted an invitation from the Western Pacific to untangle its affairs. The WP had enjoyed a golden age of prosperity in the 1950s and early 1960s, but had stumbled on hard times in the late 1960s. Perlman's reputation as a master fixer of broken railroads still shone despite the Penn Central disaster. In his typical way, he went out on the road, covering the entire length of the WP, spotting dozens of problems to solve and errors to correct. Within three months he had the railroad profitable and paying dividends again; by the end of his first year he had reduced its operating ratio thirteen points.

Perlman retired in 1976, although he continued to keep an unofficial finger on the railroad's pulse. He and his lieutenant, later successor, Mike Flannery, are generally credited with bringing the WP to a level, physically and financially, that made it an attractive merger partner for the Union Pacific, a merger consummated in December 1982. He died in San Francisco on April 30, 1983.

There were times during Perlman's career when he was abrasive and an egotist; that side of his personality was most evident in the B&O proxy fight. Around the Red Team of the Pennsylvania Railroad he had carried a chip on his shoulder, feeling himself a Jewish technician who loved the trains plunged in among Protestant Brahmins who seemed to him to care more about their investments and their country clubs.

But Perlman was also a mild-mannered man who talked to everyone on his railroad, from directors to dining car waiters, to see what was on their minds; who walked into hopeless situations and almost always turned them around, never losing his nerve and never looking back. Even in his latter years on the Western Pacific, he never got stuck in old ways. "When you do something do it right," he used to say, "and in two years look it over carefully; in five years look it over with suspicion; and in ten years, throw it out and start over." All of railroading's problems, he thought, could be solved with common sense and modern technology.

References:
Robert Bedingfield, "Young Wins Fight for the Central," *New York Times,* June 12, 1954, pp. 1, 27;

Joseph Borkin, *Robert R. Young: The Populist of Wall Street* (New York: Harper & Row, 1969);

Joseph Daughen and Peter Binzen, *The Wreck of the Penn Central* (Boston: Little, Brown, 1971);

"The Denver & Rio Grande," *Fortune,* 40 (November 1949): 97-105, 210-216;

David P.Morgan, "Alfred Perlman, 1902-1983," *Trains,* 43 (July 1983): 4;

Morgan, "A Conversation with A. E. Perlman," *Trains,* 34 (August 1974): 42-45;

Richard Saunders, *The Railroad Mergers and the Coming of Conrail* (Westport, Conn.: Greenwood Press, 1978);

U.S. Congress, Senate, Committee on Commerce, *The Penn Central and Other Railroads,* 92nd Congress, 2d sess., 1972.

Archives:
Some New York Central Railroad and Penn Central papers are at Eleutherian Mills Historical Library, Wilmington, Delaware.

Piggyback/Trailers-on-Flatcars

A Chicago Great Western Railroad "piggyback," circa 1936 (Courtesy Roger Grant)

The idea of the railroad "piggyback," the popular name for the intercity transportation of truck trailers or containers on specially equipped flatcars, dates from the 1920s. Although steam railroads had hauled loaded wagons on flatcars in the nineteenth century, it was the electric interurban industry that popularized the modern concept. The Chicago, North Shore & Milwaukee, a Samuel Insull property, led the way in 1926, when it began to transport specially designed truck trailers on modified flatcars to compensate for its inability to bring freight into Chicago's Loop over the local elevated system. A year later another Insull "juice" line, the Chicago, South Shore & South Bend, proudly introduced its "ferry truck" service: "Trailers left at your door for loading, shipped overnight on special flat cars." In 1935 the Chicago Great Western (CGW) became the first steam railroad to emulate the Insull roads. Initially the CGW carried trailers on an experimental basis, but on July 7, 1936, the company established daily "trailer trains" between Chicago and St. Paul. By World War II the CGW had expanded the service throughout its 1,500-mile system. A few other Class I carriers followed suit: the New York, New Haven & Hartford, for example, found piggybacking ideal for its territory, where trucks had seriously damaged railroad freight revenues. In the late 1950s the concept became more widely employed; thirty years later it was nearly universal. By 1984 piggyback movements ranked second only to coal in number of carloadings, accounting for 13.3 percent of all traffic. Newer versions of piggybacking have been devel-

oped: in 1984, for instance, the Chicago & North Western and the Union Pacific introduced "stack" unit trains, which permit two layers of marine containers to be stacked on specially designed low-profile rail cars.

Reference:

H. Roger Grant," Chicago Great Western Railroad: Piggyback Pioneer," *Trains,* 46 (January 1986): 31-34.

—H. Roger Grant

Pittsburgh & Lake Erie Railroad

by Michael Bezilla

Pennsylvania State University

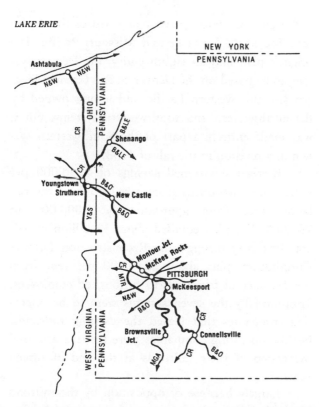

Map of the Pittsburgh & Lake Erie Railroad (1983)

A group of Pittsburgh businessmen formed the Pittsburgh & Lake Erie Railroad (P&LE) in 1875 to con-

nect their city with Youngstown, Ohio, thus giving shippers a western outlet independent of the Pennsylvania Railroad (PRR) and the Baltimore & Ohio. Much of the money to build the line was furnished by the New York Central (NYC), which by 1889 held two-thirds of the P&LE's capital stock and exercised firm control over the road. For the next seventy-nine years the Central operated the P&LE as a semi-autonomous subsidiary, using it to gain entry to the industrial heartland of its arch-rival, the PRR.

From Youngstown, where interchange with the parent was made, the P&LE stretched southeastward into the Ohio and Monongahela valleys of Pennsylvania, rich with coal mines, steel mills, and heavy manufacturing. The railroad enjoyed a stable and prosperous existence as it hauled millions of tons of coal each year from mines on its southern extremities to the mills of Pittsburgh or to the Youngstown gateway. Steel products, limestone, and coke accounted for most of the remaining traffic, which crested at 3.2 billion ton-miles in 1923. The P&LE preferred to allot switching and branch-line chores to subsidiaries of its own; most of its approximately 225 route-miles were main line—a not inconsequential factor in explaining the company's prosperity.

The P&LE's fortunes were inextricably tied to those of the steel and coal industries of western Pennsylvania, and as that industrial base gradually eroded, the amount of freight moved by the railroad declined. By 1962 the P&LE was generating about 1.2 billion ton-miles annually. Nevertheless, it continued to provide handsome dividends for its parent and was one of the few financial bright spots for the Penn Central, whose subsidiary it became following the 1968 NYC-PRR merger.

The P&LE operated for the most part independently of the Penn Central. Shortly after the latter declared bankruptcy in 1970 the two roads brought suit against one another for alleged unpaid debts; the claims were eventually settled out of court. In 1976 the P&LE fought successfully against inclusion in Conrail, arguing that Congress intended that newly formed system to encompass only financially ailing railroads. In 1979 the Penn Central—by then essentially a real estate firm—sold the P&LE to an independent party of investors. Within a few years, however, the railroad's economic condition deteriorated rapidly as a deep recession permanently closed many of the Pittsburgh area's steel mills. By the mid 1980s, the P&LE hovered on the brink of insolvency.

References:

Harrington Emerson, *Col. J. M. Schoonmaker and the Pittsburgh and Lake Erie Railroad* (New York: Engineering Magazine, 1913);

Lee Gregory, "The Little Giant, Free at Last," *Trains*, 41 (July 1981): 36-47;

Harold H. McLean, *Pittsburgh and Lake Erie Railroad* (San Marino, Cal.: Golden West Books, 1980).

Prince Plan of Railroad Consolidation

The Prince Plan of Railroad Consolidation was the most important of several proposals for cost reduction by consolidation of railroad facilities that were advanced during the Depression. The plan, which was solicited by President Franklin D. Roosevelt from financier F. H. Prince and formulated by John W. Barriger III early in 1933, sought to produce eight systems based on acceptance of the existing division of the industry into eastern, southern, and western regions. The eastern region was to have a northern system based on the New York Central and the four railroads controlled by the Van Sweringen brothers of Cleveland: the Chesapeake & Ohio, New York, Chicago & St. Louis (Nickel Plate), Pere Marquette, and Erie. The southern system in the eastern region was based on the Pennsylvania Railroad, Baltimore & Ohio, and Norfolk & Western. The southern region was to be served by a southeastern system based on the Atlantic Coast Line and Seaboard Air Line, and a Mississippi Valley system organized around the Illinois Central. The western region was to have a northwestern system comprising the Great Northern, Northern Pacific, Chicago, Milwaukee, St. Paul & Pacific, and Chicago, Burlington & Quincy; a central system based on the Union Pacific and Southern Pacific; and a southwestern system composed of the Atchison, Topeka & Santa Fe and Missouri Pacific. The original plan had an eighth entity, the Denver system, to be based on the Denver & Rio Grande Western and the Western Pacific and jointly owned by the northwestern and southwestern systems, but it was made entirely a part of the Southwestern system in a revision in the fall of 1933.

Barriger envisioned savings of $740,000 per year, about two-thirds from a reduction of the rail labor force from approximately 1,000,000 to 700,000. The plan entailed about $1 billion in federal financing through the Reconstruction Finance Corporation, plus about $250,000 per year from the Treasury in payments to furloughed employees. Transitionally the seven systems were to be operating companies that leased the existing railroads, but the operating companies were to have acquired ownership of their railroads at the end of fifteen years.

Largely because of opposition by the railroad brotherhoods to the prospect of massive reduction in employment, the Roosevelt administration had abandoned the Prince Plan by the end of 1933.

References:
"The Prince Plan of Railroad Consolidation" (1933), mimeograph, Interstate Commerce Commission Library, Washington, D.C.;

"Prince Rail Consolidation Plan Somewhat Modified," *Railway Age,* 95 (1933): 506;

"Railroad Plan Nears Completion," *Railway Age,* 94 (1933): 509-514.

—George W. Hilton

William J. Quinn

(May 8, 1911-   )

by Carlos A. Schwantes

University of Idaho

William J. Quinn (Kalmbach Publishing Company)

CAREER: Attorney in private practice (1935-1937); assistant U.S. district attorney for Minnesota (1937-1940); attorney, Minneapolis, St. Paul & Sault Ste. Marie Railroad (1940-1942); special agent, Federal Bureau of Investigation (1942-1945); assistant commerce counsel (1945-1946), commerce counsel (1946-1952), general counsel (1952-1953), vice president and general counsel (1953-1954), Minneapolis, St. Paul & Sault Ste. Marie Railroad; general soliciter (1954-1955), vice president and general counsel (1955-1957), president (1958-1966), Chicago, Milwaukee, St. Paul & Pacific Railroad; president, Chicago, Burlington, & Quincy Railroad (1966-1970); vice president, Burlington Northern Railroad (1970); chief executive officer, Chicago, Milwaukee, St. Paul & Pacific Railroad (1970-1978); president and chairman, Chicago Milwaukee Corporation (1971-1978).

William J. Quinn headed the Chicago, Milwaukee, St. Paul & Pacific Railroad (Milwaukee Road) from 1958 to 1966 and again from 1970 until late 1978. A handsome, affable man, he was only forty-six years old when he became president of the carrier, making him the youngest person ever to head the Milwaukee Road and one of the nation's youngest chief executives.

Born in St. Paul, Minnesota, in 1911 to William and Celina LaRoque Quinn, William John Quinn graduated from St. Thomas College in St. Paul with a bachelors degree in 1933 and from the University of Minnesota with a degree in law two years later. He served as assistant United States district attorney for Minnesota from 1937 to 1940.

The grandson of a locomotive engineer and the son of a prominent trial lawyer, Quinn joined the legal department of the Minneapolis, St. Paul and Sault Ste. Marie Railroad (Soo Line) in 1940. In 1942 he married Floy Isabel Heinen; they had eight children. After serving as a special agent for the Federal Bureau of Investigation during World War II he moved through the ranks of the Soo Line, becoming a vice president in 1953. The following year he joined the Milwaukee Road as general counsel, rising to president in 1958. In 1966 he departed for the Chicago, Burlington & Quincy Railroad, where he succeeded L. W. Menk as president. When the Burlington became part of the Burlington Northern Railroad in 1970, however, Quinn held only the post of vice president in the new company, a status that no doubt contributed to his willingness to return to the Milwaukee Road as chief executive officer on March 16, 1970.

When Quinn became president of the Milwaukee Road in 1958, he was widely hailed as one of the railway industry's bright new breed of lawyer-executives. Both he and the Milwaukee Road were viewed as progressive in matters of race relations and won commendations for "observing the fundamental right of equality of opportunity of employment" from a prominent Chicago civic group. Quinn's management style was characterized as "low profile." *Railway Age* in 1975 described him as a quiet and conservative Irishman, not given to making rash pronouncements. It observed that Quinn had earned the trust and respect of his peers as a spokesman for Western railroads.

Quinn was the author of the Quinn Plan, proposed in 1975 as a way for the federal government to restructure and rationalize the overbuilt and underutilized physical plant of America's Western railroads. The plan died in Congress. Its demise was but one more disappointment for Quinn during the 1970s, the most notable being the bankruptcy of the Milwaukee Road in December 1977. The bankruptcy gave rise to a number of criticisms of Quinn.

He was accused of having placed too much faith in merger as the best means to save the carrier. During his first tenure as head of the Milwaukee Road, Quinn had unsuccessfully sought a merger with the Chicago & North Western; during his second term he tried to merge with the Burlington Northern, but that attempt also failed.

The 1970s were exceedingly difficult years for the Milwaukee Road—made more difficult, said the critics, by the failure of Quinn and Presidents Curtiss E. Crippen and Worthington L. Smith to exploit the railroad's advantages. The Milwaukee's advantages, apart from its natural resource holdings, were few, but they included a line that after 1973 could offer through service from Louisville, Kentucky, to Portland, Oregon. In the eyes of critics, Milwaukee Road management appeared provincial and ingrown when compared to that of its competitors, the Chicago & North Western and the Burlington Northern; it was slow to respond to changing circumstances or to the liability of having too many miles of marginal line.

The 1977 bankruptcy, the third in fifty-two years, was perhaps inevitable and probably would have come earlier had the railroad not tapped the resources of its land company. Anything Quinn could have done, short of a merger with the Burlington Northern or some other strong line, would likely have only postponed the Milwaukee Road's final bankruptcy.

Quinn served as the Milwaukee Road's chief executive officer until his retirement in October 1978. He also held the post of president and chairman of the Chicago Milwaukee Corporation, a holding company formed in 1971, and was a director of Amtrak.

A critical essay in *Forbes* after Quinn's retirement noted that during only two of his last eight years as head of the Milwaukee Road had the company turned even a meager profit, and that while stockholders were forced to swallow their losses Quinn's salary had jumped more than 45 percent. His salary of $190,000 just prior to retirement was higher than that of the chief executives of such solvent companies as Holiday Inns and Trans World Airlines, the article observed.

References:

"I'm All Right, Jack," *Forbes*, 122 (October 30, 1978): 178;

"Mergers: The 'Quinn Plan' Goes to Washington," *Railway Age*, 176 (September 29, 1975): 30, 53;

"Mergers: What Ever Happened to the Quinn Plan?," *Railway Age*, 177 (March 29, 1976): 19-20;

Thomas H. Ploss, *The Nation Pays Again* (N.p.: Thomas H. Ploss, 1984);

"Railroads: Presidential Turntable," *Time*, 8 (October 21, 1966): 105.

Railroad Land Grants

Railroad land grants were the major form of congressional grants of land from the public domain, far exceeding land grants for schools, colleges, roads, canals, river improvement, and reclamation combined. Land grant policy rested on the assumption that the social rate of return on aided railroad investment would exceed the opportunity cost of capital in the economy. Congress saw railroad construction as a means of speeding economic growth and development; the land donations were to provide an asset upon which capital to construct the railroads could be borrowed. Almost 19,000 miles of railroad, about 40 percent of mileage built during the major grant period between 1850 and 1871, received federal land grant aid. Net land grant proceeds represented about one-third of the cost of construction west of the Mississippi River up to 1882.

Federal railroad land grants went through two phases. In the first phase, beginning in 1830, grants were made to the states, which parceled the land out to railroads. By 1859 fifty railroads, representing almost 9,000 miles of construction, had received 33 million acres.

In the second phase, grants went directly to specific railroads. This phase began with the 1850 Illinois Central and Mobile & Ohio land grant. The Pacific Railway Acts of 1862 and 1864 continued this trend, giving land to the Union Pacific and Central Pacific and creating the first transcontinental rail link. Numerous grants, primarily to the Pacific railroads, followed. The railroads received alternate sections of land, on each side of the right-of-way, within the limits of the particular act: six miles, ten miles, twenty miles, or forty miles. Growing public opposition led to the end of federal land grants after the 1871 Texas & Pacific grant. Federal and state grants totaled 179 million acres. Fourteen of the seventy recipients received 90 percent of the total. Four Pacific systems—the Union Pacific, the Southern Pacific, the Northern Pacific, and the Atchison, Topeka & Santa Fe—received about 73 percent of the 130 million acres of federal land grants patented by the railroads.

Starting with the Illinois Central grant, the federal government required recipients to transport government freight and troops at 50 percent and mail at 80 percent of established rates. Competitive pressures led almost all non-land-grant railroads in the land grant regions to join in the rate reductions to the federal government. The Transportation Act of 1940 rescinded reduced rates for freight and mail; reduced rates for troops and military supplies continued until October 1, 1946. Mail savings totaled over $60 million. Troop and military supply savings were immensely bloated by World War II: rate reductions totaled $580 million and ran about $20 million per month by June 1943; the total by September 1946 is estimated to have been $1 billion.

If 1870 is taken as the average year lands were received under the grants, the rate reductions were received on average about seventy years later. The $440 million the railroads received from the federal land grants came on average at least ten years after the grants were given. Comparison of revenues and paybacks requires both to be put in terms of 1870. Discounting by a conservative estimate of 2 percent, the rate reductions were worth $250 million and the revenues $360 million in 1870; thus, over the long term, the land grants involved a significant net subsidy to the railroads.

Land grant policy was generally nonoptimal: either too much or too little aid was provided to specific railroads. But while land grants were theoretically not the most efficient means of aiding railroad construction, they were the only politically feasible means at the time. Recent research supports the conclusion that land-grant policy was rational in terms of economic efficiency for several of the aided systems and made a positive contribution to the economic growth of the nation.

Reference:
Lloyd J. Mercer, *Railroads and Land Grant Policy* (New York: Academic Press, 1982).

–Lloyd J. Mercer

Railroad Unions and Brotherhoods

A track crew composed of Navajo Indians tamping ballast on the Atchison, Topeka & Santa Fe Railway line near Boron, California (Santa Fe Railway photo)

Trade unionism has been an integral component of railroad operations in the United States practically since the inception of the industry. In no other trade has labor been organized in such a persistent and comprehensive fashion. In the second half of the twentieth century, between 80 and 90 percent of all railway workers in the country were employed under union contract and were members of a broad range of craft organizations. Variously called brotherhoods, orders, or unions, by 1987 many of the associations had represented their respective constituencies for more than a century.

Operating trainmen were the first to organize. Engine drivers founded the Brotherhood of Locomo-

tive Engineers in 1863, conductors the Order of Railway Conductors & Brakemen (ORCB) in 1868, firemen the Brotherhood of Locomotive Firemen & Engineers (BLF&E) in 1873, switchmen the Switchmen's Union of North America (SUNA) in 1877, and brakemen the Brotherhood of Railroad Trainmen (BRT) in 1883. Typically these organizations began as mutual aid or fraternal societies and were quickly transformed into bargaining agents. Guaranteed-income agreements to combat irregular work schedules, wage-rate increases, shorter hours, the abrogation of capricious rule-making by supervisors, grievance procedures, seniority systems, and insurance protection emerged as early demands of the unions.

In the late nineteenth century and the first decades of the twentieth century nonoperating service and maintenance railroad workers followed the lead of the trainmen either by forming their own protective associations or by joining already existing craft unions. In 1987 the major nonoperating unions included the International Brotherhood of Boilermakers, Iron Shipbuilders, Blacksmiths, Forgers and Helpers, founded in 1881; the Brotherhood of Maintenance of Way Employees (BMWE) and the Order of Railroad Telegraphers, both founded in 1886; the International Association of Machinists and Aerospace Workers, founded in 1888; the Hotel and Restaurant Employees and Bartenders International Union, founded in 1890; the Sheet Metal Workers' International Association and the International Brotherhood of Electrical Workers, both founded in 1891; the International Brotherhood of Firemen and Oilers, founded in 1898; the Brotherhood of Railway, Airline & Steamship Clerks, Freight Handlers, Express & Station Employees, founded in 1899; the Brotherhood of Railroad Signalmen, founded in 1908; the American Train Dispatchers Association, founded in 1917, the Railroad Yardmasters of America, founded in 1918; the Brotherhood of Sleeping Car Porters, founded in 1925; and the American Railway and Airline Supervisors Association, founded in 1934. Unlike the original trainmen's unions, organizations of nonoperating railroad workers have with few exceptions been associated from their very beginnings with the American Federation of Labor and later the American Federation of Labor-Congress of Industrial Organizations (AFL-CIO).

Reorganizations and name changes were a constant feature of the brotherhoods in the twentieth century. The Brotherhood of Maintenance of Way Employees, for example, was established in 1886 as the Brotherhood of Railway Section Foremen of North America. In 1891 this small organization merged with the Order of Railway Trackmen to form the International Brotherhood of Railway Track Foremen of America. In 1896 and 1899, respectively, the Independent Brotherhood of Railway Trackmen of America and the United Brotherhood of Railway Trackmen of Canada were absorbed. The union was chartered by the AFL in 1900 as the Brotherhood of Railway Trackmen of America; in 1918 it became the United Brotherhood of Maintenance of Way Employees & Railway Shop Laborers. Its present title was adopted in 1925. In 1921 and 1937, respectively, the union absorbed the Order of Skilled Maintenance of Way Employees and the Pennsylvania System Fraternity, both of which had previously seceded from the parent organization. In the mid 1980s the Brotherhood of Maintenance of Way Employees (AFL-CIO) counted 119,184 members organized in 1,040 locals. Similarly complicated histories could be related for other brotherhoods.

Divided craft unionism has remained a notable feature of the railroad industry; extreme occupational diversity, the perennial problem of which workers are to be furloughed in slack times, and jurisdictional rivalries and bureaucratic politics have fixed craft practices and traditions in the trade and doomed repeated attempts at industrial unionism to failure. Railroad company consolidations, managerial associationalism, and increased government intervention in railway labor relations, however, have demanded more cooperative approaches on the part of railway unions and the practical jettisoning of pure craft policies.

Nonoperating unions associated with the American Federation of Labor adopted joint action strategies as early as the 1890s. Such efforts led in 1908 to the creation within the AFL of the Railway Employee's Department, an agency which has ex-

isted in one form or another since then to coordinate railroad craft union activities. In the first decade of the twentieth century officials of the trainmen's brotherhoods likewise entered into compacts to resolve jurisdictional disagreements and present common demands to sets of companies, though many of these arrangements proved to be short-lived. In general, a system of labor relations developed in which groups of unions commonly petitioned regionally based groups of carriers for contracts or contract changes. Expansion in union membership, the spread of locals, government mediation services, and the creation of managerial associations all contributed to a new structure of labor-management dealings.

Interunion cooperation in the twentieth century led to important consolidations that went beyond simple mergers and absorptions of related occupational groups. At a time when technological improvements, competition from other forms of transportation, and cutbacks in rail service were vastly reducing railway employment and when management was becoming increasingly resistant to strong brotherhood control of work rules (most notably on the number of workers on train runs), trainmen's union officials began seriously to consider the possibility of officially joining forces. In 1963 an attempt to merge the Brotherhood of Locomotive Engineers and the Brotherhood of Locomotive Firemen & Enginemen failed; the president of the firemen's union, a group severely threatened by the diesel engine's elimination of the position of fireman, then proposed a merger with the conductor's, brakemen's, and switchmen's brotherhoods. On January 1, 1969, after several years of discussion and negotiations, the BLF&E, BRT, ORCB, and SUNA were formally merged into the United Transportation Union (UTU), consisting of 250,000 members organized in 2,500 locals. Eighty years after the Knights of Labor and Eugene Victor Debs and his American Railway Union attempted to undo craft practice and bring one big union to the trade, industrial unionism finally had come to the railroad industry. The creation of the UTU and the continuing cooperative efforts of the AFL-CIO nonoperating railway unions left the Brotherhood of Locomotive Engineers with its 36,000 members and 851 locals in a singular position. The oldest brotherhood, it also remains the only one to be both unchanged in organization and name over its long history and an independent trade union unassociated with any federated labor organization or other railway labor group.

A most critical ingredient in railroad industrial relations has been the evolving and growing role that the federal government has played in structuring and mediating disputes. The first intervention of federal officials into railroad labor affairs occurred during the Civil War, when President Lincoln ordered the seizure of the Philadelphia & Reading Railroad by the military after a strike by the newly created Brotherhood of Locomotive Engineers had closed the line. During the great railroad strikes of July 1877, when the commerce of the nation was crippled, President Rutherford B. Hayes ordered troops to quell disturbances and federal judges began enjoining strike actions. After further crippling strikes in 1885 and 1886 Congress began considering legislation to establish arbitration procedures for railway labor disputes. The result was the Act of 1888, the first of a series of measures creating governmental agencies to mediate labor relations within the rail industry. The law allowed for the creation of three-member panels to air contract differences between unions and employers when both parties volunteered to participate; no enforcement powers were granted. Congress was forced to amend the act following the great Pullman strike of 1894, which proceeded despite possibilities for negotiation afforded by the Act of 1888. In 1898 Congress passed the Erdman Act, applying only to trainmen, which established a series of steps to avoid work stoppages. The commissioner of labor and the chairman of the Interstate Commerce Commission were delegated authority to establish boards of arbitrators; participation in the proceedings still remained voluntary and enforcement of proposed settlements ambiguous, however. The brotherhoods welcomed passage of the Erdman Law, which also outlawed the use of yellow-dog contracts and blacklists by managers.

In 1913 Congress revised the Erdman Law with the Newlands Act, which established a permanent Board of Mediation and Conciliation that could offer its services on its own initiative during disputes. The next seven years witnessed a vast expansion of governmental activity in railway affairs in general and railway industrial relations in particular. On the eve of a threatened strike by the five biggest trainmen's brotherhoods in 1916 Congress adopted the Adamson Act, which established eight hours as the standard workday for American railwaymen. During World War I the railroads were placed under the direction of the United States Railroad Administration, which created adjustment boards to deal with labor impasses. Under rulings issued during the war, the Railroad Administration also guaranteed all railway workers the rights to organize and join labor unions and made interference with such rights a federal offense. Railway union membership during the war doubled as a result.

Many of the labor practices established during the war were codified in the Transportation Act of 1920, which also returned the railroads to private management despite a campaign by the brotherhoods to further their nationalization. The act created a Railroad Labor Board with a regional system of boards of adjustment to settle disputes. The Railroad Labor Board had the authority to establish guidelines for wage rates and working conditions to apply during negotiations.

The legislative search for peaceful means to settle railway labor conflicts reached a final stage with passage of the Railway Labor Act of 1926, which, in amended form, remains the basic law today. The law, which aimed at the complete prevention of strikes, detailed procedures for the initiation of contract talks between unions and carriers and for later mediation and then arbitration by government-sponsored boards of conciliation. A thirty-to-sixty-day cooling-off period was also provided for, and the president was given last-resort emergency powers to settle disputes. In 1934 Congress passed the Railroad Retirement Act, which created a government-administered pension program for workers in the industry. With the passage of federal mediation laws and particularly the Railroad Labor Act of 1926, the railway brotherhoods became involved in a bureaucratic and legal maze. Federal agencies and courts have taken an increasing role in determining union jurisdictions; in establishing guidelines for wages, work loads, grievance procedures, and other working conditions; and in structuring the behaviors of both unions and management during disputes. Government intervention has had a significant impact in curtailing railroad work stoppages.

From the great railroad strikes of 1877 to the nationwide strike of shopmen in 1922, the railroads served as sites for the most dramatic confrontations between labor and capital in the period. The railroad brotherhoods rarely participated in such headline-capturing events as the Pullman Strike of 1894; the momentous strikes of the era were either largely unorganized or led by dissident groups such as the Knights of Labor and the American Railway Union. From the creation of the Brotherhood of Locomotive Engineers brotherhood officials have generally been among the more conservative leaders in the American trade union movement both tactically and politically. Brotherhood spokesmen warned their members against participation in the famous strikes of the late nineteenth and early twentieth centuries; and with the exception of a brief period in the early 1920s when the brotherhoods championed nationalization of the rail lines, railroad unions have not played a notable role in American politics.

As a result of government intervention, a nationwide railroad work stoppage has not been allowed to occur since the shopmen's strike of 1922. On ten occasions during the twentieth century individual companies or the nationwide system of rail carriers have been officially seized by the military through presidential order to prevent strikes; these actions occurred during times of national emergency. Other threatened large-scale strikes have been postponed through mediation processes. There have been strikes against individual carriers: between 1935 and 1969, 409 work stoppages on the railroads were recorded by the Department of Labor. Yet the estimated working time lost during these job actions by the brotherhoods was substantially lower than for other trades: the average railroad strike lasted only 15.5 days, government arbitration proceedings curtailing their impact and duration. Railroad trade unions in the twentieth century have thus operated under unique circumstances.

References:

Harry E. Jones, *Railroad Wages and Labor Relations, 1900-1952* (Washington, D.C.?: Bureau of Information of the Eastern Railways, 1953);

Walter Licht, *Working for the Railroad: The Organization of Work in the Nineteenth Century* (Princeton: Princeton University Press, 1983);

Howard W. Risher, Jr., "The Crisis in Railroad Collective Bargaining: A Study of the Institutional Impediments to Change in the Industrial Relations Systems," Ph.D. dissertation, University of Pennsylvania, 1972.

—Walter Licht

Ratemaking

Railroad freight rates in the nineteenth century were based neither on the cost of the service performed nor on a simple weight-and-mileage formula, but on what railroad managers thought the value of the service was to the shipper. This approach produced an inconsistent, unfair, and chaotic system of thousands of rates, which in a monopoly situation encouraged excessive transportation and maximized railroad profits. With tremendous investments in roadbeds, rolling stock, and stations, railroads had high fixed costs whether they ran one or a hundred trains a day. Since the cost differential between underutilized and fully utilized equipment was virtually zero, railroads lowered rates where freight was needed to fill empty cars. Railroads also penetrated underdeveloped areas and, hoping to reap freight harvests, hauled the cheap bulk products of those regions—ore, coal, grain, lumber—at low rates to encourage economic growth.

By the late nineteenth century, however, railroads were competing among themselves and with water carriers for freight between most metropolitan areas. Savage rate wars led railroads to discriminate against shippers from rural areas where the roads had a monopoly (the long-short-haul abuse) and against small shippers by means of rebates to large shippers. Railroads tried to avoid rate wars by dividing freight; after the 1887 Interstate Commerce Act outlawed pools, they used rate setting associations and bureaus. But they continued to adhere to value-of-service rates. Discrimination led to federal regulation in 1887 by the Interstate Commerce Commission (ICC). Although under a value-of-service system it was difficult, if not impossible, to define the "reasonable and just" rates Congress required, the ICC left that system intact.

In the twentieth century the ICC, having been given control over maximum rates in 1906 and over minimum rates in 1920, in effect froze value-of-service rates. The results were disastrous for railroads. The public thought railroads were charging all the traffic would bear and railroads, though they could demonstrate their overall operating costs and revenues, had difficulty justifying specific rate increases to the ICC because their existing rates had nothing to do with the actual cost of service. In 1956 there were 75,000 railroad tariffs ranging from those covering 15 percent of fully distributed costs to those covering 566 percent. As a result, valuable manufactured goods, which usually paid high shipping rates, were moved by trucks (which provided better service than trains), while cheap bulk commodities were moved at a loss by railroads. In 1961, 22 percent of all railroad freight paid rates that failed to cover costs. Value–of–service ratemaking aggravated a massive misallocation of transportation resources and destroyed a large segment of the rail system. Critics in the 1960s and 1970s advocated deregulation and cost-of-service ratemaking to revitalize what was left of the railroad system.

References:

Robert C. Fellmeth, project director, *The Interstate Commerce Omission: The Public Interest and the ICC* (New York: Grossman, 1970);

Ann F. Friedlaender, *The Dilemma of Freight Transport Regulation* (Washington: Brookings Institution, 1969);

Ari and Olive Hoogenboom, *A History of the ICC: From Panacea to Palliative* (New York: Norton, 1976);

Edward C. Kirkland, *Industry Comes of Age: Business, Labor, and Public Policy, 1860-1897* (New York: Holt, Rinehart & Winston, 1961);

Albro Martin, *Enterprise Denied: Origins of the Decline of American Railroads, 1897-1917* (New York: Columbia University Press, 1971);

John R. Meyer, *The Economics of Competition in the Transportation Industries* (Cambridge: Harvard University Press, 1959);

Merton J. Peck, "Competitive Policy for Transportation?," in Almarin Phillips, ed., *Perspectives on Antitrust Policy* (Princeton: Princeton University Press, 1965), pp. 247-249;

Ernest W. Williams, Jr., *The Regulation of Rail-Motor Rate Competition* (New York: Harper, 1958).

—Ari Hoogenboom

Samuel Rea

(September 21, 1855-March 24, 1929)

by Michael Bezilla

Pennsylvania State University

Samuel Rea in 1916 (James J. Hill Reference Library)

CAREER: Rodman, Pennsylvania Railroad (1871-1873); bookkeeper, Hollidaysburg Iron and Nail Company (1873-1875); assistant engineer, Pennsylvania Railroad (1875-1877); assistant engineer, Pittsburgh & Lake Erie Railroad (1877-1879); assistant engineer, (1879-1888), assistant to the second vice president (1888-1889), Pennsylvania Railroad; vice president, Maryland Central Railroad and chief engineer, Baltimore Belt Railroad (1889-1891); assistant to the president (1892-1899), fourth vice president (1899-1905),

third vice president (1905-1909), second vice president (1909-1911), first vice president (1911-1913), president (1913-1925), Pennsylvania Railroad.

Had Samuel Rea never achieved the presidency of the Pennsylvania Railroad (PRR)—the nation's largest rail carrier by nearly every measure—he nonetheless would be worthy of historical note, for his accomplishments as a bridge and tunnel builder rank him as one of America's premier civil engineers. His engineering achievements did much to advance his progress through the management ranks of the Pennsylvania Railroad, culminating in a twelve-year term as president. In that office, he succeeded in bringing about substantial improvements to the property, in spite of the constraints imposed by World War I and its aftermath.

Samuel Rea was born in Hollidaysburg, Pennsylvania, on September 21, 1855, to James D. and Ruth Moore Rea. His great-grandfather and namesake had migrated to America from Scotland in 1754, and his grandfather, John Rea, had served as a major general in the Continental Army and later, after settling in Chambersburg, Pennsylvania, for five terms in the United States House of Representatives. But Sam Rea was born into relatively humble circumstances. When his father died in 1868, the boy had to leave school and find employment in a general store to support the family. Hollidaysburg, once a bustling canal center, by the mid nineteenth century had been eclipsed by the nearby Pennsylvania Railroad town of Altoona. Rea applied to the PRR for a job and was hired in 1871 as a rodman or surveyor's helper by assistant engineer James McCrea—the man he would one day succeed as chief executive of the giant railroad.

Rea worked for the PRR for two years before being laid off in the Panic of 1873. After working as a bookkeeper for the Hollidaysburg Iron and Nail Company, he rejoined the railroad in 1875 as an assistant engineer in building a bridge across the Monongahela River at Pittsburgh. But the economy had not yet fully recovered from the effects of the depression, and when the span was completed, Rea was again furloughed. In 1877 he joined the Pittsburgh & Lake Erie Railroad (soon to become a New York Central subsidiary), then constructing a line from Youngstown, Ohio, through Pittsburgh to the southwestern Pennsylvania coalfields. When that project was finished in 1879 Rea returned to the PRR yet another time, still as an assistant engineer. His most important assignment involved the construction of the subsidiary Western Pennsylvania Railroad, intended to be a low-grade freight line passing to the north of the mountainous mainline between Pittsburgh and Altoona. Now more certain of his future, in 1879 Rea married Mary Black of Pittsburgh. They had a son (who would precede his father in death) and a daughter.

Vice President J. N. DuBarry, the Pennsylvania's chief civil engineering officer, noticed Rea's extraordinary self-taught abilities as an engineer and brought him to the railroad's Philadelphia general offices in 1883 as his principal assistant. Five years later Rea was made assistant to the second vice president, but the position was still one of subordinate engineer and not the promotion that Rea believed he deserved. He soon resigned from the PRR to accept an offer from the Baltimore & Ohio Railroad (B&O) to become vice president of one of its subsidiaries, the Maryland Central, and chief engineer of another, the Baltimore Belt Railway.

The B&O's line through the city of Baltimore was divided by the Patapsco River, necessitating a slow and expensive car float operation. The railroad wanted to eliminate the ferry in favor of an all-rail route and at the same time divert its main line away from the congested downtown and waterfront areas. It fell to Rea to supervise the planning and construction of a belt railway around the city.

A section of the new railroad included a heavily graded, 7,000-foot tunnel. Long before the bore was completed—a prodigious engineering feat given the local geology and the problems associated with tunneling beneath an urban area—Rea recognized that coal-burning locomotives could not be used safely within it. He therefore made preparations to use electric traction, a form of motive power thereto-

fore used only by light-duty street and interurban railways. Overwork and resultant ill health forced Rea to leave the B&O in 1891, but his vision became a reality four years later when an electric locomotive pulled the first train through the tunnel. The B&O, thanks in large measure to Rea, thus earned the distinction of becoming the first North American steam railroad to electrify. The operation was to continue for another fifty-seven years, amply demonstrating the wisdom inherent in Rea's innovative approach.

After taking a year off to rest, Rea went back to the Pennsylvania Railroad for the fourth and final time as assistant to President George B. Roberts. On the very day of his appointment he departed for London to gather information on that city's railway terminals and underground railway lines. The Pennsylvania was pondering whether to extend its eastern terminus from Jersey City to a new station in Manhattan, on the other side of the Hudson River. Roberts believed that the company could benefit from Rea's experience in tunnel and bridge building—to say nothing of his open-mindedness toward electric traction, which was anathema to many steam men.

Meanwhile, Vice President DuBarry died, and upon returning from abroad, Rea was assigned those duties of his late mentor that involved system-wide construction and related real estate and financial work. Finances were hardly mysterious to Rea. While living in Pittsburgh he had helped establish and had become a partner in the investment house of Rea Brothers, through which he became personally acquainted with the prominent bankers of the day.

With the elevation of Alexander J. Cassatt to the PRR presidency in 1899, Rea's fortunes also rose. Both men had been arguing for several years in favor of undertaking the ambitious New York extension. As chief executive, Cassatt moved to implement the project, estimated to cost more than $100 million. He made Rea fourth vice president and charged him with overseeing the extension's engineering work.

This work entailed the construction of twin tubes beneath the Hudson River, a subterranean approach to the magnificent new Pennsylvania Station in mid Manhattan, and four tunnels under the East River to connect the station with the Long Island Rail Road, a commuter-hauling PRR subsidiary. All trains to and from Pennsylvania Station were to be electrically powered. Six years into the project Rea was promoted to third vice president, but his responsibilities remained essentially the same.

Cassatt died suddenly in December 1906, with the extension still several years from completion. Wall Street considered Rea, Cassatt's closest associate, to be a prime candidate to become the new president, but within a week the PRR's board of directors instead elevated Vice President James McCrea.

McCrea was in many respects the opposite of Rea—aloof, imperious, extremely conservative in finances and in politics, and frail in health. His subordinate, on the other hand, delighted in being on first-name terms with many employees, made no secret of his Democratic leanings (he opposed the Republicans' high protective tariff), and boasted a robust physique. (He preferred chopping wood to the more accepted managerial pastime of playing golf.) In spite of the absence of a close personal relationship between the two men, McCrea retained Rea as the PRR's chief construction and civil engineering officer and head of the New York tunnel extension. Trains finally commenced running through the Hudson tubes in November 1910. Over the decades that followed, the efficiencies and conveniences of the extension rewarded the Pennsylvania many times over for its stupendous investment.

Rea was made second vice president in 1909. Cognizant of his subordinate's unique combination of talents, McCrea put Rea in charge of the railroad's accounting department as well as its construction activities. In 1911 the board elected Rea first vice president, seemingly all but confirming the fact that he was to be the Pennsylvania's next president.

There was no doubt in Rea's mind that he deserved the job. He had turned down the presidencies of the Southern Pacific Railroad in 1899 and the New Haven in 1905, ostensibly because he preferred to follow the New York project through to completion but probably also because he realized that settling for the presidency of another road would dash all prospects of ever heading "the Standard Railroad of the World." He counted heavily on support from those PRR directors who were dissatisfied with McCrea's cautious spending policies and wished to see a more growth-minded man in the president's office.

The more conservative directors, however, expressed contentment with McCrea's policies, especially after the unprecedented expenditures of the Cassatt administration. Moreover, they recoiled at the prospect of turning over railroad affairs to any person who had not pledged allegiance to Republican politics and who was not even an Episcopalian (Rea was a Presbyterian). Consequently, when McCrea's health waned early in 1912 and talk of retirement surfaced, there was speculation that Rea would again be passed over, this time in favor of second vice president John B. Thayer.

But in April 1912 Thayer went down on the *Titanic*. In December, plagued by a kidney ailment that would soon kill him, McCrea resigned. Rea was thereupon elected the Pennsylvania Railroad's ninth president, effective January 1, 1913.

Rea took over a railroad whose total route mileage had not grown appreciably since around 1900. Rather than expand by taking over smaller lines, as some other railroads were doing, Rea desired to concentrate on making the existing property more efficient. Chief among early projects with this aim was the conversion of commuter service between Philadelphia's Broad Street Station and Paoli, some twenty miles distant, from steam to electric propulsion. Complete in 1915, the Paoli electrification marked the first phase in the conversion of nearly all the Philadelphia suburban routes to electric traction, a goal accomplished by 1925. This suburban service used the latest high-voltage, alternating-current technology and gave the PRR the experience and confidence it needed to electrify its entire 245-mile New York-Washington main line, beginning in 1928. That project put the Pennsylvania in the forefront of electrification and, at $250 million, ranked as the largest capital improvement program undertaken up to that time in the American railroad industry. It was accomplished during the presidencies of W. W. Atterbury and Martin W. Clement, but the foundation—the engineering studies, the planning, the marshaling of finances—was a product of the Rea administration.

Also under Rea, the railroad adopted on a prodigious scale more modern classes of steam locomotives (the L1s 2-8-2, the I1s 2-10-0, and the K4s 4-6-2) after many years of trying to improve obsolete types or make do with less efficient engines. Other notable improvements included the construction in cooperation with three other railroads of the $70-million Union Station in Chicago and modernization of several Lake Erie ports.

These and other improvements were effected in spite of the hardships wrought by World War I and the confusion and uncertainty that plagued the railroad industry during and immediately after the war. World War I had an especially severe effect on the PRR because of the railroad's strategic location. Not only did it serve the nation's industrial heartland; it relayed foodstuffs from the Midwest to Eastern ports and funneled troops from all parts of the country to mid-Atlantic points of embarkation. America entered the war in April 1917, and as the nation mobilized, the PRR's east-west main line between Pittsburgh and Philadelphia became increasingly congested. Traffic elsewhere on the system and on other railroads also approached a standstill. Rea and executives from other lines formed the Railroad War Board to promote increased cooperation among the carriers in order to get the trains moving again and to ward off possible federal intervention.

The board's efforts proved fruitless, and on December 26, 1917, President Woodrow Wilson proclaimed that the railroads would thenceforth be operated by the government through the new United States Railway Administration (USRA). Rea and other top railroad officials were relegated to the sidelines for the duration of the emergency. The USRA had the authority to make decisions regarding labor policies and capital investments as well as operations, and to charge the costs to the railroads. Federal control succeeded in avoiding a total breakdown of the national rail network, leading some political and labor union leaders to demand that the government retain permanent ownership of the railroads after peace returned.

Rea and his counterparts on other roads vehemently opposed this idea; and after debating the issue at length, Congress in March 1920 decreed that private operation would be restored by the end of the year. Impressed by the efficiency resulting from USRA-enforced cooperation among lines, however, Congress also directed the Interstate Commerce Commission (ICC) to study the feasibility of consolidating the nation's railroads into a few large systems.

Rea spent much time trying to develop proposals for consolidation less detrimental to the PRR's well-being than the ICC's plan; other railroad presidents were doing the same thing. In the end, neither the ICC's plan nor any conceived by the industry was adopted.

Rea gave even more attention to undoing what he saw as damage done to the Pennsylvania by USRA rule. To avoid labor problems and work stoppages, the federal government had recognized the shopcraft unions of the American Federation of Labor (AFL), recognition the AFL had long sought in vain from the PRR's owners. The USRA had also greatly enlarged the Pennsylvania's labor force during the war but had failed to trim it once peace returned. Thus, while the PRR had employed 233,000 men and women in the spring of 1917, it had a payroll of 280,000 through eight months of USRA rule in 1920, although traffic levels were about the same. Not coincidentally, the Pennsylvania posted a $62 million operating deficit in 1920. Rea clung to the PRR's longstanding opposition to collective bargaining on a national, industry-wide basis, which had been granted under the USRA; he argued that each railroad should negotiate with its own employees. He was often heard to remark, possibly in reference to his own experience, that "no man should ask for more than employment. When that is given, it is up to him to do the rest."

The president preferred not to involve himself directly with the labor question—perhaps foreseeing that the situation could only tarnish his image among the railroad's work force—and delegated that responsibility to Vice President Atterbury. In 1921 the Pennsylvania unilaterally withdrew recognition of the AFL shopcraft unions (a move later upheld by the courts) and proceeded to form company unions. The PRR had always prided itself on the high morale of its workers, but the arbitrary manner in which the union contracts were negated cast a pall over labor-management relations that would last for decades. Nevertheless, the company unions did give their members enough satisfaction that when the AFL shopcraft unions staged a nationwide strike in July 1922, the Pennsylvania was little affected. Rea's reputation as "the grand old man of the PRR" survived intact.

Rea devoted most of the remainder of his tenure to improving the company's financial status so that by the end of the decade it would once again be in a position to launch a major program of improvements (especially electrification). He also did away with the old Lines East/Lines West dichotomy, having seen from wartime experience that it impeded the smooth flow of traffic through the Pittsburgh gateway. Net operating income rose from $37 million in 1921 to $100 million in 1925.

When Rea retired on October 1, 1925, he became the first president to live long enough to invoke the railroad's mandatory rule that employees retire at age seventy (a regulation Rea himself had helped draft while still a vice president). The presidency of the Pennsylvania was widely regarded as a "man-killing" job. All of Rea's predecessors since 1852 had died in office or within months of leaving it. Rea enjoyed nearly four years of retirement, spent mostly at his home in Gladwyne in the Philadelphia suburbs. He took an active role in urban and regional planning—a role consistent with his development of an electrified commuter railroad network for Philadelphia—but attracted public attention only when he headed a group of Delaware Valley businessmen in support of Al Smith's unsuccessful run for the White House in 1928. (Like Smith, Rea detested Prohibition.) Rea died on March 24, 1929, succumbing to a heart attack following a long bout with influenza. Twenty-five years later the Pennsylvania Railroad opened in Hollidaysburg what was then the world's largest railcar building and repair facility and christened it the Samuel Rea Shop in his honor.

Rea was the epitome of the self-made man. Although he had scant formal schooling, throughout his life he devoured books on history, biography, and economics. Upon his retirement, when asked by newspaper reporters what advice he might give to youths who would emulate his heroic life, he gave a one-word response: "Read!" His self-education served the Pennsylvania Railroad well. Besides supervising some of its most important engineering projects, he led the railroad on an ambitious but carefully considered course of improvements and modernization and swiftly returned it to prosperity after the ordeal of World War I and government operation.

Publications:
Statement of Mr. Samuel Rea, President, Pennsylvania Railroad System, before the Interstate Commerce Commission, 7 May 1917 (Philadelphia: Pennsylvania Railroad, 1917);

"Engineering Reminiscences," *Journal of the Franklin Institute*, 202 (August 1926): 165-172.

References:
George H. Burgess and Miles C. Kennedy, *Centennial History of the Pennsylvania Railroad* (Philadelphia: Pennsylvania Railroad, 1949);

"McCrea Resigns as President of Pennsylvania Railroad, Samuel Rea to Succeed Him," *New York Times*, November 24, 1912, p. 1;

"Rea Retires from Pennsylvania Railroad," *New York Times*, October 1, 1925, p. 7;

"Samuel Rea," *Railway Age Gazette*, 53 (November 22, 1912): 993-994;

"Samuel Rea New Pennsylvania Railroad President, McCrea Resigns," *Philadelphia Public Ledger*, November 24, 1912

"Samuel Rea Retires as PRR President," *Philadelphia Inquirer*, October 1, 1925;

H. W. Schotter, *The Growth and Development of the Pennsylvania Railroad Company* (Philadelphia: Allen, Lane & Scott, 1927).

Archives:
The disposition of Samuel Rea's personal and family papers is unknown. His business papers relating to the Pennsylvania Railroad are in the PRR archives held by the Pennsylvania Historical and Museum Commission, Harrisburg. These archives have not been catalogued and are not open to researchers.

Reading Company

by James N. J. Henwood

East Stroudsburg University of Pennsylvania

Map of the Reading Company system

The development of the anthracite fields in northeastern Pennsylvania was the stimulus for the chartering of the Philadelphia & Reading Railroad (P&R) in 1833. By 1842 a line had been constructed along the Schuylkill River between Philadelphia and Pottsville, where connections were made to various "lateral" or feeder lines, which eventually became branches of the P&R.

In 1863, the company emerged victorious in a struggle with Schuylkill Navigation Company for dominance in the coal trade. The company expanded by leasing or buying adjoining roads, which enabled it to reach Harrisburg and Allentown, and later Bethlehem; Shippensburg, where connections would provide much bridge traffic; Bound Brook, New Jersey, which became part of a New York route in conjunction with the Jersey Central; Port

Reading, New Jersey, on the Arthur Kill, which gave direct access to New York City; and South Jersey, through the purchase of the Atlantic City Railroad, which was rebuilt and extended to Cape May.

Until 1869, the P&R had been conservatively managed, but in that year the flamboyant, thirty-four-year-old Franklin B. Gowen became president. Forceful, daring, and egotistical, he initiated an aggressive program of expansion which eventually ended in receivership for the railroad. Gowen purchased vast amounts of coal lands, borrowing heavily to do so, and organized the Philadelphia and Reading Coal and Iron Company to manage them. He also improved the road physically and developed a large tidewater terminal at Port Richmond in Philadelphia.

The P&R was twice in receivership between 1880 and 1888, when J. P. Morgan effected a reorganization. Speculation again was dominant under President Archibald A. McLeod, who attempted to extend Reading power to New England and leased the Lehigh Valley and the Central Railroad of New Jersey. The P&R could not support this ambitious undertaking and once more entered receivership in 1893.

In 1897, Morgan again reorganized the line, establishing a holding company, the Reading Company, to manage the properties. In a last spate of expansion, the Reading reached Wilmington, Delaware, in 1898 and once more acquired control of the Jersey Central in 1901. At the same time, the Baltimore & Ohio gained control of the Reading.

In the twentieth century, the Reading remained a major anthracite carrier and developed considerable bridge (through) and terminal traffic. In

1923, the Reading Company merged with the P&R and a number of other wholly owned lines and became an operating company. An extensive commuter network was operated out of Philadelphia; most of these lines were electrified by 1933. That year, the Atlantic City Railroad was merged into a new corporation, the Pennsylvania-Reading Seashore Lines, owned one-third by the Reading and two-thirds by the Pennsylvania. The common ills of northeastern railroading beset the Reading after World War II: the collapse of anthracite, modern highways, industrial decay, passenger losses, and high taxes and terminal expenses. The Reading declared bankruptcy in 1971 and was taken over in 1976 by Conrail, which still operates much of the property.

References:

Jules I. Bogen, *The Anthracite Railroads* (New York: Ronald Press, 1927);

George H. Drury, *The Historical Guide to North American Railroads* (Milwaukee: Kalmbach, 1985), pp. 275-277;

Bert Pennypacker, *Reading Power Pictorial* (Rivervale, N.J.: Carleton, 1973);

This Is the Reading (Philadelphia: Reading, 1951).

Rebates

With enormous investments in roadbeds, rolling stock, and stations, nineteenth-century railroads had high fixed costs, whether they ran one or a hundred trains a day. Since the cost differential between under utilized and fully utilized equipment was virtually nil, railroads were willing to offer discounts on their rates to attract large shippers. Such a deduction was called a rebate, which meant returning part of the payment. Even if fully distributed costs, including fixed charges, were not met after a rebate was given, the railroad's overall revenues would increase as long as out-of-pocket costs for the shipment were covered.

Rebates were illegal: railroads were public carriers, and their charters required that all shippers must pay the same rate for the same service. Nevertheless, in the late nineteenth century, with railroads competing strenuously for freight between most metropolitan areas, large shippers extracted rebates from carriers and felt justified because railroads could handle a huge shipment more economically than they could handle numerous smaller shipments adding up to the same tonnage. Rebates to Standard Oil ran as high as 50 percent on shipments from Cleveland to New York City. Small shippers and their congressional representatives were understandably hostile to rebates. Rebates were outlawed in the Interstate Commerce Act (1887); when the practice continued, vigorous enforcement by the Theodore Roosevelt administration of the Elkins Antirebating Act (1903), which made rebating a criminal violation for both shippers and railroad managers, finally stopped the practice.

Reference:

Ari and Olive Hoogenboom, *A History of the ICC: From Panacea to Palliative* (New York: Norton, 1976).

—Ari Hoogenboom

John S. Reed

(June 9, 1917-   )   by Keith L. Bryant, Jr.

Texas A&M University

John S. Reed (Santa Fe Railway photo)

CAREER: Test assistant (1939-1940), special representative to general superintendent of transportation (1946-1948), trainmaster (1949-1951), superintendent (1952-1954), assistant to vice president (1954-1957), executive assistant to the president (1957-1959), vice president–finance (1959-1964), vice president, executive department (1964-1967), president (1967-1978), chief executive officer (1968-1982), chairman (1973-1983), Atchison, Topeka & Santa Fe Railway; president (1968-1978),

chairman and chief executive officer, Santa Fe Industries (1973-1983).

Rising through the ranks of the operating department of the Atchison, Topeka & Santa Fe Railway to the executive offices in Chicago, John S. Reed played a conspicious role in the rapid modernization of the railroad. He participated in the formation of Santa Fe Industries as a holding company for the carrier and its petroleum, real estate, pipeline, mineral, and lumber subsidiaries. An ardent "Santa Fe" man, Reed rebuffed until the end of his tenure efforts by other railroads to merge with the railway in the era of megamergers. He sought to maintain the Santa Fe's independence as he redeployed assets and expanded nonrail business activities.

John Shedd Reed was born in Chicago in 1917 to Kersey Coates and Helen May Shedd Reed. His grandfather, John Graves Shedd, had donated the famous Shedd Aquarium to the city. Reed attended the Chicago Latin School, the Los Alamos Ranch School, and the Hotchkiss School in Connecticut before entering Yale University. Graduating with a degree in industrial administration in 1939, Reed joined the Santa Fe's testing department. Undoubtedly a young man with his education, military experience, and family connections could have entered any number of firms, but Reed was a "rail fan" who fondly remembered the long train trips of his youth on the California Limited to the West Coast. With the outbreak of World War II he enlisted in the navy, attended the V-7 program at Annapolis, and was commissioned an ensign in 1941. He rose to the rank of lieutenant commander before returning to civilian life and the Santa Fe's operating department in 1946. He served in various capacities in Amarillo and Slaton, Texas; Pueblo,

Colorado; and Marceline, Missouri, before moving to Chicago in 1957 as executive assistant to the president. He became vice president for finance in 1959 and vice president of the executive department in 1964.

Reed made railroading and the Santa Fe his life's work. A "no-nonsense" executive who banned liquor from his private car, Reed came to believe that the Santa Fe should develop long-range plans to gain efficiency and greater profitability, but he refused to cut corners in terms of maintenance and the acquisition of new technologies.

Reed succeeded Ernest S. Marsh as president of the the railway in 1967. After a decade of service in the executive department he had a thorough knowledge of the company's operations and its potential. In less than two years the railway formed Santa Fe Industries, restructured all the major units into that holding company, and staved off an effort by the Missouri Pacific to force an unfriendly merger. Reed established new directions for the railway and for Santa Fe Industries, demanding greater utilization of equipment, more highly trained executives, and adoption of new technologies. The data processing center in Topeka, Kansas, and the computerized inventory control system for purchasing in Chicago received special attention. The acquisition of equipment for the trailers-on-flatcars (TOFC or piggyback) program accelerated as TOFC business soared. Containers-on-flatcars traffic increased also, especially to and from Japan.

The railway embarked on an extensive effort to improve its trackage. A welded-rail program covered most main lines, and major traffic bottlenecks on the branch to Phoenix and across Cajon Pass in California were improved with curve and grade reductions. A huge new computerized yard opened in Kansas City, and a computerized center in Chicago was established to control the allocation and use of locomotives and cabooses on the entire system. In 1968 Reed announced the introduction of the Super C, an all-TOFC-and-container freight train that ran from Chicago to Los Angeles on a thirty-four and a half hour schedule which bettered the time of the famous Super Chief passenger train. Expedited shipments from Chicago to New York meant that a trailer could be moved from coast to coast in fifty-four hours.

The Santa Fe also turned to unit trains to generate traffic and revenues. For example, coal was hauled from New Mexico to California for Kaiser Steel; together with the Duval Corporation the company developed a means of transporting molten sulphur in unit trains from the mines in west Texas to the docks of Galveston.

While the railway had acquired some minor lines after 1945, its only major efforts at expansion had been aborted by the Interstate Commerce Commission. Proposals to obtain an entrance into St. Louis and to acquire the Western Pacific were denied. While the Santa Fe actively opposed the acquisition and dismemberment of the Chicago, Rock Island & Pacific by its arch rivals, the Southern Pacific and the Union Pacific, it did not vigorously pursue large-scale merger partners of its own. There were talks with the Missouri Pacific and with the St. Louis-San Francisco (Frisco), but disagreements over terms and the value of securities precluded mergers. Reed appeared determined to keep the Santa Fe a major independent carrier. But even as the Penn Central and other eastern carriers collapsed and the government formed Conrail in the 1970s, the railway map in the West was also changing. The formation of the Burlington Northern (BN) in 1970 created a giant that competed directly with the Santa Fe in the Midwest. When the BN acquired the Frisco in 1980, that competition extended to much of the Southwest as well. The merger of the Union Pacific, Missouri Pacific, and Western Pacific in 1981 forced the Santa Fe to reexamine its position. It had become clear that merger with the Southern Pacific was dictated by the emergence of powerful rivals throughout the company's territory. The Santa Fe Southern Pacific Corporation was formed in 1983.

Santa Fe Industries expanded rapidly under Reed though the railway did not. As prices for petroleum rose, the company's subsidiaries in that industry enlarged their exploration and production programs. Santa Fe Industries entered, then left, the air freight business, and a massive pipeline system for anhydrous ammonia was built from Louisiana to the Midwest. In 1972 Santa Fe Industries bought Robert E. McKee, a large general contractor in the Southwest. As economic growth in the Sunbelt accelerated, Santa Fe Industries developed a number of major real estate projects in San Diego, Los Angeles, and the San Francisco Bay area.

John S. Reed represented a new generation of railroader. His education and ideas were different from those of the men who had led the Santa

Fe before 1945. Yet he remained firmly committed to the railway as executives on other carriers engaged in massive mergers, downgraded the importance of the railroad units, or even spun off the railway portions of their holding companies. In 1983 he retired as an executive of the railway, though he continued to serve as director of Santa Fe Southern Pacific Corporation and to play an active role in numerous civic and charitable organizations in Chi-

cago and across the country. He had married Marjorie Lindsay in 1946, and they had five children. In 1987 the Reeds resided in Lake Forest, Illinois.

References:

Keith L. Bryant, Jr., *History of the Atchison, Topeka and Santa Fe Railway* (New York: Macmillan, 1974);

Fred Frailey, "Keeping a Railroad on the Right Track," *Chicago Sun-Times,* December 6, 1970.

W. Thomas Rice

(June 13, 1912-)

by James A. Ward

University of Tennessee at Chattanooga

CAREER: Engineer (1934-1936), assistant supervisor (1936-1940), supervisor of track (1940-1942), Pennsylvania Railroad; officer, U.S. Army Railway Corps (1942-1946); supervisor of track, superintendent of Potomac Yard, superintendent, general superintendent (1946-1955), president (1955-1957), Richmond, Fredericksburg & Potomac Railroad; president and director, Atlantic Coast Line Railroad (1957-1967); president and chief executive officer (1967-1970), chairman of the board and president (1970-1972), chairman of the board and chief executive officer (1972-1977), chairman of the board and member of the executive committee (1977-1981), chairman emeritus (1981-1983), Seaboard Coast Line Railroad; chairman emeritus, Seaboard System (1983-).

W. Thomas Rice is a classic example of a twentieth-century railway executive: he began in a railroad engineering corps and with the exception of World War II stayed in the industry throughout his career, slowly working his way up to the executive offices. Railroads had become so technical by their 100th anniversary that the typical men who reached their upper ranks were formally trained engineers, like Rice, familiar with all operational and maintenance phases of the business.

William Thomas Rice was born in Hague, Vir-

ginia, on June 13, 1912, to John and Elizabeth Conway Snow Rice. After graduation from Cople High School in 1929 he attended Virginia Polytechnic Institute, where he earned a bachelor of science degree in civil engineering in 1934.

Rice received his early training right after graduation on the Pennsylvania Railroad, where he was an assistant in the engineering corps stationed at Elmira, New York. Promising young engineers on large roads were moved frequently to acquaint them with various divisions, and Rice followed this pattern for years. He was soon posted to the Maryland Division at Wilmington, Delaware, and from there to the engineering office in Philadelphia. During his professional peregrinations, Rice married Jacqueline Johnson on September 14, 1935; they had two children.

Appointed an assistant supervisor of the Williamsport Division at Sunbury and Lock Haven, Pennsylvania, on February 15, 1936, Rice was soon transferred to the same position on the Maryland Division. He was promoted on April 1, 1940, to supervisor of track for the Delmarva Division at Clayton, Delaware, and from there to the same job at Logansport, Indiana, where he worked from August 1, 1941, until April 9, 1942.

Rather than interrupting Rice's career, World War II afforded him additional training and experi-

W. Thomas Rice

ence. In April 1942 he entered the army as a first lieu-tenant in the 730th Railway Operations Battalion. Between January 1943 and June 1945 he rose to company commander, battalion executive officer, and finally battalion commander of the 791st and 711th Railway Operations Battalions, stationed in Iran. There Rice kept supplies of Lend-Lease war material flowing to the Soviet Union. At the end of the European war, Rice was immediately sent to Sixth Army headquarters in the Philippines, and later to Japan, as a rail officer. In March 1945 he was promoted to lieutenant colonel. For his war efforts, Rice was awarded the Legion of Merit with Oak Leaf Cluster.

After mustering out in early 1946 Rice took a position with the Richmond, Fredericksburg & Potomac Railway (RF&P), part of the Atlantic Coast Line (ACL) serving successively as supervisor of track at Fredericksburg, as superintendent of the Potomac Yard at Alexandria, and as superintendent.

By 1951 Rice had finished his apprenticeship, and he began a meteoric rise through the ranks of the RF&P and its parent company, starting as general superintendent. Four years later he was named president of the RF&P. In 1957 he became president and a member of the board of directors of the Atlantic Coast Line, which stretched from Richmond to south Florida.

As president of the ACL Rice maintained a first-class property that was well organized and well operated. He expanded it slightly in 1958 with the acquisition of the Franklin & Carolina Railroad in Virginia, but he disposed of the ACL's holdings in the Peninsular & Occidental Steamship Company in 1960 and a year later sold the road's investment in the Baltimore Steam Packet Company (Old Bay Line) and discontinued all railway service on Chesapeake Bay. He also moved the corporate offices from Norfolk to Jacksonville, Florida, in 1960. Despite technical advances such as dieselization, the

ACL was faced with severe competition from other railways and nonrailway carriers. During Rice's tenure his road's tonnage increased, but its gross revenues lagged. When congressional committee hearings in 1958 demonstrated that no political solution to the industry's problems was forthcoming, Rice began talking with President John Smith of the competing Seaboard Air Line Railroad about a merger. They reached an agreement in 1960, attended Interstate Commerce Commission hearings the following year, and received permission to merge in December 1963. When consolidation finally took place on July 1, 1967, Rice became president and chief executive officer of the newly organized Seaboard Coast Line. In 1970 he became chairman of the board, retaining both posts until he reached retirement age in 1977. That year he relinquished daily oversight of the business but retained his seat as chairman of the board and member of the executive committee. In 1981 he became chairman emeritus.

Rice maintains memberships in a long list of organizations, including the American Society of Civil Engineers, Army Railway Engineering Association, American Association of Railroad Superintendents, Association of American Railroads, Transportation Association of America, National Defense Transportation Association, National Freight Traffic Association, and the U.S. Chamber of Commerce. He also sits on boards of banks, land companies, steamship companies, and other railroads. A major general in the reserves, he is an Episcopalian and an independent in politics. He was a prominent figure in the railroad merger movement that swept the country in the 1950s and 1960s, and through his efforts the SCL (after 1983 the Seaboard System, a component of CSX) took its place as one of three or four southern consolidated rail systems that serve larger territories, control greater financial resources, face less rail competition, and enjoy a greater measure of security than was the case in earlier times.

Edward P. Ripley

(October 30, 1845-February 4, 1920)

by Keith L. Bryant, Jr.

Texas A&M University

Edward P. Ripley (Santa Fe Railway Photo)

CAREER: Clerk, dry goods business, Boston (1862-1866); contracting agent, Star Union Line, Boston (1866-1870); clerk (1870-1872), northeastern agent (1872-1875), general eastern agent (1875-1886), traffic manager (1887-1888), general manager (1888-1890), Chicago, Burlington & Quincy Railroad; third vice president, Chicago, Milwaukee & St. Paul Railway (1890-1895); president (1896-1919), chairman of the board (1920), Atchison, Topeka & Santa Fe Railway.

In 1918 the *New York Times* hailed Edward P. Ripley as "the greatest living railroad man."

Such an accolade in an era of railway giants reflected Ripley's leadership of the Atchison, Topeka & Sante Fe Railway. He had turned a bankrupt ruin into one of the most profitable carriers in the nation through careful, controlled expansion, rapid modernization, and concern for economic development in its territory. As a national leader of the rail industry, Ripley strongly opposed government regulation of the railroads, and he fought the railway unions through the establishment of company-paid benefits, strict discipline, and a system of work incentives and bonuses. In twenty-four years he created an efficient, profitable railroad that was the envy of managers and owners throughout the industry.

Born in Dorchester, Massachusetts, in 1845, the son of Charles Pinckney and Anne Robinson Payson Ripley, Edward Payson Ripley received a good common-school education. Ripley's father was a merchant in Dorchester, but the son, after clerking in a dry-goods store for four years, found employment as a clerk in the Boston office of the Star Union Line. He quickly mastered the detail of the office, and when an opportunity came for a better-paying job on the Chicago, Burlington & Quincy Railroad (CB&Q), he joined that carrier.

Boston financial interests dominated the CB&Q, as they did the Atchison, Topeka & Santa Fe Railroad and other Western lines, and Ripley's talents became obvious to the leaders of the Burlington. Ripley believed in service and stability, and he dedicated himself to the railroad. He solicited traffic and developed rates as the northeastern agent from 1872 to 1875 and general eastern agent from 1875 to 1886 before transferring to Chicago to become traffic manager. When Ripley became general manager in 1888 the CB&Q was facing a period of tense labor relations, and he had to cope with strikes and the reputation the carrier had earned as militantly antilabor. In 1890 Charles Elliott Perkins, president of the railroad, tried to make Ripley vice president of traffic; but Ripley did not approve of the new organizational scheme and resigned.

Almost immediately the Chicago, Milwaukee & St. Paul Railroad, offered Ripley a position as third vice president. The Milwaukee Road, as the carrier later came to be known, found itself constantly fighting for a larger share of the market in the upper Midwest and between Chicago and Omaha. Ripley, with his knowledge of traffic and rate structures, provided the railroad with an experienced hand. For five years Ripley labored to generate traffic and revenues for the Milwaukee Road. A dynamic and vigorous man, Ripley took a leading role in civic affairs in Chicago, which had become his home, and in 1893 he helped to organize the Columbian Exposition there.

His work brought him to the attention of investors in the financially wracked Atchison, Topeka & Santa Fe, which had fallen into bankruptcy in 1893 through overexpansion and fiscal mismanagement. A lengthy and tortuous reorganization followed, with groups of security holders fighting to protect their interests. Foreign investors, mainly English and Dutch bondholders, wanted Ripley for the new company's president, and they found allies among Boston investors and in J. P. Morgan. When "Railway" replaced "Railroad" in the reorganized carrier's name in December 1895, Ripley was named president; he took office on January 1, 1896.

The security holders who controlled the Santa Fe found in Ripley a strong and dedicated leader with a reputation for honesty, integrity, and outstanding managerial skills. The reorganization had led to decisions to drop the Colorado Midland and the St. Louis-San Francisco (Frisco) as subsidiaries, and fixed charges had been greatly reduced through the elimination of some security issues and the lowering of interest rates on certain classes of bonds. The Santa Fe Ripley inherited was leaner, but it was not a first-class property.

Immediately upon being named to the presidency, Ripley moved to create a new corporate management team. Aldace Walker, a nationally recognized industry leader, had been elected chairman of the board, and a well-known lawyer, Victor Morawetz, served as general counsel. Walker's presence would strengthen Ripley's efforts to sell securi-

ties to raise capital for improvements and a slow and controlled expansion. Morawetz worked to clear titles to various properties, especially the Atlantic & Pacific (A&P) trackage from Albuquerque to Needles, California. Ripley's major rival for the presidency, Daniel B. Robinson, became first vice president. Ripley put together a group of executives who responded quickly to his decisions, and he delegated considerable authority to subordinates in whom he had confidence. An operations expert, Ripley turned the legal and financial problems over to Morawetz and concentrated on revitalizing the company and raising employee morale.

Ripley's team estimated that $250 million needed to be spent over twenty-five years to modernize the company; the bankers who dominated the board approved the program, though without enthusiasm. The A&P was rebuilt, not abandoned as some had counseled, and Ripley traded the Santa Fe's line into Mexico, the Sonora Railway, to the Southern Pacific in exchange for trackage from Needles to Mojave, California. New steel rails were laid, bridges were rebuilt, and new facilities were constructed in Galveston and Dallas. The operating ratio for the second year of Ripley's tenure fell from 82.9 to 74.68 and a profit of $1.6 million was promptly reinvested in the property.

Ripley acted quickly to reduce costs. The mechanical department experimented with oil as a fuel for locomotives to replace coal and, after several successful tests, began a conversion program. Petroleum had been discovered on Santa Fe lands in California and in several areas of Oklahoma and Texas. Having fuel on line meant reduced transportation costs in addition to basic savings in operating expenses. The Santa Fe expanded its major shops, rebuilt or scrapped older equipment, and improved main-line operations with modern signal systems. Ripley ordered new locomotives as well as new freight and passenger cars, and he mounted a crash program to install safety couplers and air brakes on all equipment. Earnings rose and in 1899 the board of directors ordered a dividend paid on preferred stock.

The financial success of the rehabilitation program restored confidence on Wall Street and allowed Ripley to begin a modest expansion program. In 1898 he purchased the San Francisco, San Joaquin Valley Railway (SF&SJV) in order to gain access to San Francisco and the Bay area. In order to reach the SF&SJV, the Santa Fe obtained trackage rights over the Southern Pacific from Mojave to Bakersfield over Tehachapi Pass. On San Francisco Bay the Santa Fe built terminals and acquired ferryboats to reach the city from Point Richmond. Thus the carrier, having entered Los Angeles and San Diego earlier, had access to all three major ports in California.

By 1915 the railway had grown to 11,000 miles of track versus 6,400 in 1896, and a net loss of $4 million in 1896 had become a profit of $20 million nineteen years later. Ripley and Vice President Paul Morton raised operating efficiency, generated new traffic, purchased a railroad to Phoenix, and built a cutoff from central Arizona to the main line in California. Another subsidiary was organized to extend a branch to the Grand Canyon, where a hotel was developed. Within a brief period the Santa Fe came to dominate rail traffic in northern Arizona.

The carrier built a second north-south line through Oklahoma Territory with branches to Tulsa and throughout central Oklahoma, thus dominating much of the new Sooner State. Through construction and purchases Ripley acquired trackage extending deep into east Texas, with a broadly curving line north to Longview. This route provided access to the forests of that region, and the Santa Fe later purchased the Kirby Lumber Company and became a major lumber producer. Together with the Southern Pacific, the Santa Fe pushed construction of a branch north from San Francisco Bay almost to the Oregon border. To reach the farming and ranching areas of southeastern New Mexico another line was built down the Pecos River Valley to Pecos, Texas.

Ripley's expansion program had two goals: to open new areas to generate traffic without invading the territory of another railroad and to reduce mileage and grades. The latter effort included the Belen Cutoff across central New Mexico to move freight on a low-grade line rather than across Raton Pass to the north. While the mileage difference for traffic from Chicago to California would be slight, the difference in grades would produce significant operating savings. To link the major trackage in Texas to the main line to California another cutoff, the Coleman, was constructed from Brownwood northwest through Lubbock to Texico on the Texas-New Mexico border. The Coleman Cutoff made the Santa Fe a major competitor for Texas-California

traffic and opened vast areas of the plains to ranchers and farmers. Line improvements accelerated as profits rose, and the company rapidly gained a reputation as a first-class railway.

Ripley also launched programs to generate new revenues along the entire system. The Santa Fe's agriculture department promoted the settlement of lands, particularly in west Texas and southeastern New Mexico. The company sent agricultural experts into farm areas to give advice and to counsel diversification of crops. Free seeds were distributed to encourage the cultivation of alfalfa, milo, barley, and other grains. The railway dispatched demonstration trains with blooded livestock and agricultural exhibits carrying the slogan "A Cow, Sow and Hen," and the Santa Fe sponsored chapters of organizations of young farmers. Some lands were sold to farmers, particularly in southwest Kansas, but the emphasis was not on land sales but on increased and more diversified production. In 1902 the company created an industrial department to solicit new on-line industries, but it did not become significant until the 1920s.

From 1895 to 1912 Ripley worked a virtual miracle on the system. Revenues, profits, mileage, and equipment all increased at a rapid rate. Some stockholders grumbled, but Ripley urged patience as profits were reinvested in improvements. In 1915 the *Railway Age Gazette* reviewed Ripley's work and noted that $298 million had been invested in the property, much of it financed through short-term bonds paid off out of earnings. As a result, revenue per train mile exceeded that of comparable carriers, traffic was more diversified and less subject to fluctuation, and capitalization per mile had actually *declined*. Management had begun to compensate shareholders with dividends, and the Santa Fe became a "blue chip" stock; one analyst called it "the Pennsylvania of the West." Other evaluations praised the road's conservative fiscal policies. As representatives of E. H. Harriman and the Rockefellers came on the board of directors, Ripley successfully fought to maintain the Santa Fe's independence.

Much Populist opposition to corporations in the 1890s was generated by complaints against the railroads; the Santa Fe was the "whipping boy" in Kansas, for example. As demands for effective regulation of railroad rates grew louder in the Progressive Era after 1900, Ripley sought freedom from government interference; one Progressive writer found his views "medieval." Privately Ripley counseled his fellow executives to accept federal ratemaking, but to push for a form of government rate setting that would still provide the carriers with some flexibility. Ripley used company annual reports, newspaper and magazine articles, speeches, regulatory hearing testimony, and other forums to carry his views to the public. Audiences responded well to Ripley, a large man with an athletic body, sharp grey eyes, and sizeable walrus mustache. He pointed to rising costs—taxes, wages and employee benefits, and interest rates—and to capital needs for betterment programs, even as efforts by state agencies and the Interstate Commerce Commission (ICC) to hold or even reduce rates continued. Investors were afraid to purchase securities issued by the carriers under these conditions; in the absence of long-range rate stabilization, the railways would not find the capital to carry on major modernization efforts. He urged an open rate structure and the end of rebates; Ripley wanted "free competition." Conflicts with state governments in Kansas and Texas followed, and for a while he stopped construction programs in the latter state. In 1910 Ripley told an ICC hearing in Chicago that the best way to set rates was to charge "what the traffic will bear." His blunt, outspoken manner outraged Progressives who believed in "scientific" federal ratemaking. Ripley explained that he did not mean that railroads should charge all that could be "extorted" or "squeezed" from the traffic but, rather, the least possible burden on shippers and consumers, or rates based on "the value of the service"; but the damage had been done. While one member of the ICC called Ripley's testimony "most statesmanlike," many Progressive found evidence to "prove" greed on the part of the railroads.

Ripley discovered that his worst fears had become realities as the ICC refused to grant general rate increases. He denounced the commission, terminated some major construction projects, and reported to stockholders in 1913, "Our troubles are with various government bodies." Ripley and other railroad leaders met with President Woodrow Wilson in September 1914 and urged him to stop the administration's verbal abuse of the industry. Ripley admitted that railway manager's had made major mistakes, but pointed out that the hostility of certain political leaders and journalists was undermining public confidence in the industry and that the

consequences could be damaging. The president agreed, but others in the administration, such as William Jennings Bryan, and supporters of the administration, such as Louis Brandeis, pushed for even greater regulation. Ripley could not stem the tide that swept the nation from 1900 to 1917, and the Elkins Act, Hepburn Act, Mann-Elkins Act, and Valuation Act of 1913 shaped the future of the railroads for the next fifty years. Ripley's hopes for cooperation between the industry and government were dashed. He advocated regional boards to set rates with a federal veto, a plan he believed would guarantee a significant return on investment; his scheme gained little attention.

Ripley decided that the Santa Fe needed to generate public support to offset the negative publicity that had produced cries for regulation. The railroad had been caught granting rebates, and former Vice President Morton, who had become a member of President Theodore Roosevelt's cabinet, had been forced to resign his cabinet post. Ripley tried to "sell" the railway to its customers and to the people in its territory. The Santa Fe's managers would go to the people, answer questions, present their case, and listen to shipper complaints. One week each month the company sent a special train, the Harmony Special, over part of the system. Santa Fe executives toured the line, attended town meetings, met with business people and farmers, held open forums, and gave interviews to the press. Civil engineers from the engineering department offered advice and aid on community services. Representatives of the agriculture department met with farmers and their families and provided advice on diversification, insect problems, and soil erosion. Ripley sought the friendship of the people living along line, and the image of the carrier did improve markedly.

Ripley had far less success in labor relations. He fought unionization and the growth of the railroad brotherhoods even as he demanded total loyalty to the Santa Fe. He ordered the creation of new railroad YMCAs for off-duty crews. The railway built dormitories, reading rooms, recreational facilities, and even, at some desert division points, swimming pools. The company created a pension system, expanded Santa Fe hospitals, and provided other benefits. Ripley desired to "foster a spirit of teamwork," recognize merit, and place confidence in his men, for he believed that they would respond to fair treatment with pride and loyalty. Labor relations under Ripley did not, however, enter a "golden age" of teamwork, happy workers, and intense loyalty to the firm.

Labor strife was often bitter, and the company used Oriental strikebreakers and several times broke unions. The "Brown System" of discipline created detailed records for each employee based upon merits and demerits. This system of discipline was supposed to create greater efficiency and give the employees a sense of job security; the results were otherwise. Ripley then introduced a "betterment" system leading to automatic and unlimited wage increases based upon performance. Bonuses would stimulate outstanding efforts, so Ripley believed, and in 1916 all workers earning less than $2,000 yearly received a 10 percent bonus. Efficiency experts were hired to create standards of effort, and under the new approach wages did rise and savings were made. An extensive apprenticeship system was instituted to bring in younger workers with high skill levels. Ripley sought to create a sense of esprit de corps through a company magazine and increased employee benefits. He hoped that company loyalty would transcend the worker's commitment to unionism, but it did not. While many of the employees affectionately referred to Ripley as "the old man" and did take pride in working for the railway, labor problems continued into the 1920s.

Under Ripley the Santa Fe had almost doubled in size and had become one of the nation's most modern and profitable railways. It was prepared, as some carriers were not, to participate in the rapid effort to mobilize for war in 1917. Nevertheless, the federalization of the railroads by the government removed Ripley, "the stern old lion," from command. He died on February 4, 1920, in Santa Barbara, California, shortly before the Santa Fe was returned to private hands. He was survived by his wife, Francis E. Harding Ripley, whom he had married in 1871, and their four children. The Ripleys had wintered in southern California for several years, but made their home in Riverside, Illinois. Throughout his career Ripley maintained, "I just happened into the railway business."

Publications:

"The Railroads and the People," *Atlantic Monthly*, 107 (January 1911): 12-23;

"How I Got Customers to See My Side," *System*, 29 (April 1916): 339-345.

References:

Keith L. Bryant, Jr., *History of the Atchison, Topeka and Santa Fe Railway* (New York: Macmillan, 1974);

James H. Ducker, *Men of the Steel Rails: Workers on the Atchison, Topeka & Santa Fe Railroad, 1869-1900* (Lincoln: University of Nebraska Press, 1983);

Edward Hungerford, "Edward Payson Ripley," *System*, 27 (February 1915): 155-159;

"Ninteen Years' Development Work on the Santa Fe," *Railway Age Gazette*, 58 (June 18, 1915): 1403-1406; (June 25, 1915): 1465-1468;

L. L. Waters, *Steel Trails to Santa Fe* (Lawrence: University of Kansas Press, 1950).

Donald J. Russell

(January 3, 1900-December 13, 1985)

by Don L. Hofsommer

Augustana College

Donald J. Russell (courtesy Southern Pacific Company)

CAREER: Timekeeper for maintenance-of-way gang (1920), instrumentman (1920-1923), assistant engineer (1923-1926, project engineer (1926-1927), roadmaster, Portland Division (1927-1928), assistant trainmaster (1928-1929), trainmaster (1929-1934), assistant superintendent, Portland Division (1934-1937), general manager (1937-1939), superintendent, Los Angeles Division (1939-1941), assistant to the president (1941), vice president (1941-1951), executive vice president (1951), president (1952-1964), chairman (1964-1972), Southern Pacific Company; chairman of the board, St. Louis Southwestern Railway and other Southern Pacific subsidiaries (1952-1964).

Donald J. Russell began his railroad career as a lowly timekeeper and ended it as chairman of the sprawling Southern Pacific Company (SP) fifty-two years later. His rise through the ranks was nothing short of spectacular, and the quality of his managerial skill was widely recognized at a time when few observers had kind things to say about the railroad industry.

Donald Joseph Russell was born in Denver, Colorado, on January 3, 1900, to Donald McKay and Josephine Nunan Russell, and grew up in Oregon and California. He served in the Canadian air force during World War I, attended Stanford University, and entered the employ of the Southern Pacific as a timekeeper for a maintenance-of-way gang in 1920. The following year he married Mary Louise Herring. Russell held numerous positions in the engineering and operating departments before his appointment as assistant to the president in 1941; there was little doubt that he was headed for the corner suite in the executive department, and in January 1952 he became president of the SP.

Russell's views on managing the property were simple and clearly stated. "Railroading is like athletics—you eat it and sleep it 24 hours a day or you go to work elsewhere." He held tenaciously to that standard for himself and expected it of others. "The company—he lived and breathed it," recalled an associate. Others remembered that his was an imperial style, that he rarely delegated authority, that he was an awesome figure. They also recalled, however, that his "bark was worse than his bite," that he was firm but fair, and that he was an aggressive, capable, and inventive manager. Subordinates were especially impressed by Russell's "hands-on feel" for the railroad. Indeed nobody doubted his knowledge of the property or his ability to spend the company's money to the greatest advantage.

An operating officer once told a magazine editor how upset the general office became over a snow blockade in the mountains. The rationality of this reaction was lost on the journalist, who protested that a heavy snowfall represented "an Act of God." Replied the trainmaster, "Mr. Russell doesn't believe in Acts of God." Thus, when one of the company's premier passenger trains became stuck during a blizzard in the Sierra Nevada, Russell praised the unceasing efforts of company personnel to free the train, but nobody doubted that he was sorely displeased that the honor and reputation of the SP had been besmirched. It was much the same when a devastating earthquake hit south central California on July 21, 1952. Over 1,000 men and approximately 175 heavy machines toiled for twenty-five days and more than $2 million was expended before the line could be reopened. Russell himself spent considerable time "on the scene" to "expedite matters." He was clearly proud of the way the company had responded to this emergency, but he also expected that kind of response as a matter of routine: "The things that people look on as great catastrophes," he said, "are commonplace with us. We get out and fix them."

It was that kind of mentality—"no problem is too big to overcome"—that Russell wished to see in his subordinates. But the first requisite of a successful manager, he told students at Stanford University's Graduate School of Business in the summer of 1956, was "the ability to grasp specific situations quickly and relate them to broad, long-range considerations." Russell perceived that these skills, inadequately developed in otherwise talented officers, might be made to flourish by sending the executives to college for what he called "broadening," and the SP paid full salaries as well as all expenses for managers selected for the program. "We are happy of course, to be able to give more education to some of our people," Russell noted, but the program was primarily a hardheaded business effort.

Russell was an early pessimist regarding the future of railroad passenger business; this pessimism was based on his perception of the relative advantages enjoyed by the train's principal competitors— the automobile and the airliner. "There will never be a thing as valuable as rubber tires going where the people are," Russell said in noting the flexibility of the automobile for the short haul. Moreover, Congress had established the first federal highway program in 1916 and forty years later passed the Federal-Aid Highway Act, inaugurating the interstate highway network and giving the automobile an advantage for long-distance-travel as well. Similarly, commercial aviation, which profited greatly from technological advances made during World War II, grew astonishingly through the late 1940s and the following decade. Russell's views, molded in part by his experiences in the Canadian air force, were in advance of conventional wisdom. As early as 1942 he had warned that passenger revenues provided only a small portion of the SP's income but consumed a disproportionate percentage of management's time and the company's resources. In 1956 Russell observed that losses in passenger patronage came despite the millions of dollars expended after the war to provide the finest trains in the country. In 1955 alone, he continued, the SP had lost $4 million on the dining car service because the company "tried to give the best we could for what people could afford to pay." Yet the slippage in passenger numbers continued. "It's just a change in the American way of life," said the SP president. "You can't make people do what they don't want to." The "jet plane will spell the end of the transcontinental (passenger) train"; "The Pullman car will be extinct within 20 years," Russell predicted in 1957.

It was Russell's task to preside over the conversion from steam to diesel power at the SP. The capital requirements necessary for dieselization were stupendous, but Russell correctly observed that "the investment was worth every cent." The diesel proved to be more efficient than steam but, more important, steam required massive service facilities and a huge attending labor force that the diesel did not. Steam power, in fact, served to point up one of the industry's major liabilities—railroading was at once capital intensive *and* labor intensive. Russell saw no immediate way to avoid the constant need for massive infusions of capital, but he did set out to "get rid of bodies." Dieselization certainly reduced the number of employees, and Russell looked elsewhere for opportunities to trim the work force. He was enraged when an internal study showed that an average of thirty-three persons handled—or, in Russell's word, "touched"—a company requisition. A streamlined system, instituted shortly thereafter, reduced the number who "touched" the requisition to five—with a correspondingly smaller number of persons on the payroll. "A large number of employees," said Russell, was "fine in a time when wages were low" and when there was little competition from other modes of transportation. It was not fine, however, in an era of escalating wages and intense modal competition.

Russell constantly looked for better ways to do business. He complained bitterly that "the rail-

road industry was far behind others" in the area of research, and under his direction the SP's Bureau of Transportation Research and Department of Research and Mechanical Standards were nurtured. Additionally, he engaged Stanford Research Institute (SRI) in 1953 to search for a cure to the constant problem of freight claims. "I wanted PhDs who knew nothing about railroads to study the problem," Russell explained. Two years later the institute and the SP's Sacramento shops unveiled the prototype of the Hydra-Cushion freight car, which featured hydraulic dampening devices to reduce coupling and train-slack impact. During a six-month test in which the car hauled only automobile windshields, no claims were filed by shippers. Early in 1958 the SP sold the Hydra-Cushion rights and patents to other manufacturers; consequently, the entire national car fleet benefited from the new technology. Russell also looked to SRI for advice on the application of magnetic-drum data storage devices to various accounting and car reporting functions.

Of the many betterment projects approved during the Russell years, none was more dramatic than the Salt Lake fill. The SP's impressive cross-lake trestle, in use since 1904, had incurred increased maintenance problems with age, and if the company chose to renew it, the work would have to be done "under traffic." SP engineers and outside consultants considered various alternatives, among them renewing the old trestle, but eventually they concluded that a fill would be the best choice. Work began in 1955 and required a prodigious effort. The top of the fill would be 38 feet wide; its length was 12.68 miles; its maximum height was 97 feet. Material handled totaled 60,832,000 cubic yards. Work on the project went well and on July 27, 1959, almost a year ahead of schedule, the first revenue train passed over the fill.

Russell was a firm believer in advertising and did not hesitate to authorize expenditures to publicize the new fill and other SP programs or developments; the company won many awards for its promotional activities. On the other hand, one advertising campaign was immediately controversial. Early in 1954 the SP placed a huge, two-dimensional lighted display sign atop its general office building in San Francisco. Each evening it blinked the company slogan—"SP, Your Friendly Railroad." The public's response was anything but friendly. Letters to editors of the city's newspapers charged the SP with callous disregard for the integrity of San Francisco's skyline. The photographer Ansel Adams was one of many prominent persons who complained of the SP's "arrogance." Russell assured the environmentalist that "railroad people are not a breed apart" and that "we of the Southern Pacific are just as proud of San Francisco . . . and its beauties as you and other citizens." In spite of the protests, the sign remained until 1961, when it was quietly dismantled. Russell later admitted that "it was a lousy thing."

Nothing loomed so large on the Southern Pacific during the 1960s as Donald J. Russell himself. "With the railroadman's traditional gold watch chain slung across his vest" he "looks every inch the old-time railroad boss," wrote one observer in 1965. Russell was, indeed, a railroader's railroader– "the most dedicated railroadman I ever knew," said the St. Louis Southwestern Railway's Harold J. McKenzie. Russell possessed a commanding presence: no subordinate ever thought of calling him anything but "Mr. Russell."

Russell's success as a manager sprang from his character. The *San Francisco Examiner* called him "an unpretentious realist"; an associate referred to him as an "uncomplicated purist." Subordinates clearly respected his integrity, his honesty, and his unfailing ability to make decisions. Nobody had to guess where Russell stood on issues. As his wife once said, he was "seldom wrong and never in doubt." Sternly self-disciplined, fearsome, and blunt nearly to rudeness, Russell was an aggressive, capable, and inventive manager whose mind was restlessly independent. His style was at once traditional and unorthodox. He was, for the SP, the right man at the right time.

Russell was not without humor, but often it was sardonic. Russell showed no humor on one issue, however: he was emphatic in his belief that one of top management's major responsibilities was that of locating and cultivating talent for executive leadership. His views regarding desirable characteristics were typically straightforward. He looked for the person who could "gear his imaginative process to cold facts," who could "grasp specific situations quickly and relate them to broad, long-range considerations," who was an "innovatist" as opposed to a "repeater." Additionally, he placed high value on a person's ability to make decisions and on his "courage to think out recommendations and then stand up for them." Equally important were emotional

stamina, ambition, "a real love for the activity in which the company is engaged," and an "interest in affairs outside the company." Finally, the future executive must be "interested in people." He had to be "consistently fair"; he must "be able to see the other person's point of view," "understand the emotional reasons behind it," and "find a common ground for understanding." After all, said Russell, "his most important task will be to build a team which will do the job for him, and he will be able to do this only by motivating and inspiring the people around him."

In 1957, Russell received the National Defense Transportation Association's annual award, and the same year he was honored by *Forbes Magazine* as one of the fifty "foremost business leaders of America." Russell's countenance graced the cover of *Time* for August 11, 1961 and *Forbes* for November 1, 1965.

In an industry that many saw as disintegrating and demoralized and others saw as dying, the SP's star seemed to shine brightly. Russell had provided the company with personal and determined leadership, had demanded innovation and imagination from subordinates, and had forced the SP, as one writer phrased it, to "discard its conservatism." The same observer praised Russell and the SP for realizing "sooner than most that the rails were caught up in a fight for survival." *Time* called the SP "aggressively modern," and *Forbes* said it was "one of the best-run railroads in the U.S."

Russell did not shrink from large price tags. "Capital expenditures are the prerequisite of profits," he was fond of saying, but he was not a spendthrift. To those who advanced proposals for improvements or capital expenditures, Russell posed his classic question: "What will your project do to improve earnings per share?" Well-conceived and economically justifiable plans were approved.

One of these projects was the 78.3-mile Palmdale Cut-off in California, designed to provide a shortcut between the SP's Sunset-Golden State Route at Colton and its San Joaquin line at Palmdale. Work began early in 1966; on July 11, 1967, the Palmdale Cut-off was placed in service. It was the longest domestic construction project undertaken by any railroad in many years and cost $22 million. The price was justified, Russell thought, for the new route enabled the SP to save time and ton-miles while avoiding the congestion of Los Angeles.

Russell was an early and energetic advocate of the diversified transportation company. In his view, "such a company would offer movement by rail, by air, by highways, by water, or by pipeline, in any combination best tailored to individual need." Russell contemplated the acquisition of the Railway Express Agency, which, if merged with the SP's Pacific Motor Trucking subsidiary, "would provide a very attractive operation" since Railway Express "had rights to go to so many places." The railroad or another subsidiary could provide trailers and flatcars for the far-flung operation that Russell envisioned. The plan was dropped after Russell concluded that the Interstate Commerce Commission would not approve the idea.

This failure did not end Russell's interest in a fully integrated transportation network under one management. There was one opportunity immediately at hand: the SP, like other rail carriers, had watched in dismay as unregulated truckers captured a large portion of the petroleum products business that previously had gone by rail. "Why not lose the business to ourselves" Russell asked. Thus was born, in 1953, Southern Pacific Pipe Lines, Incorporated.

Russell chafed under restrictions that prevented the SP from creating "a transportation supermarket" which would benefit the public interest. Frustrated in his greater goals, Russell nevertheless pressed for a policy of "trying to get into businesses that are related to transportation—that is

what we know something about—rather than spread out into areas where we are not familiar."

Russell left the presidency in 1964 to become chairman of the SP. He retired effective May 17, 1972. His mark on the Southern Pacific was indelible. He took justifiable pride in the performance of SP system railways, especially during the 1960s, when revenue ton miles increased by 51 percent, gross ton-miles per train hour grew by 49 per cent, and revenue tons per car rose by 35 percent. Russell thought that the key to his success was "a lot of hard work and God-given faculty to think a little bit." His most prized accomplishment was "raising the overall quality of the property" and "reducing the debt of the company." As his successor, Benjamin F. Biaggini, put it, "The vision of his leadership will have a continuing effect on the Company for years to come." The outstanding characteristic of Russell's stewardship was his ability to make progressive decisions on major issues or projects. Russell died on December 13, 1985 at the age of eighty-five.

References:

Don L. Hofsommer, *The Southern Pacific 1901-1985* (College Station: Texas A&M University Press, 1986);

Francis B. O'Gara, "S. P. Head Sees Passenger Travel Fade," *San Francisco Examiner*, July 12, 1956;

"Railroads: Healthy among the Sick," *Time*, 78 (August 11, 1961): 57-62;

"The Southern Pacific Co.," *Forbes*, 96 (November 1, 1965): 24-29.

St. Louis-San Francisco Railway Company

by Martin M. Pomphrey

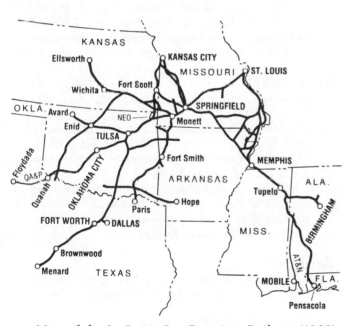

Map of the St. Louis-San Francisco Railway (1980)

The name of the St. Louis-San Francisco Railway Company (Frisco) represented aspirations rather than eventualities, as Frisco tracks extended west scarcely within half a continent of the Golden Gate.

With St. Louis the scene of a great railroad convention in 1849, enthusiasm was high for a railroad spanning the continent. The Frisco's story starts in March of that year, when the Missouri legislature granted a charter to the Pacific Railroad Company of Missouri to build a railroad from St. Louis to the western boundary of the state.

On July 23, 1852, the first division of the Pacific Railroad opened from St. Louis to Franklin (now Pacific), Missouri. By this time it had already obtained authority to construct a branch line from Franklin to Springfield and southwest Missouri. The new line—the Southwest Branch of the Pacific Railroad—became the nucleus of the Frisco system. It opened to Rolla, Missouri, in 1860.

The Pacific Railroad main line was completed to Kansas City, Missouri, by 1865, but Rolla remained the Southwest Branch terminus. After default on indebtedness caused by the road's devastation during the Civil War, the Southwest Branch was sold and reorganized as the Southwest Pacific Railroad in 1866. It failed financially in 1868. A new company, the South Pacific Railroad, was formed to extend the line from Rolla to Lebanon, Springfield, and Pierce City, Missouri, in 1869-1870.

On October 26, 1870, the Atlantic & Pacific Railway (A&P) gained control of the South Pacific. The A&P completed the line to Vinita, Indian Territory (now Oklahoma), and continued to operate the South Pacific in conjunction with its lines until its bankruptcy in 1875. In September 1876 the South Pacific was sold at public auction and conveyed to the newly organized St. Louis & San Francisco Railway.

At this stage the corporate history of the Frisco becomes complex. The stock or properties of many companies were acquired; corporate control shifted from group to group; subsidiary companies were formed to construct new sections of road. All in all, there were approximately 145 corporations involved in forming the system.

The new Frisco became owner of nearly a million acres of land, including the original A&P land grant. Through stock ownership the Frisco controlled the only remaining A&P property–trackage from the Missouri border to Vinita–and the A&P franchise from the Missouri border to San Francisco. By its charter, the Frisco was formed to build its road to the Pacific coast, but trouble with Indian nations and stock control of the Frisco from 1879 to 1896 by the Atchison, Topeka & Santa Fe Railroad intervened. The Santa Fe used the A&P franchise and the major portion of the A&P land grant to construct a line from Albuquerque to Los Angeles; the line was partly paid for by the Frisco, which derived little benefit from all it put into the venture. In 1890 the Frisco came directly under the management of the Santa Fe. In 1893 the Santa Fe and the Frisco went into receivership, but management continued under the Santa Fe until reorganization of a new Frisco–the St. Louis-San Francisco Railroad–in 1896.

Acquisitions continued under the new company, including the St. Louis, Memphis & Southeast in 1902; the Quanah, Acme & Pacific in 1903; and the Kansas City, Fort Scott & Memphis in 1928 (the Frisco had leased this company since 1901). These acquisitions extended the Frisco to Birmingham, Alabama, and eventually to the port of Pensacola, Florida.

Under the leadership of B. F. Yoakum from 1900 to 1913, the Chicago, Rock Island & Pacific, the Chicago & Eastern Illinois (C&EI), and the Frisco railroads were welded into one system; the 1913-1914 depression, however, cast the Frisco and the C&EI into receivership, ending the Rock Island operating agreement. In a reorganization in 1916 the Frisco's name was changed to St. Louis-San Francisco Railway.

After government operation during World War I, the Frisco resumed its expansion until the Great Depression brought about its bankruptcy in 1932, followed by trusteeship until January 1947.

The period after the trusteeship ended was one of building and modernization. Traffic records were set; control of the Alabama, Tennessee & Northern Railroad was acquired, giving the Frisco its second port city–Mobile, Alabama; dieselization was completed on February 28, 1952; and passenger service was terminated in December, 1967.

From 1963 until 1980 the Frisco engaged in several merger studies, culminating in merger with the Burlington Northern Railroad on November 21, 1980.

Unpublished Document:

Clair V. Mann, "Frisco First: A Source Materials History of the St. Louis & San Francisco Railroad, 1845-1945," 4 volumes. Unpublished typescript, Phelps County Historical Society, Rolla, Missouri.

References:

Joe G. Collias, *Frisco Power* (Crestwood, Mo.: MM Books, 1984);

H. Craig Miner, *The St. Louis-San Francisco Transcontinental Railroad, the Thirty-Fifth Parallel Project, 1853-1890* (Lawrence, Manhattan & Wichita: University Press of Kansas, 1972);

G. C. Swallow, *Geological Report of the Country along the Line of the Southwestern Branch of the Pacific Railroad, State of Missouri–with Memoir of the Pacific Railroad* (St. Louis: Knapp, 1859).

Archives:

Corporate documents of the St. Louis–San Francisco Railway Company are at the St. Louis Mercantile Library.

St. Louis Southwestern Railway

by Don L. Hofsommer

Augustana College

Map of the St. Louis Southwestern Railway (1930)

The St. Louis Southwestern Railway (SSW or Cotton Belt) began life in 1871 as the 3-foot gauge Tyler Tap Railroad between Tyler and Big Sandy, Texas, after disappointed citizens of Tyler learned that their community would not be served by regional trunk roads. It was rechartered in 1879 as the Texas & St. Louis Railway, and by the end of 1883 its service area ranged from central Texas to southeastern Missouri. It was reorganized in 1886 as the St. Louis, Arkansas & Texas Railway, and its lines were converted to standard gauge (4 feet

8½ inches). Additional mileage was added, and in 1891 the road was incorporated in Missouri as the St. Louis Southwestern and under the laws of Texas as the St. Louis Southwestern of Texas.

The SSW eventually passed to the control of Edwin Gould, who gained access for the road to the important gateways of St. Louis, Memphis, and Dallas. In addition, Gould promoted local projects, authorized a major demonstration farm in Texas, and took an active role in a campaign to control mosquitoes and thus malaria.

Not a great money-maker during the first quarter of the twentieth century, the Cotton Belt was nevertheless attractive to larger railroads because of its strategic value. For a short period in 1925 the company was under control of the Chicago, Rock Island & Pacific, which sold its interest to Leonor F. Loree of the Kansas City Southern. In 1932 the giant Southern Pacific (SP) acquired nearly all of the SSW's capital stock. The Cotton Belt was a "good fit" for the SP, giving the larger road effective connections with Eastern roads at Memphis and East St. Louis.

The Southern Pacific's strategy was sound but its timing was awful: the country was in the midst of the Great Depression. Reflecting the fate of the territory it served, on December 12, 1935, the SSW filed for reorganization under Section 77 of Bankruptcy Act. The company completed a voluntary adjustment program, paid all interest and principal in default, and emerged from bankruptcy in 1947 with its property intact.

During hard times and good times alike, the Cotton Belt aggressively solicited both through and local freight, and its reputation among shippers was positive. It established the Blue Streak Merchandise train in 1931, and later extended the train's route over parent SP to Los Angeles. Moreover, the SSW pursued dynamic property improvement and advertising programs. The rewards were an increased market share and enhanced profitability. For the fifteen-year period beginning in 1954 the SSW's operating ratio averaged only 63.74, and in 1967 the company provided an impressive 12.11 percent return on investment.

During 1980 trackage from New Mexico to Kansas City and St. Louis—acquired from the moribund Rock Island—was added to the Cotton Belt, but its resident management was gradually elimi-

nated and the general office building at Tyler was sold. The Cotton Belt and its parent, the Southern Pacific, both faced an uncertain future in what industry analysts had come to call the era of the megamerger.

References:

80 Years of Transportation Progress: A History of the St. Louis Southwestern Railway (Tyler, Tex.: St. Louis Southwestern Railway, n.d.);

Don L. Hofsommer, *The Southern Pacific, 1901-1985* (College Station: Texas A&M University Press, 1986);

Joseph A. Strapac, *Cotton Belt Locomotives* (Huntington Beach, Cal.: Shade Tree Books, 1977).

Archives:

There are no archives of the corporate records of the St. Louis Southwestern Railway.

Fred W. Sargent

(May 26, 1876-February 4, 1940)

by H. Roger Grant

University of Akron

CAREER: Private practice of law, Sioux City, Iowa (1901-1912); attorney, Chicago, Rock Island & Pacific Railroad (1912-1920); general solicitor, (1920-1923), vice president and general counsel 1923-1925), president (1925-1939), Chicago & North Western Railway .

Fred Wesley Sargent, who would guide the sprawling Chicago & North Western Railway (C&NW) system through the halcyon years of the late 1920s and the Depression of the 1930s, was born on May 26, 1876, in the Plymouth County community of Akron, Iowa, which his father, Edgar Wesley Sargent, a miller and landowner, had founded. His mother was Abbie Haskell Sargent. After completing high school in Akron, Sargent matriculated at the nearby University of South Dakota in Vermillion. He later transferred to the State University of Iowa College of Law in Iowa City, where he received the LL.B. degree in 1901. Sargent opened a law office in bustling Sioux City, northwestern

Iowa's foremost city. On January 9, 1902, he married Mary Minier; they had three children. In 1906 and again in 1908 he won election on the Republican ticket as city attorney. During this period he had his first professional contact with the railroad industry when he took the C&NW and its affiliate, the Chicago, St. Paul, Minneapolis & Omaha (Omaha Road), as clients. In 1912 the Chicago, Rock Island & Pacific appointed Sargent to head its legal operations in the Hawkeye State; he served that company from offices in Des Moines until 1920, when he joined the C&NW as its general solicitor. Three times during the next four years he turned down offers of the vice presidency. In 1923 he finally accepted the promotion and took the title of vice president and general counsel. A year later, upon the resignation of President William H. Finley, Sargent became the road's tenth president.

As head of the 10,129–mile Chicago & North Western system, Sargent generally continued the policies of his predecessors, striving to please shippers.

Fred W. Sargent

He also sought to improve the property: rehabilitation of the Proviso Yards near Chicago and construction of the Wood Street Yards in the city were two of the leading betterments he carried out. But he approved the expenditure of $1,265,000 to build a thirty-four mile extension between the South Dakota communities of Winner and Wood in 1929, only to see drought and soil erosion cut the agricultural traffic to virtually nothing once the line opened. A happier event was the debut of the "400" passenger trains between Chicago and the Twin Cities via Milwaukee on January 2, 1935: "400 miles in 400 minutes . . . the fastest train on the American continent." Using refurbished Class E-2a Pacifics and standard heavyweight passenger equipment, these crack trains captured and maintained a good percentage of the market until the company could afford to purchase state-of-the-art diesel-powered streamlined train sets from Pullman-Standard in 1939.

Sargent's accomplishments on the Chicago & North Western were negated by the Great Depression. Gross revenues remained rather constant from

1925 through 1929, averaging about $148 million annually, but dropped dramatically after 1930, hitting a low in 1932 of about $75 million. Because the road's earnings could not support its capital structure, Sargent, with board approval, ordered a petition filed with the federal court in Chicago in June 1935 for reorganization under Section 77 of the Bankruptcy Act.

Although depressed conditions overwhelmed Sargent's presidency, he was a bright, thoughtful, and perceptive railroad leader who sensed the inherent weaknesses of the industry. Sargent blasted needless federal supervision and suggested that deregulation would benefit companies and shippers alike. He endorsed the provision of the Transportation Act of 1920 that called for carrier consolidation, but he thought it foolish of Washington to demand that "competition not be materially lessened." Sargent realized that by the 1930s trucks, buses, automobiles, barges, and airplanes had ended any possibility of railroads dominating intercity transport. "To adhere to the old conception that rail carriers have a monopoly of transportation is to fail to recognize the great change that has come upon us," he told the American Railway Magazine Editors' Association in 1938. "It is a reactionary attitude and a removal from the spirit of progress of these modern times. The premise of monopoly now having failed, the whole plan and scheme of regulation is no longer tenable." The mood of the country during the New Deal, however, was against Sargent's sentiments, and his ideas had virtually no impact. Sargent was fifty years ahead of his time.

Sargent did his best to energize the Chicago & North Western system, but he failed. Sargent's health began to decline about the time the railroad entered receivership, and on June 1, 1939, he resigned the presidency. He spent his brief retirement on his farm near Mount Vernon, Iowa, where he pursued his only hobby, gardening. He died on February 4, 1940.

Unpublished Document:

"The State of the Industry," October 14, 1938, in the Chicago & North Western Railway Historical Society Papers, Northern Illinois University, DeKalb, Illinois.

References:

"Fred W. Sargent Resigns," *Railway Age*, 106 (June 3, 1939): 945;

"Hughitt and Finley Retire," *Railway Age*, 78 (June 27, 1925): 1641-1642.

Stuart T. Saunders

(July 16, 1909 - February 8, 1987)

by Richard Saunders

Clemson University

Stuart T. Saunders

CAREER: Lawyer, Washington, D.C. (1934-1939); assistant general solicitor (1939-1947), assistant general counsel (1947-1954), vice president and general counsel (1954-1956), executive vice president (1956-1958), president and chief executive officer (1958-1963), Norfolk & Western Railway; chairman and chief executive officer, Pennsylvania Railroad (1963-1968); chairman and chief executive officer, Penn Central (1968-1970).

Stuart T. Saunders will no doubt be remembered primarily for leading the Penn Central to debacle and bankruptcy amid charges of mismanagement and deception and investigations by the Interstate Commerce Commission (ICC), the Securities and Exchange Commission (SEC), and Congress into his conduct of the company's affairs. Earlier he had cut through the political and institutional logjam to make possible, for better or worse, the Penn Central merger, which laid the groundwork for the creation of Conrail and the radical rationalization of railroad service in the Northeast. On the Pennsylvania Railroad (PRR), and before that on the Norfolk & Western (N&W), he practiced a style of management then becoming common in other industries but new to railroading, in which chief executive officers divorce themselves from their company's operations, conventions, and traditions and concentrate on finance, legal and political matters, and diversification.

Stuart Thomas Saunders was born in McDowall, West Virginia, in 1909 to William Hamett and Lucy Smith Saunders, and grew up on a dairy farm in Bedford County, Virginia, near Roanoke. He was a star debater and valedictorian of the class of 1926 at Bedford High School. He graduated from Roanoke College at Salem, Virginia, in 1930, and from Harvard Law School in 1934. He practiced law in Washington, D.C., for two years before joining the firm of Douglas, Obear and Campbell in that city in 1936.

He married Dorothy Davidson in 1939. It is said that it was at her urging that he took a position as assistant general solicitor with the Norfolk & Western Railway that year so that the newlywed couple could return to the area around Roanoke, where they had both grown up. He became assistant general counsel in 1947, vice president and general counsel in 1954, and executive vice president in 1956. On April 1, 1958, he succeeded Robert H. Smith as president of the N&W.

Saunders was the first president at the N&W, and one of the first in railroading, to become a chief executive officer through sheer brilliance and ambition, without having started on the tracks or the trains and working his way up through the ranks. There was a sense in the business community that railroad leadership tended to be too insular, too wedded to railroading's traditions, and that this new kind of executive was a good thing.

His first move as president was to push ahead, quickly and decisively, with dieselization. No railroad in the United States had stuck with steam as long as the N&W, which had done so out of loyalty to the coal industry that was its main customer; it had built new steam locomotives as late as 1952. There was a strong professional and emotional attachment to steam on the N&W, and this intellectual nonrailroader who eliminated it with such ruthlessness caused great dismay among many of the railroad's employees. The episode set the tone for Saunders's style of management: profits mattered; sentiment did not.

After dieselization, Saunders tended to stay out of running trains. The N&W was rich—its rate of return was regularly the highest, or next to the highest, of any railroad in the country. It could hire the best professionals to run the railroad and provide them with the tools to do the job. Saunders put in twelve-hour days and often took work home at night. He was articulate, well-prepared, self-assured, and persuasive.

Saunders attracted the attention of the railroad industry by his daring and brilliant takeover of the Virginian Railway in 1959. The Virginian, the newest (it was founded in 1909) and leanest of the Pocahontas coal roads, had lower grades over two of the three mountain ridges that both carriers crossed on their way to the sea. By building a few simple connecting links between them, it was possible to create a railroad with the lowest possible ruling grade. The Koppers Company, which owned the Virginian, was happy to trade it for a substantial stake in the N&W.

This consolidation was the first of the "modern" (post-1955) mergers of financially unrelated, parallel railroads, and it raised questions of reduced competition. In addition, it was fraught with implica-

tions for all eastern railroading. The N&W was controlled by the Pennsylvania Railroad, although neither railroad publicly admitted it, and Saunders sat on the PRR's board of directors. The Virginian, on the other hand, was regarded by the New York Central as its friendly connection into the coalfields. The New York Central's president, Alfred Perlman, saw the merger as a grab by the Pennsylvania for a railroad that was vital to the Central, and thus as a betrayal by the very company with which he was just beginning merger negotiations. He was furious at the Pennsylvania and at Saunders.

Saunders convinced coal operators that the N&W-Virginian merger, rather than restricting competition, would open new marketing possibilities for them. He convinced the United Mine Workers that the welfare of the coal industry, and therefore the security of their jobs, would be enhanced by stronger railroads. He tirelessly gave talks in school gymnasiums and church basements across Virginia and West Virginia to convince the people that the merger was good for them. Though he had been raised in these hills, he was urbane, sophisticated, and aristocratic in bearing; but he was effective. The support he won from the industry and the people who would be most affected by the merger undermined whatever antitrust objections the ICC or the Justice Department might raise.

His settlement with labor was regarded as brilliant in some quarters, disastrous in others, but broke what was probably a crucial obstacle to the merger. The railroad at first asked for complete freedom to rearrange its work force as it pleased after merger; the brotherhoods asked for ironclad protection. It was expected that the ICC would grant a compromise of four years' protection, as prescribed in the New Orleans Union Passenger Terminal Case of 1954. But on the way to that compromise, labor's lawyers were likely to cross-examine the railroad so intensely that the whole merger plan might unravel. Saunders went to Washington to deliver to the Railway Labor Executives' Association, the agency that would fight the battle for the railroad's unions, the pep talk he had given so successfully to the folks in West Virginia. As a closing flourish, he added that no employee would lose a job as a result of merger. That meant an "attrition" agreement—everything labor had asked for. Dumbfounded, the labor lawyers adjourned to discuss the offer. Saunders insisted that his workers had job security, but that he had the right to move them to any point on the railroad—though not to any job—where they were needed.

Next Saunders undertook a much more ambitious and much more complex merger with the Wabash and the New York, Chicago & St. Louis (Nickel Plate). Those railroads complemented each other as perfectly as the Virginian did the N&W. Both were profitable, the Nickel Plate more so than the Wabash. Both could funnel export traffic to the Port of Norfolk and free the N&W from its dependence on coal. Both the N&W and the Wabash were financially related to the Pennsylvania, and so, like the Virginian merger, this consolidation was thought in railroad circles to be another imperial move by the Pennsylvania. The merger would not have been possible if the Pennsylvania had not agreed to sell the N&W its line between Sandusky and Columbus, Ohio; otherwise, the N&W would not connect with the Wabash or the Nickel Plate at any point. Saunders was seen as a key lieutenant in the Pennsylvania's expansive empire.

As the head of one of Virginia's most profitable and most important corporations, Saunders had considerable influence in the state's affairs. He publicly chastized the state government for failing to make Virginia as attractive for investment as neighboring North Carolina, prompting Governor Lindsay Almond to call him "the Patrick Henry of Virginia's industrial revolution." Saunders kept a high public profile and was active in civic affairs, serving as chairman of the Virginia Foundation for Independent Colleges, trustee of Hollins College, and chairman of the board of trustees of Roanoke College. He was the recipient of the Hampton Roads Maritime Association Award for 1961 in recognition of his success in developing coal traffic and general cargo at the port, and was cochairman with Henry Ford II of the Businessmen's Committee for Tax Reduction in 1963. He was active in the Democratic party, with influence at the Democratic National Committee (DNC). President John F. Kennedy, eager to cultivate executives who were Democrats—especially after his confrontation with U.S. Steel in 1962 made the business community wary of him—named Saunders to the President's Advisory Board on Labor-Management Relations and to the board of directors of the National Cultural Center.

Saunders did not stay at the N&W to see the Wabash-Nickel Plate merger completed. In the spring of 1963 he was invited to succeed James Symes as chairman and chief executive officer of the Pennsylvania, with his duties to begin on October 1. His selection was a break with PRR tradition: he had not come up through the PRR ranks; he was not a railroader; he was not a Philadelphian; he was not a Republican. But the PRR's directors evidently saw merger with the New York Central as the company's top priority and regarded Saunders as the man with the demonstrated ability to get a merger through. He was respected in the financial community. He was a politician, and steering mergers past the shoals of regulation and antitrust law was a political endeavor. He was a Democrat with ties to the Kennedy administration, something the traditionally Republican PRR needed very badly at a time when it appeared that the Democrats would be in power for years to come. And he was socially acceptable, a matter of more than passing interest to the men who ran the Pennsylvania Railroad.

Unlike the N&W, the Pennsylvania was no longer rich. It suffered from a declining traffic base, passenger and commuter operations that lost huge amounts of money, and an aging physical plant characterized by poorly-maintained track, derailments, and locomotives out-of-service awaiting repairs. The morale of its workers was low and its management was lacking in new ideas. Saunders had been a brilliant choice to head the N&W but was probably the wrong man for the Pennsylvania at a point in its history when it needed an expert railroader to make the machinery work again. It is not clear whether Saunders understood, or even cared about, the company's railroad-related problems.

He arrived in Philadelphia acting every bit the part of the chairman of a blue-chip firm. He was invited to the city's most prestigious clubs, including the Philadelphia Club. He played bridge and enjoyed French cooking. He was driven to work from his home in one of the Main Line's most exclusive suburbs in a limousine, which did not endear him to the riders of the "red rattlers," the railroad's aging commuter cars.

Very early in his tenure in Philadelphia he became fascinated with diversification, with taking the railroad's assets and paltry profits and putting them into high-yield investments. Milton Shapp, then a Philadelphia industrialist and later governor of Pennsylvania, told reporters Joseph Daughen and Peter Binzen that Saunders wanted to get out of the railroad business, that after a few drinks he would start talking about how Litton Industries was putting money to good use and getting good returns. "He said he wanted to keep the money for real estate investments instead of putting it in the fucking railroad. That's what he said, the fucking railroad."

Soon after Saunders's arrival on the Pennsylvania, the Justice Department determined that the PRR did control the N&W and that for the N&W-Wabash-Nickel Plate merger to be approved the PRR would have to get rid of its N&W holdings. That N&W stock was the PRR's last money making asset. Saunders's old friends from the N&W came to Philadelphia to persuade him and his board to divest. These former colleagues were his adversaries now and the sessions were painful. Reluctantly, the PRR decided to divest. Saunders thought the money from the sale of the N&W stock could go for diversification. Buckeye Pipeline was purchased, as were real estate development companies in Florida, Texas, and California, and a money-losing airline, Executive Jet Aviation, whose president was diverting company funds to his personal use.

After the divestiture of the N&W, it was more important than ever for the PRR that the merger with the New York Central go through. Saunders swung into action and the opposition melted away, just as it had in the Virginian case. He made speeches in towns across Pennsylvania, where popular opposition to the merger was most intense because of plans to divert traffic from the PRR to the Central's water-level route. He used a combination of persuasiveness, personal charm, and political clout to win over Pennsylvania's outgoing Democratic governor, David Lawrence; its incoming Republican governor, William Scranton; Philadelphia's Democratic mayor, James Tate; and the Democratic administration in New Jersey.

Shapp, a Democrat, was a particularly delicate problem. A millionaire with political ambitions, he hoped to combine popular antagonism to the "Republican" railroad with fears that the merger was a grab by New York interests for a railroad that was rightfully Pennsylvania's into an issue that would win him public office. Shapp had not counted on the arrival of Saunders, an influential

Democrat, as the head of the "Republican" railroad, nor had Saunders counted on Shapp, an opponent who also had friends in the Democratic party. Saunders had to bring Arthur Krim, finance chairman of the Democratic National Committee, to Philadelphia to make it clear to Shapp that the Johnson administration favored the merger and that if Shapp would drop his opposition, his campaign would receive a big contribution from the DNC.

Labor's lawyers, Albert Brandon for the Pennsylvania Federation of Labor and William Mahoney for the Railway Labor Executives' Association, had exacted some devastating admissions in early testimony before the ICC on the deficiency of planning for the merger, and had shown that many of the railroads' assertions about regulation, taxes, and labor costs were not correct. Labor knew that Saunders would be good for an attrition agreement, just as he had been in the Virginian case, and so held out for a little more. On May 20, 1964, Saunders signed an agreement promising that all employees *on the date the agreement was signed* were guaranteed lifetime job protection. Saunders gambled that the merger would be consummated quickly; in fact, it would be nearly four years before all the legal hurdles were cleared. On merger day, Penn Central had to take back hundreds of people who had been employed on May 20, 1964, but who had long since become redundant and had been laid off. The labor agreement was probably not the fatal blow to the Penn Central, as some analysts have tried to portray it, but it was certainly one of the nails in its coffin.

The highest price Saunders paid for the merger was his agreement to absorb the New York, New Haven & Hartford Railroad, which he had to do to get the Justice Department to withdraw from the case. Attorney General Robert Kennedy was concerned about the fate of the New Haven, which served Massachusetts: the railroad was bankrupt, with no hope of reorganizing on its own, and was threatened with the diversion of what was left of its freight traffic to an all-Penn Central route if the merger went through. Saunders initiated negotiations with the New Haven's trustees; he was the only officer of either the Pennsylvania or the New York Central who showed any enthusiasm for the road. On August 24, 1964, he was assured by the attorney general that if satisfactory arrangements were made with the New Haven, Justice would drop its opposition. Ultimately the ICC made it clear that the *only* reason it approved a Pennsylvania-New York Central merger was because that was the *only* private enterprise solution it could find for the New Haven. Even without the New Haven, Penn Central might not have succeeded; but the weight of this decaying passenger carrier was clearly more than it could bear.

On merger day, February 1, 1968, Saunders was at the pinnacle of his career. He was on the cover of *Time* and would be the *Saturday Review*'s businessman of the year. He was the recipient of honorary degrees from the University of Maryland and from Washington and Lee University and other Virginia colleges. He was on the boards of directors of the Chase Manhattan Bank, United States Steel, the Equitable Life Assurance Society, and other banks and corporations. He was the recipient of the Salzberg Medal for a Distinguished Contribution to Transportation.

In the structure of Penn Central that had finally been agreed upon, Saunders, as chairman and chief executive officer, was to concentrate on finances, diversification, regulation, and politics; Perlman would be president and chief operating officer, which meant that he ran the railroad. Both men could be steely in their own ways. (The often-cited example from Saunders's side was his response to a reporter's question about his favorite game of bridge. Did he enjoy it? "I play to win," he had said.) Saunders, the Episcopalian socialite, and Perlman, the Jewish technical ace, did not appear to like each other, nor did either appear to respect the other's area of responsibility within the company. Perlman saw diversification as siphoning money away from the railroad and even believed that Saunders was deliberately starving the road. Saunders acted as though he thought the railroad was dragging down what could be a glittering financial empire. The inability of the two spheres of management to communicate effectively was disastrous, especially when each had friendly ears on the board of directors.

Through the 1960s, as negotiations and court cases over the merger had dragged on, it had become necessary for the Pennsylvania Railroad to put the best face on—actually, to misrepresent—its true financial status. The fortunes of the Central under Perlman's management had been rising in this period vis-à-vis the Pennsylvania's; if this fact

had become known, it might have been necessary to renegotiate the complicated stock exchange ratio, which would have given the Central a greater—even a dominant—influence in the merged company. The misrepresentation had been accomplished through accounting sleights of hand that the PRR's vice president for finance, David Bevan, called in a 1966 memo "imaginative accounting." Bevan insisted that Saunders had demanded the accounting tricks. After the merger, it was necessary to misrepresent the Penn Central's financial position because its solvency depended on its ability to borrow large sums of money. Dividends were paid regularly, though with borrowed funds, and the robust figures on the balance sheet seldom represented hard cash. That the deception worked as long as it did was a credit to Saunders's persuasiveness and the confidence he inspired in the banking community, for all those bankers had to do was look out the window of a PRR passenger train to see a dying railroad.

After the merger, apparently at Saunders's urging, the two giant railroads were hastily thrown together to bring the savings that were supposed to result from the merger down to net as quickly as possible. No time was allowed to prepare employees; there was no money for the capital improvements necessary to tie the two roads together. The result was the complete breakdown of operations. By the beginning of 1970 management had lost control of the railroad, and a brutal winter finished the job. The railroad was losing a million dollars a day. After the first-quarter report came out in early May, the financial community and the railroad's own directors began to pierce the veil of Saunders's misleading financial figures. At the board meeting of June 8, 1970, Saunders, Perlman, and Bevan were called in and summarily fired. Saunders was stunned; he had expected Perlman and Bevan to be dismissed, but not himself. Two weeks later the company declared bankruptcy and sought the protection of the courts.

Saunders was given a pension of $114,000 a year, approximately half his previous salary; a court later ordered it substantially reduced. His peace was interrupted by summonses to testify before the Securities and Exchange Commission, the ICC, and Congress. In 1972 he was hired by Wheat First Securities of Richmond, Virginia, as a consultant on coal resources and coal transportation. In 1974 the SEC filed suit against him and others for false and misleading statements about the company's condition and for the improper diversion of funds to a Liechtenstein bank. He signed a consent decree, neither an admission nor denial of guilt. In 1975 a settlement of $12.6 million was reached between a group of plaintiffs, including the trustees of the Penn Central and the holders of Pennsylvania Railroad debentures, and the railroad's former officers and auditors, who were accused of dereliction of duty and issuing false financial statements and misleading proxy material. Saunders was one of the defendants who had to contribute to the settlement fund. While some of the defendants' contributions were made public (Perlman had to contribute $25,000, for example), Saunders's was not.

Stuart Saunders died on February 8, 1987, in Richmond. In a eulogy in *Trains* magazine, David Morgan said: "Seldom in the industry had a man risen so rapidly, rearranged the rail map more, or fallen from favor faster." He added: "None can question Saunders' behavior after the fall from grace . . . . in which he lost his personal wealth and made no excuses."

References:

Robert Bedingfield, "$12.6 Million Settlement Proposed in Pennsy Suits," *New York Times*, September 4, 1975, p. 1;

Felix Belair, Jr., "Ex-Pennsy Head Consents to Restrictions by S.E.C.," *New York Times*, July 30, 1974, p. 43;

Joseph Daughen and Peter Binzen, *The Wreck of the Penn Central* (Boston: Little, Brown, 1971);

Stephen Salisbury, *No Way to Run a Railroad: The Untold Story of the Penn Central Crisis* (New York: McGraw-Hill, 1982);

Richard Saunders, *The Railroad Mergers and the Coming of /Conrail* (Westport, Conn.: Greenwood, 1978);

Robert Sobel, *The Fallen Colossus* (New York: Weybright & Talley, 1977);

U.S. Congress, Senate, Committee on Commerce, *The Penn Central and Other Railroads*, 92nd Congress, 2d sess., 1973.

Archives:

Some Pennsylvania Railroad records are at Eleutherian Mills Historical Library, Wilmington, Delaware.

Henry A. Scandrett

(April 8, 1876-March 20, 1957)

by Carlos A. Schwantes

University of Idaho

Henry A. Scandrett

CAREER: Claim adjuster (1901), assistant attorney for Kansas and Missouri (1901-1911), Union Pacific Railroad; assistant interstate commerce attorney (1911-1912), attorney (1912-1913), Union Pacific and Southern Pacific systems; interstate commerce attorney (1913-1918), assistant director of traffic (1918), Union Pacific Railroad; traffic assistant, Central Western Region, United States Railroad Administration (1918-1920); valuation and commerce counsel (1920-1925), vice president in charge of valuation, commerce matters, and land and public relations departments (1925-1928), Union Pacific Railroad; president (1928-1936), trustee (1936-1945), president (1945-1947), Chicago, Milwaukee, St. Paul & Pacific Railroad.

Henry A. Scandrett served as president and trustee of the Chicago, Milwaukee, St. Paul & Pacific Railroad (Milwaukee Road) during the troubled years from 1928 until 1947. Like many railroad leaders of his era, Scandrett had worked his way up through industry ranks, beginning as a claim adjuster for the Union Pacific in 1901.

Born in Faribault, Minnesota, in 1876 to Henry Alexander and Jane Whipple Scandrett, the younger Henry Alexander Scandrett attended a military academy in Faribault and later the University of Minnesota, where he was captain of the football team. Graduating in 1900 with a degree in law, he joined the Union Pacific the following year. He went on to hold a series of increasingly important posts with the railroad, becoming a vice president in 1925.

Scandrett succeeded Harry E. Byram as president of the Milwaukee Road when the railroad emerged from bankruptcy proceedings in January 1928. On March 11 of that year he married Frances Hochstetler; they had one son.

Scandrett's first two years at the Milwaukee Road were relatively prosperous ones for the railroad. He led efforts to improve the railroad's physical structure: new rail was laid and stations and other structures were refurbished. But with the onset of the Great Depression in 1930 it became obvious that Scandrett was president of a weak company that would only grow weaker during the lean years to come. The Milwaukee Road suffered from declining freight revenues and grievous losses in the local passenger business. In 1932 alone passenger revenues declined by 28 percent.

The Milwaukee Road filed for bankruptcy in 1936, and Scandrett was appointed one of its trustees. Despite the hard times, the Milwaukee Road began to acquire a progressive new image. Scandrett was especially proud of the inauguration in 1937 of the Hiawathas, high-speed streamlined passenger trains operating between Chicago and Minneapolis.

During Scandrett's trusteeship the company suffered the worst accident in its history: on June 19, 1938, near Saugus, Montana, the Olympian plunged through a bridge weakened by a cloudburst. Forty-four passengers and four employees lost their lives and seventy-five people were injured. Critics claimed that the financially ailing company had skimped on track maintenance, but that allegation was never proved.

On October 1, 1945, the Milwaukee Road emerged from its second bankruptcy and Scandrett again became president, a post he held until retirement in May 1947. Succeeding him was Charles H. Buford, an Arkansan who began with the Milwaukee Road as an instrument man in 1907 and was the first Milwaukee president since Albert J. Earling to have worked his way up through the railroad's ranks.

Scandrett served as a director of the Association of American Railroads from its formation in 1934 until his retirement in 1947. Active in civic and educational affairs, he described himself as an Episcopalian and Republican. He died in Chicago in 1957.

Reference:

August Derleth, *The Milwaukee Road: Its First Hundred Years* (New York: Creative Age Press, 1948).

Seaboard Air Line Railroad

by James A. Ward

University of Tennessee at Chattanooga

Map of the Seaboard Air Line Railroad (1930)

After the Civil War, Northern capitalists gained control of the Seaboard & Roanoke Railroad. Its president, John M. Robinson of Baltimore, added the Raleigh & Gaston and the Raleigh & Augusta Air Line to his small system in the 1870s to create a 280-mile road running from Portsmouth toward Atlanta. During the following decade, Robinson bought the Carolina Central and built the Georgia,

Carolina & Northern Railway which, when completed in 1892, gave his roads access to Atlanta. By then his little empire of five lines, known as the Seaboard Air–Line System, consisted of over 800 miles of track with steamship service north to Portsmouth, Norfolk, Baltimore, and New York.

At the end of 1898 John L. Williams and Sons of Richmond and Middendorf, Oliver and Company of Baltimore, owners of the Georgia & Alabama Railway between Savannah and Montgomery, purchased the Seaboard. The new owners almost doubled its size in February 1899 when they purchased the 940-mile long Florida Central & Peninsular Railroad from W. Bayard Cuttings and R. Fulton Cuttings. Williams and Middendorf added other short lines to their holdings and built the Richmond, Petersburg & Carolina to improve connections with Raleigh and the old Confederate capital. Finally, after a protracted fight with J. P. Morgan, the two men won an agreement in October 1899 with the Richmond, Fredericksburg & Potomac to use that road's facilities to connect with Washington, D.C., and New York City. Six months later the Seaboard's owners organized a new corporation, the Seaboard Air Line Railway, that consolidated their twenty separate companies and 2,600 miles of road.

The Seaboard's golden spike ceremony and special trains to Tampa masked the desperate financial straits caused by the road's rapid expansion. Competition from the Atlantic Coast Line (ACL) and the Southern Railway dampened the Seaboard's business and in 1903 Williams was forced to go to New York City and Boston for funds to keep his company afloat. A Wall Street syndicate led by Thomas F. Ryan wrested control of the Seaboard from Williams and added managerial instability to the road's troubles. The Ryan interests also pushed expansion, purchasing four short lines and constructing a new road to fill the gaps between Atlanta and the mineral-rich area around Birmingham, the "Pittsburgh of the South." The Seaboard struggled along until the 1907 panic, and went into receivership in January 1908. As the panic's grip weakened, the road's prospects improved and it emerged from receivership on November 4, 1909.

After receivership, the Seaboard expanded in Florida to develop agricultural and mining lands, pushing its rails down the west coast. In 1915 these lines, with new extensions in South Carolina, were merged with the Seaboard in a new corporate entity, the Seaboard Air Line Railroad Company, which billed itself as "The Progressive Railway of the South." Three years later S. David Warfield—a former financial partner of Williams; organizer of the Continental Trust Company of Baltimore, the Seaboard's receiver in 1908-1909; and an uncle of Wallis Warfield Simpson (who later became the Duchess of Windsor)—became the road's president. He, too, energetically pushed Florida expansion in the 1920s to take advantage of the real estate boom in the state. His principal project was a 300-mile extension from Coleman to West Palm Beach and Miami that enabled the Seaboard to advertise that it was the only railroad to serve both Florida coasts. He also laid heavier rail, increased ballast, installed automatic block signals, and double-tracked much of the mainline. Warfield died in 1927 and his successor, Legh R. Powell, Jr., continued his projects. The work, however, strained the company's slender resources and the 4,500-mile Seaboard survived the stock market crash for only a little over a year, declaring bankruptcy in December 1930. It stayed under Powell's receivership for fourteen and a half years, during which it bought new equipment with loans from the Reconstruction Finance Corporation. It sustained the heavy traffic generated by

World War II, although not without several serious accidents in places where the double track and automatic block signaling had not been installed.

On May 31, 1945, the Seaboard's assets were auctioned off to the road's bondholders for $52 million. The road was reorganized the following year as the Seaboard Air Line Railroad. Powell resumed its presidency and held the post until he was succeeded by John W. Smith in 1952. The company prospered, earning $16.1 million or $3.30 a share in 1966, its last full year of operation as an independent; but it faced heavy competition from other railways, from trucks for the citrus trade, and from airlines for the Florida tourist traffic. With rising gross revenues but with net income lagging behind, Smith started merger talks in 1958 with Thomas Rice of the Atlantic Coast Line. Within two years they submitted a plan to the Interstate Commerce Commission, which held hearings in 1961 and gave its permission for the merger in December 1963. The two roads became the Seaboard Coast Line on July 1, 1967, the first time two prosperous competing roads had been allowed to consolidate. The commission agreed that competition among railroads was not as important as competition with alternate forms of transport and that the railways were entitled to a fair return on their investments. On January 1, 1983, the Seaboard Coast Line became part of the Seaboard System.

References:

Richard E. Prince, *Seaboard Air Line Railway* (Green River, Wyo.: Published by the author, 1969);

"Seaboard and Coast Line: A Billion-Dollar Merger," *New York Times*, July 1, 1967, pp. 1, 26;

John F. Stover, *The Railroads of the South, 1865-1900.* (Chapel Hill: University of North Carolina Press, 1955), pp. 270-274:

Archives:

The merger papers of the Seaboard Air Line Railroad and the Atlantic Coast Line Railroad are in the Thomas Fuller Collection, University of Oregon Library, Eugene. Other papers are at Seaboard System general offices in Jacksonville, Florida.

Seaboard Coast Line Railroad

by James A. Ward

University of Tennessee at Chattanooga

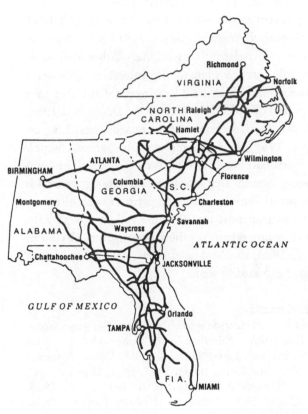

Map of the Seaboard Coast Line Railroad (1967)

The Seaboard Coast Line Railroad was created on July 1, 1967, through the merger of two southeastern competitors, the Atlantic Coast Line (ACL) and the Seaboard Air Line (SAL). John Smith of the SAL and Thomas Rice of the ACL began discussing the merger in 1958 after it became apparent that Congress would not help the railroads. The two roads were not in immediate financial trouble, but

their long-range prospects were not bright after they lost much of their citrus, peach, and potato business to trucks and their Florida tourist traffic to the airlines. Citing the wastefulness of parallel roads between Richmond and south Florida, their fears of eventual nationalization, and their belief that a lack of rail competition would not adversely affect the region, the two companies petitioned the Interstate Commerce Commission for permission to merge. The commission held hearings in 1961 and gave its consent in December 1963. The new company controlled 9,624 miles of road with assets of $1.2 billion and gross revenues of over $400 million.

The Mercantile Safe-Deposit Trust Company of Baltimore owned 56 percent of the ACL and controlled the Louisville & Nashville Railroad (L&N). Under the merger the trust company retained control of the Seaboard and the L&N. The Seaboard Coast Line merged with the L&N to become the Seaboard System on January 1, 1983.

References:

Richard Saunders, *The Railroad Mergers and the Coming of Conrail* (Westport, Conn.: Greenwood Press, 1978), pp. 202-209;

"Seaboard and Coast Line: A Billion-Dollar Merger," *New York Times*, July 1, 1967, pp. 1, 26.

Archives:

Merger papers of the Seaboard Air Line Railroad and the Atlantic Coast Line Railway are in the Thomas Fuller Collection, University of Oregon Library, Eugene. Other papers are at the Seaboard System general offices, Jacksonville, Florida.

Perry Shoemaker

(July 15, 1906-   )

by Richard Saunders

Clemson University

Perry Shoemaker

CAREER: Laborer, freight checker, foreman, terminal yardmaster (1929-1931), general yardmaster (1931-1932), Erie Railroad; research assistant (1934-1938), superintendent of freight transportation (1938-1941), New York, New Haven & Hartford Railroad; transportation assistant to president (1941), superintendent of mechanical and engineering division (1941-1942), general superintendent, superintendent (1943-1946), general manager (1946-1947), vice president of operations (1948-1952),

president, director, and chairman of the executive committee (1953-1960), Delaware, Lackawanna & Western Railroad; vice chairman (1960-1961), chairman (1961-1962), Erie-Lackawanna Railroad; president (1961-1967), trustee (1967-1968), Central Railroad of New Jersey; transportation consultant (1968-   ).

Perry Monroe Shoemaker was born in Elmira, New York, in 1906 to J. Raymond and Mabel Perry Shoemaker. He worked as a track laborer on the Pennsylvania Railroad and as an assistant on a dynamometer car on the Erie Railroad while he attended the University of Michigan. He graduated in 1928 with a degree in mechanical engineering and went to Yale, where, a year later, he earned a master's degree in transportation engineering. In 1930 he married Emily Hane; they had four children. As the Depression gathered, he stayed on the Erie, becoming a general yardmaster in 1931. In 1934 he joined the New York, New Haven & Hartford Railroad as a research assistant. In 1938 he became superintendent of freight transportation.

William White became president of the Delaware, Lackawanna & Western Railroad in January 1941, and in June he hired Shoemaker as his personal assistant. During the White presidency, Shoemaker progressed through a series of ever more responsible positions, becoming vice president of operations in 1948. The Lackawanna, once an incredibly wealthy, aristocratic symbol of the days of New York's economic and cultural dominance of the continent, had fallen on hard times with the decline of two of its most important sources of revenue: anthracite coal and passengers. White revitalized the railroad and restructured its corporate organization, making it, by the year of its centennial in 1951, as fine a dieselized, double-tracked, high-speed, high-capacity railroad as one could find. When White left in 1952 to begin his short and unhappy stint as the head of the New York Central, Shoemaker became president of the Lackawanna.

Under Shoemaker, the Lackawanna remained an excellent railroad in the face of mounting adversity. It pioneered piggyback service and contract rates, yet still offered a full line of traditional freight and passenger service. To the end, it operated scrupulously on time, a call from the president's office checking each day on the performance of the company's flag-bearer, the New York–to–Buffalo streamliner Phoebe Snow. Until austerity forced cutbacks in the spring of 1960, the morale of all who worked for the Lackawanna remained high with the enthusiasm that comes from confidence in leadership and from doing a job well.

But the Lackawanna was beset with changing economic conditions. Anthracite, the railroad's original reason for being, vanished utterly as a space-heating fuel. Long-haul passenger service, a promising investment as late as the inauguration of the Phoebe Snow in 1949, became a millstone. Commuter service, operated close to the break-even point as long as midday shopping and evening theater crowds rode the trains, sank deeply into the red as shopping malls invaded the suburbs and non-rush–hour traffic vanished. Finally, the St. Lawrence Seaway, which opened in 1958, diverted traffic from the five Great Lakes-to-the-sea railroads; and the Lackawanna, along with Lehigh Valley, was nothing but a Great Lakes-to-the-sea road.

In addition, Shoemaker had to face several specific crises. One was merger negotiations with the New York, Chicago & St. Louis Railroad (Nickel Plate). White had committed a significant portion of the Lackawanna's liquid assets to the purchase of Nickel Plate stock, then had jeopardized the merger by his inept handling of sensitive personalities on the Nickel Plate board. Shoemaker, realizing that with the coming of the Seaway the Lackawanna had to expand west of Buffalo or die, asked for two Lackawanna nominees to be seated on the Nickel Plate board. But Nickel Plate opponents of the merger, regarding the Lackawanna as an arrogant has-been, hardened their position. The accession of Lynne White to the Nickel Plate presidency in 1949 probably doomed the Lackawanna's efforts, for he had been close to the anti-Lackawanna

faction on the Nickel Plate board. The Nickel Plate petitioned the Interstate Commerce Commission to declare the Lackawanna illegally in control. The Lackawanna, fearing that it might be forced to sell its Nickel Plate stock–which was, by the late 1950s, its last money-making asset–put the stock in trust. In l960 it sold the stock to pay its bills.

On the night of August 19-20, 1955, Hurricane Diane ripped through northeastern Pennsylvania, obliterating nearly seventy miles of the Lackawanna's main line. Service on the main line east of Binghamton was suspended indefinitely. Bethlehem Steel gave the railroad's order for 3,000 tons of rail the emergency designation "rights above everything." The cost of repairs was $8 million, which the railroad paid out of cash, and a month's revenues were lost while the line was rebuilt. The hurricane left a financial wound that would require at least five good years to heal, but two years later the company had to endure the opening of the Seaway, labor disruptions that would shut down first New York Harbor and then the steel industry, and the onset of recession. Then, in l957, the Army Corps of Engineers determined that the railroad's bridge across the Hackensack River, on the main line's final approach to New York Harbor, was a danger to shipping, and the Lackawanna was forced to borrow $5 million to make repairs.

In 1956 the Lackawanna and the Erie consolidated their passenger facilities on the New Jersey waterfront in the Lackawanna's Hoboken Terminal, bringing 32,000 daily Erie passengers to mingle with the Lackawanna's 56,000. In 1959 the Lackawanna ripped up seventy miles of its main line between Binghamton and Corning and moved its trains to the parallel Erie line. These projects were so successful that, in 1959, plans were made to merge the two railroads. The concept of the Erie-Lackawanna may have originated with William White who initially intended to make his Delaware & Hudson part of a three-way merger. When that was not possible, Shoemaker became one of the Erie-Lackawanna's creators.

He negotiated for the Lackawanna as good a deal as he could, given that it was only half the size of the Erie and otherwise had no trumps. The Lackawanna's stockholders would own 35 percent of the merged company and name one third of the directors. He was hounded throughout the negotiations by a gaggle of dissident stockholders who wanted the company to purchase their shares at above-market prices.

While the merger talks were continuing, the Lackawanna intervened unsuccessfully in a Mohawk Airlines mail rate case that would skim away profitable first-class mail and leave the railroad with break-even second and third class. Shoemaker took pride in providing services the public wanted, but the high taxes imposed by New Jersey politicians forced him to file petitions to end suburban service on the railroad's electric line. He also initiated the legal action that would eventually bring a Supreme Court ruling that the taxes Hudson County, New Jersey, imposed on the railroad—a 100 percent assessment, while everyone else was assessed at 33 percent—were confiscatory and unconstitutional. He was concerned, especially after executive pay cuts were forced in 1960, that his most talented people would leave. He understood but was disappointed when his ace traffic man, William G. White, left for (and eventually headed) Consolidated Freightways.

The Lackawanna's executive committee met for the last time on October 13, 1960. As the meeting drew to a close, Shoemaker's directors presented him with the regulator clock made in England in 1853 that had stood for years in the president's office. On merger day, October 17, Shoemaker left New York aboard the Westerner to assume his new duties in Cleveland as vice chairman of the Erie–Lackawanna (the hyphen was dropped in 1963). As the train gathered speed into the twilight, every locomotive whistle in the Hoboken Terminal blew in salute.

Extracting the savings that were supposed to flow from merger eluded the old Erie management, and in 1961 the company turned to Shoemaker and the Lackawanna management. His tenure as chairman was short and unpleasant, made difficult by the fact that the capital to make the physical changes necessary to get the savings, such as a new classification yard at Buffalo, was not there. In February 1962 he accepted the invitation of the Central Railroad of New Jersey to become its president upon the retirement of E. T. Moore. The move meant a reduction in salary from $91,000 to $63,000.

The Jersey Central was not a happy place to be in the 1960s, with short hauls, dwindling anthracite traffic, money-losing commuter operations, and New Jersey taxes. No help was forthcoming from the Jersey Central's parent, the Reading, or from the Reading's parent, the Baltimore & Ohio (B&O), or from the B&O's parent, the Chesapeake & Ohio, or from the state of New Jersey, despite the protestations of Governor Hughes that service on the Central had to be maintained. Bankruptcy was declared in 1967. Shoemaker served as trustee for a year, then resigned in April 1968 to open a consulting business in Florida.

Shoemaker's first wife had died in 1964. In 1965 he had married Vivien Bulloch Keatley. After her death in 1972, he married Iva Brown Corcoran.

References:

"Erie's Chairman Changing Roads," New York Times, February 28, 1962, p.41;

"Jersey Central Head Quits," New York Times, April 21, 1958, p. 82;

Richard Saunders, The Railroad Mergers and the Coming of Conrail (Westport, Conn.: Greenwood Press, 1978);

Thomas Taber and Thomas Taber III, The Delaware, Lackawanna & Western Railroad in the Twentieth Century, 2 volumes (Muncy, Pa.: Privately printed, 1980).

Archives:

Delaware, Lackawanna & Western Railroad papers are at Syracuse University Library and the Eleutherian Mills Historical Library in Wilmington, Delaware.

Matthew S. Sloan

(September 5, 1881-June 14, 1945)

by Don L. Hofsommer

Augustana College

Matthew S. Sloan

CAREER: Manager, electric light plant, Dothan, Alabama (1902); employee, Nashville, Tennessee, street railway (1902); apprentice in railway motor testing department, supervisor of turbine installations, General Electric Company (1902-1906); chief engineer, general superintendent, assistant to president, Birmingham Railway Light and Power Company (1906-1914); vice president and general manager, New Orleans Railway and Light Company (1914-1917); assistant to vice president and general manager, New York Edison Company (1917-1919);

president, Brooklyn Edison Company (1919-1932); treasurer, Electrical Testing Labs (1919-1932); president, Amsterdam Electric Light, Heat and Power Company (1920-1932); president, New York Edison Company and affiliates (1928-1932); co-chairman, Share the Work Movement (1932-1934); chairman of the board and president, Missouri-Kansas-Texas Railroad (1934-1945).

Matthew Scott Sloan came to railroading late in his career. He had served with distinction in the electrical power industry; and, in the darkest hours of the Great Depression was named to head the greatly distressed Missouri-Kansas-Texas Railroad (M-K-T or Katy).

Sloan was born to Matthew Scott and Mary Elizabeth Scott Sloan in Mobile, Alabama, on September 5, 1881. His father was the chief of the Mobile Fire Department. Sloan attended Alabama Polytechnic Institute, where he earned a B.S. in 1901, an M.S. in 1902, and an E.E. in 1911.

Sloan began his career during the summer of 1902 as manager of the light plant in Dothan, Alabama. From there he moved briefly to a street railway system in Nashville, Tennessee. From 1902 to 1906 Sloan worked for the General Electric Company in Schenectady, New York, rising from an apprenticeship in the railway motor testing department to supervisor of turbine installations. In 1906 he returned to Alabama as chief engineer and assistant to the president of the Birmingham Railway Light and Power Company. In 1911 he married Lottie Everard Lane. Three years later he became vice president and general manager of the New Orleans Railway and Light Company; in 1917 he was named assistant to the vice president and general manager of the New York Edison Company. Shortly after World War I the Brooklyn Edison Company recruited him as its head. In 1928 Sloan became president of the huge New York Edison Company, which had resulted from the consolidation of the old New York Edison, Brooklyn Edison, and other utilities firms.

During the 1920s Sloan was one of the best-known businessmen in America. A large, handsome man, Sloan was a frequent subject of articles in magazines and journals, and he himself wrote for publication on topics close to his heart.

Sloan was a capable and aggressive leader who believed in expansion through cutting rates and increasing efficiency. He also advocated intelligent integration or combination within the electrical utilities industry. Most of all, he was an enthusiastic exponent of effective public relations and good will. Indeed, few American industrialists better understood the basic need for amicable relations between companies and their constituencies.

While Sloan was a skillful manager, he ultimately failed in the corrupt political environment of New York City by insisting on efficiency instead of cooperating with the spoils system. In 1932 his political enemies convinced the board of New York Edison to demand his resignation.

Sloan spent the next two years as treasurer of Electrical Testing Labs. In 1933 he became a director of the M-K-T, and in April 1934 he was named chairman of the board. Two months later he also assumed the presidency.

It was a dubious honor; the Katy was nearly moribund. The press, however, expected the road to have a new lease on life under Sloan's dynamic leadership. Sloan immediately set out to evaluate the property, to meet the Katy's employees and customers, to study the service area, and to otherwise build confidence. He retained his residence in New York City but pledged that his headquarters would be "on the line." He found the Katy's properties in deplorable condition and its financial condition even worse. In fact, the company was desperate after the economic downturn of 1938, and its common stock sold at a mere twenty-five cents per share.

Something more than Sloan was required to save the Katy. In any event, traffic resulting from World War II provided salvation for the M-K-T and much of the railroad industry. As business improved, Sloan poured profits into the company's track, locomotives, and cars, into painting and repairing its structures, and into retiring debts and thus reducing fixed charges. In 1944 the company earned a profit of $6.1 million.

The press noted that the Katy had been near bankruptcy when Sloan took over in 1934, but that it was now a handsome and attractive property. On the other hand, the railroad's resurrection also attracted the rapacious Edward N. Claughton, who owned 11 percent of the Katy's stock and who complained that if shareholders did not receive dividends during war years they could expect even less thereafter. Sloan insisted, though, that money should not yet be paid out for dividends but should continue to be employed in a program of improvement and debt reduction. A bitter proxy fight followed; M-K-T management was ultimately victorious, but in the meantime Sloan died on June 14, 1945.

Publications:

"Diogenes Had the Right Idea," *American Magazine*, 13 (June 1927): 42-43;

"A Policy That Has Tripled Sales in 8 Years," *Magazine of Business*, 52 (November 1927): 549-551, 634-637;

"Electricity–Mankind's Universal Servant," *Annals of the American Academy of Political and Social Science*, 159 (January 1932): 140-147.

Reference:

V. V. Masterson, *The Katy Railroad and the Last Frontier* (Norman: University of Oklahoma Press, 1952).

John Walter Smith

(July 20, 1900-May 3, 1972)

by James A. Ward

University of Tennessee at Chattanooga

John Walter Smith

CAREER: Engineering inspector (1924), maintenance of way department (1924-1932), division engineer (1932-1936), operating and engineering department (1936-1944), assistant chief engineer and assistant general superintendent (1944-1946), assistant to the president (1946-1950), vice president for administration (1950-1952), president, director, member of executive committee (1952-1967), Seaboard Air Line Railroad; chairman of the board, member of executive committee (1967-1971), direc-

tor, (1971-1972), Seaboard Coast Line Railroad.

John Walter Smith was born in Baltimore, Maryland, on July 20, 1900, to James Goldfinch and Christina Reif–Schneider Smith. He attended the University of Maryland, where he received his B.S. in civil engineering in 1921.

Smith joined the Seaboard Air Line Railroad (SAL) in 1924 as an engineering inspector of construction work. He performed those duties less than a year before he was appointed to the maintenance of way department. On September 4, 1926, he married Mary Elizabeth Appel; they had two children. In 1932 the SAL, in receivership due to the Depression, made Smith a division engineer. Four years later he was given responsibilities in the operating and engineering departments. In 1944 he was promoted to assistant chief engineer and assistant general superintendent.

Legh R. Powell, Jr., had been the SAL's president from 1927 until it entered receivership in 1930, and had been the company's receiver since then. After the SAL reorganized in 1946 and Powell again became president, he chose Smith as his assistant. In 1950 Powell named Smith vice president for administration. When Powell became chairman of the board in 1952, Smith took over the presidency. Smith inherited a railway that had been sold to its bond-holders only six years earlier and built it into a profitable company able to compete with the rival Atlantic Coast Line (ACL).

The Seaboard's new president was a technician rather than an innovator. Well schooled in railroad fundamentals, he attempted to strengthen his property through conventional means popular in his day. He improved and updated the road, installing Centralized Traffic Control throughout the system by 1965 and completing its dieselization program. Smith donated obsolete steam locomotives from the Gainesville Midland Railroad, which he purchased in 1959, to exhibitors throughout the country. A year earlier he had added the Macon, Dublin & Savannah to the SAL, but the great expansionist impulse of earlier decades had been spent by the time of Smith's tenure.

Smith realized by the mid 1950s that the SAL was continuing to lose much of its lucrative citrus and peach traffic to trucks and its Florida tourist trade to airplanes. No amount of internal corporate economy and modernization could ever compensate for lost revenue from those sources. When congressional hearings in 1958 indicated that government regulatory policies were not going to change, Smith met with his counterpart on the Atlantic Coast Line, Thomas Rice, to talk about merging the two properties. Within two years they had outlined an agreement and presented it to the Interstate Commerce Commission (ICC), which took testimony in 1961 and gave its assent in December 1963. The ICC set new precedents with the SAL-ACL case: it was the first time the commission had allowed two prosperous roads, that were more competitive than complementary to merge. Smith and Rice convinced the ICC that even though both roads were profitable, they were earning less than a fair return and that competition with each other was less important than competition with other means of transport. On the eve of the final merger on July 1, 1967, Smith's road had just posted a quarterly net income of $1.4 million or 30 cents a share; in the previous year it had had net earnings of $16.1 million or $3.30 a share. The ACL had done even better, netting $22 million the year before the merger. The combined company, the Seaboard Coast Line (SCL), was a Southern giant.

Smith, at sixty-six was past retirement age at the time of the merger; Rice was twelve years his junior. Smith became the SCL's chairman of the board, while Rice became president and chief executive officer. Smith turned the chairman's duties over to Rice in 1971 but remained a member of the board.

When he stepped down as chairman of the board, Smith held an impressive number of positions with other railroads and businesses. He was chairman of the board and a member of the executive committee of the Taveres & Gulf Railroad, president and director of the Georgia, Florida & Alabama Railroad Company and the Southeastern Investment Company, chairman of the boards of the Gainesville Midland Railroad and the Clinchfield Railroad, director of six railroads and a bank, and trustee of Richmond Memorial Hospital. He was also a member of the American Railway Engineering Association and the National Defense Transportation Association. Smith also belonged to what must have been a record number of clubs for such a busy man. They were located all over the territory his railroads served and ranged from the University, Traffic, and Links in New York City to Deerwood and Hidden Hills in Jacksonville, Florida.

Smith died on May 3, 1972. He had taken a railroad that had recently emerged from receivership and built it into a formidable competitor; he had taken the longer view of the railway industry's future and acted on that view. He had convinced the ICC to allow mergers that would create financial strength even if they lessened competition between railroads. Through his efforts the Seaboard Coast Line (which on January 1, 1983, merged with the Louisville & Nashville Railroad to become the Seaboard System, a component of CSX) became one of the giant combinations in the South.

References:

Richard E. Prince, *Seaboard Air Line Railway* (Green River, Wyo.: Published by author, 1969);

"Seaboard and Coast Line: A Billion-Dollar Merger," *New York Times*, July 1, 1967, pp. 1, 26.

Robert H. Smith

(March 10, 1888-June 18, 1960)

by Keith L. Bryant, Jr.

Texas A&M University

Robert H. Smith

CAREER: Chainman, axeman (1910), masonry inspector and transitman (1911-1913), assistant roadmaster (1913-1914), roadmaster (1914-1916), assistant division superintendent (1917-1922), division superintendent (1922-1931), general superintendent (1931-1936), general manager (1936-1939), vice president and general manager (1939-1942), vice president, operations (1942-1946), president (1946-1958), Norfolk & Western Railway.

Robert Hall Smith followed a career path that was typical in American railroading in the first half of the twentieth century. He entered service with the Norfolk & Western Railway (N&W) after graduating from college, and for the next thirty-five years he moved up through the ranks until he reached the company presidency. Smith worked for a prosperous, medium-sized, coal-hauling carrier that was dominated financially by the Pennsylvania Railroad.

The N&W was fiercely independent in operations, however, and was a strenuous competitor of the Chesapeake & Ohio, the Baltimore & Ohio, and the Virginian in hauling coal from West Virginia to the Atlantic Seaboard and the Midwest.

Born in Baltimore, Maryland, in 1888 to Robert H. and Margaret B. Clark Smith, he was educated at the Tome School in Maryland, and Princeton University, where he was an "oar" on the rowing crew. In 1910 he obtained a summer job as an axeman and chainman with the Norfolk & Western, and after graduation from Princeton in 1911 with a degree in civil engineering he returned to the railroad as a masonry inspector and transitman. He was promoted to assistant roadmaster in 1913 and to roadmaster in 1914. He married Mary Elizabeth Wysor in 1916, and they had five children. A leading citizen of Roanoke, Virginia, where he lived most of his adult life, Smith served on the boards of regional banks and as a trustee of Hollins College. He was an Episcopalian. Throughout his life, Smith's primary interest was the Norfolk & Western Railway, and he served as an executive of the firm in a critical period.

Smith's career paralleled that of his predecessor, William J. Jenks: they both served as general superintendent, general manager, and vice president for operations before being elevated to the presidency. They established the basic strategy for the N&W: the company would emphasize efficiency and prudent management, build the finest physical plant funds would allow, seek to develop a diversified traffic while recognizing that coal was the premier cargo, and maintain the firm's independence despite the dominant financial position of the Pennsylvania Railroad. Jenks and Smith brought the N&W through the Great Depression in good shape. Because of its efficient plant and fiscal conservatism the carrier remained profitable and in the late 1930s took advantage of low costs to make significant improvements. Heavier rails were installed on the mainline and on branches that carried major traffic; a program to construct modern steam locomotives at the Roanoke shops produced some of the finest power ever built; and the movement of freight was enhanced with the expansion of the Centralized Traffic Control system, new yards, and more efficient coal piers at Norfolk. Thus, when traffic began to grow at a rapid rate in 1939, the year Smith became operations vice president, the carrier was in good physical condition.

As vice president during World War II, Smith was responsible for developing plans to move vast wartime tonnage with fewer locomotives, cars, and employees than the N&W had had during World War I. True, the motive power was heavier and more efficient, grades and curves had been reduced, and freight car capacities had increased, but the level of traffic was tremendous. Employees frequently saw "Racehorse" Smith on the system as he dealt with growing problems. Distinguished in appearance, wearing a three-piece suit with a gold watch chain stretched across his vest, Smith was a formidable figure. He was popular with the workers even though he was considered very strict, and he knew the N&W property mile-by-mile. An inveterate walker, he literally walked the line on foot and gained a detailed knowledge of the railway. Approachable, cordial, and always a gentleman, Smith was a good listener who accepted suggestions and listened to grievances.

In 1946 Smith accepted the presidency of the N&W, and for the next twelve years he led the firm through a period of dramatic change for American railroading. Nearly all of the nation's other railroads were shifting rapidly to diesel power, but the N&W had an enormous investment in its steam engines and was reluctant to upset the coal companies by converting from steam, which used coal for fuel, to diesel. The N&W stayed with steam as long as it could, even buying used steam switchers from the Chesapeake & Ohio as that firm bought diesels. In 1952 the N&W tested diesel freight units in the mountainous Pocahontas Division, but when the tests proved inconclusive, Smith decided to develop even more efficient steam power. A giant, coal-fired, steam turbine, electric-drive locomotive, the Jawn Henry, was developed with the Baldwin-Lima-Hamilton Company; it was successful on the road,

but its power plant was too complex and expensive to maintain. Steam stayed longer on the N&W than on other major carriers, but the cost of wages, materials, and support facilities dictated dieselization. Smith placed the N&W's first diesel orders in 1955 and launched a motive power revolution on the system.

Smith headed the N&W at a time when the railroads needed higher rates in order to rehabilitate their properties, but the Interstate Commerce Commission refused requests for general rate hikes. The operating ratio rose as a coal strike of 110 days reduced traffic in 1949, and many homes and factories in the East began to convert heating and power systems to natural gas. During the 1950s coal traffic fell and wage agreements produced higher labor costs. The operating ratio of 52 in 1950 rose to 65.4 in 1958, a respectable figure compared to the rest of the industry but of grave concern to Smith. He could report to the board of directors in Philadelphia that profits and dividends would continue, but clearly, significant changes had to be made.

Smith ordered dieselization to be accelerated and petitioned to discontinue most of the unprofitable passenger service, and the traffic department sought additional freight movements. The westward movement of coal began to be exceeded by eastbound traffic for export as the closing of the Suez Canal created a demand for coal abroad, and the volume shipped through Norfolk grew. Smith's responses to the railroad's problems were of the traditional sort: he pushed for greater efficiency, traffic growth, and rate adjustments, just as his predecessors had. After he retired as president in 1958, his successors turned to mergers and vast territorial expansion, and they transformed the moderate-sized N&W into one of the nation's largest carriers.

Smith was a temperate man who ordered buttermilk rather than wine or martinis with his seafood in the N&W's business car. He would read a book while traveling to Philadelphia, not engaging in idle talk when he could be learning more about the business. The N&W was a fairly simple railroad to operate compared to most, and Smith excelled at doing things as they had always been done on the carrier. He died in 1960.

Reference:

E. F. Pat Striplin, *The Norfolk & Western: A History* (Roanoke: Norfolk & Western Railway, 1981).

Soo Line Railroad Company

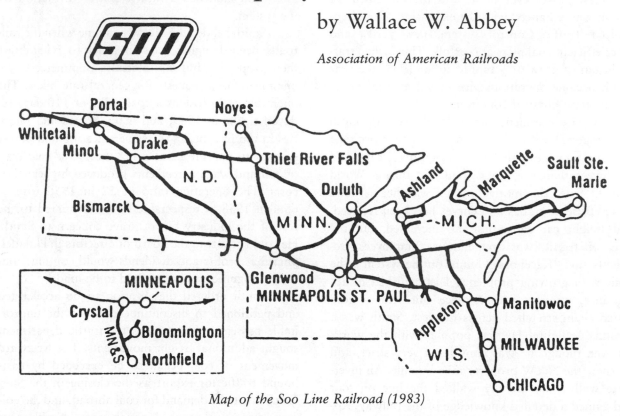

by Wallace W. Abbey

Association of American Railroads

Map of the Soo Line Railroad (1983)

Soo Line Railroad Company, the principal subsidiary of Soo Line Corporation, operated 7,750 miles of route in the midwestern United States in 1987. The Soo has had a volatile financial record and, until the 1980s, a history of conservatism. It has grown from a modest regional carrier to become the nation's tenth largest rail system.

The Soo is the result of the combination of many individual railroad corporations. Almost from the beginning, it has had one predominant stockholder: the giant Canadian Pacific Railway (CP) or the CP's holding company, Canadian Pacific Ltd.

Prior to 1960 the predecessor companies of the Soo distilled themselves into three: the Duluth, South Shore & Atlantic (DSS&A), which traversed Michigan's Upper Peninsula and dated from 1857; the Wisconsin Central (WC), born of local pride in its namesake state between 1871 and 1910; and the Minneapolis, St. Paul & Sault Ste. Marie (MStP&SSM), incorporated in 1883 by Minneapo-

lis millers to gather grain and to ship their produce (while avoiding the high rates charged by the lines that ran through Chicago) by way of a connection with the Canadian Pacific at Sault Ste. Marie, Michigan. The MStP&SSM also connected with the Canadian Pacific at Portal, North Dakota, and Noyes, Minnesota. None of the three was a wealthy property, although the MStP&SSM managed well enough in good wheat years; each company had been bankrupt once. All three had their headquarters in Minneapolis. The MStP&SSM and the Wisconsin Central were operated together as the original "Soo Line" (from Sault—pronounced "soo"—Ste. Marie); the DSS&A was operated separately, in competition with the Soo.

The three railroads were merged on December 30, 1960, into the 4,700-mile Soo Line Railroad Company. Few of the traditional cost savings associated with railroad mergers were available to the "new" Soo, since the constituent companies had not duplicated each other's services, but by effective marketing and efficient operation the new Soo was able to produce consistent profits and high returns on investment. The 1960s and 1970s were marked not only by a vastly improved balance sheet but by modest capital improvements to fixed plant and rolling equipment. The company seemed content with its traditional service territory and its role as a strong United States connection for the Canadian Pacific.

By about 1970, however, other American railroads had begun to acknowledge their shrinking transportation-market shares by merging, by significantly "downsizing" themselves, or by going bankrupt. Fearful of being boxed into its traditional territory, the Soo sought to extend itself to Kansas City. Failing in 1983 to acquire the Minneapolis-to-Kansas City line of the bankrupt and lifeless Chicago, Rock Island & Pacific, the Soo in 1984 sought the "viable core" of the Chicago, Milwaukee, St. Paul & Pacific (Milwaukee Road). The Milwaukee Road had been in bankruptcy reorganization since 1977 and had reduced itself from a hopeless 11,000 miles to a self-sustaining property of 3,100 miles. The Soo acquired the Milwaukee Road's rail assets on February 19, 1985, for $659 million, doubling its revenue base and greatly expanding its territory.

Having thus opened its own routes to Kansas City and Louisville, the Soo arranged in 1985 for its trains to serve Detroit from Chicago over the tracks of another railroad, establishing a new and more efficient connection with eastern Canada. The Soo was also able to integrate former Milwaukee Road lines into its own route structure, resulting in operating economies.

Also in 1985 the Soo spun off 2,000 miles of lightly trafficked lines, primarily in Wisconsin and Upper Michigan, to an autonomous subsidiary, Lake States Transportation Division. After an unsuccessful attempt to persuade its unions to grant concessions that would reduce operating costs, it sought buyers for this sizable system. An unaffiliated company coincidentally named Wisconsin Central Ltd. was expected to become the owner of Lake States in 1987.

The plant rationalization prompted by the purchase of the Milwaukee Road and the changing eco-

nomics of railroad operation signaled the Soo's shift from a regional carrier able to live comfortably with relatively short hauls on light-density lines to one that would concentrate its efforts on longer hauls over high-density lines.

The burden of the Milwaukee Road's debt, coupled with a long downturn in rail traffic generally, adversely affected the Soo's profitability. After years of consistent profits, the company recorded heavy losses in 1985 and 1986. The 1986 loss of $43 million was due in large part to a charge of $82 million associated with reductions in physical plant and employment.

The Soo at the time was by no means the only railroad to show a loss. Its return to financial health would await a reduction in its debt load, a continuation of the downsizing trend that began in earnest with the creation of Lake States, and much the same kind of dollar-stretching management that the company had practiced in the 1960s and 1970s—but on a considerably larger scale.

References:
Wallace W. Abbey, *The Little Jewel; Soo Line Railroad and The Locomotives That Make it Go* (Pueblo, Col.: Pinon Productions, 1984);
Patrick Dorin, *The Soo Line* (Seattle: Superior, 1979);
Aurele A. Durocher, *The Duluth, South Shore, and Atlantic Railway Company*, Bulletin 111, Railway & Locomotive Historical Society, Inc. (Boston: Baker Library, Harvard Business School, 1964);
Roy L. Martin, *History of the Wisconsin Central*, Bulletin 54, Railroad & Locomotive Historical Society, Inc. (Boston: Baker Library, Harvard Business School, 1941);
Charles C. Nelson, *Wisconsin & Northern Railroad*, Bulletin 116, Railway & Locomotive Historical Society (Boston: Baker Library, Harvard School of Business, n.d.);
Leslie V. Suprey, *Steam Trains of the Soo: Golden Centennial Edition* (Fortuna, Cal.: Steam Trains of the Soo Publishers, 1983).

Archives:
Milwaukee Road reorganization documents were donated by the debtor company to the Milwaukee Public Library and were being catalogued in 1987. The Soo Line Historical & Technical Society, (Willis J. Ehlert, Archives Chairman, 4022 Paunak Avenue, Madison, Wisconsin 53707), in 1987 was developing an archive of materials concerning the Soo Line Railroad Company and its predecessors.

Southern Pacific Company

by Don L. Hofsommer

Augustana College

SP

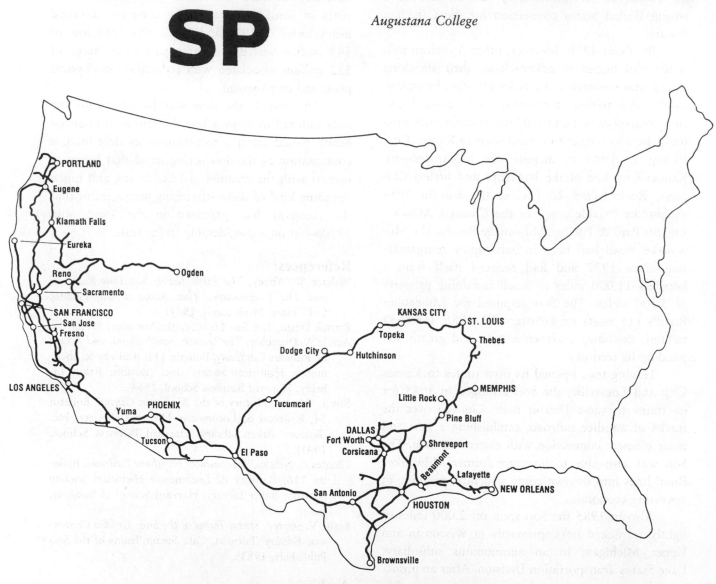

Map of the Southern Pacific system (1983)

Promoters of the Union Pacific Railroad had anticipated that their company would build the nation's first transcontinental railroad. Consequently, they were surprised and displeased when four Californians formed the Central Pacific Rail Road on June 28, 1861, and then convinced Congress and President Abraham Lincoln to support their company in construction from the West Coast to join with the Union Pacific at some unspecified location along the selected route.

Success followed the linkup at Promontory, Utah on May 10, 1869, and the Californians—Charles Crocker, Mark Hopkins, Leland Stanford, and Collis P. Huntington—soon became known as the "Big Four." Additional construction and acquisition of other lines quickly added to their influence. In 1884 many of the constituent roads were consolidated as the Southern Pacific Company (SP), although the Central Pacific remained as a leased property. By 1900 the SP consisted of 8,206 route miles stretching in the form of a crescent southward from Portland, Oregon, through Los Angeles and then eastward to El Paso, San Antonio, Houston, and New Orleans, with the original mainline jutting over the Sierra Nevada and across Nevada and Utah to meet the Union Pacific at Ogden. In addition, the SP boasted its own steamship company linking New York and other points with the railroad at New Orleans.

In 1900 Edward H. Harriman gained control of the SP, spent massively to make it an even more impressive property, and placed it under common management with the Union Pacific, of which he had also gained control. Even before he died in 1909, however, the federal government threatened to break up the arrangement, and did so in 1913. Soon thereafter, government attorneys also pledged to strip away the SP's Central Pacific Overland Route from Oakland to Ogden plus valuable terminals and secondary lines, and place these with the Union Pacific. The matter was resolved in the SP's favor in 1923, but the episode cost the company untold money and lost opportunities.

Additional expansion occurred during the 1920s, especially in Oregon and Arizona, and in 1932 the SP acquired the 1,700-mile St. Louis Southwestern Railway, giving it access to the primary gateways of St. Louis and Memphis.

World War II provided the SP with its finest hour. Because of its network of lines to and from the major ports of California, Texas, and Louisiana, the SP became the primary artery of transportation for the Pacific theater.

The same route structure favored the company when the West and Southwest boomed in the postwar era. The SP made every effort to locate new shippers along its lines and in many seasons was the industry leader in doing so. At the same time, the SP's management ordered track improvements, high-horsepower motive power, and computer technology. Many observers considered the SP the country's premier railroad during the mid 1960s and applauded the railroad's diversification program during the following decade.

By the 1980s the movement to giant mergers in the railroad industry was in full flower. In 1983 the Southern Pacific Company and Santa Fe Industries were merged to form Santa Fe Southern Pacific Corporation, and the new holding company went before the Interstate Commerce Commission with a plan to merge its railroad companies.

References:

Don L. Hofsommer, *The Southern Pacific, 1901-1985* (College Station: Texas A&M University Press, 1986);

Neil C. Wilson and Frank J. Taylor, *Southern Pacific: The Roaring Story of a Fighting Railroad* (New York: McGraw-Hill, 1952).

Archives:

Some corporate records have been deposited at the California State Railroad Museum at Sacramento.

Southern Railway

by Keith L. Bryant, Jr.

Texas A&M University

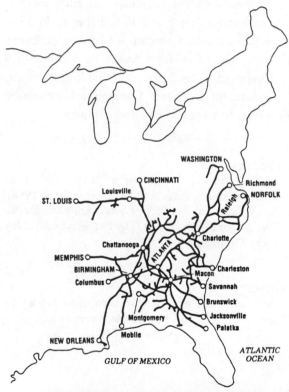

Map of the Southern Railway (1983)

Incorporated in Virginia on June 18, 1894, the Southern Railway was formed by the J. P. Morgan interests as a successor to the failed Richmond & West Point Terminal Railway and its major subsidiaries, including the Richmond & Danville and the East Tennessee, Virginia & Georgia Railway. Within four years the Southern operated a system extending south and west from Washington, D.C., through Richmond, Charlotte, and Atlanta to New

Orleans; a line south from Cincinnati to Atlanta; a route west to Memphis; and extensive branches in the Carolinas, Georgia, and Alabama. The companies absorbed by the Southern Railway, such as the Mobile & Ohio, included some of the most significant of the antebellum railways of the South and some of the major carriers created between 1865 and 1890.

The new company's leadership, especially President Samuel Spencer, believed that the railway's future depended upon the economic development of the region and upon the railway's ability to rehabilitate its trackage and equipment. During the firm's first two decades profits were reinvested to replace an outdated locomotive fleet, to rebuild or replace bridges inadequate to support heavier locomotives and cars, to improve steel rails and roadbeds for faster speeds and greater safety, and to acquire new freight and passenger cars. Simultaneously the carrier embarked on a program to encourage farmers in the South to diversify their crops rather than rely on cotton and tobacco, to reduce soil erosion, and to use improved seeds and farming techniques. The railway created departments to solicit traffic and to develop industrial sites.

Spencer purchased a line between St. Louis and Louisville in 1901, and the next year the Southern and the Louisville & Nashville jointly purchased the Chicago, Indianapolis & Louisville (Monon Route) between Louisville and Chicago. Additional infusions of capital allowed the Southern to develop yards and terminals in Louisville, Jacksonville, and New Orleans. This program of improvement accelerated after 1911 with the introduction of oil-burning locomotives, block signaling, and train dispatching by telephone. Some of the carrier's success resulted from the improvement of the regional economy, but much can be attributed to Spencer and to his successor, William W. Finley, who served from 1906 to 1913.

With the return of the Southern Railway to private hands after World War I, another significant era of expanded services and modernization was initiated. By 1920 the Southern was 8,000 miles long and entered every state south of the Potomac River except West Virginia. Fairfax Harrison, who served as president from 1913 to 1937, introduced the new Ps4 Pacific locomotives to the Southern's engine fleet. Luxury passenger trains were placed in service to capture the lucrative Florida traffic. A new company headquarters building was opened in Washington only two months before the stock market crashed in 1929.

The railway faced economic disaster during the Depression. The South was the "nation's number one economic problem," according to President Franklin D. Roosevelt, and that meant declining traffic, revenues, and profits for the railway. As the Depression deepened, the Southern missed bankruptcy only because of loans from the Reconstruction Finance Corporation. The railway lost its investments in the Mobile & Ohio and the Monon, and was forced to make massive reductions in services and expenses.

Because of large-scale military expenditures in the South and a general return to prosperity in the region during World War II, the Southern made a dramatic fiscal comeback under President Ernest E. Norris. Dieselization began in the early war years and was completed in 1955. After the war the company introduced a number of streamlined passenger trains on faster schedules made possible by significant trackage improvements. Some lines received double track or Centralized Traffic Control (CTC), and there was a massive program to rebuild the route from Cincinnati to Atlanta. Management embarked on a twofold response to strong competitive pressures from truck lines, barge operators, airlines, and pipelines: mechanization to greatly reduce labor costs and a vigorous marketing of transportation with innovative equipment and lower rates.

Presidents Harry DeButts, who served from 1952 to 1962, and D. William Brosnan, whose term lasted from 1962 to 1967, carried out a bold program that turned the Southern Railway into a major rail innovator. They introduced huge grain carriers, the "Big John" hoppers, to cut rates on wheat from the Midwest to the Southeast. Brosnan pioneered in the mechanization of track maintenance with specially designed equipment and crews dispatched in trucks over a wide territory. Efforts to end the use of firemen in diesel locomotives led to mixed results and confrontations with the railroad brotherhoods, but overall labor costs fell. In the shops, yards, and offices new technologies were introduced, with computerization of record keeping and inventories substantially reducing costs. The railway terminated most of its passenger services, but maintained the Southern Crescent as one of the nation's finest passenger trains. (Indeed, the railway initially refused to join Amtrak in order to maintain control of the train and its quality of service.) By the 1960s the leading financial journals were lauding the Southern as one of the best-managed firms in America.

In 1967 the Seaboard Air Line and the Atlantic Coast Line merged and the resulting Seaboard Coast Line controlled both the Louisville & Nashville and the Clinchfield. The Southern had acquired the Central of Georgia in 1963 but found itself surrounded by the "Family Lines" of the Seaboard Coast Line. In an effort to protect its position, the Southern Railway announced plans in 1980 for a merger with the Norfolk & Western, and in 1982 the two carriers became the Norfolk Southern Corporation. Norfolk Southern subsequently acquired a large position in Piedmont Airlines and purchased North American Van Lines. These investments were part of a concerted effort to create a fully integrated transportation network. Efforts to purchase Conrail from the federal government were unsuccessful, however, and in 1986 that offer was withdrawn.

Reference:
Burke Davis, *The Southern Railway: Road of the Innovators* (Chapel Hill: University of North Carolina Press, 1985).

Archives:
The corporate records of the Southern Railway are at the company's headquarters in Atlanta.

Spokane, Portland & Seattle Railway

by Dan Butler

Westark Community College

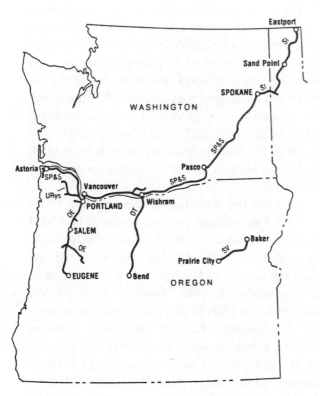

Map of the Spokane, Portland & Seattle Railway (1930)

The Portland & Seattle Railway was founded in 1905 by James J. Hill to compete with the Southern Pacific and Union Pacific for control of rail traffic in Oregon. A secondary consideration was to prevent the Chicago, Milwaukee & St. Paul from building along the north bank of the Columbia River to Portland. The railroad changed its name in 1908 to the Spokane, Portland & Seattle Railway (SP&S). The same year the line was completed between Pasco, Washington, and Portland, and the next year it reached Spokane from Pasco.

The Spokane, Portland & Seattle was the joint property of the Northern Pacific and the Great Northern throughout its history; the line never developed a clear separate identity, despite an attempt to portray itself as the "Northwest's Own Railroad."

Completion of the main line in 1909 was followed by the acquisition of trackage to Astoria and Seaside, Oregon. This line had connecting service with Hill's passenger ships to California. The Oregon Electric Railway, which gave the SP&S access to the rich Willamette valley of central Oregon, was acquired in 1910; and the Oregon Trunk Railway between Wishram, Washington, and Bend, Oregon, which later became a source of bridge traffic (traffic transported by a railroad between two other railroads) between California and the Northwest, was opened in 1911.

Freight traffic on the SP&S was heaviest between Pasco and Portland, with most tonnage moving between Wishram and Portland. Passenger traffic consisted largely of connecting sections of the transcontinental trains of the parent companies. These connections were made at Pasco and Spokane. After World War II, improved track and level gradients aided the road in maintaining fast running times for all of its main line trains. The company generated substantial amounts of wood products from western Oregon and agricultural commodities from eastern Washington, and generally prospered during the postwar years.

The Spokane, Portland & Seattle ceased to function as a separate railroad in 1970 when it merged with the Great Northern, Northern Pacific, and Chicago, Burlington & Quincy to form the Burlington Northern.

Reference:
Donald Sims, "The SP&S Story," *Trains Magazine*, 20
    (March 1960): 35-41; (April 1960): 27, 34.

Archives:
    The corporate records of The Spokane, Portland & Se-
attle Railway are located in the Burlington Northern collection at the Minnesota Historical Society, St. Paul,
Minnesota.

Lucian C. Sprague

(September 29, 1885-August 3, 1960)

by Don L. Hofsommer

Augustana College

Lucian C. Sprague (Kalmbach Publishing Company)

CAREER: Call boy (1899), block, operator, machinist apprentice, fireman, brakeman, engineer
(1899-1911), Chicago, Burlington & Quincy Railroad; locomotive expert and air brake inspector, International Correspondence Schools (1911-1912);
supervisor of air brakes, Great Northern Railway
(1912-1915); general mechanical inspector, Baltimore & Ohio Railroad (1915-1917); general sales

manager and general manager of railroad department, Chicago Pneumatic Tool Company
(1917-1920); consulting engineer (1920-1923); superintendent (1923-1924), general manager and
vice president (1924-1929), Uintah Railway; executive vice president, Dardelet Threadlock Corporation (1929-1932); executive representative, Missouri-
Kansas-Texas Railroad (1932-1935); receiver
(1935-1943), president (1943-1954), Minneapolis
& St. Louis Railway.

Lucian C. Sprague was a classic example of
one who started at the bottom rung of the railroad
industry's ladder and rose to the top. He began his
career at age thirteen as a call boy on the Chicago,
Burlington & Quincy Railroad and ended it as president of the 1,600 mile Minneapolis & St. Louis Railway (M&StL).

Lucian Charles Sprague was born in Serena, Illinois, on September 29, 1882, to Horatio Cobb
Sprague, a mechanical engineer, and Julia Keegan
Sprague. He studied mechanical engineering
through the International Correspondence Schools
and took a business course at the Alexander Hamilton Institute. He married Ruth McKee in 1924;
they had two children. Sprague was a Methodist
and a Republican. His hobby was the breeding and
training of trotting horses and he owned several
world champions.

Sprague learned railroading from the roundhouse to the corporate offices, on both sides of the locomotive cab and as an inspector of air brakes and
general mechanics. As a consultant to the Denver

& Rio Grande in the early 1920s he dealt with the operating problems of that carrier. In 1923 he became superintendent of the Uintah Railway, sixty-eight mile-long, narrow-gauge ore line desperately in need of modernization. The dynamic Sprague immediately decided that heavier motive power—articulated Mallets—was needed, but railroaders said that sharp curves on the Uintah precluded the use of such engines. With the help of designers from the Baldwin Locomotive works, Sprague proved the nay-sayers wrong. The new locomotives moved ore trains over 7 1/2 percent grades and made the carrier economically viable. When he went to the Missouri-Kansas-Texas Railroad (Katy) as executive representative in 1932, Sprague faced the challenge of soliciting traffic for a weak railroad in a highly competitive territory. By selling reliable service, the genial Sprague helped bolser the Katy's revenues. In 1935 Walter W. Colpitts, of the engineering firm of Coverdale & Colpitts, insisted that Sprague be named co-receiver of the Minneapolis & St. Louis Railway if he, Colpitts were to serve as Chairman of the bondholder's committee.

Sprague's varied background prepared him well for his greatest challenge and greatest reward—resurrecting the moribund Minneapolis & St. Louis, a company which had been in receivership since 1923. The M&StL's assets, such as they were, had been put up for auction with regularity but no buyers had appeared. It fell to Sprague, who became known as "the doctor of sick railroads," and his backers to make something of what many called the "Maimed and Still Limping."

Sprague obtained court permission to scrap obsolete motive power and equipment as well as marginal branches. The money saved was spent immediately to improve the main line from Minneapolis to Peoria, to modernize the company's best locomotives, and to purchase new equipment. These improvements lifted the morale of company employees and prepared the property for the flood of business that came as the result of World War II. The property was finally returned to its owners on December 1, 1943, and Sprague was named president of the company.

Sprague was an outgoing, sentimental man who was utterly devoted to the M&StL. He was charismatic and an excellent salesman. Each fall the road operated "Sprague Specials" to carry important shippers and friends of the railroad on a pheasant-hunting expedition along the M&StL in South Dakota. During these trips Sprague would promote the company's improved plant, reliable service, and lack of bonded indebtedness. M&StL, he argued, now stood for "Modern & Streamlined."

Sprague's flamboyant style and heavy spending for entertainment left him open to periodic criticism by shareholders, and his success in resurrecting the M&StL made the company a prize target for corporate raiders. After a bitter proxy fight in 1954, Sprague was unseated by a group of insurgents. He died six years later.

References:

Frank P. Donovan, *Mileposts on the Prairie: The Story of the Minneapolis & St. Louis Railway* (New York: Simmons-Broadman, 1950);

David Karr, *Fight for Control* (New York: Ballantine Books, 1956), pp. 105-117.

William Sproule

(November 25, 1858-January 1, 1935)

by Don L. Hofsommer

Augustana College (Sioux Falls)

William Sproule

CAREER: Clerk, American News Company (*circa* 1876); clerk, mercantile firms in Sacramento and San Francisco, California (1876-1882); freight clerk (1882-1887), assistant general freight agent (1887-1897), general freight agent (1897-1898), general traffic manager (1898-1906), Southern Pacific Company; director, member of the executive committee, and traffic manager, American Smelting and Refining Company (1906-1910); president, Wells Fargo Company (1910-1911); president, Southern Pacific Company (1911-1917); chairman of Western department, Railroads' War Board (1917); director of Western district of Central Western region, United States Railroad Administration (1918); president, Southern Pacific Company (1920-1928); president, Central Pacific Railroad (1928-1935).

Few immigrants rose to the presidency of any major American corporation, but William Sproule became the leader of two: the Wells Fargo Company and the Southern Pacific Company (SP). Born in County Mayo, Ireland, on November 25, 1858, Sproule was tutored at home by his father, a schoolmaster and graduate of Trinity College, Dublin. When he was about eighteen, Sproule migrated to New York City, where he took a job with the American News Company. Six months later he traveled to California, finding employment as a clerk in the mercantile business. Sproule worked for firms in Sacramento and San Francisco before joining the Southern Pacific Railroad in 1882 as a freight clerk. Thus began an active career of over forty years with one of the nation's leading carriers.

Sproule became known in the industry as a "traffic man." From 1882 to 1887 he labored for the SP as a freight clerk and then moved through the ranks as an assistant freight agent, general freight agent, and general traffic manager. He gained an intimate knowledge of the railroad's traffic potential and competitive position. Sproule's abilities attracted the attention of one of the carrier's major customers, the American Smelting and Refining Company, which lured him away from the SP in 1906.

While serving as American Smelting's traffic manager, Sproule also filled positions on the firm's executive committee and board of directors, acquiring experience at a higher corporate level. His positions also gave him other business contacts and led to an offer in 1910 of the presidency of Wells Fargo Company. Sproule held this position only briefly, for after the death of E. H. Harriman, the Harriman Lines were reorganized and restaffed, and Sproule was offered the presidency of the Southern Pacific Company.

The new managerial team for the Harriman properties included a variety of men with railway and financial experience, but Sproule alone had the connections to develop the traffic potential of the SP. A retiring and reserved man, Sproule avoided personal publicity to the point of keeping his age secret. On the other hand, he was a consummate public relations man for the railroad. He proved to be a talented public speaker who attempted to generate favorable accounts about the carrier in the press and to present a positive view to chambers of commerce, fraternal groups, and civic clubs. Overcoming his reluctance to make himself a public figure, Sproule would eventually serve as president of the Bohemian Club of San Francisco, director of the

Twelfth Federal Reserve District, and member of the Golden Gate Park Commission in San Francisco.

Soon after he became president of the Southern Pacific, the government forced the SP to separate from the Union Pacific, with which the SP connected at Ogden, Utah, to form the famous Overland Route. After World War I the government filed suit demanding that the Central Pacific, an SP subsidiary which actually owned the trackage from Ogden to Oakland as well as important terminals and secondary routes, be given to the Union Pacific. This case was settled in favor of the SP in 1923, but it preoccupied the SP's management throughout the period.

Sproule was the spokesman who put forward the SP's position on a variety of issues. This duty included urging investment in California and elsewhere in the SP's vast service domain, pointing out the negative impact of "Progressive" legislation on business in general and the railroads in particular, and advocating an adequate return on investment for the nation's rail carriers.

Although he had risen through the ranks of the sales department and generally understood the need for positive public relations, Sproule could be obtuse. A case in point involved the SP's purchase of fifty locomotives in 1922 and the desire of Baldwin Locomotive Works to publicize that fact. Baldwin wanted to ship the entire consignment in one train and focus public attention on it as a visible symbol of a rebounding postwar economy. Sproule, however, worried that "if anything happened to the solid engine train we [SP] would be exposed to criticism not only for the accident, but for having promoted it." Representatives of Baldwin and the Pennsylvania Railroad—which happily agreed to handle the train of locomotives westward from the plant near Philadelphia—continued to plead the case with Sproule, and the Pennsylvania arranged to print and distribute 10,000 impressive broadsides calling attention to "The Prosperity Special." The idea struck a responsive chord in the public, and the media enthusiastically reported the movements of the novel train as it rolled toward the SP. Sproule was astonished at the response and was finally forced to capitulate; the train moved as a solid unit to Los Angeles, where thousands of persons inspected it at Exposition Park. President Warren G. Harding sent a telegram thanking the SP for supporting the campaign to "restore permanent prosperity to all our people."

Sproule retired as president of the SP on December 31, 1928, retaining the largely honorary title of president of the Central Pacific Railroad, an SP subsidiary. He had married Mary Louise Baird-Baldwin in 1905; the union was childless. Sproule died on January 1, 1935. His public service was recognized during World War II, when a Liberty Ship was named for him.

Reference:
Don L. Hofsommer, *The Southern Pacific, 1901-1985* (College Station: Texas A&M University Press, 1986).

Archives:
Sproule materials can be found in the corporate archives of the Southern Pacific Transportation Company, San Francisco.

Staggers Rail Act of 1980

The Staggers Rail Act of 1980 bears the name of Harley O. Staggers (D-W.Va.), who was about to retire after long service as chairman of the House Commerce Committee. The act was the Carter administration's effort at partial deregulation of the railroad industry. It represented a compromise between the interests of those who sought decartelization of the industry and shippers who wanted to retain maximum-rate control for commodities—mainly coal and bulk grains—for which they considered themselves still captive to the railroads. The act, consequently, deregulated movements for which the rates were below 160 percent of variable cost. In 1984 this percentage was to rise to a range of 170 to 180 percent at the discretion of the Interstate Commerce Commission (ICC). This provision was expected to deregulate about two-thirds of rail traffic, but to retain maximumrate control for captive commodities. Railroads were allowed to raise rates by 6 percent per year, plus the inflation rate, until 1984; and thereafter by no more than 4 percent, and then only if they were revenue-inadequate. The ICC interpreted revenue-adequacy as the ability to earn the cost of capital; but the cost of capital was about double the industry's rate of return. In consequence, almost all railroads were considered revenue-inadequate.

In an effort to improve Conrail's performance, the act allowed revenue-inadequate railroads to add surcharges for unprofitable interline movements, and also for movements on unprofitable lightly trafficked lines. Rates might be canceled if they did not cover 110 percent of variable costs. Rate bureaus might not allow discussion or voting on single-line rates, or on joint rates except to carriers that might reasonably participate in the movement. Rules for abandonment of lines were liberalized, with expanded options for transfer of branch lines to local operators.

Most important, the act explicitly legalized rates negotiated between railroads and individual shippers for habitual or continual movements. Modeled on a successful Canadian enactment of 1967, this provision made such rates free of regulation, except where they might be protested as discriminatory or violative of common carrier obligations.

The provisions of the act that sought decartelization have, in general, been outstandingly successful. The act has turned the great majority of rates over to market determination, accelerated the decline of mileage, encouraged diversion of unremunerative traffic, and raised the industry's rate of return. Those who sought retention of maximumrate regulation for coal and agricultural products have generally been dissatisfied with the act, arguing that the ICC's definition of revenue-adequacy has allowed excessive escalation of rates on such commodities. Spokesmen for such groups have generally sought either reregulation or passage of a bill to enable the building of interstate slurry pipelines.

The legalization of contractual rates in the Staggers Act, combined with a provision of the Shipping Act of 1984 allowing American shipping companies to quote rates to inland points, has produced a major change in American rail technology and economic organization. In 1985 American steamship operators began contracting for trainload movement of containers to Chicago and other inland cities. Such movements are mainly made in five-car articulated units in a double-stacked configuration. This improvement will probably lead to distributed power in trains, slack-free coupling, and electric braking, all technological changes that are thought to have been inhibited by the traditional economic organization of the railroads. Similarly, the placing of responsibility for carriage in the hands of the steamship companies is probably the beginning of train operation by specialized carriers distinct from the owners of the rails, the economic organization thought most compatible with a competitively organized railroad industry.

–George W. Hilton

A. B. Stickney

(June 27, 1840-August 9, 1916)

by H. Roger Grant

University of Akron

A. B. Stickney

CAREER: Postal clerk (1861); school teacher (1861-1863); editor, *Stillwater* (Minnesota) *Messen-*

ger (1863); law practice (1863-1871); organizer, North Wisconsin Railway Company (1871-1873); vice president, general manager, and chief counsel, St. Paul, Stillwater & Taylor's Falls Railroad (1872-1879); president, St. Croix Railway & Improvement Company (1872-1879); construction superintendent, St. Paul, Minneapolis & Manitoba Railway (1879-1880); general superintendent, western division, Canadian Pacific Railroad (1880-1881); vice president, Minneapolis & St. Louis Railway (1881-1883); president, Minnesota & Northwestern Railroad (1883-1887); president, Chicago, St. Paul & Kansas City Railway (1887-1892); chairman of the board (1892-1908), president (1894-1900), receiver (1908-1909), Chicago Great Western Railway.

Alpheus Beede Stickney was born in Upper Wilton Village in the township of Wilton, Franklin County, Maine, the son of Daniel and Ursula Beede Stickney. His parents, of old Puritan stock, were never prosperous. The senior Stickney sought to support the household, which consisted of a boy and girl from a previous marriage and A. B. (he refused to use Alpheus) and his three sisters, through farming and occasional Universalist preaching and newspaper editing. In 1847 the Stickneys relocated to the Lee Community in Penobscot County, and two years later they moved to Dixfield in Oxford County.

These formative years of Stickney's life were not pleasant. Daniel deserted the family when Stickney was about ten, and Ursula turned to piecework in her home for a local shoe manufacturer. Stickney and some of the other children joined in these laborious tasks. Fortunately for the family, Alpheus Beede, Stickney's much beloved uncle, persuaded Ursula in the spring of 1850 to join her father on his farm in Carroll County, New Hampshire. For the next six years Stickney worked for his grandfather, Aaron Beede, and also in a nearby shoe factory. Still, he was able to attend a public school during the winter months (probably in Center Sandwich), and in the autumn of 1856 he enrolled in a Freewill Baptist academy in New Hampton. He continued his education there for another two years, although he interrupted it with stints of school teaching during the winter months. In 1858 Stickney left New Hampshire for Maine. Conditions there were no less difficult. As he recalled in an unpublished autobiography written for his children in the 1880s, "Life . . . was not very agreeable wandering from place to place and earning a subsistence by teaching country schools etc., studied one or two terms at Foxcroft Academy [Maine] . . . and finally entered as a student in the law office of Josiah Crosby in the Village of Dexter, Penobscot County, Maine." After completing his legal training, Stickney decided to follow a brother to the beckoning opportunities of the Minnesota frontier. He selected the thriving St. Croix River settlement of Stillwater and arrived there in June 1861 "in poor health [possibly consumption] and poor in purse."

No stranger to hard work, this "tall and dignified uprooted New Englander with gray eyes and red hair" (later a "subdued mouse-colour") earned his first money as a postal clerk. Soon he became employed by the Stillwater Public Schools and also won admission to the Washington County bar. In 1863 he served briefly as editor of the *Stillwater Messenger*, "but [I] never was very proud of [my] success in the Editorial business." After ending his journalism career, Stickney successfully turned his energies to the legal profession and land speculation. On October 2, 1863, he married the bright and attractive Kate W. H. Hall of Collinsville, Illinois. In a year the first of Stickney's eight children was born.

An individual who demonstrated signs of living the Horatio Alger "rags-to-riches" story,

Stickney soon sought the greater challenges and advantages of Minnesota's capital city. In 1869 he moved to St. Paul and eventually to a mansion at 288 Summit Avenue. While still dabbling in the law, Stickney accelerated his real-estate activities, purchasing large parcels of timber and raw agricultural lands. But his most important work involved railroads.

In the fall of 1871 Stickney became one of several organizers of the North Wisconsin Railway Company. Soon this little pike opened between the communities of Hudson and New Richmond, and later it reached the northern part of the state. Although his association with the North Wisconsin did not prove profitable and he liquidated his interests after two years, his enthusiasm for railroads did not flag. In June 1872 Stickney assumed the management of the recently opened St. Paul, Stillwater & Taylor's Falls Railroad Company, and he subsequently launched the St. Croix Railway & Improvement Company, which involved more railroad construction in the Stillwater area. Then, in 1879, Stickney broadened his horizons when he accepted an offer from St. Paul's premier railroad figure, James J. Hill, to become the construction superintendent of Hill's rapidly expanding St. Paul, Minneapolis & Manitoba Railway, the core of the future Great Northern Railway. A year later Stickney took on the general superintendency of the Canadian Pacific Railroad's western division. Hill, too, had already become deeply involved in this operation. Stickney's work in the rough-and-tumble environment north of the border tested his friendship with Hill. As the Canadian Pacific pushed westward from Winnipeg, several high-ranking employees apparently exploited opportunities to reap personal profits from townsite speculation. Stickney was one of those accused. The affair cost the chief engineer his job, but Hill accepted Stickney's word that he had not committed any conflict of interest. Hill's intercession kept Stickney with the company and also undoubtedly strengthened his affection toward Hill.

Stickney returned to St. Paul in 1881 and joined the inner circle of the Minneapolis & St. Louis Railway Company, a road that tapped prosperous sections of southern Minnesota and northern Iowa for Minneapolis industrialists. His tasks included supervising the building of the subsidiary Minnesota Central. In 1883 Stickney resigned, probably because of a burning desire to create his own railroad.

In the autumn of 1883 Stickney became involved in a railroad project that would occupy the rest of his business career. With the backing of a group of English investors headed by Robert Benson of London, and some American investors, Stickney between 1884 and 1888 turned the charter of the "paper" Minnesota & Northwestern Railroad into an operating road that linked St. Paul with Chicago. Soon this firm pushed to St. Joseph and Kansas City, Missouri, through acquisitions of the Wisconsin, Iowa & Nebraska Railway (Waterloo to Des Moines, Iowa) and a combination of new line construction and leased properties. In 1887 the assets of the Minnesota & Northwestern were transferred to the freshly created Chicago, St. Paul & Kansas City Railway, which in turn emerged as the Chicago Great Western in 1892. By 1903 the company, commonly called the "Maple Leaf Route," reached Omaha through the purchase of a Hill firm, the Mason City & Fort Dodge Railroad, and more building. Stickney thus headed a 1,500-mile regional transportation network that would change remarkably little until its sale to the Chicago & North Western Railway in 1968.

Stickney demonstrated considerable skill as an entrepreneur. Like other good businessmen, he was an innovator in the sense of taking a lead in changing policies rather than imitating well-established practices. Stickney effectively used various construction syndicates, especially the Minnesota Loan & Debenture Company, to build the Chicago Great Western's lines and to maximize profits for himself and investor friends. To generate much-needed traffic, he became one of the region's earliest promoters of scientific agriculture, particularly purebred livestock and potato culture. And he nearly single-handedly launched the famed South St. Paul stockyards in the late 1880s and the Omaha Grain Exchange in the early twentieth century. (Omaha emerged almost overnight as the nation's fourth largest grain center.) Stickney was, as a contemporary remarked, "a man who has the courage to gamble on himself." But he understood most of the economic and political forces at play. He had the good sense to realize that future prosperity of the Chicago Great Western lay with trunk lines that linked such vital, thriving gateways as the Twin Cities, Chicago, Kansas City, and Omaha and not with roads like the Minne-

apolis and St. Louis that wandered through the hinterlands of a single urban center.

While Stickney gained considerable recognition for his forceful style of railroading, he became something of a celebrity among contemporary reformers. He differed from his colleagues when he dared to endorse federal regulation of the transportation enterprise. In 1891 his 249-page book *The Railway Problem* appeared, in which he urged lawmakers to fashion a rate structure that would be equitable for both shippers and security holders. Specifically, Stickney advocated a national schedule based upon types of commodities hauled and average line-haul and terminal expenses. "It must be conceded that rates thus established would fit together all over the United States with mathematical precision," he wrote. Stickney held this unorthodox position for a rail industry leader because the Chicago Great Western had well-entrenched rivals: between the Twin Cities and Chicago alone it faced six competitors. Since the Chicago Great Western relied heavily on traffic in this competitive market, any prolonged slashes in through-traffic charges devastated earnings. Hill, who strongly resisted federal intervention, once chided Stickney, "If you had my railroad [the robust Great Northern], I would expect you to have my thoughts."

While railroad associates commonly viewed Stickney as an iconoclast, they shared many of his assumptions about the world of business. Most admired his frugality, hard work, and daring. And in a society which prized the self-made man, colleagues and the general public, too, applauded his remarkable rise.

Stickney possessed a warm and likable personality. He was a doting husband and father. The surviving correspondence between Stickney and his children reveals a man who did what he could to make life satisfying, whether it be sound words of advice and encouragement or the payment of medical bills or even the purchase of a house or business. This thoughtfulness carried over into the running of the Chicago Great Western. When the company opened its massive shops complex in Oelwein, Iowa, in 1898, Stickney contributed more than a workplace designed for safety and efficiency; he also underwrote construction of Liberty Hall, an employees' center. "It is better to have men reading and talking than drinking and whoring," he said. Also in the 1890s he introduced an unusual program of profit-sharing. Although this scheme never attracted much worker enthusiasm, Stickney's paternalistic efforts generally yielded good results. Labor problems on the road proved to be minimal, and workers often spoke of "The Stickney" or "our railway and not that d--d railway."

Kate, Stickney's wife of thirty-six years, died of cancer on December 2, 1899. On New Year's Day, 1901, Stickney, at the age of sixty, married the daughter of his legal mentor, forty-eight-year-old Mary Crosby of Dexter, Maine. This relationship proved unsatisfactory; his second wife preferred to be with her family and not with Stickney.

The brief but severe panic of 1907 so badly disrupted the Chicago Great Western that the company entered its first receivership in 1908. Stickney became a coreceiver, but he served in that capacity for only a few months. At age sixty-eight he decided to retire to his summer place on White Bear Lake outside St. Paul. While not fabulously wealthy, he could afford to pursue his favorite pastime, civic betterment activities, including a plan to improve St. Paul's public parks. He also took considerable pleasure from watching his children mature and their families develop. Only his eldest son, Samuel Crosby Stickney, followed a career in transportation, first with the Chicago Great Western and then with the Erie Railroad.

His children and grandchildren cared for him during his twilight years. The creator of the Chicago Great Western Railway died peacefully of heart problems at age seventy-six on August 9, 1916, only a few weeks after the death of his neighbor and fellow "empire-builder," James J. Hill.

Publications:

The Railway Problem (St. Paul, Minn.: Merrill, 1891);

The Economic Problems Involved in the Election of 1896 (Chicago [?], 1896 [?]);

The Defects of the Interstate Commerce Law (Washington, D.C. [?], 1905);

Railway Rates: A Discovery and Demonstration in Schedule Making, with an Appendix Containing a Concrete Illustration of the New-Method Universal Schedule (St. Paul, Minn.: McGill-Warner Co., Printers, 1909);

Shall Theoretical and Practical Agriculture and the Physical Development of Childhood Be Added to the Curriculum of the City Public Schools? A Paper Read at a Meeting of the American Association for Advancement of Science Held in Minneapolis, Minnesota, December 28, 1910 (St. Paul, Minn.: McGill-Warner, 1910).

References:

H. Roger Grant, "A. B. Stickney and James J. Hill: The Railroad Relationship," *Railroad History*, 146 (Spring 1982): 9-22;

Grant, *The Corn Belt Route: A History of the Chicago Great Western Railroad Company* (De Kalb: Northern Illinois University Press, 1984).

Archives:

The principal bodies of A. B. Stickney's materials are held by the Minnesota Historical Society in St. Paul and by Stickney's granddaughter, Emily Stickney Spencer, of Goleta, California.

Arthur E. Stilwell

(October 21, 1859-September 26, 1928)

by Keith L. Bryant, Jr.

Texas A&M University

Arthur E. Stilwell (Courtesy Kansas City [Missouri] Public Library)

CAREER: Salesman, Travelers Insurance Company (1882-1886); vice president, Kansas City Suburban Belt Railroad (1889-1900); president, Kansas City, Pittsburg & Gulf Railroad (1897-1899); president, Missouri, Kansas and Texas Trust Company (1891-1900); president, National Surety Company (1893-1897); president, Kansas City, Mexico & Orient Railway (1900-1912).

Arthur E. Stilwell promoted two major railroads in the south central states between 1889 and 1912: the Kansas City, Pittsburg & Gulf Railroad

(KCP&G), which later became the Kansas City Southern Railway, and the Kansas City, Mexico & Orient Railway (KCM&O), which later became part of the Atchison, Topeka & Santa Fe Railway. Gifted with the ability to persuade reluctant investors to place capital in his visionary schemes, Stilwell built a beltline railway in Kansas City, developed townsites along the routes of his railroads, and founded Port Arthur, Texas. Many of his projects proved to be entrepreneurial errors, at least at the time he promoted them, but several subsequently became valuable commercial properties. After his retirement from business, Stilwell wrote books attacking financiers and advocating world peace, as well as poetry and fiction.

Born in 1859 in Rochester, New York, to Charles Herbert Stilwell and Mary Augusta Pierson Stilwell, Arthur Edward Stilwell came from an upper-middle-class family. His grandfather, Hamblin Stilwell, was a leading Democratic politician in Rochester and served as major in 1852-1853. Charles Herbert Stilwell graduated from the Columbia University College of Physicians and Surgeons but apparently did not practice medicine; instead, he became a partner in an unsuccessful jewelry store. Arthur Stilwell attended public school only through the fourth grade and received the balance of his education at home. After his father's store failed in 1875, Stilwell ran away from home to enter the world of business. He traveled to St. Louis and then to New York City, and got a job selling advertising in railroad timetables. On a trip to Virginia he met Jennie A. Wood, whom he married on June 10, 1879. In the next few years Stilwell operated a print shop in Kansas City and then sold insurance in Chicago for the Travelers Insurance Company. In 1886 he returned to Kansas City, where he embarked on a career as a railroad promoter.

At least six feet in height and weighing between 180 and 200 pounds, Stilwell presented an athletic appearance. A rather handsome man with light brown hair and a fair complexion, he wore a thick mustache throughout most of his adult life. He dressed impeccably and was known as a "figure of elegance." He carried a gold-headed cane and "affected the mannerisms of an English Duke." He became a devout Christian Scientist after a practitioner of that belief was credited with curing a spinal ailment he contracted. An eternal optimist, Stilwell conveyed to friends and strangers his infectious enthusiasm for life.

In Kansas City Stilwell used the small amount of capital he possessed to form a trust company and then, with funds secured locally and in St. Louis and Philadelphia, began to create a myriad of firms to build a belt railway, a hotel, an office building, grain elevators, and a joint passenger station. With seemingly no limits to his talent for raising funds, Stilwell formed the Kansas City, Pittsburg & Gulf Railroad to build a line from Kansas City to the Gulf of Mexico. The concept of linking the agricultural Midwest to the closest port on the Gulf was an old one. Stilwell's original intent was to build to Sabine Pass, Texas, but the destination soon became a new townsite, Port Arthur, on Sabine Lake. From 1890 to 1897 Stilwell sold securities, issued contracts, developed townsites, purchased equipment, and drove the KCP&G south toward the Gulf. A substantial portion of the capital came from Holland, and Stilwell named townsites for his investors—Mena and De Queen, Arkansas; De Ridder and De Quincy, Louisiana; and Nederland, Texas, among others. Complications developed in dredging the ship channel from Sabine Pass to Port Arthur, however, and rail traffic failed to develop as Stilwell had hoped. While he devoted his attention to forming a new company to operate a railway north and east from Kansas City to Omaha, Nebraska, and Quincy, Illinois, the KCP&G failed and entered receivership. John W. Gates and E. H. Harriman took over the railroad and created its successor, the Kansas City Southern Railway. After Stilwell lost control of the KCP&G, oil was discovered at Spindletop near Port Arthur, causing the town to mushroom and providing substantial traffic for the railway.

Undismayed by the loss of his trust company and his railroad, Stilwell announced in 1900 the formation of another trust company and another railway, the Kansas City, Mexico & Orient, to construct a line from Kansas City across Kansas, Oklahoma Territory, and Texas to the Rio Grande and then through Mexico to Topolobampo on the Gulf of California, where he intended to found Port Stilwell. The idea of a line from Kansas City to a Pacific port south of California had been discussed since the 1870s. During the next decade Stilwell raised capital, largely in England, and built a route from Wichita, Kansas, through Oklahoma to San Angelo, Texas. As in his earlier promotions, Stilwell generated a vast array of publicity with his schemes, and articles about him and the KCM&O were found frequently in leading newspapers and magazines. Three isolated segments were constructed in Mexico, but the KCM&O did not yield profits. The "Orient" had been aided by the government of President Porfirio Díaz, but when the Mexican Revolution began the government was not able to protect the railway from the depredations of the revolutionists. Unable to generate sufficient agricultural traffic in the United States and faced with huge losses in Mexico, the KCM&O failed in 1912 and Stilwell was ousted as president. A lengthy receivership followed until 1928, when the company was purchased by the Atchison, Topeka & Santa Fe Railway; the Santa Fe then sold the lines in Mexico to an American investor. In 1940 the Mexican government purchased the property in that country, construction resumed, and, as the Ferrocarril de Chihuahua al Pacifico, the entire route from the Rio Grande to Topolobampo was completed.

Following the loss of the "Orient," Stilwell and his wife moved to France, where he wrote books attacking the "cannibals of finance" who had taken his enterprises from him. He also wrote books pleading for peace a few years before World War I broke out. By 1920 he was writing fiction and nonfiction works dealing with spiritualism, in which he claimed that his railroads and urban promotions were the consequences of dreams, "fairies," and "brownies"; he also wrote poetry. Publicity about him continued during the 1920s, and he published his memoirs serially in the *Saturday Evening Post* in 1927-1928. The Stilwells had returned to New York City, and Stilwell died there on September 26, 1928, of pulmonary edema and cerebral embolism. Thirteen days later his wife leaped to her death from a window of their apartment.

Arthur Stilwell made significant contributions to the development of railways in the south central states; some of his urban promotions proved successful as well. He committed serious errors of judgment about the economic workability of his schemes, but raised millions of dollars in capital to carry out his plans. Able to sell securities in the most speculative of ventures, he proved incapable of managing the enterprises he created.

Publications:

The World by the Tail with a Down Hill Pull, edited by Stilwell and J. E. Roberts (Kansas City: Stilwell & Roberts, 1896);

The Wise Men of Kansas, edited by Stilwell and Roberts (Kansas City: Stilwell & Roberts, 1896);

The Mystic 16 to 1, edited by Stilwell and Roberts (Kansas City: Stilwell & Roberts, 1896);

The Demonetization of the Mule, edited by Stilwell and Roberts (Kansas City: Stilwell & Roberts, 1896);

Confidence or National Suicide? (New York: Bankers, 1910);

Universal Peace-War is Mesmerism (New York: Bankers, 1911);

Cannibals of Finance: Fifteen Years' Contest with the Money Trust (Chicago: Farnum, 1912);

To All the World (except Germany) (London: Allen & Unwin, 1915);

The Great Plan: How to Pay for the War (London & New York: Hodder & Stoughton, 1918);

The Light That Never Failed (London: Jarrolds, 1920);

Live and Grow Young (New York: Youth, 1921);

Forty Years of Business Life (New York, 1926);

"I Had a Hunch" by Stilwell and James R. Crowell, *Saturday Evening Post*, 200 (December 3, 1927): 3-4, 161-162, 165-166, 168; (December 17, 1927): 24, 26, 96, 98, 101-102; (December 31, 1927): 24, 26, 77-79; (January 14, 1928): 31, 70, 72, 77-78; (January 28, 1928): 26, 83, 86, 89-91, 94; (February 4, 1928): 38, 44, 46.

References:

Keith L. Bryant, Jr., *Arthur E. Stilwell: Promoter with a Hunch* (Nashville: Vanderbilt University Press, 1971);

John Leeds Kerr and Frank Donovan, *Destination Topolobampo: The Kansas City, Mexico & Orient Railway* (San Marino, Cal.: Golden West Books, 1968);

David M. Pletcher, *Rails, Mines and Progress: Seven American Promoters in Mexico, 1867-1911* (Ithaca, N.Y.: Cornell University Press, 1958).

Archives:

There is no substantial collection of Stilwell papers. The minute books and related documents of Stilwell's Kansas City projects are located at the headquarters of the Kansas City Southern Railway in Kansas City, Missouri. Some materials on the Kansas City, Mexico & Orient Railway are to be found at the Baylor University Library, Waco, Texas.

James M. Symes

(July 8, 1897-August 3, 1976)

by Michael Bezilla

Pennsylvania State University

James M. Symes (Photo by Fabian Bachrach; courtesy Kalmbach Publishing Company)

CAREER: Clerk and car tracer (1916-1920), statistician (1920-1922), freight movement director (1922-1923), train movement director (1923-1927), chief assistant to general manager, Western Region (1927-1928), superintendent, passenger transportation, Western Region, (1928-1929), superintendent, passenger transportation, Eastern Region (1929-1934), chief of freight transportation (1934-1935), Pennsylvania Railroad; vice president of operations and maintenance, Association of American Railroads (1935-1939); general manager, Western Region (1939-1941), vice president, Western Region (1942-1946); assistant vice president of operations (1946-1947), vice president of operations (1947-1952), executive vice president (1952-1954), president (1954-1959), chairman of the board, (1959-1963), Pennsylvania Railroad; member of board of directors, Penn Central Transportation Company (1968-1969).

James M. Symes, the penultimate chief executive of the Pennsylvania Railroad (PRR) and the last one to be a product of the railroad's up-from-the-ranks operating tradition, was the initiator and chief architect of the merger between the PRR and the New York Central System (NYC) to form the Penn Central Company (PC). He pursued this merger single-mindedly once he had satisfied himself that even after completion of the Pennsylvania's massive post-World War II modernization program, which he oversaw, the railroad would not long remain a profitable enterprise.

Born on July 8, 1897, in Glen Osborne, Pennsylvania, a suburb of Pittsburgh, James Miller Symes (pronounced "sims") was a son of Frank H. and Clara Heckert Symes. His father was a lifelong PRR employee, retiring as a baggage master after fifty years' service. Symes considered employment with the railroad after graduating from Sewickley (Pennsylvania) High School in 1914 but was deterred by the low starting salaries. While working for the West Penn Power Company, he enrolled in an evening secretarial course at the Carnegie Institute of Technology, feeling that such training would prepare him for a job with the Pennsylvania

Railroad—a dream he had not given up—at an acceptable wage. Before he had finished the course, Symes was approached by the manager of a semiprofessional baseball team that the PRR sponsored. A star shortstop in high school, Symes reached an agreement with the manager to take a twenty-five-dollar-a-month job with the railroad as a clerk and car tracer, and play the infield for the PRR's ball team for fifteen dollars monthly. In 1919 he married Fern E. Dick, who also worked for the PRR as a clerk.

In 1920, four years after starting his railroad career, Symes became a statistician in the Lake division superintendent's office in Cleveland, Ohio. In 1922 he was promoted to freight movement director, a post that took him away from bookkeeping and put him in the operating department. Here he gained the attention of his future mentor, division superintendent Martin W. Clement. One evening Symes filled a request for light engines in direct disregard of the trainmaster's standing order that no engines without trains were to be dispatched from Cleveland. A verbal brawl ensued, in which Symes contended that his actions carried the authority of the superintendent and therefore superseded that of the trainmaster. The matter eventually reached Clement, who supported Symes and marked him as a man to be watched for future promotion. In 1923, when Clement was named general manager of the Central Region with offices in Pittsburgh, Symes was transferred there to become the region's train movement director. Four years later, after Clement had gone to the company's Philadelphia general offices to become assistant vice president in charge of operations, Symes went to Chicago, first as chief assistant to the Western Region general manager and then as the region's superintendent of passenger transportation—his first real managerial assignment.

In 1929 Symes was given a similar position in the Eastern Region, headquartered at Philadelphia. Five years later, when Clement moved up to become the road's acting president, Symes was designated chief of freight transportation for the entire PRR system.

In that capacity, Symes also represented his railroad on the so-called Eastman committee—a group created by federal coordinator of transportation Joseph B. Eastman to comply with the Emergency Railroad Transportation Act of 1933, through which the Roosevelt administration hoped to secure voluntary industry action to reduce the nation's overbuilt and inefficient system of rail lines and terminals. Symes's growing interest in a national approach to rail problems led him to take a leave of absence from the PRR in 1935 to join the newly formed Association of American Railroads (AAR) in Washington, D.C., as vice president of operations and maintenance. One of the AAR's early goals was to promote its own version of industry cooperation, thereby avoiding undue influence by the government on such matters as mergers, joint trackage and terminal rights, and physical plant rationalization. Such cooperation was slow in coming, but Symes's Washington experience nevertheless impressed deeply upon him the benefits inherent in joint operation and use of facilities. He listened as industry leaders, academics, and politicians extolled the virtues of consolidation, which would make the railroads more effective in battling competition from highway vehicles and airplanes. It was perhaps here that the seeds of the Penn Central merger were sown.

Symes returned to the Pennsylvania in 1939 as general manager of the Western Region. In 1942 he became the region's vice president—its chief operating officer—a post he occupied until President Clement brought him back to Philadelphia in 1946 as assistant vice president of operations. The following year he was elevated to vice president of operations, traditionally one of the final stepping stones to the road's presidency.

But Symes had to wait his turn. Clement had already groomed Walter S. Franklin, a career PRR man from the traffic department, to be his immediate successor. Thus, when Clement moved up to the newly created position of chairman of the board in 1949, the directors elected Franklin president. The chairman was to be the company's chief spokesman on financial and governmental issues while the president oversaw the railroad's business affairs.

When he had joined the operations department in Philadelphia in 1946, Symes had made no secret of his desire to emulate the example of certain other roads and replace the PRR's 4,100-unit steam locomotive fleet with diesels. The more conservative members of the mechanical department and even President Clement wavered on the issue, on the one hand believing that the railroad ought to remain loyal to its friends in the coal industry and on the other expressing enthusiasm for Symes's estimates of how much money would be saved by dieselization. By elevating Symes to the operations vice presidency, Clement in effect approved his subordinate's ten-year, $400-million program to dieselize the entire system except for that portion east of Harrisburg, Pennsylvania, operated by electric traction.

Clement retired in 1951, and the board chairmanship was temporarily eliminated. When Franklin stepped down three years later, Symes—who had been the official heir apparent since being named executive vice president in 1952—was elected the thirteenth president of the railroad.

The PRR was huge by any measure. It carried 10 percent of the nation's rail freight traffic and 15 percent of its passengers. The value of its physical plant and rolling stock exceeded $3 billion—fully 10 percent of the American railroad industry's capital investment. Its 25,000 track miles accounted for a similar share of the industry's total, and its 126,000 employees dwarfed the work forces of most other roads. Since the close of World War II, however, the mighty Pennsylvania had fallen on hard times. It had recorded its first net annual operating deficit in 1946 (ironically, its centennial year), and its net income for 1954 was only $18 million, from gross receipts of $70.8 million. First the Great Depression and then World War II had prevented it from carrying out much-needed modernization programs (aside from electrification), and the wear and tear caused by wartime traffic further underscored the necessity for substantial improvements.

In one of his first directives as president, Symes forbade further use of the phrase "Standard Railroad of the World," an accolade the PRR had bestowed on itself in the 1890s, until such time as the company could again live up to it. (The slogan never returned to official use.) He also pressed forward as vigorously as the railroad's finances would permit with the modernization programs inaugurated by Clement and Franklin.

These programs included closing many smaller classification yards and increasing the size and efficiency of the larger ones, chief among which was the sprawling facility at Conway, Pennsylvania, not far from Symes's boyhood home. The world's largest car building and repair plant, the Samuel Rea Shop, was opened at Hollidaysburg, Pennsylvania. Innovative marketing concepts were utilized in an attempt to recapture lost freight and passenger traf-

fic. The PRR pioneered in the use of TrucTrain or trailer-on-flatcar service, for example, and experimented with the lightweight, all-coach Aerotrain for travelers between New York and Chicago. Symes gave financial vice president David Bevan a free hand in reorganizing the accounting department, resulting in the adoption of modern statistical practices that put the Pennsylvania in the forefront among railroads in the ability to trace cash flows and predict financial outcomes. Under Symes's leadership the PRR finally began a diversification program, taking steps in joint ventures aimed at redeveloping prime downtown real estate in Philadelphia (where the Penn Center office complex replaced Broad Street Station), New York, Chicago, and Pittsburgh.

The positive effects of these and other components of the drive to modernize were in many cases slow to be realized or were never realized at all, and Symes finally abandoned hope that the Pennsylvania could ever return to the kind of prosperity it had enjoyed before World War II. A nationally recognized spokesman for railroads before numerous government panels in the 1950s, Symes gained a reputation for being a prophet of doom for the industry. He warned that if strict federal regulatory practices were not relaxed to make railroads more competitive with other modes of transport, widespread bankruptcy and nationalization would by inevitable. Most of the problems the PRR faced, he avowed, plagued railroads from coast to coast.

In the absence of any fundamental change in government policy, Symes sought salvation for the Pennsylvania through a merger with its bitter arch rival, the New York Central. He first broached the idea in 1957, and it remained uppermost in his thoughts for the rest of his career.

The notion of consolidating the two roads, which served much the same territory between New York, Chicago, and St. Louis, was a radical one. All previous consolidation schemes put forth since the 1920s had envisioned the PRR and the NYC remaining independent and dividing up the remaining smaller northeastern lines among them. But Symes contended that combining the two roads was the best solution to the economic woes of each. "There are no two railroads in the country in a better position than the Pennsylvania and the Central, by reason of their location, duplicate facilities and services, and similarity of traffic patterns," he said in a hearing before the Interstate Commerce Commission (ICC) in 1961, "to consolidate their operations and substantially increase efficiency and provide an improvement in service at lower cost."

By September 1957 Symes had won the support of NYC board chairman Robert R. Young. But Young was neither a veteran Central man nor even a professional railroader. After his death in January 1959, the NYC management headed by Alfred Perlman—a lifelong railroad man with little use for the Pennsylvania's conservative ways—refused to participate in any further discussions about a merger.

The Central reversed its attitude once again early in 1960. By that time the Chesapeake & Ohio Railroad was effecting a takeover of the Baltimore & Ohio. If the PRR took similar control of the Norfolk & Western, in which it had invested heavily, the New York Central could find itself without a friendly northeastern partner. Perlman therefore reopened negotiations with Symes, who since May 1959 had been the Pennsylvania's chairman of the board (reviving Clement's tradition at a most opportune time). In the spring of 1962 the directors and stockholders of both companies overwhelmingly voted in favor of the merger, and hearings commenced before the Interstate Commerce Commission. Symes was persuaded to stay on past normal retirement age in order to see the proposed merger through what were expected to be its most difficult times. He retired on September 30, 1963, one day before the ICC hearings concluded.

The commission approved the consolidation in principle, but nearly five years of litigation had to be endured before the two lines finally came together on February 1, 1968, to form the Penn Central. Symes had remained a PRR director during this period and served an additional year on the Penn Central's board. His most noteworthy action was to oppose (unsuccessfully) the government-mandated inclusion of the bankrupt New York, New Haven & Hartford Railroad in the PC in 1969.

The Penn Central never realized the efficiencies Symes had predicted for it. Indeed, instead of solving the problems of the PRR and NYC, it seemed to compound them. In June 1970 the PC declared bankruptcy in the largest business failure in American history up to that time. After failing to reorganize, it formed the core of the new Consolidated Rail Corporation (Conrail), created by Congress in 1976 from the ruins of a half-dozen bankrupt northeastern rail lines.

The factors that led to the downfall of Penn Central were too complex to permit any brief assessment of Symes's judgment in seeking the merger in the first place. It is worth noting, however, that the PC's chief executive officer—the man who more than any other individual bore the responsibility for the railroad's collapse—was handpicked by Symes. Stuart T. Saunders had taken over as head of the PRR in 1963 on the basis of Symes's recommendation that he would make an ideal choice to preside over the merged companies. Although Saunders had previously been president of the Norfolk & Western, he had come up through its legal department and possessed virtually no knowledge of railroading as a business. It is ironic that Symes, himself a first-class operating man, failed to comprehend how great a liability the lack of familiarity with even the fundamentals of railroading would be to the man charged with merging two of the world's largest and most complex (not to mention mutually hostile) rail systems.

In retirement, as in his professional life, Symes moved easily in the upper echelons of Philadelphia society, his humble origins and lack of a college education notwithstanding. He never regretted failure to earn a degree, telling reporters in 1963 that "the experience I got on the job working with tough old timers gave me more than I would have gotten from four years of college." He qualified the remark by noting, "I don't believe it could be done today. The opportunity is not as great." Symes's trusting, easygoing personality—in contrast to the starchiness of his predecessors, Clement and W. W. Atterbury—made him one of the PRR's most popular presidents. Some observers thought that in fact he was too good-natured, that he was not tough enough to squelch the petty politicking among subordinates that by the 1950s was sapping the vitality of the railroad's managerial ranks.

Symes lived to see the coming of Conrail. He died on August 3, 1976, in a nursing home in Feasterville, a suburb of Philadelphia. His wife had died two years earlier. They were survived by a daughter, Jeanne Doris Symes.

The Pennsylvania's decline in the 1950s and early 1960s probably would have occurred regardless of who was at its head, given the unfavorable regulatory climate, the general decline of industry in the Northeast, and the high costs of terminating freight traffic and carrying millions of passengers each year. Symes was correct in devoting his energies to seeking a merger for the PRR, but he chose the wrong partner—he did not realize that the New York Central was even weaker in most respects than his own company and that it would only magnify the Pennsylvania's weaknesses. That fatal error in judgment cast a giant shadow over the half-century of service he otherwise rendered so competently.

References:

George H. Burgess, and Miles C. Kennedy, *Centennial History of the Pennsylvania Railroad* (Philadelphia: Pennsylvania Railroad, 1949);

Joseph R. Daughen, and Peter Binzen, *The Wreck of the Penn Central* (Boston: Little, Brown, 1971);

"The Future.... What Jim Symes Is Doing about It," *Railway Age,* 136 (June 14, 1954): 63-66;

"J.M. Symes To Be Next President of Pennsylvania," *Railway Age,* 136 (May 17, 1954): 134;

Herrymon Maurer, "New Signals for the Pennsy," *Fortune,* 52 (November 1955):111-117, 159-171;

Stephen Salsbury, *No Way to Run a Railroad* (New York: McGraw-Hill, 1982);

"Symes' New President of Pennsylvania RR," *Philadelphia Inquirer,* May 12, 1954, p. 17;

"Symes Retirement Set," *New York Times,* September 29, 1963, III: 3;

"Symes Steps Down," *Railway Age,* 155 (October 7, 1963): 191;

"Symes to Succeed Franklin as President of PRR," *New York Times,* May 12, 1954, p. 47.

Archives:

The corporate documents of the Pennsylvania Railroad have been divided among several northwestern universities and museums, with the core materials—including presidential correspondence and directors' meeting minutes—going to the Pennsylvania Historical and Museum Commission, Harrisburg. None of these materials have been catalogued or opened to researchers.

Texas & Pacific Railway

by George H. Drury

Trains *Magazine*

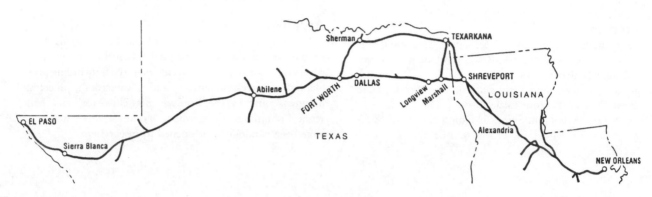

Map of the Texas & Pacific Railway (1930)

Of the transcontinental routes surveyed between 1853 and 1856, the southernmost was across central Texas. It was the shortest of the routes and involved less climbing and less exposure to winter weather than the others. During the Civil War, though, it lay in Confederate territory, so the route through Omaha and Ogden won the backing of the federal government. After the Civil War the Texas route was again considered for a railroad. Congress chartered the Texas Pacific Railroad in 1871 to construct a line from Marshall, Texas, through El Paso to San Diego, California. The name of the undertaking was soon changed to Texas & Pacific Railway (T&P). Its first president was Thomas Scott, formerly of the Pennsylvania Railroad, and its first chief engineer was Grenville M. Dodge, who had been chief engineer of the Union Pacific.

The T&P began by purchasing the franchises and properties of two small railroads: the Southern Pacific Railroad (no relation to the modern Southern Pacific), which was already in operation between Shreveport, Louisiana, and Longview, Texas; and the Southern Transcontinental Railway, which had not begun construction. Construction of the

T&P began at Longview in October 1872, and even with such hindrances as low water in the Red River, which halted the boats carrying supplies, an epizootic which killed the mules, and yellow fever which threatened the men, the line reached Dallas within a year.

By the beginning of 1874 the T&P had lines in operation from Shreveport to Dallas, from Marshall to Texarkana, and from Sherman to Brookston, near Paris. The line was pushed on to Fort Worth in July 1876 (to keep the road's charter alive, the Fort Worth representative kept the Texas legislature in session until the railroad reached the town), and the Texarkana-Sherman line was completed less than a month later.

In January 1880 Jay Gould and Russell Sage gained seats on the T&P's board of directors, and in April 1881 Gould purchased Scott's interest in the company and named himself president. Meanwhile, construction had resumed westward from Fort Worth; the line met the (modern) Southern Pacific, which had been building east from El Paso, at

Sierra Blanca on December 15, 1881. The nation had acquired its second transcontinental rail route.

By purchase and construction the T&P reached New Orleans from Shreveport in September 1882, completing the basic shape of the T&P map.

The Texas & Pacific underwent a receivership from 1885 to 1888 and entered another in 1916. The Texas oil boom returned financial strength to the road in the early 1920s; oil was a major part of the road's traffic until the 1940s, when pipelines took away much of the business. During the reorganization of 1923, which ended the receivership of

1916, the T&P issued preferred stock to the Missouri Pacific (MP or MoPac) in exchange for mortgage bonds. By 1930 the MP owned all of the Texas & Pacific's preferred stock and more than half of its common stock. MoPac control culminated in the merger of the T&P into the MP on October 15, 1976. MP is now part of Union Pacific.

References:

George H. Drury, *The Historical Guide to North American Railroads* (Milwaukee: Kalmbach, 1985), pp. 321-323;

Don Watson and Steve Brown, *Texas & Pacific* (Cheltenham, Ontario: Boston Mills Press, 1978.

Isaac B. Tigrett

(September 15, 1879-May 2, 1954)

by James H. Lemly

Isaac B. Tigrett (Kalmbach Publishing Company)

CAREER: Cashier, Bank of Halls, Tennessee (1899-1903); cashier, Union Bank and Trust, Jackson, Tennessee (1903-1912); president, Mercantile Union Trust Company, Jackson, Tennessee (1912-1923); treasurer (1911), president (1912-1927), Birmingham & Northwestern Railroad; president, Gulf, Mobile & Northern Railroad (1919-1940); president (1940-1952), chairman (1952-1954), Gulf, Mobile & Ohio Railroad.

Isaac Burton (Ike) Tigrett (pronounced *tie-gret*) was a railroad president or chief executive officer for over forty-two years. Almost all of this serv-

ice was with the Gulf, Mobile & Ohio Railroad (GM&O) and its predecessor and "parent," the Gulf, Mobile & Northern (GM&N); few business executives have had such a span of successful leadership. Tigrett's chief claim to recognition however, rests not on his railroad expertise but on the traits of character and ability which allowed him to serve as a significant business, civic, and cultural promoter and as a developer and leader of his community, his company, and especially his employees. One of his protégés admitted, however, that Tigrett demanded such loyalty and effectiveness that he was at times impossible to live with. Tigrett himself belittled his railroad operating skills throughout his career. He was quoted as saying, "If I had not begun my career as a president, I probably never would have risen to that position."

Tigrett's most valued qualities came out in his sense of dedication to his tasks, both business and civic, and his ability to communicate with his employees and the customers and supporters of his various rail lines. He had an uncanny knack of making himself liked and respected by almost everyone with whom he came in contact and he somehow projected these qualities through his work force.

Tigrett was born in Friendship, Tennessee, on September 15, 1879, to Samuel King Tigrett, a pioneer Baptist preacher, and Elizabeth Alice Nunn Tigrett. The family moved to Halls, Tennessee, when Tigrett was about seven, and he lived there through his public school years. He attended college at Southwestern Baptist University, now Union University, in Jackson, Tennessee. Although he was small of frame and stature he was an ardent tennis and football player. Some of his leadership ability must have been evident in college, for he was quarterback of his team, which somehow arranged a game with Yale University. His team played Yale on even terms–a fact about which Tigrett boasted whenever he had an opportunity. Throughout his adult years he was an active golfer; indeed, he said that one reason he continued to live in Jackson was that he could reach the golf course from his office in five minutes.

After earning his B.A. degree, Tigrett returned to Halls in 1898. In 1899, using most of the $800 insurance money he received after his father's death, he opened the only bank in town. In 1903 he was elected cashier of the Union Bank and Trust Company at Jackson, where he resumed friendships and civic contacts he had made in college.

The Mercantile Union Trust Company of Jackson elected him president in 1912, and he retained that post until 1923. During the 1920s he gave his name and some attention to I. B. Tigrett & Company, Investment Bankers. He was never its major executive, but when it became insolvent in 1931, he led the effort to pay all of its debt to clear his name.

For many years he was an officer in the Jackson Publishing Company, and he held innumerable civic appointments; for a time he was interim president of Union University. He was in many respects Jackson's leading citizen, and his most enduring memorial is the Isaac Burton Tigrett High School of Jackson. In 1904 Tigrett married Mary Sue Kennedy of Tuscaloosa, Alabama. They had no children.

Tigrett's professional career had begun in banking at the youthful age of twenty. His vigor and enthusiasm so influenced his associates that he was elected treasurer and then president of the Tennessee Bankers Association. In 1911 he was selected as vice president for Tennessee of the American Bankers Association.

His civic leadership and banking experience led him into the railroad world, which dominated the remainder of his life. The Birmingham & Northwestern (B&NW), a forty-eight mile local railroad, was started in 1911 by a promoter from Halls. The road was intended to connect Birmingham, Alabama, to Kansas City, Missouri, by way of Jackson and Dyersburg, Tennessee. Its growth centered on the segment between Dyersburg and Jackson, and a friendly banker was needed in Jackson. After Tigrett was persuaded to become the railroad's treasurer and then, in 1912, its president, the community invested $125,000 to complete the line. Tigrett retained his banking positions, however, and was only a financial overseer of the railroad. He re-

mained president of the Mercantile Bank after he became president of the Gulf, Mobile & Northern Railroad (GM&N) in 1919 and only resigned from the bank in 1923, when it became evident that the railroad would survive.

When Tigrett became head of the GM&N he took along Frank Hicks, a young friend who had held several significant positions on the B&NW, to be comptroller and his assistant. The 409-mile GM&N was a collection of bits and pieces of track linked together over the previous twenty years. The track closest to Jackson, Tennessee, had been built to serve the upper hill country of northeast Mississippi. Soon after the close of the Civil War Col. William Faulkner, grandfather of the noted Mississippi author, had begun this segment at his hometown of Ripley. South of this region extensive stands of virgin pine were available, and other developers were active in constructing local lines in those areas.

Many more miles to the south, promoters had started a great scheme to build a railroad from Mobile, Alabama, to Kansas City via Hattiesburg and Jackson, Mississippi. The motivation for this effort was to gain access to the fine pine stands in southern Mississippi and to expand traffic patterns to and from the port at Mobile. This line, reorganized in 1890 into a new company, the Mobile, Jackson & Kansas City Railroad (MJ&KC), grew slowly. Eventually, it gave up its northwestward thrust and turned north toward Laurel, Mississippi, as its first goal.

By 1902 the company had a new plan to build northward through Mississippi to join with Colonel Faulkner's line, renamed the Gulf & Chicago (G&C), and thus create a north-south line anchored on the Port of Mobile. Construction moved ahead through 1905 and 1906 to complete the G&C southward to Decatur, Mississippi. Decatur was not far west of Meridian, a junction point on the successful east-west route of the Vicksburg & Alabama Railroad and the equally effective Mobile & Ohio Railroad, which ran north and south from Mobile to Paducah, Kentucky, through Jackson, Tennessee. The MJ&KC was being constructed at the same time from Laurel north to Decatur. In 1906 the lines were joined, forming an operating unit which extended from Mobile to Middleton, Tennessee.

The two companies tried to operate cooperatively, but they both failed and a new company, the

New Orleans, Mobile & Chicago Railroad Company, was created in 1909. It, too, failed in 1913. The experts who were brought in to form its successor—the Gulf, Mobile & Northern—were tough-minded and experienced New Yorkers: W.H. Coverdale, a highly regarded rail management consultant and engineer, and R. H. Brown, a representative of the banking firm of Kuhn, Loeb. The GM&N corporation began its existence under wartime federal railroad control on January 1, 1917.

With expansion in mind, Coverdale quickly found Tigrett in Jackson and persuaded him to serve as a director and local promoter to help build into Jackson. With Coverdale's support, Tigrett was elected president of the railroad in October 1919.

The GM&N was a lean if not efficient company. Its former bondholders had been forced to give up their securities for preferred stock which would have no value if some way was not found to make the line into a workable business entity. The company had two short-term objectives: to build into Jackson and to stay alive. The extension was built by 1919, and the task of survival really began. This corporation was to occupy most of Tigrett's time and energy for many years.

Tigrett was not a railroad operator, but by 1920 he had the ability to manage money and people. These skills were to make him famous over the next thirty years. He begged, pleaded, wheedled, and cajoled his customers, employees, and backers into supporting the existence and growth of "their" railroad into a strong corporate servant of the region, even though it never became a financial giant. This it could not do because its southern territory was essentially weak and had been handicapped by the devastation of the cotton economy of the region by the boll weevil.

Competent rail operating managers were sought and found as the road slowly improved in 1920. Hicks worked on traffic solicitation and internal financial problems. Tigrett, while closely overseeing his operating managers, turned his attention primarily to financial problems, for which he had been employed, and to human relations, for which he had great talent. Among his major tasks were to beg for patience from the federal government, which, while relinquishing control of the nation's rail lines, had also provided funds for rebuilding run-down segments of track; from stockholders, who dreamed of a future payout; and from the banks,

which had advanced new loans to keep the road operating.

Tigrett also had to persuade his employees that they could better their lives by making the railroad prosper. Speeches were made to employees all along the road and a concerted drive began to communicate with the company work force. An in-house newspaper, the *GM&N News*, was started. At the same time, shippers and passengers who patronized the road, as well as all local government agencies, were asked to support the rebuilding of the line. In this drive Tigrett, and eventually the entire work force, used all avenues available to them, including letters to newspapers and a continuing stream of press releases. The term *media blitz* had not yet been coined, but Tigrett and his team carried one out from 1920 to 1925.

Poor passenger train service was the most visible evidence of the weakness of the GM&N in 1920. Efforts were made to clean up equipment (new rolling stock was out of the question) and the roadbed was slowly but steadily improved. One small "betterment" was made in passenger comfort: the company stopped charging one cent for each paper drinking cup in its cars!

Nothing could be done to truly reverse the overall poor service, and complaints were frequent. One newspaper editor attacked the road unmercifully and Tigrett felt that he had to reply. In an open letter he said:

> The editorial which appeared in the last issue of your esteemed paper furnishes cause for sincere regret both to our management and to our employees.
>
> I regret very much that it was necessary to delay for an hour one of our trains on which you were a passenger. . . .
>
> Your statement that we are acting independently and unmindful of the interests of our patrons is certainly a very erroneous interpretation of the purposes and intentions of either the management or the employees, and I am very hopeful that the occasion which called forth your criticism will appear to you in a different light in view of the statements herewith given.
>
> You, yourself, are engaged in conducting an enterprise which is at least semi-public. You have, no doubt, in building up your paper, sustained embarrassments and misfortunes which do not come to those who publish larger papers and who have a larger income. You have, no doubt, expected and received the forbearance and co-operation of the public whom you serve. I most sincerely ask for the

same forbearance and co-operation from you and the public generally whom we serve.

The years from 1923 to 1928 were good to Tigrett's railroad. As employee morale and performance continued to improve, earnings became sufficient to look to the future and the management team felt able to turn to external problems. Damage suits, especially in Mississippi, were numerous, time-consuming, and costly. The company struggled with the problem in the courts, in the press, and at public gatherings. Early in the 1920s little could be done but talk. The damage suit challenge was confronted firmly and vigorously, but with Tigrett's brand of dry humor. When a Newton, Mississippi, banker sued the railroad over an accident with a freight train, the court awarded what seemed excessive damages. Tigrett published an open letter which politely chided the court for the size of the award and castigated the judge for instructing the jury to find the railroad responsible, but his deepest cut was for his fellow banker:

This advertisement is . . . an appeal to the automobile owners and drivers for a more careful approach to railroad crossings. . . .
   Again, it is a special appeal to bankers to use our crossings as little as possible. If our enginemen and trainmen could have some notice of their intention to drive across our line at some particular time, we could well afford to suspend operations entirely for that day. . . .
   We again appeal to every citizen along our line for aid and co-operation.

From the standpoint of basic survival, the GM&N seemed to have "turned the corner" with the waning of the postwar recession. Major improvements in morale and job performance had become evident. The tracks and equipment were as well kept as funds would allow and the attitude of the public had shown a major change. Encouraged by the general financial improvement, in 1924 the GM&N bought the B&NW and began the expansion envisioned by Coverdale and Brown in 1917 and nurtured through the years by Tigrett and his staff.

In 1926 the GM&N purchased control of the Jackson & Eastern Railroad and began to build into Jackson, Mississippi, to allow consolidated operations with the New Orleans Great Northern Railroad, giving access to the port of New Or-

leans. This combination offered a much longer haul for both lines.

A second part of the expansion plan was to add mileage on the northern end of the line. The Nashville, Chattanooga, and St. Louis Railroad (NC&StL) had trackage between Jackson and Paducah which could be used by the GM&N, and at Paducah the Chicago, Burlington & Quincy would provide a friendly link to St. Louis and the upper Midwest. The GM&N reached an agreement with the NC&StL in 1926, and began to run its trains the extra 145 miles into Paducah. The GM&N used its own equipment and crews and paid car mile fees for the use of the track. The extension allowed the Burlington to become a major traffic partner of the GM&N, which vastly irritated the Illinois Central (IC). Tigrett and his team became a group to be reckoned with and were recognized as leaders in the railroad world. The GM&N effectively controlled and operated over 1,000 miles of line, more than double the weak 409 miles of 1920.

The program to find a longer-haul pattern was completed in 1927 when the link to New Orleans was completed. This accomplishment effectively ended an era for the GM&N employee family. During the years 1920 to 1925 a small, poor rural line had struggled to become an effective, if low-key, operation. The people of the GM&N with their leadership had brought about growth and effectiveness which seemed to some a modern miracle. When this feat was achieved and the road began to reach out into new territory, some of the camaraderie which had been evident on the "old" GM&N began to fade; but the old loyalties and the respect for a job well done remained a glowing memory for those involved. Glen Brock, who joined the GM&N rail family in 1922 and was honorary chairman of the merged Illinois Central Gulf Railroad at the time of his death in 1987, wrote in 1979:

I am familiar with what actually took place from 1922. . . . It was a gradual improvement in the physical condition of the property. . . . The improvement and recognition of the individual officers and employees brought a spirit of optimism in the future. It brought about a togetherness and a spirit of importance to each officer and employee. . . .
There was faith and belief in the management by the employees. There was a remarkable attitude of cooperation between labor and management. It was really one of

those situations that Mr. Tigrett constantly dwelt on, that we would sink or swim together. We would succeed or fail, depending upon how well each one of us would give the best that we had to the property. It was a spirit that was real, genuine and pleasing. It forced an increase in productivity. It was a tremendous experience in faith and confidence between one and another, job satisfaction and pride. . . .

Our public relations were excellent, brought about by Mr. Tigrett's constant stream of information concerning the railroad to the public and to the local and state governments—wide open and aboveboard.

The actual respect, admiration and affection that existed between the employees and the management was unbelievable. . . . Everyone had a desire to be the best in his line, because he knew and she knew each would be recognized, on account of the three "R's"—recognition, responsibility and reward. The first was considered the most important. It was a well coached team and a beautiful performance.

The Great Depression hurt the GM&N and created special problems. Early in 1932 the unions on the NC&StL demanded that their crews be put on GM&N trains, which the GM&N felt that it could not do. By this time the Illinois Central was in trouble too, however, so it agreed to allow the GM&N to use its tracks, which were shorter than the NC&StL route. Later, the IC unions rebelled, and the GM&N was given a dismissal notice. While the case was in court, the GM&N continued to operate on the IC tracks.

Tigrett and his team knew that they would lose the IC trackage rights eventually, and they did in 1938. The answer was to merge with the moribund Mobile & Ohio, which roughly paralleled the GM&N out of Mobile but ran on north to St. Louis. After two years of hearings the merger was approved by the Interstate Commerce Commission

(ICC) and completed with the formation of Gulf, Mobile & Ohio Railroad in 1940.

Not content with terminating in St. Louis, Tigrett and his staff in 1944 turned to the task of assimilating the Alton Railroad into the corporate structure. Adding the venerable but bankrupt line from St. Louis and Kansas City to Chicago would give the GM&O over 2,800 miles of main line. This merger was approved by the ICC in 1945, but the final work was not completed until May 1947.

By 1952 Tigrett was weary and had begun to suffer minor health problems; he felt that his part of the work was largely finished. When A. C. Goodyear retired as chairman of the board in November Tigrett was named to replace him. Hicks, Tigrett's friend and coworker for thirty-five years, succeeded Tigrett as president. Tigrett died on May 2, 1954.

Tigrett had stepped into a difficult rail management task in an era when many railroads were either declining or collapsing. He had led the rejuvenation of not one but three significant rail properties and the formation of one strong operating unit. He had lived most of his life in a small town but had been involved with activities and issues of great import. He had been liked, respected, and helped by major business executives and government officials throughout the United States. And, significantly, almost every one of these people felt that in 1950, he was the same friendly small-town businessman he had been in 1920.

Reference:
James H. Lemly, *The Gulf, Mobile and Ohio: A Railroad That Had to Expand or Expire* (Homewood, Ill.: Irwin, 1953).

Archives:
A significant amount of material relating to the Gulf, Mobile & Ohio Railroad prior to its 1972 merger with the Illinois Central is at the University of South Alabama, Mobile.

William H. Truesdale

(December 1, 1851 - June 2, 1935)

by Richard Saunders

Clemson University

William H. Truesdale

CAREER: Clerk in auditor's office (1869), transfer agent (1869-1873), purchasing agent (1873-1874), Rockford, Rock Island & St. Louis Railroad; lawyer, Osborne & Curtis, Rock Island, Illinois (1874-1876); assistant to receiver and treasurer (1876-1879), general freight agent (1879-1881), Logansport, Crawfordsville & Southwestern Railroad; assistant traffic manager, Chicago, St. Paul, Minneapolis & Omaha Railway (1881-1883); assistant to the president (1883), vice president (1883-1887), president (1887-1894), receiver (1888-1894), Minne-

apolis & St. Louis Railway; third vice president and general manager (1894- 1897), second vice president and general manager (1897-1898), first vice president and general manager (1898-1899), Chicago, Rock Island & Pacific Railroad; president (1899-1925), chairman (1925-1930), Delaware, Lackawanna & Western Railroad.

William Haynes Truesdale was born near Youngstown, Ohio, in 1851 to Calvin and Charlotte Haynes Truesdale. After completing high school in Rock Island, Illinois, where his family had moved, he was hired as a clerk in the auditor's office of the Rockford, Rock Island & St. Louis, a local road that became a component of the Chicago, Burlington & Quincy. In 1872 he was made cashier. That year he was sent to Frankfurt, Germany, as transfer agent in the hoped-for sale of securities to German investors. He returned to Rock Island in 1874 to work for the law firm of Osborne and Curtis and then went briefly to the Logansport, Crawfordsville & Southwestern Railroad in Indiana. He married Annie Topping in Terre Haute in 1878; they had three children. He joined the Chicago, St. Paul, Minneapolis & Omaha Railway as assistant traffic manager in 1881. In 1883 he moved to the Minneapolis & St. Louis Railway as assistant to the president. He was made a vice president the same year and became president in 1887. When the road was forced into bankruptcy in 1888 he was appointed receiver.

To that point his experience had been in the business-financial-traffic side of railroading. But when he accepted the position of third vice president and general manager of the Chicago, Rock Island & Pacific Railroad on June 6, 1894, he moved into the construction end of the business. Though he was not an engineer, he could conceive and direct large projects. Though the Rock Island had been the first to bridge the Mississippi in the 1850s, it had failed to round out its system. In the 1890s, with Truesdale as the responsible officer, it rebuilt its line across Kansas and pushed it into New Mexico to a connection with the El Paso & Southwestern (which later became part of the Southern Pacific). It also built south across Indian Territory (Oklahoma) and into Texas. Wrote Robert J. Casey and W. A. S. Douglas, "He . . . negotiated canyons, circled mountains or dug through them, . . . spanned waters which in summer were trickles of damp sand but which in winter became raging torrents. . . . truss-tamed the Red River, the Cimarron and the Canadian. . . ."

Early in 1899, when Samuel Sloan, the builder of the modern Delaware, Lackawanna & Western Railroad (DL&W) and its anthracite coal empire, decided to step down, it was assumed that he would be succeeded by W. F. Hallstead, the company's chief operating officer, who had spent his life in the service of the DL&W. But the directors passed him over and on February 14, 1899, announced they had selected the Rock Island's young bridge builder as president.

After three tumultuous months in office, Truesdale told reporters that he had not found his new position "more rocky than a man should expect." But in the heyday of yellow journalism the papers were filled with gossip from the railroad's headquarters at 140 Cedar Street in New York's financial district. Truesdale fired Hallstead along with most of the rest of Sloan's "old-timers," many of whom were not all that old. Undiplomatically, he told reporters that "no *good* man has or will be dropped." Relations between Truesdale and Sloan became strained, but Truesdale denied that there was any friction. On the road, employee morale suffered. A strike was threatened after an engineer named George Stitcher, deemed by Truesdale to be sowing seeds of discontent, was demoted to the Hoboken roundhouse "for reasons satisfactory to the directors of the road." Truesdale made it clear that he would break the strike without remorse, and there was no strike. "The Lackawanna," he said succinctly, with both the competence and the arrogance that would come to symbolize him and the railroad, "is being put into business shape."

Truesdale rebuilt the Lackawanna into a road of engineering excellence, perhaps the most techni-

cally perfect railroad in the United States. It was rich from mining anthracite coal in its own mines and hauling it to market but had not straightened out the many curves and steep grades in its mountainous line. Truesdale initiated a series of massive realignment and reengineering projects to correct this problem.

The first was the Slateford Cutoff across northwestern New Jersey between Port Morris and Slateford Junction, Pennsylvania, that cut eleven miles and steep grades and sharp curves out of what had been the principal bottleneck in the main line. This project included massive and graceful viaducts across the Paulin's Kill and the Delaware River, and the mighty Pequest Fill, which provided a level bed for a double-track, seventy-mile-per-hour railroad, four miles in length and 110 feet above the valley floor, in violently undulating territory. Opened in 1911, the line was abandoned by Conrail in the early 1980s to make sure that it would never be extracted in any future reorganization of northeastern railroading to form some sort of competition for Conrail's monopoly.

The second project was the Nicholson Cutoff west of Scranton, between Hallstead and Clark's Summit, Pennsylvania. This line, running high along the ridges of the Pocono Mountains, was meant to reduce grades and curvature rather than mileage; 50 percent of the original forty-three-mile line was curving grades. This project involved construction of the 1,600-foot Martin's Creek Viaduct and the 2,800-foot Tunkhannock Viaduct, both of concrete arch construction, so graceful that for years they were pictured in basic civil engineering texts as the quintessence of the bridge builder's art.

Truesdale built stations, individually designed of brick, stone, or, preferably, concrete, including the palatial, marble-interiored terminals at Buffalo, Scranton, and Hoboken. The latter handled, at its peak in the 1950s, 446 trains a day for the Lackawanna and Erie Railroads, along with ferryboats and tube trains for Manhattan. Smaller replicas of these stations dotted smaller towns as the Lackawanna's massive investment in suburban services opened up the New Jersey suburbs as comfortable bedroom communities for Newark and New York. Truesdale built the Bergen Tunnels that carried a four track main line through the solid rock of the Palisades. And he planned the electrification of the suburban line from Hoboken to Denville/

Dover via Summit (freights took the four-track Boonton line), which was pushed to completion in 1930 after he had left the presidency to become chairman, and as darkness began to gather around the Lackawanna Railroad.

Truesdale said he saw "no reason why railway employees should not have increased wages. We are willing to pay them provided only that the efficiency of labor is kept up." That was the catch: he was convinced that increased wages reduced productivity. "We find by actual experience that increased pay is not compensated by better service." He opposed the eight-hour day and unions. He regarded what he perceived as the conspiratorial labor lobby in Washington as "pernicious, demonological and harmful to the best interests of the country. Persons who comprise it pursue methods that are as questionable and as dangerous as the most unscrupulous politician. They do not represent the real interests of the working man but more often foster their own private advantage." He railed against government for being in league with labor and for confusing the desires of mere common people with the true interests of the country. He was furious when, under the commodities clause of the Hepburn Act, the railroad was forced to sell the Lackawanna Coal Company, its mining subsidiary. (It may have been some consolation to him that Lackawanna Coal paid a final dividend to the railroad's stockholders of 50 percent, or that when the Glen Alden Coal Company was created to take over its assets, its stock was sold to the railroad's stockholders for $5 a share and shot immediately to $150 a share on the open market.)

Under Truesdale's management the Lackawanna Railroad, with a valuation of $50 million, paid out $192 million in dividends. Much of this money went to big financial interests, but much of it also went to small investors, for securities of the Lackawanna Railroad were among the very issues that gave "widow and orphan stock" its name.

Truesdale was the epitome of the conservative opposition against which Progressives like Theodore Roosevelt and Woodrow Wilson fought. His conservatism was arrogant and insensitive but was based on the knowledge that he had done an important job that had benefited the lives (and pocketbooks) of millions and done it to the highest standards of excellence. His simple statement, "Railroads are the greatest factor in the upbuilding of the nation," captured the spirit of his faith in the iron rail as the source of strength and nationhood. Miss Phoebe Snow, the mythical lady in white (whose gown was never dirtied by the clean hard-coal-burning locomotives of the Lackawanna), was the creation of his publicity department and, in her Gibson Girl finery, symbolized the graciousness of train travel in its grandest age. One of her advertising jingles could have been an epitaph for William Truesdale: "I won my fame and wide acclaim / For Lackawanna's splendid name."

Truesdale stepped up from the presidency to the chairmanship in 1925. He retired in 1930 due to ill health and died in 1935 at the age of eighty-three at his home in Greenwich, Connecticut. The rector of St. Thomas Episcopal Church in Manhattan came out to deliver the funeral oration, for Truesdale was an important man from what was still an important company.

References:

Robert J. Casey and W. A. S. Douglas, *The Lackawanna Story* (New York: McGraw-Hill, 1951);

"Lackawanna's New President," *New York Times*, February 15, 1899, p. 4;

"No Strike on the D. L. and W.," *New York Times*, April 27, 1899, p. 14;

Thomas Taber and Thomas Taber III, *The Delaware, Lackawanna & Western Railroad in the Twentieth Century*, 2 volumes (Muncy, Pa.: Thomas Taber III, 1980).

Walter J. Tuohy

(March 12, 1901-May 12, 1966)

by Charles V. Bias

Marshall University

Walter J. Tuohy (CSX Corporation)

CAREER: Clerk, Illinois Central Railroad (1917-1921); office manager in a Chicago manufacturing plant (1921-1922); district passenger agent, Pennsylvania Railroad, Chicago (1922-1923); salesman, Radio Coal Company (1923-1924); salesman, coal department (1924-1926), manager, coal department (1926-1930), Wisconsin Lime and Cement Company; manager, wholesale sales, Consumers Company, Chicago (1930-1934); assistant to the vice president, then vice president, Shippers Fuel Corporation (1934-1939); president, Globe Coal Company, Chicago (1939-1943); vice president (1943-1948), president (1948-1964), chief executive officer (1964-1966), Chesapeake & Ohio Railway;

chairman of the board, Baltimore & Ohio Railway (1964-1966).

Born in Chicago on March 12, 1901, Walter Joseph Tuohy was the son of Lawrence J. and Margaret Freeman Tuohy. After attending parochial schools in Chicago, he obtained a bachelor of arts degree from De Paul University in 1925 by attending night school. While working in a succession of jobs, Tuohy went on to complete a bachelor of law degree from De Paul in 1929. In the same year he was admitted to the Illinois bar, but never practiced law. He married Mary Frances Curry on June 20, 1931; the couple had four children.

Tuohy was the embodiment of Irish charm, a raconteur, and a student of Tennyson. He was a slight, thin-faced man who, despite his stern qualities as a businessman, always had a smile on his face; he was described as looking like a smiling falcon. His favorite hobbies were playing the fiddle and golfing.

Tuohy's business career began in 1917, when the Illinois Central Railroad hired him as a clerk, a position he held until 1921. Tuohy then served in numerous capacities with several companies, becoming president of the Globe Coal Company in 1939. In 1943 Robert R. Young, chairman of the board of the Chesapeake & Ohio Railway (C&O), recognizing the need for an expert in coal development, hired Tuohy as vice president in charge of coal traffic and development for the C&O. From July 1 to October 31, 1943, he assumed additional duties as associate deputy to the coal mines administrator for the United States Department of the Interior during the period of government control of the nation's coal mines. On July 20, 1943, the C&O promoted Tuohy to first vice president, and he was given full authority over operations of the company during any absence of the C&O's president, Robert J. Bowman.

The C&O's coal tonnage increased from 73,372,420 tons in 1943 to 92,738,921 tons in 1947. All-time loading records were set and ninety-one new mines were opened in southern West Virginia and eastern Kentucky, areas serviced by the Chesapeake & Ohio.

Tuohy remained first vice president until October 1948, when he replaced Bowman as president. Tuohy was the first coal specialist to hold that position; but, despite his nontraditional background, he was perhaps the C&O's most able president in the post-World War II era.

During Tuohy's eighteen-year tenure the company continued to expand and modernize its holdings. One of the most popular acquisitions of the C&O during Tuohy's presidency was the Greenbrier resort in White Sulphur Springs, West Virginia, where Tuohy frequently golfed on the Old White Course with Sam Snead, the course pro.

Under Tuohy's leadership the C&O completed the installation of Centralized Traffic Control over the entire mainline and on many branch lines. In an attempt to compete with the avalanche of truck traffic, the C&O initiated a highly successful piggyback service. In 1957, in order to maintain up-to-date information on shipments, the C&O established a Car Location Information Service in Huntington, West Virginia, which electronically pinpointed the location of a shipment or car at any given time. In 1963 the company added a piggyback control center to the Car Location Information Service.

While these improvements were important to the continued growth and prosperity of the C&O, the most important accomplishment of Tuohy's presidency occurred on February 1, 1963, with the acquisition by the Chesapeake & Ohio of the Baltimore & Ohio Railroad. This consolidation combined two major eastern railroads with a total trackage of 11,015 miles and assets totaling $2.3 billion.

Cyrus S. Eaton continued as chairman of the C&O's board of directors while Jervis Langdon, Jr., remained president of the B&O. On December 16, while continuing as president of the C&O, Tuohy became chairman of the board of directors of the B&O. He continued in these dual positions until April 20, 1964, when the C&O's board of directors elected him chief executive officer of the C&O. Gregory S. DeVine replaced Tuohy as president of the C&O and as a director of the B&O.

In taking over the B&O, the C&O also acquired control of the Western Maryland Railroad, which was largely owned by the B&O. In 1966 the C&O took control of the Chicago, South Shore & South Bend Railway. Shortly before his death on May 12, 1966, Tuohy received word from Herman Pelver, president of the Norfolk & Western Railway Company (N&W), that the N&W's stockholders had approved a merger with the Chesapeake & Ohio. Although this merger failed to materialize, Tuohy had laid the groundwork for a rail system that would have been competitive with the Penn Central System.

On the negative side of the ledger, not all of Tuohy's policies were popular. Over strenuous objections of coal operators and miners in West Virginia and Kentucky, Tuohy dieselized the C&O's locomotive fleet. Tuohy proceeded slowly, dieselizing the main line before introducing diesels into the coalfields. Despite dire predictions of retaliatory action, the operators and miners acquiesced in the change. Another unpopular development under Tuohy's leadership was the decline of the C&O's passenger service. When he became president, the C&O had one of the most modern passenger train systems in the nation. Gradually, Tuohy allowed the system to decline, particularly after Young left the company in 1954.

The Chesapeake & Ohio Railway Company prospered under the leadership of Walter J. Tuohy despite the decline of railroads nationally. Of course, the C&O had the good fortune of serving the lucrative coalfields of southern West Virginia and eastern Kentucky, but Tuohy added to its prosperity by continuing the company's policy of acquiring additional mileage through stock control, consolidations, and mergers. By most standards, Tuohy must be judged one of the best presidents in the history of the C&O.

References:

Charles V. Bias, "A History of the Chesapeake and Ohio Railway Company, 1836-1877," Ph.D. dissertation, University of West Virginia, 1979;

"Chessie's Merger Master," *Time*, 77 (February 17, 1961): 86;

Edith L. Fisch and others, *Lawyers in Industry* (Dobbs Ferry, N.Y.: Oceana Press, 1956), pp. 118-119.

Archives:

Papers of Walter J. Tuohy are at the offices of CSX System in Jacksonville, Florida.

Frederick D. Underwood

(February 1, 1849-February 18, 1942)

by James N. J. Henwood

East Stroudsburg University

CAREER: Brakeman to division superintendent, Chicago, Milwaukee & St. Paul Railroad (1867-1886); general superintendent (1886), general manager (1886-1888), Minneapolis & Pacific Railroad; general manager, Minneapolis, St. Paul & Sault Ste. Marie Railroad (1886-1899); general manager (1899), vice president (1899-1901), Baltimore & Ohio Railroad; president, Erie Railroad (1901-1926).

Frederick D. Underwood, longtime president of the Erie Railroad, achieved recognition as a self-made, energetic administrator who physically rehabilitated the properties with which he was associated. An operating man, who was as comfortable beside the track as he was in the boardroom, Underwood helped transform the Erie from a run-down, financially weak line into a strong regional freight carrier.

Born in Wauwatosa, Wisconsin, on February 1, 1849, to Enoch Downs Underwood, a farmer and a Baptist minister, and Harriet Denny Underwood, Underwood was the third of five children. After being educated at Wayland Academy, he was hired at age eighteen by the Chicago, Milwaukee & St. Paul Railroad as a brakeman. He climbed through the ranks until he became division superintendent.

By the 1880s the millers of Minneapolis, led by Senator Albert B. Washburn, were seeking a rail outlet to the east as an alternate to the route through Chicago. They planned a road due east from the Twin Cities to Sault Ste. Marie, where it could connect with the Canadian Pacific. To accomplish this, they organized two railroads, the Minneapolis, Sault Ste. Marie & Atlantic and the Minneapolis & Pacific, which were consolidated in 1888 to become the Minneapolis, St. Paul & Sault Ste.

Marie Railroad (Soo Line). In 1886 Underwood joined the Minneapolis & Pacific as general superintendent, becoming general manager the same year, and supervised the construction of nearly 1,300 miles of Soo Line track. This expansion was initially opposed by James J. Hill's St. Paul, Minneapolis & Manitoba Railway, but from this rivalry Hill came to know and respect Underwood.

The Baltimore & Ohio Railroad (B&O) entered receivership in 1896; two years later, a group of Chicago investors asked Hill to join them in reorganizing the company. Hill agreed, with the blessings of J. P. Morgan, and traveled east to examine the property. He recommended improved operating methods and the rebuilding of large sections of the road to reduce grades and curves and to increase traffic flow. He also persuaded Underwood to leave the Soo and to become general manager of the B&O in 1899. Later that year Underwood was promoted to vice president.

Underwood stayed with the B&O for two years. He gained a reputation for being efficient, a skilled administrator, and a good judge of character. He was a "hands-on" railroader who mixed with the men in the ranks and gained their respect. He began the work of transforming the B&O into a modern carrier.

After emerging from receivership late in 1899, the B&O attracted the attention of the Pennsylvania Railroad, which began quietly to buy the stock of its southern neighbor. By 1901 the Pennsylvania had effectively gained control of the B&O, and in May it sent Leonor F. Loree to be president. It was time for Underwood to move on.

The Erie Railroad, extending from the Hudson River to Chicago, was an even more woebegone property than the B&O had been. After a history marked by financial upheavals, the Erie had fallen on hard times. J. P. Morgan had reorganized it in 1895, but the property was still physically decrepit, financially weak, and low in public esteem. After consulting with Hill, Morgan offered the presidency of the Erie to Underwood. During the next quarter of a century Underwood made dramatic improvements to the Erie and kept the railroad afloat financially. He sometimes made poor judgments, however; one instance occurred in 1905, when he arranged for the Erie to purchase control of the Cincinnati, Hamilton & Dayton Railroad and its affiliate, the Pere Marquette. Impressed with a statement Morgan had secured from the current owners of the lines describing their good condition, Underwood persuaded the Erie board to buy control of the companies for approximately $12 million. When Underwood later personally inspected the properties, he was shocked to discover that they were in poor condition and were not even earning their fixed charges. Returning to Morgan, Underwood complained of errors in the statement Morgan had given him. The financier immediately repurchased the stock himself, at the same price the Erie had paid for it, and then placed the lines in receivership.

Underwood's friendship with Edward H. Harriman also proved helpful. In 1908, when the Erie needed $5.5 million to redeem short-term notes, Harriman averted a possible bankruptcy by arranging to lend the entire amount himself, with the stipulation that Underwood should remain as president for the three-year term of the loan.

Underwood is remembered most for his physical rehabilitation of the Erie. The Graham cutoff, which required a mile-long tunnel and the high Moodna Viaduct, added miles but provided a low-grade freight line near Middletown. A second cutoff reduced grades on a section of line in western New York. Still another cutoff near the New York-Pennsylvania line reduced grades in that area. Much double track was installed, a new route through Bergen Hill in northern New Jersey was constructed, new and more powerful locomotives were added to the roster, shops were consolidated and rebuilt, and terminals were improved.

New ideas appealed to Underwood. He ordered the first gasoline-powered passenger car and started the first railroad employees' magazine. Less successful was his use of outside contractors to perform jobs normally done by Erie workers. Although personally popular and sympathetic to labor, he opposed what he called the extreme demands of the unions. In 1907, in a public debate with Samuel Gompers, president of the American Federation of Labor, he maintained that wages should be cut if earnings fell.

Under Underwood's regime, Erie freight traffic almost doubled to over 9 million ton-miles in 1926. Annual revenues rose from $40 million to over $118 million, while operating costs fell because of longer and heavier trains. Over $174 million was spent on improvements, and the Erie wound up with more low-grade trackage than any other eastern trunk line except the New York Central.

Underwood enjoyed life and he lived in fine style. He married Sara Virginia Smith in 1875; they were divorced in 1886. In 1893, he married Alice Stafford Robbins. They had two sons. A licensed captain, he owned three yachts in succession; he was also an automobile fancier. In addition to his New York home, he had farms in Wisconsin and Minnesota, where he raised cattle and spent his summers.

In the 1920s the Van Sweringen brothers of Cleveland began to buy Erie stock, and by 1926 they had gained control. Underwood retired on December 26 of that year, although he retained an office and his favorite chair in the Erie building in New York City. He died in 1942 at the age of ninety-three.

References:

Edward Hungerford, *Men of Erie* (New York: Random House, 1946);

Hungerford, *The Story of the Baltimore and Ohio Railroad, 1827-1927*, 2 volumes (Freeport, N.Y.: Books For Libraries Press, 1972);

Albro Martin, *James J. Hill and the Opening of the Northwest* (New York: Oxford University Press, 1976);

Herbert L. Satterlee, *J. Pierpont Morgan* (New York: Arno Press, 1975).

Union Pacific Railroad

by Maury Klein

University of Rhode Island

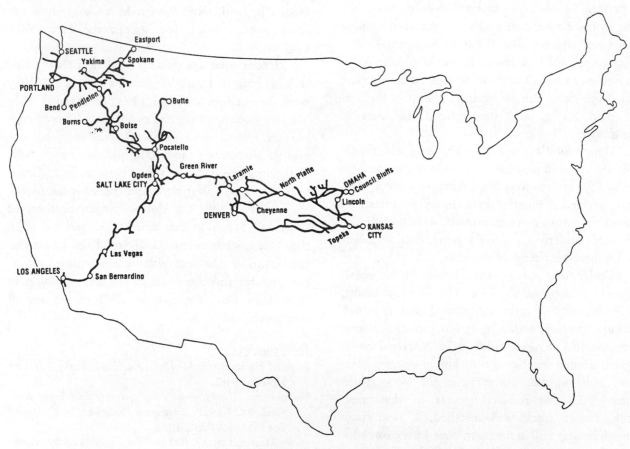

Map of the Union Pacific Railroad (1983)

The Union Pacific Railroad was a unique company from its inception as part of the nation's first transcontinental railroad. Chartered under the Pacific Railroad Acts of 1862 and 1864, the company built 1,085 miles westward from Omaha to a connection with the Central Pacific Railroad at Promontory, Utah. The celebrated driving of the golden spike joining the two roads took place on May 10, 1869. An unbroken rail route from the Atlantic to the Pacific coast did not actually occur until 1871, however,

The Union Pacific Railroad's City of San Francisco (U.P.R.R. Museum Collection)

when the company opened its bridge over the Missouri River at Omaha.

Every step of the road's progress west was marked by impressive performances by the engineers and crews and by squabbling and intrigues among factions within the management. More than once avarice and ineptness in the front office nearly brought the project to ruin. Gen. Grenville M. Dodge stood out not only for his superb work as chief engineer but also for smoothing over much of the friction that plagued the enterprise.

Contrary to myth, federal subsidies played a minor role in building the road. The company received aid in two principal forms: a land grant of more than 11 million acres, which ultimately proved valuable but contributed little toward construction, and a loan (*not* subsidy) in the form of bonds given only after completion of twenty-mile sections of road. To raise funds for the work the direc-

tors resorted to a construction company, Credit Mobilier. In 1872 a bitter national election campaign elevated questionable practices by this company into one of the major scandals of the era.

The internecine warfare among the Union Pacific's managers continued after the road opened. After running through three presidents in four years, the Union Pacific was already flirting with bankruptcy when a major depression struck in 1873. At this low ebb in its fortunes Jay Gould bought control of the company. Within two years he had revitalized its finances, overhauled its management, and launched an ambitious expansion program. Despite his unsavory reputation, Gould transformed the Union Pacific into a strong and growing system. He pushed its development in Utah, Colorado, and Wyoming, and in 1880 merged it with the rival Kansas Pacific. From his efforts evolved the basic system that exists today.

Gould surrendered control of the Union Pacific in 1880 after his lengthy campaign to reach a settlement with the federal government failed. Vague language in the acts of 1862 and 1864 kept the company embroiled in disputes with Washington. As long as it remained a creature of Congress, the Union Pacific was a target for constant political and financial attacks. When repeated negotiations to discharge the federal loan proved futile, the company drifted from one crisis to another during the 1880s, first under Sidney Dillon and then under a reform administration headed by the well-meaning but inept Charles Francis Adams, Jr. In 1890 Gould again stepped in to rescue the Union Pacific from bankruptcy, but his death two years later left the company without strong leadership just before the depression of 1893 hit the country.

In October 1893 the Union Pacific sank into a receivership that lasted for four years and dismembered the original system. After a protracted fight over reorganization, a syndicate eliminated the government as a creditor by repaying the entire federal loan with interest and forming a new company under a Utah charter. During the spring of 1898 an obscure financier named E. H. Harriman emerged as the dominant figure in the new management. Over the next decade he transformed the Union Pacific into the strongest railroad in the West and made himself the most powerful railroad man in America.

Harriman put most of the original system back together and rebuilt it into a modern, efficient road capable of handling the huge traffic that returned with prosperity in 1898. After gaining firm control of the company's former lines in the strategic Northwest, he bought control of the Southern Pacific system in 1901, reconstructed the line, and unified its operation with that of the Union Pacific until the combination was dissolved by the Supreme Court in 1913. An attempt by Harriman to gain control of the Northern Pacific in 1901 led to the creation of the Northern Securities Company, which the Supreme Court ruled illegal in 1904. In 1902 Harriman gained control of the Los Angeles & Salt Lake Railroad, then under construction, giving the Union Pacific a direct line into southern California when the road was completed in 1907.

By the time of his death in 1909, Harriman had left a deep and lasting imprint on the Union Pacific. The system embraced 6,062 miles of track and was imbued with traditions of efficiency, service, and safety that still endure. A succession of capable presidents sought to preserve and extend the Harriman legacy during the troubled years after World War I. For sixty years the road's management was in large measure a family affair. Judge Robert S. Lovett, Harriman's counsel, held major positions in the company until his death in 1932. During the next thirty-five years his son, Robert A. Lovett, and Harriman's sons, W. Averell and E. Roland, alternated as dominant figures in the New York management.

Under their administration the Union Pacific prospered at a time when other railroads were falling victim to new modes of competition. The original land grant proved increasingly valuable as a source of mineral and industrial development. A thriving tourist traffic was built up by the founding of Sun Valley and expansion of parks in Utah. The company was among the first to use streamliners, and moved to dieselization after World War II despite its enormous coal holdings. During the 1950s and 1960s it was quick to adopt such innovations as unit trains, Centralized Traffic Control (CTC), microwave communication, computers, piggyback, and a host of other technical, mechanical, and structural improvements. During the merger mania of the 1960s a proposed consolidation with the Chicago, Rock Island & Pacific fell through after thirteen years of Interstate Commerce Commission hearings and delays.

Aware that its mineral, oil, land, and industrial activities were becoming increasingly important, the company reorganized in 1969 as the Union Pacific Corporation, a holding company with four divisions, one of which was the Union Pacific Railroad. In 1981 the latter merged with the Missouri Pacific and the Western Pacific, giving the newly formed Union Pacific System a total mileage of 21,500.

References:
Maury Klein, *The Life and Legend of Jay Gould* (Baltimore: Johns Hopkins University Press, 1986);

Klein, *Union Pacific: Volume 1: The Birth of a Railroad 1862-1893* (New York: Doubleday, 1987);

Nelson Trottman, *History of the Union Pacific* (New York: Ronald, 1923).

United States Railroad Administration

by William R. Doezema

Houghton College

The United States Railroad Administration (USRA) was a national agency created to oversee federalization of the railroads during World War I. Certain steamship lines, canals, and the American Express Company also fell under its purview. It represented a governmental effort to overcome rail service problems—especially congestion and freight car shortages—resulting from the dramatically increased freight demands of the war. Previous private and public attempts to resolve the problems had been thwarted by numerous factors, including antitrust and antipooling laws, Interstate Commerce Commission (ICC) decisions against rate increases in the previous decade, undermaintenance, conflicting and exorbitant "priority" shipping orders from different government bodies, high rail labor turnover, and severe winter weather.

To reduce the threat these rail service problems posed to the Allies and to American mobilization, President Woodrow Wilson, acting under authority of the Army Appropriation Act of August 29, 1916, proclaimed on December 26, 1917, that on December 28 operation of the railroads would be assumed by the USRA. In effect, ICC regulation temporarily ended, and the government leased the railroads. The Railroad Control Act of March 21, 1918, guaranteed the roads compensation based on an income average for the three years ending June 30, 1917. This law also established $500 million for federal control expenses and promised a return to private control no later than twenty-one months after ratification of a peace treaty. President Wilson selected his secretary of the treasury (and son-in-law), William G. McAdoo, to be director general of the USRA, a post taken over by assistant director general Walker D. Hines when McAdoo resigned on January 11, 1919. The director general position was retained until 1939, when its functions were

transferred to the secretary of the treasury for liquidation and final settlement.

Empowered with greater authority over an industry than any other war-born agency, freed from antitrust prohibitions, and staffed largely with railroad men, the USRA effected major changes in the nation's rail operations. Through eight main divisions at its headquarters in Washington, D.C., and seven regional offices, the USRA abandoned the enforced competition of the past in favor of cooperation, unification, and centralized control. It made important strides toward elimination of duplicate services, reduction of indirect shipping, consolidation of facilities, and standardization of rail equipment and procedures. These changes and the acquisition of additional railroad equipment rapidly ended congestion and car shortages.

Other major USRA initiatives included raising wages and freight rates substantially. The war's inflation and the postwar recession, however, together with the decision to forgo additional rate increases, left the USRA about $900 million in debt when the twenty-six months of federal control expired on March 1, 1920; the figure is $1.2 billion if one adds the amount paid to the railroads for undermaintenance claims.

While federal control accomplished its immediate war-related objectives, perhaps more important was the long-term effect it and the war had on the climate of opinion about regulation. For half a century before the war, antipathy to the roads had produced restrictions on them with few compensating governmental responsibilities toward them. The war demonstrated what some individuals had long contended: that more positive regulation would benefit the public as well as the railroads. While many railroads would, with some justice, contend that federal control had fallen short of its responsibilities—

in rail maintenance and higher rates to cover wage gains, to mention two prominent examples—clearly regulation under the USRA was significantly more salutary than under the restrictive regulatory system in place before the war. The Transportation Act of 1920 solidified the new era of positive rail regulation begun under the USRA, even as that agency and its experiment in government enterprise became a distant memory.

References:
William J. Cunningham, *American Railroads: Government Control and Reconstruction Policies* (Chicago: A. W. Shaw, 1922);

K. Austin Kerr, *American Railroad Politics, 1914-1920: Rates, Wages, and Efficiency* (Pittsburgh: University of Pittsburgh Press, 1968);

I. Leo Sharfman, *The American Railroad Problem: A Study in War and Reconstruction* (New York: Century, 1921).

Archives:
The Records of the United States Railroad Administration are in Record Group 14, National Archives of the United States, Washington, D.C.

Unit Trains

A unit train is a grouping of identical or nearly identical freight cars assigned to shuttle cargo between its point of origin and its destination. Coal, for example, is carried from a mine to a generating plant in trains of hopper cars that move in a round-robin fashion. Ore and grain are also commonly moved by unit trains. Unit train operations have several advantages over conventional rail freight shipments. Delivery is faster because classification, weighing, and other terminal delays are avoided. Equipment and crews are more efficiently used because of rapid turnaround and avoidance of normal train makeup and breakup procedures: turnaround time for unit train equipment is seven to ten days, while a freight car in ordinary service requires thirty days. Freight cars normally suffer from gross underutilization, spending far more time standing in yards or sidings than moving over the line earning income; a well-managed unit train can be in operation almost continuously and will pause only to load and unload. The productivity of unit trains has helped keep bulk shippers loyal to railroad transportation. The cars are sometimes owned by the shippers, particularly in the electric power industry.

For decades the Interstate Commerce Commission (ICC) would not permit trainload rate discounts, feeling that they benefited large shippers at the expense of their smaller competitors. But in 1958, as cheap oil and projected coal slurry lines threatened to reduce the shipment of coal by rail,

the ICC at last allowed multiple car rates, which encouraged unit train shipments. Modern railroaders claim that unit trains were introduced early in 1960 when the Southern Railway began operations for an Alabama power company, using 100-ton capacity aluminum hopper cars.

The unit train in all its refinements of diesel locomotive and enormous cars is a creation of recent decades, yet the essential concept is far older. By the late 1840s a large volume of coal was moving by rail from inland mines to Atlantic ports. The Reading, for example, carried 1,115,918 tons of coal in 1849 from central Pennsylvania mines to its massive coal wharf at Port Richmond, where tiny wooden hopper cars unloaded directly into sailing ship holds for transshipment to far distant consumers. Late in the nineteenth century other commodities were handled in block trains. Produce traveled the continent in trains called "fruit blocks" to facilitate icing en route as well as speed deliveries. Silk trains operated both to speed and protect a valuable cargo. Even logging trains foretold the unit train's productivity by taking logs directly from the forest to the mill; once unloaded, the train of flat cars returned directly to the cutting site. None of these examples agree exactly with all the details of present-day unit trains but the similarities are worthy of study in an industry that tends so consistently to overlook its past.

References:
John H. Armstrong, *The Railroad—What It Is, What It Does* (Omaha: Simmons-Boardman, 1977);

Paul W. MacAvoy and James Sloss, *Regulation of Transport Innovation* (New York: Random House, 1967).

—John H. White, Jr.

Valuation Act of 1913

In most surveys of interstate commerce regulation in the United States, the Valuation Act of 1913 has received sparse attention. The Hepburn Act of 1906 had taken the crucial step of granting the Interstate Commerce Commission (ICC) railroad rate-making powers, which the 1910 Mann-Elkins Act had extended to authorize the setting of rates without a shipper's prior complaint. Even so, the commission still lacked effective means to determine what "just and reasonable rates" might be. At the urging of Commissioner Charles A. Prouty, the lame-duck session of the sixty-second Congress finally addressed the issue.

Introduced on December 3, 1912, by the Commerce Committee's chairman, William C. Adamson of Georgia, House Bill 22593 amended the 1887 Interstate Commerce Act "by providing for physical valuation of the property of carriers subject thereto and securing information concerning their stocks and bonds and boards of directors." Inspired by the widespread belief among Progressives that the nations' railroads were overcapitalized, this measure passed the House two days later with few changes and little debate. Consideration on the Senate floor was also brief. Wisconsin's Robert M. La Follette argued for the need for valuation of all railroad property if the ICC were to set "reasonable rates"; that same day, February 24, 1913, the Senate passed the bill with minor amendments in which the House speedily concurred. On March 1 President Taft approved it as Public Law 400.

The implementation of the measure required creation of a Division of Valuation (it became the Bureau of Valuation in 1917) whose staff and expenditures soon exceeded those of all the rest of the ICC. Prouty resigned as commissioner in 1914 in order to direct this new agency, which was to devote almost two decades to painstaking development of the primary valuations as of dates between 1914 and 1921. Antiregulation, pro-carrier scholars have cited these extensive studies to prove that "by the time the Progressive era arrived, water had been squeezed from railroad stock," but I. L. Sharfman's five-volume history of the ICC (1931-1937) concludes that the Valuation Act met a real need in the "trial and error" development of a method of control that after 1920 moved away from a restrictive spirit toward a more affirmative approach.

References:
Ari and Olive Hoogenboom, *A History of the ICC: From Panacea to Palliative* (New York: Norton, 1976);
I. L. Sharfman, *The Interstate Commerce Commission,* 5 volumes (New York: The Commonwealth Fund, 1931-1937).

—G. Wallace Chessman

Oris Paxton Van Sweringen

(April 24, 1879-November 23, 1936)

Mantis James Van Sweringen

(July 8, 1881-December 12, 1935)

by Herbert H. Harwood, Jr.

CSX Transportation (Ret.)

Oris Paxton Van Sweringen and Mantis James Van Swerengen (courtesy CSX Corporation)

CAREERS: Partnership of O. P. and M. J. Van Sweringen (*circa* 1900-1935); began development of Shaker Heights, Ohio (1906); formed and controlled holding companies: Nickel Plate Securities Corporation (1916-1922), Vaness Company (1922-1935), Alleghany Corporation (1929-1936), Pittston Company (1930-1936); through holding companies, acquired control of the New York, Chicago & St. Louis Railroad (1916-1936), Toledo, St. Louis & Western Railroad (1922-1923), Lake Erie & Western Railroad (1922-1923), Chesapeake & Ohio Railway-Hocking Valley Railway system (1923-1936), Erie Railroad (1924-1936), Pere Marquette Railway (1924-1936), Wheeling & Lake Erie

Railroad (1929-1936), Missouri Pacific Railroad-Texas & Pacific system (1930-1936), Chicago & Eastern Illinois Railroad (1930-1936).

They were one of the stranger business phenomena of the 1920s—two prim, reserved bachelor brothers who seemingly came out of nowhere and suddenly controlled the country's largest railroad network. Enigmas then and virtually unknown now, their personal lives and thoughts never have been well documented and probably never will be.

The Van Sweringen brothers of Cleveland are conventionally viewed as leading examples of that ephemeral breed of businessman who pyramided paper empires during the heady Harding-Coolidge era, only to see them vaporize in the Depression. They were that, but they were something more substantial, too. They were builders, and their physical creations have endured remarkably long and well. In their time, their companies were among the best managed and most efficient in the business; more than fifty years later, most of them remain healthy and vigorous.

Oris Paxton Van Sweringen and Mantis James Van Sweringen were native Ohioans who began as Cleveland real estate promoters at the turn of the century. For what appeared to be whimsical reasons, they bought a 523-mile secondary railroad in 1916. Fourteen dazzling years later they controlled a 23,000-mile rail system reaching from the Atlantic to the Rockies and from Ontario to the Gulf of Mexico. And while doing so, they did not forget their roots in real estate. They gave Cleveland its most lasting landmarks: the pioneering planned suburb of Shaker Heights, its rapid transit system, a strong downtown commercial core, and the city's symbol—the slim, soaring Terminal Tower building.

As entrepreneurs they were an unlikely pair. Genuinely modest and intensely private, they were most often described as shy, quiet, and well mannered. They never made public speeches and they shunned large gatherings of all kinds, including almost any social activities. Their personal habits were rigidly conservative, and their aesthetic tastes were refined but unadventurous.

Yet they conceived bold, innovative, and often risky plans. Once set on a course, they moved swiftly and aggressively through the jungles of politics and powerful commercial rivalries. They dealt deftly and calmly with complex and frighteningly precarious financing methods. And when called upon to sell themselves and their ideas, they did so articulately and persuasively. Little wonder that they baffled their contemporaries and left later historians with the impossible challenge of understanding them.

Their abilities were clearly unequal, but the brothers complemented one another and worked as a unit. Oris, the older, was the creative thinker, the strategic planner, and—when necessary—the speaker and negotiator. He had a quick, flexible mind capable of cutting through complexities, and could accurately predict the results of any action. Mantis, more pragmatic and less imaginative, took care of day-to-day details and Oris's personal affairs; he was, quite literally, his brother's keeper. Oris was serious, deliberate, and physically slow; Mantis was quick, alert, and nervous. The two shared abundant ambition, an almost total devotion to work, and a unique personal bond. They lived together, had one career together, and died almost together.

Their first names apparently derived from some whimsy of their mother, Jennie Curtis Sweringen; even they never knew where the names came from. But to their friends and the business community they were most often simply "O. P." and "M. J."—and always in that order. Once they became well known, Clevelanders quickly simplified them to "the Vans." (The family name had originally been Van Sweringen, but the "Van" had later been dropped; the brothers reinstated it for themselves.)

They had come out of the purest pluck-and-luck tradition. Sons of a rootless father, James Tower Sweringen, who produced six children but minimal income, they spent their childhoods in borderline poverty, being moved from spot to spot in northern Ohio. O. P. had been born outside Wooster, Ohio, in 1879 and M. J. in another small community near Wooster in 1881. Their mother died in 1886, when O. P. was six and M. J. was four. What was left of the family finally settled in Cleveland in about 1890. There an older brother provided most of the support while two older spinster sisters raised the boys. The brothers finished the eighth grade but then had to go to work, passing through an aimless succession of jobs in several different businesses. O. P., however, saw opportunities in real estate as Cleveland rapidly industrialized and prospered; in 1900, at age twenty-one, he and

land Heights, a pleasant, sparsely populated plateau six miles southeast of the city's center. They seemed to have a touch for this type of market and, helped by their low-key approach and self-assurance, became modestly successful.

Adjacent to their Cleveland Heights properties was a 1,366-acre block of vacant land which originally had been a Shaker farm colony. By then it was owned by a Buffalo investor syndicate which saw its possibilities for future suburban subdivision but had been unaggressive in exploiting them. The brothers bought a few single lots from the owners and gradually resold them, but soon O. P. evolved a much more elaborate scheme: conversion of the entire tract—and more—into a carefully planned community, based on aesthetic appeal and long-run stability, for Cleveland's swiftly multiplying business elite.

The brothers used as their model a revolutionary concept of community planning and control created for Baltimore's Roland Park development in the 1890s. The Roland Park plan was built on deed restrictions dictating house size and architectural style, combined with planned amenities, landscap-M. J. set up a partnership and started dealing in residential property.

Success was erratic until 1904, when they began trading in lots for high-priced homes in Cleveing, aesthetically designed street layouts, and an exclusive electric railway giving quick access to downtown. They refined and magnified the Roland Park principles and ultimately made their settlement, called Shaker Heights, a landmark in suburban planning and an upper-income community of national stature. It was the first application of a key Van Sweringen talent: while not original thinkers, they were gifted adapters and embellishers of significant new ideas.

The Vans committed themselves to the old Shaker property in 1906, and gradually bought surrounding land so that the original 1,366 acres eventually expanded to about 4,000. The brothers had little capital of their own, but they quickly exhibited a second talent: the ability to devise financing methods which allowed them to control an enterprise while others supplied the money.

The most critical problem was downtown transportation. The brothers visualized something faster than an ordinary trolley line, and in 1910 they announced plans for a rapid transit line from Shaker Heights directly to Public Square,

Cleveland's historic center. A year before, they had quietly begun buying terminal property at the Square. They then made a momentous friendship. While picking up additional land in 1913 to expand their Shaker development, they bought a small farm from Alfred H. Smith. Smith was a former Clevelander who had made good as senior vice president of the New York Central railroad system; a year later, in fact, he moved up to the presidency of the vast Vanderbilt company. A dynamic, aggressive, up-from-the-ranks railroader, Smith was an exceptionally capable executive who saw farther and moved faster than most of his peers in the business. The encounter between the driving fifty-year-old Smith and the quietly creative young O. P. Van Sweringen apparently produced a chemical reaction and a close relationship began. Smith helped the brothers build part of their rapid transit line, then proceeded to transform them from local real estate entrepreneurs into national economic powers.

The first step was modest enough. Smith's New York Central was the dominant carrier in Cleveland, but it had several serious facilities problems there. Most notably, it needed a larger, better-located freight-handling terminal in the downtown area. Smith saw the brothers' projected rapid transit route as a means to reach a new freight terminal site without the delays and political problems involved in the Central's trying to obtain its own right-of-way. He and the Vans agreed to build a major section of the line jointly, using the Van Sweringens' name but with the Central advancing the needed funds.

Due in large part to this financing, the Vans finished their rapid transit line to within two miles of Public Square in 1920; city streetcar tracks were used to complete the trip. Once service started, Shaker Heights grew quickly. But even before that, the brothers' activities had begun to grow and multiply. Among other things they had entered a wholly new business—railroading.

The railroad was the New York, Chicago & St. Louis, universally known by its odd nickname, the Nickel Plate Road. Despite its ambitious corporate title, the 523-mile Nickel Plate owned only a single line between Buffalo and Chicago, passing through Cleveland. The railroad almost precisely paralleled part of the New York Central's main line and was widely viewed as a classic example of late nineteenth-century commercial blackmail. Nobody had been surprised when, immediately after the Nickel Plate opened in 1882, the Central's William H. Vanderbilt announced that he had bought control of it. The Nickel Plate's route through Cleveland crossed the brothers' Shaker Heights rapid transit line and passed close to Public Square; thus, using its right-of-way seemed to be the most practical method of completing the "rapid's" last leg into the Square.

Coincidentally, Smith faced a severe strategic dilemma with the Nickel Plate. When he and the Van Sweringens met, the Central still firmly controlled the railroad but, for obvious reasons, did little to nurture it. But passage of the 1914 Clayton Anti-Trust Act had made this control of a direct competitor untenable, and Smith somehow had to dispose of the Nickel Plate while minimizing the potential damage to the Central. Despite its dubious origin, the Nickel Plate was a well-built, strategic line which could be extremely dangerous in the hands of some powerful competitor such as the Pennsylvania Railroad. But there were few alternatives.

In the Van Sweringens he found one. In their dealings with him, the ambitious brothers had impressed Smith as capable, aggressive in their own way, and trustworthy. Private negotiations were conducted and on July 5, 1916, the Vans owned the Nickel Plate. The public was told that the brothers had bought the railroad as a by-product of their rapid transit and Public Square plans, which was indeed true—up to that point.

Typically, the brothers had scant capital of their own for the purchase. They negotiated a favorable installment payment plan with the Central, borrowed the down payment, and created a holding company to own the stock and pay for it. This company, the Nickel Plate Securities Corporation, became a prototype for the Vans' future financing methods: most of its funds came from nonvoting preferred shares sold to outsiders, while the brothers personally held the majority of the voting common stock at a minimal investment. The preferred stockholders were paid a fixed dividend which in turn came from the railroad's dividends; the remaining railroad dividend payments would go to the brothers. This highly leveraged design promised large profits to the brothers provided that the railroad's earnings grew beyond what was needed to cover the preferred dividend requirements. For virtually full control of the $8.5 million Nickel Plate

investment—plus several other enterprises also put into the holding company—the Vans actually paid only $520,000, which itself was borrowed.

Knowing nothing about the railroad business and needing a manager who could produce results quickly, the brothers asked Smith to provide a president for the Nickel Plate. Smith nominated John J. Bernet, the Central's resident vice president at Chicago. At age forty-eight, the direct, decisive Bernet was one of the company's youngest and ablest executives.

Bernet unhesitatingly accepted the Vans' offer and over the next several years built the neglected Nickel Plate into a remarkably efficient, premium-service carrier. And as the brothers' acquisitions grew, Bernet became their chief railroad executive, moving from one Van Sweringen railroad to another as his skills were needed. Although sometimes criticized for questionable traffic solicitation methods, he revitalized each of the railroads with modern physical plants, innovative equipment designs, and high service standards. Bernet also illustrated another of the brothers' operating methods: not managers themselves, they picked an unusually high quotient of capable people to run their businesses, gave them a free hand, and provided them with money for first-class facilities.

The Van Sweringens had entered the railroad business as it was in the midst of transition from a growth industry to a "mature" one; it was a coincidence which carried them farther into railroading than they had ever planned. The free-spirited competition of the late nineteenth century had produced too many rail lines operated by too many companies. Expensive but immovable, these railroads represented large sunk investments which could not be supported by traffic levels yet also could not be liquidated easily. Thus the weak companies continued to compete with, and depress the earnings of, the stronger ones, and the industry as a whole was having problems attracting the large capital funds it needed. Increasing regulation was further limiting the managerial and financial options.

One solution was to rationalize the overbuilt national rail system by consolidating the multiplicity of strong and weak companies into large systems designed for competitive and financial balance. To do so, the 1920 Transportation Act ordered the Interstate Commerce Commission (ICC) to develop an industry-wide consolidation plan. But along with its benefits, any such large-scale restructuring inevitably would alter existing railroad market relationships and traffic flows. As a result, individual companies—particularly the already strong ones—approached the planning process with some fears; the ICC was no less hesitant about its controversial mission.

Characteristically, Smith saw the implications and determined to take the initiative to protect the Central's interests before the process went too far. Three railroads then dominated the Eastern region: his New York Central, the stronger Pennsylvania Railroad, and the weaker Baltimore & Ohio (B&O). Already big and powerful enough, the Central likely would gain little in any consolidation plan; on the other hand, it could lose much if its smaller competitors and feeders were welded into large, strong, and more hostile systems. Feeling that consolidations were inevitable in any event, Smith decided to shape them to his advantage. Already he had sold the Nickel Plate to the Van Sweringens; now he saw the brothers as instruments to put together another major eastern system informally allied to the Central.

The brothers' operating methods were ideal for accomplishing Smith's goals. Their tightly controlled holding company technique allowed quick decisions and actions, unencumbered by a large corporate organizational structure or many of the regulatory procedures which bound the railroads. Smith's plan would be attractive to the financial community, too: profits could be made from new securities issues, and a Van Sweringen-sponsored system would provide a market for anyone wanting to liquidate railroad investments. Finally, the brothers would need little capital themselves, but could reap their leveraged profits.

Thus, soon after the 1920 act was passed, the Van Sweringen-Smith relationship expanded dramatically. Essentially Smith supplied the strategic guidance, the entrée to the New York financial institutions, and the Central's tacit support. The Vans provided their skills in creating the necessary corporate and financing devices plus their quiet, confidence-inspiring manner. It helped too that, thanks to Bernet's work with the Nickel Plate, they were becoming accepted as competent railroad operators.

The team worked astonishingly quickly—particularly considering the complex negotiations, in-

tricate financing, and political pitfalls involved. Within four years—from 1921 through 1924—the Vans' railroad control had grown from the 523-mile Nickel Plate to a 9,145-mile eastern system made up of four major companies and several subsidiaries. Even more surprisingly, it had been done at a time when national policy logically would have dictated a delay while the ICC struggled to put together its own plan.

When the dust settled in 1924, the Vans had made their Nickel Plate into a 1,700-mile system by acquiring and merging two other lines—the Toledo, St. Louis & Western (Clover Leaf Route) and the Lake Erie & Western. They also had working control of the Chesapeake & Ohio system (C&O), the Erie Railroad, and the Pere Marquette Railway. What had emerged was the makings of a fourth large Eastern trunk line—not quite the equal of the New York Central, the Pennsylvania, or even the B&O, but nonetheless a soundly designed, coherent, and viable network with a few advantages the bigger systems lacked. At its east end were two Atlantic ports, New York and Hampton Roads; on the west it reached the primary gateways of Chicago and St. Louis, plus Peoria, Louisville, and three ports on Lake Michigan's west shore. In between it served many Midwestern industrial cities and was especially strong in Michigan's budding auto production centers. Additionally, the C&O gave it deep roots in the rich, rapidly emerging West Virginia and eastern Kentucky bituminous coalfields. In all, traffic flows and markets meshed well. Smith and the brothers had picked the cream of what had been available. Only the perenially weak Erie—which had been a reluctant choice—was a worry.

But at this point the brothers had only a group of controlled railroads, not a single system. Their actions so far had bypassed the ICC's jurisdiction, and in some cases their working control was precariously based. To put the Nickel Plate, C&O, Erie, and Pere Marquette together as one corporate unit would require ICC permission and additional stock purchases. The immediate goal had been achieved, however; the brothers' system was accepted as a fait accompli by both the ICC and the railroad industry for all subsequent consolidation planning.

This snowballing railroad empire ostensibly had its genesis in the brothers' need to get a short rapid transit right-of-way into Cleveland's Public

Square in 1916. And while it was rolling along, the Square terminal plans were far from forgotten. They too began to change and grow, aided again by Smith.

Another of Smith's Cleveland problems was pressure to replace the grossly outmoded 1866 Union Depot, the city's principal passenger station, located on the lakefront about five blocks from the Square. A new lakefront station had been planned as a part of a grandiose city-sponsored mall plan inspired by the City Beautiful vision from the 1893 Columbian Exposition in Chicago. In 1902 Cleveland had hired the Exposition's chief architect, Daniel H. Burnham, to design a complex of neoclassical public buildings in a formal mall setting between Public Square and the lake. The first new civic building was finished in 1908 and others followed, but by 1916 the station existed only in drawings.

Also by 1916, O. P.'s ever-expansive mind had transformed the Public Square rapid transit terminal idea into a combined commercial and transportation center. The Square was still the center of the city's extensive streetcar system, but the commercial center had shifted almost half a mile eastward. With Square property relatively cheap, the brothers saw another opportunity. In 1916 they started building the thousand-room Hotel Cleveland, and also talked with four of Cleveland's smaller railroads about building a joint passenger terminal on their Square site. At the same time, however, they had begun dealing with Smith of the Nickel Plate purchase, and by some process—perhaps as a sweetener in the negotiations—Smith became interested in using the Square terminal, too. In 1918 he formally requested that the brothers include the New York Central in their Public Square railroad terminal planning.

Smith's decision transformed the brothers' Square site into the focal point for almost all of Cleveland's intercity travel—which in turn would create an enormously strong magnet for a new commercial complex. It also meant that the Central would provide the financial underpinning upon which the Van Sweringen development could be built.

The foundation of the terminal plan was the use of air rights above the railroad station for commercial structures. It was a new concept for urban railroad terminals, which traditionally had been monumental stand-alone structures expressing civic pride and corporate ego. Smith's New York Central had pioneered the idea with its Grand Central Termi-

nal in New York, opened in 1913. Although Grand Central itself was monumental in the old mold, its under-street platform and yard areas were designed for what later became an extremely profitable overhead development.

The Van Sweringens carried the concept several steps farther: at Cleveland there would be no visible station whatever; its facilities would be entirely below street level. Above it and around it would be an interconnected complex of office buildings, stores, banks, restaurants, and access streets—plus the already completed hotel. Furthermore, it would be a comprehensive transportation center, incorporating all of Cleveland's intercity railroads, its electric interurban lines, the Shaker Heights "rapid," and a planned city rapid transit system. The city's streetcar lines outside on the Square would be connected by underground walkways. In short, the terminal pulled together all components of city commerce in a single planned unit—a concept which remains unique in urban design. In its time it was never exactly duplicated; now, with most intercity travel by air and auto, it never could be.

The brothers announced their expanded terminal plan in 1918. Predictably, a political tangle ensued over the conflicting lakefront and Public Square station proposals, but a voter referendum in 1919 gave the Vans their go-ahead. Construction started in 1923, but even afterward the complex changed and grew as the brothers conceived new ideas. The most memorable of these transformed the originally planned squat fourteen-story central office building into a spectacular 708-foot, fifty-two-story skyscraper, to be called the Terminal Tower.

Beset by plan changes and engineering difficulties, the terminal complex was not completed until 1930, and was far costlier than planned—particularly for the railroad access routes and facilities. But when it finally opened, the Terminal Tower was the country's second tallest building, and for thirty-seven years it was the tallest outside New York City. And although portions of the complex were never completed, it accomplished its purpose of stopping the dispersion of Cleveland's downtown commerce and pulling it back to a central point.

The early 1920s had been a time of unremitting success for the brothers, but by mid-decade events subtly began to turn against them. The first blow hit suddenly on March 8, 1924, when Smith was killed in a horseback riding accident. Smith's successor at the New York Central, Patrick E. Crowley, not only lacked Smith's personal tie to the brothers but also much of Smith's vision and fire. Afterward the brothers' relationships with the Central would be mostly cordial but at arm's length.

There were internal problems, too. In April 1925 the brothers went before the ICC for its blessing on their plan to put together the Nickel Plate, C&O, Erie, and Pere Marquette. To their surprise the hearings turned out to be long and brutal, primarily because of opposition from an angry group of C&O minority stockholders. In March 1926 the commission turned down the proposal.

Although the denial was seemingly only a temporary setback, viewed with hindsight it was a crucial loss. The brothers would never accomplish a full-scale merger of their railroads. Other needs intervened; they had to refinance their heavy borrowings and also make large new stock purchases to solidify control of their railroads. As a stopgap they created a complex array of holding companies which could continue to circumvent the ICC's authority while generating new funds. Large loans were also negotiated with the J. P. Morgan group, which had become the brothers' major backer. A less comprehensive merger proposal was presented to the ICC in 1927, but after deliberating for a year the commission allowed only a portion of it.

By then the railroad consolidation scene had turned turbulent. Unenthusiastic about its planning mandate and slow to act, the ICC had let the Vans preempt whatever eastern plan it might have created. By the mid 1920s it still had no firm plan, and others were moving to expand or protect their domains by picking up uncommitted railroads.

One of those who did so was Leonor F. Loree, the ambitious and awe-inspiring president of the small Delaware & Hudson (D&H). Starting in 1924, Loree gradually patched together a shaky fifth eastern system based on the D&H, Lehigh Valley, and Wabash. By 1927, with the covert backing of the Pennsylvania Railroad, he was moving to get more railroads and enter new territories. In turn, the Vans, New York Central, and Baltimore & Ohio formed a loose alliance to stop Loree and any other interlopers. One railroad which Loree, the Central, and the B&O all coveted was the Buffalo, Rochester & Pittsburgh (BR&P), a strategic north-south line in western Pennsylvania and New York State. Another key company was the Wheeling & Lake Erie (W&LE), running diagonally across northern

Ohio and providing a western access to Pittsburgh through a close connection.

Working quickly together, the Vans, Central, and B&O bought three-way control of the W&LE in 1927. On their own, the brothers snapped up the BR&P in October 1928; five months later, in early 1929, they traded it to the B&O for the B&O's share of the Wheeling & Lake Erie. At the same time the brothers bought the New York Central's W&LE interest outright. The net result of this confusing shuffle was one more railroad in the Van Sweringen fold—the 530-mile W&LE. Although the acquisition had been primarily defensive, this railroad also nicely complemented their system by giving it a link to Pittsburgh and the Ohio valley.

Temporarily frustrated in their attempt to merge their railroads but with their horizons still expanding, the brothers then formed a new master holding company to gather in all of their railroad interest. The euphoric stock market of 1928-1929 was an ideal environment for allowing an eager public to provide them with more capital, and in January 1929 the Alleghany Corporation came into being. (The odd spelling commemorated Alleghany, Virginia, the summit of the C&O's main line over the Alleghenies and the highest point on the Van Sweringen system.) In typical Van Sweringen fashion, Alleghany was designed to give the brothers direct personal control while its large capital came from bonds and nonvoting preferred stock.

Scarcely had Alleghany appeared when it suddenly began gathering in a vast new addition: the 12,000-mile Missouri Pacific system (MP), which spread from St. Louis into the Southwest and Far West. By April 1930 the brothers had amassed a majority control at a total cost of almost $100 million and at one stroke had more than doubled the size of their railroad empire. Immediately after the MP purchase they also bought the small but strategic Chicago & Eastern Illinois (C&EI), which gave the Missouri Pacific a route from its St. Louis terminal into Chicago and tied together the western extremities of their eastern system.

The popular press quickly picked up the possibility of a coast-to-coast Van Sweringen system. O. P. vigorously denied any such intentions, stressing that the brothers were merely investing in a growing region of the country and had no plans to merge the Missouri Pacific with their eastern lines.

At the least, however, by buying the MP they were also buying traffic for their eastern system—particularly petroleum from the Gulf coast and meat from Kansas City.

One Van Sweringen associate later observed that "if wearied by overconcentration on his railroads, O. P. would shift his interest to another activity. . . . These shifts of attention from one enterprise to another refreshed and relaxed him." If so, O. P. had lots of relaxation in the late 1920s. Despite the massively increasing complexities of his railroad world, he seemed to pour even more energy into his other businesses.

In 1926, for example, the brothers decided to double the size of the successful Shaker Heights development by adding 4,000 acres stretching six miles to the east. Called Shaker Country Estates, the new area was designed for a top-income clientele. Its main boulevard was an astounding 600 feet wide, limited-access roadways, local roadways, and a grade-separated rapid transit line—an extremely visionary design for 1926. And at the west end of Shaker Heights they built Shaker Square, reputedly the country's first planned shopping center, consisting of harmoniously designed neo-Georgian buildings grouped around an idealized New England common.

In 1929 the brothers took control of the Cleveland Railway Company, operator of the city streetcar network. Extensive work was also done on a city rapid transit system feeding into the Terminal development.

Then, suddenly, everything stopped. With far greater vision than foresight, the brothers had made some of their largest investments as the economy began collapsing in 1930. Labyrinthine and varied as it was, the brothers' financial structure basically was built on fixed-payment obligations—bonds, preferred stocks, and loans. Such a structure demanded regular dividends from the operating companies to cover the fixed payments. But the brothers' major businesses—railroads and real estate—were among the Depression's worst casualties.

For the railroads, the combination of low business levels, high fixed costs, and the loss of high-revenue freight to trucks quickly cut away profits. By 1931 most Van Sweringen railroads were showing deficits, which continued through 1932 and 1933. The expensively bought Missouri Pacific

turned into a catastrophe; in 1933 it was forced to declare bankruptcy. The C&EI followed it the same year, and the Erie wavered on the brink. The brothers' single blessing was the Chesapeake & Ohio, whose relatively stable and profitable coal business continued to give them some support.

If anything, their real estate was worse. The high-income residential market virtually evaporated. Shaker Heights land sales ceased and the vast new Shaker Country Estates never had a chance. Partly because of the many Van Sweringen companies, the Terminal office complex was somewhat more viable, but the four large new buildings were still too much for the thin market.

The years from 1930 to 1935 were a nerve-wracking succession of crises all through the intricate holding company network, as payments fell due and as dropping stock prices destroyed the value of collateral. But O. P.'s creative mind seemed to work as well going downhill as up. By refinancing loans, moving funds from one company to another, and negotiating payment deferrals, he somehow held the severely shaking structure together.

He was helped by the C&O's cash and credit and by the sheer size and power of what he had created. With so much investment sunk and so many important businesses affected, the New York banks which had supported the brothers found it difficult to abandon them. In one typically adroit and key maneuver, the brothers negotiated a $39.5 million loan from the Morgan group in late 1930. Herbert Hoover's new Reconstruction Finance Corporation lent $75 million to various Van Sweringen railroads, almost half of it to the doomed Missouri Pacific and its affiliates.

Thus in 1935, to almost everyone's surprise, the entire structure was still intact. But it was more illusion than reality. Legally, the brothers had lost their empire; they continued to manage it only by the forbearance and courtesy of their creditors, who recognized that leaving the Vans in charge was their best alternative. The brothers had pledged all their personal assets, too; their living expenses were also covered by their creditors.

On May 1, 1935, the $39.5 million Morgan loan of 1930 came due; with interest, the amount owed was more than $50 million. Virtually all of the Van Sweringens' holdings had been pledged as collateral for the loan. But by then the New York banks could no longer afford to carry the brothers and decided to sell the assets and take their substantial losses. They did agree, however, to cooperate in keeping the brothers in control of their companies if a way could be worked out.

O. P. found a way. With no banking credit anywhere, he desperately canvassed Cleveland businessmen for support. Finally George A. Tomlinson, a Great Lakes shipping operator and occasional business associate, took O. P. to his close friend George A. Ball, the Mason jar manufacturer in Muncie, Indiana. Together the three created a new holding company, Midamerica Corporation, which would buy the Van Sweringen holdings from the New York bank group. Ball contributed most of the capital, Tomlinson the rest, and it was agreed that the brothers would operate the company with an option to buy back its assets later.

On September 30, 1935, the Van Sweringen assets were auctioned in New York. Midamerica bid $3.1 million and, amid sighs of relief from everyone, received the entire Van Sweringen empire—worth over $3 billion at its peak in 1929. The brothers were still in business.

The Midamerica sale was another triumph, but the last. The stress and humiliation of the past six years had literally drained the life from the brothers. Already, in July 1935, they had lost Bernet, who had still been struggling in poor health at age sixty-seven to revive the railroads. M. J., hypertensive and exhausted, died in Cleveland on December 12, 1935. Left alone, O.P. lasted less than a year; on November 23, 1936, while en route to New York, he succumbed to a heart attack. M. J. had died at fifty-four; O.P. was fifty-seven.

Tomlinson and Ball, both elderly and wealthy enough on their own, wanted no part of the seething serpents' nest which unexpectedly had dropped in their laps; they arranged to sell Midamerica as quickly as practical. By then the Cleveland real estate and transit holding companies were in bankruptcy and eventually went into other hands, but the centerpiece—Alleghany, with its rail system—remained. A buyer quickly appeared in the form of a syndicate headed by stockbroker Robert R. Young. After one false start, Young, backed by Woolworth heir Allan P. Kirby, bought Alleghany in April 1937.

The flamboyant, Wall Street-baiting Young was the antithesis of the Van Sweringens, but his story is ultimately equally tragic. Like the brothers, Young was seldom static for long; progressively he took Alleghany in other directions and slowly the original Van Sweringen rail system broke apart. But most of its components vindicated the brothers' management and judgment by remaining strong through the 1980s—although all had been merged into larger systems by then. In Cleveland, where the Terminal Group and Shaker Heights continued to be stable and successful landmarks despite significant changes in the urban and suburban environments, the Van Sweringen name is occasionally mentioned vaguely, but it is unknown elsewhere. That seemed to be the way they wanted it.

References:

George E. Condon, *Cleveland: The Best Kept Secret* (Garden City: Doubleday, 1967);

Joseph F. Doherty, "Smooth is the Road," *Tracks* (September 1955–April 1958);

Ian S. Haberman, *The Van Sweringens of Cleveland* (Cleveland: Western Reserve Historical Society, 1979);

(Virginia) Taylor Hampton, "Cleveland's Fabulous Vans," *Cleveland News*, August 2-19, 1955;

Louise Jenks, *O. P. and M. J.* (Cleveland: Privately printed, 1940);

John A. Rehor, *The Nickel Plate Story* (Milwaukee, Wis.: Kalmbach, 1965);

U.S. Congress, Senate, Committee on Banking and Currency, *Stock Exchange Practices,* Hearings Report No. 56, 73rd Congress, 1st sess., 1933;

U.S. Congress, Senate, Committee on Interstate Commerce, *The Van Sweringen Corporate System: A Study in Holding Company Financing,* Report No. 714, 77th Congress, 1st sess., 1941.

Virginian Railway

by George H. Drury

Trains Magazine

Map of the Virginian Railway

The Virginian Railway was created by Henry Huttleston Rogers to carry coal from mines in West Virginia to ships at Norfolk, Virginia. The Virginian had its beginning in the Deepwater Railway, a four-mile line connecting coal mines and lumber mills with the Chesapeake & Ohio (C&O) at Deepwater, West Virginia, thirty miles southeast of Charleston. By 1902 Rogers, a vice president of Standard Oil, had acquired an interest in the road. He was unable to reach agreement on freight rates with either the C&O or the Norfolk & Western (N&W) and decided to build his own railroad to the coast. The Deepwater's charter was amended to permit construction to the Virginia state line, and Rogers incorporated the Tidewater Railway in February 1904 to continue the route east to Norfolk.

In 1907 the Tidewater was renamed the Virginian Railway and acquired the Deepwater. The railroad was opened between Norfolk and Deepwater in 1909. It soon became a heavy-duty road, using twelve-wheel gondolas that could carry 120 tons of coal when other roads considered the 50-ton hopper car the standard. The Virginian's roster of ever larger steam locomotives culminated in a single 2-8-8-4 that could not create steam as fast as its

six cylinders could consume it. In the 1920s the road turned to electric power for the portion of the line between Roanoke, Virginia, and Mullens, West Virginia.

During the late 1920s several larger railroads—the Norfolk & Western, New York Central (NYC), Pennsylvania, and Chesapeake & Ohio—approached the Virginian with an eye to control, lease, or merger. The Interstate Commerce Commission (ICC) denied the N&W's 1925 petition to lease the Virginian and permitted the Virginian to extend its line across the Kanawha River at Deepwater to connect with the NYC.

The attitude toward railroad mergers was considerably different in the 1950s. In 1959 the ICC approved a merger of the Virginian and the N&W, which took effect on December 1 of that year. The electrification was shut down in 1962 because the N&W had developed a one-way traffic pattern on its lines (eastbound traffic used the former Virginian route; westbound trains followed the non-electrified N&W route) and in addition was able to bypass the steepest part of the former Virginian over Clarks Gap. The only major portion of Virginian's track that has been abandoned is the main line east of Jarratt, Virginia.

References:

George H. Drury, *The Historical Guide to North American Railroads* (Milwaukee: Kalmbach, 1985), pp. 339—340;

William D. Middleton, *When the Steam Railroads Electrified* (Milwaukee: Kalmbach, 1974), pp. 180-203;

H. Reid, *The Virginian Railway* (Milwaukee: Kalmbach, 1961).

Henry Walters

(September 26, 1848-November 30, 1931)

by James A. Ward

University of Tennessee at Chattanooga

Henry Walters

CAREER: Member of engineering corps, Valley Railroad of Virginia (1875-1883); general manager (1883-1889), vice president and general manager (1889-1900), Richmond & Petersburg Railroad; president and chairman of the board, Atlantic Coast Line Company (1900-1931).

Henry Walters was born in Baltimore on September 26, 1848 to William Thompson and Ellen Harper Walters. His father was a prosperous Baltimore produce commission merchant with large financial interests in the overseas liquor trade, coastal steamers, and Southern railroads. William Walters was also a noted art collector who frequently ventured overseas on purchasing trips. His collection eventually grew to such proportions that he was forced to enlarge his home to house it. His son's career was almost a mirror image of his father's; Henry Walters expanded and consolidated his father's financial interests, especially in the South, directed his father's investment house's affairs, and added to the family's extensive art collection. The two men even looked alike, thin-featured and small in stature, although Henry was given to portliness later in life. He was quiet and soft spoken and had a propensity for wearing several gold rings.

Walters had an uneventful childhood until the outbreak of the Civil War when his father, known for his Confederate sympathies, fled to Paris with his family. Upon his return to America in 1865, Walters attended Loyola College in Baltimore and then Georgetown University in Washington, where he earned his B.A. in 1869 and his M.A. in 1871. He then went to the Lawrence Scientific School at

Harvard, where he was awarded a B.S. in 1873. He capped his education with two years of study in Paris. With a thorough grounding in technology and the arts, Walters returned to help his father achieve his plans for a consolidation of Southern railroads. His first practical experience in the railway world was in 1875, when he became a member of the Valley Railroad of Virginia's engineering corps. He then moved to a job in the operating superintendent's office on the Pittsburgh & Connellsville Railroad.

With his father's connections Walters was destined for greater responsibilities. In 1883 he joined the Richmond & Petersburg Railroad, part of the Atlantic Coast Line system his father had organized, as general manager; and six years later became vice president. In 1889 his father organized the Atlantic Improvement Construction Company, a holding company that became the Atlantic Coast Line Company in 1893. Armed with this device, Walters received Virginia's permission to combine the Petersburg Railroad and the Richmond & Petersburg Railroad as the Atlantic Coast Line Railroad Company of Virginia, with a total capitalization of $100 million and the right to purchase other railroads. William Walters died in 1894. In 1898 Henry Walters organized the 700-mile Atlantic Coast Line Railroad of South Carolina, which brought five more railroads into the firm. Two years later he changed the name of the holding company to the Atlantic Coast Line Railroad Company, becoming president at the same time, and purchased the Wilmington & Weldon system in North Carolina. He then had a total of about 2,000 miles of road.

William Walters had been financially involved with Henry Bradley Plant in various ventures in the South. When Plant died in 1899 his system of fourteen railways totaling 2,100 miles ended up in a court fight among his heirs. Henry Walters recognized the value of Plant's roads to his own system, and after Plant's widow gained court permission to sell the lines Walters bought all of them. By 1902 his growing Southern rail system stretched from Virginia to Florida and the Gulf.

Walters's next major acquisition came about almost by accident. In 1902 John "Bet a Million" Gates began speculating in Louisville & Nashville (L&N) stock and by April he had cornered the market. Speculators short in the stock were desperate, and Gates engaged J. P. Morgan to work out a solution. Morgan auctioned off control of the road's common stock; Walters, the Seaboard Air Line, and the Southern Railway bid for the stock. Walters won the right to buy the majority of the stock at the premium price of $130 a share, for a reported total of $50 million. With the L&N Walters was reputed to have become the richest man in the South; he controlled a railway empire in 1903 of almost 12,000 miles. He received much of his financial backing for the L&N takeover from the Safe-Deposit Trust Company of Baltimore, whose board he chaired.

As chairman of the ACL's board from the turn of the century until his death in 1931, Walters directed the road's policies toward reorganizing, tightening, and improving his property. He pushed the ACL into Georgia, Alabama, and Florida markets and soon gained a reputation as a builder as well as a financier. The Perry Cut-off, his most famous project, created in 1928 a new route between Chicago and Tampa-St. Petersburg. With a greater technical knowledge of railways than his father possessed, Walters insisted that the ACL have the most modern facilities; by the Great Depression most of his road was double tracked and operated by automatic block signaling. These technical improvements did not blind Walters to other aspects of the business, however; he organized the Atlantic Land and Improvement Company to develop and sell land adjacent to his road, gaining both immediate income and future business. The stock market crash of 1929 and the ensuing traffic decline curtailed many of Walters's projects, but by then he had laid the organizational, managerial, and technical foundations to make the ACL a strong competitor. His contribution was to develop the broad plans, raise the necessary monies, and provide the overall leadership while leaving details to able subordinates.

As he grew older he spent longer periods of time every year in Europe buying art. He owned paintings by Titian, Corot, Michelangelo, Bellini, Delacroix, and Raphael; Rodin's sculpture "The Thinker"; and the original manuscript of "The Star Spangled Banner." His expertise in the arts was recognized by his selection as a trustee of the Metropolitan Museum of Art and the New York Public Library. He willed his extensive collection to the city of Baltimore and left one-quarter of his estate as an endowment to maintain it. The Walters Art Gallery opened under public ownership in 1934.

Walters was an avid yachtsman and joined the syndicate that built America's Cup defenders. At the age of seventy-three on April 11, 1922, Walters married childhood friend Sarah Wharton Green Jones, a widow. Walters died in New York City on November 30, 1931 and was buried in Baltimore.

References:

Howard D. Dozier, *A History of the Atlantic Coast Line Railroad* (Boston: Houghton Mifflin, 1920);

Maury Klein, *The Louisville and Nashville Railroad* (New York: Macmillan, 1972);

John F. Stover, *Railroads of the South* (Chapel Hill: University of North Carolina Press, 1955), pp. 263–267.

Archives:

Papers of Henry Walters are at the Walters Art Gallery library, Baltimore.

Hays T. Watkins, Jr.

(January 26, 1926–)

by Richard W. Barsness

Lehigh University

Hays T. Watkins, Jr. (courtesy CSX Corporation)

CAREER: Various audit and budget staff positions (1949-1961), treasurer (1961-1963), assistant vice president (1963-1964), Chesapeake & Ohio Railway Company; vice president-finance (1964-1971), president and chief executive officer (1971-1973), Chesapeake & Ohio/Baltimore & Ohio railways; chairman and chief executive officer (1973-1975), chairman and president (1975-1980), Chessie System, Incorporated; president and co-chief executive officer (1980-1982), chairman and chief executive officer (1982-), CSX Corporation.

Hays T. Watkins, Jr., emerged as one of the most creative and successful leaders in the railroad industry during the difficult decades after World War II. Watkins's career followed the traditional model of advancing through the ranks of a single company, the Chesapeake & Ohio Railway (C&O), and its successors. But he was not bound by tradition in leading the C&O and its affiliate, the Baltimore & Ohio Railroad (B&O), through a series of major strategic changes which left the resulting firm, CSX Corporation, well positioned to meet the challenges facing the industry.

Hays Thomas Watkins, Jr., was born on January 26, 1926, on a small farm in Fern Creek, Kentucky, the only child of Hays Thomas and Minnie C. Whiteley Watkins. The elder Watkins was a local banker until the early 1930s, when the Great

Depression took its toll on the banks; the family then made its living from the farm. Watkins grew up in an environment in which there was little or no money, but ample food. He attended local schools, where he was the top student in his class. He was always good with numbers; in fact, at age four he knew the license plates of almost all the cars in the county, a feat which was written up in the local newspaper.

Watkins's ability as a student was not matched by his ability to listen. He recalled, "I was emotionally incapable of keeping my mouth shut. I got an A in my studies and a D in conduct. I have since learned to listen, because if you live very long, you find that almost everybody is smarter than you in some way."

Following graduation from New Castle High School in 1942 Watkins enrolled at nearby Bowling Green Business University (now part of Western Kentucky University). His logical, analytical mind and affinity for figures led quite naturally to a major in accounting. After completing three years of study, Watkins spent eighteen months in the United States Army. He then returned to Bowling Green, completing his B.S. degree in 1947.

Watkins developed an early fascination with railroads; he had an uncle who was a conductor and another relative who was a locomotive engineer. By 1948, when he received his master of business administration degree from Northwestern University, located on the doorstep of the nation's railroad center in Chicago, Watkins was ready to pursue a career in the industry. In 1949 he took a position as a staff analyst with the Chesapeake & Ohio Railway in Cleveland at a salary of $300 a month. The next year he married Betty J. Wright; they subsequently became parents of a son.

The industry with which Watkins cast his lot had enjoyed a final grand decade in the 1920s, when railroads were still the principal mode of intercity transportation. During the 1930s the industry suffered badly from the impact of the Depression and the rise of new competitors for passenger and freight traffic, and nearly one-third of the nation's railroad mileage went into receivership. Recovery was far from complete when World War II suddenly imposed enormous demands on the industry. Despite aging and inadequate facilities and equipment, the railroads responded remarkably well to the surge in traffic. The carriers also managed to regain a measure of financial health.

Unfortunately for the railroads, it was a brief respite. By 1950 the secular decline of the industry had resumed. Competitive modes of transportation, aided by generous public subsidies, increased their inroads into traditional rail markets and also captured much of the postwar growth in demand. Yet federal and state regulatory policies continued to treat railroads as if they were still a transportation monopoly, severely inhibiting the industry's ability to respond to the challenge from airplanes, trucks, barges, and pipelines.

Some railroads fared better than others. One of the more successful was the C&O, which enjoyed a solid traffic base in coal, steel, chemical, and automotive shipments. The C&O was strongly committed to managerial excellence and attracted an impressive group of young engineers, analysts, and other specialists to improve the efficiency and effectiveness of its operations. Watkins was part of this group.

Watkins advanced rapidly through a series of audit and budget staff positions, changing jobs every two years. His career and evolving management style were greatly influenced by John Kusik, the company's vice president-finance. "John Kusik was a very demanding man, but he believed in giving young people a chance," Watkins recalled. "He moved us around and gave us all kinds of opportunities. . . . He challenged me when I did not want to be challenged, and I will never forget what he taught me. As I rose through the ranks to the position of chairman, I tried to challenge others and to give those reporting to me a similar chance. . . ."

In 1961 Watkins was appointed treasurer of the C&O and two years later became an assistant vice president. In 1964, at the unusually young age of thirty-eight, he was promoted to vice president-finance for the recently affiliated Chesapeake & Ohio and Baltimore & Ohio railways. This corporate arrangement, which intentionally stopped short of outright merger, had been initiated by the C&O in 1961 as part of a widespread restructuring of the nation's railroads. The declining fortunes of the industry, especially in the East and Midwest, prompted even reasonably healthy carriers such as the C&O to pursue new combinations which would improve their future prospects.

During his seven years as chief financial officer, Watkins continued to build his reputation as an unusually thoughtful and talented executive. He was personable, highly intelligent, and had a disciplined, orderly mind capable of almost total recall. He was skillful at analyzing problems and recommending creative solutions. Watkins did not hesitate to define his principles or make unpopular decisions, and he clearly knew how to motivate people. These attributes, together with his dedication to the railroad industry and to vigorous competition made Watkins in 1971 the choice to succeed Gregory S. DeVine as president and chief executive officer of the C&O/B&O combination. Watkins was the fourteenth president of the C&O and the twentieth in the B&O's line of succession. At age forty-five he was one of the youngest major chief executives in the industry's history.

The railroad industry in the early 1970s remained distressed. The continuing decline in both maintenance expenditures and traffic left many carriers in poor shape physically as well as financially. The Interstate Commerce Commission (ICC) and many railroad managers continued to adhere to obsolete views of the industry's needs and problems. Meanwhile, the Federal Railroad Administration, a unit of the recently established United States Department of Transportation, struggled to establish economically feasible regulations to correct a serious deterioration in railroad safety.

Watkins's philosophy for addressing the industry's problems became apparent from the outset of his presidency of the C&O/B&O. He believed that carriers had to make rail service much more reliable and customer oriented, that railroad management had to become sensitive to profits as well as traffic volume, and that the entire range of assets of railroad companies had to be utilized much more productively. Breakthroughs in the quality, reliability, and profitability of rail service required new attitudes and relationships among carrier marketing, financial, and operating personnel. Better asset utilization required changes in corporate structure because regulatory constraints prevented carriers from making fully productive use of non-transportation assets. Toward this end the Chessie System, Incorporated, was formed in mid 1973 as a holding company parent of the C&O. The Chesapeake & Ohio Railway, the Baltimore & Ohio Railroad, and the Western Maryland Railway, which was owned by the C&O and B&O, continued as a transportation system under the name Chessie System.

The parent corporation became the focal point for Watkins's goal of developing the full economic potential of an impressive roster of assets, which had a book value of $2.6 billion. These assets included more than 500,000 acres of coal and timber lands; 11,000 miles of railroad right-of-way, much of which was suitable for pipeline and power transmission line development; and nearly 50,000 acres of real estate, the most valuable portions of which were located in Chicago, Richmond, Detroit, Baltimore, and Washington. When Chessie System, Incorporated, was established, Watkins stated that it was clear that the new holding company might facilitate diversification in the future, but that management had "no present plans for diversification."

Although formation of Chessie System, Incorporated, constituted a strategic move in the right direction, the company's fortunes remained tied to the railroad industry, which continued to suffer from excess capacity, intense competition from other modes of transportation, and inadequate profitability. Watkins felt that more decisive steps were needed both at the corporate and the federal levels.

In Washington, administrative and legislative developments during the late 1970s held out the possibility of a substantial reduction of federal economic regulation of the railroads. Many rail executives opposed this prospect because the quid pro quo for deregulation included the loss of antitrust immunity for collective rate setting. Watkins was part of a minority which strongly favored the deregulatory Staggers Rail Act of 1980. Watkins argued that the industry's only hope for survival lay in freedom to compete vigorously against other modes of transportation. He believed that the inherent advantages of railroads would enable them to succeed in the marketplace, provided that management effectively met the challenge.

While the federal government embarked on deregulation of railroads and other modes of transportation, Watkins began a series of strategic moves at the corporate level to enhance the Chessie System's ability to prosper in this new environment. To increase the geographic scope of Chessie's operations, broaden its range of transportation services, and increase opportunities for diversification into other lines of business, especially natural resources, Watkins in 1980 brought the company into an alliance with another strong rail system, Seaboard Coast Line Industries, Incorporated. As equal partners, on November 1 they formed a new holding company, CSX Corporation, with headquarters in Richmond, Virginia. Watkins was named president and co-chief executive officer and Prime F. Osborn III of Seaboard was named chairman and co-chief executive officer. Seaboard Coast Line Industries, Incorporated, was the product of a series of postwar rail mergers involving the Seaboard Railroad, Atlantic Coast Line, Louisville & Nashville, and other carriers. Its operations were concentrated in the Southeast and its headquarters were in Jacksonville, Florida.

The railroads brought together under CSX represented a nearly 28,000-mile system serving twenty-one states and one province of Canada. Because the system included an important jointly owned bridge line (a railroad connecting two other railroads), the Richmond, Fredericksburg & Potomac, CSX was in an excellent position to handle the rapidly growing volume of north-south traffic as well as the more traditional flow between the East Coast and the Midwest. Another significant opportunity for traffic growth lay in "piggyback" traffic (joint truck-rail shipments). To compete more effectively in this market, CSX in 1981 formed Chessie Motor Express to originate and deliver shipments to and from Chessie's and Seaboard's forty-seven intermodal terminals. Chessie Motor Express combined the flexibility of short-haul trucking with economics of long-haul movement by rail, and with its nationwide traffic authority could contract with other carriers for shipments outside CSX territory.

Watkins believed that CSX must be a market-driven company and provide fully integrated customer services. Railroads were in a new era and needed to change their perspective: "We are no longer just railroads, but total distribution systems. . . . Railroads can—and are—getting into related lines of business like trucking, warehousing and bulk distribution."

When Osborn retired in 1982, Watkins was appointed chairman and sole chief executive officer. His next strategic move, a successful tender offer in 1983 for Texas Gas Resources Corporation, significantly augmented CSX's transportation and natural resource capabilities. It was a controversial move in some quarters, however, for in addition to Texas

Gas Corporation's 6,000-mile Gulf-to-Midwest pipeline network, the firm also owned the nation's leading common-carrier barge line, American Commercial Lines, Incorporated. The barge-rail aspects of the merger required the approval of the Interstate Commerce Commission, and the stock of American Commercial Lines was placed in an independent voting trust while the ICC considered the case.

Watkins's objective in offering coordinated multimodal transportation and distribution services ("One Stop Shipping") did not please some parties. Competing barge lines and a variety of shipper and other transportation interests opposed the barge-rail merger as anticompetitive. This argument would have been a powerful one decades earlier, when railroads were the dominant mode of transportation, but by the 1980s technological change and the decline of the railroad industry made rail ownership of other transport modes more likely to increase than diminish competition. The Interstate Commerce Commission approved the merger of American Commercial Lines and CSX Corporation in late 1984.

By 1985 it was clear that Watkins, more than any other rail executive, had successfully moved his company through the bleak 1970s and into the promising era of deregulation. An inveterate optimist, he instilled a sense of opportunity throughout CSX in meeting the new challenge. A financial expert by instinct and training, he never lost sight of the need to control costs, improve profits, and enhance shareholder value. At the same time, he demonstrated an impressive grasp of marketing strategy. Several national business publications recognized his achievements, including *Modern Railroads* magazine, which in 1984 named Watkins "Man of the Year."

Watkins was not permitted to rest on his laurels, however, for many difficult problems remained. A secure future for CSX or any other transportation-based company proved to be a rapidly moving target. Coal shipments, the leading commodity movement for CSX, did not grow as anticipated because of instability in world energy markets. Manufacturing activity in the United States, especially "smokestack" industries served by railroads, declined sharply as production shifted to foreign producers with lower costs. Railroad labor unions proved less responsive than other transport labor groups to the need for wage restraint and increased productivity. Finally, the Reagan Administration's plan to sell the federally rehabilitated Consolidated Rail Corporation (Conrail) to the Norfolk Southern Corporation posed a serious threat to the future of CSX, because the two companies were CSX's principal competitors.

In his continuing drive to improve asset utilization and sharpen CSX's competitive edge, Watkins in 1985 restructured the corporation's activities into four lines of business: transportation, energy, properties, and technology. The transportation segment was also significantly restructured to complete the unification of former Chessie and Seaboard marketing activities and operations. Rail system mileage, which had already been cut from 27,906 in 1980 to 24,058 at the end of 1985, was to be reduced an additional 4,000 miles by 1990. The shedding of unproductive or marginal branch lines and other rail assets, together with a continuing reduction in rail employment, was designed to achieve a significant increase in productivity. Rail employment, which was 71,336 when CSX was formed in 1980, had been reduced to 48,086 by the end of 1985 and was scheduled to drop to 38,000 by 1990 through a voluntary retirement incentive program.

Meanwhile, in Washington Watkins and his staff lobbied vigorously against the proposed sale of Conrail to the Norfolk Southern, arguing that the combination would effectively eliminate rail competition in much of the eastern United States to the detriment of shippers as well as CSX. Many shippers and other parties agreed, and brought the proposed transaction to an impasse in Congress. In August 1986 the Norfolk Southern conceded defeat and withdrew its purchase offer.

Watkins's other strategic move in response to the changing economy was to make a successful tender offer in 1986 for Sea-Land Corporation, a leading United States flag ocean shipping company. Sea-Land's fifty-seven vessels served seventy-six world ports, and it had revenues of $1.6 billion in 1985. Watkins contended that a merger between CSX, the nation's second largest rail system, and Sea-Land did not threaten competition because they were end-to-end participants in movements of containerized international traffic: "We are simply going where the business is and trying to do it in the most efficient way." The Interstate Commerce Commission began its review of the proposed combination in July 1986 and in February 1987 declared that it lacked jurisdiction over the merger.

When Watkins started with the Chesapeake & Ohio in 1949, the railway's revenues were about $300 million annually. By the mid 1980s CSX had become a multimodal transportation and natural resources company with annual revenues in excess of $7 billion. Watkins had played a major part in most of the changes which occurred in the intervening period, during which the company remained consistently, if not always adequately, profitable. Watkins and his staff made a number of what he called "fortunate decisions," helping to shape strategy and organize and reorganize the company as growth proceeded. His creativity and skill in successfully bringing a tradition-bound company into a new era served as a model for the entire transportation industry. During his career Watkins has also served as a director of four other corporations and has shared his talents with many educational and civic organizations. His deep interest in higher education includes active roles with the College of William and Mary, Northwestern University, and Johns Hopkins University.

Publications:

"Railroads Can Be a Growth Industry," *Railway Age*, 171 (August 30, 1971): 5, 20–23;

"Chessie System, Inc. As Parent Company," *Transportation Research Forum Proceedings–Fourteenth Annual Meeting*, 14, no. 1 (1973): 525–527.

References:

George DeMare, "How to Become a CEO: Hays Watkins," *Financial Executive*, 1 (June 1985): 24–27;

Robert Roberts, "Hays Watkins: Man of the Year," *Modern Railroads*, 39 (January 1984): 18–21;

Carol H. Wesselmann, "CSX: Transportation Supermarket," *Modern Railroads*, 40 (November 1985): 20–39.

Archives:

There appear to be no archives of the papers of Hays T. Watkins, Jr. Corporate documents of the CSX Corporation are at the company's offices in Richmond, Virginia.

Western Maryland Railway

by James N. J. Henwood

East Stroudsburg University

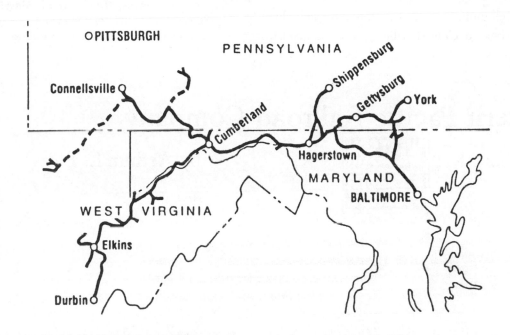

Map of the Western Maryland Railway (1930)

The Baltimore, Carroll & Frederick Rail Road was chartered on May 27, 1852, to build a line from Baltimore to the Cumberland Valley near Hagerstown. It soon became the Western Maryland Rail Road (WM), and began operations to Owings Mills in 1859. In 1862, it reached Union Bridge and ten years later, Hagerstown.

During the presidency of John Mifflin Hood from 1874 to 1902, the line attained a mileage of 270 and reached Hanover, Gettysburg and Shippensburg in Pennsylvania and Cherry River, West Virginia, where it connected with the Baltimore & Ohio (B&O). The WM was to serve as a link between the B&O and the Philadelphia & Reading, via Shippensburg.

From its founding, the WM had depended heavily on the city of Baltimore for financial sup-

port, but in 1902, the city sold its interests to a syndicate headed by George Gould, who wanted the WM as the eastern link in his projected transcontinental system. Gould built a tidewater terminal at Port Covington and extended the WM to Cumberland by 1906. A number of short roads were acquired, pushing the WM to the Elkins, West Virginia, area, which allowed it to tap coal deposits and timberlands. But Gould had overextended himself by his aggressive policies and his empire began to crumble.

The WM entered receivership in 1908; two years later it emerged as the Western Maryland Railway. In 1912, the new management completed an eighty-six-mile line from Cumberland to Connellsville, Pennsylvania, where it connected with the

Pittsburgh & Lake Erie. A considerable growth in traffic resulted.

In 1927, the B&O bought a major interest in the WM, but its stock was placed in a nonvoting trust. Coal, timber, ore, and "fast freight" took the line through the 1950s, but the decline of the first two commodities and the merger movement of the 1960s undermined the WM's traffic and profits. The solution was to consolidate with the B&O and the Chesapeake & Ohio, which was accomplished in 1967. Duplicate facilities, such as Port Covington, were eliminated, and 125 miles of main line from Hancock to Connellsville were abandoned in

1975. Eight years later, what was left of the WM was formally merged into the B&O.

References:

Roger Cook and Karl Zimmermann, *The Western Maryland Railway* (San Diego: Howell-North, 1981);

George H. Drury, *The Historical Guide to North American Railroads* (Milwaukee: Kalmbach, 1985), pp. 349–351;

Edward M. Killough, *A History of the Western Maryland Railway Company, Including Biographies of the Presidents*, revised edition (Baltimore: Western Maryland Railway, 1940);

Harold A. Williams, *The Western Maryland Railway Story: A Chronicle of the First Century, 1852-1952* (Baltimore: Western Maryland Railway, 1952).

Western Pacific Railroad Company

by Arthur L. Lloyd

Amtrak

On March 3, 1903, the Western Pacific Railroad Company (WP) was organized by Arthur W. Keddie and Walter J. Bartnett and articles of incorporation filed with the county clerk of the City and County of San Francisco. This action marked the beginning of a new transcontinental railroad extending from San Francisco/Oakland to Salt Lake City, connecting at the latter point with the Denver & Rio Grande Railroad (D&RG). Backing the company was George Gould, who already controlled the D&RG and had the ambition of building a line from coast to coast.

The line was incorporated three days later, and construction started soon thereafter. The route would be over Beckwourth Pass, lowest crossing of the Sierra Nevada, following a survey made forty years earlier by W. H. Kennedy that utilized a gradient of 1% through the Feather River Canyon. The first spike was driven at Third and Union Streets in Oakland on January 2, 1906. It was November 1,

1909, when the track gangs from east and west met on the steel bridge across Spanish Creek near Keddie, California. There was not big celebration, no decorated locomotives meeting headend, no magnums of champagne, and no cheering crowd. The only spectators were two local wives and their little girls.

The Western Pacific was part of a 13,708-mile nationwide railway system that reached from San Francisco to Baltimore, with the exception of a short gap between Wheeling, West Virginia, and Connellsville, Pennsylvania. Gould's dream of a transcontinental system was about to be realized.

Through freight service was inaugurated on December 1, 1909. Prior to that, local freight and passenger runs had been made triweekly from Salt Lake City to Shafter, Nevada, connecting with the Nevada Northern Railway, which tapped the extensive copper deposits at Ely, Nevada. Passenger ser-

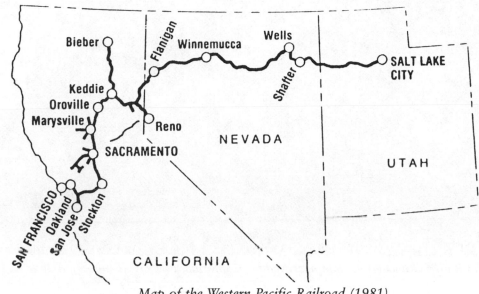

Map of the Western Pacific Railroad (1981)

vice started on August 22, 1910, and this time, extensive celebrations were enacted all along the route.

The early years were not easy. Terms of the mortgage prohibited the building of any branch lines or acquisition of other roads to help feed traffic, and the lack of any on-line industries severely hampered business. The Rio Grande, which had guaranteed the Western Pacific's mortgage bonds, defaulted on March 1, 1915, forcing the Western Pacific into receivership. The Gould empire was crumbling as the Wabash and the Denver & Rio Grande both went into bankruptcy. With the San Francisco Exposition in 1915 and the advent of World War I, however, traffic on the WP began to boom. The property was sold on the steps of the Oakland station on June 28, 1916, and the Western Pacific Railroad Company emerged.

The new company was not hampered by the original guarantee against branch lines and acquisitions. A 75 percent interest in the Tidewater Southern Railway extending from Stockton to Turlock was purchased, and this valuable line is part of today's Union Pacific System, feeding traffic to and from the San Joaquin Valley. A narrow-gauge line from Reno to Lakeview, Oregon, by way of Northern Cali-

fornia, the Nevada-California-Oregon Railway, was purchased between Reno and the WP main line and converted to standard gauge, providing entrance to the Nevada city. Construction of a branch line to San Jose was started from Niles (now Fremont); this move was proven to be a wise one, for in the early 1950s Ford Motor Company located a major assembly plant on this line at Milpitas. On December 23, 1921, the Sacramento Northern Railroad, an electric interurban line extending from Sacramento to Chico, Woodland, Oroville, and Colusa was purchased. In August 1927 the San Francisco-Sacramento Railroad, another electric line, was acquired; in 1929 it was merged into the Sacramento Northern, creating a 175-mile line from Oakland to Chico.

In 1926 Arthur Curtiss James, probably the last of the great railroad financial giants, had added control of Western Pacific to his holdings in the Great Northern, Northern Pacific, Chicago, Burlington & Quincy, and other Western railroads. James had immediately embarked on building a connection between Keddie, California, and Klamath Falls, Oregon, joining the Western Pacific to the Great Northern. The WP built north 112 miles to Bieber,

Western Pacific Railroad excursion train near Keddie, California, in 1950 (Courtesy Arthur L. Lloyd)

while the Great Northern built 88 miles south from Klamath Falls, and the two were joined on November 10, 1931. This expansion was to be the last, as the nation was in the throes of the Great Depression. The Western Pacific defaulted on its bond interest on March 1, 1935, and filed a petition and plan for voluntary reorganization. It did not emerge until 1944, when the courts finally approved a stringent plan to cut the debt.

The Western Pacific prospered during World War II and started on an extensive modernization program in 1945. In the ensuing years heavier rail was laid, continuous welded rail was introduced, Centralized Traffic Control was placed over the entire 924-mile main line (except for the paired track territory in Nevada), and dieselization of motive power was completed. The WP had been a pioneer in introducing diesels, being the second major railroad in the United States to do so.

On March 20, 1949, the Vista-Dome California Zephyr was placed into service in partnership with the Rio Grande and the Burlington. The "most talked-about train in the country" was discontinued on March 22, 1970.

The Western Pacific continued to do well through the 1950s and 1960s and fought off merger efforts in the early 1960s by the Southern Pacific and the Atchison, Topeka & Santa Fe. Changing freight traffic patterns, heavy truck competition, and other factors weakened the road and, though remaining modern and competitive at all times, the WP allowed itself to be purchased by the Union Pacific Railroad in 1981. By 1987 little was left of the "Feather River Route" except as an integral part of the gigantic Union Pacific System.

References:

Gilbert H. Kneiss, "Fifty Candles for Western Pacific," *Western Pacific Mileposts*, 4 (March 1953): 1–20, 45–65;

Bruce A. MacGregor and Ted Benson, *Portrait of a Silver Lady* (Boulder, Col.: Pruett, 1977);

J. A. Strapac, *Western Pacific's Diesel Years* (Muncie, Ind.: Overland Models, 1980).

Archives:

The corporate records of the Western Pacific Railroad Company are at the headquarters of the Union Pacific System, Omaha, Nebraska.

William White

(February 3, 1897-April 6, 1967)

by Richard Saunders

Clemson University

William White (Kalmbach Publishing Company)

CAREER: Clerk (1913-1916), secretary to vice president (1916-1917), Erie Railroad; secretary to assistant director, eastern region, and secretary to New York District Conference Committee, United States Railroad Administration (1917-1920); office manager (1920-1923), trainmaster (1923-1926), assistant superintendent (1926-1927), superintendent (1927-1929), assistant general manager (1929-1934), assistant to vice president for operations (1934-1936), general manager, eastern district (1936-1938), Erie Railroad; general manager (1938), vice president and general manager (1938-1941), Virginian Railway; president, Delaware, Lackawanna & Western Railroad

(1941-1952); president, New York Central System (1952-1954); president, Delaware & Hudson Railroad (1954-1962); chairman, Delaware & Hudson Company (1960-1966); chairman, Erie Lackawanna Railroad (1963-1967).

William White will probably be remembered as the man who lost the great proxy battle for control of the New York Central to Robert Young in 1954. More significantly, he was the quintessential railroad manager of the 1940s and 1950s, "a railroad man's railroad man," as he was described in the advertising industry magazine *Tide* (May 22, 1954, page 26) during the fight for the Central. First on the Erie, then on the Virginian, the Delaware, Lackawanna & Western, the New York Central, the Delaware & Hudson (D&H), and the Erie Lackawanna (EL), he was a builder of morale and a master of operating details who was trusted by those who depended on him and who, within railroading's traditional practices and values, made the companies he ran productive and profitable. At the time of his death in 1967, he was regarded as nothing less than the man who saved the Erie Lackawanna.

White was born in 1897 at Midland Park, New Jersey, the son of Garrett White, a mechanic, and Anna Amos White. He left school at age sixteen to clerk in the New York freight accounts office of the Erie Railroad. He worked his way up quickly, becoming secretary to the vice president by the time he was nineteen. In 1918 he married Margaret Elizabeth Crane; they had two children. He went out on the road to learn about operations at age twenty-three. He was trainmaster of the Kent Division at twenty-six and superintendent of the Mahoning Division, the Erie's busy line through the Ohio steel belt, at twenty-nine. He went on to be assistant general manager and general manager, and in 1938 the Virginian Railway, the newest and leanest of the Pocahontas coal roads, hired him as its general manager. His mastery of the art of traditional railroading was noted in the trade press and he was quickly made a vice president of the Virginian. In 1941, when he was forty-three, the Delaware, Lackawanna & Western, aristocrat of the anthracite roads, selected him to be its new president.

If one had looked out the windows of the Lackawanna Limited in those last days before World War II, one would have seen a multitracked, high-speed railroad that looked strong and healthy. But hidden from the view of the packed commuter trains on the electric line and the thundering Pocono class steam locomotives leading long freights over the mountains was the fact that the road had failed to meet its fixed charges in the waning years of the Great Depression. A high proportion of those fixed charges were guaranteed dividends that had to be paid on the stock of the local railroads the Lackawanna had acquired as its system expanded in the nineteenth-century—dividends that ran at 7 percent and more, higher than the going interest rate and more than the railroad was earning.

It was White's task to shake the complacency of the owners of these "widow-and-orphan" issues from the Gilded Age and convince them that the security of the parts was no greater than the strength of the whole. It was a delicate task, but he succeeded. The debt structure was streamlined; the cash was re-invested in plant and equipment, notably diesel locomotives. The Lackawanna rolled its war-time freights without interruption and was in good condition to brave the postwar world. It even began paying dividends again in 1948. White persuaded his board to buy streamlined passenger cars for a new train, christened the Phoebe Snow in honor of the Lackawanna's legendary lady-in-white advertising symbol. It was one of North America's great trains in what turned out to be the Lackawanna's final years.

White failed, however, in his attempt to take over the New York, Chicago & St. Louis Railroad (Nickel Plate) and make the Lackawanna into an east-west trunk line. The two railroads were each other's best connections; they solicited freight together and had honed their interchange procedures at Buffalo to eleven minutes for transfer from one railroad to the other. The Nickel Plate had been part of the Van Sweringen railroad empire and was controlled by the Chesapeake & Ohio (C&O). In 1947 Robert Young, furious at a clique of Nickel Plate preferred stockholders who had blocked a merger of the Nickel Plate and the C&O, distributed the C&O's Nickel Plate stock as a bonus to C&O stockholders. Control of the Nickel Plate was thus scattered into thousands of private portfolios. White had the Lackawanna buy as much as it could, as anonymously as it could. In January 1948 he summoned the Nickel Plate's directors to New York, seated them in the Lackawanna's sumptuous boardroom, and demanded their resignations. They were dumbfounded. When they regained their composure, they refused. White told them that they were mere humans and would die, but the Lackawanna was a corporation that would outlive them all, and could wait.

But it could not wait. History was turning against it; its heavy anthracite and passenger traffic would vanish and there would be nothing to replace it. The Nickel Plate directors perceived this fact. Whether or not their attitude would have been different if White had handled the matter more diplomatically can never be known nor can it be known whether, if such a Nickel Plate-Lackawanna combination had come about, the later configuration of northeastern railroading would have been substantially different.

Despite this setback, White's reputation as a superlative railroad manager was undiminished. In 1952 the New York Central hired him to succeed President Gustav Metzman. It was hoped that he could work the same miracles for the Central that he had for the Lackawanna, and do it, as he had done it there, within the framework of traditional railroading. For although the New York Central was one of the blue chips of American industry, it, too, was deeply in debt, borrowing Niagaras of money in an effort to spend its way to profitability.

White pushed ahead with dieselization, but otherwise tried to hold the line on capital spending. He mastered a myriad of operating details in order to squeeze every ounce of profitability out of existing plant. He initiated steps to bring fixed charges under control. And, like the true railroad man that he was, he insisted that the track be restored to its Golden Era standards. When the work was done and the Central seemed to be responding, he had the Twentieth Century Limited placed back on its sixteen-hour schedule and made it run on time, a symbol to employees and the public that the Central was whole again.

But White never questioned the basic premises of the old New York Central—never considered that maybe it ought to get out of the commuter and long-haul passenger services that tied up a disproportionate share of the company's assets, or that it should abandon branch lines that had little earning potential. He was a traditional railroader who accepted all of these nineteenth century services and obligations as given and tried to minimize losses by making the services as efficient as possible. He was as quick to invest in money-losing commuter operations as in money-making freight operations.

In 1954 he was ousted from the Central after Young won what was billed as the proxy battle of the century. Young's onslaught had been expected ever since the Interstate Commerce Commission (ICC) had denied him a seat on the Central board in 1948. Rumors that Young was about to make a move had been reported in the trade press at regular intervals, and White had been selected as the man who could best fend off a Young attack.

White had earned enormous respect from the railroad industry, from the business community generally, and from bankers. He was a director of the Manufacturers' and Traders' Trust Company of Buffalo, the First National Bank of the City of New York (Citibank), and American Telephone & Telegraph (AT&T), and a member of the latter's executive committee. He was part of the establishment, and the establishment rallied behind him—which gave Young an opening to accuse him of being a tool of the banker clique that wanted the railroads to remain in debt so that they could continue to charge exorbitant interest rates.

Young was a celebrity, articulate and flashy, and he talked about flashy things, like super passenger trains with domes and lounges. This sort of talk intrigued the press and the public. White was stiff, almost to the point of cloddishness. The battle was not for public opinion, but it seemed to be because each side had to reach thousands of Central shareholders whose stock was held in street names and who could therefore not be identified. Ads had to be placed in newspapers, which invited news stories about the issues the ads had raised. Before long, the two men were on the covers of magazines and featured in articles. On "Meet the Press," Young's visions of fancy streamliners seemed exciting and modern. White pleaded that he liked streamliners, too, that he had nurtured the Phoebe Snow, but that these were the frosting, not the substance of railroading. He sounded defensive and unimaginative. Young insisted that the little people who had invested their money in the New York Central, the "Aunt Janes," would rise up behind him and take control of their railroad away from the monied interests who ran it with uninspired managers like White.

When it was over, the "Aunt Janes," a majority of stockholders—as opposed to a majority of shares—had voted their confidence in White and in traditional management. A large majority of the Central's employees had also expressed their support of White. White took comfort in that support and said so in a moving valedictory that appeared in the railroad's house organ, the *Headlight*. Young won a majority of shares, his total swelled by the 800,000 shares previously owned by the C&O that were bought for him by his rich friends, Texas oilmen Sid Richardson and Clint Murchison. Big money, admittedly not the Wall Street money that Young despised but oil money, helped to change the course of eastern railroading.

It was White, not Young, who understood the immensity of the Central's problems. "If we should get licked in this fight," he had told newsmen two days before the stockholders' meeting in Albany that unseated him, "I want to see Mr. Young up here on the 32nd floor [of the New York Central Building] meeting our day-to-day problems. I'd just like to see him sit down, by God, and stick it out for five years." At the moment of Young's election as chairman of the board, the Central had barely enough cash in its accounts to meet the next week's payroll. Its legal department was already deep in its study of the bankruptcy laws.

Good luck and good times got Young through the initial crisis and enabled him to play with his passenger trains for a few years. The recession that began in the fall of 1957 ended Young's luck; it was widely believed that the Central's mounting problems were the reason Young took his own life in January 1958. He had not "stuck it out," in White's phrase, for five years. Alfred Perlman, the man Young had brought in to replace White as president, began immediately after Young's death to transform the Central into a lean freight line and to eliminate the passenger, commuter, and branch line operations—the steps that White had shown no inclination to take.

A certain stigma clung to the loser of so public a battle, but White was still an excellent railroad manager. When Joseph Nuelle reached mandatory retirement age as president of the Delaware & Hudson in 1954, the D&H immediately hired White to succeed him.

White's tenure at the D&H was marked not by showmanship but by competence. Through the 1960s the D&H was the only railroad east of Buffalo and Pittsburgh that was making solid profits and paying solid dividends. The D&H was small, certainly compared to the Central, and had certain significant advantages in post-1950s railroading: no commuters, few passengers, and plenty of bridge traffic that it received from and delivered to its connections with a minimum of terminal expense at either end. White retained all his respect in the business community; he remained a director of Citibank and AT&T and was chairman of the Greater New York Red Cross. Though he never graduated from high school, he was granted honorary degrees by Thiel College and Syracuse University for exhibiting the highest qualities of integrity in the management of American business.

Like many railroaders of the 1950s, White foresaw consolidation as the industry's salvation. In 1956 the D&H, the Erie, and the Lackawanna began talks about the possibility of merger; it is believed that White was the instigator. He was still close to his old colleagues at the Lackawanna, and many of the Erie's top management people had come up through the ranks on that railroad at the same time he did. The three railroads complemented each other perfectly; a combination of the Erie and the Lackawanna would make possible extensive coordination in the territory east of Buffalo, and the D&H's main source of traffic was the interchange it received from both the Erie and the Lackawanna at Binghamton. The railroads hired Wyer, Dick and Company, a consulting firm, to make studies of possible savings from a three-way merger. When the studies were nearing completion, and were indicating that important savings were indeed possible, White suggested calling in financial consultants to see if the three companies' financial structures could fit together as neatly as their operations.

The investment firm of First Boston Company was hired and, as White had suspected, found that the D&H was too rich to join in such troubled company. Each share of dividend-paying D&H stock was worth so much more than the shares of the other two that any equitable arrangement would give D&H shareholders a 67 percent stake in the merged company, Erie holders 27 percent and Lackawanna holders 13 percent despite the fact that the D&H was one quarter the size of the Erie and one half the size of the Lackawanna. It was certain that neither Erie nor Lackawanna shareholders would approve such an arrangement, and so the D&H bowed out. The other two railroads completed their merger in 1960 amid great hope that consolidation would renew the strength of two proud companies.

But the merger did not work as planned. The savings that were anticipated in the Wyer, Dick report were to come from hundreds of projects—some major, such as rerouting Lackawanna trains over the Erie into Buffalo, and many small, such as less steam needed to heat waiting sleeping cars when passenger services were combined. It would take a master manager to realize these savings. In addition, some of the projects that promised great economies later on, such as the new consolidated classification yard at Buffalo, required major outlays of capital, which the Erie Lackawanna road did not have and could not borrow. Some of its best executives, particularly from the somewhat younger Lackawanna management, left before the merger for more secure jobs elsewhere. Former Erie management tried its hand at running the line, with disappointing results; then former Lackawanna management took over, but the results were only slightly better.

Then they turned to White. White could master the myriad of operating details necessary to make the merger work. He had the confidence of the financial community, and could therefore raise the capital the Erie Lackawanna needed. He had the prestige to convince government bodies—the ICC and the State of New Jersey—to give the railroad relief from its commuter operations. And he had the respect in railroad circles to win for the Erie Lackawanna a secure niche in the emerging consolidation picture in the East: the creation of a Norfolk & Western (N&W) that would include the Lackawanna's historic connection, the Nickel Plate, could rob the Erie Lackawanna of its most lucrative traffic; so could a Pennsylvania-New York Central merger, unless either those merged companies were prohibited from hurting the Erie Lackawanna or the Erie Lackawanna was included in those mergers. White was offered the chairmanship of the Erie Lackawanna in 1963.

White was not willing to give up his post at the D&H, so special permission had to be obtained from the ICC for him to serve two railroads simultaneously. "I did not seek the position," said White to the *Wall Street Journal*, "but on Erie Lackawanna's board are old friends and associates who thought I could help them. One doesn't easily refuse a request from those with whom he has always had pleasant relations."

In May 1963 the railroad was on the brink of bankruptcy. It was holding $2.5 million in bills it could not pay; $4.5 million in New Jersey taxes were due the next month; $11.5 million was due on Erie Railroad bonds in a few months with better than even odds that the company would have to default. "How would you like to be in the shoes of William White?" asked David Morgan in *Trains*. "Luckless Erie Lackawanna, the problem child of the East . . . is the road for which merger has yet to write a miracle."

Some thought White chose an odd place to start. The traditionless Erie Lackawanna Limited was rechristened Phoebe Snow. The old Phoebe Snow's tavern-observation cars were ordered out of storage and back into service. The whole train was fixed up and made lovely again. All the newspapers up and down the line carried articles about it. It was a master stroke: the train became the company's flagbearer and the morale of employees, customers, and creditors rallied.

White turned the Erie Lackawanna around. The New Jersey tax bill was paid, even though it drew working capital down to the danger level. White managed to convince the holders of the Erie bonds, First National City Bank and Metropolitan Life, to postpone the due date. Equipment trusts were secured for new locomotives and cars. New Jersey was persuaded to subsidize the commuter operations. All of these actions made the EL more attractive for inclusion in the emerging Norfolk and Western. By 1965 the road reported a profit; it was not large—$3.8 million—but it was the first since 1956. "In mid-1963, when we set for ourselves the goal of getting in the black by 1965," said White in

the company's 1965 annual report, "we knew it would be difficult to accomplish . . . and there were times in late 1963 and early 1964 when we feared bankruptcy could not be avoided because the cash available was $1 million less than the bills we were holding unpaid. We weathered those bad times, and favored by good times, and by running a tight ship, the company in 1965 turned a profit. It is a big boost to the morale of our entire staff." ICC Commissioner Charles Webb, one of the activists on the commission who had challenged the railroads' optimistic forecasts for their mergers, praised White for his "superb management" and as representing the very best in business management with honor and integrity.

White died suddenly on April 6, 1967, on a business trip to Cleveland. He was survived by his second wife, Ruth Dougherty White, whom he had married in 1948, following the death of his first wife in 1947. His death was a blow to the Erie Lackawanna. He alone, with his skill and his spirit, had kept it together through its darkest hour. Its fortunes would never ride so high again: it soon came under the control of the N&W, which never wanted it, let it slide into bankruptcy, and conveyed it to Conrail in 1976. Most of its routes, except the Buffalo-Jersey City main line of the former Erie Railroad, were subsequently abandoned.

Publications:

The Lackawanna, the Route of Phoebe Snow: A Centenary Address New York: Newcomen Society 1951).

References:

Joseph Borkin, *Robert Young: The Populist of Wall Street* (New York, Harper & Row, 1969);

Herrymon Maurer, "The Central Rolls Again," *Fortune*, 50 (May 1954): 86–93, 139–148;

David Morgan, "EL Remains a 'Formidable Task,'" *Trains,* 25 (January 1965): 9;

Richard Saunders, *The Railroad Mergers and the Coming of Conrail.* (Westport, Conn.: Greenwood Press, 1978);

"White, D&H Chairman, Formally Named Head of Lackawanna," *Wall Street Journal,* June 14, 1963, p. 14.

Archives:

The Delaware, Lackawanna & Western Railroad Company Papers are at Syracuse University Library, Syracuse, New York; Erie Lackawanna Railroad Company papers are at the Eleutherian Mills Historical Library, Wilmington, Delaware.

Frederic B. Whitman

(September 1, 1898-April 30, 1982)

by Arthur L. Lloyd

Amtrak

Frederic B. Whitman (courtesy Arthur L. Lloyd)

CAREER: Fireman, Fort Worth & Denver City Railway (1919-1921); assistant trainmaster, trainmaster, assistant superintendent (1921–1939), division superintendent (1939-1945), general superintendent, Western District (1945-1948), Chicago, Burlington & Quincy Railroad; executive vice president (1948-1949), president (1949-1963), Western Pacific Railroad.

Frederic Bennett Whitman was born in Cambridge, Massachusetts, on September 1, 1898 to Edmund Allen and Florence Josephine Whitman. He was educated in Cambridge grade, high, and Latin schools. He received his bachelor's degree from Harvard University in 1919.

Whitman began his railroad career in 1919, while still attending school, as a locomotive fireman for the Fort Worth & Denver City Railway. In 1921, following receipt of the M.B.A. degree cum laude from the Harvard Graduate School of Business Administration, he went to the parent railroad, the Chicago, Burlington & Quincy. He worked his way through various operating department positions, including division superintendent at St. Joseph, Missouri, from 1939 to 1945 and general superintendent for the Western District, headquartered in Lincoln, Nebraska, from 1945 to 1948.

Meanwhile, the Western Pacific Railroad (WP), which had prospered during World War II and had emerged from bankruptcy in 1944, was looking for a top official to replace Harry A. Mitchell, who was scheduled to retire in 1949. Mitchell and his predecessor, Charles Elsey, had nursed the Western Pacific through the Great Depression and the war with an aging physical plant, and the railroad was ripe for innovation and improvement.

Whitman joined the Western Pacific on October 1, 1948 as executive vice president and director. On March 20, 1949, Mitchell inaugurated the Vista-Dome California Zephyr streamliner, which would revolutionize postwar passenger rail transportation and would call the attention of the 1,200-mile property to freight traffic managers.

Whitman replaced Mitchell as president on July 1, 1949. He was also appointed president of Western Pacific subsidiaries and affiliates: the Oakland Terminal Railway, Alameda Belt Line, Salt Lake City Union Depot & Railroad Company, and Standard Realty and Development Company. He served on the boards of directors of the Sacramento Northern Railway, the Tidewater Southern Railway, and the Central California Traction Company.

Whitman placed into effect at the WP many concepts that were revolutionary from a railroad standpoint. He knew that a modern property must have an active sales organization, and made sales calls with his marketing staff. He was not bashful about asking for business from the top industrial and manufacturing companies in the United States. Whitman recognized the importance of the passenger train as a showcase for the capabilities of the railroad, and the California Zephyr was well supported under his leadership. The train remained strong and earned more money than the top trains of the competing Southern Pacific (SP) and Atchison, Topeka & Santa Fe.

One of Whitman's goals was to meet all 10,000 Western Pacific employees. The railroad's public relations and personnel departments organized a program of breakfasts, lunches, and dinners along the railroad during early 1950 so that the boss and his vice president and general manager, Harry Munson, who had come from the Chicago, Milwaukee, St. Paul & Pacific at the same time as Whitman came from the Burlington, could talk to the workers. The event, dubbed "Operation Nosebag," was repeated in 1952 with eleven dinners in the top hotels of on-line cities. Whitman and Munson outlined company goals and reported on progress to date.

Whitman's tenure saw a complete transformation of the Western Pacific. From a railroad which was content to live on the leavings of the more powerful Southern Pacific and Santa Fe lines, the company became a serious competitor able to match transit times, provide new equipment, take the lead in innovative concepts, and capture over 50 percent of the transcontinental passenger traffic to and from northern California. Centralized Traffic Control (CTC) was placed into effect over all 924 main line miles from Oakland to Salt Lake City, except for the paired-track portion between Weso and Alazon, Nevada, where all WP and SP trains went eastbound on WP rails and westbound on SP trackage. CTC gave the road nearly the capability of double track without the expense.

In the 118-mile Feather River Canyon, which was beset by winter slide problems, extensive slide-detector fencing was installed and most tunnels were lined with concrete, replacing wood siding. In one particularly slide-prone area, near milepost 250, a new 3,100-foot tunnel was bored behind the unstable canyon wall. The Western Pacific was a pioneer in replacing jointed rail with continuously welded rail, which allowed for smoother and safer operations. New, innovative "Compartmentizer-Equipped" and "Damage Free" boxcars were placed in service, giving shippers more security that their goods would arrive safe and undamaged.

As railroads began to de-emphasize passenger service after 1958, Whitman would not allow the California Zephyr to deteriorate. Service remained top-flight and efforts were made to attract as much business as possible to the train during the off-peak winter months. Summer traffic continued to be strong and overall occupancy remained close to 80 percent on a year-round basis.

Whitman also found time for civic activities. He served on the San Francisco Federated Fund and the Oakland Community Chest and merged all of the San Francisco Bay Area Community Chests into the United Bay Area Crusade, of which he was the first president. The United Bay Area Crusade is now the United Way.

Whitman married Gertrude Bissell June 13, 1927; they had two children. He retired as president of Western Pacific in 1963, remaining on a consulting basis for two years. He died at his home in Oakland in 1982, leaving a legacy as one of the most progressive and innovative railroad presidents in modern times.

Reference:

Bruce A. MacGregor and Ted Benson, *Portrait of a Silver Lady* (Boulder, Col.: Pruett, 1977).

Daniel Willard

(January 28, 1861-July 6, 1942)

by John F. Stover

Purdue University

Daniel Willard (Kalmbach Publishing Company)

CAREER: Section hand, Vermont Central Railroad (1879); fireman (1879-1880), locomotive engineer (1880-1883), Connecticut & Passumpsic Rivers Railroad; locomotive engineer, Lake Shore & Michigan Southern Railroad (1883-1884); brakeman, locomotive engineer, roundhouse foreman (1884-1890), trainmaster, traveling engineer, assistant superintendent, acting superintendent (1890-1894), division superintendent (1894-1899), Minneapolis, St. Paul, Sault Ste. Marie & Atlantic Railway; assistant general manager, Baltimore & Ohio Railroad (1899-1901); first vice president and general manager, Erie Railroad (1901-1904); vice president-

operation and maintenance, Chicago, Burlington & Quincy Railroad (1904-1910); president (1910-1941), chairman of the board (1941-1942), Baltimore & Ohio Railroad.

Daniel Willard was born on January 28, 1861, in North Hartland, Vermont, the only son of three children of Daniel Spaulding Willard and Mary Anna Daniels Willard. As a young man, Willard's father spent three years at sea before returning to the ancestral farm. Daniel Spaulding Willard was a stern man, and Willard was taught to say "Yes, *Sir*" in response to any question from his father. Willard's mother died when he was five.

As the only boy in the family Willard, although never a robust youth, soon learned the chores that were a part of a 250-acre Vermont farm; it seemed to the boy that there was no bottom to the large kitchen wood box that he had to keep filled. He was an avid reader and still found time in the long winter evenings to play his fiddle or knit himself a pair of red woolen socks. As a youth Willard attended the Methodist Church, but as an adult he became a Unitarian. At age sixteen, even before graduating from high school, he taught in the district school at nearby Hartland Hill, where he had room and board with Mrs. Samuel Taylor, a retired teacher with an extensive library in her home. The novels, essays, and biographies he read there gave the young man an interest in good literature that would continue for the rest of his life. After graduating from the Windsor, Vermont, high school in 1878, Willard had the ambition to be a doctor. His father could not afford to send his son to Dartmouth, which Willard favored, but found sufficient funds to send the boy to the Massachusetts State Agricultural College at Amherst. Willard had attended college for only six months when eye trouble, later diagnosed as astigmatism, forced him to return to his father's farm in the spring of 1879.

Willard was fascinated by the Vermont Central Railroad, which ran across the family farm. He was further inclined toward a railroad career by the fact that an uncle was a locomotive engineer and several cousins had railroad jobs. In April 1879 a friend of the family offered him a job as a section hand at a dollar a day, and Willard quickly accepted. The pay was cut to ninety cents before he started work, but $5.40 a week was still fair pay for a Vermont farm boy in the 1870s. Even though Willard weighed little more than 125 pounds he stayed with the job, and soon was helping the section boss make out his daily reports at the end of the ten-hour day. Within a few months Willard heard of a job opening as a fireman on the Connecticut & Passumpsic Rivers Railroad, a line running from White River Junction to the Canadian line.

Willard applied for the job and was soon assigned to firing on freight trains. The pay was $1.40 a day for throwing ten to twelve cords of wood into the firebox of a twenty-ton locomotive. Additional duties, such as polishing the brass and shining the engine, might be assigned by the engineer, and there was no extra pay for overtime. But Willard liked the new job and began to dream of moving across the cab to the position of engineer. During his first winter with the Connecticut & Passumpsic Rivers Willard fired a donkey engine on a piledriver, and later was promoted to firing on a passenger run. After a year Willard turned down the offer of a clerkship in the Lyndonville headquarters because of his desire to be a locomotive engineer. Before he was twenty he was promoted to the right-hand side of the cab as an engineer of a wood-burning 4-4-0 (four-wheel pilot truck, four driving wheels, no trailing truck) in freight service at a wage of $2.00 per day. Willard later said that the promotion was the greatest thrill of his life. During his remaining months on the small Vermont line Willard became a member of the Brotherhood of Locomotive Engineers.

In 1883 Willard found work as a locomotive engineer on the Lake Shore & Michigan Southern in Elkhart, Indiana, on the advice of a friend who pointed out that good engine men on the Lake Shore were receiving $3.00 a day. But a business depression soon caused Willard to be furloughed. In the spring of 1884 he found employment as a brake-man on a construction train on the Minneapolis, St. Paul, Sault Ste. Marie & Atlantic Railway (Soo Line), which was being built in northern Wisconsin. Soon he was again a locomotive engineer and a little later was made foreman of a three-stall roundhouse at Turtle Lake, Wisconsin, the headquarters of the growing line. Willard returned to Vermont to be married on March 2, 1885, to Bertha Leone Elkins of North Troy. He brought his bride back to Turtle Lake, but before long the couple moved to Minneapolis, where their two sons were born.

During his first half-dozen years on the Soo Willard held a variety of jobs—brakeman, fireman, conductor, engineer, telegraph operator, and roundhouse foreman. He carried a pocket-sized memorandum book filled with facts and figures under alphabetical headings—for example, A—airbrakes, accidents; B—ballast, boilers, bolts, bridges; C—Canadian railroads, cars, coaches, coal. Willard was clearly preparing himself for larger and more important positions.

Shortly after Willard joined the Soo the owners had appointed a new general manager, Frederick D. Underwood, a former division superintendent on the Chicago, Milwaukee & St. Paul Railway. Willard's first contact with Underwood had come when the new general manager made an inspection visit of the Soo facilities at Turtle Lake. Willard had felt that he had the roundhouse in first-class shape, only to have the official comment on the icy condition of the outside steps and the total absence of barrels filled with water for fire protection. But Underwood became well aware of Willard's record as the Vermonter worked his way up to be the second ranking member on the roster of Soo engineers. In 1890 Underwood promoted him to trainmaster. Underwood believed in discipline and suggested that Willard might have to put a bit of distance between himself and some of his old cronies. As Willard left his office Underwood told the new trainmaster, "From this time on, you will be *Mister* Willard."

During the 1890s Underwood continued to promote Willard to positions of higher responsibility. In turn he became traveling engineer, assistant superintendent, acting superintendent, and finally, after fifteen years of railroading, division superintendent. The pay was never much above $200 a month during the decade. The chief engineer of the Soo called upon Willard for assistance in preparing specifications and purchasing equipment; he also prepared memoranda concerning the growing need of the Soo Line for new motive power. Increasingly through the 1890s Willard became a firm friend and able advisor to Underwood.

On February 1, 1899, Underwood became the second vice president and general manager of the Baltimore & Ohio Railroad (B&O); soon he asked Willard to come to Baltimore as assistant general manager. Willard was given supervision over many major purchases for the B&O; Underwood also expected his new assistant to be his eyes and ears, saying to Willard: "I want to know all about this road; I am terribly ignorant about it." As a result, Willard spent four or five days of every week out on the road, traveling by train, by horseback, and on foot. He gave Underwood detailed written and oral reports on the problems, the strengths, and the weaknesses of the 2,300-mile system, gaining an intimate knowledge of the physical character, equipment, and personnel of the road against the day, a decade later, when he would return as its president. In the spring of 1901 Underwood was elected president of the Erie Railroad, and at once John K. Cowen, president of the Baltimore & Ohio, offered Willard the position of general manager. Willard declined the offer; he had promised Underwood that he would become his assistant at the Erie. Willard had been in New York City only a short time before Underwood made him first vice president and general manager of the Erie.

Underwood and Willard were soon making plans to upgrade the freight service on the Erie. Their line provided a more direct route to many midwestern cities than the New York Central, and was far less mountainous than the Pennsylvania. Willard recruited executives from other roads to help rebuild certain lines in order to improve the freight operations. When there were labor problems with the Erie firemen, Willard drew up new work rules which were acceptable to the union workers. Having worked his way up through the ranks, it was easy for Willard to understand the viewpoint of labor.

James J. Hill, who controlled the well-built Great Northern and was soon to have a dominant interest in both the Northern Pacific and the Chicago, Burlington & Quincy, had been a member of the Erie board since 1900. Willard and Hill became good friends, and late in 1903 Hill offered Willard the operating vice presidency of the Burlington at a salary of $30,000 a year. Willard declined, but Hill was a hard man to refuse. Soon he again approached Willard, offering $50,000 a year plus a bonus. Underwood urged his assistant to accept the offer, and Willard became vice president in charge of operation and maintenance of the Burlington in January 1904. Hill reportedly told his new vice president that he expected him to save a million dollars a year without losing one shipper, stockholder, or employee. Hill had the reputation of being a hard and autocratic boss, but the two men found little difficulty in working together.

When Willard moved to Chicago he became a member of a three-man executive team which also included George B. Harris, president of the Burlington, in charge of finance and corporate development, and Darius Miller, vice president in charge of traffic. Hill expected the three to create more traffic and to move it with a maximum of efficiency. Willard did his share to improve the operation of the Burlington during his six years with the road. Much new double track was built between Chicago and Omaha and many passing tracks were lengthened. Since the cost of railroad ties had increased greatly, Willard had ties of inferior woods chemically treated to bring them up to the quality of the ties formerly made of oak. Tie-treating plants were established at Galesburg, Illinois, and Sheridan, Wyoming.

Discovering that the quality of the water in much of the Burlington territory was so bad that engine failure and service disruption had become fairly frequent, Willard had dozens of wells dug and reservoirs constructed to bring good water to the railroad. Where good water could not be obtained, he had water-treating plants installed. Willard strongly urged the purchase of a 100 Prairie type locomotives (2-6-2 [a two-wheel pilot truck, six drivers, and a two-wheel trailing truck]). Hill favored the Consolidation type (2-8-0), which had been so successful on the Great Northern, but Willard finally sold him on the Prairie engine type. Willard's improvements paid off: by 1906 the average freight train load on the Burlington had climbed to 376 tons compared to 200 tons in 1901.

Willard ended the long-standing rule of laying off workers for minor offenses; instead, he started a demerit system, with an entry placed on a man's record for a rule infraction. The man stayed on the payroll and, through good conduct, could clear his record of earlier demerits. The new plan was popular with the men and Willard was again shown to be a friend of railroad labor.

Late in 1909 the Baltimore & Ohio was looking for a new president. Judge Robert S. Lovett, the president of the Union Pacific and a director of the Baltimore & Ohio, asked Underwood to suggest a candidate for the position, and Underwood named Willard as the best possible choice. Willard was approached and accepted the offer. Hill did his best to retain Willard on the Burlington, even offering him the presidency of the line.

Willard became the president of the Baltimore & Ohio on January 15, 1910. As one who had known the labor of laying track and shoveling coal into a locomotive firebox, Willard was noted for his ability to work with subordinates without friction. At the same time his fellow workers soon learned that while he rarely gave direct orders, Willard expected that his suggestions would be followed. The Baltimore & Ohio president had an insatiable curiosity and a passion for exact information, and was a great reader. In commenting on his election the editors of the *Railroad Gazette* wrote that Willard: "not only works hard, but works fast . . . he has been a student all his life."

The Baltimore & Ohio was a historic and proud line. Chartered in 1827, it had reached Wheeling in 1852 and Chicago in 1874. It was not as large or rich a trunk line as either the New York Central or the Pennsylvania, but since 1900 its system had grown from 2,300 to 4,000 miles and its yearly revenue had increased from $42 million to $71 million. It had paid yearly dividends of $4 to $6 since the turn of the century. In 1909, however, there were growing complaints about both the passenger and the freight service on the line.

Willard started at once to upgrade and rebuild the Baltimore & Ohio. In the first year of his presidency his board approved $43 million in expenditures for line improvement and new equipment. Willard soon realized that the mountains of Maryland, West Virginia, and Pennsylvania would require a heavier engine than the Prairie, and by 1913 he had purchased 512 Mikado type (2-8-2) locomotives. By that year he had also purchased 27,000 new freight cars. In 1909 less than 800 miles of the road was laid with steel rail weighing 90 to 100 pounds per yard; by 1913 this figure had

more than tripled. Many bridges were rebuilt, and some single-track spans were replaced with double tracks. Some tunnels had their roofs blasted off and their grades lowered, while other single-track tunnels were replaced with new double-track bores. Soon Willard had completed plans to double-track the entire main line from Philadelphia through Baltimore, Washington, and Pittsburgh to Chicago. Between 1910 and 1917 Willard spent $139 million for additions, betterments, extensions, and new equipment.

Early in his presidency Willard announced that he would not advertise B&O passenger service until the road's tracks, engines, and cars were equal to the best in the nation. By 1913 he had added 150 new passenger cars to the equipment roster. The Pennsylvania Railroad had started to use steel passenger cars in 1898, but few such cars were seen on the Baltimore & Ohio until Willard became president. In 1911-1912 Willard ordered 78 steel passenger cars, and by 1917 nearly three-quarters of all B&O passenger traffic moved in steel cars and all first-class trains were described as electric-lighted vestibuled steel cars. On the eve of World War I B&O passengers did not travel as fast as those on the Pennsylvania or the New York Central, but they were as safe and comfortable.

Shortly after assuming the B&O presidency Willard was elected president of the American Railway Association. He was also chosen to represent the Eastern railroads in 1912 in settling a labor controversy with the locomotive engineers. The next year Willard spoke for the railroads as they sought a rate increase from the Interstate Commerce Commission (ICC).

The new president spent much of his time in inspection trips over his 4,000-mile system; some weeks found him out on the road two days for every one in the office. His business car, No. 99—the same number he had used on the Burlington—was always parked at the Camden Station, ready for use. The 99 was a "rolling office" filled with company records, files, and maps. The car steward and galley chef always had the car fully stocked with food and supplies for any length of trip.

No. 99 left on one of its longest trips on a Sunday evening in March 1913, taking Willard to a flood-stricken area in the Midwest. A tornado had brought torrential rains to the Ohio Valley; hundreds of lives were lost and nearly all the rail lines in Indiana, Ohio, and western Pennsylvania were ravaged by the high water. For several days only a single rail route was in operation between New York City and Chicago. Some 170 miles of the B&O main line were washed out, and over 400 miles were under water. Total property damage to the B&O exceeded $3 million and the loss in revenue was at least $1.5 million. Three days before leaving for the flood area Willard, who liked a good cigar, had given up smoking for a month in an annual exercise to maintain his self-discipline. As he moved from one emergency to another many of his co-workers offered him cigars, but the president kept the pledge he had made to himself.

By 1916 the B&O's total revenue had increased nearly 50 percent over that of 1910; this rise represented a real increase in traffic, since freight rates and passenger fares were quite stable during the period. Much of the increase in traffic occurred because the European nations fighting World War I were seeking more and more food and military supplies from America.

Late in October 1916 President Woodrow Wilson appointed Willard to the advisory commission to the newly established Council of National Defense. Willard moved into the Willard Hotel in Washington and was soon spending more time considering such subjects as wartime food control, conscription, and daylight-saving time than he was directing the Baltimore & Ohio. In March 1917 he was elected chairman of the advisory commission.

On April 6, 1917, the United States declared war on Germany. As the nation turned from neutrality to an all-out war effort the expanding economy quickly put a strain on the railroads. The increased regulation of the Progressive Era had made it difficult for the railways to obtain rate increases: the general price level had risen 30 percent between 1900 and 1915 but average freight rates had remained unchanged. Many lines had delayed maintenance and improvement programs, and in 1916 nearly a sixth of the national rail network was under receivership. Under the Federal Possession and Control Act of 1916 the president could take over the railways in an emergency; wishing to avoid such action, shortly after the declaration of war Willard invited fifty railroad presidents to meet in Washington to discuss the role of American railways in the war. The result was the creation of the Railroads' War Board, consisting of five railroad presidents with Fairfax

Harrison of the Southern Railway as chairman and Willard as an ex-officio member.

The Railroads' War Board sought to operate the rail system of America as if it were "a continental railway system." The board suggested the reduction of duplicate passenger services and heavier loading of freight cars, and set up pools of freight equipment to reduce car shortages. The problem was compounded by the fact that the railroads had fewer freight cars and engines in 1917 than in 1914. Bad planning, the issuance of too many "preference tags," the fact that most shipments were headed for Atlantic ports, and severe winter weather late in 1917 all combined to cause a major traffic crisis and a shortage of 158,000 freight cars. The ICC recommended that the government take over the railroads, and President Wilson ordered federal operation of the lines effective December 28, 1917, with William G. McAdoo as director general. The United States was the last of the warring nations to take such action. Willard was unhappy with government control, believing that his line had been prepared to meet almost any increased war traffic. During the twenty-six months of federal control Willard remained president of the B&O, but actual operation of the line was in the hands of men responsible to McAdoo.

With the increased war traffic the B&O's employment roster grew from 60,000 to 70,000 workers between 1916 and 1918. Total revenue increased from $117 million in 1916 to $140 million in 1917, $175 million in 1918, and $182 million in 1919, but operating expenses climbed faster than freight rates or total revenue: between 1916 and 1919 the average wages for labor, for example, rose from $891 to $1,485 per year. As a result the operating ratio of the B&O climbed from 72 in 1916 to 77 in 1917, 92 in 1918, and 93 in 1919.

In October 1918 General Pershing cabled the War Department that he needed a top railroad executive to straighten out the French railways in the American sector of the western front. Secretary of War Newton D. Baker invited Willard to go to France, and a colonel's commission was sent to Baltimore. At the end of October Willard's son Harold and Harold's wife died of influenza within twenty-four hours of one another. This double tragedy kept Willard from going to France.

In the early postwar years a great variety of opinion could be found about the future of the railroads. The most extreme suggestion was that of Glen E. Plumb, legal counsel for the operating unions, who proposed that the federal government purchase all the lines. Government ownership of railways was gaining acceptance in much of the world but the American public generally did not favor the idea. Willard, like most rail executives, favored private ownership with improved federal regulation. Wilson supported this view, and signed the Transportation Act of 1920 the day before the railroads were returned to private control on March 1. The legislation increased the size of the ICC and gave it increased control over railroad security issues, mergers, and efforts of the railways to earn a "fair rate of return."

The first two years of private operation were difficult for the B&O. Somehow the increased operating expenses and the 1920 operating ratio of 98 had to be reduced. Fortunately for the railroads, in the late summer of 1920 the ICC increased passenger fares and freight rates. Between 1920 and 1922 the cost of living declined 20 percent and the new Railroad Labor Board cut railroad wages by 12 percent, effective in July 1921. The B&O labor force dropped from 72,000 to 59,000 workers between the spring of 1920 and the spring of 1921. As a result, operating expenses declined from $226 million in 1920 to $165 million 1922, and the operating ratio fell to 82.

The Baltimore & Ohio faced a coal strike from April to August 1922, which caused a serious decline in coal traffic. Railroad shop craft workers refused a 10 percent wage cut ordered by the Railway Labor Board and walked off their jobs on July 1, 1922; Willard made a settlement with his shop men more easily than some of the other lines did with theirs, and the strike against the B&O ended in September.

Even though passenger traffic was declining on the Baltimore & Ohio in the 1920s, Willard believed that a first-class passenger service was essential to the prosperity of the line. In 1923 he told some long-time B&O workers that the essentials of good passenger service were: "1. To go safely—2. to go comfortably—3. to go on time." Two all-Pullman trains were inaugurated in the decade—the Capitol Limited to Chicago in May 1923 and the National Limited to St. Louis in April 1925. Each of the luxury trains provided such amenities as a lounge car, valet, maid, train secretary, manicure, and shower

bath. At the same time, Willard admitted that since 80 percent of his passengers did not ride the Pullmans, the B&O really was a "day coach road." The B&O president was proud of his railroad's reputation for fine food, and when No. 99 was at the rear of a passenger train Willard sometimes had food from the dining car sent back to the business car. If the president and his guests gave a favorable verdict on the Chesapeake Bay fish, or the crisp corn meal muffins, a personal thank-you note from Willard, and possibly his signed photograph, were often sent forward to the chef.

Much new motive power for both passenger and freight trains was acquired during the 1920s. The heavier steel passenger equipment purchased before World War I required more powerful engines, and between 1911 and 1917 Willard ordered 80 Baldwin Pacific type (4-6-2) locomotives for passenger service. The best-known B&O Pacific engines were the 20 ordered from Baldwin in 1927 and named for American presidents from Washington through Arthur; the olive green, gold-striped locomotives had 80-inch drivers and weighed 163 tons. Most of the freight engines purchased in the decade were Mikados (2-8-2), Santa Fes (2-10-2), or articulated Mallets. By 1927 the B&O included 600 sturdy Mikados in its roster. Most of the Mallets had a (2-8-8-0) wheel arrangement with 58-inch drivers, and weighed up to 250 tons. Willard's road was operating 135 of the huge engines by 1927.

Willard was certain that his line had suffered from undermaintenance during the twenty-six months of federal control and was not in the top-grade condition in 1920 that it had enjoyed on the eve of the war. During the 1920s more than $90 million was spent for additions and betterments for the line. Bridges were upgraded, the entire Metropolitan Branch northwest of Washington was improved, and grade crossings were eliminated or safeguarded throughout the system. A huge vegetable and produce terminal was constructed in Philadelphia and grain elevators and yard facilities were built at Locust Point in Baltimore.

During the decade Willard found time for things other than his railroad. In 1921 he was the chairman of the board of directors of the American Railroad Association, and in 1926 he was made a member of the board of American Telephone & Telegraph Company. President Hoover appointed him to the board of visitors of the U.S. Naval Academy.

Willard had been on the board of trustees of Johns Hopkins University since 1914, and in 1926 was elected president of that board. With his dark suits, derby or homburg, and sober haberdashery Willard could easily have been taken for a professor himself. He would send his steward, Jim Ennis, to a men's shop for an assortment of neckties, select one from the group, and send Ennis back to purchase a dozen of that style.

A major event of the decade was the celebration of the railroads's centennial in 1927; since the B&O was the first American railroad to offer scheduled freight and passenger service to the public, the celebration also marked the centennial of the entire rail industry. In 1925 Willard had employed Edward Hungerford, an author with long experience in public relations and advertising, to direct the year-long birthday party. The first event of importance in 1927 was the centenary dinner on February 28, 1927, 100 years after the Maryland legislature had granted a charter for the founding of the railroad. More than 950 guests, all male, crowded the main floor and boxes of the Lyric Theater plus the ballroom of the nearby Belvedere Hotel. The guest list included civic leaders from Baltimore, the entire Maryland legislature, important politicians from Washington, top B&O officials, representatives of railroad labor, and presidents of several railroads. With the Belvedere guests seated in the Lyric balcony, Willard called the meeting to order by ringing a silver-plated locomotive bell and introduced the speaker of the evening, former secretary of war Baker, a longtime friend of Willard and a director of the Baltimore & Ohio since 1923. The program concluded with a brief three-act pageant reviewing key events in the early history of the railroad. By 11:00 the party had ended, and special trains were soon leaving Mount Royal Station returning guests to Washington and New York City.

The other major event of the year was the Centenary Exhibition and Pageant of the Baltimore & Ohio Railroad, which came to be known as the Fair of the Iron Horse, in September and October. A site for the fair was selected near Halethrope, eight miles out of Baltimore on the B&O main line to Washington. A 500-foot-long Hall of Transportation contained a variety of railway exhibits, including thirty-two full-sized wooden models of early European and American locomotives. Two large miniature railroad layouts showed the development of the Baltimore & Ohio. Other exhibits covered developments in signals, brakes, track, bridges, and other rail equipment. Many historic American locomotives were on display in front of the exhibit hall. A parade track surrounded the exhibit area, permitting the movement and storage of rail equipment used in the pageant. Facing the pageant stage was an 800-foot-long grandstand with a seating capacity of 12,000. Willard and Hungerford had expected that daily attendance at the fair might be 20,000 to 25,000 people; in fact, the total attendance for the free twenty-three-day fair was over 1.25 million, or more that 50,000 a day.

The Baltimore & Ohio was a prosperous road in the 1920s and could easily afford the million dollars the centennial cost. During the decade revenue ranged between $200 million and $250 million a year, with annual net revenue between 1923 and 1929 of $50 million to $65 million. Between 1923 and 1929 the operating ratio ranged from 73 to 78. Dividends on the common stock were resumed in 1923; the stock had been as low as $27 a share in the early 1920s but was over $145 in the summer of 1929. In 1929 the National City Bank of New York wrote of the B&O: "It has also been demonstrated that its present heavy traffic is being handled with great efficiency and with a lower trend of costs of operation." That year the Baltimore & Ohio board reelected Willard at an annual salary of $150,000.

More than 1,600 men and women honored Willard at a testimonial dinner at the Lord Baltimore Hotel in Baltimore on January 13, 1930. The banquet was sponsored by the B&O's unions in recognition of Willard's score of years as president of the railroad. Labor leaders, railroad presidents, and government officials all praised Willard during the festive evening. William Green, president of the American Federation of Labor, was unable to be present at the party, but his telegram of congratulations concluded: "No man is more deserving than Mr. Willard of the honor and tribute which you and the representatives of labor will pay him." A few weeks later *Time* magazine endorsed the accolades given Willard when it wrote: "He has a conscience in dealing with labor. Any man can go directly to him with his troubles." Thirteen colleges and universities granted honorary degrees to Willard during his years with the Baltimore & Ohio.

But the euphoria did not last long. Monthly traffic reports throughout 1930 were not encouraging. Total revenues were only $206 million, nearly $40 million below those of 1929. Car loadings and revenue fell even faster the following year, and the total revenue for 1931 was more than $48 million below that of 1930. Expenses were cut, repairs and maintenance were delayed, and workers were laid off, but the operating ratio still climbed—from 73.6 in 1929 to nearly 76 in 1931. At the same time the interest charges on the funded debt increased from $29 million to $31 million a year. During this decline, on January 28, 1931, Willard reached the age of seventy; he submitted his resignation to his board of directors, but they would not consider his leaving the presidency.

Early in 1931 Willard discussed the financial problems facing the industry with several other railroad presidents. They agreed that a major boost in freight rates plus a pay reduction for labor would be required to solve the financial woes of the industry. Their request for a 15 percent increase in freight rates was denied, but the Interstate Commerce Commission finally approved a selective 3 percent boost. Few rail executives thought that labor would stand for any reduction in wages. Railroad labor leaders in the summer of 1931 were planning to ask Congress for legislation adopting a six-hour workday with no reduction in pay, and were pointing out that total railroad employment had dropped from 1,858,000 in 1923 to 1,661,000 in 1929 and 1,259,000 in 1931. Average annual pay of rail workers had declined from $1,744 in 1929 to $1,664 in 1931, but this reduction was caused not by a drop in pay scales but rather by a decline in hours of work. Between 1929 and 1931 the cost of living in the nation had dropped more than 10 percent.

Willard still thought that the brotherhoods might consider a voluntary cut in wages. In a meeting in October 1931 with several railroad presidents and the leaders of the operating unions he discovered that the labor leaders were at least willing to discuss the subject. Preliminary sessions were held late in 1931, with Willard the chairman of the carriers and David B. Robertson of the firemen's union the chairman for labor. It was agreed to hold a mammoth negotiating conference in Chicago during January 1932. For three weeks 1,500 leaders of twenty-one unions and nine railroad presidents

with all their assistants met in large and small sessions in the Palmer House and the Congress Hotel. Robertson, who had known Willard since their days on the Erie, told his fellow union leaders that Willard could be trusted to treat labor fairly. When asked about a reduction in the salaries of rail officials, Willard said his own salary had been cut 20 percent and that on November 1, 1931, all other B&O officials had taken reductions of at least 10 percent. Willard told the labor leaders he was confident that a wage reduction of 10 percent would mean that few additional workers would be laid off. Finally, late on Sunday evening, January 31, the labor leaders and the railroad presidents signed a document providing for a 10 percent wage reduction. When Willard started to return home to Baltimore he found that the labor leaders had placed a huge basket of flowers in his business car.

During the first year of the new wage agreement the railroads saved about $200 million; the savings on the B&O in 1932 were between $5 million and $6 million. But even with these savings 1932 was a crisis year for the Baltimore & Ohio. Total revenue was under $126 million, a decline of $32 million for the year; gross corporate income was about $6 million less than the fixed charges for the year. The financial deficit was compounded by the fact that the B&O had $63 million in twenty-year 4 1/2 percent convertible bonds that would mature on March 11, 1933; Willard and his top officials knew that the poor stock market conditions of 1932-1933 would make it next to impossible to refund or refinance the maturing securities. After lengthy negotiations in the summer and fall of 1932 with the ICC and the Reconstruction Finance Corporation (RFC) a refunding plan was approved on November 15. The RFC lent the B&O sufficient funds to repay half of the maturing bonds, with the bondholders accepting new 5 percent refunding and general mortgage bonds for the other half.

Since Willard and his top officials believed that the traffic drop in the winter of 1929-1930 was only temporary, no reduction was made in the improvement program for 1930. In 1931 few improvements were made and no money was spent on new equipment. During the rest of the 1930s few years saw more than one or two million dollars spent for improvements, and the total for the decade was little more than 30 percent of that spent during the 1920s. Ordinary track maintenance declined greatly; between 1930 and 1932 the man-hours of labor per mile of track fell by 60 percent. Far more equipment was retired than purchased between 1930 and 1940; the locomotive roster dropped from 2,364 to 2,065, freight cars from 102,000 to 83,000, and passenger cars from 1,732 to 1,274, while only 44 locomotives, nearly 13,000 freight cars, and 95 passenger cars were purchased. No new equipment was acquired during 1931, 1933, or 1934.

Even with the shortages of money Willard managed some innovations and improvements in service on his railroad during the decade. Of the forty-four locomotives purchased, thirty-seven were diesels, including several new passenger units plus twenty-five switch engines. (The first diesel owned by the B & O—a small sixty-ton, 300-horsepower switcher purchased in the 1920s for use in Manhattan—had been one of the first diesels in the nation.) Willard was also a pioneer in the introduction of air conditioning for passenger trains. On May 24, 1931, the B&O began operating the first completely air-conditioned passenger train, the Columbian, between Washington and New York City. The *Los Angeles Times* remarked that in the West, "we refrigerate our fruit but roast our passengers." By 1936 the B&O had air conditioning in 275 of its passenger cars. Willard insisted that he would permit air conditioning in his No. 99 only after it was installed in all principal through trains. In the middle 1930s Willard introduced two new streamliner passenger trains with air conditioning and diesel power. A survey of businessmen gave B&O passenger service high marks for cleanliness, temperature control, service, food, and equipment. B&O passenger travel was also safe: in 1935 the *Baltimore & Ohio Magazine* pointed out that no B&O passenger had lost his life since May 1919. Even so, Willard knew that his passenger trains were in a losing battle with the family automobile. In 1931 he said, "The railroads will never get back the travel constantly turning to private automobiles. The public likes to ride in its own car."

Improvements were also made in freight service. A free pickup and delivery service for some less-than-carload freight shipments was put into effect in 1936 by the B&O and other eastern railroads. Since World War I the operating efficiency of freight service on the Baltimore & Ohio had greatly increased. Such gains helped offset losses to trucks in the 1930s in shipments of automobiles, citrus fruit, livestock, and less-than-carload freight.

Willard's road enjoyed a modest growth in traffic in the mid 1930s and between 1932 and 1937 annual revenues grew each year, increasing a total of more than 30 percent in the six years. Additional help was obtained from the Reconstruction Finance Corporation and by 1937 the RFC debt had climbed to $87 million. The greatest financial crisis for Willard came in 1938, when gross revenue dropped nearly $35 million, the operating ratio rose to 78, and the deficit for the year was a record $13 million. Even worse was the fact that debt obligations of $185 million (including the RFC debt) were due to nature by 1942.

But Willard had some good friends in his time of need. Whenever President Roosevelt journeyed to Hyde Park he took the B&O, which he considered his favorite railroad. Willard also had many friends in Congress who viewed the B&O executive as a liberal with a good railway labor record. In January 1938 Willard obtained another RFC loan of more than $8 million, and in November the ICC permitted him to initiate a plan for a moratorium on bond interest payments. As Congress considered the proposed plan in the spring of 1939 Willard declared: "If I thought business conditions were to remain as bad as they are, I would say put us in receivership." In July Congress passed and President Roosevelt signed the Chandler Bill, which provided for a modification of interest on B&O securities and lowered annual fixed charges to $19 million for eight years. A large majority of the bondholders approved the modification plan. The federal government had saved the railroad from receivership. Willard's confidence seemed justified, for B&O revenues bounced back to $161 million in 1939 and $179 million in 1940.

When World War II started in Europe in 1939 President Roosevelt asked Willard and Carl Gray, the retired president of the Union Pacific, to study the capacity of the country's rail system to handle the traffic that would result from a defense buildup. A year later, on May 17, 1940, Willard's second son, Daniel, Jr., died at the age of forty-six.

Every year after his seventieth birthday, except for the financial crisis year of 1938, Willard had placed his resignation before his board. Each time it was unanimously declined. Since he loved his job and his health was good, Willard did not press the matter. In May 1941, a few months after his eightieth birthday, Willard once again offered his resignation, with the strong suggestion it should be accepted. The board acceded to his request with reluctance, and on June 1, 1941, elected him chairman. He was to receive the same salary for the chairmanship, $60,000 a year, that he had been paid as president; his pay had been cut to that figure in 1937-1938 when the line was near receivership. In 1941 Willard owned 1,005 shares of common stock that had paid no dividends for a decade. As he gave up the presidency he had held for thirty-one years Willard said: "I wish I were only sixty and could keep on, I love it."

The former president served only thirteen months as chairman of the Baltimore & Ohio board. After being ill about six weeks, Willard died in Union Memorial Hospital in Baltimore on July 6, 1942. He was buried in the family plot at Hartland, and was survived by his wife and four grandchildren. His fellow board members wrote of Willard: "His leadership in employer-employee relations was an asset not only to the Baltimore & Ohio but redounded also to the benefit of industry generally and to the country as a whole." In his note of condolence President Roosevelt wrote: "Daniel Willard was one of the great figures in modern railroading."

Willard's long career spanned the years from the days of Jay Gould and James J. Hill to an era of strict federal regulation and the New Deal. In his more than six decades of railroad service he moved from the woodburner to the diesel—from the Golden Age of railroading to the beginning of decline for the industry. Throughout his long life Willard remained a Vermonter with the traits of the people of that state—the self-reliance, independence, honesty, and integrity so well known by his associates. Willard was not a railroad owner but an operator and executive—a "railroad man," as his fellow B&O workers viewed him. His successful career owed much to the nearly twenty years of managerial apprenticeship under Frederick D. Underwood and James J. Hill. Though conservative in politics, Willard was liberal in his relations with labor. His passion for exact information and his deep-seated curiosity helped give substance to the cool-headed persuasiveness which was so successful with both labor and management. Upon his retirement from active management of the Baltimore & Ohio he was one of the most widely known and respected of all American railway executives.

References:

"Great Northern Pacific," *Time*, 15 (March 3, 1930): 45;

Edward Hungerford, *Daniel Willard Rides the Line. The Story of a Great Railroad Man* (New York: Putnam's, 1938);

Hungerford, *The Story of the Baltimore & Ohio Railroad, 1827-1927* (New York: Putnam's, 1928);

Richard C. Overton, *Burlington Route: The History of the Burlington Lines* (New York: Knopf, 1965);

John F. Stover, *History of the Baltimore & Ohio Railroad* (West Lafayette, Ind.: Purdue University Press, 1987).

Robert E. Woodruff

(11 September 1884–21 September 1967)

by Richard Saunders

Clemson University

Robert E. Woodruff in 1944, explaining an instructional chart used in the Erie Railroad's training program for supervisory personnel (AP/Wide World Photos)

CAREER: Track laborer, foreman, transitman, inspector (1905-1906), assistant division engineer (1906), division engineer (1906-1908), trainmaster (1908-1909), general agent (1909-1910), superintendent (1910-1917), superintendent of transportation, Lines West of Salamanca, New York (1917–1918), general superintendent, Lines West of Salamanca, New York (1918-1920), regional manager (1920-1922), superintendent (1922-1927), general manager, Eastern District (1927–1928), assistant vice president, system (1928-1929), vice president in charge of operations and maintenance (1929-1939), trustee and chief executive officer (1939-1941), president (1941–1949), chairman of the board (1949-1956), director (1956-1959), Erie Railroad.

Robert Eastman Woodruff was born on a farm near Green Bay, Wisconsin, on September 11, 1884, to Walter Harold and Bel Eastman Woodruff. The family moved to Benton Harbor, Michigan, where Woodruff finished high school in 1901. After receiving a bachelor of science degree in civil engineering from Purdue University in 1905 he was offered a job in the engineering department of the Erie Railroad; but Woodruff sensed that regardless of his degree, he should start on the track in traditional railroad fashion. His great sense of tradition was a hallmark of his career and would prove to be both a strength and a weakness.

He rose quickly, becoming an inspector at the Kent, Ohio, roundhouse and then at the Cleveland ore docks. A year after he hired on, he was made assistant division engineer, first on the Mahoning Division, then on the Meadville Division, and then at the Chicago terminals. In 1910 he was made superintendent of the Rochester Division, which was off the mainline and burdened with an interurban commuter operation. In 1912 he became superintendent of the Kent Division on the most difficult section of the main line, where the railroad crossed the hills and valleys of eastern Ohio in the old Connecticut Western Reserve on almost continuous 1 percent grades. During World War I he returned as superintendent to the Mahoning Division, the road's busy line into Cleveland, and then was made general superintendent of all lines west of Salamanca, New York.

In 1920, in one of Erie president Frederick Underwood's attempts to restructure his administration, Woodruff was sent to Hornell, New York, to become manager of the newly created Hornell Region. Hornell was a bustling little silk- and beer-making city of 15,000 in the Allegheny foothills of New York's southern tier. It was also the nexus of the Erie Railroad—the site of its major locomotive shops, the junction of three divisions, and the point where the Great Lakes-to-the-sea line to Buffalo diverged from the New York-Chicago main line. The Erie was the town's largest employer; Erie men tended to swagger and the young Woodruff was the up-and-coming prince of the town's most elite organization. His neighbors in Hornell recalled later that they always knew he was destined to move up. He was friendly and always had a healthy sense of modesty, but was treated with a certain deference even by the heirs of pioneer families at the Presbyterian Church he attended.

The concept of the Hornell Region was short-lived, however, and in 1922 Woodruff was sent to Buffalo to take charge of the railroad's busy interchange and lake terminal operations. Though a branch, this was one of the key divisions of the Erie. While there, he wrote *The Making of a Railroad Officer*, his philosophy of what it took to run a mighty artery of transportation—work hard, have respect for those below, and get out on the line and know the operation. He stayed in Buffalo until 1927, when, with the road under Van Sweringen control and John J. Bernet as president, he became regional manager of all lines east of Buffalo. He was made assistant vice president of the Erie system in 1928. On May 28, 1929, he succeeded John Denney, who had moved up to the presidency, as vice president of operations and maintenance.

Denney and Woodruff guided the Erie through the Great Depression. The railroad tightened its belt; it made the "Van Sweringen" Berkshire steam locomotive (designed by the Van Sweringen roads' joint Advisory Mechanical Committee) the workhorse of its freight fleet; and, under Woodruff's direction, it double-tracked much of its line across eastern Ohio to eliminate what was, even at Depression levels of traffic, a bottleneck. That the Erie might be included in a grand consolidation with the Chesapeake & Ohio and other Van Sweringen railroads was a constant possibility. It was not clear, if that happened, how much of the Erie's management would be retained; but despite the uncertainty about his future, Woodruff married Marian Clough in 1936. They had two daughters.

The Erie might have survived the Depression had it not been for its enormous debt, the legacy of the Erie Ring of the nineteenth century, which two subsequent bankruptcies had failed to reduce. The railroad entered receivership on January 18, 1938, and on October 18, 1939, with Denney departing for the presidency of the Northern Pacific, Woodruff was named trustee and chief executive officer.

As part of the retrenchment imposed by bankruptcy, Woodruff did his best to prune the railroad of marginal operations. He extricated it from the Rochester commuter business and eliminated most branch line passenger service except that from New York to Cleveland and Buffalo, but failed to win Interstate Commerce Commission approval to abandon a portion of the Rochester Division that was deemed redundant. Concessions were extracted from key creditors, and the Erie's complex debt structure, which consisted of nine separate, overlapping bond issues on the original mainline across New York State, was simplified into two, the first not due until 1964. The Erie had seemed destined to a decade of wrangling by creditors, but it emerged from receivership on December 22, 1941, with Woodruff as president.

In retrospect, however, it can be seen that the debt was not reduced nearly enough. The Erie's leveraged debt per mile remained well above the industry average, a burden that became a terrible impediment in the merger discussions of the late 1950s and precluded the railroad from finding a safe haven in the Norfolk & Western in the 1960s. The question must be raised whether Woodruff might have spoken more forcefully for the needs of the railroad as opposed to the needs of creditors, or whether he was too eager to become master in his own house.

Nevertheless, with reorganization behind it, the Erie under Woodruff appeared to prosper. During World War II it fielded two railroad battalions for the army, the 735th and the 765th, both of which played important roles in the push across the Rhine. In 1944 Woodruff solved the road's perennial problems across eastern Ohio by buying four-unit diesel locomotives that could move 5,000-ton trains across the hilly terrain. The cost was $3 million for the locomotives and another $1 million for servicing facilities; the alternative was the construction of new alignments and multiple tracks for $16 million. Everyone seemed pleased at how inexpensively the problem was solved. When the war was over and restrictions on the purchase of new locomotives ended, Woodruff plunged the Erie into full dieselization.

In the Woodruff years, the Erie was perhaps the quintessential American railroad. Its track was excellent; the morale of its people was high; its tonnage was increasing, particularly its share of the prestige perishable traffic from the West; its passenger service was modest but conducted with pride, while the more than 30 million commuters a year that passed through its Jersey City Terminal gave at least the illusion that it was a major passenger carrier; it advertised regularly in national and local publications; it covered fixed charges; and on June 19, 1942, for the first time in sixty-nine years, it paid dividends on its common stock.

Woodruff loved the railroad, and by all accounts, loved and was loved by the people who worked for it. He had a warm personality, preferred first names, and reflected the values of the small towns from which he came and which the Erie served. He took pride in the classes he set up to further the skills of his employees. He was so proud of the number of former Erie men who went on to become officers and even presidents of other railroads that he gave out I-Worked-for-the-Erie Club pins and held reunion dinners. The success of his former employees reinforced his sense that the Erie way of running a railroad was the best way. He had good words for labor unions, telling a convention of his undergraduate fraternity, Theta Xi, that labor did not get enough in the old days and that the unions had helped to rectify the situation. But he deplored socialism in articles in *Railway Age* and elsewhere, apparently believing that the United States was about to recklessly turn to it. His fears, about which he was outspoken, reflected the paranoia that gripped many American railroad executives in the wake of British railway nationalization following World War II.

Woodruff retired from the presidency on October 1, 1949, and became chairman of the board. He was a fatherly presence in the summer-long celebrations in 1951 that marked the railroad's centennial. His 1945 address on the beginnings of the Erie was updated and reprinted for the occasion. He was immensely proud of what he had built.

But all was not well: the Erie was, in fact, on the eve of a painful decline that would lead to a weak-sister merger with the Lackawanna in 1960, a court-ordered guardianship by the Norfolk & Western (under its Dereco subsidiary) in 1967, bankruptcy in 1972, inclusion in Conrail in 1976, and dismemberment by Conrail thereafter. The decline was not all Erie's fault, and certainly not all Woodruff's. But it must be asked what might have been done during the railroad's brief "Indian summer" of prosperity to forestall its subsequent decline, and whether, in the long run, the Erie would have been better served by being led by men with new ideas rather than men steeped in the Erie way of doing things.

Woodruff stepped down as chairman on October 24, 1956, when Paul W. Johnston left the presidency to become chairman and Harry von Willer became president. He remained on the board until 1958, when he retired to Delray Beach, Florida. He died on September 21, 1967.

Publications:

The Making of a Railroad Officer (Chicago: Simmons-Boardman, 1925);

Erie Railroad–Its Beginnings! 1851 (New York: Newcomen Society of England, American Branch, 1945); reprinted as *Erie Railroad: Its Beginnings and Today* (Cleveland [?]: Railroad, 1951);

"Preserving the American Way," *The Unicorn of Theta Xi*, 48 (October 1951): 20-21.

References:

"A Brief Look at the Erie Today," *Railway Age*, 31 (May 14, 1951: 86-87;

Edward Hungerford, *Men of Erie* (New York, Random House, 1946);

Henry S. Sturgis, *A New Chapter of Erie: The Story of Erie's Reorganization, 1938-1941* (New York, 1948).

"R. E. Woodruff Becomes Erie Chairman Oct. 1; P. W. Johnston Will Be New President," *Railway Age*, 127 (September 24, 1949): 56-57.

Archives:

Erie Railroad papers are at Syracuse University Library, Syracuse, New York, and at Eleutherian Mills Historical Library, Wilmington, Delaware.

Benjamin Franklin Yoakum

(August 20, 1859-November 28, 1929)

by Don L. Hofsommer

Augustana College

Benjamin F. Yoakum

CAREER: Freight clerk, Southern Pacific Railroad (circa 1877); rodman, general passenger agent, division freight agent, International & Great Northern Railroad (*circa* 1878-*circa* 1883); chief clerk and head of sales, traffic manager, assistant general manager (1884-1888), general manager (1888-1890), receiver (1890-1893), San Antonio & Aransas Pass Railway; general manager and third vice president, Gulf, Colorado & Santa Fe Railway (1893-1896); vice president and general manager (1896-1900), president (1900-1904), St. Louis & San Francisco Railroad; president and chairman of the board, Chicago & Eastern Illinois Railroad (1902-1905); chairman of the executive committee, St. Louis & San Francisco Railroad and Kansas City, Fort Scott & Memphis Railway (1904-1914); chairman of the board of directors and of the executive committee, St. Louis, Brownsville & Mexico Railway (1905-1914); chairman of the executive committee, Chicago & Eastern Illinois Railroad (1905-1909); chairman of the executive committee, Chicago, Rock Island & Pacific Railway (1905-1909); chairman of the board of directors, St. Louis & San Francisco Railroad and Chicago & Eastern Illinois Railroad (1909-1913); director, Seaboard Air Line Railway (1914-1922); chairman of the board, Empire Bond and Mortgage Corporation (1924-1929).

In 1912 *The World's Work* called Benjamin Franklin Yoakum "the empire builder of the Southwest," and clearly Yoakum cut a wide swath in the railroad industry during the early years of the twentieth century. But his star was tarnished by overexpansion and fell as quickly as it rose.

Born in Limestone County, Texas, in 1859, the son of Franklin Yoakum, a country physician who gave up his practice to become president of what became Trinity University, and Narcisus Teague Yoakum. Neither the halls of ivy nor the practice of medicine beckoned to the young man, however; instead, the call of the iron horse attracted him. His first job was as a freight clerk in Houston for the Southern Pacific. He soon became a chain bearer in a surveying party locating the International & Great Northern Railroad into Palestine, Texas, and moved up to the position of division freight agent in San Antonio.

Even as a youth, Yoakum exhibited an unbounded enthusiasm for Texas and the opportunities to be found there. This attribute attracted the attention of Jay Gould, who hired him as a "land-boomer," steering immigrants from Europe to farm lands being opened along the Gould lines. Yoakum's exuberance about the Lone Star State also appealed to Uriah Lott, who hired Yoakum away from Gould to become chief clerk and head of sales for the fledgling San Antonio & Aransas Pass (SAP) — Lott's new road pledged to link San Antonio with the Gulf. Yoakum became traffic manager of the SAP in 1884. The following year he married Elizabeth Bennett of San Antonio; they had two daughters. Yoakum was made general manager of the SAP in 1888 and, when the road went bankrupt in 1890, he was named one of its receivers. After holding that position for two years, Yoakum went to the Gulf, Colorado & Santa Fe as general manager and third vice president. In 1896 he was named vice president and general manager of the St. Louis & San Francisco Railroad (Frisco); he became president in 1900 and chairman of the executive committee in 1904.

Under Yoakum's leadership the Frisco experienced a meteoric rise. He pushed massive construction projects, purchased a number of important short lines, and in 1902 gained control of the Chicago & Eastern Illinois (C&EI) for the Frisco. In 1901 control of the Chicago, Rock Island & Pacific Railway had passed to William B. Leeds, Daniel Reid, and W. H. and J. H. Moore — a combination known as the Reid-Moore syndicate — who were determined to expand the Rock Island's dominion. Yoakum's Frisco checkmated the Rock Island in several skirmishes, and in 1903 he and the Reid-Moore forces reached an accommodation that placed him on the Rock Island's board of directors. A year later Yoakum's man, Benjamin L. Winchell, became the Rock Island's president.

Yoakum's burning desire to reach Dallas and Fort Worth with the Frisco had been satisfied in 1902, but that success only fueled his ambitions. Houston, the Rio Grande Valley, and several locations in Louisiana appeared tantalizingly on maps adorning his office. Should he move toward any of these areas, he would court the wrath of a jealous Edward H. Harriman; but Yoakum plunged ahead. In 1905 he took control of the Trinity & Brazos Valley Railroad, which, with additional construction and trackage rights, offered a new line competitive with one of Harriman's roads between Dallas and Houston. Harriman had sought to forestall this eventuality and had even urged Yoakum to take a half-interest in his company rather than prosecute new construction, but the State of Texas would not allow the arrangement. The Trinity & Brazos Valley served as a funnel for both the Rock Island and the Frisco and, after the Colorado & Southern and the Fort Worth & Denver City came under the wing of the Chicago, Burlington & Quincy, for that system as well. Yoakum formed the Houston Belt & Terminal to provide yard facilities for the Trinity & Brazos Valley at Houston and also to compete further with the Harriman roads.

Another of Yoakum's projects was the Gulf Coast Lines, which, he hoped, would link Memphis and New Orleans with Houston and the Rio Grande Valley. Harriman, whose lines in Louisiana would be hurt by this competition threatened to build "mile-for-mile" parallel lines in the Rio Grande Valley. Yoakum was better connected politically in Texas, however, and he prevailed. Work began just west of Corpus Christi in 1903 and the first train entered Brownsville in 1904; through service between Houston and the Rio Grande Valley began in 1907. Additional construction, acquisition of short lines, and trackage agreements finally gave the Gulf Coast Lines a somewhat indirect route to New Orleans by the end of 1907.

Yoakum instituted the Frisco System Land and Immigration Association to promote settlement in the Rio Grande Valley; in 1906 alone it brought in 11,700 homeseekers with special round — trip fares of $15 from Minneapolis, Chicago, or St. Louis. At the same time Yoakum paid agricultural educators from all over the country to evaluate the territory and make recommendations. Out of this project came the truck farming and fruit growing businesses that have made the Rio Grande Valley famous.

Yoakum was considered a good manager. He spent time on the property, becoming familiar with its characteristics and getting to know his officers as well as the rank and file. He also visited with shippers and learned their needs.

At the apex of his power and prestige between 1903 and 1913, Yoakum's views on a variety of subjects were sought by the popular media. *The World's Work* noted in 1912 that Yoakum had "devoted a large share of his thought to the problem of the high cost of living and . . . has formulated practical suggestions for solving it." Yoakum was particularly concerned with the problems of farmers. "The foundations of a permanent agriculture in any country," he argued, would be "laid only when the land is made to support as many families, owning their own land, as that land can support." Therefore, the central question was whether the individual farmer was being supplied with ample capital at reasonable rates. The answer in the United States, Yoakum believed, was no. The conclusion, he feared, was that the development of agricultural sections could not reach "full strength or work out to anything approximating final destiny." Yoakum advocated the creation in the federal government of a bureau of marketing to "collect accurate and complete records of the prices of farm products in all markets of the country and distribute these records in the form of bulletins to farmers of the country." He toyed with the notion of farmers' cooperatives — especially applauding efforts of that type in Denmark — and, to save lives and enhance property values, he urged that machinery used in constructing the Panama Canal be returned to the United States for use in federally sponsored flood-control projects along the Mississippi River.

Yoakum also addressed issues involving the railroad industry. Like many other rail leaders, he worried that "continual agitation against the railroads" would result in the decline of business and national prosperity. The crucial issue, he felt, was ignorance: the people of the country simply did not have the facts. Had they such accurate information they would render proper judgments. Consequently, this husky, broad-shouldered Texan set out on the "sawdust trail" to take his "new religion" to clubs, societies, labor unions, and any other audience that would have him. He had no quarrel with the underlying principles of the Theodore Roosevelt administration toward business, he told *Harper's Weekly* in 1908, and declared that the Hepburn Act was "not burdensome." No new rules or regulations were required, though, and any minor adjustments in the laws could be taken car of over time "through cooperation of the railroads with the Interstate Commerce Commission." He believed that railroad company accounts should be "subject to inspection by the Government, as openly and as freely as the accounts of a national bank." This practice, he felt, would result in "fair rates and equitable dealings" and afford the investor a "proper test of value for the securities he buys or owns."

By late 1912 Yoakum was less sanguine. He noted that in the United States railroad business was the largest industry, that it supported 1.7 million employees, and that it was the largest consumer of manufactured products. Yet the industry was increasingly out of favor with investors, who pointed to the "high cost of railroading" and wondered if "new railroads can be operated at a profit." Ever the expansionist, Yoakum was deeply troubled by this attitude. East of the Mississippi, he observed, the ratio of acres of land to miles of railroad was 5,000-to-1, but in the West it was 13,000-to-1. "Oklahoma is only half supplied with railroads," he believed. "Arkansas is barely prospected, Louisiana is short of transportation to develop the state." Worst of all, he fretted, "Texas needs very badly at least 10,000 miles of new line." Attracting monies for such expansive undertakings, Yoakum noted, would be difficult under the current conditions. Some legislation dealing with railroads in the last dozen years had been "salutary," but most of it, he increasingly believed, had been "restrictive, prohibitive, regulative."

There was good reason for Yoakum to be concerned — not just at an abstract level, but more immediately. In 1909 the Rock Island ran into financial difficulties as bonds that had facilitated expansion came due. A rift developed between Yoakum and the Reid-Moore syndicate, the association between the Rock Island and the Frisco was dissolved, and both roads tottered toward financial disaster. The Frisco and the C&EI entered separate bankruptcies in 1913, and the Rock Island followed two years later.

Yoakum argued that the Frisco's problems were the result of natural disaster; increased costs of labor, taxes, and materials; restrictive government regulations; and the inability to raise rates to protect the credit of the company. Others pointed to the Frisco's excessive use of junior bonds (bonds following those issued earlier) and short-term notes, and to the fact that the company's bond and note obligations represented a disproportionate part of debt. The financial analyst John Moody asserted that the Frisco under Yoakum's leadership had taken on too much debt in acquiring "feeders" that had probably future value but represented poor sources of immediate traffic and income. A particular liability, Moody charged, was Yoakum's grand

project in the Gulf coast region of Texas and Louisiana. Most damaging of all to Yoakum's reputation was an accusation by the Interstate Commerce Commission that he had made substantial profits in directing the affairs of the Frisco at the expense of the company.

Yoakum was a director of the Seaboard Air Line Railway from 1914 to 1922 and chairman of the board of the Empire Bond and Mortgage Corporation from 1924 until his death. He died in New York City in 1929, largely a forgotten man in the American railroad industry.

References:

James L. Allhands, *Looking Back Over 98 Years: The Autobiography of James L. Allhands* (Malibu, Cal.: Pepperdine University, 1978);

"The High Cost of Farming," *The World's Work*, 24 (September 1912): 474, 519 – 533;

St. Clair Griffin Reed, *A History of the Texas Railroads and of Transportation Conditions Under Spain and Mexico and the Republic and the State* (Houston: St. Clair, 1941).

Robert R. Young

(February 14, 1897–January 25, 1958)

by Charles V. Bias

Marshall University

Robert R. Young (Courtesy CSX Corporation)

CAREER: Rifle powder cutter (1916), shift clerk (1916-1917), junior engineer (1917), assistant treasurer (1917-1920), E. I. du Pont de Nemours Company; treasurer, Domestic Dehydrator Corporation (1921-1922); assistant treasurer, Allied Chemical and Dye Company (1922-1923); financial department (1923-1928), assistant treasurer (1928), General Motors; treasurer, Equishares Corporation (1928-1931); founder and head, Young, Kolbe and Company (1931-1937); chairman of the board, Alleghany Corporation (1937-1958); chairman of the board, Chesapeake & Ohio Railway Company (1942-1954); chairman of the board, New York Cen-

tral Railroad System (1954-1958).

Robert R. Young was a brilliant Wall Street financier who became one of America's most colorful railroad men by taking control of the Alleghany Corporation, a holding company that controlled the Chesapeake & Ohio Railway (C&O), the New York, Chicago & St. Louis Railroad (Nickel Plate or NKP), and the Pere Marquette Railway (PM). He extended and improved those lines and tried for years to merge the C&O with the New York Central System (NYC) to create a great Eastern trunk line. He failed in that attempt, as he did in his efforts to revitalize rail passenger service in the United States, but went on to become chairman of the NYC and preside over the beginning of a return to prosperity for that road. National economic conditions, however, caused a downturn in the fortunes of the Central and of Young himself, and he ended his life a suicide.

Born in the frontier village of Canadian in the Texas panhandle on February 14, 1897, Robert Ralph Young was the son of David John Young, a banker, and Mary Arabella Moody Young. Even though his family was relatively wealthy, Young was not reared in a plush environment. The youngest of three children, Young grew up accustomed to a free, out-of-doors life, which included hunting prairie chickens and cottontail rabbits; at an early age he became an expert rifleman. His mother, who had lived the harsh life of a pioneer woman, regaled him with stories of fighting Indians and Mexicans. It was from his mother, who spent many evenings reading poetry to the children, that he acquired a taste for books.

Smaller than other boys his age, Young tried to dominate them with his wit, imagination, and skill. Because of his disproportionately large round head, yellow hair, and ruddy complexion, always badly burned by the Texas sun, he received the nickname "Punkin Head," later shortened to "Punk." Another, more prophetic nickname, based on his initials, was "Railroad" Young. After his mother died when he was ten years old, Young would hike or ride alone over the "golden billows" of the prairies following great "shining dust clouds," as he afterwards phrased it in the poems that he wrote; for the rest of his life, he was subject to periods of deep depression.

The schools in Canadian did not challenge Young's superior intelligence; the local Baptist Academy judged him "to be sharp as a tack but wild." Therefore, his father sent him to Culver Military Academy in Indiana in an attempt to eliminate his "misbehavior." At Culver he frequently received demerits for his "devilish conduct," which included shooting pool and drinking beer, but he finished at the head of his class, excelling in mathematics and English. At graduation he was offered the opportunity to be the class valedictorian, but, in an uncharacteristic display of shyness, Young declined the honor.

His academic record at Culver earned him a scholarship to the University of Virginia. Again, however, his "devilish" conduct emerged. Only seventeen years of age and freed of the discipline of the military school, his scholastic record declined. He rivaled most of his classmates in the extracurricular arts of poker and crapshooting and became a promising member of the University of Virginia Drinking Society. At the end of his sophomore year, Young failed to appear for his final examinations, thus ending his college career in the spring of 1916. Later he remarked, "I just cracked up."

Meanwhile, he had fallen in love with the beautiful Anita O'Keeffe, whom he had met at a university social function; she was the sister of the painter Georgia O'Keeffe. In April 1916, without parental approval, they were married.

A few weeks later, Young returned to Texas without his bride, fearing that his marriage might alienate his father. In the event, it was Young who terminated relations with his father. He did not relish the idea of working in his father's bank, and he did not like the woman his father had recently married. Within two weeks after his return to Canadian, he left to rejoin his wife in Virginia.

World War I had begun, and Young took a job cutting rifle powder at the E. I. du Pont de Nemours plant in Carney's Point, New Jersey. At the end of six months he was promoted to shift clerk, and within another year he was transferred to the mechanical department as a junior engineer. At the end of 1917 the company assigned him to its main plant in Wilmington, Delaware, as assistant treasurer.

In the autumn of 1920 he quit du Pont and moved to New York City, where he invested $5,000 that he had inherited from his mother's estate in an independent business venture, the Domestic Dehydrator Corporation. The business failed six months later. In 1921 he found a position similar to the one he had held at du Pont with the Allied Chemical and Dye Company. The following year he moved to the financial department of General Motors, starting at $100 a week and becoming an assistant treasurer at a salary of $35,000 a year in 1928. Later, Young stated that in this position "I received a training in corporate finance and accounting practices which could have been equalled in almost no other job in the country."

When John J. Raskob, chairman of the General Motors financial committee, resigned at the end of 1928, he offered Young employment as treasurer of his Equishares Corporation, in which Pierre S. du Pont was also involved. Young accepted the offer, feeling that with General Motors he had reached the position of waiting for someone to die so that he could become a vice president.

As the person in charge of Raskob's stock market operations and his representative in many corporations, Young developed an astute knowledge of the stock market. He illustrated his expertise by recommending in June 1929 that Raskob sell many of his stock holdings before stock prices began to decline. Raskob ignored Young's advice and lost much of his fortune. Young, on the other hand, sold practically all of his holdings while prices were still high.

In 1931 Young formed his own firm, Young, Kolbe and Company, and acquired a seat on the New York Stock Exchange. His junior partner, Frank F. Kolbe, who had worked with Young in the financial department of General Motors, was a perspicacious analyst of the securities of corporations that had fallen into receivership. Following Kolbe's advice, the new company purchased bankrupt firms and managed their successful reorganization.

In the autumn of 1934 the Alleghany Corporation went into receivership; a year later, on September 30, 1935, the controlling stock in Alleghany, owned by O. P. Van Sweringen, was sold at a forced auction by J. P. Morgan, to whom Van Sweringen's securities had been pledged. Young was eager to gain control of the Alleghany: although the corporation was insolvent at that time, it controlled a rail system of 23,000 miles through the heart of America as well as many other companies, most of which were bankrupt. When the bidding was over, a new holding company, the Midamerica Corporation, headed by George A. Ball of Muncie, Indiana, a manufacturer of canning jars, had purchased control of Alleghany for approximately $3.1 million. But Van Sweringen had devised a plan whereby Ball would buy Alleghany and Van Sweringen would continue to run the companies involved.

Young had been buying Alleghany's preferred stock and closely watching its affairs since 1933. His forecast that the company's stock would have a sensational rise was proven accurate during the recovery markets of 1935 and 1936. By December 1936 Alleghany's receivership had ended.

Van Sweringen had died in November, leaving the aging Ball in charge of the company. Ball decided to sell his interest, and in April 1937 a group consisting of Young, Kolbe, and Allan P. Kirby, heir to the Woolworth fortune, acquired 43 percent of the stock of the Alleghany Corporation, which controlled the Chesapeake & Ohio, Pere Marquette, Nickel Plate, Wheeling & Lake Erie, and Missouri Pacific railroads. Young was elected chairman of Alleghany. On December 13, 1967, Kolbe sold his interest in Alleghany to Young and Kirby. Finally, in 1942, after five years of negotiations and litigation, the George A. and Francis Ball Foundation transferred its holdings in the Alleghany Corporation to Young and Kirby, giving them majority control. The C&O's board of directors elected Young chairman. Young then ousted the president of the C&O, George D. Brooke, and replaced him with his own lawyer, Carl E. Newton.

The acquisition of the Chesapeake & Ohio, Nickel Plate, and Pere Marquette by Young and Kirby did not go unchallenged. In March 1944 E. E. Boles, assistant director of the Bureau of Finance of the Interstate Commerce Commission (ICC), recommended that the commission declare the Alleghany Corporation's control of the three rail-roads illegal and the order the company to divest itself of these holdings. Boles charged that Alleghany had gained control of the railroads without the ICC approval required by the Transportation Act of 1940.

At the ICC's hearings on the charges, Young and Kirby marshaled a mountain of evidence showing that since they assumed majority control of the lines, management had been consistent with the public interest. A battery of shippers, economists, railroad officials, analysts, and union officials supported their contention. The Alleghany exhibit revealed that between 1923 and 1942 inclusive, the C&O, Nickel Plate, and Pere Marquette had increased their investments in transportation property by 64 percent, 51 percent, and 37 percent, respectively, compared with an increase of 24 percent for all Class 1 railroads. Furthermore, between 1923 and 1943 the three railroads spent nearly $600 million for major improvements. All but a small part of the $395 million expended by the C&O directly contributed to increasing the volume and speed of service rendered to the public. Young and Kirby emphasized that many of the advances had occurred after 1937, when they acquired partial interest in the Alleghany Corporation. In addition, Alleghany's management in 1938 had persuaded the holders of unsecured Nickel Plate notes to extend the notes' expiration date, thereby avoiding receivership or reorganization of the Nickel Plate.

The arguments presented by Young and Kirby were successful, and on June 5, 1945, the Interstate Commerce Commission ruled that the Alleghany's control of the C&O, NKP, and PM was legal and in the public interest. Moreover, the ICC concluded that Alleghany operated the three railroads with greater efficiency than the average Class 1 railroad in the United States.

While Young was chairman of the board of the Chesapeake & Ohio, three presidents served the company: Newton from 1942 to 1946, Robert Bowman from 1946 to 1948, and Walter Tuohy from 1948 to 1966. Bowman served adequately, continuing the policies of his predecessors; Newton and Tuohy, were outstanding presidents. Strictly from a financial standpoint, Tuohy was the most successful of the three, but this success partially resulted from the general prosperity of the nation.

To provide better service to its customers, the Chesapeake & Ohio continued to improve its physical facilities. These betterments included a tunnel improvement program, the completion of many second and third tracks, the construction of additional switching facilities and side tracks, bridge repairs, and the implementation of Centralized Traffic Control (CTC). The C&O completed an $11.7 million classification yard at Russell, Kentucky, and refurbished its docking facilities in Toledo, Newport News, and Chicago. To develop new coal areas and encourage the opening of new mines to replace worked-out mines, the Chesapeake & Ohio organized a Coal Development Department in 1943, the only such department operated by an American railroad company. The C&O added many branch lines; one of these, a twenty-three-mile extension of the Elkhorn & Beaver Valley Branch from Wayland to Dean, Kentucky, tapped an area containing 200 million tons of recoverable coal with an expected yield of 1.5 million tons annually.

One of the most popular acquisitions of the C&O after World War II was the purchase of the Greenbrier resort at White Sulphur Springs, West Virginia. After being used as a military hospital during the war, the property was acquired for $1.95 million in December 1946. The C&O immediately began a $4 million modernizing and refurbishing program, and the Greenbrier reopened on April 19, 1948.

In January 1947, operating through the Alleghany Corporation, the C&O purchased 400,000 shares of New York Central stock. The *New York Herald Tribune* noted that control of the far-flung New York Central System (NYC), operating nearly 11,000 miles of line and with assets of about $1.75 million, had apparently passed into Young's hands, since the purchase made the Alleghany Corporation the largest single NYC stockholder. In February the *Wall Street Journal* contended that Young's goal was the merger of Eastern roads into three systems headed by the Pennsylvania, Baltimore & Ohio, and Chesapeake & Ohio-New York Central. Although Young had discussed the possibility of such a merger at the time of the purchase, he stated in 1948 "that while he believed the NYC had a great future and potential, he had no plans to merge the two companies until such time as the restoration of the earnings and credit position of the NYC indicated the wisdom of such a course."

On June 6, 1947, the C&O merged with the Pere Marquette, creating a system of 5,122 miles of

main line. It embraced lines from Newport News and Washington, D.C., to Toledo and Chicago; and a line north of Lake Erie and Buffalo, New York, extending throughout Michigan, with a ferryboat line across Lake Michigan from Ludington, Michigan, to Kewaunee, Manitowac, and Milwaukee, Wisconsin. Bowman, head of the Pere Marquette, became president of the combined companies, succeeding Newton, and the consolidated board of directors of the merged companies elected Young chairman.

Young believed that despite the ever-increasing competition from other means of transportation, the railroads could still generate a profit from their passenger trains if they would modernize their service and equipment. To illustrate his point, in 1946 Young ran advertisements in newspapers headlined "A Hog Can Cross the Country Without Changing Trains—You Can't!" After the Chesapeake & Ohio's acquisition of New York Central stock, he attempted to convince Central officials that new lightweight trains, which could operate safely at speeds in excess of 100 miles per hour, could make the company's passenger service profitable. But Young's importuning fell on deaf ears.

In January 1954 Young resigned as chairman of the C&O because of Interstate Commerce Commission regulations prohibiting interlocking directorates. His resignation ended his struggle to merge the C&O and the NYC. But in attempting to gain control of the Central for the C&O, Young had obtained proxies representing enough voting shares to control the NYC, and in July he became board chairman of the Central. He immediately hired Alfred E. Perlman of the Denver & Rio Grande Western Railroad as president, and Perlman proceeded to trim and revitalize the Central.

After his resignation as chairman of the C&O, Young seemed to lose his enthusiasm for business. In the 1950s, railroading sank into the doldrums. Passengers rode airplanes or buses, or drove themselves. Trucks replaced the railroads as freight haulers. Featherbedding, bureaucratic routines, overcapitalization, high taxes, and government regulation sapped the energy of the industry, and decaying facilities signaled the decline of the railroads.

On Monday, January 10, 1958, Young presided over a meeting of the board of directors of the NYC. The meeting was gloomy; financial reports for the year were poor, and Central stock had fallen in the recession that had started in 1957. Moreover, Young himself had suffered reverses in the stock market, forcing him to sell part of his Alleghany stock to raise cash.

On the morning of the twenty-fifth, Young rose early, as was his habit; he ate breakfast at 8:00 and retired to the billiard room of the twenty-five-room house he had built in Palm Beach, Florida. When Young failed to appear at noon for an appointment, members of the household went looking for him. He was found slumped in a chair with a twenty-gauge shotgun between his knees. Police estimated that he had committed suicide around 10:00 A.M. No note was found, and no inquest was held. In addition to his wife, Young was survived by a daughter.

References:

Charles V. Bias, "A History of the Chesapeake and Ohio Railway Company, 1836-1977," Ph.D. dissertation, West Virginia University, 1979;

Joseph Borkin, *Robert R. Young, the Populist of Wall Street* (New York: Harper & Row, 1969);

Matthew Josephson, "The Daring Young Man of Wall Street," *Saturday Evening Post*, 218 (August 11, 1945): 12-13; (August 18, 1945): 22-23; (August 25, 1945):35;

David A. Monroe, "An Exclusive Interview With Robert R. Young," *New Republic*, 117 (September 8, 1947): 24-26;

"Robert R. Young," *Fortune*, 35 (May 1947): 96-103;

"Robert R. Young Dies of Suicide," *New York Times*, January 26, 1958, p. 1.

Archives:

Materials relating to Robert R. Young are at Chessie System offices in Jacksonville, Florida.

Contributors

Wallace W. Abbey–*Association of American Railroads*
Richard W. Barsness–*Lehigh University*
Michael Bezilla–*Pennsylvania State University*
Charles V. Bias–*Marshall University*
Seth H. Bramson–*Miami Shores, Florida*
John J. Broesamle–*California State University, Northridge*
Keith L. Bryant, Jr.–*Texas A&M University*
Dan Butler–*Westark Community College*
G. Wallace Chessman–*Denison University*
William R. Doezema–*Houghton College*
George H. Drury–*Trains Magazine*
John F. Due–*University of Illinois*
Albert S. Eggerton, Jr.–*Southern Railway (Retired)*
John Fahey–*Eastern Washington University*
Robert L. Frey–*Wilmington College of Ohio*
H. Roger Grant–*University of Akron*
Herbert H. Harwood, Jr.–*CSX Transportation (Retired)*
James N. J. Henwood–*East Stroudsburg University of Pennsylvania*
David H. Hickcox–*Ohio Wesleyan University*
George W. Hilton–*University of California, Los Angeles*
Don L. Hofsommer–*Augustana College*
Ari Hoogenboom–*Brooklyn College and the Graduate Center, City University of New York*
Maury Klein–*University of Rhode Island*
James H. Lemly–*Atlanta, Georgia*
Walter Licht–*University of Pennsylvania*
Arthur L. Lloyd–*Amtrak*
Albro Martin–*Bradley University*
Lloyd J. Mercer–*University of California, Santa Barbara*
George H. Merriam–*Fitchburg State College*
Craig Miner–*Wichita State University*
Charles O. Morgret–*Morgret, Inc.*
Douglas C. Munski–*University of North Dakota*
Martin M. Pomphrey–*St. Louis, Missouri*
Richard Saunders–*Clemson University*
Carlos A. Schwantes–*University of Idaho*
Vernon Gladden Spence–*George Mason University*
John F. Stover–*Purdue University*
Roger L. Sullivan–*Union Pacific Railroad*
James A. Ward–*University of Tennessee at Chattanooga*
John H. White, Jr.–*National Museum of American History*
W. Thomas White–*James Jerome Hill Reference Library*

Index

The following index includes names of people, corporations, government agencies, organizations, laws, and technologies. It also includes key terms such as *bridges, safety,* etc.

A page number in *italic* type indicates the first page of an entry devoted to the subject. *Illus.* indicates a picture of the subject. *Map* indicates the depiction of the route of a railroad at a given point in its history.

Index